KNOWING AND WRITING

New Perspectives on Classical Questions

ROBERT REILLY
ANNE T. SALVATORE

Rider College

■ HarperCollins*Publishers*

Sponsoring Editor: Patricia Rossi
Development Editor: David Munger
Project Editor: Karen Trost
Design Supervisor: Heather A. Ziegler
Text Design: North 7 Atelier Ltd.
Cover Design: Circa 86, Inc.
Cover Photo: Window with pyramid/butterfly/ivy, Ellen Schuster/Image Bank
Production: Beth Maglione/Kathleen Donnelly
Compositor: Circle Graphics
Printer and Binder: R. R. Donnelley & Sons Company
Cover Printer: The Lehigh Press, Inc.

For permission to use copyrighted material, grateful acknowledgment is made to the copyright holders on pp. 681–685, which are hereby made part of this copyright page.

KNOWING AND WRITING: New Perspectives on Classical Questions

Library of Congress Cataloging-in-Publication Data

Knowing and writing: new perspectives on classical questions/
  [edited by] Robert Reilly, Anne T. Salvatore.
      p. cm.
   Includes bibliographical references and index.
   ISBN 0-06-045352-4 (student ed.)—ISBN 0-06-500478-7
(instructors ed.)
    1. College readers.   2. English language—Rhetoric.   I. Reilly,
Robert, 1933- .   II. Salvatore, Anne T., 1941- .
PE1417.K66   1992
808'.0427—dc20   91-15825
                                                     CIP

91 92 93 94 9 8 7 6 5 4 3 2 1

Contents

UNIT TWO
PERSONAL RELATIONSHIPS
Understanding Love, Sex, and Marriage **151**

UNIT THREE
FREE CHOICE
The Nature of Freedom and Responsibility   331

UNIT FOUR
TECHNOLOGY
External Reality and the Human Person   507

Preface

Composition theory is galloping ahead of most available textbooks. Not only do professors themselves crave a body of knowledge and ideas to discuss; students, the new research reveals, have the same need, though for a different reason. *Studies in cognitive psychology now suggest that what professors recognize as "good" academic writing by students depends on a context supported by a real knowledge base.* We explore some of this compelling research in our Instructor's Manual.

Unfortunately, many students have not had the opportunity to develop such a context and knowledge base. Part of our purpose, therefore, is to provide a *body of knowledge* that will present a topic in all its complexity, encourage in-depth thinking, generate ideas, and, as a context builds, produce more substantial, interesting, truly engaged academic writing.

To assert that this knowledge may be missing, however, is not at all to imply a lack of *ability* in today's students. Indeed, the research points to a difference between ability and the demonstration of ability. We assume that our students possess a basic competence, too often untapped. The opposite assumption, we feel, has seriously damaged our education system as well as our own morale; it has reinforced the unwarranted conclusion that we ought to supply students with general-level texts as writing sources. This book proposes to move them ahead. Though some of the selections can be challenging, we believe that the features we describe below will help to make these readings accessible and enjoyable.

FEATURES

1. **Four Timeless Issues:** To encourage depth, we have selected only four issues; this strategy allows us to offer a variety of perspectives on each issue. We have included not only classic statements of these issues, but contemporary responses as well. The opportunity to read many pieces that relate to a single topic enables students to gain a more comprehensive picture of the ideas involved. They can identify the relevant questions and begin to formulate their own positions on these questions. To spark interest, we have chosen issues that are relevant to students' personal lives yet are also crucial for contemporary society: Prejudice, Personal Relationships, Free Choice, and Technology. For example, while great strides have been made toward eliminating ethnic, racial, and religious

prejudices, these social ills still exercise tremendous power in our society. Our students may recognize this festering problem in a subliminal way, but few have come to grips with it. In addition, most students have great interest in their own personal relationships, and can profit considerably from studying the implications of their own behavior and exploring ways of enhancing their relationships. Free choice is a topic that students may not have considered, even subliminally. Assuming their own freedom, they often overlook the various guises that "imprisonment" might wear; this unit offers forms of empowerment about which many have never dreamed. Finally, even though we live in an age of astonishing scientific and technological advancement, few of us comprehend it, with resultant feelings of confusion and alienation. We believe this unit will help many students appreciate the impact of science and technology on their lives, and will better enable them to articulate their responses to this technology. As students discover the importance of these issues to their own well-being, they often invest more of themselves in writing about the topics.

2. **Cross-Disciplinary Selections:** We have chosen selections for each unit from as many disciplines as possible: Certain disciplines, of course, are more relevant to particular units. We include a significant number of literary readings because both instructors and students enjoy them and because they encourage affective responses, interpretive thinking, and original ideas about a topic. We have also incorporated two illustrations in each unit, representing various media such as painting, drawing, photography, and even a cartoon. Like the literary selections, the illustrations prompt creative thinking, and they demonstrate how different modes of expression can suggest similar ideas. Each piece of art is integrally related to the unit's theme, sometimes complementing a subtopic already present in a prose selection, and sometimes suggesting a new subissue that broadens the discussion.

3. **Flexibility:** Given the various levels and types of composition courses, the range of instructors' teaching experience, and the diverse philosophies of composition pedagogy currently being practiced, we have aimed to provide the maximum flexibility by offering alternate *structures*:

   a. Each unit contains more than enough material to permit the teacher to deal with the same topic throughout an entire semester or quarter. In addition, some of the selections can easily be transposed from one unit to another. For instance, Keller's essay in the Technology unit, "Women in Science: An Analysis of a Social Problem," can also be used in the Prejudice unit; Menninger's "Decisions in Sexuality: An Act of Impulse, Conscience, or Society?" is included in the unit Personal Relationships, but it is also appropriate for the Free Choice unit. Thus, the instructor can choose among readings as he or she thinks best. For yearlong composition sequences the book can be used in both terms by covering different units during each term.

b. For those who prefer not to follow our topical approach, we offer other options through two additional tables of contents at the back of the book. One of these arranges the selections by academic disciplines. Those who are interested in writing across the curriculum will find this table of contents particularly useful. For instructors oriented toward writing technique, we have included a rhetorical table of contents, which organizes the readings by rhetorical strategies, such as narration, description, example, argument, and others.

4. **An Introduction to Instructors: A Theoretical Rationale:** Providing the scholarly foundation that informs the book's title, this rationale for *Knowing and Writing* (in the Instructor's Manual) offers the instructor an overview of relevant cognitive and writing theory. Several theorists offer compelling reasons for providing a knowledge base; others encourage writing assignments that include emotional and informal responses to texts as well as the use of collaborative learning. A *bibliography* is appended for those who wish to study the topic further.

5. **To Our Student Writers: How to Survive and Prosper in a College Composition Class:** This introduction to critical reading and writing not only speaks directly to students but insists that they participate actively even as they read the introduction. Thus, instead of asking them to read about how other students before them have responded, as most introductions do, we ask them questions, then leave space where they can write their own responses; afterward, we discuss with them the ways in which they may have reacted to our prompts and the implications of their reactions. In other words, we treat reading as an interactive process right from the start. Moreover, we ask them to summarize what they have learned about active reading from the introduction, and encourage them to return to it to refresh their memories later. Other topics discussed in the student introduction include overcoming writer's block, the conventions of different disciplines, the writing process, and seeking assistance through writing centers.

6. **Unit and Entry Introductions:** Each unit is preceded by an overview that prepares students to think about relevant issues, definitions, historical context, or disciplinary approaches to the topic. Moreover, each reading entry within a unit includes biographical information on the author, date of publication, and some helpful leads into the selection.

7. **Broad Perspectives:** At the end of each unit, we encourage students to reconsider all the readings in that unit in order to create relationships among them. This broad question is followed by a series of "cluster" questions, which draw explicit relationships among smaller groups of readings for that unit. Finally, at the end of the text, we include a "CrossViews" section to connect ideas among the four units.

8. **Glossary:** To make the text even more user-friendly, we offer definitions of

important rhetorical and literary terms. Many of these terms, or derivatives of them, are used in the text and are highlighted in bold print.

Each reading is accompanied by the following aids:

Previews: To encourage active engagement with the text, one or more prereading questions are strategically placed before the selection. Students can write brief, informal answers before approaching the text.

Journal Writings: These questions following each reading ask for relatively brief, informal responses of a paragraph or two. Often aimed at eliciting the student's personal knowledge or experience, they emphasize narration, description, or fairly simple exposition.

Brainstorming and Drafting: These relatively brief assignments generally require critical thinking and in-depth analysis. Sometimes they build on Previews or Journal Writings; often they attempt to broaden and deepen the student's knowledge base by asking about comparisons, contrasts, or applications of ideas among the unit's readings. While generally limited to a few sentences or at most a couple of paragraphs, these questions can also function as prewriting for more extended papers.

The Authors' Methods: These questions call the student's attention to writing techniques employed by the authors. The instructor can use these to focus on the effectiveness and appropriateness of different methods in context. The student is often asked to imitate the method with a paragraph of his or her own.

Creative Projects: These projects are occasionally included to give students the opportunity to create imaginative texts. While such writing is required only infrequently in academia, the task itself is important because it values creative talent and stimulates original thinking.

Formal Writing and Research Papers: Requiring polished, extended papers, these projects emphasize analysis and argument; comparisons among readings are encouraged when possible. For most selections, at least one question will require research of some type: interviewing, field research, library sources. Specific library tools are often suggested.

Footnotes: Technical terms and difficult allusions are explained in footnotes.

ACKNOWLEDGMENTS

We wish to thank Rider College for supporting our work through Summer Fellowship awards. We are also grateful to all our colleagues in the English department who discussed their ideas about composition, responded to our surveys, and offered their encouragement. Among these, particular recognition is due to those who suggested topics or material for the text, or responded graciously to our work in progress: Gary Barricklow, Virginia Cyrus, James

Guimond, Judith Johnston, Mary O'Reilly, Roberta Sethi, Jack Sullivan, and Arlene Wilner. Colleagues in other departments who kindly contributed their expertise include William Amadio (Computer Information Systems), Marvin Goldstein (Psychology), and Robert Good (Philosophy). Rider College reference librarian Kathryn Holden and Bensalem School District librarian Helen Londergan offered many helpful suggestions for articles and illustrations. Toby Fulwiler (University of Vermont) responded to an early draft of the proposal with insightful comments that prompted us to change the nature of the apparatus.

Many of our students aided directly in putting together this text by suggesting articles they discovered in their own research, proposing subtopics, and writing journal questions: Ray Agliata, John Annasenz, Maria De Frank, Desiree Feo, Michael Fox, Valiere Frantzeskos, Adam Gee, Beth Gerber, Tara Kurzinsky, Kimberly Lutz, Marlana Mazmanian, John Murray, Jennifer Pogge, and David Salemme.

Editors Patricia Rossi, David Munger, Lucy Rosendahl, and assistant editor Mark Paluch provided excellent advice as well as support and friendly encouragement. Project editor Karen Trost was a knowledgeable, well-organized, and understanding administrator; copy editor Harriet Sigerman contributed many perceptive suggestions for editing the text. Susie Geraci was a prompt and accurate assistant with permissions and clerical tasks.

We wish to thank all of our reviewers: Libby Bay, Rockland Community College; Jon Bouknight, University of Washington; Duncan Carter, Portland State University; John Clifford, University of North Carolina at Wilmington; Ruth Greenberg, Jefferson Community College; Elizabeth Hodges, Virginia Commonwealth University; Kathy McClelland, University of California, Santa Barbara; Terry Otten, Wittenburg University; Randall Popkin, Tarleton State University; Michael Sita, Pima Community College; Margaret Smith, University of Texas–El Paso; Myrna Smith, Raritan Valley Community College; Margot Soven, LaSalle University; John Trimbur, Worcester Polytechnic Institute; and Nancy Yee, Fitchburg State University.

Finally, Lola, Eric, and Dede Reilly and Nick, Scott, Kevin, and Kristin Salvatore are the patient, understanding family members who kept us smiling while we wrestled with the arduous but ultimately satisfying tasks of thinking, planning, writing, and revising.

Robert Reilly
Anne T. Salvatore

INTRODUCTION: TO OUR STUDENT WRITERS

How to Survive and Prosper in a College Composition Class

Once upon a time, two college composition teachers were feeling frustrated. They had just finished writing a textbook. "You need to add an introduction for the students," their publisher told them. "Introductions are boring," the professors said to each other. They grumbled. They complained. They rationalized. They procrastinated. Then they began to worry about the fast-approaching deadline. But deadlines have a way of facilitating action. The professors began to scribble a few silly ideas on their yellow legal pads. Suddenly, the reluctant professors made an important discovery: Their own behavior was strikingly similar to the behavior of many of the students who are required to take their composition classes!

We, the editors, are those two professors. We'd like to emphasize that we, too, are human beings who sometimes yield to the tempting bliss of passivity. Often, we don't feel like writing. And as long as we find excuses to remain inactive, nothing happens. But when we *must* act, ideas are finally born. We find that we like very much *to have written.* Recognizing that activity is essential to any accomplishment, we'd like to invite you to participate actively in this course, starting now. We're asking you to begin a collaborative journey toward an understanding of why you might want to read, write, and think deeply—the activities assumed by this book—and how you as students and we as professors can assume coresponsibility for promoting success in those activities.

We will ask you to write impromptu but thoughtful and honest answers to the questions that appear in the next few pages. No one will grade you on these answers. In fact, most likely, no one will see them except yourself, though your instructor may discuss them with you. But we do ask that you answer each question as you come to it, *before you read the paragraph that follows it.* In fact, whenever you see some blank lines provided for your response, we ask that you cover the next paragraph with some blank paper until you have finished writing.

1

Why do you think your college requires you to take a writing course?

_____

_____

_____

_____

_____

_____

Did you say that probably college teachers want you to communicate your ideas better? Do they think you need to improve your grammar and spelling? Do they want you to impress other teachers and future employers with your capabilities? Or was your answer somewhat more cynical—because English teachers need their jobs? We'd agree with all of those, although we'd probably insist that the last assertion, though true in itself (most of us _do_ need our jobs), is not directly related to the question.

But recently other reasons have come to light. Many professors of biology, history, psychology, education, accounting, and computer science, for example, believe that writing can be a powerful tool in learning all kinds of material; they tell us that, through writing, their students discover new insights, recall material better, sometimes even find answers to their own questions. In addition, teachers want you to take composition because you learn firsthand how writers behave: how they progress, often slowly, from draft to draft; how they change ideas; reorganize; add new material; refine style; correct spelling, punctuation, and grammar; eliminate typing errors.

Well, if this is a writing class, why do you suppose your teacher wants you to do all this reading?

_____

_____

_____

_____

_____

_____

_____

Did you answer that the readings will give you ideas? We agree—maybe. Reading _can_ be a source of knowledge. Think about our title: _Knowing and_

Writing. Yes, reading can help you "know" by offering you information: established facts or other people's ideas. Certainly we agree that gathering a good base of information is indispensable if you are to write cogently about a topic that you have never studied before. As literary specialists, for example, we might be able to write meaningfully and perhaps insightfully about a poem by Chaucer or a novel by Dickens. But if you asked us to write about managerial accounting or a chemical compound, we would need to gather information first; otherwise, our writing would be drivel. Yet gathering information is not sufficient either. Unless we interpret or process the information somehow, there is little reason for anyone to read our report instead of the original piece of writing. Thus, gathering facts and collecting others' ideas provides only one kind of knowledge. While such knowledge is important and necessary as background, we need also to progress toward other kinds of knowledge if we want our writing to be fresh and interesting. **Before we can write perceptively in response to a reading, we need to process the information we receive: That is, we need to start behaving like "good" readers.**

CONQUERING YOUR TEXTS

List some of the things that "good" readers do to process what they read.

_____

_____

_____

_____

_____

_____

_____

_____

_____

_____

Surveying the Text

You probably said that good readers survey the entire text, searching for the main idea, and of course you are right—assuming that there is a "main" idea. (Occasionally, you will find an exploratory or meandering piece that presents many ideas without singling one out.) Much academic writing, however, makes a claim or assertion about something—has a "thesis." A claim is not the same as a topic, which tells you only the specific subject matter being discussed; a topic usually does not reveal the author's belief about this subject matter. For example, in the following paragraph from Simone de Beauvoir's "The Woman in Love," in the Personal Relationships unit, the *topic* is women's attitudes in romantic love situations.

> Men have found it possible to be passionate lovers at certain times in their lives, but there is not one of them who could be called "a great lover"; in their most violent transports, they never abdicate completely; even on their knees before a mistress, what they still want is to take possession of her; at the very heart of their lives they remain sovereign subjects; the beloved woman is only one value among others; they wish to integrate her into their existence and not to squander it entirely on her. For woman, on the contrary, to love is to relinquish everything for the benefit of a master.

What does de Beauvoir assert about her topic in this paragraph?

_____

_____

_____

_____

_____

_____

While there are many ways of stating her claim, de Beauvoir believes that men, considering themselves sovereign beings, treat love for women as only one of many values in their lives, while women, according men supreme importance, consider love for men the highest value of their lives. Or, you could say (somewhat more generally) that men and women think and behave differently in love situations at least partially because of their beliefs about gender rankings. In some readings, you can underline the author's exact words as a thesis. In de Beauvoir's essay, however, no single sentence captures the thesis; therefore, we have constructed an implied claim for the whole paragraph. We asked about only one paragraph because you have not read the entire essay; if you consult the essay as it appears later in this book, however, you will see that this claim also represents her thesis for the entire reading.

What are some clues that signal a thesis or claim in a reading?

_____

_____

_____

_____

_____

_____

Did you suggest looking at the title first? Generally this is a good place to start, as authors often deliberately choose titles that hint at their claims. In de Beauvoir's case, though, the essay title, "The Woman in Love," provides only the *topic*, not the *claim*. But this essay is taken from a chapter in her book entitled *The Second Sex*. Here we find a strong hint about the general claim of the book: The "traditional" male believes that the male sex is primary and dominant, while the "traditional" female believes that her sex is secondary and subservient. This general thesis then becomes more specific according to the topic of each chapter.

Did you also recommend checking the first few paragraphs for another clue? How about the last few paragraphs? In academic writing, an author may try to create some suspense about his or her claim by posing it tentatively or suggesting it as a question in the introduction and then offering some resolution, specification, or deeper meaning to it in the conclusion. For example, in the introduction to his essay in the Technology unit Langdon Gilkey asks whether a scientific culture can "show itself to be in need of religion"; his conclusion implies a positive answer to his question and presents his specific claim about the type of religion that can best serve the modern technological world. Thus, **good readers begin by surveying the entire text, especially the title, introduction, and conclusion, for other clues about the thesis.**

In short stories and poems, a thesis will rarely be stated explicitly. Instead, the characters, setting, situation, outcome, and symbols imply some statement about the human condition, which we call a theme. Because such themes are implicit rather than explicit, readers are less likely to agree on what the "central" theme might be. In fact, stories and poems of any artistic complexity usually contain several possible themes, none of which can be simply reduced to a moral. For example, in Tillie Olsen's "I Stand Here Ironing," in the Free Choice unit, you as the reader may decide that the theme involves a real difficulty in evaluating where a parent's influence begins and ends; another reader may argue that the story emphasizes how social and historical influences determine our choices; a third reader may even decide that these two themes are equally important in the story. In other words, **with imaginative writing, the clues are more subtle: Good readers of literature need to interpret the theme from a personal understanding of the story's evidence.**

Let's return to your **list of things good readers do.** Did you point out that they also search for subtopics and related ideas? This is crucial for comprehending an author's logic, especially in an argumentative piece. For instance, in Martin Luther King's "Letter from Birmingham Jail," in the Prejudice unit, the subtopics include King's reasons for being in Birmingham, his reasons for choosing direct action, the timeliness of the action, the rationale behind breaking the law, and other subtopics. Many of these subtopics are stated in the first sentences of paragraphs, a good place to look for clues, though not every author states a subtopic there. Sometimes the clues appear at the ends of paragraphs; sometimes the ideas are only implied.

In science or social science writing in particular, the author often makes things easier for us by devising bold headings to indicate subtopics. For example, in "Some Conditions of Obedience and Disobedience to Authority," Stanley

Milgram includes the following headings in a report of his experimental study: "Terminology," "Subject Population," "The General Laboratory Procedure," "Pilot Studies," etc. **Good readers survey paragraphs and headings to isolate subtopics; they may also wish to jot down an outline as an aid to remembering the ideas.**

Personalizing the Text

A fairly quick overview, of course, is only the beginning. What else is on your list? Making notes? We prefer note-taking over simply underlining or highlighting, because notes (annotations) help us understand and remember the material; they force us to concentrate; they allow us to personalize the text.

Let's try annotating de Beauvoir's paragraph:

[Marginal annotations: "Very long sentence"; "Different attitudes: male, dominant female, submissive"; "supreme ruler"; "How would she define great lover? How different from passionate lover?"; "give up authority"; "Not true for all women— would I give up my career?"]

Men have found it possible to be passionate lovers at certain times in their lives, but there is not one of them who could be "a (great) (lover") in their most violent transports, they never (abdicate) completely; even on their knees before a mistress, what they still want is to take possession of her; at the very heart of their lives they remain (sovereign) subjects; the beloved woman is only one value among others; they wish to integrate her into their existence and not to squander it entirely on her. For (woman,) on the contrary, to love is to (relinquish everything) for the benefit of a master.

As you can see from the marginal notes, annotations can take the form of summary, interpretation, definition of difficult words, questions about the text, and challenges to the author—whatever the reader finds helpful in making the text his or her own. Try annotating the following passage, also from de Beauvoir:

> The psychoanalysts are wont to assert that woman seeks the father image in her lover; but it is because he is a man, not because he is a father that he dazzles the girl child, and every man shares in this magical power. Woman does not long to reincarnate one individual in another, but to reconstruct a situation: that which she experienced as a little girl, under adult protection. She was deeply integrated with home and family, she knew the peace of quasi-passivity. Love will give her back her mother as well as her father, it will give her back her childhood. What she wants to recover is a roof over her head, walls that prevent her from feeling her abandonment in the wide world, authority that protects her against her liberty.

What should a good reader annotate? We do not know. Every reader brings his or her own experiences, beliefs, values, uncertainties, and sense of priorities to a passage. Because psychology interests us, we might comment that this paragraph takes the traditional psychoanalytical approach. Examining our own family backgrounds, we might want to jot down some reasons why little girls desire this passivity and why they allow boys the active role. Feeling rebellious, we might even begin thinking of the many contemporary women we know who assume an active role in contradiction to de Beauvoir's assertion. (We especially enjoy contradicting an author, and we suspect that you do too. It's exciting to discover that you don't need to accept everything you read in print.) If we were puzzled, we could consult a dictionary to figure out why the author used "quasi-passivity."

All of this, of course, has taken more time than you might expect to give to a paragraph. But a note or annotation can be one small step on the way to a fresh, effective, individual idea for a paper. **Good readers of college texts, like good drivers, begin by surveying the road (text) ahead. Good readers move quickly when they can, more slowly when they need to ponder; they are careful, active, involved. From the information offered, they begin to build a new, personalized knowledge that includes a part of themselves.**

Finally, did you include making connections on your **list of things good readers do?** In this course, you will be asked to read several selections on the same topic in order to extend and deepen your knowledge of that topic. In general, the more connections you are able to make among these readings, the richer your knowledge will be, and the more substantial and impressive your writing will become. For example, suppose you are writing a paper using some of Rita Freedman's ideas (in the Free Choice unit) about women who buy more and more makeup because they are enslaved by society's definition of beauty. You can enhance your discussion by alluding to Alice Walker's moving account (in the same unit) of a young girl who reacted to life very differently after she sustained an eye injury that she thought destroyed her beauty. As part of your discussion, you might wish to propose a way of breaking free from such enslavement. Perhaps you will decide to include some ideas from your psychology class about the need for a strong sense of self to free us from the imprisonment of society's definitions. You may even be able to recount a personal incident illustrating how such a limitation can be overcome. In other words, **good readers make connections among readings; they examine their own life experiences and the experiences of people around them as rich sources of material to write about.**

We have been chatting for several pages here about the things that good readers do. As an aid to your memory, list below the methods we have discussed. Check back to this page several times during the semester.

_____

_____

_____

_____

_____

_____

_____

_____

_____

_____

_____

_____

_____

_____

_____

_____

CONQUERING THE BLANK PAGE

For three minutes, write without stopping about what worries you the most when you are asked to write.

_____

_____

_____

_____

_____

_____

_____

_____

_____

_____

———————————————————————————

———————————————————————————

———————————————————————————

When we ask our students this question, some say they worry about grammar and spelling. Others find organization difficult. But perhaps the greatest concern is finding ideas to write about. We took some time to write about our worries too. You may be surprised to discover our biggest fear: that we won't have anything important to say. Maybe that's why we procrastinated so long in writing this introduction for you. But we started scribbling on our yellow pads *before* we knew what we wanted to say. After a while, we discovered that we had plenty of things we wanted to tell you. In fact, by now you may be wishing that we hadn't discovered quite so much!

Why do so many people become fearful when they stare at a blank page? One reason may be that, when asked to write, we tend to think immediately of the end **product**—the ideal: a beautifully organized, correct, fresh and creative, idea-filled text that now looks so effortless to us as readers. But is it truly so effortless? Do "real" writers simply wait for inspiration and then, trancelike, sit at their typewriters or computers and let their fingers type out the **product?**

For most writers, the answer is no. Even as eminent a writer as Gustave Flaubert, the author of *Madame Bovary,* had difficulty getting his thoughts onto paper. In a February 1852 letter to Louise Colet describing his problems with composing *Madame Bovary,* Flaubert complains of the same malady that many of us have experienced:

> Bad week. Work didn't go; I had reached a point where I didn't know what to say . . . I was completely in the dark: it is very difficult to clarify by means of words what is still obscure in your thoughts. I made outlines, spoiled a lot of paper, floundered and fumbled. Now I shall perhaps find my way again.

Another professional writer, contemporary Scottish playwright Marcella Evaristi, tells us how she solves this kind of problem:

> Overcoming a block for me is often about overcoming a ridiculously stern intolerance of first ideas. (If only I could stop being so hard on myself, I think; let myself play around with my thoughts.) . . . I mostly hate Stage One of writing where you can still change your mind about your subject; perhaps great unconscious strides are being made but what it feels like is neurotic shadow boxing. So . . . bully or trick yourself however you can into Stage Two. I find it sickeningly difficult. It feels as if I have a highly suspicious jury inside my head whose strictures I would dismiss out of hand when applied to other writers but their judgements on me and my work leave me cowed. . . . Getting the jury to disappear for long enough to let you begin, that's the trick. That beautiful moment when you click into Work Proper . . . time speeds up and you lose yourself in the work.

We each have our own "jury," someone in our heads judging everything we write. Let's promise ourselves right now that we'll ignore that jury long enough to "flounder and fumble" as Flaubert did through at least one sheet of blank paper. That is, we will start with one small step, one part of the **writing process.**

Of course, if you duplicate the method of active reading that we have been suggesting, you will probably collect at least enough thoughts to fill a sheet about every reading. Our **Preview** question, which appears right before each reading, will help you to begin the process. When you complete each reading, you will be able to "click into Work Proper" more easily if you consult our questions at the end. They are intended to help you progress further with the composing process. **Give yourself permission to write down even your most ordinary reaction.**

The **Journal Writings** section is a particularly appropriate place to begin, since many of its questions call on your personal experience or observation, rather than on a specialized knowledge. In general, the writing task is to narrate, describe, or explain some incident or reaction you have about the reading. Since the writing task is "informal," you are free to think mostly about your ideas; don't worry about organization, grammar, or spelling—you can deal with these later in the process.

The **Brainstorming and Drafting** activities continue the fight against the blank page by suggesting some ideas for you to ponder and react to on a higher level of critical thinking. For example, these questions may ask you to generalize after considering several concrete examples. Or, you may be asked to apply some abstract principle to other concrete situations. Some of these questions reinforce connections you may already have made or suggest new connections among several readings. Other questions give you the opportunity to discuss your thoughts with your peers—another way to stimulate ideas to help you move along in the process. The task in these activities remains informal, though you may decide later to turn such paragraphs into a formal—that is, revised and polished—paper.

Studying and imitating the **Author's Methods** will give you more ammunition against writer's block by developing your confidence about rhetorical methods. These questions enable you to understand a particular method easily by isolating it from other concerns; you can then reconnect the method to the issues at hand as you practice your own version of it.

Sometimes we include **Creative Projects,** opportunities for you to compose your own imaginative literature on a topic. Even though most college writing involves nonfiction or academic prose, you may want to develop your own talent by selecting these questions. If your college has a literary magazine, you may wish to submit your finished piece for publication.

By the time you reach the **Formal Writing and Research** section, you will already have thought and written about the reading in some depth—excellent preparation for any writing task. Yet these questions sometimes create the most anxiety because they require you to take a giant step forward in the writing process. That is, they ask you to prepare a finished essay in your best academic prose—using a logically organized, well-developed, mature style, with fresh ideas and specific examples, correct grammar, spelling, and punctuation; some of these assignments also require library or field research. But once again, focusing immediately on the ideal—the **product**—is likely to cause paralysis. Try, instead, to focus on one step of the **process** at a time.

What shall we call these "steps" in the writing process that we've been talking about? As we identify each by its professional name, we ask you to try it as your introduction to the process. Remember, however, that sometimes you will find yourself activating two or more stages simultaneously; you may not always want to follow them in the same order.

Considering the Assignment What type of writing is required? For example, should you narrate (tell a story), describe (recount details), report (indicate facts or others' ideas), explain (demonstrate how to do something or how an idea works), argue (state a position and give reasons for it)? Some assignments will specify the task; others may not. If you are uncertain, ask your instructor.

Defining the Audience Are you writing solely for your instructor? Will your peers be included? Does the assignment stipulate some other fictional audience, such as a group of parents, public school teachers, employees of a computer firm? What is the educational level of this proposed audience? What do they already know? What will they need to find out? Will they understand professional terms or will you need to define these for them, or should you not even use these terms? Does your audience have strong opinions that you want to change? Needless to say, a computer manual that you write for a novice user would be very different from one that you write for longtime users.

Inventing This is any activity that helps you think of ideas, such as reading, making lists, free writing, constructing a "tree" of ideas with branches showing related topics, outlining, etc. This is sometimes called the "prewriting" stage.

Try making a list of some ways that males or females behave when they are in love.

_____

_____

_____

_____

_____

_____

_____

_____

_____

_____

Drafting This involves putting some sentences and paragraphs together in a preliminary way. You may wish to explore a tentative thesis, or you may even discover a new thesis as you are writing. Don't worry too much if your ideas aren't in order yet: You can move them around later. Like Flaubert, you might even decide to throw this draft away. Since you are not sure whether these sentences will appear in the final draft, you don't need to worry yet about style and mechanics.

Using your list above as a basis, try drafting one paragraph in which you make a claim (assert a thesis) about male or female behavior in love situations. Write for an audience of students in another composition class who have not read de Beauvoir's article.

_____

_____

_____

_____

_____

_____

_____

Revising This involves changing the nature or the order of ideas, or adding or subtracting ideas, evidence, or examples.

Try revising the paragraph you drafted. But first, show it to a friend. Ask: What can I do to make this paragraph better? Besides your friend's advice, consider the paragraph yourself: Is your claim specific enough? Do you want to place it elsewhere in the paragraph? Can you add some more relevant examples? Should you rearrange the order of your sentences? Can you use evidence from de Beauvoir's paragraph? Of course, if this were an actual assignment, you would probably want to set it aside after revising, and consider additional revisions later.

_____

_____

_____

_____

_____

_____

_____

Editing Check for complete sentences; Improve the sentence structure; use precise vocabulary and eliminate unnecessary "jargon"; correct grammar, spelling, and punctuation.

Try editing your revision above. Use a different color pen or pencil to make your corrections.

Proofreading Check for typing errors. You don't need to do this now, since your copy is not yet typed. But when you do a writing assignment for any class, you need to correct your final copy after it is typed or word-processed. Otherwise, your instructor may count a typing error as though it were a spelling error.

WRITING BEHAVIOR FOR ALL DISCIPLINES

The process we have been talking about will help you conquer the blank page not only in your composition class but for your other subjects as well. Even if your instructors do not specify that readings and drafts are due before the final copy, don't skip these crucial parts of the process. Most successful student writers do not skip them. Most successful professional writers do not skip them either.

Besides applying your writing *behaviors* to other courses, you will be able to apply the *general skills* that you learn. For example, your instructors will expect your papers to have a main idea, thesis, or claim. They will evaluate your work for its accuracy and its logical order. They will expect you to generate valid ideas and to support them with relevant examples, experimental data, statistics, and secondary sources. They will want you to write complete sentences of varying complexity, and they will insist that you use correct grammar, spelling, and punctuation—even when they have not explicitly mentioned these points in their assignments. Certainly, they will expect you to follow assignment directions precisely.

DIFFERENCES IN WRITING ACROSS THE DISCIPLINES

To become a successful writer in a subject area or "discipline," you will need first to develop some knowledge of the subject matter. You will, of course, learn subject matter by reading your text actively, studying lecture notes, participating in class discussions, talking informally with your peers, and reading other sources. This knowledge base will enable you to begin to think more critically and to write with some authority in the discipline. Naturally, the more courses you take in a field, the more authoritative your writing will become.

To be fully successful in your writing, though, you must also become aware of each discipline's writing "conventions." Just as the various countries of the world have different customs and cultural practices, so different subject areas, or disciplines, have different writing conventions. While we cannot describe these in depth for every discipline here, we have listed a few questions to consider before writing a paper in a subject area that is new for you.

Genres of Writing

What types of papers are usually done in this field? For example, will your professor expect a lab report, experimental study, review of previous research, personal essay, interpretation of literary texts, or something else? What specific kinds of writing are appropriate for these different types of papers? If you are asked for a research report in a psychology class, should you state your position on a controversial issue? Should a science lab report include your interpretive comments? In a philosophical position paper, would you include both sides of the issue? When you are uncertain of the answers to these questions, ask your instructor.

Formats of Writing

What is the structure of the paper? Should its organization be narrative, logical, chronological? Are an introduction, body, and conclusion expected? Is a stipulated list of headings always used? Are there other parts to be included?

Methods of Development

How do writers in this field develop their ideas? Do they use examples from a text, anecdotes about a particular case, statistical evidence, experimental studies, statements from other authorities, field research, visual evidence such as charts and graphs, logical reasoning, descriptive details? Which research indexes are likely to help you find articles in the field?

Styles of Writing

Is the use of "I" acceptable in papers for this field? Should you choose words that sound objective? Are the verbs generally active or passive? Is humor permitted in any academic writing? Can you include personal examples? Which bibliographical style does your professor prefer? What specific terms do professionals in the field habitually use?

SEEKING HELP WITH YOUR WRITING

We have listed some of the important questions that students have. Ask your instructor about them if you are unsure of how to proceed. In addition, many instructors will be happy to discuss your paper in its topic or draft stages. As you move through the writing process in any discipline, take time to discuss your paper with your peers, and perhaps to consult someone in your writing or skills center, if your college has such a resource. Ultimately, of course, you become an effective writer only if you take control of your own reading and writing behavior. We hope this text will be your first major step toward succeeding in these endeavors. If you've read this far, chances are that your own motivation will be instrumental in helping you succeed!

UNIT
One

PREJUDICE

Clarifying and Challenging Biased Attitudes

*N*o one can say with certainty when prejudice began. Yet it seems reasonable to assume that it originated very early in human history. Possibly it had its beginnings in humanity's early struggle for survival, when Cro-Magnon man competed with his Neanderthal rivals for the best hunting and gathering grounds. No doubt the development of speech had an influence, giving human-kind the ability to articulate the differences that defined groups and led one group to assert its superiority over another.

The influence of speech is clearly indicated in the attitude of the Greeks of classical times toward their neighbors, whom they called barbarians. The word *barbarian* itself has an echoic quality; it imitates the sounds of the non-Greek languages and indicates the condescension felt toward the speakers of those languages. The condescending attitude of those ancient Greeks exemplifies the attitude of superiority. Somehow *we* are always, in some way or another, better than *they* are. If the reasons for this superiority are not self-evident, *we* will invent (read rationalize) reasons that are sufficiently self-justifying.

Consider some statements reflecting the forms that the alleged superiority of various groups takes:

Men are stronger and braver than women.

That nationality or ethnic group is dirty.

People who worship that way or in that church or temple are not as moral as we are.

We are more intelligent than members of that race.

Peasants are so inferior to us nobles.

Such statements hardly begin to suggest the range and complexity of prejudice. Almost any sort of difference—racial, religious, ethnic, social, sexual, or eco-nomic—may well become the basis for prejudice against an identifiable group. There seem to be few limits.

One might go so far as to say that prejudice underlies much of the long history of "man's inhumanity to man." Personal enmities, family feuds, tribal clashes, and outright wars between nations might all have roots in this one cause. Yet the concept of prejudice seems to have attracted little attention before the Renaissance. In fact, during the Middle Ages theologians ignored the Gospel exhortation to "love thy neighbor as thy self" by expressing the most prejudicial opinions about both Jews and Moslems, which the Moslems, at least, returned with bloody interest.

After the raging religious wars sparked by the Reformation, some philosophers began to consider what might be done about religious prejudice. How much allowance ought one give to those who firmly hold different faiths? This question, which asked not only how much ought to be tolerated but who ought to receive toleration, ultimately led to applications beyond the religious sphere. As the question of toleration began to be examined, so did the rights of other humans. If one respects those rights, one must adopt a tolerant attitude toward the person—an attitude likely to reduce or preclude prejudice.

The stories and essays in this unit deal with prejudice in different ways. Allport is concerned with defining it, but others, such as Mebane and Kureishi, are more interested in showing it in action, directly affecting people's lives. Some writers, such as Prager and Telushkin (not to mention Chaucer), are interested in its religious aspects, while others, like Nager, emphasize its political impact. Baldwin and Gordimer, among others, are concerned with individual responses to it. Sanchez, Hooks, and Luke suggest some things that can be done about it. However much their approaches differ, the authors of all the essays ask us to take a new look at the questions prejudice raises.

Once we begin to grapple with issues relating to prejudice, each of us is likely to make the not-very-pleasant discovery that we harbor, perhaps more deeply than we imagined, negative feelings or opinions about some particular group. The readings in this section are designed to help each individual understand the nature of prejudice, sympathize with the feelings of those who suffer oppression because of it, and ultimately begin the struggle with some questions of toleration: (1) The question put to Jesus, "And who is my neighbor?" When we have answered that, we can go on to (2): "What responsibilities does the 'neighbor' relationship impose on both of us?"

We may not be able to find complete and final answers to these questions, but we may well become better people—people who try to understand and empathize with our neighbors—because we have examined the questions thoughtfully and comprehensively.

Gordon W. Allport

The Nature of Prejudice

(1954)

Gordon W. Allport (1897–1967) was educated at Harvard University and did postgraduate work in Berlin and Hamburg. Profoundly influenced by meeting Sigmund Freud in 1920, he chose to pursue a career in psychology. After brief appointments at Robert College and Dartmouth, he returned to Harvard as a member of the faculty. Most of his work was in social psychology. Two of his important works are *Personality: A Psychological Interpretation* and *The Nature of Personality.* He gained worldwide recognition for his books on prejudice and rumors.

In this selection, from his book *The Nature of Prejudice,* Allport is primarily concerned with defining prejudice in all its various manifestations— racial, ethnic, religious, and sexual. But he also explores the implications and results of various ways of defining the term.

PREVIEWS

A. **Define** prejudice for yourself without looking in a dictionary. Perhaps thinking of some examples (from your own direct experience or what you have read or heard from others) will help you gather ideas for your definition.

B. List several groups of people whom you think are the object of prejudice. Try to think of a reason for the prejudice against each group on your list.

For myself, earth-bound and fettered to the scene of my activities, I confess that I do feel the differences of mankind, national and individual. . . . I am, in plainer words, a bundle of prejudices—made up of likings and dislikings—the veriest thrall to sympathies, apathies, antipathies.   CHARLES LAMB

In Rhodesia a white truck driver passed a group of idle natives and muttered, "They're lazy brutes." A few hours later he saw natives heaving two-hundred-pound sacks of grain onto a truck, singing in rhythm to their work. "Savages," he grumbled. "What do you expect?"

In one of the West Indies it was customary at one time for natives to hold their noses conspicuously whenever they passed an American on the street. And in

England, during the war, it was said, "The only trouble with the Yanks is that they are over-paid, over-sexed, and over here."

Polish people often called the Ukrainians "reptiles" to express their contempt for a group they regarded as ungrateful, revengeful, wily, and treacherous. At the same time Germans called their neighbors to the east "Polish cattle." The Poles retaliated with "Prussian swine"—a jibe at the presumed uncouthness and lack of honor of the Germans.

In South Africa, the English, it is said, are against the Afrikaner; both are against the Jews; all three are opposed to the Indians; while all four conspire against the native black.

In Boston, a dignitary of the Roman Catholic Church was driving along a lonesome road on the outskirts of the city. Seeing a small Negro boy trudging along, the dignitary told his chauffeur to stop and give the boy a lift. Seated together in the back of the limousine, the cleric, to make conversation, asked, "Little Boy, are you a Catholic?" Wide-eyed with alarm, the boy replied, "No sir, it's bad enough being colored without being one of those things."

Pressed to tell what Chinese people really think of Americans, a Chinese student reluctantly replied, "Well, we think they are the best of the foreign devils." This incident occurred before the Communist revolution in China. Today's youth in China are trained to think of Americans as the *worst* of the foreign devils.

In Hungary, the saying is, "An anti-Semite is a person who hates the Jews more than is absolutely necessary."

No corner of the world is free from group scorn. Being fettered to our respective cultures, we, like Charles Lamb, are bundles of prejudice.

TWO CASES

An anthropologist in his middle thirties had two young children, Susan and Tom. His work required him to live for a year with a tribe of American Indians in the home of a hospitable Indian family. He insisted, however, that his own family live in a community of white people several miles distant from the Indian reservation. Seldom would he allow Tom and Susan to come to the tribal village, though they pleaded for the privilege. And on rare occasions when they made the visit, he sternly refused to allow them to play with the friendly Indian children.

Some people, including a few of the Indians, complained that the anthropologist was untrue to the code of his profession—that he was displaying race prejudice.

The truth is otherwise. This scientist knew that tuberculosis was rife in the tribal village, and that four of the children in the household where he lived had already died of the disease. The probability of infection for his own children, if they came much in contact with the natives, was high. His better judgment told him that he should not take the risk. In this case, his ethnic avoidance was based on rational and realistic grounds. There was no feeling of antagonism involved.

The anthropologist had no generally negative attitude toward the Indians. In fact he liked them very much.

Since this case fails to illustrate what we mean by racial or ethnic prejudice, let us turn to another.

In the early summer season two Toronto newspapers carried between them holiday advertisements from approximately 100 different resorts. A Canadian social scientist, S. L. Wax, undertook an interesting experiment. To each of these hotels and resorts he wrote two letters, mailing them at the same time, and asking for room reservations for exactly the same dates. One letter he signed with the name "Mr. Greenberg," the other with the name "Mr. Lockwood." Here are the results:

> To "Mr. Greenberg":
> 52 percent of the resorts replied;
> 36 percent offered him accommodations.
> To "Mr. Lockwood":
> 95 percent of the resorts replied;
> 93 percent offered him accommodations.

Thus, nearly all of the resorts in question welcomed Mr. Lockwood as a correspondent and as a guest; but nearly half of them failed to give Mr. Greenberg the courtesy of a reply, and only slightly more than a third were willing to receive him as a guest.

None of the hotels knew "Mr. Lockwood" or "Mr. Greenberg." For all they knew "Mr. Greenberg" might be a quiet, orderly gentleman, and "Mr. Lockwood" rowdy and drunk. The decision was obviously made not on the merits of the individual, but on "Mr. Greenberg's" supposed membership in a group. He suffered discourtesy and exclusion *solely* because of his name, which aroused a prejudgment of his desirability in the eyes of the hotel managers.

Unlike our first case, this incident contains the two essential ingredients of ethnic prejudice. (1) There is definite hostility and rejection. The majority of the hotels wanted nothing to do with "Mr. Greenberg." (2) The basis of the rejection was categorical. "Mr. Greenberg" was not evaluated as an individual. Rather, he was condemned on the basis of his presumed group membership.

A close reasoner might at this point ask the question: What basic difference exists between the cases of the anthropologist and the hotels in the matter of "categorical rejection"? Did not the anthropologist reason from the high probability of infection that it would be safer not to risk contact between his children and the Indians? And did not the hotelkeepers reason from a high probability that Mr. Greenberg's ethnic membership would in fact bring them an undesirable guest? The anthropologist knew that tubercular contagion was rampant; did not the innkeepers know that "Jewish vices" were rampant and not to be risked?

This question is legitimate. If the innkeepers were basing their rejection on facts (more accurately, on a high probability that a given Jew will have undesirable traits), their action would be as rational and defensible as the anthropologist's. But we can be sure that such is not the case.

Some managers may never have had any unpleasant experiences with Jewish guests—a situation that seems likely in view of the fact that in many cases Jewish guests had never been admitted to the hotels. Or, if they have had such experiences, they have not kept a record of their frequency in comparison with objectionable non-Jewish guests. Certainly they have not consulted scientific studies concerning the relative frequency of desirable and undesirable traits in Jews and non-Jews. If they sought such evidence, they would . . . find no support for their policy of rejection.

It is, of course, possible that the manager himself was free from personal prejudice, but, if so, he was reflecting the anti-Semitism of his gentile guests. In either event our point is made.

DEFINITION

The word *prejudice*, derived from the Latin noun *praejudicium*, has, like most words, undergone a change of meaning since classical times. There are three stages in the transformation.

1. To the ancients, *praejudicium* meant a *precedent*—a judgment based on previous decisions and experiences.
2. Later, the term, in English, acquired the meaning of a judgment formed before due examination and consideration of the facts—a premature or hasty judgment.
3. Finally the term acquired also its present emotional flavor of favorableness or unfavorableness that accompanies such a prior and unsupported judgment.

Perhaps the briefest of all definitions of prejudice is: *thinking ill of others without sufficient warrant*. This crisp phrasing contains the two essential ingredients of all definitions—reference to unfounded judgment and to a feeling-tone. It is, however, too brief for complete clarity.

In the first place, it refers only to *negative* prejudice. People may be prejudiced in favor of others; they may think *well* of them without sufficient warrant. The wording offered by the *New English Dictionary* recognizes positive as well as negative prejudice:

> *A feeling, favorable or unfavorable, toward a person or thing, prior to, or not based on, actual experience.*

While it is important to bear in mind that biases may be *pro* as well as *con*, it is none the less true that *ethnic* prejudice is mostly negative. A group of students was asked to describe their attitudes toward ethnic groups. No suggestion was made that might lead them toward negative reports. Even so, they reported eight times as many antagonistic attitudes as favorable attitudes. . . . [A]ccordingly, we shall be concerned chiefly with prejudice *against*, not with prejudice *in favor of*, ethnic groups.

The phrase "thinking ill of others" is obviously an elliptical expression that must be understood to include feelings of scorn or dislike, of fear and aversion, as well as various forms of antipathetic conduct: such as talking against people, discriminating against them, or attacking them with violence.

Similarly, we need to expand the phrase "without sufficient warrant." A judgment is unwarranted whenever it lacks basis in fact. A wit defined prejudice as "being down on something you're not up on."

It is not easy to say how much fact is required in order to justify a judgment. A prejudiced person will almost certainly claim that he has sufficient warrant for his views. He will tell of bitter experiences he has had with refugees, Catholics, or Orientals. But, in most cases, it is evident that his facts are scanty and strained. He resorts to a selective sorting of his own few memories, mixes them up with hearsay, and overgeneralizes. No one can possibly know *all* refugees, Catholics, or Orientals. Hence any negative judgment of these groups *as a whole* is, strictly speaking, an instance of thinking ill without sufficient warrant.

Sometimes, the ill-thinker has no first-hand experience on which to base his judgment. A few years ago most Americans thought exceedingly ill of Turks—but very few had ever seen a Turk nor did they know any person who had seen one. Their warrant lay exclusively in what they had heard of the Armenian massacres and of the legendary crusades. On such evidence they presumed to condemn all members of a nation.

Ordinarily, prejudice manifests itself in dealing with individual members of rejected groups. But in avoiding a Negro neighbor, or in answering "Mr. Greenberg's" application for a room, we frame our action to accord with our categorical generalization of the group as a whole. We pay little or no attention to individual differences, and overlook the important fact that Negro X, our neighbor, is not Negro Y, whom we dislike for good and sufficient reason; that Mr. Greenberg, who may be a fine gentleman, is not Mr. Bloom, whom we have good reason to dislike.

So common is this process that we might define prejudice as:

> an avertive or hostile attitude toward a person who belongs to a group, simply because he belongs to that group, and is therefore presumed to have the objectionable qualities ascribed to the group.

This definition stresses the fact that while ethnic prejudice in daily life is ordinarily a matter of dealing with individual people it also entails an unwarranted idea concerning a group as a whole.

Returning to the question of "sufficient warrant," we must grant that few if any human judgments are based on absolute certainty. We can be reasonably, but not absolutely, sure that the sun will rise tomorrow, and that death and taxes will finally overtake us. The sufficient warrant for any judgment is always a matter of probabilities. Ordinarily our judgments of natural happenings are based on firmer and higher probabilities than our judgments of people. Only rarely do our categorical judgments of nations or ethnic groups have a foundation in high probability.

Take the hostile view of Nazi leaders held by most Americans during World War II. Was it prejudiced? The answer is No, because there was abundant available evidence regarding the evil policies and practices accepted as the official code of the party. True, there may have been good individuals in the party who at heart rejected the abominable program; but the probability was so high that the

Nazi group constituted an actual menace to world peace and to humane values that a realistic and justified conflict resulted. The high probability of danger removes an antagonism from the domain of prejudice into that of realistic social conflict.

In the case of gangsters, our antagonism is not a matter of prejudice, for the evidence of their antisocial conduct is conclusive. But soon the line becomes hard to draw. How about an ex-convict? It is notoriously difficult for an ex-convict to obtain a steady job where he can be self-supporting and self-respecting. Employers naturally are suspicious if they know the man's past record. But often they are more suspicious than the facts warrant. If they looked further they might find evidence that the man who stands before them is genuinely reformed, or even that he was unjustly accused in the first place. To shut the door merely because a man has a criminal record has *some* probability in its favor, for many prisoners are never reformed; but there is also an element of unwarranted prejudgment involved. We have here a true borderline instance.

We can never hope to draw a hard and fast line between "sufficient" and "insufficient" warrant. For this reason we cannot always be sure whether we are dealing with a case of prejudice or nonprejudice. Yet no one will deny that often we form judgments on the basis of scant, even nonexistent, probabilities.

Overcategorization is perhaps the commonest trick of the human mind. Given a thimbleful of facts we rush to make generalizations as large as a tub. One young boy developed the idea that all Norwegians were giants because he was impressed by the gigantic stature of Ymir in the saga, and for years was fearful lest he meet a living Norwegian. A certain man happened to know three Englishmen personally and proceeded to declare that the whole English race had the common attributes that he observed in these three.

There is a natural basis for this tendency. Life is so short, and the demands upon us for practical adjustments so great, that we cannot let our ignorance detain us in our daily transactions. We have to decide whether objects are good or bad by classes. We cannot weigh each object in the world by itself. Rough and ready rubrics, however coarse and broad, have to suffice.

Not every overblown generalization is a prejudice. Some are simply *misconceptions,* wherein we organize wrong information. One child had the idea that all people living in Minneapolis were "monopolists." And from his father he had learned that monopolists were evil folk. When in later years he discovered the confusion, his dislike of dwellers in Minneapolis vanished.

Here we have the test to help us distinguish between ordinary errors of prejudgment and prejudice. If a person is capable of rectifying his erroneous judgments in the light of new evidence he is not prejudiced. *Prejudgments become prejudices only if they are not reversible when exposed to new knowledge.* A prejudice, unlike a simple misconception, is actively resistant to all evidence that would unseat it. We tend to grow emotional when a prejudice is threatened with contradiction. Thus the difference between ordinary prejudgments and prejudice is that one can discuss and rectify a prejudgment without emotional resistance.

Taking these various considerations into account, we may now attempt a final definition of negative ethnic prejudice. . . . Each phrase in the definition represents a considerable condensation of the points we have been discussing:

> Ethnic prejudice is an antipathy based upon a faulty and inflexible generalization. It may be felt or expressed. It may be directed toward a group as a whole, or toward an individual because he is a member of that group.

The net effect of prejudice, thus defined, is to place the object of prejudice at some disadvantage not merited by his own misconduct.

IS PREJUDICE A VALUE CONCEPT?

Some authors have introduced an additional ingredient into their definitions of prejudice. They claim that attitudes are prejudiced only if they violate some important norms or values accepted in a culture. They insist that prejudice is only that type of prejudgment that is ethically disapproved in a society.

> One experiment shows that common usage of the term has this flavor. Several adult judges were asked to take statements made by ninth-grade children and sort them into piles according to the degree of "prejudice" represented. It turned out that whatever a boy may have said against girls as a group was not judged to be prejudice, for it is regarded as normal for an early adolescent to heap scorn on the opposite sex. Nor were statements made against teachers considered examples of prejudice. This antagonism, too, seemed natural to this age, and socially unimportant. But when the children expressed animosity toward labor unions, toward social classes, races or nationalities, more judgments of "prejudice" were given.
>
> In brief, the social importance of an unfair attitude entered into the judges' view of its prejudiced character. A fifteen-year-old boy who is "off" girls is not considered as biased as one who is "off" nationalities other than his own.

If we use the term in this sense we should have to say that the older caste system in India—which is now breaking down—involved no prejudice. It was simply a convenient stratification in the social structure, acceptable to nearly all citizens because it clarified the division of labor and defined social prerogatives. It was for centuries acceptable even to the untouchables because the religious doctrine of reincarnation made the arrangement seem entirely just. An untouchable was ostracized because in previous existences he failed to merit promotions to a higher caste or to a supermortal existence. He now has his just desserts and likewise an opportunity through an obedient and spiritually directed life to win advancement in future reincarnations. Assuming that this account of a happy caste system really marked Hindu society at one time, was there then no question of prejudice?

Or take the Ghetto system. Through long stretches of history Jews have been segregated in certain residential zones, sometimes with a chain around the region. Only inside were they allowed to move freely. The method had the merit of preventing unpleasant conflict, and the Jew, knowing his place, could plan his life with a certain definiteness and comfort. It could be argued that his lot was much more secure and predictable than in the modern world. There were periods in history when neither the Jew nor gentile felt particularly outraged by the system. Was prejudice then absent?

Were the ancient Greeks (or early American plantation owners) prejudiced against their hereditary class of slaves? To be sure they looked down upon them, and undoubtedly held fallacious theories concerning their inherent inferiority and "animal-like" mentality; but so natural did it all seem, so good, so proper, that there was no moral dilemma.

Even today, in certain states, a *modus vivendi** has been worked out between white and colored people. A ritual of relations is established, and most people abide unthinkingly by the realities of social structure. Since they merely follow the folkways they deny that they are prejudiced. The Negro simply knows his place, and white people know theirs. Shall we then say, as some writers have, that prejudice exists only when actions are *more* condescending, *more* negative, than the accepted culture itself prescribes? Is prejudice to be regarded merely as deviance from common practice?

Among Navaho Indians, as in many societies on earth, there is belief in witchcraft. Whoever is accused of being a witch is earnestly avoided or soundly punished on the basis of the prevailing erroneous conceptions concerning the dark powers of witches. Here, as in our preceding illustrations, all the terms of our definition of prejudice are met—but few members of the Navaho society make a moral issue of the matter. Since the rejection of witches is an accepted custom, not socially disapproved, can it be called prejudice?

What shall we say about this line of argument? It has impressed some critics so much that they hold the whole problem of prejudice to be nothing more than a value-judgment invented by "liberal intellectuals." When liberals do not approve of a folkway *they* arbitrarily call it prejudice. What they should do is to follow not their own sense of moral outrage, but consult the ethos of a culture. If the culture itself is in conflict, holding up a higher standard of conduct than many of its members practice, then we may speak of prejudice existing within the culture. Prejudice is the *moral evaluation* placed by a culture on some of its own practices. It is a designation of attitudes that are disapproved.

These critics, it would seem, confuse two separate and distinct problems. Prejudice in the simple psychological sense of negative, overgeneralized judgment exists just as surely in caste societies, slave societies, or countries believing in witchcraft as in ethically more sensitive societies. The second problem—whether prejudice is or is not attended by a sense of moral outrage—is a separate issue altogether.

To be sure, countries with a Christian and democratic tradition view ethnic prejudice with disfavor more often than do countries without this ethical tradition. And it is also probably true that "liberal intellectuals" are more likely than most people to become emotionally aroused by the problem.

Even so, there is not the slightest justification for confusing the objective facts of prejudice with cultural or ethical judgment of these facts. The unpleasant

---

* modus vivendi—manner of living, mutual accommodation. [Eds.]

flavor of a word should not mislead us into believing that it stands only for a value-judgment. Take the word *epidemic*. It suggests something disagreeable. No doubt Pasteur, the great conqueror of epidemics, hated them. But his value-judgment did not affect in the slightest degree the objective facts with which he dealt so successfully. *Syphilis* is a term flavored with opprobrium in our culture. But the emotional tinge has no bearing whatever upon the operations of the spirochete within the human frame.

Some cultures, like our own, abjure prejudice; some do not; but the fundamental psychological analysis of prejudice is the same whether we are talking about Hindus, Navahos, the Greeks of antiquity, or Middletown, U.S.A. Whenever a negative attitude toward persons is sustained by a spurious overgeneralization we encounter the syndrome of prejudice. It is not essential that people deplore this syndrome. It has existed in all ages in every country. It constitutes a bona fide psychological problem. The degree of moral indignation engendered is irrelevant.

FUNCTIONAL SIGNIFICANCE

Certain definitions of prejudice include one additional ingredient. The following is an example:

> Prejudice is a pattern of hostility in interpersonal relations which is directed against an entire group, or against its individual members; it fulfills a specific irrational function for its bearer.

The final phrase of this definition implies that negative attitudes are not prejudices unless they serve a private, self-gratifying purpose for the person who has them.

It will become abundantly clear . . . [M]uch prejudice is indeed fashioned and sustained by self-gratifying considerations. In most cases prejudice seems to have some "functional significance" for the bearer. Yet this is not always the case. Much prejudice is a matter of blind conformity with prevailing folkways. Some of it . . . has no important relation to the life-economy of the individual. For this reason it seems unwise to insist that the "irrational function" of prejudice be included in our basic definition.

ATTITUDES AND BELIEFS

We have said that an adequate definition of prejudice contains two essential ingredients. There must be an *attitude* of favor or disfavor; and it must be related to an overgeneralized (and therefore erroneous) *belief*. Prejudiced statements sometimes express the attitudinal factor, sometimes the belief factor. In the following series the first item expresses attitude, the second, belief:

> I can't abide Negroes.
> Negroes are smelly.

I wouldn't live in an apartment house with Jews.
There are a few exceptions, but in general all Jews are pretty much alike.

I don't want Japanese-Americans in my town.
Japanese-Americans are sly and tricky.

Is it important to distinguish between the attitudinal and belief aspects of prejudice? For some purposes, no. When we find one, we usually find the other. Without some generalized beliefs concerning a group as a whole, a hostile attitude could not long be sustained. In modern researches it turns out that people who express a high degree of antagonistic attitudes on a test for prejudice, also show that they believe to a high degree that the groups they are prejudiced against have a large number of objectionable qualities.

But for some purposes it is useful to distinguish attitude from belief. For example, . . . certain programs designed to reduce prejudice succeed in altering beliefs but not in changing attitudes. Beliefs, to some extent, can be rationally attacked and altered. Usually, however, they have the slippery propensity of accommodating themselves somehow to the negative attitude which is much harder to change. The following dialogue illustrates the point:

MR. X: The trouble with the Jews is that they only take care of their own group.

MR. Y: But the record of the Community Chest campaign shows that they give more generously, in proportion to their numbers, to the general charities of the community, than do non-Jews.

MR. X: That shows they are always trying to buy favor and intrude into Christian affairs. They think of nothing but money; that is why there are so many Jewish bankers.

MR. Y: But a recent study shows that the percentage of Jews in the banking business is negligible, far smaller than the percentage of non-Jews.

MR. X: That's just it; they don't go in for respectable business; they are only in the movie business or run night clubs.

Thus the belief system has a way of slithering around to justify the more permanent attitude. The process is one of *rationalization*—of the accommodation of beliefs to attitudes.

It is well to keep these two aspects of prejudice in mind, for in our subsequent discussions we shall have occasion to make use of the distinction. But wherever the term *prejudice* is used without specifying these aspects, the reader may assume that both attitude and belief are intended.

ACTING OUT PREJUDICE

What people actually do in relation to groups they dislike is not always directly related to what they think or feel about them. Two employers, for example, may dislike Jews to an equal degree. One may keep his feelings to himself and may hire Jews on the same basis as any workers—perhaps because he wants to gain goodwill for his factory or store in the Jewish community. The other may translate his dislike into his employment policy, and refuse to hire Jews. Both men are prejudiced, but only one of them practices *discrimination*. As a rule discrimination has more immediate and serious social consequences than has prejudice.

It is true that any negative attitude tends somehow, somewhere, to express itself in action. Few people keep their antipathies entirely to themselves. The more intense the attitude, the more likely it is to result in vigorously hostile action.

We may venture to distinguish certain degrees of negative action from the least energetic to the most.

1. *Antilocution*. Most people who have prejudices talk about them. With like-minded friends, occasionally with strangers, they may express their antagonism freely. But many people never go beyond this mild degree of antipathetic action.

2. *Avoidance*. If the prejudice is more intense, it leads the individual to avoid members of the disliked group, even perhaps at the cost of considerable inconvenience. In this case, the bearer of prejudice does not directly inflict harm upon the group he dislikes. He takes the burden of accommodation and withdrawal entirely upon himself.

3. *Discrimination*. Here the prejudiced person makes detrimental distinctions of an active sort. He undertakes to exclude all members of the group in question from certain types of employment, from residential housing, political rights, educational or recreational opportunities, churches, hospitals, or from some other social privileges. Segregation is an institutionalized form of discrimination, enforced legally or by common custom.

4. *Physical attack*. Under conditions of heightened emotion prejudice may lead to acts of violence or semiviolence. An unwanted Negro family may be forcibly ejected from a neighborhood, or so severely threatened that it leaves in fear. Gravestones in Jewish cemeteries may be desecrated. The Northside's Italian gang may lie in wait for the Southside's Irish gang.

5. *Extermination*. Lynchings, pogroms, massacres, and the Hitlerian program of genocide mark the ultimate degree of violent expression of prejudice.

This five-point scale is not mathematically constructed, but it serves to call attention to the enormous range of activities that may issue from prejudiced attitudes and beliefs. While many people would never move from antilocution to avoidance; or from avoidance to active discrimination, or higher on the scale, still it is true that activity on one level makes transition to a more intense level easier. It was Hitler's antilocution that led Germans to avoid their Jewish neighbors and erstwhile friends. This preparation made it easier to enact the Nürnberg laws of discrimination which, in turn, made the subsequent burning of synagogues and street attacks upon Jews seem natural. The final step in the macabre progression was the ovens at Auschwitz.

From the point of view of social consequences much "polite prejudice" is harmless enough—being confined to idle chatter. But unfortunately, the fateful progression is, in this century, growing in frequency. The resulting disruption in the human family is menacing. And as the peoples of the earth grow ever more interdependent, they can tolerate less well the mounting friction.

JOURNAL WRITINGS

1. Write a paragraph in which you **describe** a case of prejudice—one that you experienced yourself or one that you witnessed. Use detail that will make the case perfectly clear to a reader.
2. In some notes written purely for yourself, explore your own emotional responses to people who express prejudice. What are those responses? **Describe** what these responses lead you to say or do.

BRAINSTORMING AND DRAFTING

3. In a group, share the paragraph you have written for question 1 above. Explain how the case you have described fits into one of Allport's five classes of discrimination.
4. Consider Allport's **example** of the hostile view toward Nazis during World War II. He says this was not prejudice. What about the fact that many persons of German descent in this country were persecuted during this period and that the teaching of German was practically discontinued in American high schools? Write a sentence or two explaining how Allport would respond to these facts.
5. Using the library or other source, find several **definitions** of prejudice. By yourself, or in small groups, compare these definitions with Allport's. If the various definitions do not agree in all respects, draft an explanation intended to show how their differences might be reconciled; or, if they cannot be, show which version is more credible.

THE AUTHOR'S METHODS

6. After carefully examining the opening paragraphs of his essay, make a list of the means Allport uses to introduce the topic of prejudice.
7. Allport presents several definitions of prejudice. Compare some of these to see how they differ. How many different types do you find? Select the most effective and explain why you think it works well.
8. Examine the organization of Allport's essay (perhaps outlining it will help). Explain how he fits the various parts together into one large **structure.**
9. Explain why the last section (on putting prejudice into action) does or does not fit in well with his purpose of defining prejudice.

FORMAL WRITING AND RESEARCH PAPERS

10.   Consider ethnic jokes as possible **examples** of prejudice. By interviewing some friends and/or relatives, collect and **analyze** a number of such jokes. Write an essay about these jokes in which you **argue** that they are or are not examples of prejudice, basing your remarks on Allport's **definition.**

11.   Do you agree with Allport that the moral indignation engendered by prejudice is irrelevant? Write an essay of two or three fully developed paragraphs in which you explain your answer.

Geoffrey Chaucer

The Prioress's Tale

A Modernization by Robert Reilly

(ca. 1386)

Geoffrey Chaucer (ca. 1340–1400), one of the greatest poets of the English language, was the son of John Chaucer, a vintner, and Agnes de Copton. He appears to have been reared in the household of Lionel, duke of Clarence. He served in several important public capacities, both as a diplomat and civil servant. Widely read in both French and Italian, he wrote a body of poetry of which the major works are *The Canterbury Tales* and *Troilus and Criseyde.*

The Canterbury Tales is a series of stories told by pilgrims on their way from London to the shrine of St. Thomas à Becket at Canterbury. The Prioress, who is the head of a convent, tells the following story about a young boy who is murdered by Jews in an Eastern European city.

With origins as early as 1144, a strong anti-Semitic tradition persists in England. Much of this tradition focuses on accusations regarding the ritual murder of Christian children. In numerous cases the anti-Semitism resulted in riots and actual persecution of Jews; perhaps the most extreme example took place at York in 1190, when all of the members of the Jewish community were burned to death and their property seized. In 1255, ten Jews were executed for the "murder" of Hugh of Lincoln. Harsher and harsher laws were enacted against Jews. Ultimately, in 1290 (just about a century before the Prioress), King Edward I banished all Jews from England and confiscated much of their property.

PREVIEWS

A. Would you expect a nun to be prejudiced?
B. What sort of story do you think a nun on a pilgrimage might tell? Jot down some features you might expect in such a story.

PROLOG OF THE PRIORESS'S TALE

Domine dominus noster*

"O Lord, our Lord, how marvelously your name
Is spread through this large world," she said,
"Not only is your precious praise
Performed by men of dignity,
But from the mouths of children your generosity
Pours forth, for while sucking at the breast,
Sometimes they demonstrate your praise.

"Therefore, as best I'm able, in praise
Of you and of the white lily flower
Who gave you birth and remains a maid,
I'll do my best to tell a story,
Not that I may increase her honor,
For she is herself honor and the source
Of goodness, next to her Son, and the remedy of souls.

"O Mother Maiden! O Maiden Mother noble!
O bush unburned, burning in Moses' sight,
Who drew down from the Deity,
Through your humility, the Ghost who alighted in you,
Of whose power, when he enlightened your heart,
You conceived the Father's wisdom
Help me to tell a tale in your honor.

"Lady, your bounty, your magnificence,
Your virtue, and your great humility,
No tongue can express in any manner
For sometime, Lady, before men pray to you,
You anticipate in your benignity
And get us the light, by your prayer,
To guide us unto your Son so dear.

"My power's so weak, O Queen of Bliss,
To declare thy great worthiness,
That I cannot bear the burden,
But as a child of twelve months age or less
Who can scarcely express a single word,
Just so am I, and therefore I pray,
Guide the song that I shall sing of you."

---

* Lord our Lord, beginning of Psalm 8. [Eds.]

Explicit

Here begins the Prioress's Tale

There was in Asia, in a great city,
Among Christian folk, a Jewry,
Maintained by a lord of that country
For the purpose of usury and villainous gain,
Hateful to Christ and to his followers;
And through the street men might ride or walk,
For it was free and open at either end.

A little school for Christians stood
Down at the farther end, in which there were
A group of children, born of Christian blood,
Who learned in that school, year by year,
Such instruction as was the custom there,
That is to say, to sing and to read,
As small children do in their childhood.

Among these children was a widow's son
A little schoolboy, seven years of age,
Who used to go to school each day,
And also, wherever he saw an image
Of Christ's Mother, he had the custom,
As he'd been taught, to kneel down and say
His *Hail Mary*, as he goes by the way.

So this widow had taught her little son
Constantly to worship our blessed Lady,
Christ's Mother dear, and he never forgot,
For the good child will always learn quickly.
And always, when I remember this story,
Saint Nicholas stands before my eyes,
Because he, so young, did reverence to Christ.

This little child, learning his little book,
As he sat at his primer in the school,
He heard the *Alma redemptoris** sung,
As other children learned their antiphons†;
And when he could, he drew nearer and nearer,
And hearkened to every word and every note,
Until he knew the first verse by rote.

---

*A Latin hymn in honor of the Blessed Virgin Mary. [Eds.]

†A type of hymn meant to be sung alternately by two choirs. [Eds.]

He knew not what this Latin had to say,
For he was so young and tender of age,
But one day he began to beg his fellow
To explain this song in his own language,
Or to tell him why this song was used;
Very many times, upon his bare knees
He begged him to explain and declare this hymn.

His fellow, who was older than he,
Answered him thus: "This song, I have heard say,
Was made for our blissful, generous Lady
To salute her, and also to pray her
To be our help and succor when we die.
I cannot further expound this matter;
I learn the song, I know very little grammar."

"And is this song made in reverence
Of Christ's Mother?" said this innocent.
"Now, certainly, I will do my best
To learn it all before Christmas is gone.
Though I for my primer will be scolded,
And shall be beaten thrice in an hour,
I will it learn to honor Our Lady!"

His fellow taught him secretly on the way home,
Day by day, till he knew it by rote,
And then he sang it well and boldly.
From word to word, according to the notes,
Twice a day it passed through his throat,
When he went to school and homeward;
On Christ's Mother set was his intent.

As I have said, throughout the Jewry,
This little child, as he went to and fro,
Very merrily then would he sing and cry
O *Alma redemptoris* evermore.
The sweetness of Christ's Mother
So pierced his heart, that to pray to her
He could not keep from singing on the way.

Our first foe, the serpent Satan,
Who has in Jews' hearts his wasp's nest,
Swelled up and said, "O Hebrew people, alas!
Is this a thing that is honorable to you,
That such a boy shall walk as he pleases
In despite of you, and sing such sentiments,
Which are against the reverence of your laws?"

From then on the Jews conspired
To chase this innocent out of this world,
They hired a murderer for this purpose,
Who in an alley had a hidden place;
And as the child was passing by
This cursed Jew caught him, and held him fast,
And cut his throat, and cast him in a pit.

I say that in a privy they threw him
Where these Jews relieved their bowels.
O Herod's folk cursed again,
What can your evil intent avail you?
Murder will out, certainly, it will not fail,
Especially when the honor of God shall spread;
The blood cries out on your cursed deed.

O martyr, made fast to virginity,
Now you may sing, always following
The white celestial Lamb—said she—
Of which the great evangelist, Saint John,
In Patmos wrote, which says that they who go
Before this Lamb, and sing a wholly new song,
Never knew women carnally.

This poor widow waited all that night
For her little child, but he never came;
So, as soon as it was daylight,
With dreadfully pale face and busy thought,
She has at school and elsewhere him sought,
'Til finally she was able to discover
That he was last seen in the Jewry.

With mother's pity in her breast enclosed,
She goes, as if she were half out of her mind,
To every place where she supposed
It likely she might her little child find;
And ever to Christ's Mother, meek and kind,
She cried, and at last thus she did:
Among the cursed Jews she sought him.

She questions and she prays piteously
To every Jew that dwelt in that place,
To tell her if her child went by at all.
They said, "No"; but Jesus, of his grace,
Gave her the thought, within a little space,
That she cried out for her son in the place
Beside where he was cast into a pit.

O great God, that voices your praise
Through the mouths of innocents, behold your might!
This gem of chastity, this emerald,
And also of martyrdom the ruby bright,
Where he lay face up with slashed throat,
He began to sing *Alma redemptoris*
So loud that all the place began to ring.

The Christian people who were going through the street
Came to wonder about this thing
And hastily they sent for the provost;
He came at once without the least delay,
And praises Christ who is king of heaven,
And also His Mother, the honor of mankind,
And after that he had the Jews bound.

The child with piteous lamentation
Was taken up, singing his song all the time,
And with honor of great procession
They carried him into the nearest abbey.
His mother fainting by his bier lay;
Scarcely might the people who were there
Bring this new Rachel from his bier.

With torment and with shameful death
This provost put to death each Jew
At once, who of this murder knew.
He would not tolerate such cursedness.
"Evil shall have what evil shall deserve";
Therefore, he had them drawn by wild horses
And afterwards he hung them according to law.

Upon this bier lies this innocent
Before the main altar, while the mass lasts;
And after that, the abbot with his monks
Have hastened to bury him very quickly;
And when they cast holy water on him,
Yet spoke this child, when holy water was sprinkled,
And sang *O Alma redemptoris mater!*

This abbot, who was a holy man,
As monks are—or else ought to be—
Began to address this young child,
And said, "O dear child, I beseech you,
By the power of the Holy Trinity,
Tell me what is the cause of your singing,
Since it seems to me your throat is cut?"

"My throat is cut to my neck bone,"
Said this child, "and, naturally,
I should have died, yes, a long time ago.
But Jesus Christ, as you may find in books,
Wills that his glory last and be in mind,
And for the honor of his Mother dear
Yet may I sing *O Alma* loud and clear.

"Christ's Mother sweet, this well of mercy,
I always loved, after my ability;
And when I had to give up my life,
She came to me and bid me to sing
This anthem truly in my dying,
As you have heard, and when I had sung,
I thought she placed a grain upon my tongue.

"Wherefore I sing, and must certainly sing
In honor of that blessed, generous Maiden,
'Til from my tongue the grain is taken;
And after that she said this to me:
'My little child, now will I fetch you,
When the grain is taken from your tongue.
Be not afraid, I will not forsake you.'"

This holy monk, this abbot, him I mean,
Pulled out his tongue, and took away the grain,
And he gave up the ghost very quietly.
And when this abbot had this wonder seen,
His salt tears trickled down as rain,
And he fell grovelling flat upon the ground,
And he lay as still as if he had been bound.

The monks also lay on the pavement
Weeping, and praising Christ's Mother dear,
And after that rose, and went forth,
And took away this martyr from his bier;
And in a tomb of clear marble stones
They enclosed his sweet little body.
There he is now, God grant that we meet!

O young Hugh of Lincoln, slain also
By cursed Jews, as is well known,
For it is only a little while ago,
Pray also for us, we inconstant, sinful folk
That, of his mercy, God so merciful
Multiply his great mercy on us,
For reverence of his Mother Mary. Amen.

Here is ended the Prioress's Tale.

JOURNAL WRITINGS

1. Refer back to the notes you made about features that you expected to find in this tale; compare these notes with actual features that you did find in the Prioress's story. Jot down any differences.
2. Does this tale arouse feelings of sympathy or antipathy for the Jews? Explain your reasons for feeling one way or the other.

BRAINSTORMING AND DRAFTING

3. By yourself or in a group, list reasons the Prioress gives for telling this story—use these lists to **define** her purpose. Discuss the tale in the light of this purpose. How well does she do what she claims? What effects does she produce unintentionally? Begin organizing some materials for a longer paper dealing with the tale's purpose.
4. Discuss the sections of the poem that you regard as anti-Semitic. In a sentence or two, explain why you regard each section as anti-Semitic.

THE AUTHOR'S METHODS

5. Chaucer has chosen to assign this tale to the Prioress. How does the fact that she is a nun and a devout Christian affect your perception of the story?
6. Find some clues in the text that hint at Chaucer's attitude toward the Prioress. What makes his attitude difficult to define? Why might he be deliberately **ambiguous?** Answer the same questions with respect to his attitude toward the Jews.
7. Explain what sort of feelings you have about the last stanza. What does the author do in the stanza that is designed to evoke feelings?

FORMAL WRITING AND RESEARCH PAPERS

8. Identify several biblical **allusions** in this tale. Write a paragraph about each allusion, discussing its appropriateness in context. If you can detect a pattern in the allusions, perhaps you can use these paragraphs as the basis for a longer paper explaining the function of allusions in the tale.
9. Look up some of the official pronouncements of the Roman Catholic Church about Jews and Judaism. Look specifically for pronouncements in the period 1200–1400 A.D. (a Catholic encyclopedia or dictionary of Catholicism would be a good place to start). Write a paper in which you explore the relationship between the official position of the Church and the attitudes voiced by the Prioress.
10. Imagine this tale *without* the miracle of the child's song. Make a list of ways in which the story becomes more effective as a narrative because Chaucer ends it with this supernatural intervention (perhaps you will want to discuss possible benefits with your classmates or your instructor). Use your list to write an argument *in favor* of including the miracle.

Dennis Prager and Joseph Telushkin

Why Jew-Hatred Is Unique

(1983)

Dennis Prager (born 1948) is a writer and lecturer. A native of Brooklyn, New York, he received his B.A. from Brooklyn College in 1970. He has been a fellow of the School of International Affairs of Columbia University and director of the Brandeis-Bardin Institute. He and Joseph Telushkin (born 1948) have also collaborated in writing *Nine Questions People Ask About Judaism*.

In this chapter from their book, *Why the Jews?: The Reason for Antisemitism,* the authors examine the nature of Jew-hatred and argue that it is not similar to other forms of prejudice.

PREVIEWS

A.   Examine your own feelings about Jews as objectively as you can. How do you feel? What is the basis for your feelings?

B.   If you are Jewish, how do you experience the feelings of non-Jews toward you? Why do you think they feel as they do?

Hatred of the Jew has been humanity's greatest hatred. While hatred of other groups has always existed, no hatred has been as universal, as deep, or as permanent as antisemitism.

The Jews have been objects of hatred in pagan, religious, and secular societies. Fascists have accused them of being Communists, and Communists have branded them capitalists. Jews who live in non-Jewish societies have been accused of having dual loyalties, and Jews who live in the Jewish state have been condemned as "racists." Poor Jews are bullied, and rich Jews are resented. Jews have been branded as both rootless cosmopolitans and ethnic chauvinists. Jews who assimilate are often called a fifth column, while those who stay together often spark hatred for remaining different. Literally hundreds of millions of people have believed that the Jews drink the blood of non-Jews, that they cause plagues and poison wells, that they plan to conquer the world, and that they murdered God Himself.

The *universality* of antisemitism is attested to by innumerable facts, the most dramatic being that Jews have been expelled from nearly every country in which they have resided. Jews were expelled from England in 1290, France in 1306 and 1394, Hungary between 1349 and 1360, Austria in 1421, numerous localities in Germany between the fourteenth and sixteenth centuries, Lithuania in 1445 and 1495, Spain in 1492, Portugal in 1497, and Bohemia and Moravia in 1744–45. Between the fifteenth century and 1772, Jews were not allowed into Russia, and when finally admitted, they were restricted to one area, the Pale of Settlement. Between 1948 and 1967 nearly all the Jews of Aden, Algeria, Egypt, Iraq, Syria, and Yemen, though not officially expelled, fled these countries, fearing for their lives.

The *depth* of antisemitism is evidenced by the frequency with which hostility against Jews has gone far beyond discrimination and erupted into sustained violence. In nearly every country where Jews have lived, they have at some time been subjected to beatings, torture, and murder, solely because they were Jews. In the Russian Empire during the nineteenth and twentieth centuries, mass beatings and murders of Jews were so common that a word, *pogrom*, was coined to describe such incidents. And these pogroms were viewed by their antisemitic perpetrators as being of such significance that they were equated with the saving of Russia.

On a number of occasions even beating and murdering Jewish communities were not deemed sufficient. Antisemitic passions have run so deep that only the actual annihilation of the Jewish people could solve what came to be called the "Jewish Problem." The basic source of ancient Jewish history, the Bible, depicts two attempts to destroy the Jewish people, the attempt by Pharaoh and the Egyptians (Exodus 1:15–22) and that of Haman and the Persians (Book of Esther). While it is true that the historicity of these biblical accounts has not been proven or disproven by nonbiblical sources; few would dispute the supposition that in ancient times attempts were made to destroy the Jews. Indeed the first recorded reference to Jews in non-Jewish sources, the Mernephta stele, written by an Egyptian king about 1220 B.C.E.,* states "Israel is no more." Jewish writings from the earliest times until the present are replete with references to attempts by non-Jews to destroy the Jewish people. Psalms 8 3:5 describes the enemies of the Jews as proponents of genocide: "Come, and let us cut them off from being a nation, that the Name of Israel may no more be remembered." Just how precarious Jews have viewed their survival is reflected in a statement from the ancient and still recited Passover Haggadah: "In every generation they rise against us in order to annihilate us."

On two occasions in the last 350 years annihilation campaigns have been waged against the Jews: the Chmelnitzky massacres in Eastern Europe in 1648–49, and the Nazi destruction of Jews throughout Europe between 1939 and 1945.

For various reasons the Chmelnitzky massacres are today not well known

---

* [Authors' Note] Many contemporary scholars use the universal B.C.E. (Before the Common Era), rather than the Christian-based B.C. (before Christ), and C.E. (common era) instead of A.D. (*anno Domini*, "in the year of the Lord").

among Jews and virtually unknown among non-Jews; perhaps the Holocaust tends to overshadow all previous Jewish sufferings. Yet without denying the unique aspects of the Nazi Holocaust, we are obliged to cite a number of significant similarities between it and the Chmelnitzky massacres. In both instances all Jews, including infants, were targeted for murder; the general populaces nearly always joined in the attacks; and the torture and degradation of Jews were an integral part of the murderers' procedures. These characteristics are evidenced by the following contemporaneous description of a typical Chmelnitzky massacre:

> Some of them [the Jews] had their skins flayed off them and their flesh was flung to the dogs. The hands and feet of others were cut off and they were flung onto the roadway where carts ran over them and they were trodden underfoot by horse. . . . And many were buried alive. Children were slaughtered in their mothers' bosoms and many children were torn apart like fish. They ripped up the bellies of pregnant women, took out the unborn children, and flung them in their faces. They tore open the bellies of some of them and placed a living cat within the belly and left them alive thus, first cutting off their hands so that they should not be able to take the living cat out of the belly . . . and there was never an unnatural death in the world that they did not inflict upon them.

The *permanence* (as well as depth) of antisemitism is attested to by the obsessive attention given to the "Jewish Problem" by antisemites throughout history. *At one time or another nearly every one of the world's greatest powers that has had a large Jewish population has regarded this group, which never constituted more than a small percentage of the population, as an enemy.* To the Roman Empire in the first century, the Christian world for over fifteen centuries, the Nazi Reich, and to the Arabs, Muslims, and the Soviet Union today, the Jews have been or are regarded as an insufferable threat.

Jews have been perceived as so dangerous that even after their expulsion or destruction hatred and fear of them remain. The depiction of Jews as ritual murderers of young Christian children in Chaucer's "Prioress's Tale" in *The Canterbury Tales* one hundred years after all Jews had been expelled from England, and the characterization of Jews as usurers who wish to collect their interest in flesh in Shakespeare's *The Merchant of Venice* three hundred years after the Jewish expulsion, attest to the durability of antisemitism. A contemporary example is Poland in 1968 when for months the greatest issue on Polish radio, television, and in Polish newspapers was the "Unmasking of Zionists in Poland." Of the 33 million citizens of Poland in 1968, the Jews numbered about 20,000, or less than one-fifteenth of 1 percent.

How are the universality, depth, and permanence of antisemitism to be explained? Why such hatred and fear of people who never constituted more than a small minority among those who most hated and feared them? Why, nearly always and nearly everywhere, the Jews?

Many answers have been offered by scholars. These include, most commonly, economic factors, the need for scapegoats, ethnic hatred, xenophobia, resentment of Jewish affluence and professional success, and religious bigotry. But ultimately these answers do not explain antisemitism: they only explain what factors have *exacerbated* antisemitism and caused it to erupt in a given circumstance. None accounts for the universality, depth, and persistence of antisemitism. In fact, we have encountered virtually no study of antisemitism that even attempts to offer a universal explanation of Jew-hatred. Nearly every study of antisemitism consists almost solely of historical narrative, claiming implicitly that no universal reason for antisemitism exists.

We reject this approach. To ignore the question of ultimate causation, or to deny that there are ultimate causes for antisemitism, contradicts both common sense and history. Antisemitism has existed too long and in too many disparate cultures to ignore the problem of ultimate cause and/or to claim that new or indigenous factors are responsible every time it erupts. Factors specific to a given society help account for the manner or time in which antisemitism erupts, but they do not explain its genesis—why antisemitism at all? To cite but one example, the depressed economy in Germany in the 1920s and 1930s may help to explain why and when the Nazis came to power, but it does not explain why Nazis hated Jews, let alone why they wanted to murder every Jew in the world. Economic depressions do not account for gas chambers.

The very consistency of the passions Jews have aroused demands a consistent explanation. Ancient Egyptians, Greeks, and Romans, medieval and many modern Christians and Muslims, and Nazis and Communists have perhaps only one thing in common: they have all counted the Jews as their enemy, often their greatest enemy. Why?

This question has been posed only by modern Jews. From the recorded beginnings of Jewish history until the modern age, Jews never asked, "Why the Jews?" They knew exactly why. Throughout their history Jews have regarded Jew-hatred as an inevitable consequence of their Jewishness. Contrary to modern understandings of antisemitism, the age-old Jewish understanding of antisemitism does posit a universal reason for Jew-hatred: Judaism. And the historical record confirms the traditional Jewish view of antisemitism that the Jews were hated because of distinctly Jewish factors. Modern attempts to dejudaize antisemitism, to attribute it to economic, social, and political reasons, and universalize it into merely another instance of bigotry are as opposed to the facts of Jewish history as they are to the historical Jewish understanding of antisemitism.

Antisemites have not opposed Jews because Jews are affluent—poor Jews have always been as hated; or strong—weak Jews have simply invited antisemitic bullies; or because Jews may have unpleasant personalities—kindly Jews have never been spared by antisemites; or because ruling classes focus worker discontent onto Jews—precapitalist and contemporary noncapitalist societies such as those of the Soviet Union and other Communist states have been considerably more antisemitic than capitalist societies. Antisemites have hated Jews because Jews are Jewish. Christian antisemites ceased hating rich Jews when they became Christians. The same has held true for virtually all other antisemites except the Nazis, whom we shall discuss later.

The ultimate cause of antisemitism is that which has made Jews Jewish—Judaism. There are four basic reasons for this and each revolves around the theme of a Jewish *challenge* to the values of non-Jews.

1. For thousands of years Judaism has consisted of three components: God, Torah, and Israel; that is, the Jewish (conception of) God, Jewish law, and Jewish nationhood. Jews' allegiance to any of these components has been a major source of antisemitism because it has rendered the Jew an outsider, and most important, it has been regarded by non-Jews (often correctly) as challenging the validity of the non-Jews' god(s), law(s), and/or national allegiance.

By affirming what they considered to be the one and only God of all mankind, thereby denying legitimacy to everyone else's gods, the Jews entered history—and have often been since—at war with other people's most cherished values. The Jews compounded this hostility by living by their own all-encompassing set of laws in addition to or even instead of the laws of their non-Jewish neighbors. And by continually asserting their own national identity in addition to or instead of the national identity of the non-Jews among whom they lived, Jews have created or intensified antisemitic passions.

2. From its earliest days the *raison d'être** of Judaism has been to change the world for the better (in the words of an ancient Jewish prayer still recited daily, "to perfect the world under the rule of God"). This attempt to change the world, to challenge the gods, religious or secular, of the societies around them, and to make moral demands upon others (even when not done expressly in the name of Judaism) has constantly been a source of tension between Jews and non-Jews.

3. As if the above were not enough, Judaism has also held from the earliest time that the Jews were chosen by God to achieve this mission of perfecting the world. This doctrine of the Jews' divine election has been a major cause of antisemitism.

4. As a result of the Jews' commitment to Judaism, they have led higher-quality lives than their non-Jewish neighbors in almost every society in which they have lived. This higher quality of life has expressed itself in a variety of ways. To cite but a few examples: Jews have nearly always been better educated; Jewish family life has usually been far more stable; Jews aided one another considerably more than their non-Jewish neighbors aided each other; and Jews have been far less likely to become drunk, beat their wives, abandon their children, and the like. As a result of these factors, the quality of life of the average Jew, no matter how poor, was higher than that of a comparable non-Jew in that society.

This higher quality of life among Jews, which, as we shall show, directly results from Judaism, has challenged non-Jews and provoked profound envy and hostility. In this way, too, Judaism has been the source of antisemitism.

Once we perceive that it is Judaism which is the root cause of antisemitism, otherwise irrational and inexplicable aspects of antisemitism become rationally explicable.

We now understand why so many non-Jews have regarded the mere existence of Jews—no matter how few—as terribly threatening. The mere existence of the Jews, with their different values and allegiances, constituted a threat to the prevailing order.

---

* raison d'être—reason for being, cause for existence. [Eds.]

Since Judaism is the root cause of antisemitism, Jews, *unlike victims of racial or ethnic prejudice,* could in every instance of antisemitism, except Nazism, escape persecution. For thousands of years and until this day, Jews who abandoned their Jewish identity and assumed the majority's religious and national identity were no longer persecuted.*

For these reasons, Jews have always seen antisemitism as the somewhat inevitable and often quite rational, though of course immoral, response to Judaism. Thus, Jews until the modern era, and religious Jews to this day, would describe every Jew murdered by an antisemite not as a victim of ethnic prejudice but as having died *al kiddush hashem,* a martyr to the cause of Judaism, sanctifying the name of God before the world.

Once one understands why Judaism has precipitated antisemitism, the unique universality, depth, and permanence of Jew-hatred also become understandable. It takes infinitely more than economic tensions or racial prejudice to create the animosity—so often to the point of torturing children and murdering whole communities—that Jews have created throughout their long history. Only something representing a threat to the core values, allegiances, and beliefs of others could arouse such universal, deep, and lasting hatred. This Judaism has done.

That Judaism, rather than race or economics, is at the root of antisemitism also helps to explain why totalitarian regimes are inevitably antisemitic. Totalitarian regimes by definition aim to control the totality of their citizens' lives and can therefore tolerate no uncontrolled religious or national expressions, both of which are part of Judaism.

Once the Jewish bases of antisemitism are recognized, the only solutions to the "Jewish Problem," as far as antisemites are concerned, are obvious. The Jews must either convert, be expelled, or be murdered. Indeed, in the 1880s, the Russian czar's procurator of the Holy Synod and architect of Russian government policy at the time, Constantine Pobedonostsev, is said to have offered precisely this advice. One-third of the Jews living in the Russian Empire, he said, should be converted to Christianity, one-third should be expelled from the empire, and one-third should be put to death. In fact, for the last two thousand years, this has repeatedly been the chronological order of antisemitic acts. First, attempts would be made to convert the Jews. When the Jews refused, they were often expelled. And when even expulsion failed to solve the "Jewish Problem," there remained one "Final Solution," which is precisely the name the Nazis gave to their plan to murder all the Jews.

---

* [Authors' Note] There is one apparent exception to this rule, the Marranos of Spain. In the fourteenth and fifteenth centuries, Jews who converted to Christianity in Spain were not easily accepted into Christian society. But this was overwhelmingly due to the circumstances of the Jews' conversions. The Christian hierarchy was reluctant to accept these Jewish converts as genuine Christians because it knew that they had converted under threats of expulsion or death, and therefore the sincerity of the Jews' Christianity was questioned. But the Jews who proved by their behavior that they had become religious Christians were accepted. And, in fact, almost all of these tens of thousands of Marranos who remained in Spain did assimilate into Spanish society.

It is also clear that antisemitism is not ethnic or racial prejudice, though it obviously shares certain features with them. Antisemites persecuted Jews for the same reasons Romans persecuted Christians, Nazis tortured members of the Resistance, and Soviets imprison dissidents. In each instance the group is persecuted because its different beliefs represent a threat to the persecuting group. This hatred must be understood as being very different from a prejudice. Blacks in America, for example, have been discriminated against because of the physical fact of their blackness, not because of specific Black ideas or beliefs which they represent. Hatred of Blacks is racial prejudice. Blacks cannot stop being Black. But Soviet dissidents can stop being dissenters, and a Jew has always been able to, and in general still can, stop being a Jew. The single exception to this rule has been Nazi antisemitism. But even this apparent exception confirms the Jewish basis of antisemitism. The Nazis simply maintained that Jews could never really become non-Jews, that no matter how much Jews may consciously attempt to appear and behave like non-Jews, they nevertheless retain the values of Judaism. Nazi anti-Jewish "racism" emanated from a hatred of Judaism and what Jews represent. Nazi racism is *ex post facto;* first came the antisemitism, then came the racist doctrine to explain it.

Antisemitism is, therefore, as Jews have always regarded it: a response to Jews and their way of life. The charges made against Jews, that they poison wells, drink blood, plot to take over the governments of the world, or control world finance, are hallucinatory. But the roots of antisemitism are not. The real reasons antisemites hate Jews and the accusations they make against them are not necessarily the same. This is hardly uncommon. When people harbor hatreds, individually or communally, they rarely articulate rationally the reasons for their hatred.

We should not be so naive as to regard all antisemitic accusations as the reasons for the antisemitism. For example, the modern belief that economic factors cause antisemitism, besides confusing exacerbating factors with causes of antisemitism, grants the accusations of antisemites far too much credence. It is reminiscent of some historians' preoccupation with determining the historical accuracy of the Christian claim that the Jews killed Jesus, because Christian antisemites called Jews "Christ Killers," as if proving one way or another would end Christian antisemitism. The question for those wishing to understand the roots of antisemitism is not whether some Jews helped execute Jesus around the year 30 C.E. or how great a role Jews played in the German economy. The question is why, to begin with, people hate Jews. The answer is Judaism, its distinctiveness and its challenge, and we have offered four general reasons why this is so. . . .

JOURNAL WRITINGS

1.   Prager and Telushkin say the hatred of Jews is beyond prejudice. Recall Allport's **definitions** of prejudice. In light of those definitions, respond to Prager and Telushkin's assertion in a sentence or two.

BRAINSTORMING AND DRAFTING

2.   In the paragraph numbered 4 (page 42), Prager and Telushkin assert that Jews, because of their commitment to Judaism, lead "higher-quality lives." Carefully consider the points they list. Perhaps you could discuss their points with your classmates. Evaluate their case, and write a brief response to the paragraph, explaining why you agree or disagree with them.

THE AUTHORS' METHODS

3.   Outline this chapter to discover its organization. Where is the thesis? Do you find the organization effective? Write a brief critique of the organization, pointing out its strengths and weaknesses.

FORMAL WRITING AND RESEARCH PAPERS

4.   Consult *The New Cambridge Modern History* to find out about pogroms. Write a short report giving some basic facts about them.
5.   In the third paragraph Prager and Telushkin list instances of Jews being expelled from various countries. Pick one of the countries from their list. Starting with the source listed above, find out as much as possible about the particular case. Form an opinion based on the facts. Write a documented paper that presents the evidence supporting your opinion.
6.   A number of anti-Semitic groups (skinheads and others) have been active in the United States during the past few years. By using a general periodical index, identify one such group. Then consult *Psychological Abstracts* or *Sociological Abstracts* to see if any studies have been done of the group. Write a report that describes the group and analyzes the activities in a psychological or sociological context.

Langston Hughes

Haircuts and Paris

(1965)

Langston Hughes (1902–1967), famous for his stories about the character "Simple," also wrote poetry and worked as an editor and translator. Born in Joplin, Missouri, he attended Columbia University for one year and later graduated from Lincoln University in Pennsylvania. His experiences working as a seaman and living in Mexico, France, and Italy are reflected in his work. He is widely recognized for his significant contribution to the movement of black creativity known as the Harlem Renaissance.

Simple, who lives in Harlem, daydreams about the advantages of living in Paris, especially because he could go to any barbershop he might choose.

PREVIEW

Try to imagine how you would feel if you were refused service in any public place.

"If I had ever been to Paris," said Simple, "I would like to go there one more time once."

"Since you have never been in Paris, how do you know you would?" I asked.

"I know I would, because a friend of mine just came back to New York and told me all about it," said Simple. "He is as dark as me, real colored in complexion, and he said in Paris for the first time in his life, he felt like a *man*."

"I do not see why a Negro has to go all the way to Paris to feel like a man," I said.

"Some do and some don't need to go," said Simple. "Me, I feel like a man anywhere in this American country, because I feel like a man *inside* myself. But some folks are not made like that. Some black men do not feel like men when they are surrounded by white folks who look at them like as if blackness was bad manners or something. It is not bad manners to be black, any more than it is good manners to be white. God made both of us. But white folks in the U.S.A. has got the upper hand—the whip hand—which they have had since the days of slavery. White folks still have a million and one ways of keeping a Negro from feeling like a man—especially if he is a weak Negro like my friend what went to Paris and stayed a year and for the first time said he felt like a man. Me, in Paris, I would feel like *two* men. That is why I want to go, and return, then go again."

"Once you got to Paris, why would you come back?" I asked.

"To get some corn bread and pigs' feet and greens," said Simple, "which is what my friend said he missed so much in Paris. Also to see Jackie Mabley* and Pigmeat Markham[†] and Nipsey Russell[‡] at the Apollo,[§] and to hear the Caravans[||] sing gospel songs one more time. Then I would return to Paris and stay another year. My friend says the wonderful thing about Europe is that a Negro can get his hair cut anywhere. That is certainly not true in the U.S.A., where a Negro has to look for a *colored* barbershop—in spite of the Civil Rights Bill—just like in most towns down South he still has to look for a *colored* restaurant in which to eat, a *colored* hospital in which to die, and a *colored* undertaker to get buried by, also a *colored* cemetery to be buried in. They has no such jackassery in Europe."

"What?" I said.

"White folks are not jackasses in Europe," said Simple. "In Europe they accepts colored peoples as human beings. Therefore Negroes can get their hair cut anywhere in any barbershop in Paris, France, or Rome, Italy, or Madrid, Spain. Also Negroes can get shaved. Here in the United States to get shaved, a white barber is liable to cut a colored man's throat instead of trimming his beard. It would take a brave black man to set down in a white barbershop in Memphis, Jackson, Tougaloo, Birmingham, Atlanta, or anywhere else down South. With all the love he has got in his heart, I have never read in no newspaper yet where Rev. Martin Luther King has gone into a white barbershop down South and said, 'I love you, barber. Cut my hair.' Martin Luther King has got more sense than that. He knows prayer might not prevail in no white barbershop in Jackson, Birmingham, Atlanta, or Selma. Or in Boston, either."

"You are right," I said. "My dentist's son, colored, attends college in a small town in Ohio where there is no colored barbershop. This young student has to travel forty miles to Toledo to get his hair cut. The white barbershops near the college will not serve him. They politely claim they do not know how to cut colored hair."

"If white Americans can learn how to fly past Venus, go in orbit and make telestars, it looks like to me white barbers in Ohio could learn how to cut colored hair," said Simple. "But since they also might cut my throat, I prefer to go to Paris, get my hair cut there, then come home for corn bread, and return to Paris again. Even here in Harlem, I thank God for Paris barbers. Amen!"

---

*Jackie Mabley—actress and comedienne. [Eds.]

[†] Pigmeat Markham—jazz drummer. [Eds.]

[‡] Nipsey Russell—comedian. [Eds.]

[§] The Apollo—a theater in Harlem. [Eds.]

[||] The Caravans—a group of gospel singers. [Eds.]

JOURNAL WRITINGS

1. What makes this story funny? Pick a few examples of its humor and use them in a brief entry that **analyzes** its humor. You might consider, for example, how Hughes uses humor to promote understanding of the **characters** and situation or how humor is appropriate for an uncomfortable subject.
2. What is the significance of the haircuts? Barbers can no longer legally turn blacks away, but other forms of discrimination exist. Identify a few of these forms and write brief comments on their importance.

BRAINSTORMING AND DRAFTING

3. Discuss the psychology of race relations. Do you think black Americans still feel that white Americans have "the whip hand"? Why? Write about some things that individuals can do to remedy this situation.
4. " . . . he felt like a man." What does it mean to feel like a man? Why is this feeling so important to so many people? Is this an experience from which women are excluded?

THE AUTHOR'S METHODS

5. Simple lists a group of items for which he would return. What do these represent?
6. This entire story is a dialogue, a conversation between two people. How does the unnamed other speaker contribute to the effectiveness of the story? What is the significance of his having no name?
7. Notice the number of references to throat cutting in this story. Discuss their effect in a brief paragraph.

CREATIVE PROJECT

8. Write a short **short story** (no longer than Hughes's) about an incident of discrimination.

Conrad Kent Rivers

A Mourning Letter from Paris

(1968)

During his short life, Conrad Kent Rivers (1933–1968) produced a small but impressive body of poetry, including *The Still Voice of Harlem, The Wright Poems,* and several other volumes. He also wrote some short stories and one play. Born in Atlantic City, New Jersey, he graduated from Wilberforce University and became a teacher in the Chicago public schools.

In the following poem (spoken as if to his dead friend, Richard Wright), Rivers draws upon his experience as an expatriate in Paris to describe the quality of life for a black person in Paris and his own emotional state, living in a foreign country and cut off from his roots.

PREVIEWS

A. Does the idea of Paris hold a certain fascination for you? List the ideas about Paris which appeal to your imagination (be as specific and concrete as possible). If you have not read Hughes's story, do so. Are the ideas you have about Paris similar to Simple's or different?

B. Consider this statement: "A prophet is without honor in his own country." Write a sentence or two explaining what you think this statement means.

(for Richard Wright)

All night I walked among your spirits Richard:
the Paris you adored is most politely dead.

I found French-speaking bigots and some sterile blacks,
bright African boys forgetting their ancestral robes,
a few men of color seeking the same French girl.

Polished Americans watched the stark reality
of mass integration, pretending not to look homeward
where the high ground smelled of their daughters' death.

I searched for the skin of your bones, Richard.
Mississippi called you back to her genuine hard clay,
but here one finds a groove, adapts, then lingers on.

For me, my good dead friend of searing words
and thirsty truth, the road to Paris leads back home:
one gets to miss the stir of Harlem's honeyed voice,
or one forgets the joy to which we were born.

JOURNAL WRITINGS

1. What does Rivers "mourn"?
2. Have you ever wanted to run away from your own problems? Can it be
   done? Consider the works of both Hughes and Rivers as responses to the
   desire to run away from it all.

BRAINSTORMING AND DRAFTING

3. Discuss both this poem and Hughes's story with some of your classmates.
   As you talk, list whatever similarities and differences you discover. After the
   discussion, decide whether the similarities or differences are more important. Write a paper that explains why you decided in favor of similarities or
   differences.

THE AUTHOR'S METHODS

4. Write a short piece in which you explain why you think Rivers is or is not
   making a pun on "mourning."
5. What is the poetic form?
6. Look carefully at some of the words in this poem—for example, "politely,"
   "bigots," "sterile," "ancestral," "men of color," "stark," "genuine hard clay,"
   "groove," "searing," "thirsty," "honeyed." How do they work in context?
   What do they contribute to the poem's meaning? Write an essay in which
   you evaluate Rivers's use of words.
7. What is the **tone** of this poem? What evidence can you find to support your
   idea about its tone? **Describe** the tone as clearly and concisely as you can.

FORMAL WRITING AND RESEARCH PAPERS

8. Who is Richard Wright? How is the dedication of this poem appropriate?
   Write a paper in which you use biographical facts (available in a work such as
   Black American Writers) about Wright to answer the second question.
9. Research Rivers's work (again, using *Black American Writers*), read some of
   it, and write a paper interpreting another one of his poems that you find
   particularly moving.
10. **Analyze** Hughes's story and Rivers's poem, concentrating on their reasons
    for going away and for coming back. Write a paper in which you discuss the
    significance of the similarities and/or differences that you find.

Hanif Kureishi

Bradford

(1986)

Hanif Kureishi (born 1954) graduated from King's College, University of
London, and has primarily devoted himself to drama and film. He has
written eleven plays; like this article, his play *Borderline* deals with the lives
of Asian immigrants in the United Kingdom. Perhaps he is most famous for
the screenplay of *My Beautiful Laundrette.*

Bradford is a city in north central England. Formerly a major
manufacturing center, it now suffers from severe economic depression.
The author, a second-generation Pakistani immigrant, visits there to observe
and report on the political and social conditions of the Pakistani residents.

PREVIEW

Think about this situation: Some new people, who are quite different in one way or
another, move into your neighborhood. Try to imagine how you would receive them—
what your emotional response to them might be. In a few sentences, describe your
feelings and actions toward them.

Some time ago, I noticed that there was something unusual about the city of
Bradford, something that distinguished it from other northern industrial cities.

To begin with, there was Ray Honeyford. Three years ago Honeyford, the
headmaster of Bradford's Drummond Middle School, wrote a short, three-page
article that was published in the *Salisbury Review.* The *Salisbury Review* has a
circulation of about 1,000, but the impact of Honeyford's article was felt beyond
the magazine's readership. It was discussed in the *Yorkshire Post* and reprinted in
the local *Telegraph and Argus.* A parents' group demanded Honeyford's resignation. His school was then boycotted, and children, instructed by their parents not
to attend classes, gathered outside, shouting abuse at the man who weeks before
was their teacher. There were fights, sometimes physical brawls, between local
leaders and politicians. The "Honeyford Affair," as it became known, attracted so
much attention that it became common every morning to come upon national
journalists and television crews outside the school. And when it was finally

---

[Author's Note] This piece couldn't have been written without the help of Helen Jacobus.

resolved that Honeyford had to go, the Bradford district council had to pay him over £160,000 to get him to leave: ten times his annual salary.

But there were other things about Bradford. The Yorkshire Ripper was from Bradford.* The prostitutes who came down to London on the train on "cheap-day return" tickets were from Bradford. At a time when the game of soccer was threatened by so many troubles, Bradford seemed to have troubles of the most extreme kind. Days after the deaths in Brussels at the Heysel stadium, forty-seven Bradford football supporters were killed in one of the worst fires in the history of the sport. Eighteen months later, there was yet another fire, and a match stopped because of crowd violence.

There was more: there was unemployment in excess of twenty percent; there was a prominent branch of the National Front†; there were regular racial attacks on taxi drivers; there were stories of forced emigration; there was a mayor from a village in Pakistan. Bradford, I felt, was a place I had to see for myself, because it seemed that so many important issues, of race, culture, nationalism, and educa-tion, were evident in an extremely concentrated way in this medium-sized city of 400,000 people, situated between the much larger cities of Manchester and Leeds. These were issues that related to the whole notion of what it was to be British and what that would mean in the future. Bradford seemed to be a microcosm of a larger British society that was struggling to find a sense of itself, even as it was undergoing radical change. And it was a struggle not seen by the people governing the country, who, after all, had been brought up in a world far different from today's. In 1945, England ruled over six hundred million people. And there were few black faces on its streets.

The first thing you notice as you get on the Inter-City train to Bradford is that the first three carriages are first class. These are followed by the first-class restaurant car. Then you are free to sit down. But if the train is packed and you cannot find an empty seat, you have to stand. You stand for the whole journey, with other people lying on the floor around you, and you look through at the empty seats in the first-class carriages where men sit in their shirt-sleeves doing important work and not looking up. The ticket collector has to climb over us to get to them.

Like the porters on the station, the ticket collector was black, probably of West Indian origin. In other words, black British. Most of the men fixing the railway line, in their luminous orange jackets, with pickaxes over their shoulders, were also black. The guard on the train was Pakistani, or should I say another Briton, probably born here, and therefore "black."

When I got to Bradford I took a taxi. It was simple: Bradford is full of taxis. Raise an arm and three taxis rush at you. Like most taxi drivers in Bradford, the driver was Asian and his car had furry, bright purple seats, covered with the kind of material people in the suburbs sometimes put on the lids of their toilets. It

---

*The Yorkshire Ripper—Peter B. Sutcliffe, who murdered thirteen young women in northern England between 1975 and 1980. [Eds.]

†The National Front—a right-wing British political party. [Eds.]

smelled of perfume, and Indian music was playing. The taxi driver had a Brad-ford-Pakistani accent, a cross between the north of England and *Lahore,** which sounds odd the first few times you hear it. Mentioning the accent irritates people in Bradford. How else do you expect people to talk? they say. And they are right. But hearing it for the first time disconcerted me because I found that I associated northern accents with white faces, with people who eat puddings, with Geoffrey Boycott and Roy Hattersley.†

We drove up a steep hill, which overlooked the city. In the distance there were modern buildings and among them the older mill chimneys and factories with boarded-up windows. We passed Priestley Road. J.B. Priestley was born in Bradford, and in the early sixties both John Braine and Alan Sillitoe set novels here.‡ I wondered what the writing of the next fifteen years would be like. There were, I was to learn, stories in abundance to be told.

The previous day I had watched one of my favourite films, Keith Waterhouse and Willis Hall's *Billy Liar*, also written in the early sixties. Billy works for an undertaker and there is a scene in which Billy tries to seduce one of his old girlfriends in a graveyard. Now I passed that old graveyard. It was full of monstrous mausoleums, some with spires thirty feet high; others were works of architecture in themselves, with arches, urns and roofs. They dated from the late nineteenth century and contained the bones of the great mill barons and their families. In *The Waste Land* T.S. Eliot wrote of the "silk hat on a Bradford millionaire." Now the mills and the millionaires had nearly disappeared. In the cemetery there were some white youths on a Youth Opportunity Scheme, hacking unenthusiastically at the weeds, clearing a path. This was the only work that could be found for them, doing up the old cemetery.

I was staying in a house near the cemetery. The houses were of a good size, well-built with three bedrooms and lofts. Their front doors were open and the street was full of kids running in and out. Women constantly crossed the street and stood on each others' doorsteps, talking. An old man with a stick walked along slowly. He stopped to pat a child who was crying so much I thought she would explode. He carried on patting her head, and she carried on crying, until finally he decided to enter the house and fetched the child's young sister.

The houses were overcrowded—if you looked inside you would usually see five or six adults sitting in the front room—and there wasn't much furniture: often the linoleum on the floor was torn and curling, and a bare lightbulb hung from the ceiling. The wallpaper was peeling from the walls.

Each house had a concrete yard at the back, where women and young female children were always hanging out the washing: the cleaning of clothes never appeared to stop. There was one man—his house was especially run-down—who

---

* Lahore—major city in Pakistan. [Eds.]

† Geoffrey Boycott—English cricket champion; Roy Hattersley—a leader of the British Labour Party. [Eds.]

‡ J. B. Priestley—English novelist and playwright; John Braine—English novelist; Alan Sillitoe— English novelist. [Eds.]

had recently acquired a new car. He walked round and round it; he was proud of his car, and occasionally caressed it.

It was everything I imagined a Bradford working-class community would be like, except that there was one difference. Everyone I'd seen since I arrived was Pakistani. I had yet to see a white face.

The women covered their heads. And while the older ones wore jumpers and overcoats, underneath they, like the young girls, wore *salwar kamiz,* the Pakistani long tops over baggy trousers. If I ignored the dark Victorian buildings around me, I could imagine that everyone was back in their village in Pakistan.

That evening, Jane—the friend I was staying with—and I decided to go out. We walked back down the hill and into the centre of town. It looked like many other town centres in Britain. The subways under the roundabouts stank of urine; graffiti defaced them and lakes of rain-water gathered at the bottom of the stairs. There was a massive shopping centre with unnatural lighting; some kids were rollerskating through it, pursued by three pink-faced security guards in paramilitary outfits. The shops were also the same: Rymans, Smiths, Dixons, the National Westminister Bank. I hadn't become accustomed to Bradford and found myself making simple comparisons with London. The clothes people wore were shabby and old; they looked as if they'd been bought in jumble sales or second-hand shops. And their faces had an unhealthy aspect: some were malnourished.

As we crossed the city, I could see that some parts looked old-fashioned. They reminded me of my English grandfather and the Britain of my childhood: pigeon-keeping, greyhound racing, roast beef eating and pianos in pubs. Outside the centre, there were shops you'd rarely see in London now: drapers, ironmongers, fish and chip shops that still used newspaper wrappers, barber's shops with photographs in the window of men with Everly Brothers haircuts. And here, among all this, I also saw the Islamic Library and the Ambala Sweet Centre where you could buy spices: dhaniya, haldi, garam masala, and dhal and ladies' fingers. There were Asian video shops where you could buy tapes of the songs of Master Sajjad, Nayyara, Alamgir, Nazeen and M. Ali Shahaiky.

Jane and I went to a bar. It was a cross between a pub and a night-club. At the entrance the bouncer laid his hands on my shoulders and told me I could not go in.

"Why not?" I asked.

"You're not wearing any trousers."

I looked down at my legs in astonishment.

"Are you sure?" I asked.

"No trousers," he said, "no entry."

Jeans, it seems, were not acceptable.

We walked on to another place. This time we got in. It too was very smart and entirely white. The young men had dressed up in open-necked shirts, Top Shop grey slacks and Ravel loafers. They stood around quietly in groups. The young women had also gone to a lot of trouble: some of them looked like models, in their extravagant dresses and high heels. But the women and the men were not talking to each other. We had a drink and left. Jane said she wanted me to see a working men's club.

The working men's club turned out to be near an estate, populated, like most Bradford estates, mostly by whites. The Asians tended to own their homes. They had difficulty acquiring council houses or flats, and were harassed and abused when they moved on to white estates.

The estate was scruffy: some of the flats were boarded up, rubbish blew about; the balconies looked as if they were about to crash off the side of the building. The club itself was in a large modern building. We weren't members of course, but the man on the door agreed to let us in.

There were three large rooms. One was like a pub; another was a snooker room. In the largest room at least 150 people sat around tables in families. At one end was a stage. A white man in evening dress was banging furiously at a drum-kit. Another played the organ. The noise was unbearable.

At the bar, it was mostly elderly men. They sat beside each other. But they didn't talk. They had drawn, pale faces and thin, narrow bodies that expanded dramatically at the stomach and then disappeared into the massive jutting band of their trousers. They had little legs. They wore suits, the men. They had dressed up for the evening.

Here there were no Asians either, and I wanted to go to an Asian bar, but it was getting late and the bars were closing, at ten-thirty as they do outside London. We got a taxi and drove across town. The streets got rougher and rougher. We left the main road and suddenly were in a leafy, almost suburban area. The houses here were large, occupied I imagined by clerks, insurance salesmen, business people. We stopped outside a detached three-storey house that seemed to be surrounded by an extraordinary amount of darkness and shadow. There was one light on, in the kitchen, and the woman inside was Sonia Sutcliffe, the wife of the Yorkshire Ripper, an ex-schoolteacher. I thought of Peter Sutcliffe telling his wife he was the Yorkshire Ripper. He had wanted to tell her himself; he insisted on it. Many of his victims had come from the surrounding area.

The surrounding area was mostly an Asian district and here the pubs stayed open late, sometimes until two in the morning. There were no trouser rules.

During the day in this part of town the Asian kids would be playing in the streets. The women, most of them uneducated, illiterate, unable to speak English, would talk in doorways as they did where I was staying.

It was around midnight, and men were only now leaving their houses—the women remaining behind with the children—and walking down the street to the pub. Jane said it stayed open late with police permission. It gave the police an opportunity to find out what was going on: their spies and informers could keep an eye on people. Wherever you went in Bradford, people talked about spies and informers: who was and who wasn't. I'd never known anything like it, but then I'd never known any other city, except perhaps Karachi*, in which politics was such a dominant part of daily life. Apparently there was money to be made working for the police and reporting what was going on: what the Asian militants were doing; what the racists were doing; who the journalists were talking to; what attacks or demonstrations were planned; what vigilante groups were being formed.

---

* Karachi—formerly the capital of Pakistan. [Eds.]

The pub was packed with Asian men and they still kept arriving. They knew each other and embraced enthusiastically. There were few women and all but three were white. Asian men and white women kissed in corners. As we squeezed in, Jane said she knew several white women who were having affairs with Asian men, affairs that had sometimes gone on for years. The men had married Pakistani women, often out of family pressure, and frequently the women were from the villages. The Asian women had a terrible time in Bradford.

The music was loud and some people were dancing, elbow to elbow, only able in the crush to shake their heads and shuffle their feet. There was a lot of very un-Islamic drinking. I noticed two Asian girls. They stood out, with their bright jewellery and pretty clothes. They were with Asian men. Their men looked inhibited and the girls left early. Jane, who was a journalist, recognized a number of prostitutes in the pub. She'd interviewed them at the time of the Ripper. One stood by Jane and kept pulling at her jumper. "Where did you get that jumper? How much was it?" she kept saying. Jane said the prostitutes hadn't stopped work during the time of the Ripper. They couldn't afford to. Instead, they'd worked in pairs, one girl fucking the men, while the other stood by with a knife in her hand.

In 1933, when J.B. Priestley was preparing his *English Journey*, he found three Englands. There was guide-book England, of palaces and forests; nineteenth-century industrial England of factories and suburbs; and contemporary England of by-passes and suburbs. Now, half a century later, there is another England as well: the inner city.

In front of me, in this pub, there were five or six gay men and two lesbian couples. Three white kids wore black leather jackets and had mohicans: their mauve, red and yellow hair stood up straight for a good twelve inches and curved across their heads like a feather glued on its thin edge to a billiard ball. And there were the Asians. This was not one large solid community with a shared outlook, common beliefs and an established form of life; not Orwell's "one family with the wrong members in control." It was diverse, disparate, strikingly various.

Jane introduced me to a young Asian man, an activist and local political star from his time of being on trial as one of the Bradford Twelve. I was pleased to meet him. In 1981, a group of twelve youths, fearing a racial attack in the aftermath of the terrible assault on Asians by skinheads in Southall in London, had made a number of petrol bombs. But they were caught and charged under the Explosives Act with conspiracy—a charge normally intended for urban terrorists. It was eleven months before they were acquitted.

I greeted him enthusiastically. He, with less enthusiasm, asked me if I'd written a film called *My Beautiful Laundrette*. I said yes, I had, and he started to curse me: I was a fascist, a reactionary. He was shouting. Then he seemed to run out of words and pulled back to hit me. But just as he raised his fist, his companions grabbed his arm and dragged him away.

I said to Jane that I thought the next day we should do something less exhausting. We could visit a school.

I had heard that there was to be a ceremony for a new school that was opening, the Zakariya Girls School. The large community hall was already packed with three hundred Asian men when I arrived. Then someone took my arm, to eject me, I thought. But instead I was led to the front row, where I found myself sitting next to three white policemen and assorted white dignitaries, both women and men, in smart Sunday-school clothes.

On the high stage sat local councillors, a white Muslim in white turban and robes, and various Asian men. A white man was addressing the audience, the MP for Scarborough, Sir Michael Shaw. "You have come into our community," he was saying, "and you must become part of that community. All branches must lead to one trunk, which is the British way of life. We mustn't retire to our own communities and shut ourselves out. Yet you have felt you needed schools of your own . . ."

The MP was followed by a man who appeared to be a home-grown Batley citizen. "As a practising Roman Catholic, I sympathize with you, having had a Catholic education myself," he said, and went on to say how good he thought the Islamic school would be.

Finally the man from the local mosque read some verses from the Koran. The local policemen cupped their hands and lowered their heads in true multi-cultural fashion. The other whites near me, frantically looking around at each other, quickly followed suit. Then Indian sweets were brought round, which the polite English ladies picked politely at.

I left the hall and walked up the hill towards the school. The policeman followed me, holding the hands of the six or seven Asian children that surrounded him.

Batley is outside Bradford, on the way to Leeds. It is a small town surrounded by countryside and hills. The view from the hill into the valley and then up into the hills was exquisite. In the town there was a large Asian community. The Zakariya Girls School had actually been started two years ago as a "pirate" school, not having received approval from the Department of Education until an extension was built. Now it was finished. And today it became the first high school of its kind—an Islamic school for girls—to be officially registered under the Education Act. As a pirate school it had been a large, overcrowded old house on the top of a hill. Now, outside, was a new two-storey building. It was spacious, clean, modern.

I went in and looked around. Most of the books were on the Koran or Islam, on prayer or on the prophet Mohammed. The walls were covered with verses from the Koran. And despite its being a girls school there were no girls there and no Asian women, just the men and lots of little boys in green, blue and brown caps, running about.

The idea for the school had been the pop star Cat Stevens's, and he had raised most of the money for it privately, it was said, from Saudi Arabia. Stevens, who had changed his name to Yusaf Islam, was quoted as saying that he had tried everything, running the gamut of international novelties to find spiritual satisfaction: materialism, sex, drugs, Buddhism, Christianity and finally Islam. I wondered if it was entirely arbitrary that he'd ended with Islam or whether perhaps today, the circumstances being slightly different, we could as easily have been at the opening of a Buddhist school.

Yusaf Islam was not at the school but his assistant, Ibrahim, was. Ibrahim was the white Muslim in the white robes with the white turban who spoke earlier. There was supposed to be a press conference, but nothing was happening; everything was disorganized. Ibrahim came and sat beside me. I asked him if he'd talk about the school. He was, he said, very keen; the school had been the result of so much effort and organization, so much goodness. I looked at him. He seemed preternaturally good and calm.

Ibrahim was from Newcastle, and had a long ginger beard. (I remembered someone saying to me in Pakistan that the only growth industry in Islamic countries was in human hair on the face.) Ibrahim's epiphany had occurred on a trip to South Africa. There, seeing black and white men praying together in a mosque, he decided to convert to Islam.

He told me about the way the school worked. The human face, for instance, or the face of any animate being, could not be represented at the school. And dancing would not be encouraged, nor the playing of musical instruments. Surely, he said, looking at me, his face full of conviction, the human voice was expressive enough? When I said this would probably rule out the possibility of the girls taking either art or music O-Levels*, he nodded sadly and admitted that it would.

And modern literature? I asked.

He nodded sadly again and said it would be studied "in a critical light."

I said I was glad to hear it. But what about science?

That was to be studied in a critical light too, since—and here he took a deep breath—he didn't accept Darwinism or any theory of evolution because, well, because the presence of monkeys who hadn't changed into men disproved it all.

I took another close look at him. He obviously believed these things. But why was he being so apologetic?

As I walked back down the hill I thought about the issues raised by the Zakariya Girls School. There were times, I thought, when to be accommodating you had to bend over backwards so far that you fell over. Since the mid-sixties the English liberal has seen the traditional hierarchies and divisions of British life challenged, if not destroyed. Assumptions of irrevocable, useful and moral differences— between classes, men and women, gays and straights, older and younger people, developed and underdeveloped societies—had changed for good. The commonly made distinction between "higher" and "lower" cultures had become suspect. It had become questionable philosophically to apply criteria of judgement available in one society to events in another: there could not be any independent or bridging method of evaluation. And it followed that we should be able, as a broad, humane and pluralistic society, to sustain a wide range of disparate groups living in their own way. And if one of these groups wanted *halal* meat†, Islamic schools,

---

* O-Levels—examinations certifying high school competence. [Eds.]

† *Halal* meat—meat butchered according to Islamic religious principles. [Eds.]

anti-Darwinism and an intimate knowledge of the Koran for its girls, so be it. As it was, there had been Catholic schools and Jewish schools for years.

But Islamic schools like the one in Batley appeared to violate the principles of a liberal education, and the very ideas to which the school owed its existence. And because of the community's religious beliefs, so important to its members, the future prospects for the girls were reduced. Was that the choice they had made? Did the Asian community really want this kind of separate education anyway? And if it did, how many wanted it? Or was it only a few earnest and repressed believers, all men, frightened of England and their daughters' sexuality?

The house Delius* was born in, in Bradford, was now the Council of Mosques, which looked after the interests of the Bradford Muslims. There are 60,000 Muslims and thirty Muslim organizations in Bradford. Chowdhury Khan, the President of the Council, told me about the relations between men and women in Islam and the problem of girls' schools.

He said there were no women in the Council because "we respect them too much." I mentioned that I found this a little perplexing, but he ignored me, adding that this is also why women were not encouraged to have jobs or careers.

"Women's interests," he said confidently, "are being looked after."

And the girls'?

After the age of twelve, he said, women should not mix with men. That was why more single-sex schools were required in Bradford. The local council had agreed that this was desirable and would provide more single-sex schools when resources were available. He added that despite the Labour Party Manifesto, Neil Kinnock† approved of this.

I said I doubted this.

Anyway, he continued, the local Labour Party was lobbying for more single-sex schools after having tried, in the sixties, to provide mixed-sex schools. But— and this he emphasized—the Council of Mosques wanted single-sex schools *not* Islamic ones or racially segregated schools. He banged on his desk, No, no, no! No apartheid!

He wanted the state to understand that, while Muslim children would inevitably become westernized—they were reconciled to that—they still wanted their children to learn about Islam at school, to learn subcontinental languages and be taught the history, politics and geography of India, Pakistan and Bangladesh. Surely, he added, the white British would be interested in this too. After all, the relations between England and the subcontinent had always been closer than those between Britain and France, say.

I found Chowdhury Khan to be a difficult and sometimes strange man. But his values, and the values of the Council he represented, are fairly straightforward. He believes in the pre-eminent value of the family and, for example, the

---

* Delius, Frederick (1862–1934)—English classical composer. [Eds.]

† Neil Kinnock—leader of the British Labour Party. [Eds.]

importance of religion in establishing morality. He also believes in the innately inferior position of women. He dislikes liberalism in all its forms, and is an advocate of severe and vengeful retribution against law-breakers.

These are extremely conservative and traditional views. But they are also, isolated from the specifics of their subcontinental context, the values championed by Ray Honeyford, among others. There were a number of interesting ironies developing.

I sought out the younger, more militant section of the community. How did its members see their place in Britain?

When I was in my teens, in the mid-sixties, there was much talk of the "problems" that kids of my colour and generation faced in Britain because of our racial mix or because our parents were immigrants. We didn't know where we belonged, it was said; we were neither fish nor fowl. I remember reading that kind of thing in the newspaper. We were frequently referred to as "second-generation immigrants" just so there was no mistake about our not really belonging in Britain. We were "Britain's children without a home". The phrase "caught between two cultures" was a favourite. It was a little too triumphant for me. Anyway, this view was wrong. It has been easier for us than for our parents. For them Britain really had been a strange land and it must have been hard to feel part of a society if you had spent a good deal of your life elsewhere and intended to return: most immigrants from the Indian subcontinent came to Britain to make money and then go home. Most of the Pakistanis in Bradford had come from one specific district, Mirpur, because that was where the Bradford mill-owners happened to look for cheap labour twenty-five years ago. And many, once here, stayed for good; it was not possible to go back. Yet when they got older the immigrants found they hadn't really made a place for themselves in Britain. They missed the old country. They'd always thought of Britain as a kind of long stop-over rather than the final resting place it would turn out to be.

But for me and the others of my generation born here, Britain was always where we belonged, even when we were told—often in terms of racial abuse— that this was not so. Far from being a conflict of cultures, our lives seemed to synthesize disparate elements: the pub, the mosque, two or three languages, rock 'n' roll, Indian films. Our extended family and our British individuality co-mingled.

Tariq was twenty-two. His office was bare in the modern style: there was a desk; there was a computer. The building was paid for by the EEC* and Bradford Council. His job was to advise on the setting-up of businesses and on related legal matters. He also advised the Labour Party on its economic policy. In fact, although so young, Tariq had been active in politics for a number of years: at the age of sixteen, he had been chairman of the Asian Youth Movement, which was founded in 1978 after the National Front began marching on Bradford. But few of

---

* EEC—European Economic Community. [Eds.]

the other young men I'd met in Bradford had Tariq's sense of direction or ambition, including the young activists known as the Bradford Twelve. Five years after their acquittal, most of them were, like Tariq, very active—fighting deportations, monitoring racist organizations, advising on multi-cultural education— but, like other young people in Bradford, they were unemployed. They hung around the pubs; their politics were obscure; they were "anti-fascist" but it was difficult to know what they were for. Unlike their parents, who'd come here for a specific purpose, to make a life in the affluent west away from poverty and lack of opportunity, they, born here, had inherited only pointlessness and emptiness. The emptiness, that is, derived not from racial concerns but economic ones.

Tariq took me to a Pakistani café. Bradford was full of them. They were like English working men's cafés, except the food was Pakistani, you ate with your fingers and there was always water on the table. The waiter spoke to us in Punjabi and Tariq replied. Then the waiter looked at me and asked a question. I looked vague, nodded stupidly and felt ashamed. Tariq realized I could only speak English.

How many languages did he speak?

Four: English, Malay, Urdu and Punjabi.

I told him about the school I'd visited.

Tariq was against Islamic schools. He thought they made it harder for Asian kids in Britain to get qualifications than in ordinary, mixed-race, mixed-sex schools. He said the people who wanted such schools were not representative; they just made a lot of noise and made the community look like it was made up of separatists, which it was not.

He wasn't a separatist, he said. He wanted the integration of all into the society. But for him the problem of integration was adjacent to the problem of being poor in Britain: how could people feel themselves to be active participants in the life of a society when they were suffering all the wretchedness of bad housing, poor insulation and the indignity of having their gas and electricity disconnected; or when they were turning to loan sharks to pay their bills; or when they felt themselves being dissipated by unemployment; and when they weren't being properly educated, because the resources for a proper education didn't exist.

There was one Asian in Bradford it was crucial to talk to. He'd had political power. For a year he'd been mayor, and as Britain's first Asian or black mayor he received much attention. He'd also had a terrible time.

I talked to Mohammed Ajeeb in the nineteenth-century town hall. The town hall was a monument to Bradford's long-gone splendour and pride. Later I ran into him at Bradford's superb Museum of Film, Television and Photography, where a huge photo of him and his wife was unveiled. Ajeeb is a tall, modest man, sincere, sometimes openly uncertain and highly regarded for his tenacity by the Labour leader Neil Kinnock. Ajeeb is careful in his conversation. He lacks the confident politician's polish: from him, I heard no well-articulated banalities. He is from a small village in the Punjab. When we met at the Museum, we talked about the differences between us, and he admitted that it had been quite a feat for someone like him to have got so far in Britain. In Pakistan, with its petrified feudal system, he would never have been able to transcend his background.

During his time in office, a stand at the Valley Parade football ground had burned down, killing fifty-six people and injuring 300 others. There was the Honeyford affair, about which he had been notoriously outspoken ("I cannot see," he said in a speech that contributed to Honeyford's removal, "the unity of our great city being destroyed by one man"). As mayor, Ajeeb moved through areas of Bradford society to which he never had access before, and the racism he experienced, both explicit and covert, was of a viciousness he hadn't anticipated. And it was relentless. His house was attacked, and he, as mayor, was forced to move; and at Grimsby Town football ground, when he presented a cheque to the families of those killed in the fire, the crowd abused him with racist slogans; finally, several thousand football supporters started chanting Honeyford's name so loudly that Ajeeb was unable to complete his speech. He received sackfuls of hate mail and few letters of support.

Ajeeb said that no culture could remain static, neither British nor Pakistani. And while groups liked to cling to the old ways and there would be conflict, eventually different groups would intermingle. For him the important thing was that minorities secure political power for themselves. At the same time, he said that, although he wanted to become a Parliamentary candidate, no one would offer him a constituency where he could stand. This was, he thought, because he was Asian and the Labour Party feared that the white working class wouldn't vote for him. He could stand as Parliamentary candidate only in a black area, which seemed fine to him for the time being; he was prepared to do that.

There were others who weren't prepared to put up with the racism in the trade union movement and in the Labour Party itself in the way Ajeeb had. I met a middle-aged Indian man, a tax inspector, who had been in the Labour Party for at least ten years. He had offered to help canvas during the local council elections—on a white council estate. He was told that it wouldn't be to the party's advantage for him to help in a white area. He was so offended that he offered his services to the Tories. Although he hated Margaret Thatcher, he found the Tories welcomed him. He started to lecture on the subject of Asians in Britain to various Tory groups and Rotary Club dinners, until he found himself talking at the Wakefield Police College. At the Wakefield Police College he encountered the worst racists he had ever seen in his life.

He did not need to go into details. Only a few months before, at an anti-apartheid demonstration outside South Africa House in London, I'd been standing by a police line when a policeman started to talk to me. He spoke in a low voice, as if he were telling me about the traffic in Piccadilly. "You bastards," he said. "We hate you, we don't want you here. Everything would be all right, there'd be none of this, if you pissed off home." And he went on like that, fixing me with a stare. "You wogs, you coons, you blacks, we hate you all."

Ajeeb said that if there was anything he clung to when things became unbearable, it was the knowledge that the British electorate always rejected the far Right. They had never voted in significant numbers for neo-fascist groups like the National Front and the British National Party. Even the so-called New Right, a prominent and noisy group of journalists, lecturers and intellectuals, had no great popular following. People knew what viciousness underlay their ideas, he said.

Some of the views of the New Right, Ajeeb believed, had much in common with proletarian far-right organizations like the National Front: its members held to the notion of white racial superiority, they believed in repatriation and they argued that the mixing of cultures would lead to the degeneration of British culture. Ajeeb argued that they used the rhetoric of "culture" and "religion" and "nationhood" as a fig-leaf; in the end they wished to defend a mythical idea of white culture. Honeyford was associated with the New Right, and what he and people like him wanted, Ajeeb said, was for Asians to behave exactly like the whites. And if they didn't do this, they should leave.

This movement known as the New Right is grouped around the Conservative Philosophy Group and the *Salisbury Review,* the magazine that published Honeyford's article. The group is a loose affiliation of individuals with similar views. A number of them are graduates of Peterhouse, Cambridge. These include John Vincent, Professor of History at Bristol University, who writes a weekly column for the *Sun;* Colin Welch, a columnist for the *Spectator.*

Like a lot of people in Bradford, Ajeeb became agitated on the subject of the New Right and Honeyford's relationship with it. But how important was it? What did the views of a few extremists really matter? So what if they wrote for influential papers? At least they weren't on the street wearing boots. But the ideas expressed by Honeyford had split Bradford apart. These ideas were alive and active in the city, entering into arguments about education, housing, citizenship, health, food and politics. Bradford was a city in which ideas carried knives.

Ray Honeyford went to Bradford's Drummond Middle School as Headmaster in January 1980. The children were aged between nine and thirteen. At the time the school was fifty percent Asian. When he left last spring it was ninety-five percent.

Honeyford is from a working-class background. He failed his exams for grammar school, and from the age of fifteen worked for ten years for a company that makes dessicated coconut. In his late twenties, he attended a two-year teacher-training course at Didsbury College, and later got further degrees from the universities of Lancaster and Manchester. He described himself as a Marxist, and was a member of the Labour Party. But all that changed when he began teaching at a mixed-race school. He submitted an unsolicited article to the *Salisbury Review,* and the article, entitled "Education and Race—An Alternative View", was accepted.

The article is a polemic. It argues that the multi-racial policies endorsed by various members of the teaching establishment are damaging the English way of life, and that proper English people should resist these assaults on the "British traditions of understatement, civilized discourse and respect for reason." It wasn't too surprising that a polemic of this sort written by the headmaster of a school made up almost entirely of Asian children was seen to be controversial.

But the real problem wasn't the polemic but the rhetorical asides and parentheticals. Honeyford mentions the "hysterical political temperament of the Indian subcontinent," and describes Asians as "these people" (in an earlier article, they are "settler children"). A Sikh is "half-educated and volatile," and black intellectuals are "aggressive." Honeyford then goes on to attack Pakistan itself, which in a curious non-sequitur seems to be responsible for British drug problems:

> Pakistan is a country which cannot cope with democracy; under martial law since 1977, it is ruled by a military tyrant who, in the opinion of at least half his country-men, had his predecessor judicially murdered. A country, moreover, which despite disproportionate western aid because of its important strategic position, remains for most of its people obstinately backward. Corruption at every level combines with unspeakable treatment not only of criminals, but of those who dare to question Islamic orthodoxy as interpreted by a despot. Even as I write, wounded dissidents are chained to hospital beds awaiting their fate. Pakistan, too, is the heroin capital of the world. (A fact which is now reflected in the drug problems of English cities with Asian populations.)

It is perhaps not unreasonable that some people felt the article was expressing more than merely an alternative view on matters of education.

Honeyford wrote a second piece for the *Salisbury Review*, equally "tolerant," "reasonable" and "civilized," but this one was noticed by someone in Bradford's education department, and then the trouble started—the protests, the boycott, the enormous publicity. A little research revealed that Honeyford's asides were a feature of most of his freelance journalism, his most noteworthy being his reference in the *Times Educational Supplement* to an Asian parent who visited him wanting to talk about his child's education: his accent, it seems, was "like that of Peter Sellers's Indian doctor on an off day."

The difficulty about the "Honeyford Affair" was that it did not involve only Honeyford. His views are related to the much larger issue of what it is to be British, and what Britian should be in the future. And these views are, again, most clearly stated by the New Right, with which Honeyford closely identified himself. "He is," Honeyford said of Roger Scruton, the high Tory editor of the *Salisbury Review*, "the most brilliant man I have ever met."

It would be easy to exaggerate the influence of the New Right. It would be equally easy to dismiss it. But it is worth bearing in mind that shortly after Honeyford was dismissed, he was invited to 10 Downing Street to help advise Margaret Thatcher on Tory education policy. Thatcher has also attended New Right "think tanks," organized by the Conservative Philosophy Group. So too have Paul Johnson, Tom Stoppard, Hugh Trevor-Roper and Enoch Powell*.

The essential tenet of the New Right is expressed in the editorial of the first issue of the *Salisbury Review*: "the consciousness of nationhood is the highest form of political consciousness." For Maurice Cowling, Scruton's tutor at Peter-

---

* Paul Johnson—English author and editor; Tom Stoppard—English playwright; Hugh Trevor-Roper—master of Peterhouse College, Cambridge; Enoch Powell—classical scholar and Conservative politician. [Eds.]

house in Cambridge, the consciousness of nationhood requires "a unity of national sentiment." Honeyford's less elegant phrase is the "unity notion of culture." The real sense underlying these rather abstract phrases is expressed in the view the New Right holds of people who are British but not white: as Ajeeb pointed out, Asians are acceptable as long as they behave like whites; if not, they should leave. This explains why anti-racism and multi-racial policies in education are, for the New Right, so inflammatory: they erode the "consciousness of nationhood." For Scruton, anti-racism is virtually treason. In 1985, he wrote that

> Those who are concerned about racism in Britain, that call British society "racist," have no genuine attachment to British customs and institutions, or any genuine allegiance to the Crown.

The implications are fascinating to contemplate. John Casey is a Fellow of Caius College, Cambridge, and co-founded the Conservative Philosophy Group with Scruton. Four years ago, in a talk entitled "One Nation—The Politics of Race," delivered to the same Conservative Philosophy Group attended by the Prime Minister, Casey proposed that the legal status of Britain's black community be altered retroactively, "so that its members became guest workers . . . who would eventually, over a period of years, return to their countries of origin." "The great majority of people," Casey added, dissociating himself from the argument, "are actually or potentially hostile to the multi-racial society which all decent persons are supposed to accept."

This "great majority" excludes, I suppose, those who brought over the Afro-Caribbean and Asian workers—encouraged by the British government—to work in the mills, on the railways and in the hospitals. These are the same workers who, along with their children, are now part of the "immigrant and immigrant-descended population" which, according to Casey, should be repatriated. It is strange how the meaning of the word "immigrant" has changed. Americans, Australians, Italians, and Irish are not immigrants. It isn't Rupert Murdoch, Clive James or Kiri Te Kanawa who will be on their way*: it is black people.

There is a word you hear in Bradford all the time, in pubs, shops, discos, schools and on the streets. The word is "culture." It is a word often used by the New Right, who frequently cite T.S. Eliot: that culture is a whole way of life, manifesting itself in the individual, in the group and in the society. It is everything we do and the particular way in which we do it. For Eliot culture "includes all the characteristic activities of the people: Derby Day, Henley regatta, Cowes, the Twelfth of August, a cup final, the dog races, the pin-table, Wensleydale cheese, boiled cabbage cut into sections, beetroot in vinegar, nineteenth-century gothic churches and the music of Elgar."

If one were compiling such a list today there would have to be numerous additions to the characteristic activities of the British people. They would include: yoga exercises, going to Indian restaurants, the music of Bob Marley, the

---

* Rupert Murdoch—Australian publisher; Clive James—writer, broadcaster, and television critic; Kiri Te Kanawa—New Zealand opera singer. [Eds.]

novels of Salman Rushdie, Zen Buddhism, the Hare Krishna Temple, as well as the films of Sylvester Stallone, therapy, hamburgers, visits to gay bars, the dole office and the taking of drugs.

Merely by putting these two, rather arbitrary, lists side by side, it is possible to see the kinds of changes that have occurred in Britain since the end of the war. It is the first list, Eliot's list, that represents the New Right's vision of England. And for them unity can only be maintained by opposing those seen to be outside the culture. In an Oxbridge common-room, there is order, tradition, a settled way of doing things. Outside there is chaos: there are the barbarians and philistines.

Among all the talk of unity on the New Right, there is no sense of the vast differences in attitude, life-style and belief, or in class, race and sexual preference, that *already* exist in British society: the differences between those in work and those out of it; between those who have families and those who don't; and, importantly, between those who live in the North and those in the South. Sometimes, especially in the poor white areas of Bradford where there is so much squalor, poverty and manifest desperation, I could have been in another country. This was not anything like the south of England.

And of course from the New Right's talk of unity, we get no sense of the racism all black people face in Britain: the violence, abuse and discrimination in jobs, housing, policing and political life. In 1985 in Bradford there were 111 recorded incidents of racist attacks on Asians, and in the first three months of 1986 there were seventy-nine.

But how cold they are, these words: "in the first three months of 1986 there were seventy-nine." They describe an Asian man being slashed in a pub by a white gang. Or they describe a Friday evening last April when a taxi company known to employ Asian drivers received a "block booking" for six cabs to collect passengers at the Jack and Jill Nightclub. Mohammed Saeed was the first to arrive. He remembers nothing from then on until he woke seven hours later in the intensive care ward of the hospital. This is because when he arrived, his windscreen and side window were smashed and he drove into a wall. And because he was then dragged from the car, kicked and beaten on the head with iron bars, and left on the pavement unconscious. He was left there because by then the second taxi had arrived, but Mohammed Suleiman, seeing what lay ahead, reversed his car at high speed: but not before the twenty or thirty whites rushing towards him had succeeded in smashing his windows with chair legs and bats. His radio call, warning the other drivers, was received too late by Javed Iqbal. "I was," he told the *Guardian* later, "bedridden for nearly a fortnight and I've still got double vision. I can't go out on my own."

JOURNAL WRITINGS

1.   Write a paragraph **describing** Ray Honeyford that will give the reader, in the most concise and precise form, a clear picture of his personality.
2.   How does this article affect you? How might it affect an English reader differently?

BRAINSTORMING AND DRAFTING

3. Who is prejudiced against whom in this piece? Are the prejudices all limited to one side? What factors have led to your conclusion (look for evidence in the article)? Present your conclusion, with supporting evidence, in a paragraph or two.

4. Write a draft in which you discuss the status of women in this piece. How are they subject to prejudice? Explain whether this type of prejudice is covered by Allport's **classification.**

5. Identify different social classes in Bradford. Write a paragraph **describing** each class you have identified and indicating whether this class is prejudiced against another.

THE AUTHOR'S METHODS

6. Kureishi consistently relates his own experiences and **describes** what he sees and hears. Choose a passage in which he uses an example, **analyze** how it works, and write a paper telling why you think it is effective.

7. How does Kureishi indicate his feelings about the situation of Pakistanis in Bradford? What means of improvement does he suggest?

8. In part, the organization of this essay is **chronological** and geographical, but not all the parts fit into these categories. Find the parts that do not. Describe how those parts are connected to other parts of the essay and how they are integrated into the whole work.

FORMAL WRITING AND RESEARCH PAPERS

9. What city in the United States does Bradford remind you of? Write an essay (similar to Kureishi's but not so complex) in which you **describe** some aspects of the political and social life of this American city.

Nadine Gordimer

Which New Era Would That Be?

(1956)

A native of South Africa, Nadine Gordimer (born 1923) has been described as a thorn in the side of that nation's government. She has published nine volumes of short stories and four novels, including *A Guest of Honour* and *Burger's Daughter,* which are regarded as among her best.

Even though conditions in South Africa have changed substantially since the release of Nelson Mandela, the country's racial problems still persist. In this story, Gordimer depicts the visit of a liberal white woman to a group of black men in their own environment. The author is less interested in action than in character and the tensions among individuals. As you read, look for indications of prejudice in each of the characters.

PREVIEWS

A. The Republic of South Africa has long had a repressive policy toward blacks called apartheid. Try to put yourself in the position of a black person in this society, in which you are denied the right to vote and are severely restricted in other ways as well.

B. Spend a few minutes free writing about the responsibilities that any nation has to its minority citizens.

Jake Alexander, a big, fat colored man, half Scottish, half African Negro, was shaking a large pan of frying bacon on the gas stove in the back room of his Johannesburg printing shop when he became aware that someone was knocking on the door at the front of the shop. The sizzling fat and the voices of the five men in the back room with him almost blocked out sounds from without, and the knocking was of the steady kind that might have been going on for quite a few minutes. He lifted the pan off the flame with one hand and with the other made an impatient silencing gesture, directed at the bacon as well as the voices. Interpreting the movement as one of caution, the men hurriedly picked up the tumblers and cups in which they had been taking their end-of-the-day brandy at their ease, and tossed the last of it down. Little yellow Klaas, whose hair was like ginger-colored wire wool, stacked the cups and glasses swiftly and hid them behind the dirty curtain that covered a row of shelves.

"Who's that?" yelled Jake, wiping his greasy hands down his pants.

There was a sharp and playful tattoo, followed by an English voice: "Me— Alister. For heaven's sake, Jake!"

The fat man put the pan back on the flame and tramped through the dark shop, past the idle presses, to the door, and flung it open. "Mr. Halford!" he said. "Well, good to see you. Come in, man. In the back there, you can't hear a thing." A young Englishman with gentle eyes, a stern mouth, and flat, colorless hair, which grew in an untidy, confused spiral from a double crown, stepped back to allow a young woman to enter ahead of him. Before he could introduce her, she held out her hand to Jake, smiling, and shook his firmly. "Good evening. Jennifer Tetzel," she said.

"Jennifer, this is Jake Alexander," the young man managed to get in, over her shoulder.

The two had entered the building from the street through an archway lettered "NEW ERA BUILDING." "Which new era would that be?" the young woman had wondered aloud, brightly, while they were waiting in the dim hallway for the door to be opened, and Alister Halford had not known whether the reference was to the discovery of deep-level gold mining that had saved Johannesburg from the ephemeral fate of a mining camp in the nineties, or to the optimism after the settlement of labor troubles in the twenties, or to the recovery after the world went off the gold standard in the thirties—really, one had no idea of the age of these buildings in this run-down end of the town. Now, coming in out of the deserted hallway gloom, which smelled of dust and rotting wood—the smell of waiting—they were met by the live, cold tang of ink and the homely, lazy odor of bacon fat—the smell of acceptance. There was not much light in the deserted workshop. The host blundered to the wall and switched on a bright naked bulb, up in the ceiling. The three stood blinking at one another for a moment: a colored man with the fat of the man of the world upon him, grossly dressed—not out of poverty but obviously because he liked it that way—in a rayon sports shirt that gaped and showed two hairy stomach rolls hiding his navel in a lipless grin, the pants of a good suit, misbuttoned and held up round the waist by a tie instead of a belt, and a pair of expensive sports shoes, worn without socks; a young English- man in a worn greenish tweed suit with a neo-Edwardian cut to the vest that labeled it a leftover from undergraduate days; a handsome white woman who, as the light fell upon her, was immediately recognizable to Jake Alexander.

He had never met her before, but he knew the type well—had seen it over and over again at meetings of the Congress of Democrats, and other organizations where progressive whites met progressive blacks. These were the white women who, Jake knew, persisted in regarding themselves as your equal. That was even worse, he thought, than the parsons who persisted in regarding *you* as *their* equal. The parsons had had ten years at school and seven years at a university and theological school; you had carried sacks of vegetables from the market to white people's cars from the time you were eight years old until you were apprenticed to a printer, and your first woman, like your mother, had been a servant, whom you had visited in a backyard room, and your first gulp of whisky, like many of your other pleasures, had been stolen while a white man was not looking. Yet the good parson insisted that your picture of life was exactly the same as his own: *you* felt as *he* did. But these women—oh, Christ!—these women felt as *you* did. They were sure of it. They thought they understood the humiliation of the pure-blooded black African walking the streets only by the permission of a pass written out by a white person, and the guilt and swagger of the colored man light-faced enough to slink, fugitive from his own skin, into the preserves—the cinemas, bars, libraries that were marked "EUROPEANS ONLY." Yes, breathless with stout sensitivity, they insisted on walking the whole teeter-totter of the color line. There was no escaping their understanding. They even insisted on feeling the resentment *you* must feel at their identifying themselves with your feelings. . . .

Here was the black hair of a determined woman (last year they wore it pulled tightly back into an oddly perched knot; this year it was cropped and curly as a lap dog's), the round, bony brow unpowdered in order to show off the tan, the red mouth, the unrouged cheeks, the big, lively, handsome eyes, dramatically painted, that would look into yours with such intelligent, eager honesty—eager to mirror what Jake Alexander, a big, fat slob of a colored man interested in women, money, brandy, and boxing, was feeling. Who the hell wants a woman to look at you honestly, anyway? What has all this to do with a *woman*—with what men and women have for each other in their eyes? She was wearing a wide black skirt, a white cotton blouse baring a good deal of her breasts, and earrings that seemed to have been made by a blacksmith out of bits of scrap iron. On her feet she had sandals whose narrow thongs wound between her toes, and the nails of the toes were painted plum color. By contrast, her hands were neglected-looking—sallow, unmanicured—and on one thin finger there swiveled a huge gold seal ring. She was beautiful, he supposed with disgust.

He stood there, fat, greasy, and grinning at the two visitors so lingeringly that his grin looked insolent. Finally he asked, "What brings you this end of town, Mr. Halford? Sight-seeing with the lady?"

The young Englishman gave Jake's arm a squeeze, where the short sleeve of the rayon shirt ended. "Just thought I'd look you up, Jake," he said, jolly.

"Come on in, come on in," said Jake on a rising note, shambling ahead of them into the company of the back room. "Here, what about a chair for the lady?" He swept a pile of handbills from the seat of a kitchen chair onto the dusty concrete floor, picked up the chair, and planked it down again, in the middle of the group of men, who had risen awkwardly, like zoo bears to the hope of a bun, at the visitors' entrance. "You know Maxie Ndube? And Temba?" Jake said, nodding at two of the men who surrounded him.

Alister Halford murmured with polite warmth his recognition of Maxie, a small, dainty-faced African in neat, businessman's dress, then said inquiringly and hesitantly to Temba, "Have we? When?"

Temba was a colored man—a mixture of the bloods of black slaves and white masters, blended long ago, in the days when the Cape of Good Hope was a port of refreshment for the Dutch East India Company. He was tall and pale, with a large Adam's apple, enormous black eyes, and the look of a musician in a jazz band; you could picture a trumpet lifted to the ceiling in those long yellow hands, that curved spine hunched forward to shield a low note. "In Durban last year, Mr. Halford, you remember?" he said eagerly. "I'm sure we met—or perhaps I only saw you there."

"Oh, at the Congress? Of course I remember you!" Halford apologized. "You were in a delegation from the Cape?"

"Miss—?" Jake Alexander waved a hand between the young woman, Maxie, and Temba.

"Jennifer. Jennifer Tetzel," she said again clearly, thrusting out her hand. There was a confused moment when both men reached for it at once and then hesitated, each giving way to the other. Finally the handshaking was accomplished, and the young woman seated herself confidently on the chair.

Jake continued, offhand, "Oh, and of course Billy Boy"—Alister signaled briefly to a black man with sad, bloodshot eyes, who stood awkwardly, back a few steps, against some rolls of paper—"and Klaas and Albert." Klaas and Albert had in their mixed blood some strain of the Bushman, which gave them a batrachian yellowness and toughness, like one of those toads that (prehistoric as the Bushman is) are mythically believed to have survived into modern times (hardly more fantastically than the Bushman himself has survived) by spending centuries shut up in an air bubble in a rock. Like Billy Boy, Klaas and Albert had backed away, and, as if abasement against the rolls of paper, the wall, or the window were a greeting in itself, the two little colored men and the big African only stared back at the masculine nods of Alister and the bright smile of the young woman.

"You up from the Cape for anything special now?" Alister said to Temba as he made a place for himself on a corner of a table that was littered with photographic blocks, bits of type, poster proofs, a bottle of souring milk, a bow tie, a pair of red braces, and a number of empty Coca-Cola bottles.

"I've been living in Durban for a year. Just got the chance of a lift to Jo'burg," said the gangling Temba.

Jake had set himself up easily, leaning against the front of the stove and facing Miss Jennifer Tetzel on her chair. He jerked his head toward Temba and said, "Real banana boy." Young white men brought up in the strong Anglo-Saxon tradition of the province of Natal are often referred to, and refer to themselves, as "banana boys," even though fewer and fewer of them have any connection with the dwindling number of vast banana estates that once made their owners rich. Jake's broad face, where the bright pink cheeks of a Highland complexion—inherited, along with his name, from his Scottish father—showed oddly through his coarse, coffee-colored skin, creased up in appreciation of his own joke. And Temba threw back his head and laughed, his Adam's apple bobbing, at the idea of himself as a cricket-playing white public-school boy.

"There's nothing like Cape Town, is there?" said the young woman to him, her head charmingly on one side, as if this conviction was something she and he shared.

"Miss Tetzel's up here to look us over. She's from Cape Town," Alister explained.

She turned to Temba with her beauty, her strong provocativeness, full on, as it were. "So we're neighbors?"

Jake rolled one foot comfortably over the other and a spluttering laugh pursed out the pink inner membrane of his lips.

"Where did you live?" she went on, to Temba.

"Cape Flats," he said. Cape Flats is a desolate colored slum in the bush outside Cape Town.

"Me, too," said the girl, casually.

Temba said politely, "You're kidding," and then looked down uncomfortably at his hands, as if they had been guilty of some clumsy movement. He had not meant to sound so familiar; the words were not the right ones.

"I've been there nearly ten months," she said.

"Well, some people've got queer tastes," Jake remarked, laughing, to no one in particular, as if she were not there.

"How's that?" Temba was asking her shyly, respectfully.

She mentioned the name of a social rehabilitation scheme that was in operation in the slum. "I'm assistant director of the thing at the moment. It's connected with the sort of work I do at the university, you see, so they've given me fifteen months' leave from my usual job."

Maxie noticed with amusement the way she used the word "job," as if she were a plumber's mate; he and his educated African friends—journalists and schoolteachers—were careful to talk only of their "professions." "Good works," he said, smiling quietly.

She planted her feet comfortably before her, wriggling on the hard chair, and said to Temba with mannish frankness, "It's a ghastly place. How in God's name did you survive living there? I don't think I can last out more than another few months, and I've always got my flat in Cape Town to escape to on Sundays, and so on."

While Temba smiled, turning his protruding eyes aside slowly, Jake looked straight at her and said, "Then why do you, lady, why *do* you?"

"Oh, I don't know. Because I don't see why anyone else—any one of the people who live there—should have to, I suppose." She laughed before anyone else could at the feebleness, the philanthropic uselessness of what she was saying. "Guilt, what-have-you . . ."

Maxie shrugged, as if at the mention of some expensive illness, which he had never been able to afford and whose symptoms he could not imagine.

There was a moment of silence; the two colored men and the big black man standing back against the wall watched anxiously, as if some sort of signal might be expected, possibly from Jake Alexander, their boss, the man who, like themselves, was not white, yet who owned his own business, and had a car, and money, and strange friends—sometimes even white people, such as these. The three of them were dressed in the ill-matched cast-off clothing that all humble workpeople who are not white wear in Johannesburg, and they had not lost the ability of primitives and children to stare, unembarrassed and unembarrassing.

Jake winked at Alister; it was one of his mannerisms—a bookie's wink, a stage comedian's wink. "Well, how's it going, boy, how's it going?" he said. His turn of phrase was barroom bonhomie; with luck, he *could* get into a bar, too. With a hat to cover his hair, and his coat collar well up, and only a bit of greasy pink cheek showing, he had slipped into the bars of the shabbier Johannesburg hotels with Alister many times and got away with it. Alister, on the other hand, had got away with the same sort of thing narrowly several times, too, when he had accompanied Jake to a shebeen* in a colored location, where it was illegal for a white man to be, as well as illegal for anyone at all to have a drink; twice Alister had escaped a raid by jumping out of a window. Alister had been in South Africa only eighteen months, as correspondent for a newspaper in England, and because he was only two or three years away from undergraduate escapades, such incidents seemed to give him a kind of nostalgic pleasure; he found them funny. Jake, for his part, had decided long ago (with the great help of the money he had made) that he would take the whole business of the color bar as humorous. The combination of these two attitudes, stemming from such immeasurably different circumstances, had the effect of making their friendship less self-conscious than is usual between a white man and a colored one.

"They tell me it's going to be a good thing on Saturday night?" said Alister, in the tone of questioning someone in the know. He was referring to a boxing match between two colored heavyweights, one of whom was a protégé of Jake's.

Jake grinned deprecatingly, like a fond mother. "Well, Pikkie's a good boy," he said. "I tell you, it'll be something to see." He danced about a little on his clumsy toes, in pantomime of the way a boxer nimbles himself, and collapsed against the stove, his belly shaking with laughter at his breathlessness.

"Too much smoking, too many brandies, Jake," said Alister.

"With me, it's too many women, boy."

"We were just congratulating Jake," said Maxie in his soft, precise voice, the indulgent, tongue-in-cheek tone of the protégé who is superior to his patron, for Maxie was one of Jake's boys, too—of a different kind. Though Jake had decided that for him being on the wrong side of a color bar was ludicrous, he was as indulgent to those who took it seriously and politically, the way Maxie did, as he was to any up-and-coming youngster who, say, showed talent in the ring or wanted to go to America and become a singer. They could all make themselves free of Jake's pocket, and his printing shop, and his room with a radio in the lower end of the town, where the building had fallen below the standard of white people but was far superior to the kind of thing most coloreds and blacks were accustomed to.

"Congratulations on what?" the young white woman asked. She had a way of looking up around her, questioningly, from face to face, that came of long familiarity with being the center of attention at parties.

"Yes, you can shake my hand, boy," said Jake to Alister. "I didn't see it, but these fellows tell me that my divorce went through. It's in the papers today."

"Is that so? But from what I hear, you won't be a free man long," Alister said teasingly.

---

* Shebeen—an unlicensed establishment where liquor is sold illegally. [Eds.]

Jake giggled, and pressed at one gold-filled tooth with a strong fingernail. "You heard about the little parcel I'm expecting from Zululand?" he asked.

"Zululand?" said Alister. "I thought your Lila came from Stellenbosch."

Maxie and Temba laughed.

"Lila? *What* Lila?" said Jake with exaggerated innocence.

"You're behind the times," said Maxie to Alister.

"You know I like them—well, sort of round," said Jake. "Don't care for the thin kind, in the long run."

"But Lila had red hair!" Alister goaded him. He remembered the incongruously dyed, artificially straightened hair on a fine colored girl whose nostrils dilated in the manner of certain fleshy water plants seeking prey.

Jennifer Tetzel got up and turned the gas off on the stove, behind Jake. "That bacon'll be like charred string," she said.

Jake did not move—merely looked at her lazily. "This is not the way to talk with a lady around." He grinned, unapologetic.

She smiled at him and sat down, shaking her earrings. "Oh, I'm divorced myself. Are we keeping you people from your supper? Do go ahead and eat. Don't bother about us."

Jake turned around, gave the shrunken rashers a mild shake, and put the pan aside. "Hell, no," he said. "Any time. But"—turning to Alister—"won't you have something to eat?" He looked about, helpless and unconcerned, as if to indicate an absence of plates and a general careless lack of equipment such as white women would be accustomed to use when they ate. Alister said quickly, no, he had promised to take Jennifer to Moorjee's.

Of course, Jake should have known; a woman like that would *want* to be taken to eat at an Indian place in Vrededorp, even though she was white, and free to eat at the best hotel in town. He felt suddenly, after all, the old gulf opening between himself and Alister: what did *they* see in such women—bristling, sharp, all-seeing, knowing women, who talked like men, who wanted to show all the time that, apart from sex, they were exactly the same as men? He looked at Jennifer and her clothes, and thought of the way a white woman could look: one of those big, soft, European women with curly yellow hair, with very high-heeled shoes that made them shake softly when they walked, with a strong scent, like hot flowers, coming up, it seemed, from their jutting breasts under the lace and pink and blue and all the other pretty things they wore—women with nothing resistant about them except, buried in white, boneless fingers, those red, pointed nails that scratched faintly at your palms.

"You should have been along with me at lunch today," said Maxie to no one in particular. Or perhaps the soft voice, a vocal tiptoe, was aimed at Alister, who was familiar with Maxie's work as an organizer of African trade unions. The group in the room gave him their attention (Temba with the little encouraging grunt of one who has already heard the story), but Maxie paused a moment, smiling ruefully at what he was about to tell. Then he said, "You know George Elson?" Alister nodded. The man was a white lawyer who had been arrested twice for his participation in anti-discrimination movements.

"Oh, George? I've worked with George often in Cape Town," put in Jennifer.

"Well," continued Maxie, "George Elson and I went out to one of the industrial towns on the East Rand. We were interviewing the bosses, you see, not the men, and at the beginning it was all right, though once or twice the girls in the offices thought I was George's driver—'Your boy can wait outside.'" He laughed, showing small, perfect teeth; everything about him was finely made—his straight-fingered dark hands, the curved African nostrils of his small nose, his little ears, which grew close to the sides of his delicate head. The others were silent, but the young woman laughed, too.

"We even got tea in one place," Maxie went on. "One of the girls came in with two cups and a tin mug. But old George took the mug."

Jennifer Tetzel laughed again, knowingly.

"Then, just about lunchtime, we came to this place I wanted to tell you about. Nice chap, the manager. Never blinked an eye at me, called me Mister. And after we'd talked, he said to George, 'Why not come home with me for lunch?' So of course George said, 'Thanks, but I'm with my friend here.' 'Oh, that's O.K.,' said the chap. 'Bring him along.' Well, we go along to this house, and the chap disappears into the kitchen, and then he comes back and we sit in the lounge and have a beer, and then the servant comes along and says lunch is ready. Just as we're walking into the dining room, the chap takes me by the arm and says, 'I've had *your* lunch laid on a table on the stoep. You'll find it's all perfectly clean and nice, just what we're having ourselves.'"

"Fantastic," murmured Alister.

Maxie smiled and shrugged, looking around at them all. "It's true."

"After he'd asked you, and he'd sat having a drink with you?" Jennifer said closely, biting in her lower lip, as if this were a problem to be solved psychologically.

"Of course," said Maxie.

Jake was shaking with laughter, like some obscene Silenus.* There was no sound out of him, but saliva gleamed on his lips, and his belly, at the level of Jennifer Tetzel's eyes, was convulsed.

Temba said soberly, in the tone of one whose good will makes it difficult for him to believe in the unease of his situation, "I certainly find it worse here than at the Cape. I can't remember, y'know, about buses. I keep getting put off European buses."

Maxie pointed to Jake's heaving belly. "Oh, I'll tell you a better one than that," he said. "Something that happened in the office one day. Now, the trouble with me is, apparently, I don't talk like a native." This time everyone laughed, except Maxie himself, who, with the instinct of a good raconteur, kept a polite, modest, straight face.

"You know that's true," interrupted the young white woman. "You have none of the usual softening of the vowels of most Africans. And you haven't got an Afrikaans accent, as some Africans have, even if they get rid of the Bantu thing."

---

* Silenus—character in Greek mythology. He was the tutor of Dionysus, who was always drunk but noted for wisdom. [Eds.]

"Anyway, I'd had to phone a certain firm several times," Maxie went on, "and I'd got to know the voice of the girl at the other end, and she'd got to know mine. As a matter of fact, she must have liked the sound of me, because she was getting very friendly. We fooled about a bit, exchanged first names, like a couple of kids—hers was Peggy—and she said, eventually, 'Aren't you ever going to come to the office yourself?'" Maxie paused a moment, and his tongue flicked at the side of his mouth in a brief, nervous gesture. When he spoke again, his voice was flat, like the voice of a man who is telling a joke and suddenly thinks that perhaps it is not such a good one after all. "So I told her I'd be in next day, about four. I walked in, sure enough, just as I said I would. She was a pretty girl, blond, you know, with very tidy hair—I guessed she'd just combed it to be ready for me. She looked up and said, 'Yes?,' holding out her hand for the messenger's book or parcel she thought I'd brought. I took her hand and shook it and said, 'Well, here I am, on time—I'm Maxie—Maxie Ndube.'"

"What'd she do?" asked Temba eagerly.

The interruption seemed to restore Maxie's confidence in his story. He shrugged gaily. "She almost dropped my hand, and then she pumped it like a mad thing, and her neck and ears went so red I thought she'd burn up. Honestly, her ears were absolutely shining. She tried to pretend she'd known all along, but I could see she was terrified someone would come from the inner office and see her shaking hands with a native. So I took pity on her and went away. Didn't even stay for my appointment with her boss. When I went back to keep the postponed appointment the next week, we pretended we'd never met."

Temba was slapping his knee. "God, I'd have loved to see her face!" he said.

Jake wiped away a tear from his fat cheek—his eyes were light blue, and produced tears easily when he laughed—and said, "That'll teach you not to talk swanky, man. Why can't you talk like the rest of us?"

"Oh, I'll watch out on the 'Missus' and 'Baas' stuff in future," said Maxie.

Jennifer Tetzel cut into their laughter with her cool, practical voice. "Poor little girl, she probably liked you awfully, Maxie, and was really disappointed. You mustn't be too harsh on her. It's hard to be punished for not being black."

The moment was one of astonishment rather than irritation. Even Jake, who had been sure that there could be no possible situation between white and black he could not find amusing, only looked quickly from the young woman to Maxie, in a hiatus between anger, which he had given up long ago, and laughter, which suddenly failed him. On his face was admiration more than anything else—sheer, grudging admiration. This one was the best yet. This one was the coolest ever.

"Is it?" said Maxie to Jennifer, pulling in the corners of his mouth and regarding her from under slightly raised eyebrows. Jake watched. Oh, she'd have a hard time with Maxie. Maxie wouldn't give up his suffering-tempered blackness so easily. You hadn't much hope of knowing what Maxie was feeling at any given moment, because Maxie not only never let you know but made you guess wrong. But this one was the best yet.

She looked back at Maxie, opening her eyes very wide, twisting her sandaled foot on the swivel of its ankle, smiling. "Really, I assure you it is."

Maxie bowed to her politely, giving way with a falling gesture of his hand.

Alister had slid from his perch on the crowded table, and now, prodding Jake playfully in the paunch, he said, "We have to get along."

Jake scratched his ear and said again, "Sure you won't have something to eat?"

Alister shook his head. "We had hoped you'd offer us a drink, but—"

Jake wheezed with laughter, but this time was sincerely concerned. "Well, to tell you the truth, when we heard the knocking, we just swallowed the last of the bottle off, in case it was someone it shouldn't be. I haven't a drop in the place till tomorrow. Sorry, chappie. Must apologize to you, lady, but we black men've got to drink in secret. If we'd've known it was you two . . . "

Maxie and Temba had risen. The two wizened colored men, Klaas and Albert, and the somber black Billy Boy shuffled helplessly, hanging about.

Alister said, "Next time, Jake, next time. We'll give you fair warning and you can lay it on."

Jennifer shook hands with Temba and Maxie, called "Goodby! Good-by!" to the others, as if they were somehow out of earshot in that small room. From the door, she suddenly said to Maxie, "I feel I must tell you. About that other story—your first one, about the lunch. I don't believe it. I'm sorry, but I honestly don't. It's too illogical to hold water."

It was the final self-immolation by honest understanding. There was absolutely no limit to which that understanding would not go. Even if she could not believe Maxie, she must keep her determined good faith with him by confessing her disbelief. She would go to the length of calling him a liar to show by frankness how much she respected him—to insinuate, perhaps, that she was *with him*, even in the need to invent something about a white man that she, because she herself was white, could not believe. It was her last bid for Maxie.

The small, perfectly made man crossed his arms and smiled, watching her out. Maxie had no price.

Jake saw his guests out of the shop, and switched off the light after he had closed the door behind them. As he walked back through the dark, where his presses smelled metallic and cool, he heard, for a few moments, the clear voice of the white woman and the low, noncommittal English murmur of Alister, his friend, as they went out through the archway into the street.

He blinked a little as he came back to the light and the faces that confronted him in the back room. Klaas had taken the dirty glasses from behind the curtain and was holding them one by one under the tap in the sink. Billy Boy and Albert had come closer out of the shadows and were leaning their elbows on a roll of paper. Temba was sitting on the table, swinging his foot. Maxie had not moved, and stood just as he had, with his arms folded. No one spoke.

Jake began to whistle softly through the spaces between his front teeth, and he picked up the pan of bacon, looked at the twisted curls of meat, jellied now in cold white fat, and put it down again absently. He stood a moment, heavily, regarding them all, but no one responded. His eye encountered the chair that he had cleared for Jennifer Tetzel to sit on. Suddenly he kicked it, hard, so that it went flying onto its side. Then, rubbing his big hands together and bursting into loud whistling to accompany an impromptu series of dance steps, he said, "Now, boys!" and as they stirred, he planked the pan down on the ring and turned the gas up till it roared beneath it.

JOURNAL WRITINGS

1. Write some answers to the question posed by the title. Explore, in one or more journal entries, the implications of this question.
2. See if you can find several **symbols** in this story (remember that actions can be symbolic). Choose the most powerful of these symbols and write a paragraph explicating its meanings.
3. How would you want Maxie to reply to Jennifer when she tells him she cannot believe his story about the lunch? Add your own paragraph to the story, containing his response to her.

BRAINSTORMING AND DRAFTING

4. In small groups, discuss the significance of Jennifer's living in Cape Flats. Explore her motivation. Would you describe her as altruistic, self-serving, or some other way? Write a paragraph that analyzes her motivation.
5. List all the **characters** in the story. Discuss their relative importance and development (which ones are well-rounded and which **stereotypes**). What sort of interactions develop and what do those interactions tell you about the characters?
6. Discuss the nature of prejudice in this story. Who is prejudiced? Who is the object of prejudice? In what ways is the real nature of equality brought into question?

THE AUTHOR'S METHODS

7. A "frame story" is one in which the setting serves to enclose one or more shorter stories. Are the real tales buried in this story? If so, what are they and what is their significance?
8. There seems to be very little action in this story. Define the real focus of interest in the story. Discuss how the reader's attention is drawn to this focus and what message it then communicates.

CREATIVE PROJECT

9. Jennifer and Alister are going to dinner afterward. Write a **short story** (sort of a continuation of this one) that shows them in the restaurant. What do they have to say about their experience with Jake and his friends? Try to convey their emotional responses.

FORMAL WRITING AND RESEARCH PAPERS

10. Find out about the nature and history of apartheid. Write an extended paper with documentation in which you explain some aspect of this policy and argue some question about its morality or political expediency.
11. See if you can find some critical interpretations of this story. Write a paper using these interpretations to support your own interpretation of the story.

James Baldwin

Notes of a Native Son

(1955)

James Baldwin (1924–1987) was born and raised in Harlem, and graduated from DeWitt Clinton High School. He became a preacher and worked at various menial jobs before publishing his first novel, *Native Son,* in 1940. In 1948 he moved to Paris, France, where he lived for ten years. While living abroad he continued to develop his skills as a novelist and essayist, publishing *Go Tell It on the Mountain* in 1953. He was the recipient of numerous literary awards.

In this autobiographical essay, Baldwin recalls his father, especially the day he died. The memories become the basis for exploring the relationship between father and son, but Baldwin also delves into the nature of his own character.

PREVIEWS

A.   In one or two sentences, **describe** your relationship to your father.
B.   Write a paragraph **narrating** an incident, involving one of your parents, that you feel deeply influenced your development.

On the 29th of July, in 1943, my father died. On the same day, a few hours later, his last child was born. Over a month before this, while all our energies were concentrated in waiting for these events, there had been, in Detroit, one of the bloodiest race riots of the century. A few hours after my father's funeral, while he lay in state in the undertaker's chapel, a race riot broke out in Harlem. On the morning of the 3rd of August, we drove my father to the graveyard through a wilderness of smashed plate glass.

The day of my father's funeral had also been my nineteenth birthday. As we drove him to the graveyard, the spoils of injustice, anarchy, discontent, and hatred were all around us. It seemed to me that God himself had devised, to mark my father's end, the most sustained and brutally dissonant of codas. And it seemed to me, too, that the violence which rose all about us as my father left the world had been devised as a corrective for the pride of his eldest son. I had declined to believe in that apocalypse which had been central to my father's vision; very well, life seemed to be saying, here is something that will certainly pass for an apocalypse until the real thing comes along. I had inclined to be contemptuous of my father for the conditions of his life, for the conditions of our lives. When his life had ended I began to wonder about that life and also, in a new way, to be apprehensive about my own.

I had not known my father very well. We had got on badly, partly because we shared, in our different fashions, the voice of stubborn pride. When he was dead I realized that I had hardly ever spoken to him. When he had been dead a long time I began to wish I had. It seems to be typical of life in America, where opportunities, real and fancied, are thicker than anywhere else on the globe, that the second generation has no time to talk to the first. No one, including my father, seems to have known exactly how old he was, but his mother had been born during slavery. He was of the first generation of free men. He, along with thousands of other Negroes, came North after 1919 and I was part of that generation which had never seen the landscape of what Negroes sometimes call the Old Country.

He had been born in New Orleans and had been a quite young man there during the time that Louis Armstrong,* a boy, was running errands for the dives and honky-tonks of what was always presented to me as one of the most wicked of cities—to this day, whenever I think of New Orleans, I also helplessly think of Sodom and Gomorrah.† My father never mentioned Louis Armstrong, except to forbid us to play his records; but there was a picture of him on our wall for a long time. One of my father's strong-willed female relatives had placed it there and forbade my father to take it down. He never did, but he eventually maneuvered her out of the house and when, some years later, she was in trouble and near death, he refused to do anything to help her.

He was, I think, very handsome. I gather this from photographs and from my own memories of him, dressed in his Sunday best and on his way to preach a sermon somewhere, when I was little. Handsome, proud, and ingrown, "like a toe-nail," somebody said. But he looked to me, as I grew older, like pictures I had seen of African tribal chieftains: he really should have been naked, with war-paint on and barbaric mementos, standing among spears. He could be chilling in the pulpit and indescribably cruel in his personal life and he was certainly the most bitter man I have ever met; yet it must be said that there was something else in him, buried in him, which lent him his tremendous power and, even, a rather crushing charm. It had something to do with his blackness, I think—he was very black—with his blackness and his beauty, and with the fact that he knew that he was black but did not know that he was beautiful. He claimed to be proud of his blackness but it had also been the cause of much humiliation and it had fixed bleak boundaries to his life. He was not a young man when we were growing up and he had already suffered many kinds of ruin; in his outrageously demanding and protective way he loved his children, who were black like him and menaced, like him; and all these things sometimes showed in his face when he tried, never to

---

* Louis Armstrong—jazz trumpeter. [Eds.]

†Sodom and Gomorrah—cities of ancient Israel, destroyed for their licentious living. [Eds.]

my knowledge with any success, to establish contact with any of us. When he took one of his children on his knee to play, the child always became fretful and began to cry; when he tried to help one of us with our homework the absolutely unabating tension which emanated from him caused our minds and our tongues to become paralyzed, so that he, scarcely knowing why, flew into a rage and the child, not knowing why, was punished. If it ever entered his head to bring a surprise home for his children, it was, almost unfailingly, the wrong surprise and even the big watermelons he often brought home on his back in the summertime led to the most appalling scenes. I do not remember, in all those years, that one of his children was ever glad to see him come home. From what I was able to gather of his early life, it seemed that this inability to establish contact with other people had always marked him and had been one of the things which had driven him out of New Orleans. There was something in him, therefore, groping and tentative, which was never expressed and which was buried with him. One saw it most clearly when he was facing new people and hoping to impress them. But he never did, not for long. We went from church to smaller and more improbable church, he found himself in less and less demand as a minister, and by the time he died none of his friends had come to see him for a long time. He had lived and died in an intolerable bitterness of spirit and it frightened me, as we drove him to the graveyard through those unquiet, ruined streets, to see how powerful and overflowing this bitterness could be and to realize that this bitterness now was mine.

When he died I had been away from home for a little over a year. In that year I had had time to become aware of the meaning of all my father's bitter warnings, had discovered the secret of his proudly pursed lips and rigid carriage: I had discovered the weight of white people in the world. I saw that this had been for my ancestors and now would be for me an awful thing to live with and that the bitterness which had helped to kill my father could also kill me.

He had been ill a long time—in the mind, as we now realized, reliving instances of his fantastic intransigence in the new light of his affliction and endeavoring to feel a sorrow for him which never, quite, came true. We had not known that he was being eaten up by paranoia, and the discovery that his cruelty, to our bodies and our minds, had been one of the symptoms of his illness was not, then, enough to enable us to forgive him. The younger children felt, quite simply, relief that he would not be coming home anymore. My mother's observation that it was he, after all, who had kept them alive all these years meant nothing because the problems of keeping children alive are not real for children. The older children felt, with my father gone, that they could invite their friends to the house without fear that their friends would be insulted or, as had sometimes happened with me, being told that their friends were in league with the devil and intended to rob our family of everything we owned. (I didn't fail to wonder, and it made me hate him, what on earth we owned that anybody would want.)

His illness was beyond all hope of healing before anyone realized that he was ill. He had always been so strange and had lived, like a prophet, in such unimaginably close communication with the Lord that his long silences which were punctuated by moans and hallelujahs and snatches of old songs while he sat at the living-room window never seemed odd to us. It was not until he refused to eat because, he said, his family was trying to poison him that my mother was forced to accept as a fact what had, until then, been only an unwilling suspicion. When he was committed, it was discovered that he had tuberculosis and, as it turned out, the disease of his mind allowed the disease of his body to destroy him. For the doctors could not force him to eat, either, and, though he was fed intravenously, it was clear from the beginning that there was no hope for him.

In my mind's eye I could see him, sitting at the window, locked up in his terrors; hating and fearing every living soul including his children who had betrayed him, too, by reaching towards the world which had despised him. There were nine of us. I began to wonder what it could have felt like for such a man to have had nine children whom he could barely feed. He used to make little jokes about our poverty, which never, of course, seemed very funny to us; they could not have seemed very funny to him, either, or else our all too feeble response to them would never have caused such rages. He spent great energy and achieved, to our chagrin, no small amount of success in keeping us away from the people who surrounded us, people who had all-night rent parties to which we listened when we should have been sleeping, people who cursed and drank and flashed razor blades on Lenox Avenue. He could not understand why, if they had so much energy to spare, they could not use it to make their lives better. He treated almost everybody on our block with a most uncharitable asperity and neither they, nor, of course, their children were slow to reciprocate.

The only white people who came to our house were welfare workers and bill collectors. It was almost always my mother who dealt with them, for my father's temper, which was at the mercy of his pride, was never to be trusted. It was clear that he felt their very presence in his home to be a violation: this was conveyed by his carriage, almost ludicrously stiff, and by his voice, harsh and vindictively polite. When I was around nine or ten I wrote a play which was directed by a young, white schoolteacher, a woman, who then took an interest in me, and gave me books to read and, in order to corroborate my theatrical bent, decided to take me to see what she somewhat tactlessly referred to as "real" plays. Theater-going was forbidden in our house, but, with the really cruel intuitiveness of a child, I suspected that the color of this woman's skin would carry the day for me. When, at school, she suggested taking me to the theater, I did not, as I might have done if she had been a Negro, find a way of discouraging her, but agreed that she should pick me up at my house one evening. I then, very cleverly, left all the rest to my mother, who suggested to my father, as I knew she would, that it would not be very nice to let such a kind woman make the trip for nothing. Also, since it was a schoolteacher, I imagine that my mother countered the idea of sin with the idea of "education," which word, even with my father, carried a kind of bitter weight.

Before the teacher came my father took me aside to ask *why* she was coming, what *interest* she could possibly have in our house, in a boy like me. I said I didn't know but I, too, suggested that it had something to do with education. And I understood that my father was waiting for me to say something—I didn't quite know what; perhaps that I wanted his protection against this teacher and her "education." I said none of these things and the teacher came and we went out. It was clear, during the brief interview in our living room, that my father was agreeing very much against his will and that he would have refused permission if he had dared. The fact that he did not dare caused me to despise him: I had no way of knowing that he was facing in that living room a wholly unprecedented and frightening situation.

Later, when my father had been laid off from his job, this woman became very important to us. She was really a very sweet and generous woman and went to a great deal of trouble to be of help to us, particularly during one awful winter. My mother called her by the highest name she knew: she said she was a "christian." My father could scarcely disagree but during the four or five years of our relatively close association he never trusted her and was always trying to surprise in her open, Midwestern face the genuine, cunningly hidden, and hideous motivation. In later years, particularly when it began to be clear that this "education" of mine was going to lead me to perdition, he became more explicit and warned me that my white friends in high school were not really my friends and that I would see, when I was older, how white people would do anything to keep a Negro down. Some of them could be nice, he admitted, but none of them were to be trusted and most of them were not even nice. The best thing was to have as little to do with them as possible. I did not feel this way and I was certain, in my innocence, that I never would.

But the year which preceded my father's death had made a great change in my life. I had been living in New Jersey, working in defense plants, working and living among southerners, white and black. I knew about the south, of course, and about how southerners treated Negroes and how they expected them to behave, but it had never entered my mind that anyone would look at me and expect *me* to behave that way. I learned in New Jersey that to be a Negro meant, precisely, that one was never looked at but was simply at the mercy of the reflexes the color of one's skin caused in other people. I acted in New Jersey as I had always acted, that is as though I thought a great deal of myself—I had to *act* that way—with results that were, simply, unbelievable. I had scarcely arrived before I had earned the enmity, which was extraordinarily ingenious, of all my superiors and nearly all my co-workers. In the beginning, to make matters worse, I simply did not know what was happening. I did not know what I had done, and I shortly began to wonder what *anyone* could possibly do, to bring about such unanimous, active, and unbearably vocal hostility. I knew about jim-crow but I had never experienced it. I went to the same self-service restaurant three times and stood with all the Princeton boys before the counter, waiting for a hamburger and coffee; it was always an extraordinarily long time before anything was set before me; but it was not until the fourth visit that I learned that, in fact, nothing had ever been set before me: I had simply picked something up. Negroes were not served there, I was told, and they had been waiting for me to realize that I was always the only Negro present. Once I was told this, I determined to go there all the time. But now they were ready for me and, though some dreadful scenes were subsequently enacted in that restaurant, I never ate there again.

It was the same story all over New Jersey, in bars, bowling alleys, diners, places to live. I was always being forced to leave, silently, or with mutual imprecations. I very shortly became notorious and children giggled behind me when I passed and their elders whispered or shouted—they really believed that I was mad. And it did begin to work on my mind, of course; I began to be afraid to go anywhere and to compensate for this I went to places to which I really should not have gone and where, God knows, I had no desire to be. My reputation in town naturally enhanced my reputation at work and my working day became one long series of acrobatics designed to keep me out of trouble. I cannot say that these acrobatics succeeded. It began to seem that the machinery of the organization I worked for was turning over, day and night, with but one aim: to eject me. I was fired once, and contrived, with the aid of a friend from New York, to get back on the payroll; was fired again, and bounced back again. It took a while to fire me for the third time, but the third time took. There were no loopholes anywhere. There was not even any way of getting back inside the gates.

That year in New Jersey lives in my mind as though it were the year during which, having an unsuspected predilection for it, I first contracted some dread, chronic disease, the unfailing symptom of which is a kind of blind fever, a pounding in the skull and fire in the bowels. Once this disease is contracted, one can never be really carefree again, for the fever, without an instant's warning, can recur at any moment. It can wreck more important things than race relations. There is not a Negro alive who does not have this rage in his blood—one has the choice, merely, of living with it consciously or surrendering to it. As for me, this fever has recurred in me, and does, and will until the day I die.

My last night in New Jersey, a white friend from New York took me to the nearest big town, Trenton, to go to the movies and have a few drinks. As it turned out, he also saved me from, at the very least, a violent whipping. Almost every detail of that night stands out very clearly in my memory. I even remember the name of the movie we saw because its title impressed me as being so patly ironical. It was a movie about the German occupation of France, starring Maureen O'Hara and Charles Laughton and called *This Land Is Mine*. I remember the name of the diner we walked into when the movie ended: it was the "American Diner." When we walked in the counterman asked what we wanted and I remember answering with the casual sharpness which had become my habit: "We want a hamburger and a cup of coffee, what do you think we want?" I do not know why, after a year of such rebuffs, I so completely failed to anticipate his answer, which was, of course, "We don't serve Negroes here." This reply failed to discompose me, at least for the moment. I made some sardonic comment about the name of the diner and we walked out into the streets.

This was the time of what was called the "brown-out," when the lights in all American cities were very dim. When we re-entered the streets something happened to me which had the force of an optical illusion, or a nightmare. The streets were very crowded and I was facing north. People were moving in every direction but it seemed to me, in that instant, that all of the people I could see, and many more than that, were moving toward me, against me, and that everyone was white. I remember how their faces gleamed. And I felt, like a physical sensation, a *click* at the nape of my neck as though some interior string connecting my head to my body had been cut. I began to walk. I heard my friend call after me, but I ignored him. Heaven only knows what was going on in his mind, but he had the good sense not to touch me—I don't know what would have happened if he had—and to keep me in sight. I don't know what was going on in my mind, either; I certainly had no conscious plan. I wanted to do something to crush these white faces, which were crushing me. I walked for perhaps a block or two until I came to an enormous, glittering, and fashionable restaurant in which I knew not even the intercession of the Virgin would cause me to be served. I pushed through the doors and took the first vacant seat I saw, at a table for two, and waited.

I do not know how long I waited and I rather wonder, until today, what I could possibly have looked like. Whatever I looked like, I frightened the waitress who shortly appeared, and the moment she appeared all of my fury flowed towards her. I hated her for her white face, and for her great, astounded, frightened eyes. I felt that if she found a black man so frightening I would make her fright worthwhile.

She did not ask me what I wanted, but repeated, as though she had learned it somewhere, "We don't serve Negroes here." She did not say it with the blunt, derisive hostility to which I had grown so accustomed, but, rather, with a note of apology in her voice, and fear. This made me colder and more murderous than ever. I felt I had to do something with my hands. I wanted her to come close enough for me to get her neck between my hands.

So I pretended not to have understood her, hoping to draw her closer. And she did step a very short step closer, with her pencil poised incongruously over her pad, and repeated the formula: " . . . don't serve Negroes here."

Somehow, with the repetition of that phrase, which was already ringing in my head like a thousand bells of a nightmare, I realized that she would never come any closer and that I would have to strike from a distance. There was nothing on the table but an ordinary watermug half full of water, and I picked this up and hurled it with all my strength at her. She ducked and it missed her and shattered against the mirror behind the bar. And, with that sound, my frozen blood abruptly thawed, I returned from wherever I had been, I *saw*, for the first time, the restaurant, the people with their mouths open, already, as it seemed to me, rising as one man, and I realized what I had done, and where I was, and I was frightened. I rose and began running for the door. A round, potbellied man grabbed me by the nape of the neck just as I reached the doors and began to beat me about the face. I kicked him and got loose and ran into the streets. My friend whispered, *"Run!"* and I ran.

My friend stayed outside the restaurant long enough to misdirect my pursuers and the police, who arrived, he told me, at once. I do not know what I said to him when he came to my room that night. I could not have said much. I felt, in the oddest, most awful way, that I had somehow betrayed him. I lived it over and over and over again, the way one relives an automobile accident after it has happened and one finds oneself alone and safe. I could not get over two facts, both equally difficult for the imagination to grasp, and one was that I could have been murdered. But the other was that I had been ready to commit murder. I saw nothing very clearly but I did see this: that my life, my *real* life, was in danger, and not from anything other people might do but from the hatred I carried in my own heart.

2

I had returned home around the second week in June—in great haste because it seemed that my father's death and my mother's confinement were both but a matter of hours. In the case of my mother, it soon became clear that she had simply made a miscalculation. This had always been her tendency and I don't believe that a single one of us arrived in the world, or has since arrived anywhere else, on time. But none of us dawdled so intolerably about the business of being born as did my baby sister. We sometimes amused ourselves, during those endless, stifling weeks, by picturing the baby sitting within in the safe, warm dark, bitterly regretting the necessity of becoming a part of our chaos and stubbornly putting it off as long as possible. I understood her perfectly and congratulated her on showing such good sense so soon. Death, however, sat as purposefully at my father's bedside as life stirred within my mother's womb and it was harder to understand why he so lingered in that long shadow. It seemed that he had bent, and for a long time, too, all of his energies towards dying. Now death was ready for him but my father held back.

All of Harlem, indeed, seemed to be infected by waiting. I had never before known it to be so violently still. Racial tensions throughout this country were exacerbated during the early years of the war, partly because the labor market brought together hundreds of thousands of ill-prepared people and partly because Negro soldiers, regardless of where they were born, received their military training in the south. What happened in defense plants and army camps had repercussions, naturally, in every Negro ghetto. The situation in Harlem had grown bad enough for clergymen, policemen, educators, politicians, and social workers, to assert in one breath that there was no "crime wave" and to offer, in the very next breath, suggestions as how to combat it. These suggestions always seemed to involve playgrounds, despite the fact that racial skirmishes were occurring in the playgrounds, too. Playground or not, crime wave or not, the Harlem police force had been augmented in March, and the unrest grew—perhaps, in fact, partly as a result of the ghetto's instinctive hatred of policemen. Perhaps the most revealing news item, out of the steady parade of reports of muggings, stabbings, shootings, assaults, gang wars, and accusations of police brutality, is the item concerning six Negro girls who set upon a white girl in the subway because, as they all too accurately put it, she was stepping on their toes. Indeed she was, all over the nation.

I had never before been so aware of policemen, on foot, on horseback, on corners, everywhere, always two by two. Nor had I ever been so aware of small knots of people. They were on stoops and on corners and in doorways, and what was striking about them, I think, was that they did not seem to be talking. Never, when I passed these groups, did the usual sound of a curse or a laugh ring out and neither did there seem to be any hum of gossip. There was certainly, on the other hand, occurring between them communication extraordinarily intense. Another thing that was striking was the unexpected diversity of the people who made up these groups. Usually, for example, one would see a group of sharpies standing on the street corner, jiving the passing chicks; or a group of older men, usually, for some reason, in the vicinity of a barbershop, discussing baseball scores, or the numbers, or making rather chilling observations about women they had known. Women, in a general way, tended to be seen less often together—unless they were church women, or very young girls, or prostitutes met together for an unprofessional instant. But that summer I saw the strangest combinations: large, respectable, churchly matrons standing on the stoops or the corners with their hair tied up, together with a girl in sleazy satin whose face bore the marks of gin and the razor, or heavyset, abrupt, no-nonsense older men, in company with the most disreputable and fanatical "race" men, or these same "race" men with the sharpies, or these sharpies with the churchly women. Seventh Day Adventists and Methodists and Spiritualists seemed to be hobnobbing with Holyrollers and they were all, alike, entangled with the most flagrant disbelievers; something heavy in their stance seemed to indicate that they had all, incredibly, seen a common vision, and on each face there seemed to be the same strange, bitter shadow.

The churchly women and the matter-of-fact, no-nonsense men had children in the Army. The sleazy girls they talked to had lovers there, the sharpies and the "race" men had friends and brothers there. It would have demanded an unquestioning patriotism, happily as uncommon in this country as it is undesirable, for these people not to have been disturbed by the bitter letters they received, by the newspaper stories they read, not to have been enraged by the posters, then to be found all over New York, which described the Japanese as "yellow-bellied Japs." It was only the "race" men, to be sure, who spoke ceaselessly of being revenged—how this vengeance was to be exacted was not clear—for the indignities and dangers suffered by Negro boys in uniform; but everybody felt a directionless, hopeless bitterness, as well as that panic which can scarcely be suppressed when one knows that a human being one loves is beyond one's reach, and in danger. This helplessness and this gnawing uneasiness does something, at length, to even the toughest mind. Perhaps the best way to sum all this up is to say that the people I knew felt, mainly, a peculiar kind of relief when they knew that their boys were being shipped out of the south, to do battle overseas. It was, perhaps, like feeling that the most dangerous part of a dangerous journey had been passed and that now, even if death should come, it would come with honor and without the complicity of their countrymen. Such a death would be, in short, a fact with which one could hope to live.

It was on the 28th of July, which I believe was a Wednesday, that I visited my father for the first time during his illness and for the last time in his life. The moment I saw him I knew why I had put off this visit so long. I had told my mother that I did not want to see him because I hated him. But this was not true. It was only that I *had* hated him and I wanted to hold on to this hatred. I did not want to look at him as a ruin: it was not a ruin I had hated. I imagine that one of the reasons people cling to their hates so stubbornly is because they sense, once hate is gone, that they will be forced to deal with pain.

We traveled out to him, his older sister and myself, to what seemed to be the very end of a very Long Island. It was hot and dusty and we wrangled, my aunt and I, all the way out, over the fact that I had recently begun to smoke and, as she said, to give myself airs. But I knew that she wrangled with me because she could not bear to face the fact of her brother's dying. Neither could I endure the reality of her despair, her unstated bafflement as to what had happened to her brother's life, and her own. So we wrangled and I smoked and from time to time she fell into a heavy reverie. Covertly, I watched her face, which was the face of an old woman; it had fallen in, the eyes were sunken and lightless; soon she would be dying too.

In my childhood—it had not been so long ago—I had thought her beautiful. She had been quick-witted and quick-moving and very generous with all the children and each of her visits had been an event. At one time one of my brothers and myself had thought of running away to live with her. Now she could no longer produce out of her handbag some unexpected and yet familiar delight. She made me feel pity and revulsion and fear. It was awful to realize that she no longer caused me to feel affection. The closer we came to the hospital the more querulous she became and at the same time, naturally, grew more dependent on me. Between pity and guilt and fear I began to feel that there was another me trapped in my skull like a jack-in-the-box who might escape my control at any moment and fill the air with screaming.

She began to cry the moment we entered the room and she saw him lying there, all shriveled and still, like a little black monkey. The great, gleaming apparatus which fed him and would have compelled him to be still even if he had been able to move brought to mind, not beneficence, but torture; the tubes entering his arm made me think of pictures I had seen when a child, of Gulliver, tied down by the pygmies on that island. My aunt wept and wept, there was a whistling sound in my father's throat; nothing was said; he could not speak. I wanted to take his hand, to say something. But I do not know what I could have said, even if he could have heard me. He was not really in that room with us, he had at last really embarked on his journey; and though my aunt told me that he said he was going to meet Jesus, I did not hear anything except that whistling in his throat. The doctor came back and we left, into that unbearable train again, and home. In the morning came the telegram saying that he was dead. Then the house was suddenly full of relatives, friends, hysteria, and confusion and I quickly left my mother and the children to the care of those impressive women, who, in Negro communities at least, automatically appear at times of bereavement armed with lotions, proverbs, and patience, and an ability to cook. I went downtown. By the time I returned, later the same day, my mother had been carried to the hospital and the baby had been born.

3

For my father's funeral I had nothing black to wear and this posed a nagging problem all day long. It was one of those problems, simple, or impossible of solution, to which the mind insanely clings in order to avoid the mind's real trouble. I spent most of the day at the downtown apartment of a girl I knew, celebrating my birthday with whiskey and wondering what to wear that night. When planning a birthday celebration one naturally does not expect that it will be up against competition from a funeral and this girl had anticipated taking me out that night, for a big dinner and a night club afterwards. Sometime during the course of that long day we decided that we would go out anyway, when my father's funeral service was over. I imagine *I* decided it, since, as the funeral hour approached, it became clearer and clearer to me that I would not know what to do with myself when it was over. The girl, stifling her very lively concern as to the possible effects of the whiskey on one of my father's chief mourners, concentrated on being conciliatory and practically helpful. She found a black shirt for me somewhere and ironed it and, dressed in the darkest pants and jacket I owned, and slightly drunk, I made my way to my father's funeral.

The chapel was full, but not packed, and very quiet. There were, mainly, my father's relatives, and his children, and here and there I saw faces I had not seen since childhood, the faces of my father's one-time friends. They were very dark and solemn now, seeming somehow to suggest that they had known all along that something like this would happen. Chief among the mourners was my aunt, who had quarreled with my father all his life; by which I do not mean to suggest that her mourning was insincere or that she had not loved him. I suppose that she was one of the few people in the world who had, and their incessant quarreling proved precisely the strength of the tie that bound them. The only other person in the world, as far as I knew, whose relationship to my father rivaled my aunt's in depth was my mother, who was not there.

It seemed to me, of course, that it was a very long funeral. But it was, if anything, a rather shorter funeral than most, nor, since there were no over-whelming, uncontrollable expressions of grief, could it be called—if I dare to use the word—successful. The minister who preached my father's funeral sermon was one of the few my father had still been seeing as he neared his end. He presented to us in his sermon a man whom none of us had ever seen—a man thoughtful, patient, and forbearing, a Christian inspiration to all who knew him, and a model for his children. And no doubt the children, in their disturbed and guilty state, were almost ready to believe this; he had been remote enough to be anything and, anyway, the shock of the incontrovertible, that it was really our father lying up there in that casket, prepared the mind for anything. His sister moaned and this grief-stricken moaning was taken for corroboration. The other faces held a dark, noncommittal thoughtfulness. This was not the man they had known, but they had scarcely expected to be confronted with *him;* this was, in a sense deeper than question of fact, the man they had not known, and the man they had not known may have been the real one. The real man, whoever he had been, had suffered and now he was dead: this was all that was sure and all that mattered now. Every man in the chapel hoped that when his hour came he, too, would be eulogized, which is to say forgiven, and that all of his lapses, greeds, errors, and strayings from the truth would be invested with coherence and looked upon with charity. This was perhaps the last thing human beings could give each other and it was what they demanded, after all, of the Lord. Only the Lord saw the midnight tears, only He was present when one of His children, moaning and wringing hands, paced up and down the room. When one slapped one's child in anger the recoil in the heart reverberated through heaven and became part of the pain of the universe. And when the children were hungry and sullen and distrustful and one watched them, daily, growing wilder, and further away, and running headlong into danger, it was the Lord who knew what the charged heart endured as the strap was laid to the backside; the Lord alone knew what one *would* have said if one had had, like the Lord, the gift of the living word. It was the Lord who knew of the impossibility every parent in the room faced: how to prepare the child for the day when the child would be despised and how to *create* in the child—by what means?—a stronger antidote to this poison than one had found for oneself. The avenues, side streets, bars, billiard halls, hospitals, police stations, and even the playgrounds of Harlem—not to mention the houses of correction, the jails, and the morgue—testified to the potency of the poison while remaining silent as to the efficacy of whatever antidote, irresistibly raising the question of whether or not such an antidote existed; raising, which was worse, the question of whether or not an antidote was desirable; perhaps poison should be fought with poison. With these several schisms in the mind and with more terrors in the heart than could be named, it was better not to judge the man who had gone down under an impossible burden. It was better to remember: *Thou knowest this man's fall; but thou knowest not his wrassling.*

While the preacher talked and I watched the children—years of changing their diapers, scrubbing them, slapping them, taking them to school, and scolding them had had the perhaps inevitable result of making me love them, though I am not sure I knew this then—my mind was busily breaking out with a rash of disconnected impressions. Snatches of popular songs, indecent jokes, bits of books I had read, movie sequences, faces, voices, political issues—I thought I was going mad; all these impressions suspended, as it were, in the solution of the faint nausea produced in me by the heat and liquor. For a moment I had the impression that my alcoholic breath, inefficiently disguised with chewing gum, filled the entire chapel. Then someone began singing one of my father's favorite songs and, abruptly, I was with him, sitting on his knee, in the hot, enormous, crowded church which was the first church we attended. It was the Abysinia Baptist Church on 138th Street. We had not gone there long. With this image, a host of others came. I had forgotten, in the rage of my growing up, how proud my father had been of me when I was little. Apparently, I had had a voice and my father had liked to show me off before the members of the church. I had forgotten what he had looked like when he was pleased but now I remembered that he had always been grinning with pleasure when my solos ended. I even remembered certain expressions on his face when he teased my mother—had he loved her? I would never know. And when had it all begun to change? For now it seemed that he had not always been cruel. I remembered being taken for a haircut and scraping my knee on the footrest of the barber's chair and I remembered my father's face as he soothed my crying and applied the stinging iodine. Then I remembered our fights, fights which had been of the worst possible kind because my technique had been silence.

I remembered the one time in all our life together when we had really spoken to each other.

It was on a Sunday and it must have been shortly before I left home. We were walking, just the two of us, in our usual silence, to or from church. I was in high school and had been doing a lot of writing and I was, at about this time, the editor of the high school magazine. But I had also been a Young Minister and had been preaching from the pulpit. Lately, I had been taking fewer engagements and preached as rarely as possible. It was said in the church, quite truthfully, that I was "cooling off."

My father asked me abruptly, "You'd rather write than preach, wouldn't you?"

I was astonished at his question—because it was a real question. I answered, "Yes."

That was all we said. It was awful to remember that that was all we had *ever* said.

The casket now was opened and the mourners were being led up the aisle to look for the last time on the deceased. The assumption was that the family was too overcome with grief to be allowed to make this journey alone and I watched while my aunt was led to the casket and, muffled in black, and shaking, led back to her seat. I disapproved of forcing the children to look on their dead father, considering that the shock of his death, or, more truthfully, the shock of death as a reality, was already a little more than a child could bear, but my judgment in this matter had been overruled and there they were, bewildered and frightened and very small, being led, one by one, to the casket. But there is also something very gallant about children at such moments. It has something to do with their silence and gravity and with the fact that one cannot help them. Their legs, somehow, seemed *exposed,* so that it is at once incredible and terribly clear that their legs are all they have to hold them up.

I had not wanted to go to the casket myself and I certainly had not wished to be led there, but there was no way of avoiding either of these forms. One of the deacons led me up and I looked on my father's face. I cannot say that it looked like him at all. His blackness had been equivocated by powder and there was no suggestion in that casket of what his power had or could have been. He was simply an old man dead, and it was hard to believe that he had ever given anyone either joy or pain. Yet, his life filled that room. Further up the avenue his wife was holding his newborn child. Life and death so close together, and love and hatred, and right and wrong, said something to me which I did not want to hear concerning man, concerning the life of man.

After the funeral, while I was downtown desperately celebrating my birthday, a Negro soldier, in the lobby of the Hotel Braddock, got into a fight with a white policeman over a Negro girl. Negro girls, white policemen, in or out of uniform, and Negro males—in or out of uniform—were part of the furniture of the lobby of the Hotel Braddock and this was certainly not the first time such an incident had occurred. It was destined, however, to receive an unprecedented publicity, for the fight between the policeman and the soldier ended with the shooting of the soldier. Rumor, flowing immediately to the streets outside, stated the soldier had been shot in the back, an instantaneous and revealing invention, and that the soldier had died protecting a Negro woman. The facts were somewhat different—for example, the soldier had not been shot in the back, and was not dead, and the girl seems to have been as dubious a symbol of womanhood as her white counterpart in Georgia usually is, but no one was interested in the facts. They preferred the invention because this invention expressed and corroborated their hates and fears so perfectly. It is just as well to remember that people are always doing this. Perhaps many of those legends, including Christianity, to which the world clings began their conquest of the world with just some such concerted surrender to distortion. The effect, in Harlem, of this particular legend was like the effect of a lit match in a tin of gasoline. The mob gathered before the doors of the Hotel Braddock simply began to swell and to spread in every direction, and Harlem exploded.

The mob did not cross the ghetto lines. It would have been easy, for example, to have gone over Morningside Park on the west side or to have crossed the Grand Central railroad tracks at 125th Street on the east side, to wreak havoc in the white neighborhoods. The mob seems to have been mainly interested in something more potent and real than the white face, that is, in white power, and the principal damage done during the riot of the summer of 1943 was to white business establishments in Harlem. It might have been a far bloodier story, of course, if, at the hour the riot began, these establishments had still been open. From the Hotel Braddock the mob fanned out, east and west along 125th Street, and for the entire length of Lenox, Seventh, and Eighth avenues. Along each of these avenues, and along each major side street—116th, 125th, 135th, and so on—bars, stores, pawnshops, restaurants, even little luncheonettes had been smashed open and entered and looted—looted, it might be added, with more haste than efficiency. The shelves really looked as though a bomb had struck them. Cans of beans and soup and dog food, along with toilet paper, corn flakes, sardines and milk tumbled every which way, and abandoned cash registers and cases of beer leaned crazily out of the splintered windows and were strewn along the avenues. Sheets, blankets, and clothing of every description formed a kind of path, as though people had dropped them while running. I truly had not realized that Harlem *had* so many stores until I saw them all smashed open; the first time the word *wealth* ever entered my mind in relation to Harlem was when I saw it scattered in the streets. But one's first, incongruous impression of plenty was countered immediately by an impression of waste. None of this was doing anybody any good. It would have been better to have left the plate glass as it had been and the goods lying in the stores.

It would have been better, but it would also have been intolerable, for Harlem had needed something to smash. To smash something is the ghetto's chronic need. Most of the time it is the members of the ghetto who smash each other, and themselves. But as long as the ghetto walls are standing there will always come a moment when these outlets do not work. That summer, for example, it was not enough to get into a fight on Lenox Avenue, or curse out one's cronies in the barber shops. If ever, indeed, the violence which fills Harlem's churches, pool halls, and bars erupts outward in a more direct fashion, Harlem and its citizens are likely to vanish in an apocalyptic flood. That this is not likely to happen is due to a great many reasons, most hidden and powerful among them the Negro's real relation to the white American. This relation prohibits, simply, anything as uncomplicated and satisfactory as pure hatred. In order really to hate white people, one has to blot so much out of the mind—and the heart—that this hatred itself becomes an exhausting and self-destructive pose. But this does not mean, on the other hand, that love comes easily: the white world is too powerful, too complacent, too ready with gratuitous humiliation, and, above all, too ignorant and too innocent for that. One is absolutely forced to make perpetual qualifications and one's own reactions are always canceling each other out. It is this, really, which has driven so many people mad, both white and black. One is always in the position of having to decide between amputation and gangrene. Amputation is swift but time may prove that the amputation was not necessary— or one may delay the amputation too long. Gangrene is slow, but it is impossible to be sure that one is reading one's symptoms right. The idea of going through life as a cripple is more than one can bear, and equally unbearable is the risk of swelling up slowly, in agony, with poison. And the trouble, finally, is that the risks are real even if the choices do not exist.

"But as for me and my house," my father had said, "we will serve the Lord." I wondered, as we drove him to his resting place, what this line had meant for him. I had heard him preach it many times. I had preached it once myself, proudly giving it an interpretation different from my father's. Now the whole thing came back to me, as though my father and I were on our way to Sunday school and I were memorizing the golden text: *And if it seem evil unto you to serve the Lord, choose you this day whom you will serve; whether the gods which your fathers served that were on the other side of the flood, or the gods of the Amorites, in whose land ye dwell: but as for me and my house, we will serve the Lord.* I suspected in these familiar lines a meaning which had never been there for me before. All of my father's texts and songs, which I had decided were meaningless, were arranged before me at his death like empty bottles, waiting to hold the meaning which life would give them for me. This was his legacy: nothing is ever escaped. That bleakly memorable morning I hated the unbelievable streets and the Negroes and whites who had, equally, made them that way. But I knew that it was folly, as my father would have said, this bitterness was folly. It was necessary to hold on to the things that mattered. The dead man mattered, the new life mattered; blackness and whiteness did not matter; to believe that they did was to acquiesce in one's own destruction. Hatred, which could destroy so much, never failed to destroy the man who hated and this was an immutable law.

It began to seem that one would have to hold in the mind forever two ideas which seemed to be in opposition. The first idea was acceptance, the acceptance, totally without rancor, of life as it is, and men as they are: in the light of this idea, it goes without saying that injustice is a commonplace. But this did not mean that one could be complacent, for the second idea was of equal power: that one must never, in one's own life, accept these injustices as commonplace but must fight them with all one's strength. This fight begins, however, in the heart and it now had been laid to my charge to keep my own heart free of hatred and despair. This intimation made my heart heavy and, now that my father was irrecoverable, I wished that he had been beside me so that I could have searched his face for the answers which only the future would give me now.

JOURNAL WRITINGS

1. Recall a day on which someone close to you died. Write a paragraph or two about what you were doing and how you were feeling on that day. Try to imitate some of the writing techniques that you observe in Baldwin's essay.
2. This is a very introspective essay. It examines, not only the events, but the way those events enable Baldwin to discover himself. Consider, for instance, the discovery of his willingness to be murdered or to commit murder. For a few days, write journal entries that attempt to delve into your own motivations and to explore your feelings about yourself and others.

BRAINSTORMING AND DRAFTING

3. Notice how Baldwin's own actions and attitudes provoke a prejudicial response. Have each member of a group present an example of actions or attitudes that provoked unwanted or unexpected responses. Discuss the significance of these examples. Write a paragraph about the significance of the example that impressed you most.
4. Baldwin talks about "the weight of white people in the world." Write a short piece in which you discuss the meaning of this phrase. Perhaps it will help to keep in mind the phrase "throwing your weight around."

THE AUTHOR'S METHODS

5. Look for instances of **irony** in this essay. Write a sentence or two about the significance of each instance. If you find a pattern of significance, perhaps you can explore in a longer paper Baldwin's use of irony throughout his essay.
6. Baldwin speaks of "schisms in the mind." Note the way in which he makes connections between (apparently) opposing pairs: for example, death (of father) birth (of sister), father's funeral/Baldwin's birthday, father/son, personal/public, black/white, interior/exterior psychological states, acceptance/fighting. Write a paper in which you show how these oppositions serve his overall purpose.

FORMAL WRITING AND RESEARCH PAPERS

7. Use a history of black Americans to find the names of several blacks who achieved success during World War II. Choose one of these. Research his or her life and write a paper that reports the sort of obstacles and opposition he or she had to overcome in order to become successful.

Malcolm Bailey

Hold: Separate but Equal

(1969)

Malcolm Bailey (born 1947), originally from Harlem, was educated at the
New Lincoln School, the High School of Art and Design, and the Pratt
Institute, where he earned his B.F.A. He has received numerous awards for
his work.

   This may strike you as a piece of draftsmanship rather than a work of
art. A mechanical drawing is really a set of directions for building
something—certainly that cannot be the case here. As you look at it, try to
discern its purpose.

JOURNAL WRITINGS

1.   Try sitting in the position of the figures in the painting. Do you find it
     comfortable? Would it be comfortable for a long period? What do your
     answers to these questions suggest about the artist's decision to paint the
     figures in this position?

BRAINSTORMING AND DRAFTING

2.   In a word or two how would you **describe** this painting? What do those few
     words tell you about the work? About your response to it?
3.   Explore some of the meanings of "hold." What sort of light do they throw on
     the painting?

THE ARTIST'S METHODS

4.   Explain why you do (or do not) find this painting **ironic.**
5.   Is this sort of drawing usually considered "art"? What do you associate it
     with? Explain why the artist has chosen it; what does he express through it?
6.   Why has the artist chosen to depict a ship? List as many reasons as you can
     and write a sentence for each reason that relates it to the meaning of the
     painting.

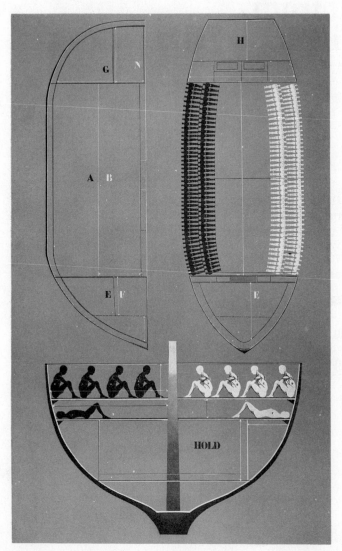

Bailey, Malcolm. *Hold, Separate but Equal* (1969). Synthetic polymer paint, presstype, watercolor, and enamel on composition board, 7' × 48". Collection, The Museum of Modern Art, New York. Mr. and Mrs. John R. Jakobson Fund.

FORMAL WRITING AND RESEARCH PAPERS

7. Look up the phrase "separate but equal." Write a paper that explains when and how it was used and relate that information to this painting.

Martin Luther King, Jr.

Letter from Birmingham Jail*

A Baptist minister from the age of eighteen, Martin Luther King, Jr. (1929–1968), was certainly the preeminent American religious leader of his generation. He graduated from Morehouse College and Crozer Theological Seminary and went on to earn a Ph.D. from Boston University and a D.D. from Chicago Theological Seminary. He founded and directed the Southern Christian Leadership Conference, an organization that was instrumental in advancing the rights of blacks during the sixties. He received many humanitarian awards, including the Nobel Peace Prize in 1964. Dr. King was murdered in 1968.

Arrested in 1963 for demonstrating without a permit, Dr. King spent several days in the jail of Birmingham, Alabama. While there, he wrote this letter in response to a full-page advertisement, run by a group of clergymen, that objected to his demonstration as untimely and provocative.

PREVIEWS

A. Write down a few things you have heard or read about the way blacks were treated in this country in the earlier part of this century.
B. How much different do you feel the treatment of blacks is today?

---

*[Author's Note] This response to a published statement by eight fellow clergymen from Alabama (Bishop C. C. J. Carpenter, Bishop Joseph A. Durick, Rabbi Hilton L. Grafman, Bishop Paul Hardin, Bishop Holan B. Harmon, the Reverend George M. Murray, the Reverend Edward V. Ramage and the Reverend Earl Stallings) was composed under somewhat constricting circumstances. Begun on the margins of the newspaper in which the statement appeared while I was in jail, the letter was continued on scraps of writing paper supplied by a friendly Negro trusty, and concluded on a pad my attorneys were eventually permitted to leave me. Although the text remains in substance unaltered, I have indulged in the author's prerogative of polishing it for publication.

April 16, 1963

MY DEAR FELLOW CLERGYMEN:

While confined here in the Birmingham city jail, I came across your recent statement calling my present activities "unwise and untimely." Seldom do I pause to answer criticism of my work and ideas. If I sought to answer all the criticisms that cross my desk, my secretaries would have little time for anything other than such correspondence in the course of the day, and I would have no time for constructive work. But since I feel that you are men of genuine good will and that your criticisms are sincerely set forth, I want to try to answer your statement in what I hope will be patient and reasonable terms.

I think I should indicate why I am here in Birmingham, since you have been influenced by the view which argues against "outsiders coming in." I have the honor of serving as president of the Southern Christian Leadership Conference, an organization operating in every southern state, with headquarters in Atlanta, Georgia. We have some eighty-five affiliated organizations across the South, and one of them is the Alabama Christian Movement for Human Rights. Frequently we share staff, educational and financial resources with our affiliates. Several months ago the affiliate here in Birmingham asked us to be on call to engage in a nonviolent direct-action program if such were deemed necessary. We readily consented, and when the hour came we lived up to our promise. So I, along with several members of my staff, am here because I was invited here. I am here because I have organizational ties here.

But more basically, I am in Birmingham because injustice is here. Just as the prophets of the eighth century B.C. left their villages and carried their "thus saith the Lord" far beyond the boundaries of their home towns, and just as the Apostle Paul left his village of Tarsus* and carried the gospel of Jesus Christ to the far corners of the Greco-Roman world, so am I compelled to carry the gospel of freedom beyond my own hometown. Like Paul, I must constantly respond to the Macedonian call for aid.

Moreover, I am cognizant of the interrelatedness of all communities and states. I cannot sit idly by in Atlanta and not be concerned about what happens in Birmingham. Injustice anywhere is a threat to justice everywhere. We are caught in an inescapable network of mutuality, tied in a single garment of destiny. Whatever affects one directly, affects all indirectly. Never again can we afford to live with the narrow, provincial "outside agitator" idea. Anyone who lives inside the United States can never be considered an outsider anywhere within its bounds.

You deplore the demonstrations taking place in Birmingham. But your statement, I am sorry to say, fails to express a similar concern for the conditions that brought about the demonstrations. I am sure that none of you would want to rest content with the superficial kind of social analysis that deals merely with effects and does not grapple with underlying causes. It is unfortunate that demonstrations are taking place in Birmingham, but it is even more unfortunate

---

* Tarsus—city in southern Turkey, birthplace of the Apostle Paul. [Eds.]

that the city's white power structure left the Negro community with no alternative.

In any nonviolent campaign there are four basic steps: collection of the facts to determine whether injustices exist; negotiation; self-purification; and direct action. We have gone through all these steps in Birmingham. There can be no gainsaying the fact that racial injustice engulfs this community. Birmingham is probably the most thoroughly segregated city in the United States. Its ugly record of brutality is widely known. Negroes have experienced grossly unjust treatment in the courts. There have been more unsolved bombings of Negro homes and churches in Birmingham than in any other city in the nation. These are the hard, brutal facts of the case. On the basis of these conditions, Negro leaders sought to negotiate with the city fathers. But the latter consistently refused to engage in good-faith negotiation.

Then, last September, came the opportunity to talk with leaders of Birmingham's economic community. In the course of the negotiations, certain promises were made by the merchants—for example, to remove the stores' humiliating racial signs. On the basis of these promises, the Reverend Fred Shuttlesworth and the leaders of the Alabama Christian Movement for Human Rights agreed to a moratorium on all demonstrations. As the weeks and months went by, we realized that we were the victims of a broken promise. A few signs, briefly removed, returned; the others remained.

As in so many past experiences, our hopes had been blasted, and the shadow of deep disappointment settled upon us. We had no alternative except to prepare for direct action, whereby we would present our very bodies as a means of laying our case before the conscience of the local and the national community. Mindful of the difficulties involved, we decided to undertake a process of self-purification. We began a series of workshops on nonviolence, and we repeatedly asked ourselves: "Are you able to accept blows without retaliating?" "Are you able to endure the ordeal of jail?" We decided to schedule our direct-action program for the Easter season, realizing that except for Christmas, this is the main shopping period of the year. Knowing that a strong economic-withdrawal program would be the by-product of direct action, we felt that this would be the best time to bring pressure to bear on the merchants for the needed change.

Then it occurred to us that Birmingham's mayoral election was coming up in March, and we speedily decided to postpone action until after election day. When we discovered that the Commissioner of Public Safety, Eugene "Bull" Connor, had piled up enough votes to be in the runoff, we decided again to postpone action until the day after the runoff so that the demonstrations could not be used to cloud the issues. Like many others, we waited to see Mr. Connor defeated, and to this end we endured postponement after postponement. Having aided in this community need, we felt that our direct-action program could be delayed no longer.

You may well ask: "Why direct action? Why sit-ins, marches and so forth? Isn't negotiation a better path?" You are quite right in calling for negotiation. Indeed, this is the very purpose of direct action. Nonviolent direct action seeks to create such a crisis and foster such a tension that a community which has constantly refused to negotiate is forced to confront the issue. It seeks so to dramatize the issue that it can no longer be ignored. My citing the creation of tension as part of the work of the nonviolent-resister may sound rather shocking. But I must confess that I am not afraid of the word "tension." I have earnestly opposed violent tension, but there is a type of constructive, nonviolent tension which is necessary for growth. Just as Socrates* felt that it was necessary to create a tension in the mind so that individuals could rise from the bondage of myths and half-truths to the unfettered realm of creative analysis and objective appraisal, so must we see the need for nonviolent gadflies to create the kind of tension in society that will help men rise from the dark depths of prejudice and racism to the majestic heights of understanding and brotherhood.

The purpose of our direct-action program is to create a situation so crisis-packed that it will inevitably open the door to negotiation. I therefore concur with you in your call for negotiation. Too long has our beloved Southland been bogged down in a tragic effort to live in monologue rather than dialogue.

One of the basic points in your statement is that the action that I and my associates have taken in Birmingham is untimely. Some have asked: "Why didn't you give the new city administration time to act?" The only answer that I can give to this query is that the new Birmingham administration must be prodded about as much as the outgoing one, before it will act. We are sadly mistaken if we feel that the election of Albert Boutwell as mayor will bring the millennium† to Birmingham. While Mr. Boutwell is a much more gentle person than Mr. Connor, they are both segregationists, dedicated to maintenance of the status quo. I have hope that Mr. Boutwell will be reasonable enough to see the futility of massive resistance to desegregation. But he will not see this without pressure from devotees of civil rights. My friends, I must say to you that we have not made a single gain in civil rights without determined legal and nonviolent pressure. Lamentably, it is an historical fact that privileged groups seldom give up their privileges voluntarily. Individuals may see the moral light and voluntarily give up their unjust posture; but, as Reinhold Niebuhr‡ has reminded us, groups tend to be more immoral than individuals.

We know through painful experience that freedom is never voluntarily given by the oppressor; it must be demanded by the oppressed. Frankly, I have yet to engage in a direct-action campaign that was "well timed" in the view of those who have not suffered unduly from the disease of segregation. For years now I have heard the word "Wait!" It rings in the ear of every Negro with piercing familiarity. This "Wait" has almost always meant "Never." We must come to see, with one of our distinguished jurists, that "justice too long delayed is justice denied."

We have waited for more than 340 years for our constitutional and God-given rights. The nations of Asia and Africa are moving with jetlike speed toward gaining political independence, but we still creep at horse-and-buggy pace

---

* Socrates—(470?–399 B.C.) Greek philosopher who trained Plato. [Eds.]

† The millennium—a period of 1000 years, time of the second coming of Christ. [Eds.]

‡ Reinhold Niebuhr—(1892–1971) American Protestant theologian. [Eds.]

toward gaining a cup of coffee at a lunch counter. Perhaps it is easy for those who have never felt the stinging darts of segregation to say, "Wait." But when you have seen vicious mobs lynch your mothers and fathers at will and drown your sisters and brothers at whim; when you have seen hate-filled policemen curse, kick and even kill your black brothers and sisters; when you see the vast majority of your twenty million Negro brothers smothering in an airtight cage of poverty in the midst of an affluent society; when you suddenly find your tongue twisted and your speech stammering as you seek to explain to your six-year-old daughter why she can't go to the public amusement park that has just been advertised on television, and see tears welling up in her eyes when she is told that Funtown is closed to colored children, and see ominous clouds of inferiority beginning to form in her little mental sky, and see her beginning to distort her personality by developing an unconscious bitterness toward white people; when you have to concoct an answer for a five-year-old son who is asking: "Daddy, why do white people treat colored people so mean?"; when you take a cross-country drive and find it necessary to sleep night after night in the uncomfortable corners of your automobile because no motel will accept you; when you are humiliated day in and day out by nagging signs reading "white" and "colored"; when your first name becomes "nigger," your middle name becomes "boy" (however old you are) and your last name becomes "John," and your wife and mother are never given the respected title "Mrs."; when you are harried by day and haunted by night by the fact that you are a Negro, living constantly at tiptoe stance, never quite knowing what to expect next, and are plagued with inner fears and outer resentments; when you are forever fighting a degenerating sense of "nobodiness"—then you will understand why we find it difficult to wait. There comes a time when the cup of endurance runs over, and men are no longer willing to be plunged into the abyss of despair. I hope, sirs, you can understand our legitimate and unavoidable impatience.

You express a great deal of anxiety over our willingness to break laws. This is certainly a legitimate concern. Since we so diligently urge people to obey the Supreme Court's decision of 1954 outlawing segregation in the public schools, at first glance it may seem rather paradoxical for us consciously to break laws. One may well ask: "How can you advocate breaking some laws and obeying others?" The answer lies in the fact that there are two types of laws: just and unjust. I would be the first to advocate obeying just laws. One has not only a legal but a moral responsibility to obey just laws. Conversely, one has a moral responsibility to disobey unjust laws. I would agree with St. Augustine* that "an unjust law is no law at all."

Now, what is the difference between the two? How does one determine whether a law is just or unjust? A just law is a man-made code that squares with the moral law or the law of God. An unjust law is a code that is out of harmony with the moral law. To put it in the terms of St. Thomas Aquinas†: An unjust law is a human law that is not rooted in eternal law and natural law. Any law that uplifts

---

* St. Augustine—(354–430) Bishop of Hippo in North Africa, theologian and philosopher. [Eds.]

† St. Thomas Aquinas—(1225?–1274) Italian scholastic philosopher and theologian. [Eds.]

human personality is just. Any law that degrades human personality is unjust. All segregation statutes are unjust because segregation distorts the soul and damages the personality. It gives the segregator a false sense of superiority and the segregated a false sense of inferiority. Segregation, to use the terminology of the Jewish philosopher Martin Buber,* substitutes an "I—it" relationship for an "I—thou" relationship and ends up relegating persons to the status of things. Hence segregation is not only politically, economically and sociologically unsound, it is morally wrong and sinful. Paul Tillich† has said that sin is separation. Is not segregation an existential expression of man's tragic separation, his awful estrangement, his terrible sinfulness? Thus it is that I can urge men to obey the 1954 decision of the Supreme Court, for it is morally right; and I can urge them to disobey segregation ordinances, for they are morally wrong.

Let us consider a more concrete example of just and unjust laws. An unjust law is a code that a numerical or power majority group compels a minority group to obey but does not make binding on itself. This is *difference* made legal. By the same token, a just law is a code that a majority compels a minority to follow and that it is willing to follow itself. This is *sameness* made legal.

Let me give another explanation. A law is unjust if it is inflicted on a minority that, as a result of being denied the right to vote, had no part in enacting or devising the law. Who can say that the legislature of Alabama which set up that state's segregation laws was democratically elected? Throughout Alabama all sorts of devious methods are used to prevent Negroes from becoming registered voters, and there are some counties in which, even though Negroes constitute a majority of the population, not a single Negro is registered. Can any law enacted under such circumstances be considered democratically structured?

Sometimes a law is just on its face and unjust in its application. For instance, I have been arrested on a charge of parading without a permit. Now, there is nothing wrong in having an ordinance which requires a permit for a parade. But such an ordinance becomes unjust when it is used to maintain segregation and to deny citizens the First-Amendment privilege of peaceful assembly and protest.

I hope you are able to see the distinction I am trying to point out. In no sense do I advocate evading or defying the law, as would the rabid segregationist. That would lead to anarchy. One who breaks an unjust law must do so openly, lovingly, and with a willingness to accept the penalty. I submit that an individual who breaks a law that conscience tells him is unjust, and who willingly accepts the penalty of imprisonment in order to arouse the conscience of the community over its injustice, is in reality expressing the highest respect for law.

Of course, there is nothing new about this kind of civil disobedience. It was evidenced sublimely in the refusal of Shadrach, Meshach and Abednego to obey the laws of Nebuchadnezzar,‡ on the ground that a higher moral law was at stake. It was practiced superbly by the early Christians, who were willing to face hungry

---

* Martin Buber—(1878–1965) Jewish religious scholar and philosopher. [Eds.]

† Paul Tillich—(1886–1965) German Protestant theologian. [Eds.]

‡ Nebuchadnezzar—(605–562 B.C.) Babylonian emperor who captured Jerusalem. [Eds.]

lions and the excruciating pain of chopping blocks rather than submit to certain unjust laws of the Roman Empire. To a degree, academic freedom is a reality today because Socrates practiced civil disobedience. In our own nation, the Boston Tea Party represented a massive act of civil disobedience.

We should never forget that everything Adolf Hitler did in Germany was "legal" and everything the Hungarian freedom fighters did in Hungary was "illegal." It was "illegal" to aid and comfort a Jew in Hitler's Germany. Even so, I am sure that, had I lived in Germany at the time, I would have aided and comforted my Jewish brothers. If today I lived in a Communist country where certain principles dear to the Christian faith are suppressed, I would openly advocate disobeying that country's antireligious laws.

I must make two honest confessions to you, my Christian and Jewish brothers. First, I must confess that over the past few years I have been gravely disappointed with the white moderate. I have almost reached the regrettable conclusion that the Negro's great stumbling block in his stride toward freedom is not the White Citizen's Councilor or the Ku Klux Klanner, but the white moderate, who is more devoted to "order" than to justice; who prefers a negative peace which is the absence of tension to a positive peace which is the presence of justice; who constantly says: "I agree with you in the goal you seek, but I cannot agree with your methods of direct action"; who paternalistically believes he can set the timetable for another man's freedom; who lives by a mythical concept of time and who constantly advises the Negro to wait for a "more convenient season." Shallow understanding from people of good will is more frustrating than absolute misunderstanding from people of ill will. Lukewarm acceptance is much more bewildering than outright rejection.

I had hoped that the white moderate would understand that law and order exist for the purpose of establishing justice and that when they fail in this purpose they become the dangerously structured dams that block the flow of social progress. I had hoped that the white moderate would understand that the present tension in the South is a necessary phase of the transition from an obnoxious negative peace, in which the Negro passively accepted his unjust plight, to a substantive and positive peace, in which all men will respect the dignity and worth of human personality. Actually, we who engage in nonviolent direct action are not the creators of tension. We merely bring to the surface the hidden tension that is already alive. We bring it out in the open, where it can be seen and dealt with. Like a boil that can never be cured so long as it is covered up but must be opened with all its ugliness to the natural medicines of air and light, injustice must be exposed, with all the tension its exposure creates, to the light of human conscience and the air of national opinion before it can be cured.

In your statement you assert that our actions, even though peaceful, must be condemned because they precipitate violence. But is this a logical assertion? Isn't this like condemning a robbed man because his possession of money precipitated the evil act of robbery? Isn't this like condemning Socrates because his unswerving commitment to truth and his philosophical inquiries precipitated the act by the misguided populance in which they made him drink hemlock? Isn't this like condemning Jesus because his unique God-consciousness and never-ceasing devotion to God's will precipitated the evil act of crucifixion? We must come to see that, as the federal courts have consistently affirmed, it is wrong to urge an individual to cease his efforts to gain his basic constitutional rights because the quest may precipitate violence. Society must protect the robbed and punish the robber.

I had also hoped that the white moderate would reject the myth concerning time in relation to the struggle for freedom. I have just received a letter from a white brother in Texas. He writes: "All Christians know that the colored people will receive equal rights eventually, but it is possible that you are in too great a religious hurry. It has taken Christianity almost two thousand years to accomplish what it has. The teachings of Christ take time to come to earth." Such an attitude stems from a tragic misconception of time, from the strangely irrational notion that there is something in the very flow of time that will inevitably cure all ills. Actually, time itself is neutral; it can be used either destructively or constructively. More and more I feel that the people of ill will have used time much more effectively than have the people of good will. We will have to repent in this generation not merely for the hateful words and actions of the bad people but for the appalling silence of the good people. Human progress never rolls in on wheels of inevitability; it comes through the tireless efforts of men willing to be co-workers with God, and without this hard work, time itself becomes an ally of the forces of social stagnation. We must use time creatively, in the knowledge that the time is always ripe to do right. Now is the time to make real the promise of democracy and transform our pending national elegy into a creative psalm of brotherhood. Now is the time to lift our national policy from the quicksand of racial injustice to the solid rock of human dignity.

You speak of our activity in Birmingham as extreme. At first I was rather disappointed that fellow clergymen would see my nonviolent efforts as those of an extremist. I began thinking about the fact that I stand in the middle of two opposing forces in the Negro community. One is a force of complacency, made up in part of Negroes who, as a result of long years of oppression, are so drained of self-respect and a sense of "somebodiness" that they have adjusted to segregation; and in part of a few middle-class Negroes who, because of a degree of academic and economic security and because in some ways they profit by segregation, have become insensitive to the problems of the masses. The other force is one of bitterness and hatred, and it comes perilously close to advocating violence. It is expressed in the various black nationalist groups that are springing up across the nation, the largest and best-known being Elijah Muhammad's Muslim movement. Nourished by the Negro's frustration over the continued existence of racial discrimination, this movement is made up of people who have lost faith in America, who have absolutely repudiated Christianity, and who have concluded that the white man is an incorrigible "devil."

I have tried to stand between these two forces, saying that we need emulate neither the "do-nothingism" of the complacent nor the hatred and despair of the black nationalist. For there is the more excellent way of love and nonviolent protest. I am grateful to God that, through the influence of the Negro church, the way of nonviolence became an integral part of our struggle.

If this philosophy had not emerged, by now many streets of the South would, I am convinced, be flowing with blood. And I am further convinced that if our white brothers dismiss as "rabble-rousers" and "outside agitators" those of us who employ nonviolent direct action, and if they refuse to support our nonviolent efforts, millions of Negroes will, out of frustration and despair, seek solace and security in black-nationalist ideologies—a development that would inevitably lead to a frightening racial nightmare.

Oppressed people cannot remain oppressed forever. The yearning for freedom eventually manifests itself, and that is what has happened to the American Negro. Something within has reminded him of his birthright of freedom, and something without has reminded him that it can be gained. Consciously or unconsciously, he has been caught up by the Zeitgeist,* and with his black brothers of Africa and his brown and yellow brothers of Asia, South America and the Caribbean, the United States Negro is moving with a sense of great urgency toward the promised land of racial justice. If one recognizes this vital urge that has engulfed the Negro community, one should readily understand why public demonstrations are taking place. The Negro has many pent-up resentments and latent frustrations, and he must release them. So let him march; let him make prayer pilgrimages to the city hall; let him go on freedom rides—and try to understand why he must do so. If his repressed emotions are not released in nonviolent ways, they will seek expression through violence; this is not a threat but a fact of history. So I have not said to my people: "Get rid of your discontent." Rather, I have tried to say that this normal and healthy discontent can be channeled into the creative outlet of nonviolent direct action. And now this approach is being termed extremist.

But though I was initially disappointed at being categorized as an extremist, as I continued to think about the matter I gradually gained a measure of satisfaction from the label. Was not Jesus an extremist for love: "Love your enemies, bless them that curse you, do good to them that hate you, and pray for them which despitefully use you, and persecute you." Was not Amos an extremist for justice: "Let justice roll down like waters and righteousness like an ever-flowing stream." Was not Paul an extremist for the Christian gospel: "I bear in my body the marks of the Lord Jesus." Was not Martin Luther an extremist: "Here I stand; I cannot do otherwise, so help me God." And John Bunyan: "I will stay in jail to the end of my days before I make a butchery of my conscience." And Abraham Lincoln: "This nation cannot survive half slave and half free." And Thomas Jefferson: "We hold these truths to be self-evident, that all men are created equal . . . " So the question is not whether we will be extremists, but what kind of extremists we will be. Will we be extremists for hate or for love? Will we be extremists for the preservation of injustice or for the extension of justice? In that dramatic scene on Calvary's hill three men were crucified. We must never forget that all three were crucified for the same crime—the crime of extremism. Two were extremists for immorality, and thus fell below their environment. The

---

* Zeitgeist—German, translated as "spirit of the times." [Eds.]

other, Jesus Christ, was an extremist for love, truth and goodness, and thereby rose above his environment. Perhaps the South, the nation and the world are in dire need of creative extremists.

I had hoped that the white moderate would see this need. Perhaps I was too optimistic; perhaps I expected too much. I suppose I should have realized that few members of the oppressor race can understand the deep groans and passionate yearnings of the oppressed race, and still fewer have the vision to see that injustice must be rooted out by strong, persistent and determined action. I am thankful, however, that some of our white brothers in the South have grasped the meaning of this social revolution and committed themselves to it. They are still all too few in quantity, but they are big in quality. Some—such as Ralph McGill, Lillian Smith, Harry Golden, James McBride Dabbs, Ann Braden and Sarah Patton Boyle—have written about our struggle in eloquent and prophetic terms. Others have marched with us down nameless streets of the South. They have languished in filthy, roach-infested jails, suffering the abuse and brutality of policemen who view them as "dirty nigger-lovers." Unlike so many of their moderate brothers and sisters, they have recognized the urgency of the moment and sensed the need for powerful "action" antidotes to combat the disease of segregation.

Let me take note of my other major disappointment. I have been so greatly disappointed with the white church and its leadership. Of course, there are some notable exceptions. I am not unmindful of the fact that each of you has taken some significant stands on this issue. I commend you, Reverend Stallings, for your Christian stand on this past Sunday, in welcoming Negroes to your worship service on a nonsegregated basis. I commend the Catholic leaders of this state for integrating Spring Hill College several years ago.

But despite these notable exceptions, I must honestly reiterate that I have been disappointed with the church. I do not say this as one of those negative critics who can always find something wrong with the church. I say this as a minister of the gospel, who loves the church; who was nurtured in its bosom; who has been sustained by its spiritual blessings and who will remain true to it as long as the cord of life shall lengthen.

When I was suddenly catapulted into the leadership of the bus protest in Montgomery, Alabama, a few years ago, I felt we would be supported by the white church. I felt that the white ministers, priests and rabbis of the South would be among our strongest allies. Instead, some have been outright opponents, refusing to understand the freedom movement and misrepresenting its leaders; all too many others have been more cautious than courageous and have remained silent behind the anesthetizing security of stained-glass windows.

In spite of my shattered dreams, I came to Birmingham with the hope that the white religious leadership of this community would see the justice of our cause and, with deep moral concern, would serve as the channel through which our just grievances could reach the power structure. I had hoped that each of you would understand. But again I have been disappointed.

I have heard numerous southern religious leaders admonish their worshipers to comply with a desegregation decision because it is the law, but I have longed to hear white ministers declare: "Follow this decree because integration is morally right and because the Negro is your brother." In the midst of blatant injustices inflicted upon the Negro, I have watched white churchmen stand on the sideline and mouth pious irrelevancies and sanctimonious trivialities. In the midst of a mighty struggle to rid our nation of racial and economic injustice, I have heard many ministers say: "Those are social issues, with which the gospel has no real concern." And I have watched many churches commit themselves to a completely otherworldly religion which makes a strange, un-Biblical distinction between body and soul, between the sacred and the secular.

I have traveled the length and breadth of Alabama, Mississippi and all the other southern states. On sweltering summer days and crisp autumn mornings I have looked at the South's beautiful churches with their lofty spires pointing heavenward. I have beheld the impressive outlines of her massive religious-education buildings. Over and over I have found myself asking: "What kind of people worship here? Who is their God? Where were their voices when the lips of Governor Barnett dripped with words of interposition and nullification? Where were they when Governor Wallace gave a clarion call for defiance and hatred? Where were their voices of support when bruised and weary Negro men and women decided to rise from the dark dungeons of complacency to the bright hills of creative protest?"

Yes, these questions are still in my mind. In deep disappointment I have wept over the laxity of the church. But be assured that my tears have been tears of love. There can be no deep disappointment where there is not deep love. Yes, I love the church. How could I do otherwise? I am in the rather unique position of being the son, the grandson and the great-grandson of preachers. Yes, I see the church as the body of Christ. But, oh! How we have blemished and scarred that body through social neglect and through fear of being nonconformists.

There was a time when the church was very powerful—in the time when the early Christians rejoiced at being deemed worthy to suffer for what they believed. In those days the church was not merely a thermometer that recorded the ideas and principles of popular opinion; it was a thermostat that transformed the mores of society. Whenever the early Christians entered a town, the people in power became disturbed and immediately sought to convict the Christians for being "disturbers of the peace" and "outside agitators." But the Christians pressed on, in the conviction that they were "a colony of heaven," called to obey God rather than man. Small in number, they were big in commitment. They were too God-intoxicated to be "astronomically intimidated." By their effort and example they brought an end to such ancient evils as infanticide and gladiatorial contests.

Things are different now. So often the contemporary church is a weak, ineffectual voice with an uncertain sound. So often it is an archdefender of the status quo. Far from being disturbed by the presence of the church, the power structure of the average community is consoled by the church's silent—and often even vocal—sanction of things as they are.

But the judgment of God is upon the church as never before. If today's church does not recapture the sacrificial spirit of the early church, it will lose its authenticity, forfeit the loyalty of millions, and be dismissed as an irrelevant social club with no meaning for the twentieth century. Every day I meet young people whose disappointment with the church has turned into outright disgust.

Perhaps I have once again been too optimistic. Is organized religion too inextricably bound to the status quo to save our nation and the world? Perhaps I must turn my faith to the inner spiritual church, the church within the church, as the true *ekklesia** and the hope of the world. But again I am thankful to God that some noble souls from the ranks of organized religion have broken loose from the paralyzing chains of conformity and joined us as active partners in the struggle for freedom. They have left their secure congregations and walked the streets of Albany, Georgia, with us. They have gone down the highways of the South on tortuous rides for freedom. Yes, they have gone to jail with us. Some have been dismissed from their churches, have lost the support of their bishops and fellow ministers. But they have acted in the faith that right defeated is stronger than evil triumphant. Their witness has been the spiritual salt that has preserved the true meaning of the gospel in these troubled times. They have carved a tunnel of hope through the dark mountain of disappointment.

I hope the church as a whole will meet the challenge of this decisive hour. But even if the church does not come to the aid of justice, I have no despair about the future. I have no fear about the outcome of our struggle in Birmingham, even if our motives are at present misunderstood. We will reach the goal of freedom in Birmingham and all over the nation, because the goal of America is freedom. Abused and scorned though we may be, our destiny is tied up with America's destiny. Before the pilgrims landed at Plymouth, we were here. Before the pen of Jefferson etched the majestic words of the Declaration of Independence across the pages of history, we were here. For more than two centuries our forebears labored in this country without wages; they made cotton king; they built the homes of their masters while suffering gross injustice and shameful humiliation— and yet out of a bottomless vitality they continued to thrive and develop. If the inexpressible cruelties of slavery could not stop us, the opposition we now face will surely fail. We will win our freedom because the sacred heritage of our nation and the eternal will of God are embodied in our echoing demands.

Before closing I feel impelled to mention one other point in your statement that has troubled me profoundly. You warmly commended the Birmingham police force for keeping "order" and "preventing violence." I doubt that you would have so warmly commended the police force if you had seen its dogs sinking their teeth into unarmed, nonviolent Negroes. I doubt that you would so quickly commend the policemen if you were to observe their ugly and inhumane treatment of Negroes here in the city jail; if you were to watch them push and curse old Negro women and young Negro girls; if you were to see them slap and kick old Negro men and young boys; if you were to observe them, as they did on two occasions, refuse to give us food because we wanted to sing our grace together. I cannot join you in your praise of the Birmingham police department.

---

* *Ekklesia*—Greek, translated as "the church." [Eds.]

It is true that the police have exercised a degree of discipline in handling the demonstrators. In this sense they have conducted themselves rather "nonviolently" in public. But for what purpose? To preserve the evil system of segregation. Over the past few years I have consistently preached that nonviolence demands that the means we use must be as pure as the ends we seek. I have tried to make clear that it is wrong to use immoral means to attain moral ends. But now I must affirm that it is just as wrong, or perhaps even more so, to use moral means to preserve immoral ends. Perhaps Mr. Connor and his policemen have been rather nonviolent in public, as was Chief Pritchett in Albany, Georgia, but they have used the moral means of nonviolence to maintain the immoral end of racial injustice. As T. S. Eliot has said: "The last temptation is the greatest treason: To do the right deed for the wrong reason."

I wish you had commended the Negro sit-inners and demonstrators of Birmingham for their sublime courage, their willingness to suffer and their amazing discipline in the midst of great provocation. One day the South will recognize its real heroes. They will be the James Merediths, with the noble sense of purpose that enables them to face jeering and hostile mobs, and with the agonizing loneliness that characterizes the life of the pioneer. They will be old, oppressed, battered Negro women, symbolized in a seventy-two-year-old woman in Montgomery, Alabama, who rose up with a sense of dignity and with her people decided not to ride segregated buses, and who responded with ungrammatical profundity to one who inquired about her weariness: "My feets is tired, but my soul is at rest." They will be the young high school and college students, the young ministers of the gospel and a host of their elders, courageously and nonviolently sitting in at lunch counters and willingly going to jail for conscience' sake. One day the South will know that when these disinherited children of God sat down at lunch counters, they were in reality standing up for what is best in the American dream and for the most sacred values in our Judaeo-Christian heritage, thereby bringing our nation back to those great wells of democracy which were dug deep by the founding fathers in their formulation of the Constitution and the Declaration of Independence.

Never before have I written so long a letter. I'm afraid it is much too long to take your precious time. I can assure you that it would have been much shorter if I had been writing from a comfortable desk, but what else can one do when he is alone in a narrow jail cell, other than write long letters, think long thoughts and pray long prayers?

If I have said anything in this letter that overstates the truth and indicates an unreasonable impatience, I beg you to forgive me. If I have said anything that understates the truth and indicates my having a patience that allows me to settle for anything less than brotherhood, I beg God to forgive me.

I hope this letter finds you strong in the faith. I also hope that circumstances will soon make it possible for me to meet each of you, not as an integrationist or a civil-rights leader but as a fellow clergyman and a Christian brother. Let us all hope that the dark clouds of racial prejudice will soon pass away and the deep fog of misunderstanding will be lifted from our fear-drenched communities, and in some not too distant tomorrow the radiant stars of love and brotherhood will shine over our great nation with all their scintillating beauty.

Yours for the cause of Peace and Brotherhood,

MARTIN LUTHER KING, JR.

JOURNAL WRITINGS

1. Think about prejudice as a learned response. Both King and Baldwin talk about the problem of rearing children in a prejudiced environment. Consider your own prejudices (face up to it, we all have them) and try to identify just where they came from. Write about how they developed and how you want to deal with them.

BRAINSTORMING AND DRAFTING

2. Religious leaders around the world consistently condemn racism. Yet some of the most racist individuals describe themselves as devoutly religious. Discuss this paradox. What, if anything, can be done about it?
3. King means to **persuade** his audience (not only the clergymen to whom the letter is directly addressed) that his position is just. Consider his tone in relation to this purpose. How does he vary his tone and how effective is tone as a persuasive instrument?

THE AUTHOR'S METHODS

4. Trace the way King responds, point by point, to the objections of the other clergymen. Perhaps outlining would help here. Characterize each of his ways of responding in a sentence or two.
5. King uses a wealth of **allusions** and citations of various authorities in this letter (remember, he was in jail so all these came from his memory). **Define** the purpose(s) and effect(s) of these allusions and citations. Write a fully developed paragraph about his use of allusion and citation.
6. **Analyze** the structure of some of Dr. King's sentences. Does he vary these structures? How do the structures he uses relate to the meaning he wants to convey? Choose several sentences that you consider particularly effective. Write sentences in the same patterns but on different topics.

CREATIVE PROJECT

7. Choose a topic about which you feel strongly (it need not be related to prejudice—the plight of the homeless, battered women, nuclear disarma-

ment are a few examples). Write an extended letter to someone who takes a different view of your topic, attempting to persuade him/her to a change of mind on the subject.

FORMAL WRITING AND RESEARCH PAPERS

8.   Research the circumstances of Dr. King's assassination. What controversy surrounded his death? Write a fully documented paper arguing one side of this controversy.

Mary E. Mebane

Incident on a Bus

(1981)

As this selection from her autobiography (*Mary,* 1981) indicates, Mary E. Mebane (born 1933) grew up in Durham, North Carolina. She graduated from North Carolina College at Durham in 1955 and earned an M.A. from the University of North Carolina in 1961. Not only has Ms. Mebane taught at all levels, elementary, secondary, and college, but she is also a writer who has published plays and essays.

Ms. Mebane evokes what it was like for a young girl to ride to her weekly music lesson on a segregated bus.

PREVIEW

Dr. King mentions that bad laws are no laws at all. Think of a law in this category that affects you somehow.

Historically, my lifetime is important because I was part of the last generation born into a world of total legal segregation in the Southern United States. When the Supreme Court outlawed segregation in the public schools in 1954, I was twenty-one. When Congress passed the Civil Rights Act of 1964, permitting blacks free access to public places, I was thirty-one. The world I was born into had been segregated for a long time—so long, in fact, that I never met anyone who had lived during the time when restrictive laws were not in existence, although some people spoke of parents and others who had lived during the "free" time. As far as anyone knew, the laws as they then existed would stand forever. They were meant to—and did—create a world that fixed black people at the bottom of society in all aspects of human life. It was a world without options.

Most Americans have never had to live with terror. I had had to live with it all my life—the psychological terror of segregation, in which there was a special set of laws governing your movements. You violated them at your peril, for you knew that if you broke one of them, knowingly or not, physical terror was just around the corner, in the form of policemen and jails, and in some cases and places white vigilante mobs formed for the exclusive purpose of keeping blacks in line.

It was Saturday morning, like any Saturday morning in dozens of Southern towns.

The town had a washed look. The street sweepers had been busy since six o'clock. Now, at eight, they were still slowly moving down the streets, white trucks with clouds of water coming from underneath the swelled tubular sides. Unwary motorists sometimes got a windowful of water as a truck passed by. As it moved on, it left in its wake a clear stream running in the gutters or splashed on the wheels of parked cars.

Homeowners, bent over industriously in the morning sun, were out pushing lawn mowers. The sun was bright, but it wasn't too hot. It was morning and it was May. Most of the mowers were glad that it was finally getting warm enough to go outside.

Traffic was brisk. Country people were coming into town early with their produce; clerks and service workers were getting to the job before the stores opened at ten o'clock. Though the big stores would not be open for another hour or so, the grocery stores, banks, open-air markets, dinettes, were already open and filling with staff and customers.

Everybody was moving toward the heart of Durham's downtown, which waited to receive them rather complacently, little knowing that in a decade the shopping centers far from the center of downtown Durham would create a ghost town in the midst of the busiest blocks on Main Street.

Some moved by car, and some moved by bus. The more affluent used cars, leaving the buses mainly to the poor, black and white, though there were some businesspeople who avoided the trouble of trying to find a parking place downtown by riding the bus.

I didn't mind taking the bus on Saturday. It wasn't so crowded. At night or on Saturday or Sunday was the best time. If there were plenty of seats, the blacks didn't have to worry about being asked to move so that a white person could sit down. And the knot of hatred and fear didn't come into my stomach.

I knew the stop that was the safety point, both going and coming. Leaving town, it was the Little Five Points, about five or six blocks north of the main downtown section. That was the last stop at which four or five people might get on. After that stop, the driver could sometimes pass two or three stops without taking on or letting off a passenger. So the number of seats on the bus usually remained constant on the trip from town to Braggtown. The nearer the bus got to the end of the line, the more I relaxed. For if a white passenger got on near the end of the line, often to catch the return trip back and avoid having to stand in the sun at the bus stop until the bus turned around, he or she would usually stand if there were not seats in the white section, and the driver would say nothing, knowing that the end of the line was near and that the standee would get a seat in a few minutes.

On the trip to town, the Mangum Street A&P was the last point at which the driver picked up more passengers than he let off. These people, though they were just a few blocks from the downtown section, preferred to ride the bus downtown. Those getting on at the A&P were usually on their way to work at the Duke University Hospital—past the downtown section, through a residential neighborhood, and then past the university, before they got to Duke Hospital.

So whether the driver discharged more passengers than he took on near the A&P on Mangum was of great importance. For if he took on more passengers than got off, it meant that some of the newcomers would have to stand. And if they were white, the driver was going to have to ask a black passenger to move so that a white passenger could sit down. Most of the drivers had a rule of thumb, though. By custom the seats behind the exit door had become "colored" seats, and no matter how many whites stood up, anyone sitting behind the exit door knew that he or she wouldn't have to move.

The disputed seat, though, was the one directly opposite the exit door. It was "no-man's-land." White people sat there, and black people sat there. It all depended on whose section was fuller. If the back section was full, the next black passenger who got on sat in the no-man's-land seat; but if the white section filled up, a white person would take the seat. Another thing about the white people: they could sit anywhere they chose, even in the "colored" section. Only the black passengers had to obey segregation laws.

On this Saturday morning Esther and I set out for town for our music lesson. We were going on our weekly big adventure, all the way across town, through the white downtown, then across the railroad tracks, then through the "colored" downtown, a section of run-down dingy shops, through some fading high-class black neighborhoods, past North Carolina College, to Mrs. Shearin's house.

We walked the two miles from Wildwood to the bus line. Though it was a warm day, in the early morning there was dew on the grass and the air still had the night's softness. So we walked along and talked and looked back constantly, hoping someone we knew would stop and pick us up.

I looked back furtively, for in one of the few instances that I remembered my father criticizing me severely, it was for looking back. One day when I was walking from town he had passed in his old truck. I had been looking back and had seen him. "Don't look back," he had said. "People will think that you want them to pick you up." Though he said "people," I knew he meant men—not the men he knew, who lived in the black community, but the black men who were not part of the community, and all of the white men. To be picked up meant that something bad would happen to me. Still, two miles is a long walk and I occasionally joined Esther in looking back to see if anyone we knew was coming.

Esther and I got to the bus and sat on one of the long seats at the back that faced each other. There were three such long seats—one on each side of the bus and a third long seat at the very back that faced the front. I liked to sit on a long seat facing the side because then I didn't have to look at the expressions on the faces of the whites when they put their tokens in and looked at the blacks sitting in the back of the bus. Often I studied my music, looking down and practicing the fingering. I looked up at each stop to see who was getting on and to check on the seating pattern. The seating pattern didn't really bother me that day until the bus started to get unusually full for a Saturday morning. I wondered what was happening, where all these people were coming from. They got on and got on until the white section was almost full and the black section was full.

There was a black man in a blue windbreaker and a gray porkpie hat sitting in no-man's-land, and my stomach tightened. I wondered what would happen. I had never been on a bus on which a black person was asked to give a seat to a white person when there was no other seat empty. Usually, though, I had seen a black person automatically get up and move to an empty seat farther back. But this morning the only empty seat was beside a black person sitting in no-man's-land.

The bus stopped at Little Five Points and one black got off. A young white man was getting on. I tensed. What would happen now? Would the driver ask the black man to get up and move to the empty seat farther back? The white man had a businessman's air about him: suit, shirt, tie, polished brown shoes. He saw the empty seat in the "colored" section and after just a little hesitation went to it, put his briefcase down, and sat with his feet crossed. I relaxed a little when the bus pulled off without the driver saying anything. Evidently he hadn't seen what had happened, or since he was just a few stops from Main Street, he figured the mass exodus there would solve all the problems. Still, I was afraid of a scene.

The next stop was an open-air fruit stand just after Little Five Points, and here another white man got on. Where would he sit? The only available seat was beside the black man. Would he stand the few stops to Main Street or would the driver make the black man move? The whole colored section tensed, but nobody said anything. I looked at Esther, who looked apprehensive. I looked at the other men and women, who studiously avoided my eyes and everybody else's as well, as they maintained a steady gaze at a far-distant land.

Just one woman caught my eye; I had noticed her before, and I had been ashamed of her. She was a stringy little black woman. She could have been forty; she could have been fifty. She looked as if she were a hard drinker. Flat black face with tight features. She was dressed with great insouciance in a tight boy's sweater with horizontal lines running across her flat chest. It pulled down over a nondescript skirt. Laced-up shoes, socks, and a head rag completed her outfit. She looked tense.

The white man who had just gotten on the bus walked to the seat in no-man's-land and stood there. He wouldn't sit down, just stood there. Two adult males, living in the most highly industrialized, most technologically advanced nation in the world, a nation that had devastated two other industrial giants in World War II and had flirted with taking on China in Korea. Both these men, either of whom could have fought for the United States in Germany or Korea, faced each other in mutual rage and hostility. The white one wanted to sit down, but he was going to exert his authority and force the black one to get up first. I watched the driver in the rearview mirror. He was about the same age as the antagonists. The driver wasn't looking for trouble, either.

"Say there, buddy, how about moving back," the driver said, meanwhile driving his bus just as fast as he could. The whole bus froze—whites at the front, blacks at the rear. They didn't want to believe what was happening was really happening.

The seated black man said nothing. The standing white man said nothing.

"Say, buddy, did you hear me? What about moving on back." The driver was scared to death. I could tell that.

"These is the niggers' seats!" the little lady in the strange outfit started screaming. I jumped. I had to shift my attention from the driver to the frieze of the black man seated and white man standing to the articulate little woman who had joined in the fray.

"The government gave us these seats! These is the niggers' seats." I was startled at her statement and her tone. "The president said that these are the niggers' seats!" I expected her to start fighting at any moment.

Evidently the bus driver did, too, because he was driving faster and faster. I believe that he forgot he was driving a bus and wanted desperately to pull to the side of the street and get out and run.

"I'm going to take you down to the station, buddy," the driver said.

The white man with the briefcase and the polished brown shoes who had taken a seat in the "colored" section looked as though he might die of embarrassment at any moment.

As scared and upset as I was, I didn't miss a thing.

By that time we had come to the stop before Main Street, and the black passenger rose to get off.

"You're not getting off, buddy. I'm going to take you downtown." The driver kept driving as he talked and seemed to be trying to get downtown as fast as he could.

"These are the niggers' seats! The government plainly said these are the niggers' seats!" screamed the little woman in rage.

I was embarrassed at the use of the word "nigger" but I was proud of the lady. I was also proud of the man who wouldn't get up.

The bus driver was afraid, trying to hold on to his job but plainly not willing to get into a row with the blacks.

The bus seemed to be going a hundred miles an hour and everybody was anxious to get off, though only the lady and the driver were saying anything.

The black man stood at the exit door; the driver drove right past the A&P stop. I was terrified. I was sure that the bus was going to the police station to put the black man in jail. The little woman had her hands on her hips and she never stopped yelling. The bus driver kept driving as fast as he could.

Then, somewhere in the back of his mind, he decided to forget the whole thing. The next stop was Main Street, and when he got there, in what seemed to be a flash of lightning, he flung both doors open wide. He and his black antagonist looked at each other in the rearview mirror; in a second the windbreaker and porkpie hat were gone. The little woman was standing, preaching to the whole bus about the government's gift of these seats to the blacks; the man with the brown shoes practically fell out of the door in his hurry; and Esther and I followed the hurrying footsteps.

We walked about three doors down the block, then caught a bus to the black neighborhood. Here we sat on one of the two long seats facing each other, directly behind the driver. It was the custom. Since this bus had a route from a black neighborhood to the downtown section and back, passing through no white residential areas, blacks could sit where they chose. One minute we had been on a bus in which violence was threatened over a seat near the exit door; the next minute we were sitting in the very front behind the driver.

The people who devised this system thought that it was going to last forever.

JOURNAL WRITINGS

1. Mebane mentions a "safety point." Write a paragraph in which you identify what it is and tell why it was important. Recall some sort of "safety point" in your own life. **Describe** it and explain how it is similar and/or different from Mebane's.
2. Recall an instance from your childhood that really frightened you. **Narrate** what happened in such a way as to make your audience understand why you were frightened.

BRAINSTORMING AND DRAFTING

3. Discuss the physical and psychological implications of living with terror. You might reconsider some of the insights that James Baldwin's piece offers.
4. Mebane talks about the seats that "by custom" could be occupied by members of either race. Discuss some of the aspects of your life that are governed by custom (as opposed to law). What are these aspects? Discuss the extent to which people should let custom dictate their responses. Write a paragraph that suggests when and how people should resist custom.

THE AUTHOR'S METHODS

5. Select some of the details in this essay that give it a sense of immediacy and reality. Write a short paper in which you explain what these details are and what effect they produce.
6. What general conclusion(s) do you draw from this very personal auto-biographical essay? Write a paper suggesting how these conclusions might apply to other situations and evaluating any dangers that might arise from such applications.
7. Analyze Mebane's vocabulary. What words seem to be appropriate for a North Carolina black girl in tenth grade? What words seem to fit an older black woman looking back on an event in her childhood? Write a paragraph about each type and a concluding paragraph discussing the significance of the differences.

FORMAL WRITING AND RESEARCH PAPERS

8. Write a paper in which you explain the motivation and significance of the old black woman's outburst.

Carol Lee Sanchez

Sex, Class and Race Intersections: Visions of Women of Color

(1983)

A native American descended from the Laguna and Sioux tribes, Carol Lee Sanchez (born 1934) is a painter as well as a poet and playwright. The mother of three children, she has published *Conversations from the Nightmare,* a book of poems.

In this short article she describes attitudes white people commonly take toward native Americans. She also explains some of the basic differences between the way that native Americans and whites relate to the world in which we all live. She concludes with an appeal for change on the part of the whites.

PREVIEW

Do you remember playing "Cowboys and Indians" when you were a child? Were there squabbles about who got to be who? Did the cowboys always win? Try to recall what sort of feelings you may have had while playing this game.

"As I understand it," said the American Indian [to one of the Puritan Fathers], "you propose to civilize me."
"Exactly."
"You want to get me out of the habit of idleness and teach me to work."
"That is the idea."
"And then lead me to simplify my methods and invent things to make my work lighter."
"Yes."
"And after that I'll become ambitious to get rich so that I won't have to work at all."
"Naturally."
"Well what's the use of taking such a roundabout way of getting just where I started from? I don't have to work now."   (AMERICAN JOKELORE)

To identify Indian is to identify with an invisible or vanished people; it is to identify with a set of basic assumptions and beliefs held by *all* who are not Indian about the indigenous peoples of the Americas. Even among the Spanish-speaking Mestizos or mezclados, there is a strong preference to "disappear" their Indian blood, to disassociate from their Indian beginnings. To be Indian is to be considered "colorful," spiritual, connected to the earth, simplistic, and disappointing if not dressed in buckskin and feathers; shocking if a city-dweller and even more shocking if an educator or other type of professional. That's the positive side.

On the negative side, to be Indian is to be thought of as primitive, alcoholic, ignorant (as in "Dumb Indian"), better off dead (as in "the only good Indian is a dead Indian" or "I didn't know there was any of you folks still left"), unskilled, non-competitive, immoral, pagan or heathen, untrustworthy (as in "Indian-giver") and frightening. To be Indian is to be the primary model that is used to promote racism in this country.

How can that happen, you ask? Bad press. One hundred and fifty years of the most consistently vicious press imaginable. Newspapers, dime novels, textbooks and fifty years of visual media have portrayed and continue to portray Indians as savage, blood-thirsty, immoral, inhuman people. When there's a touch of social consciousness attached, you will find the once "blood-thirsty," "white-killer savage" portrayed as a pitiful drunk, a loser, an outcast or a mix-blood not welcomed by, or trusted by, either race. For fifty years, children in this country have been raised to kill Indians mentally, subconsciously through the visual media, until it is an automatic reflex. That shocks you? Then I have made my point.

Let me quote from Helen Hunt Jackson's book, *A Century of Dishonor,* from the introduction written by Bishop H. B. Whipple of Minnesota, who charged that:

> [T]he American people have accepted as truth the teachings that the Indians were a degraded, brutal race of savages, who it was the will of God should perish at the approach of civilization. If they do not say with our Puritan fathers that these are the Hittites who are to be driven out before the saints of the Lord, they do accept the teaching that manifest destiny will drive the Indians from the earth. The inexorable has no tears or pity at the cries of anguish of the doomed race.

This race still struggles to stay alive. Tribe by Tribe, pockets of Indian people here and there. One million two hundred thousand people who identify as Indians—raised and socialized as Indian—as of the 1980 census, yet Cowboys and Indians is still played every day by children all over America of every creed, color, and nationality. Well—it's harmless isn't it? Just kids playing kill Indians. It's all history. But it's still happening every day, and costumes are sold and the cheap western is still rolling out of Hollywood, the old shoot-'em-up westerns playing on afternoon kid shows, late night T.V. Would you allow your children to play Nazis and Jews? Blacks and KKKs? Complete with costume? Yes! It is a horrifying thought, but in thinking about it you can see how easy it is to dismiss an entire race of people as barbaric and savage, and how almost impossible it is, after this has been inculcated in you, to relate to an Indian or a group of Indians today. For example, how many famous Indians do you know offhand? Certainly the great warrior chiefs come to mind first, and of course the three most famous Indian "Princesses"—Pocahantas, Sacajawea and La Malinche. Did you get past ten? Can you name at least five Indian women you know personally or have heard about? That's just counting on one hand, folks.

As Indians, we have endured. We are still here. We have survived everything that European "civilization" has imposed on us. There are approximately 130 different Indian languages still spoken in North America of the some 300 spoken at contact; 180 different Tribes incorporated and recognized by the Federal Government of the approximately 280 that once existed, with an additional 15 to 25 unrecognized Tribes that are lumped together on a reservation with other Tribes. We still have Women's Societies and there are at least 30 active women-centered Mother-Rite Cultures existing and practicing their everyday life in that manner, on this continent.

We have been displaced, relocated, removed, terminated, educated, acculturated and in our hearts and minds we will always "go back to the blanket" as long as we are still connected to our families, our Tribes and our land.

The Indian Way is a different way. It is a respectful way. The basic teachings in every Tribe that exists today as a Tribe in the western hemisphere are based on respect for all the things our Mother gave us. If we neglect her or anger her, she will make our lives very difficult and we always know that we have a hardship on ourselves and on our children. We are raised to be cautious and concerned for the *future* of our people, and that is how we raise our children—because *they* are *our* future. Your "civilization" has made all of us very sick and has made our mother earth sick and out of balance. Your kind of thinking and education has brought the whole world to the brink of total disaster, whereas the thinking and education among my people forbids the practice of almost everything Euro-Americans, in particular, value.

Those of you who are socialists and Marxists have an ideology, but where in this country do you live communally on a common land base from generation to generation? Indians, who have a way of life instead of an ideology, do live on communal lands and don't accumulate anything—for the sake of accumulation.

Radicals look at reservation Indians and get very upset about their poverty conditions. But poverty to us is not the same thing as poverty is to you. Our poverty is that we can't be who we are. We can't hunt or fish or grow our food because our basic resources and the right to use them in traditional ways are denied us. In order to live well, we must be able to provide for ourselves in such a way that we can continue living as we always have. We still don't believe in being slaves to the "domineering" culture systems. Consequently, we are accused of many things based on those standards and values that make no sense to us.

You want us to act like you, to be like you so that we will be more acceptable, more likeable. You should try to be more like us regarding communal coexistence; respect and care for all living things and for the earth, the waters, and the atmosphere; respect for human dignity and the right to be who they are.

During the 1930s, '40s and '50s, relocation programs caused many Indians to become lost in the big cities of the United States and there were many casualties from alcoholism, vagrancy and petty crime. Most Indians were/are jailed for assault and battery in barroom brawls because the spiritual and psychological violation of Indian people trying to live in the dominant [domineering] culture generally forces us to numb ourselves as frequently as possible. That is difficult, if not impossible, for you to understand. White science studies dead things and creates poisonous substances to kill and maim the creatures as well as the humans. You call that progress. Indians call it insanity. Our science studies living things; how they interact and how they maintain a balanced existence. Your science disregards—even denies—the spirit world: ours believes in it and remains connected to it. We fast, pray to our ancestors, call on them when we dance and it rains—at Laguna, at Acoma, at Hopi—still, today. We fight among ourselves, we have border disputes, we struggle to exist in a modern context with our lands full of timber, uranium, coal, oil, gasoline, precious metals and semi-precious stones; full—because we are taught to take only what we need and not because we are too ignorant to know what to do with all these resources. We are caught in the bind between private corporations and the government—"our guardian"—because they/you want all those resources. "Indians certainly don't need them"—and your people will do *anything* to get their hands on our mineral-rich lands. They will legislate, stir up internal conflicts, cause inter-Tribal conflicts, dangle huge amounts of monies as compensation for perpetual contracts and promise lifetime economic security. If we object, or sue to protect our lands, these suits will be held in litigation for fifteen to twenty years with "white" interests benefiting in the interim. Some of us give up and sell out, but there are many of us learning to hold out and many many more of us going back to the old ways of thinking, because we see that our ancestors were right and that the old ways were better ways. So, more Indians are going "back to the blanket," back to "Indian time," with less stress, fewer dominant (domineering) culture activities and occupations. Modern Indians are recreating Indian ways once again. All this leads to my vision as an Indian woman. It is my hope:

1. that you—all you non-Indians—study and learn about our systems of thought and internal social and scientific practices, leaving your Patriarchal Anthropology and History textbooks, academic training and methodologies at home or in the closet on a dusty shelf.
2. that your faculties, conference organizers, community organizers stop giving lip service to including a "Native American" for this or that with the appended phrase: "if we only knew one!" Go find one. There are hundreds of resources lists or Indian-run agencies, hundreds of Indian women in organizations all over the country—active and available with valuable contributions to make.
3. that you will strongly discourage or STOP the publication of any and all articles *about* Indians *written by non-Indians,* and publish work written by Indians about ourselves—whether you agree with us, approve of us or not.
4. that you will *stop colonizing us* and reinterpreting *our* experience.

5. that you will *listen* to us and *learn* from us. We carry ancient traditions that are thousands of years old. We are modern and wear clothes like yours and handle all the trappings of your "civilization" as well as ours; maintain your christianity as well as our ancient religions, and we are still connected to our ancestors, and our land base. You are the foreigners as long as you continue to believe in the progress that destroys our Mother.

You are not taught to respect our perfected cultures or our scientific achievements which have just recently been re-evaluated by your social scientists and "deemed worthy" of respect. Again, let me re-state that 150 years of bad press will certainly make it extremely difficult for most white people to accept these "primitive" achievements without immediately attempting to connect them to aliens from outer space, Egyptians, Vikings, Asians and whatever sophisticated "others" you have been educated to acknowledge as those who showed the "New World" peoples "The Way." Interestingly, the only continents that were ever "discovered" (historically) where people already lived are North and South America. Who discovered Europe? Who discovered Africa? Who discovered Asia? Trade routes, yes—continents, no. Manifest Destiny will continue to reign as long as we teach our children that Columbus "discovered" America. Even this "fact" is untrue. He actually discovered an island in the Caribbean and *failed* to discover Cathay!

When we consistently make ourselves aware of these "historical facts" that are presented by the Conqueror—the White Man—only then can all of us benefit from cultural traditions that are ten to thirty thousand years old. It is time for us to *share* the best of all our traditions and cultures, all over the world; and it is our duty and responsibility as the women of the world to make this positive contribution in any and every way we can, or we will ultimately become losers, as the Native Race of this hemisphere lost some four hundred years ago.

JOURNAL WRITINGS

1. Which part of Ms. Sanchez's article do you find most **persuasive?** Why?
2. Consider the paragraph that begins "As Indians, we have endured." Write down your immediate and unreflective response to the facts in this paragraph. After a day or two, review what you have written and record whether your response is different.

BRAINSTORMING AND DRAFTING

3. Try Sanchez's test—"how many famous Indians do you know offhand?" Evaluate your own response. Would you do better or worse with some other ethnic group? Write a few sentences appraising the adequacy of this test and describing your own emotional response to it.

THE AUTHOR'S METHODS

4.   Reread the next-to-last paragraph. **Describe** the author's view of history in this paragraph. **Explain** why you agree or disagree with it.

5.   Carefully consider the tone of this article. What words and idiomatic expressions does she use to develop this tone? Write a paper that describes the tone of the article and the way it affects you as a reader.

CREATIVE PROJECT

6.   Write a poem that expresses your feelings about some aspect of the natural world and your relationship with it.

FORMAL WRITING AND RESEARCH PAPERS

7.   " . . . at Laguna, at Acoma, at Hopi . . . " Consult an atlas (for instance, *The Atlas of North American Indians*) to find out where these places are. Then look up each of them in *The Encyclopedia of Anthropology* to find out what importance these places have for native Americans. Choose one of the three. Write a report about its significance.

8.   Consult *Abstracts in Anthropology* to find some articles about the status of women in native American tribal organizations. Select a tribe or nation. Write a paper that **describes** the status of women in that tribe or nation and **compares** it to the status of women in contemporary American society as a whole.

Betye Saar

The Liberation
of Aunt Jemima

(1972)

Betye Saar (1926–), who was born in Los Angeles, graduated from Pasadena City College in 1949. She is best known for her constructions in boxes, which she produced during the 1960s.

   This construction loses some of its effect in a photograph. Remember that it is a box (2³/₄ inches deep and about the size of an ordinary sheet of paper). Look carefully at the three different images of Aunt Jemima that it presents.

JOURNAL WRITINGS

1.   What feelings does the picture on page 125 stimulate? Describe your feelings and explain what aspects of the picture give rise to those feelings.

BRAINSTORMING AND DRAFTING

2.   Free associate as you look at this construction; note down whatever comes to mind. Look over the notes you have written and write a few sentences explaining whatever patterns you find.

THE ARTIST'S METHODS

3.   Repetition is a significant part of this work. Examine the parts that are repeated and write a paragraph commenting on the purpose of repeating parts within the work as a whole.
4.   Write a paragraph explaining the **symbolism** of the objects that the statue of Aunt Jemima is holding.
5.   What parts of this construction use **stereotypes?** Determine to your own satisfaction how and why these stereotypes are used. Write a paragraph that relates the use of stereotypes to the effect of the whole work.
6.   How does the fact that this work is a "box" contribute to its impact on the viewer?

FORMAL WRITING AND RESEARCH PAPERS

7.   Find out as much as you can about Aunt Jemima. Carefully define the **connotations** that became linked to this logo. In a paper, relate these connotations to the history of Aunt Jemima and **argue** that this construction is an effective and appropriate response to these connotations.

Norma Nager

Racism and White Women: Keeping Sexism Intact

(1984)

Norma Nager (born 1936) is a native of rural Wisconsin who began her education by studying nursing. She became a registered nurse in 1957 and earned a certificate in Public Health Nursing and a B.S. from the University of Minnesota in 1961. She then switched to sociology, receiving her M.A. (1967) and Ph.D. (1978) from the University of Wisconsin at Madison. Since then she has been teaching at the college level.

Nager points out that white feminists, while struggling for the improvement of women, often take racist positions. She believes that this contributes to implicit forms of oppression.

PREVIEW

What does the term *sexist* bring to mind? Recall and describe a specific action or situation that you would describe as sexist.

Recently, a friend and colleague—a Black man—was walking down a New York City street behind a white woman. She saw his reflection in the store window and grabbed her purse to her side. Basically, it irritated him. This had happened to him before and he decided that if the woman behaved this way unconsciously he would be doing her a favor by making her aware of what it meant to him. If she was consciously doing it, it was insulting and he wanted to let her know that. So he quickened his pace and as he got to her side he said, "Excuse me . . . "—as he spoke the woman ran screaming across the street.

In the 1970s and '80s the fears of white women about Black men are expressed not just in their faces on city streets, but are reflected in literary terms in such works as Susan Brownmiller's *Against Our Will*. This perception of sexual violence is only one of the ways that racism and sexism are perpetuated and intensified, effectively preventing cooperation between women's rights groups and Black rights groups. Just as women's rights were pitted against voting rights in the 1800s to destroy alliances between Abolitionists and white suffragists, in the 1970s and 1980s issues of employment, wages, occupational distribution, and crime rates have been used to manipulate white women into taking extremely racist stands against minorities, and especially against Blacks.

According to recent reports of the Bureau of Census, whites, both male and female, earn more than Blacks. Since the material conditions of the lives of people are critical considerations in determining their attitudes, the fact that the vast majority of whites have a material life-style far different from the vast majority of Blacks in this country perpetuates separatist attitudes. Most white women who have been involved in women's organizations come from the middle class; thus, the additional privilege of class has made it impossible for them to unite with other women in forging alliances for the liberation of women and of other people struggling for self-determination. As Karl Marx* has pointed out, the consciousness of people does not determine their being; on the contrary, their social being, or position, determines their consciousness.

If women are defined in terms of their race, sex, and class, then class relations, race relations, and patriarchal relations define their consciousness, and have implications which are different for different groups of women by race and by class. It means, therefore, that the objective position of Black women, and of white women *who predominate* in the women's movement are quite different. These genuine differences must be acknowledged. We still hear about Blacks being killed or jailed by the police for little, if any, reason; about the high infant mortality rates for Blacks and Native Americans; and about the disproportionately high unemployment rates among Blacks. But what does it mean to white women concerned about women's issues and the liberation of women? One thing it clearly demonstrates is that the major issues addressed by the women's movement are not the same issues as those listed above.

While Black women and men must be concerned with the very critical issues of surviving in a racist world, the white women's movement is concerned with such individualized issues as equal pay for equal work, sexual abuse, and so on. One need only peruse current women's publications such as *Ms. Magazine* and *Working Woman* to document this. It is not that these issues are unimportant; it is simply that if they remain in an individualized context, very little will be accomplished for people other than middle-class white women, and for them the gains will be temporary until the broader economic and political context is changed. Until the "survival issues" most relevant to Black people are solved, the "success issues" of the women's movement cannot be resolved.

To overcome barriers that separate them from other women, white women must first confront the reality of racism—not simply racism as a general evil in society but racial hatred and stereotypes in themselves and in their communities. It is precisely the racism and classism of members of white women's rights groups that have caused the majority of Black women to suspect motives and to reject active participation.

---

* Karl Marx—(1818–1883) German socialist philosopher, author of *Communist Manifesto*. [Eds.]

There are many examples of how women's organizations ignore racist policies. The jailing and retention in New York City of Ms. Jerry Gaines, a Black woman from Mississippi and mother of eight, for refusing to collaborate with the authorities concerning a Nyack, New York, bank robbery is one instance. I have not heard of an organized protest from any women's organization, but would be delighted to learn that I am wrong and that there is fundraising and picketing by NOW or some other feminist group.

Another area overlooked by women's groups is the employment and occupational picture for Blacks, particularly for young women. According to the Bureau of Labor Statistics, the unemployment rate is almost 50 percent for teenage Black males, and it is even higher for teenage Black females. While some of this is due to changes in occupational structure, unemployment for these groups has always been extremely high. We can be sure that with organized coalitions, demands for fundamental changes in these conditions would be effected. The same kinds of changes can be brought about with the coalitions of people bent on liberation—women's liberation, Black liberation, Native-American liberation—changes in displacement from homes and neighborhoods, changes in health care, and changes in quality of education.

However, none of these struggles will include white women unless we acknowledge and work through our own ideological blindness toward the unification of the real women's liberation movement: the struggle toward self-determination and human dignity is not simply for middle-class white women, or for women only, but for all people. Until we understand the interrelatedness of oppression—by race, sex, and class, and how that oppression, in turn, is related to the universal problems of potential destruction of all life—we will continue to cooperate in our own sexual and class oppression.

JOURNAL WRITINGS

1. In a few sentences, describe your initial reaction to this article; include both intellectual and emotional responses.
2. What connection is Nager making between sexism and racism? Define this connection as briefly and precisely as possible.

BRAINSTORMING AND DRAFTING

3. Should the women's movement address the issues of justice and infant mortality that Nager cites? Discuss this question in a group, giving each person an opportunity to express and support an opinion. Note down the reasons given for and against. Write a short paper arguing your own opinion, refuting at least one opinion that you disagree with.

THE AUTHOR'S METHODS

4. Nager's main assertion seems to be in the sentence at the end of the second paragraph. Do you believe that she adequately supports this assertion? If you do, make an outline of her main supporting points. If you do not, decide what would be adequate support and make an outline of those points.

5. Study the opening paragraph. What purpose does this example serve? In a few sentences, explain this purpose and the relationship of the example to the remainder of the article.

6. Reread the paragraph that begins "Another area overlooked by . . . " Focus your attention on the last two sentences. Are they clear? Rewrite them to make the whole paragraph more clear.

CREATIVE PROJECT

7. Use the example in the first paragraph as the situation for a short story. What happens next? How do the characters feel and react? What in their backgrounds has led to this situation?

FORMAL WRITING AND RESEARCH PAPERS

8. Nager mentions Ms. Jerry Gaines as an example of racist policies. Use the *New York Times Index* for 1984 to find out just what happened to Gaines. Write a report on this case, restricting yourself to the facts of the matter. Later, you may want to expand this report into an argument that the Gaines case did or did not exemplify racist policies.

9. Compare Nager's position with the position articulated by Bell Hooks on Black women and Black liberation (see page 139). Write a paper in which you point out their similarities and differences and argue that one author presents her position more persuasively.

Nina Hibbin

Sexist Scenes
from Office Life

(1986)

Nina Hibbin (born 1922) says, in a letter to the editors, that she "died of a heart attack 1988, but [was] brought back to life by marvels of modern science." After she left school at age 16, she became an investigator for Mass-Observation during the London blitz. During the remainder of WWII she served as a flight mechanic with the Royal Air Force. She taught in state infant and junior schools after the war, but left that in 1957 to take up freelance journalism, specializing in film criticism and history. In the 1970s she held two administrative positions related to film-making. Nina Hibbin published more than twenty articles on women, social issues, and television criticism for the *New Statesman* during 1985 and 1986. She is the author of *Eastern Europe* (1966) and co-author of *What A Carry On* (1988).

PREVIEW

Have you ever been sexually harassed (or observed anyone else being harassed)? Just how significant do you regard such behavior?

It's incredible what women have to contend with from some of their male associates at work. In the 1970s, when I was first an "officer" in a regional arts association and then went on to run a large and rapidly expanding film organisation, I came slap up against it. Win some, lose some, as the following examples (with altered names) demonstrate.

Phone call from manager of consultancy firm:

HE: Is there anybody there?
ME: Yes, I'm here. I'm the director—remember? I asked you to ring.
HE: But is there anybody there I can speak to?
ME: You can speak to me.
HE: I mean on technical matters.
ME: You can speak to me.
HE: Well, I spoke to the other young lady and she didn't seem to know anything about it . . .

The "other young lady" is a temp who has started that day. "I'm not young and I'm no lady," I tell the manager—and prove it with a few choice words.

From the Regional Secretary of the Boilermakers' Union
To the Director of TSC
> For the attention of Miss Hibbin
> Dear Sir . . .

From the Director of TSC
To the Regional Secretary of the Boilermakers' Union
> For the Attention of Master Knowles
> Dear Madam . . .

I'm invited to be the Chair of a small area group I've helped to set up. I receive a copy of the draft Articles of Association for amendment. Letter from me to the group's solicitor:

> . . . Apart from my own position, women contending for office or trusteeship in the future may be inhibited by the exclusive "he" and "him" language used throughout the draft. Please delete all reference to "Chairman" and substitute "Chairperson" and use the he/she and his/her form . . .

Reply to me from group's solicitor:

> . . . We do not think that "Chairperson" is an appropriate term for this document. We are, however, prepared to add a rider stating that "he" or "him" may be read as "she" or "her" . . .

Letter from me to solicitor:

> . . . I must insist on "Chairperson". I am prepared, however, to accept a rider, provided that female pronouns (she/her) are used in the Articles. The rider will then state that "she" or "her" may be read as "he" or "him" . . . A few weeks later I receive an amended copy, with "Chairperson", "he/she" and "him/her", as originally requested throughout.

President of the Local Businessman's Club:

> HE: . . . We have a monthly luncheon with a speaker. I know you ladies don't go in much for public speaking, but would you like to give it a try?
> ME: Why me?
> HE: We're having our Ladies Invitation Luncheon next month—you know, the wives come along, too; we feel they deserve a treat once a year. We thought it would be a novelty to have a lady speaker.
> ME: Don't you ever have women speakers at your men-only do's?
> HE: It wouldn't be quite proper would it?

City Hall. Meeting with the Director of Arts and Leisure. He comes behind me and pinches my bottom.

> ME: Mr. Williams—do you do that to my male colleagues when they visit you?
> HE: Good heavens—no! I'm not one of those!

I receive an unsolicited "Dear Sir" letter and brochure about office equipment. As usual, it's all about the "businessman" and "his" interests. I send the letter back with I DON'T DO BUSINESS WITH FIRMS THAT ASSUME ALL POTENTIAL CUSTOMERS ARE MEN scrawled across it. Managing director of the office equipment on the phone (long distance):

> HE: When I received your comment I thought it was some kind of joke. I showed it to my wife for a laugh. But she said you were quite right. In fact, she's made me promise to revise all my publicity and letter styles to appeal to both sexes.
> ME: Good for her—and for you. I'm delighted.
> HE: Fine. Now that we've got that out of the way, when may I expect your order?

Coffee-making rota in the general office notice-board. Everyone, as agreed at staff meeting, to take a turn.

> ME: Where's the coffee, Gary? It's your turn today.
> HE: Can't one of the girls do it?

A fortnight later. Gary's turn again.

> HE: I've decided not to have coffee any more. Bad for digestion. So you can cross me off the rota.

A few days later, Joanna's turn.

> GARY: Joanna love, seeing that you've got some coffee over—do you think I might have a drop?

Extract from internal job description for proposed post of administrator sent to me for approval by Jim, secretary of a film theatre struggling along with voluntary labour:

> . . . He or she (but in this case it would be better to have a "he") will be expected to . . .

Letter to Jim:

> . . . As the administrator who has worked her guts out to get you the funding for a full-timer, I take your expressed preference for a man as a personal insult. Unless you delete this notion from the job description—and from your mind—I will withdraw from the project and will advise the sponsors to do so, too . . .

Reply from Jim:

> Well, well, well! Fancy anyone accusing me, of all people, of being a male chauvinist pig. It so happens that in this particular instance I really did think that a man would be more suitable. However, in deference to your strong opinions . . .

> BETTY: (helping me with correspondence) Men! They're all the same. They'll never change. I wonder you bother to try.

JOURNAL WRITINGS

1. Write a little vignette similar to the ones in Hibbin's article. If you cannot think of one with sexist overtones, write one dealing with any form of prejudice.
2. Respond to some of the various types of sexist behavior that Hibben has written about.

BRAINSTORMING AND DRAFTING

3. Interview one of your classmates about his/her on-the-job experiences. Find out what sort of professional relationships between the sexes he/she experienced. Use the material from this interview to write a **description** of these experiences.
4. Discuss the causes of sexist behavior. What possible cures can you think of? Write a short paragraph about one of the causes and a possible cure for it.

THE AUTHOR'S METHODS

5. The author uses an almost telegraphic **style** (very brief, lots of ellipses) and a dramatic format. Write a paragraph in which you **describe** the effect of these techniques on you as a reader.
6. This piece might well be regarded as a **satire.** If it is, what or who is being satirized? Explain, in a paragraph or two, why you think it is, or is not, likely to produce any changes in the readers.

FORMAL WRITING AND RESEARCH PAPERS

7. Use the *New York Times Index* for the past year to find reports on sexual harassment in the workplace. Use the information you obtain to write a paper that discusses the frequency of such conduct and evaluates the magnitude of the problem.

Bell Hooks

Homophobia in Black Communities

(1989)

Bell Hooks is the pseudonym used by Gloria Watkins (born 1952). Originally from Kentucky, she attended Stanford University, where she received her B.A. in 1973. She did her graduate work in English at the University of Wisconsin and the University of California, Santa Cruz, earning her Ph.D. in 1983. She has taught at several colleges, including Yale, and is currently a member of the faculty at Oberlin. Among her many publications are *Feminist Theory: From Margin to Center* and *Ain't I a Woman: Black Women and Feminism.*

After examining some of the different attitudes toward gays that she has encountered in black communities, Ms. Hooks deals with the charge that black communities are more homophobic than others. She then argues that it is important to challenge homophobic attitudes.

PREVIEW

Look up "homophobia." Write down some homophobic expressions or examples of some actions that reflect this attitude.

Recently I was at my parents' home and heard teenage nieces and nephews expressing their hatred for homosexuals, saying that they could never like anybody who was homosexual. In response I told them, "There are already people who you love and care about who are gay, so just come off it!" They wanted to know who. I said, "The who is not important. If they wanted you to know, they would tell you. But you need to think about the shit you've been saying and ask yourself where it's coming from."

Their vehement expression of hatred startled and frightened me, even more so when I contemplated the hurt that would have been experienced had our loved ones who are gay heard their words. When we were growing up, we would not have had the nerve to make such comments. We were not allowed to say negative, hateful comments about the people we knew who were gay. We knew their names, their sexual preference. They were our neighbors, our friends, our family. They were us—a part of our black community.

The gay people we knew then did not live in separate subcultures, not in the small, segregated black community where work was difficult to find, where many of us were poor. Poverty was important; it created a social context in which structures of dependence were important for everyday survival. Sheer economic necessity and fierce white racism, as well as the joy of being there with the black folks known and loved, compelled many gay blacks to live close to home and family. That meant however that gay people created a way to live out sexual preferences within the boundaries of circumstances that were rarely ideal no matter how affirming. In some cases, this meant a closeted sexual life. In other families, an individual could be openly expressive, quite out.

The homophobia expressed by my nieces and nephews coupled with the assumption in many feminist circles that black communities are somehow more homophobic than other communities in the United States, more opposed to gay rights, provided the stimulus for me to write this piece. Initially, I considered calling it "homophobia in the black community." Yet it is precisely the notion that there is a monolithic black community that must be challenged. Black communities vary—urban and rural experiences create diversity of culture and lifestyle.

I have talked with black folks who were raised in southern communities where gay people were openly expressive of their sexual preference and participated fully in the life of the community. I have also spoken with folks who say just the opposite.

In the particular black community where I was raised there was a real double standard. Black male homosexuals were often known, were talked about, were seen positively, and played important roles in community life, whereas lesbians were talked about solely in negative terms, and the women identified as lesbians were usually married. Often, acceptance of male homosexuality was mediated by material privilege—that is to say that homosexual men with money were part of the materially privileged ruling black group and were accorded the regard and respect given that group. They were influential people in the community. This was not the case with any women.

In those days homophobia directed at lesbians was rooted in deep religious and moral belief that women defined their womanness through bearing children. The prevailing assumption was that to be a lesbian was "unnatural" because one would not be participating in child-bearing. There were no identified lesbian "parents" even though there were gay men known to be caretakers of other folks' children. I have talked with black folks who recall similar circumstances in their communities. Overall, a majority of older black people I spoke with, raised in small, tightly knit southern black communities, suggested there was tolerance and acceptance of different sexual practices and preferences. One black gay male I spoke with felt that it was more important for him to live within a supportive black community, where his sexual preferences were known but not acted out in an overt, public way, than to live away from a community in a gay subculture where this aspect of his identity could be openly expressed.

Recently, I talked with a black lesbian from New Orleans who boasted that the black community has never had any "orange person like Anita Bryant*

---

*Anita Bryant—(born 1940) singer and film star, strong opponent of the gay rights movement.[Eds.]

running around trying to attack gay people." Her experience coming out to a black male roommate was positive and caring. But for every positive story one might hear about gay life in black communities, there are also negative ones. Yet these positive accounts call into question the assumption that black people and black communities are necessarily more homophobic than other groups of people in this society. They also compel us to recognize that there are diversities of black experience. Unfortunately, there are very few oral histories and autobiographies which explore the lives of black gay people in diverse black communities. This is a research project that must be carried out if we are to fully understand the complex experience of being black and gay in this white-supremacist, patriarchal, capitalist society. Often we hear more from black gay people who have chosen to live in predominantly white communities, whose choices may have been affected by undue harassment in black communities. We hear hardly anything from black gay people who live contentedly in black communities.

Black communities may be perceived as more homophobic than other communities because there is a tendency for individuals in black communities to verbally express in an outspoken way anti-gay sentiments. I talked with a straight black male in a California community who acknowledged that though he has often made jokes poking fun at gays or expressing contempt, as a means of bonding in group settings, in his private life he was a central support person for a gay sister. Such contradictory behavior seems pervasive in black communities. It speaks to ambivalence about sexuality in general, about sex as a subject of conversation, and to ambivalent feelings and attitudes toward homosexuality. Various structures of emotional and economic dependence create gaps between attitudes and actions. Yet a distinction must be made between black people overtly expressing prejudice toward homosexuals and homophobic white people who never make homophobic comments but who have the power to actively exploit and oppress gay people in areas of housing, employment, etc. While both groups perpetuate and reinforce each other and this cannot be denied or downplayed, the truth is that the greatest threat to gay rights does not reside in black communities.

It is far more likely that homophobic attitudes can be altered or changed in environments where they have not become rigidly institutionalized. Rather than suggesting that black communities are more homophobic than other communities, and dismissing them, it is important for feminist activists (especially black folks) to examine the nature of that homophobia, to challenge it in constructive ways that lead to change. Clearly religious beliefs and practices in many black communities promote and encourage homophobia. Many Christian black folks (like other Christians in this society) are taught in churches that it is a sin to be gay, ironically sometimes by ministers who are themselves gay or bisexual.

In the past year I talked with a black woman Baptist minister, who, although concerned about feminist issues, expressed very negative attitudes about homosexuality, because, she explained, the Bible teaches that it is wrong. Yet in her daily life she is tremendously supportive and caring of gay friends. When I asked her to explain this contradiction, she argued that it was not a contradiction, that the Bible also teaches her to identify with those who are exploited and oppressed, and to demand that they be treated justly. To her way of thinking, committing a sin did not mean that one should be exploited or oppressed.

The contradictions, the homophobic attitudes that underlie her attitudes, indicate that there is a great need for progressive black theologians to examine the role black churches play in encouraging persecution of gay people. Individual members of certain churches in black communities should protest when worship services become a platform for teaching anti-gay sentiments. Often individuals sit and listen to preachers raging against gay people and think the views expressed are amusing and outmoded, and dismiss them without challenge. But if homophobia is to be eradicated in black communities, such attitudes must be challenged.

Recently, especially as black people all over the United States discussed the film version of Alice Walker's novel *The Color Purple,* as well as the book itself (which includes a positive portrayal of two black women being sexual with each other), the notion that homosexuality threatens the continuation of black families seems to have gained new momentum. In some cases, black males in prominent positions, especially those in media, have helped to perpetuate this notion. Tony Brown stated in one editorial, "No lesbian relationship can take the place of a positive love relationship between black women and black men." It is both a misreading of Walker's novel and an expression of homophobia for any reader to project into this work the idea that lesbian relationships exist as a competitive response to heterosexual encounters. Walker suggests quite the contrary.

Just a few weeks ago I sat with two black women friends eating bagels as one of us expressed her intense belief that white people were encouraging black people to be homosexuals so as to further divide black folks. She was attributing the difficulties many professional heterosexual black women have finding lovers, companions, husbands, to homosexuality. We listened to her and then the other woman said, "Now you know we are not going to sit here and listen to this homophobic bull without challenging it."

We pointed to the reality that many black gay people are parents, hence their sexual preference does not threaten the continuation of black families. We stressed that many black gay people have white lovers and that there is no guarantee that were they heterosexual they would be partnered with other black people. We argued that people should be able to choose and claim the sexual preference that best expresses their being, suggesting that while it is probably true that positive portrayals of gay people encourage people to see this as a viable sexual preference or lifestyle, it is equally true that compulsory heterosexuality is promoted to a far greater extent. We suggested that we should all be struggling to create a climate where there is freedom of sexual expression.

She was not immediately persuaded by our arguments, but at least she had different perspectives to consider. Supporters of gay rights in black communities must recognize that education for critical consciousness that explains and critiques prevailing stereotypes is necessary for us to eradicate homophobia. A central myth that must be explored and addressed is the notion that homosexuality means genocide for black families. And in conjunction with discussions of this issue, black people must confront the reality of bisexuality and the extent to which the spread of AIDS in black communities is connected to bisexual transmission of the HIV virus.

To strengthen solidarity between black folks irrespective of our sexual preferences, allegiance must be discussed. This is especially critical as more and more black gay people live outside black communities. Just as black women are often compelled to answer the question—which is more important: feminist movement or black liberation struggle?—women's rights or civil rights?—which are you first: black or female?—gay people face similar questions. Are you more identified with the political struggle of your race and ethnic group or gay rights struggle? This question is not a simple one. For some people it is raised in such a way that they are compelled to choose one identity over another.

In one case, when a black family learned of their daughter's lesbianism, they did not question her sexual preference (saying they weren't stupid, they had known she was gay), but the racial identity of her lovers. Why white women and not black women? Her gayness, expressed exclusively in relationships with white women, was deemed threatening because it was perceived as estranging her from blackness.

Little is written about this struggle. Often black families who can acknowledge and accept gayness find inter-racial coupling harder to accept. Certainly among black lesbians, the issue of black women preferring solely white lovers is discussed but usually in private conversation. These relationships, like all cross-racial intimate relationships are informed by the dynamics of racism and white supremacy. Black lesbians have spoken about absence of acknowledgement of one another at social gatherings where the majority of black women present are with white women lovers. Unfortunately, such incidents reinforce the notion that one must choose between solidarity with one's ethnic group and solidarity with those with whom one shares sexual preference, irrespective of class and ethnic difference or differences in political perspective.

Black liberation struggle and gay liberation struggle are both undermined when these divisions are promoted and encouraged. Both gay and straight black people must work to resist the politics of domination as expressed in sexism and racism that lead people to think that supporting one liberation struggle diminishes one's support for another or stands one in opposition to another. As part of education for critical consciousness in black communities, it must be continually stressed that our struggle against racism, our struggle to recover from oppression and exploitation are inextricably linked to all struggles to resist domination—including gay liberation struggle.

Often black people, especially non-gay folks, become enraged when they hear a white person who is gay suggest that homosexuality is synonymous with the suffering people experience as a consequence of racial exploitation and oppression. The need to make gay experience and black experience of oppression synonymous seems to be one that surfaces much more in the minds of white people. Too often, it is seen as a way of minimizing or diminishing the particular problems people of color face in a white-supremacist society, especially the problems encountered because one does not have white skin. Many of us have been in discussions where a non-white person—a black person—struggles to explain to white folks that while we can acknowledge that gay people of all colors are harassed and suffer exploitation and domination, we also recognize that there is a significant difference that arises because of the visibility of dark skin. Often homophobic attacks on gay people occur in situations where knowledge of sexual preference is indicated or established—outside of gay bars, for example. While it in no way lessens the severity of such suffering for gay people, or the fear that it causes, it does mean that in a given situation the apparatus of protection and survival may be simply not identifying as gay.

In contrast, most people of color have no choice. No one can hide, change, or mask dark skin color. White people, gay and straight, could show greater understanding of the impact of racial oppression on people of color by not attempting to make these oppressions synonymous, but rather by showing the ways they are linked and yet differ. Concurrently, the attempt by white people to make synonymous experience of homophobic aggression with racial oppression deflects attention away from the particular dual dilemma that non-white gay people face, as individuals who confront both racism and homophobia.

Often black gay folk feel extremely isolated because there are tensions in their relationships with the larger, predominately white gay community created by racism, and tensions within black communities around issues of homophobia. Sometimes, it is easier to respond to such tensions by simply withdrawing from both groups, by refusing to participate or identify oneself politically with any struggle to end domination. By affirming and supporting black people who are gay within our communities, as well as outside our communities, we can help reduce and change the pain of such isolation.

Significantly, attitudes toward sexuality and sexual preference are changing. There is greater acknowledgement that people have different sexual preferences and diverse sexual practices. Given this reality, it is a waste of energy for anyone to assume that their condemnation will ensure that people do not express varied sexual preferences. Many gay people of all races, raised within this homophobic society, struggle to confront and accept themselves, to recover or gain the core of self-love and well-being that is constantly threatened and attacked both from within and without. This is particularly true for people of color who are gay. It is essential that non-gay black people recognize and respect the hardships, the difficulties gay black people experience, extending the love and understanding that is essential for the making of authentic black community. One way we show our care is by vigilant protest of homophobia. By acknowledging the union between black liberation struggle and gay liberation struggle, we strengthen our solidarity, enhance the scope and power of our allegiances, and further our resistance.

JOURNAL WRITINGS

1. You discover that your roommate is gay. Describe how you would feel. What would you do?
2. What did you find surprising in this essay about gay people? Why did it surprise you? Describe how your previous opinions or ideas have changed after reading this essay.

BRAINSTORMING AND DRAFTING

3. Interview some of your peers, both men and women. Ask questions that will reveal their knowledge about and attitudes toward gay persons. What conclusions do you reach from these interviews? Summarize the information gathered through your interviews and use it as support in a paper which presents your conclusions.
4. Consider the case of the Baptist minister. Do you find her actions and attitudes contradictory as Hooks does? Write a paragraph about the possibility of "condemning the sin, but not the sinner."

THE AUTHOR'S METHODS

5. Hooks begins her essay with an anecdotal example. Think of a similar example of prejudice from your own experience. Write an opening paragraph for an essay using your own example.
6. Hooks describes America as a "white-supremacist, patriarchal, capitalist society." What does this tell you about her attitudes? Explain why you would or would not call her attitudes prejudiced.
7. Summarize Hooks' conclusion. Explain why you agree or disagree with what she wants.

FORMAL WRITING AND RESEARCH PAPERS

8. "There is greater acknowledgment that people have different sexual preferences and diverse sexual practices." Argue that this acknowledgment does or does not mean that these different preferences and practices are all morally and socially acceptable.
9. Find out about Anita Bryant's opposition to the gay rights movement (start with the *New York Times Index* for 1977). In a documented paper, evaluate her action, showing how it may have been shaped by a larger historical context.
10. If you have read David Leavitt's story "Territory" in the unit on Personal Relationships, describe the attitude toward homosexuality in that story and compare it to the attitude that Hooks expresses in her essay.

Emma Lazarus

The New Colossus

(1883)

Emma Lazarus (1849–1887), the daughter of a wealthy family of Sephardic Jews, grew up and was privately educated in New York. A cultivated and widely traveled person, she translated Heinrich Heine's poetry and wrote a romance based on Goethe's life. Eventually she moved in the most exclusive literary circles of her time, becoming a friend of Ralph Waldo Emerson. Her most important collection of poetry is entitled *Song of a Semite*. The following short poem, written to raise money for construction of the base of the Statue of Liberty (and later enscribed there), is the work for which she is best known.

PREVIEW

List some associations that the Statue of Liberty brings to your mind.

Give me your tired, your poor,
Your huddled masses yearning to breathe free,
The wretched refuse of your teeming shore
Send these, the homeless tempest-tost to me,
I lift my lamp beside the golden door!

JOURNAL WRITINGS

1. **Describe** your initial emotional response to this poem. Try to explain what stimulated this response.
2. Write a paragraph in which you relate the attitude expressed in this poem to the prejudicial attitudes described in "Bradford" by Hanif Kureishi or in "Incident on a Bus" by Mary Mebane.

BRAINSTORMING AND DRAFTING

3. Discuss the attitude toward immigrants expressed in the poem—**define** it as precisely as you can. Think of terms that are frequently applied to ethnic

groups or immigrants—for example, "spick" or "wop." Are these terms mostly positive or negative? Write a paragraph in which you discuss the attitude of the poem and **compare/contrast** it with the attitude suggested by your collection of terms.

THE AUTHOR'S METHODS

4.   Who is the speaker in this poem? How did you reach your conclusion? How does this affect your response to the poem?
5.   What are the **connotations** of the word "refuse" in line three? Explain how these connotations work in the context of the poem, and in the physical context of its inscription on the base of the Statue.
6.   What is suggested by the words "golden door" in the last line of the poem?

FORMAL WRITING AND RESEARCH PAPERS

7.   Look up information about the Colossus of Rhodes. Write a paper in which you **explain** what the Colossus of Rhodes was and discuss the appropriateness of the **analogy** in the title of the poem. Find other points in the poem at which the analogy is also used.
8.   Do some research about Ellis Island. Write a documented paper about the way immigrants were treated as they arrived in this country. Perhaps you will be able to draw some conclusions about the difference between the ideal picture of immigration and the historical reality.

Dudley Randall

The Melting Pot

(1968)

A native of Washington, D.C., Dudley Randall (born 1914) is a poet, librarian, and editor. Randall has received degrees from Wayne State University and the University of Michigan. In addition to publishing several significant volumes of poetry (among them *Cities Burning* and *A Litany of Friends*), he has edited several anthologies of black poetry.

Randall presents "the melting pot" from his own black perspective.

PREVIEW

America is often referred to as a "melting pot." Write down a few notes telling what this phrase means to you. This can be an intellectual or emotional response.

There is a magic melting pot
where any girl or man
can step in Czech or Greek or Scot,
step out American.

Johann and Jan and Jean and Juan,
Giovanni and Ivan
step in and then step out again
all freshly christened John.

Sam, watching, said, "Why, I was here even
before they came,"
and stepped in too, but was tossed out
before he passed the brim.

And every time Sam tried that pot
they threw him out again.
"Keep out. This is our private pot.
We don't want your black stain."

At last, thrown out a thousand times,
Sam said, "I don't give a damn.
Shove your old pot. You can like it or not,
but I'll be just what I am."

JOURNAL WRITING

1. Many American families retell stories about the coming of their ancestors to this country. Interview an older member of your family and try to elicit such a story. Record it in writing as accurately as you can. According to your interviewee, were the persons involved well received here? Did they easily become Americanized?

BRAINSTORMING AND DRAFTING

2. In a group, share some of the stories you have recorded from your families. What common features do these stories have? What conclusions about the myth of the melting pot can you draw from the common features? Summarize your conclusions in a brief paragraph.
3. Evaluate Sam's decision in the last line of the poem. What might it mean in his life? What advantages or disadvantages might he realize as a result of this decision?

THE AUTHOR'S METHODS

4. When we speak, we control our tone of voice—angry, sad, cool, or whatever. Poets also control tone in their poems. Describe the tone of this poem. What aspects of its language lead to your conclusion about its tone?

CREATIVE PROJECT

5. This poem tells a story in ballad stanzas. Try writing a poem in this form about some interesting current event.

FORMAL WRITING AND RESEARCH PAPERS

6. Do some research (the *Dictionary of American History* might be a good source) about the beginnings of slavery in this country. Write a documented paper about those beginnings in which you explain some of the reasons slavery was established here.
7. Write a fully developed paper in which you compare the attitudes expressed in this poem with those in "The New Colossus." Use the comparison to reach a conclusion about the "melting pot" idea.
8. Research the ways in which groups easily identifiable as "outsiders" have become accepted as immigrants to the United States, for example, the Irish in New England and Chinese and Japanese on the West Coast. Write a documented paper that explains how they gained acceptance.

Luke 10:25–37 (King James Version)

Parable of the Good Samaritan

(ca. 80 A.D.)

The author of one of the four gospels, Luke (1st century A.D.–date uncertain) is reputed to have been born at Antioch in Syria. He was a physician and perhaps a painter. Born a gentile, he was one of the earliest converts to Christianity and accompanied Paul of Tarsus on several of his missionary journeys.

Confronted with a self-justifying trick question, Jesus responded with this parable of a man traveling on the very dangerous road from Jerusalem to Jericho. The traveler receives help where it might least be expected after being spurned by those who might have been expected to aid him.

PREVIEWS

A. Jot down a few acts that you would consider neighborly.
B. The noun *neighbor* derives from a Middle English word meaning "near dweller." Ask yourself if it is merely that; write a sentence or two explaining your response.

And, behold, a certain lawyer stood up, and tempted him, saying, Master, what shall I do to inherit eternal life? He said unto him, What is written in the law? how readest thou? and he answering said, Thou shalt love the Lord thy God with all thy heart, and with all thy soul, and with all thy strength, and with all thy mind; and thy neighbour as thyself. And he said unto him, Thou hast answered right: this do, and thou shalt live. But he, willing to justify himself, said unto Jesus, And who is my neighbour? and Jesus answering said, A certain man went down from Jerusalem to Jericho, and fell among thieves, which stripped him of his raiment, and wounded him, and departed, leaving him half dead. And by chance there came down a certain priest that way: and when he saw him, he passed by on the other side. And likewise a Levite, when he was at the place, came and looked on him, and passed by on the other side. But a certain Samaritan, as he journeyed, came where he was: and when he saw him, he had compassion on him, and went to him, and bound up his wounds, pouring in oil and wine, and set him on his own beast, and brought him to an inn, and took care of him. And on the morrow when he departed, he took out two pence, and gave them to the host, and said unto him, Take care of him; and whatsoever thou spendest more, when I come again, I will repay thee. Which now of these three, thinkest thou, was neighbour unto him that fell among the thieves? And he said, He that shewed mercy on him. Then said Jesus unto him, Go, and do thou likewise.

JOURNAL WRITINGS

1.   "Don't get involved!" is a fairly common piece of modern folk wisdom. Make two lists: why one should and should not "get involved" with helping a perfect stranger.

BRAINSTORMING AND DRAFTING

2.   In a group, compare the lists you made about "getting involved." Discuss the risks that the Samaritan took in helping the man who had been mugged. Write a paragraph about the relationship of those risks to his moral stature.

THE AUTHOR'S METHODS

3.   Look up *parable* in a dictionary of literary terms. How do the characteristics of the definition fit this story?
4.   Why has the author chosen a "priest" and a "Levite" as the two persons who "passed by on the other side"? Write a paragraph explaining these choices and another in which you justify their action.

CREATIVE PROJECT

5.   Write a modern parable about someone in trouble who gets help from an unexpected source.

FORMAL WRITING AND RESEARCH PAPERS

6.   Do some research about the Samaritans (consult *A Reader's Guide to the Great Religions* or *Encyclopedia Judaica* to get started). Try to discover why there was enmity between them and the Jews. Draw on your research to explain why the Samaritan is the central figure in this parable.

BROAD PERSPECTIVES ON PREJUDICE

OverView of the Unit

While the causes of prejudice are various, the result always leads to some form of human suffering. Reexamine the essays, stories, and poems that you have read in this unit. Look for ways of subdividing prejudice and for relationships among the various readings. When you have found a subdivision with several relationships, explore the type of human suffering that you find described. Write a paper designed to elicit the reader's sympathy for those suffering from this particular subcategory of prejudice; suggest some sort of positive action that the reader can take to reduce or eliminate both the prejudice and the suffering.

ClusterWritings

1. Look at the two pictures in this unit. Are both stereotyped views of the condition of blacks? Do you find such stereotypes in some of the essays as well? Write an essay drawing on several readings from the unit to support your views about the relationship between stereotyping and prejudice.
2. In their autobiographies, Baldwin and Mebane present very personal views of the effects of prejudice. Martin Luther King, Jr., does the same in his letter. Look at these pieces in light of the effects they describe. Write an essay on the effects of prejudice, using **examples** from these essays to support your assertions.
3. Chaucer's Prioress clearly demonstrates the persistence of anti-Semitic ideas. Prager and Telushkin assert that these ideas are unique. But look at Luke's account of the Good Samaritan. Here the Jews are the prejudiced parties. Consider the other two pieces in the light of Luke's. Write an essay showing what conclusions you reach.
4. Emma Lazarus asserts that the United States is ready to accept all comers into the promised land. Randall replies that the promise applies to anyone but blacks. Write an essay in which you **argue** that *neither* assertion is completely true. You may want to collect some additional information to support your position.
5. In spite of the struggle for women's rights which dates back to the early nineteenth century), women have not yet achieved equality in all the ordinary aspects of political, economic, and social life. Find material in several of the readings (perhaps you could use some from the unit on Personal Relationships as well) concerning the relationships between the sexes (and the possible prejudices connected with these relationships). Use this material to formulate a **thesis** about such relationships. Write a paper in which you present evidence to support your thesis.
6. Sometimes location becomes an important factor in the development of prejudice. At times one hears statements such as "If they would only stay in their own place." Hughes and Rivers have written about the desire to move

to another place; Kureishi depicts people who have moved from Pakistan to England. Using material from these three essays for support, write an essay in which you argue that people who move to different environments may become objects of prejudice because they are not understood and do not understand their new environment.

7. What can be done about prejudice? Nager, Hooks, and Luke all offer suggestions. You may find others in different readings or have ideas of your own. Write an essay that suggests some answers to this question.

PERSONAL RELATIONSHIPS

Understanding Love, Sex, and Marriage

"*L*ove conquers all," the Latin poet Virgil once pronounced, with apparent ease. But authentic personal relationships—that is, intimate connections between human beings—are rarely achieved with ease. Even social acceptance of serious, knowledgeable discussion about personal relationships has not been easily won. For many years, such talk was considered the preoccupation of idle women or, at times, a thinly disguised homily delivered by a religious authority or a concerned parent. In the academic world, with the exception of literary and graphic artists whose ideas about love were presented imaginatively, "real" scholars, it was assumed, devoted their time to more serious matters.

In recent decades, though, the essential seriousness of the topic has gained recognition by both male and female scholars from many disciplines. While they do not always agree with one another's conclusions, these researchers often make valuable contributions to their respective fields by defining the questions that need to be investigated. What are some of these questions? Many of them, of course, overlap several disciplines; nevertheless, the following discussion offers some general indications of the issues and questions posed by each academic discipline.

Philosophers such as Plato and Simone de Beauvoir attempt to define the nature and purpose of love and sex. For instance, is love an instantaneous response or something that builds slowly and solidly into a "true" stage? Is it temporary or permanent? Must sex involve an emotional response or can it be a purely physical satisfaction? Will a long-term married love differ essentially from a passionate love? Philosophers theorize, too, about the role of love in human life; some, like Robert Solomon, examine the language we apply to love and sexuality to determine the meanings we attach to them. Contemplating ideal situations, these thinkers contrast our interpretations with reality. Others view relationships as the ultimate fulfillment of the ideal or spiritual self. Philosophers also consider the role of any pain or suffering involved.

While psychologists also explore the role of the self, they, like Roy W. Menninger, are more likely to focus on self as the expression of personality and to emphasize the need for self-esteem as the basis of a satisfying relationship. Studying our complex, sometimes contradictory motives, psychologists trace patterns of individual behavior, including what Sigmund Freud defined as infantile sexual traits, as well as deeply rooted sex-role stereotypes, which may prompt individuals to act in particular ways in a relationship. Psychology is interested in the spectrum of intimate relationships, from heterosexual, to homosexual and bisexual responses, as well as extra-marital affairs; it seeks to define differences between what it considers "normal," healthy relationships and pathological ones.

Sociologists, too, examine these various forms of inter-relating, but usually in the context of a group or through a person's interactions with the outside world. For example, how does family background, the peer group, or society at large affect the way we form relationships? Sociology studies the nature of marriage as a social institution: Do monogamous relationships work best or should we abandon monogamy in favor of many sex partners? Sociologists evaluate the stability of marriage as a social institution by examining statistics on divorce. They also investigate alternative forms of relationships, such as living together and communal households. Finally, they explore various reasons why human beings become attracted to one another: Do we search out someone with similar traits and background, or are we more likely to find differences attractive?

History and anthropology awaken us to the realization that our own romantic, sexual, and marital practices are not necessarily common to all historical eras and cultures. In many parts of the world, for example, romantic love, if recognized at all, is still not considered an appropriate reason for marriage; instead, considerations of social class and economic means lead parents to arrange a union for their child. Some previous civilizations encouraged extra-marital sex and even granted it a religious rationale; in other countries, it was quietly tolerated or sometimes punishable by death. Thus, historians like John D'Emilio and Estelle B. Freedman, as well as anthropologists, show us differences among peoples and periods, and imply, philosophically, that romantic love may be a learned behavior.

Early Christian theologians, represented by Saint Augustine, introduced a moral component that connected human love with divine love, but also attempted to restrict sexual practice to marriage and procreation. Many contemporary theologians, however, have explored the notion that sex is an expression of love. The concepts of "sin" and "virtue" inform the thinking and language of theological commentary, and all theologians use a value system as the basis for their ideas.

Values are often, though not always, inherent in the literary and graphic representations of love and sex. But artists and writers usually convey their ideas subtly, through characters, symbols, settings, and narrative tone. In their work, they may simply pose a question, or they may postulate a number of possible "answers." Raymond Carver, Joyce Carol Oates, and Remedios Varo are artists who have explored personal relationships in thought-provoking ways without prescribing answers.

Through these varying perspectives, we hope to suggest that this topic is both complex and broad, yet certainly not "settled." We offer, therefore, no final definitions or untouchable conclusions of our own about love, sex, or marriage. Instead, we encourage you to examine the varying positions, explore additional research, and think critically about where you stand on each issue. We trust that knowing more about the topic will not only help you to write more cogently about it, but may also aid you in making more informed, and therefore freer choices, about love, sex, and marriage in your own life.

Plato

Aristophanes' Definition of Love

(ca. 380 B.C.)

Plato (ca. 427–347 B.C.), a Greek philosopher who profoundly influenced Western thought, was educated as a noble Athenian. Though politics interested him, he chose instead to study philosophy under Socrates. After Socrates was executed for allegedly neglecting the gods of the state, Plato fled from Athens, but later returned to found his own school, the Academy—an early prototype of what we would call a university. He taught in the school and wrote extensively until his death. Besides the *Symposium,* his works include the *Apology* (a defense of his teacher, Socrates), the *Republic,* and *Laws.*

Many of Plato's philosophical beliefs are creatively presented in the form of "dialogues" or discussions. The *Symposium,* from which this excerpt was taken, describes an extended dinner and drinking party, during which several speakers compete on the topic of love. Aristophanes, a Greek comic dramatist, is one of these speakers who, after missing his turn because he has the hiccups, recovers and narrates the following story, dramatizing one of the classical and popular beliefs about the origin of love and sexuality.

PREVIEWS

A. In a sentence or two, write your own **definition** of love.
B. List the characteristics of the person you would ideally love.

Aristophanes professed to open another vein of discourse; he had a mind to praise Love in another way, unlike that either of Pausanias or Eryximachus. Mankind, he said, judging by their neglect of him, have never, as I think, at all understood the power of Love. For if they had understood him they would surely have built noble temples and altars, and offered solemn sacrifices in his honour; but this is not done, and most certainly ought to be done: since of all the gods he is the best friend of men, the helper and the healer of the ills which are the great impediment to the happiness of the race. I will try to describe his power to you, and you shall teach the rest of the world what I am teaching you. In the first place, let me treat of the nature of man and what has happened to it; for the original human nature was not like the present, but different. The sexes were not two as they are now, but originally three in number; there was man, woman, and the union of the two, having a name corresponding to this double nature, which had once a real existence, but is now lost, and the word "Androgynous" is only preserved as a term of reproach. In the second place, the primeval man was round, his back and sides forming a circle; and he had four hands and four feet, one head with two faces, looking opposite ways, set on a round neck and precisely alike; also four ears, two privy members, and the remainder to correspond. He could walk upright as men now do, backwards or forwards as he pleased, and he could also roll over and over at a great pace, turning on his four hands and four feet, eight in all, like tumblers going over and over with their legs in the air; this was when he wanted to run fast. Now the sexes were three, and such as I have described them; because the sun, moon, and earth are three; and the man was originally the child of the sun, the woman of the earth, and the man-woman of the moon, which is made up of sun and earth, and they were all round and moved round and round like their parents. Terrible was their might and strength, and the thoughts of their hearts were great, and they made an attack upon the gods; of them is told the tale of Otys and Ephialtes who, as Homer says, dared to scale heaven, and would have laid hands upon the gods. Doubt reigned in the celestial councils. Should they kill them and annihilate the race with thunderbolts, as they had done the giants, then there would be an end of the sacrifices and worship which men offered to them; but, on the other hand, the gods could not suffer their insolence to be unrestrained.

At last, after a good deal of reflection, Zeus discovered a way. He said: "Methinks I have a plan which will humble their pride and improve their manners; men shall continue to exist, but I will cut them in two and then they will be diminished in strength and increased in numbers; this will have the advantage of making them more profitable to us. They shall walk upright on two legs, and if they continue insolent and will not be quiet, I will split them again and they shall hop about on a single leg." He spoke and cut men in two, like a sorb-apple which is halved for pickling, or as you might divide an egg with a hair; and as he cut them one after another, he bade Apollo give the face and the half of the neck a turn in order that the man might contemplate the section of himself: he would thus learn a lesson of humility. Apollo was also bidden to heal their wounds and compose their forms. So he gave a turn to the face and pulled the skin from the sides all over that which in our language is called the belly, like the purses which draw in, and he made one mouth at the centre, which he fastened in a knot (the same which is called the navel); he also moulded the breast and took out most of the wrinkles, much as a shoemaker might smooth leather upon a last; he left a few, however, in the region of the belly and navel, as a memorial of the primeval state. After the division the two parts of man, each desiring his other half, came together, and throwing their arms about one another, entwined in mutual embraces, longing to grow into one, they were on the point of dying from hunger and self-neglect, because they did not like to do anything apart; and when one of the halves died and the other survived, the survivor sought another mate, man or woman as we call them, being the sections of entire men or women,—and clung to that.

They were being destroyed, when Zeus in pity of them invented a new plan: he turned the parts of generation round to the front, for this had not been always their position, and they sowed the seed no longer as hitherto like grasshoppers in the ground, but in one another; and after the transposition the male generated in the female in order that by the mutual embraces of man and woman they might breed, and the race might continue; or if man came to man they might be satisfied, and rest, and go their ways to the business of life: so ancient is the desire of one another which is implanted in us, reuniting our original nature, making one of two, and healing the state of man. Each of us when separated, having one side only, like a flat fish, is but the indenture of a man, and he is always looking for his other half. Men who are a section of that double nature which was once called Androgynous are lovers of women; adulterers are generally of this breed, and also adulterous women who lust after men: the women who are a section of the woman do not care for men, but have female attachments; the female companions are of this sort. But they who are a section of the male follow the male, and while they are young, being slices of the original man, they hang about men and embrace them, and they are themselves the best of boys and youths, because they have the most manly nature. Some indeed assert that they are shameless, but this is not true; for they do not act thus from any want of shame, but because they are valiant and manly, and have a manly countenance, and they embrace that which is like them. And these when they grow up become our statesmen, and these only, which is a great proof of the truth of what I am saying. When they reach manhood they are lovers of youth, and are not naturally inclined to marry or beget children,—if at all, they do so only in obedience to the law; but they are satisfied if they may be allowed to live with one another unwedded; and such a nature is prone to love and ready to return love, always embracing that which is akin to him.

And when one of them meets with his other half, the actual half of himself, whether he be a lover of youth or a lover of another sort, the pair are lost in an amazement of love and friendship and intimacy, and will not be out of the other's sight, as I may say, even for a moment: these are the people who pass their whole lives together; yet they could not explain what they desire of one another. For the intense yearning which each of them has towards the other does not appear to be the desire of lover's intercourse, but of something else which the soul of either evidently desires and cannot tell, and of which she has only a dark and doubtful presentiment. Suppose Hephaestus, with his instruments, to come to the pair who are lying side by side and to say to them, "What do you people want of one another?" they would be unable to explain. And suppose further, that when he saw their perplexity he said: "Do you desire to be wholly one; always day and night to be in one another's company? for if this is what you desire, I am ready to melt you into one and let you grow together, so that being two you shall become one, and while you live live a common life as if you were a single man, and after your death in the world below still be one departed soul instead of two—I ask whether this is what you lovingly desire, and whether you are satisfied to attain this?"—there is not a man of them who when he heard the proposal would deny or would not acknowledge that this meeting and melting into one another, this becoming one instead of two, was the very expression of his ancient need. And the reason is that human nature was originally one and we were a whole, and the desire and pursuit of the whole is called love.

JOURNAL WRITINGS

1. **Paraphrase** Aristophanes' **definition** of love. In a paragraph, explore the similarities and differences between Aristophanes' definition and the one you composed in Preview question A. Then, revise your definition if you wish.
2. Aristophanes' story implies that men and women will be happy only if they find their ideal "other halves." Play the devil's advocate (that is, one who deliberately advances the opposing view) against Aristophanes and **argue** that searching for an ideal can become a liability in a potential relationship. To dramatize your argument, include a brief **narrative** that illustrates this liability, just as Aristophanes' story illustrates the ideal.

BRAINSTORMING AND DRAFTING

3. Read the introduction to the Free Choice unit in this text, together with the selection from Erich Fromm's *Escape From Freedom*. How might believing in Aristophanes' **definition** of love affect our freedom as human beings? Consider also whether such a belief would make us more or less like Fromm's automatons.
4. Sociologists and psychologists have different ways of accounting for the attractions that human beings have for one another. (For example, they theorize that some of us are attracted to people like ourselves in various ways.) In groups of three or four, each member should list some possible reasons, conscious or unconscious, for an attraction that may become a love relationship. The group leader will **synthesize** the separate lists into one composite list. After discussing all of the reasons in some depth, each person should draft a paragraph explaining how one or more of these reasons for attraction is/are embedded in Aristophanes' narrative. (Or, you may choose to work individually by simply making your own list, then choosing one item to write about.)

THE AUTHOR'S METHODS

5. Plato chose the great comic dramatist, Aristophanes, to present this theory of love. Just before Aristophanes begins his tale, we are told that he has the hiccups, often seen as a comic malady. Find and mark a passage in the

reading that could be interpreted comically. Draft a paragraph explaining how a humorous interpretation of the passage would affect the meaning of the whole story.

6.   In the story, Aristophanes uses **narrative** writing—that is, he tells a story— to dramatize a popular **definition** of love. Find and mark a passage in which he uses **descriptive** details to make his narrative more real, more convincing, or more colorful. Draft a paragraph in which you include **specific** details about the personality of someone you like.

CREATIVE PROJECT

7.   While **mythological** stories often contain unrealistic events, these **narratives** may represent real wishes, fears, or beliefs that human beings have about their world. Plato's narrative, for example, may indicate our wish to believe in the existence of an ideal mate. Using a series of events as your framework, write your own mythological story to illustrate the wishes, fears, or beliefs behind *your* definition of love. Include specific details about each of your events. **Conclude,** as Aristophanes does, with a **general** statement of your definition.

FORMAL WRITING AND RESEARCH PAPERS

8.   The concept of power informs Plato's **narrative** through a source external to the love relationship: the thoughts and actions of the god Zeus, who manipulates human beings. Write a paper in which you **define** the concept of power, **analyze** its effects on the characters, and speculate on one or more sources of external "power" that might affect a contemporary love relationship. Evaluate the effects of these external power sources on the relationship.

9.   Using some indexes such as *Historical Abstracts* and the *Humanities Index,* or the card or computer catalog, find some information on the attitude of the ancient Greeks toward homosexuality. Read also David Leavitt's short story, "Territory." Write a paper in which you compare and/or contrast the Greek attitude, as evidenced by Plato's **narrative,** with the contemporary attitude as demonstrated by Leavitt's story. Include **specific** details to prove your points. Use your research to support your interpretation.

Robert C. Solomon

Models and Metaphors: "The Game of Love"

(1981)

Robert Solomon was born in 1942 in Detroit, Michigan. He received a B.A. from the University of Pennsylvania and an M.A. and Ph.D. from the University of Michigan. After holding teaching posts at several universities, he accepted a position at the University of Texas at Austin in 1972, where he is currently professor of philosophy. His many published works cover a variety of philosophical concerns such as existentialism, phenomenology, German idealism, and philosophical psychology. His recent works include *Above the Bottom Line: An Introduction to Business Ethics* and a volume he edited, *What is an Emotion?: Classical Readings in Philosophical Psychology.*

The selection below, from *Love: Emotion, Myth, and Metaphor,* combines historical and psychological perspectives with a philosophical examination of the language of love. Through a careful consideration of the words we often use to describe relationships, Solomon draws implications about our definitions of love.

PREVIEWS

A. Complete the following sentence in at least three different ways: "Love is like . . . "
B. Write for five minutes about what you consider to be the single most important feature of a love relationship.

We look at love, as we look at life, through a series of metaphors, each with its own language, its own implications, connotations and biases.

For example, if someone says that love is a game, we already know much of what is to follow: relationships will tend to be short-lived. Sincerity will be a strategy for winning and so will flattery and perhaps lying. ("All's fair . . . ") The person "played with" is taken seriously only as an opponent, a challenge, valued in particular for his or her tactics and retorts, but quickly dispensable as soon as someone has "won" or "lost." "Playing hard to get" is an optional strategy, and being "easy" is not immoral or foolish so much as playing badly, or not at all.

On the other hand, if someone sees love as "God's gift to humanity," we should expect utter solemnity, mixed with a sense of gratitude, seriousness and self-righteousness that is wholly lacking in the "love is a game" metaphor. Relationships here will tend to be long-lasting, if not "forever," fraught with duties and obligations dictated by a "gift" which, in the usual interpretations, has both divine and secular strings attached.

The "game" metaphor is, perhaps, too frivolous to take seriously. The "gift of God" metaphor, on the other hand, is much too serious to dismiss frivolously. . . . What I would like to do is display the variety and richness of the metaphors through which we tend to talk about, and experience, love. Not surprisingly, these love metaphors reflect our interests elsewhere in life—business, health, communications, art, politics and law as well as fun and games and religion. But these are not mere "figures of speech"; they are the self-imposed structures that determine the way we experience love itself. (For this reason, we should express some pretty strong reservations about some of them.)

TIT FOR TAT: LOVE AS A FAIR EXCHANGE

One of the most common love metaphors, now particularly popular in social psychology, is the *economic* metaphor. The idea is that love is an exchange, a sexual partnership, a trade-off of interests and concerns and, particularly, of *approval*. "I make you feel good about yourself and in return you make me feel good about myself." Of course exchange rates vary—some people need more than others—and there is a law of diminishing returns; that is, the same person's approval tends to become less and less valuable as it becomes more familiar. (This law of diminishing returns, which we experience as the gradual fading of romantic love, has been explored by the psychologist Eliot Arenson of the University of California at Santa Cruz. His theory has been aptly named by his students "Arenson's Law of Marital Infidelity.") In some relationships the balance of payments may indeed seem extremely one-sided but the assumption is, in the words of the Harvard sociologist Homans, that both parties must believe they are getting something out of it or they simply wouldn't stay around.

Now this economic model has much to offer, not least the fact that it gives a fairly precise account of the concrete motivation for love, which is left out of more pious accounts that insist that love is simply good in itself and needs no motives. But the problem is that it too easily degenerates into a most unflattering model of mutual buying and selling, which in turn raises the specter that love may indeed be, as some cynics have been saying ever since Marx (Karl) and Engels, a form of covert prostitution, though not necessarily—or even usually—for money. "I will sleep with you and think well of you or at least give you the benefit of the doubt if only you'll tell me good things about myself and pretend to approve of me."

It may be true that we do often evaluate our relationships in this way, in terms of mutual advantage and our own sense of fairness. The question, "What am I getting out of this, anyway?" always makes sense, even if certain traditional views of love and commitment try to pretend that such selfishness is the very antithesis of love. But the traditional views have a point to make too, which is, simply, that such tit-for-tat thinking inevitably undermines a relationship based on love, *not* because love is essentially "selfless" but because the bargain table is not the place to understand mutual affection. Love is not the exchange of affection, any more than sex is merely the exchange of pleasure. What is left out of these accounts is the "we" of love, which is quite different from mere "I and thou." This is not to say that fairness cannot be an issue in love, nor is it true that "all's fair" in love. But while the economic exchange model explains rather clearly some of the motives for love, it tends to ignore the *experience* of love almost altogether, which is that such comparisons and evaluations seem at the time beside the point and come to mind only when love is already breaking down. It is the suspicion, not the fact, that "I'm putting more into this than you are" that signals the end of many relationships, despite the fact that, as business goes, they may have been "a good arrangement."

THE JOB OF LOVING: THE WORK MODEL

A very different model is the *work* model of love. The Protestant ethic is very much at home in romance. (Rollo May calls love the Calvinist's proof of emotional salvation.) And so we find many people who talk about "working out a relation-ship," "working at it," "working for it" and so on. The fun may once have been there, of course, but now the real *job* begins, tacking together and patching up, like fixing up an old house and refusing to move out until the roof caves in. This is, needless to say, a particularly self-righteous model, if for no other reason than that it begins on the defensive and requires considerable motivation just to move on. Personal desires, the other person's as well as one's own, may be placed behind "the relationship," which is conceived of as the primary *project*. Love, according to the work model, gets evaluated above all on its industriousness, its seriousness, its success in the face of the most difficult obstacles. Devotees of the work model not infrequently choose the most inept or inappropriate partners, rather like buying a run-down shack—for the challenge. They will look with disdain at people who are merely happy together (something like buying a house from a tract builder). They will look with admiration and awe at a couple who have survived a dozen years of fights and emotional disfigurements because "they made it work."

A MADNESS MOST DISCRETE:
THE (MELO) DRAMATIC MODEL

In contrast to the work model, we can turn with a sense of recreation to the *dramatic* model of love, love as theater, love as melodrama. This differs from the game model in that one's roles are taken *very* seriously, and the notions of winners and losers, strategy and tactics, are replaced by notions of performance, catharsis, tragedy and theatricality. Roles are all important—keeping within roles, developing them, enriching them. The dramatic model also tends to play to an audience, real (whenever possible) or imagined (when necessary). Fights and reconciliations alike will often be performed in public, and an evening at home alone may often seem pointless. Some dramatic lovers are prima donnas, referring every line or part back to themselves, but one can be just as theatrical by being visibly selfless, or martyred, or mad. Lunt and Fontanne or Bogart and Bacall might well be models, and lovers will strain without amusement to perfect for the appropriate occasion someone else's drawl, insult, posture or sigh. Unfortunately the dramatic model too easily tends to confuse interpersonal problems with theatrical flaws, to praise and abuse itself in those mincing terms that are, appropriately, the vocabulary of the theater critic. (Clive Barnes as Cupid?) The worst that one could say of such love, therefore, is that it's "boring" or "predictable."

"RELATIONSHIPS": BANALITY AS METAPHOR

Blandness can be just as significant as profundity and excitement, and a metaphor may be intentionally noncommittal as well as precise. Thus we find the word "thing" substituted as a grammatical stand-in for virtually everything from sexual organs (a young virgin gingerly refers to her first lover's "thing") to jobs, hang-ups and hobbies (as in "doing your own thing"). Where love is concerned, the most banal of our metaphors, so pervasive and so banal that it hardly seems like a metaphor, is the word "relating," or "relationship" itself. There's not much to say about it, except to ponder in amazement the fact that we have not yet, in this age of "heavy relationships," come up with anything better. There is a sense, of course, in which any two people (or two things) stand in any number of relationships to one another (being taller than, heavier than, smarter than, more than fifteen feet away from . . . etc.). The word "relations" was once, only a few years ago, a polite and slightly clinical word for sex (still used, as most stilted archaisms tend to be, in law). People "relate" to each other as they "relate a story," perhaps on the idea that what couples do most together is to tell each other the events of the day, a less than exciting conception of love, to be sure. But metaphors can be chosen for their vacuousness just as for their imaginative imagery, and the fact that this metaphor dominates our thinking so much (albeit in the guise of a *meaningful* relationship) points once again to the poverty of not only our vocabulary but our thinking and feeling as well. Anyone who's still looking for a "meaningful relationship" . . . may have a lot to learn about love, or not really care about it at all.

LOVE AND ELECTRONICS: THE COMMUNICATION METAPHOR

A powerful metaphor with disastrous consequences that was popular a few years ago was a "communication" metaphor, often used in conjunction with a "relating" metaphor, for obvious reasons. Both were involved with the then hip language of media and information theory: "getting through" to each other and "we just can't communicate any more" gave "relationships" the unfortunate appearance of shipwrecked survivors trying to keep in touch over a slightly damaged shortwave radio. The information processing jargon ("input," "feedback," "tuning in" and "turning off") was typically loaded with electronic gadget imagery, and good relationships appropriately were described in terms of their "good vibrations." But, like all metaphors, this one revealed much more than it distorted, namely, an image of isolated transmitters looking for someone to get their messages. It was precisely this milieu that gave birth to Rollo May's *Love and Will*, and his concern that we had rendered love between us impossible. Love was thought to be mainly a matter of self-expression, largely but not exclusively verbal expression. Talk became enormously important to love; problems were talked over, talked through and talked out. The essential moment was the "heavy conversation" and, appropriately, talk about love often took the place of love itself. Confession and "openness" (telling all) became the linchpins of love, even when the messages were largely hostility and resentment. Psychotherapist George Bach wrote a number of successful books, including *The Intimate Enemy* (with Peter Wyden), which made quite clear the fact that it was expression of feelings, not the feelings themselves, that made for a successful relationship. On the communication model, sex too was described as a mode of communication, but more often sex was not so much communicating as the desire to be communicated with. Sex became, in McLuhanesque jargon, a "cool" medium. And, like most modern media, the model put its emphasis on the medium itself (encounter groups, etc.) but there was precious little stress on the *content* of the programming. Not surprisingly, love became an obscure ideal, like television advertisements full of promise of something fabulous yet to come, hinted at but never spoken of as such. In fact the ultimate message was the idea of the medium itself.

THE ONTOLOGY OF LONELINESS: LOVE AND ALONENESS

In our extremely individualistic society we have come to see isolation and loneliness as akin to "the human condition," instead of as by-products of a certain kind of social arrangement, which puts mobility and the formation of new interpersonal bonds at a premium. This individualistic metaphor, which I call "the ontology of loneliness," is stated succinctly, for example, by Rollo May: "Every person, experiencing as he [sic] does his own solitariness and aloneness, longs for union with another" (*Love and Will*, p. 144). Similarly, Erich Fromm preoccupies himself with "our need to escape the prison of our aloneness," and the radical feminist Shulamith Firestone complains about the same need "to escape from the isolation of our own solitude." Love, then, is a refuge from an otherwise intolerable existence. Our "natural" state is aloneness; our escape from this state, hopefully, is love. "Love," writes the poet Rilke, "is two solitudes reaching out to greet each other."

This is a viewpoint that has been argued by many philosophers under the name of "solipsism" ("the only sure thing is one's own existence") and has been developed by the vulgar philosopher Ayn Rand into an argument for selfishness:

"Each of us is born into the world alone, and therefore each of us is justified in pursuing our own selfish interests." But the premise is false and the inference is insidious. Not even Macduff (who was not, strictly speaking, "of woman born") came into the world by himself. And not only in infancy but in adulthood we find ourselves essentially linked to other people, to a language that we call our own, to a culture and, at least legally, to a country as well. We do not have to find or "reach out" to others; they are, in a sense, already *in us*. Alone in the woods of British Columbia, I find myself still thinking of friends, describing what I see as if they were there—and in their language. The idea of the isolated self is an American invention—reinforced perhaps by the artificially isolated circumstances of the psychiatrist's office and our fantasies about gunfighters and mountain men, but this is not true of most of us. And this means that love is not a refuge or an escape either. Our conception of ourselves is always a social self (even if it is an antisocial or rebellious self).

Our language of love often reflects this idea of natural isolation, for example in the "communication" metaphor in which isolated selves try desperately to "get through" to one another. But this is an unnecessarily tragic picture of life and love, and its result is to make love itself seem like something of a cure for a disease, rather than a positive experience which already *presupposes* a rather full social life. Indeed, it is revealing that, quite the contrary of social isolation, romantic love is usually experienced only *within* a rather extensive social nexus. "Sure, I have lots of friends and I like my colleagues at work but, still, I'm lonely and I want to fall in love." But that has nothing to do with loneliness. It rather reflects the tremendous importance we accord to romantic love in our lives, not as a cure for aloneness, but as a positive experience in its own right, which we have, curiously, turned into a need.

"MADE FOR EACH OTHER": THE METAPHYSICAL MODEL

Standing opposed to the "ontology of loneliness" is an ancient view which takes our *unity,* not our mutual isolation, as the "natural" state of humanity. The classic statement of this view, brilliant in its poetic simplicity, is Aristophanes' speech in the *Symposium,* in which he describes our "natural" state as double creatures, cleft in two by Zeus for our hubris, struggling to be reunited through love. Our own image of two people "being made for each other" is also an example of the metaphysical model, together with the idea that marriages are "made in heaven" and the idea that someone else can be your "better half." The metaphysical model is based not on the idea that love is a refuge from isolated individualism but, quite the opposite, on the idea that love is the realization of bonds that are already formed, even before one meets one's "other half."

The ontology of loneliness treats individuals as atoms, bouncing around the universe alone looking for other atoms, occasionally forming more or less stable molecules. But if we were to pursue the same chemical metaphor into the metaphysical model, it would more nearly resemble what physicists today call "field theory." A magnetic field, for instance, retains all of its electromagnetic properties whether or not there is any material there to make them manifest. So too, an individual is already a network of human relationships and expectations, and these exist whether or not one finds another individual whose radiated forces and properties are complementary. The old expression about love being a matter of "chemical attraction" (from Goethe to Gilbert and Sullivan*) is, scientifically, a century out of date; "attraction" is no longer a question of one atom affecting another but the product of two electromagnetic fields, each of which exists prior to and independently of any particular atoms within its range. So too we radiate charm, sexiness, inhibition, intelligence and even repulsiveness, and find a lover who fits in. The problem with this viewpoint, however, is that it leaves no room for the *development* of relationships but rather makes it seem as if, if the love is there at all, it has to be there, and be there in full, from the very beginning.

LOVE AND DISEASE: THE MEDICAL METAPHOR

"Love's a malady without a cure," wrote Dryden, and today, our favorite metaphor, from social criticism to social relationships, has become the disease metaphor, images of health and decay, the medicalization of all things human, from the stock market to sex and love. Not surprisingly, a large proportion of our books about love and sex are written by psychiatrists and other doctors. (They used to be written by priests and theologians.) Our society is described in terms of "narcissism" (a clinical term), as an "age of anxiety," and as "decadent" (the negative side of the biological process). For Rollo May and Erich Fromm, lack of love is the dominant disease of our times. For others, *Love and Addiction* author Stanton Peele, for instance, love is itself a kind of disease, an "addiction," waiting to be cured. Some feminists have seized on the disease metaphor (a disease invented by and carried by men): Ti-Grace Atkinson (in *Amazon Odyssey*) calls love "a pathological condition," and Erica Jong (in *Fear of Flying*) calls it "the search for self-annihilation." But whether love is the disease or love is the cure, what is obvious is that this model turns us all into *patients*, and one might well ask—the professional interests of the A.M.A. aside—whether that is the arena within which we want to talk about love.

THE ART IN LOVING: THE AESTHETIC MODEL

Perhaps the oldest view of love, the pivot of Plato's *Symposium*, is an *aesthetic* model: love as the admiration and the contemplation of *beauty*. The emphasis here is on neither relating nor communicating (in fact, unrequited love and even voyeurism are perfectly in order). On this model, it is not particularly expected that the lover will actually *do* much of anything except, perhaps, to get within

---

* [Author's Note] Hey diddle diddle with your middle-class kisses.
It's a chemical reaction, that's all. (Gilbert and Sullivan)

view of the beloved at every possible opportunity, as one might stand before the fireplace and admire one's favorite painting over the mantel. It is this model that has dominated many of our theories about love, though not, luckily, our actual practices. It is this model that best fits the moaning troubadours in twelfth-century France, composing poetry about the inaccessible beauty of the maiden up there on the tower balcony, visible but untouchable. It is this model that feminists rightly complain about when they accuse men of "putting them up on a pedestal," a charge that too often confuses the idealization that accompanies it with the impersonal distancing that goes along with the pedestal. The objection is not to the fact that it is a pedestal so much as the fact that it is usually a very *tall* pedestal, so that any real contact is pretty much out of the question and the fear of falling is considerable. Or else it is a very *small* pedestal, "and like any small place," writes Gloria Steinem, "a prison."

LOVE AND COMMITMENT: THE CONTRACT MODEL

An old view of love, which dominated much of the eighteenth and nineteenth centuries, was a *contract* model, a specific instance of a more general "social contract" theory that was then believed by most people to be the (implicit) basis of society itself. Contracts in love were exemplified, of course, by the quite explicit and wholly legal contract of marriage, but even then, and especially now, the idea of implicit contracts was taken for granted too. (*Cosmopolitan* magazine last year reran one of its most popular pieces, about "secret" contracts in love, two hundred years too late to be in vogue.) What is crucial to this metaphor, however, is the fact that *emotion* plays very little part in it. One accepts an obligation to obey the terms of the contract (implicit or explicit) whether or not (though hopefully whether) one wants to. The current term for this ever popular emasculation of emotion is *commitment*. In fact there seems to be an almost general agreement among most of the people I talk to that "commitment" is what constitutes love. (The contrast is almost always sexual promiscuity or purely "casual" affairs.) But commitment is precisely what love is *not* (though of course one can and often does make commitments on the basis of the fact that he or she loves someone). A commitment is an obligation sustained *whether or not one has the emotion that originally motivated it.* And the sense of obligation isn't "love."

FREUDIAN FALLACIES: THE BIOLOGICAL METAPHOR

The idea that science itself can be but a metaphor strikes us as odd, but much of what we believe about love, it seems, is based on wholly unliteral biological metaphors. For example, we believe that love is "natural," even an "instinct," and this is supported by a hundred fascinating but ultimately irrelevant arguments about "the facts of life": the fact that some spiders eat their mates, that some birds mate for life, that some sea gulls are lesbians, that some fish can't mate unless the male is clearly superior, that chimpanzees like to gang bang and gorillas have weenies the size of a breakfast sausage, that bats tend to do it upside down and porcupines do it "carefully." But romantic love is by no means "natural"; it is not an instinct but a very particular and peculiar attitude toward sex and pair-bonding that has been carefully cultivated by a small number of modern aristo-cratic and middle-class societies. Even sex, which would seem to be "natural" if anything is, is no more mere biology than taking the holy wafer at high mass is just eating. It too is defined by our metaphors and the symbolic significance we give to it. It is not a "need," though we have certainly made it into one. Sex is not an instinct, except in that utterly minimal sense that bears virtually no resemblance at all to the extremely sophisticated and emotion-filled set of rituals that we call—with some good reason—"making love." And where sex and love come together is not in the realm of nature either, but in the realm of expression, specific to a culture which specifies its meaning.

There is one particular version of the biological metaphor, however, which has enjoyed such spectacular scientific airplay, ever since Freud at least, that we tend to take it as the literal truth instead of, again, as a metaphor. It is the idea that love begins in—or just out of—the womb, and that our prototype of love—if not our one "true" love—is our own mother.

This would suggest indeed that love is, if not an instinct, common to all human beings. But the argument turns on a number of obvious fallacies, starting from the premise that, because of the extraordinarily slow development of human infants, all of us, from our very birth (and perhaps before), need love. But . . .

1. This isn't romantic love, in any case, and romantic love is in no way reducible to mere dependency. In fact, despite its "baby" imagery, ro-mantic love presupposes just what infancy lacks: a sense of selfhood and a high degree of mobility and independence. Moreover, the view expresses an obvious male bias and leaves the romantic desires of women something of a mystery (for Freud in particular).

2. To need love is not to need *to* love. Some people need desperately to be loved but have no inclination whatever to love in return.

3. Babies need care and comfort, not necessarily love. In fact regular tender care is far more desirable than adoring but erratic attention. Romantic love, of course, thrives on the latter, gets too easily bored with the first.

4. In few societies is the care of a particular mother expected by either the infant or society, and the idea that one has special affection for one person exclusively is an anthropologically peculiar notion which in fact is disin-tegrating in our society too. In most societies, increasingly in our own, an infant is cared for by any number of different people, male as well as female, and the idea of a single utterly dominant dependency figure—which so obsessed Freud—is a peculiarity of the Victorian Viennese middle-class ethic, not a universal human characteristic.

5. It is most implausible that any adult emotion is simply reducible to an infantile need. To identify a radical politician's moral indignation with infantile rage would be offensive as well as simply wrong; to think of sexual jealousy as merely an adult extension of a child's possessiveness is not only

to misunderstand jealousy but to misunderstand children as well. And even in those relatively few cases in which the so-called "Oedipal complex" reigns supreme, it is a mistake to reduce all subsequent affections to a mere repetition of family dynamics. Some psychologists, Gordon All- port for example, have come to refer to this rejection of Freudian reduc- tionism as "the autonomy of motives." No matter how revealing the origins of one's affections, it is their development and differences that define them. We think it noteworthy when a man dates a woman who resembles his mother, not when he does not. The Oedipal complex is desperately looking for an occasional instance as if to confirm it.

We sometimes plague ourselves with the idea that we are "hung up" on Oedipal images. In high school I worried about the fact that the girls I "dated" bore a sometimes striking resemblance to my mother. (They were usually short, bright, creative and Caucasian.) I had read enough Freud for this to worry me. Many years later a psychotherapist convinced me, or I "discovered," that, indeed, I was looking for a woman who was more like my father, which confused me considerably, needless to say, but worried me too. But this limited number of alternatives, always clouded by the threat of "neurosis," turns out to be non- sense, or worse—it is the Freudian doctrine of original sin, a new source of unnecessary guilt and just as much a myth as the original Original Sin. In fact our models and prototypes of love include not only our parents but brothers, sisters, teachers in junior high school, first dates, first loves, graduating-class heroes and heroines, hundreds of movie stars and magazine pictures as well as a dozen considerations and pressures that have nothing to do with prototypes at all. Indeed, even Freud insists that it is not a person's *actual* parent who forms the romantic prototype but rather a phantom, constructed from memory, which may bear little resemblance to any actual person. But if this is so, perhaps one's imagined mother is in fact a variation on one's first girl friend, or a revised version of Myrna Loy. Why do we take the most complex and at times exquisite emotion in most of our lives, and try to reduce it to the first and the simplest?

Or, if the Oedipal theory is right, why didn't Romulus, raised by a she-wolf, rape his dog, instead of the Sabine women? Mere motherhood is not everything, even in ancient mythology.

"THE FLAME IN MY HEART": THE EMOTION METAPHOR

Love is an emotion. But the way we talk about emotions is itself so pervaded by metaphors that one begins to wonder whether there is anything there to actually talk about. We talk about ourselves as if we were Mr. Coffee machines, bubbling over, occasionally overflowing, getting too hot to handle, and bursting from too much pressure. We subscribe in metaphor if not in medicine to the medieval theory that the seat of the emotions is in the heart, and in love it is the heart that pounds, beats, breaks and is bound and occasionally butchered. We describe love in terms of heat, fire, flame—all of which are expressive and poetic but, it is sometimes hard to remember, metaphors all the same. But is love really that sense that one is going to burst? The warm flush that pours through one's body when *he* or *she* walks into the room: is that love? And if so, why do we set so much store by it? It is for this reason, no doubt, that the age-old wisdom about love has made it out to be more than a mere emotion—a gift from God, a visitation from the gods, the wound of Cupid's arrow, the cure for a disease or a disease itself, the economics of interpersonal relations or even "the answer" to all life's problems. But then again, maybe we underestimate our emotions.

What is love? It seems to be almost everything except, perhaps, "never having to say you're sorry." Love is a series of metaphors, which we glorify selectively, picking one out and calling it "true" love, which itself is another metaphor.

Not all metaphors are created equal. Some are profound, some are banal, some increase our self-confidence, others make us feel slimy, defensive or sick. There is no "true" love, for there is no singly true metaphor, but this does not mean that one should not choose carefully. For choosing one's metaphor is, in fact, choosing one's love life as well.

JOURNAL WRITINGS

1. **Describe** in some detail a relationship of your own, or of someone you know, that contains features from one or more of Solomon's **metaphors.**
2. Choose the model Solomon writes about that *least* appeals to you as a **definition** of love. In a paragraph explain some of the problems people might have if they base a relationship primarily on this metaphor.

BRAINSTORMING AND DRAFTING

3. Look up a **definition** of **metaphor** in the glossary and write it down. In this article, Solomon begins with the metaphor "love is a game"; he then discusses other metaphors that he thinks people use to define the features important to them in a love relationship. Apply one of Solomon's metaphors to a *sexual* relationship (or create a metaphor of your own that will apply). For example, what if "sex is a game"? Provide some details, as Solomon does, to explain how the metaphor works. Optional: Ask members of a small group to comment on the problems of applying your metaphor to a true-life relationship.
4. Re-read Plato's **narrative** in this unit. Pretend that you are Aristophanes; write a letter to Robert Solomon in which you defend yourself against his objection that the "metaphysical model" leaves no room for the *development* of a relationship.
5. In his discussion of some of the **metaphors,** Solomon appears to be objecting to an exaggerated use of a particular feature of a relationship. Choose

one model or metaphor, and **argue** that the same feature, rightly used, could *benefit* a relationship. Support your **argument** with **examples** from relationships familiar to you.

THE AUTHOR'S METHODS

6. For many of the models, Solomon does not merely explain the **metaphor** in an objective manner. He also chooses his **diction,** his **analogies,** and even his punctuation very deliberately in order to convey his negative attitude toward the metaphor. In a well-detailed paragraph, show how Solomon creates **tone** by manipulating language either in "The Work Model" or in "The Communication Metaphor."

7. One of Solomon's interesting stylistic devices is the use of "interrupters" (words, phrases, or clauses often surrounded by commas which interrupt another grammatical unit). The following sentence, for example, contains one of these interrupters: "In some relationships the balance of payments may indeed seem extremely one-sided but the assumption is, *in the words of the Harvard sociologist Homans,* that both parties must believe they are getting something out of it or they simply wouldn't stay around." How does the device enhance this sentence? Find at least two other sentences in which Solomon uses the device. Then write several sentences about someone you love using your own "interrupting" devices.

FORMAL WRITING AND RESEARCH PAPERS

8. Solomon **argues** that no *one* of these metaphors defines "true love." Write a paper in which you attempt to formulate a working **definition** of love by explaining several features of a good love relationship. Include **examples** of these features from films you have seen, or from novels, short stories, or poems you remember. You may also wish to refer to the selections by Plato, Solomon, and Carver to support your ideas.

9. Do some research on the customs or practices that surround romantic love or marriage in an African country. (Consult, for example, the *Social Sciences Index* and the card or computer catalog.) Write a paper describing these customs and **analyzing** the beliefs about love that lie behind them. Provide specific **examples** to support your ideas.

Raymond Carver

What We Talk About When We Talk About Love

(1981)

A contemporary American short-story writer and poet, Raymond Carver (1938–1988) was born in Clatskanie, Oregon, received an A.B. from California State University, Humboldt, and studied at the University of Iowa. He taught creative writing in California and New York, and received the National Endowment for the Arts Award in fiction. His work has been translated into many languages.

A husband and father early in life, Carver at first found little time for writing, but he was able to turn out poems and short stories quickly. Critics noted the complex artistry and deep emotional undertone in his first short-story collection, *Will You Please Be Quiet, Please?* (1976). His recent work includes *Cathedral* (1984), a short-story collection, and *Ultramarine* (1986), a collection of poems. The following selection is the title story from his 1981 collection, in which he examines the harmony and discord in several types of human love relationships. This story poses the ultimate questions about love—what is it, and how do we know when we have found it?

PREVIEW

Is it possible to experience "true love" with more than one person in our lives? Explain why or why not.

My friend Mel McGinnis was talking. Mel McGinnis is a cardiologist, and sometimes that gives him the right.

The four of us were sitting around his kitchen table drinking gin. Sunlight filled the kitchen from the big window behind the sink. There were Mel and me and his second wife, Teresa—Terri, we called her—and my wife, Laura. We lived in Albuquerque then. But we were all from somewhere else.

There was an ice bucket on the table. The gin and the tonic water kept going around, and we somehow got on the subject of love. Mel thought real love was nothing less than spiritual love. He said he'd spent five years in a seminary before quitting to go to medical school. He said he still looked back on those years in the seminary as the most important years in his life.

Terri said the man she lived with before she lived with Mel loved her so much he tried to kill her. Then Terri said, "He beat me up one night. He dragged me around the living room by my ankles. He kept saying, 'I love you, I love you, you bitch.' He went on dragging me around the living room. My head kept knocking on things." Terri looked around the table. "What do you do with love like that?"

She was a bone-thin woman with a pretty face, dark eyes, and brown hair that hung down her back. She liked necklaces made of turquoise, and long pendant earrings.

"My God, don't be silly. That's not love, and you know it," Mel said. "I don't know what you'd call it, but I sure know you wouldn't call it love."

"Say what you want to, but I know it was," Terri said. "It may sound crazy to you, but it's true just the same. People are different, Mel. Sure, sometimes he may have acted crazy. Okay. But he loved me. In his own way maybe, but he loved me. There was love there, Mel. Don't say there wasn't."

Mel let out his breath. He held his glass and turned to Laura and me. "The man threatened to kill me," Mel said. He finished his drink and reached for the gin bottle. "Terri's a romantic. Terri's of the kick-me-so-I'll-know-you-love-me school. Terri, hon, don't look that way." Mel reached across the table and touched Terri's cheek with his fingers. He grinned at her.

"Now he wants to make up," Terri said.

"Make up what?" Mel said. "What is there to make up? I know what I know. That's all."

"How'd we get started on this subject, anyway?" Terri said. She raised her glass and drank from it. "Mel always has love on his mind," she said. "Don't you, honey?" She smiled, and I thought that was the last of it.

"I just wouldn't call Ed's behavior love. That's all I'm saying, honey," Mel said. "What about you guys?" Mel said to Laura and me. "Does that sound like love to you?"

"I'm the wrong person to ask," I said. "I didn't even know the man. I've only heard his name mentioned in passing. I wouldn't know. You'd have to know the particulars. But I think what you're saying is that love is an absolute."

Mel said, "The kind of love I'm talking about is. The kind of love I'm talking about, you don't try to kill people."

Laura said, "I don't know anything about Ed, or anything about the situation. But who can judge anyone else's situation?"

I touched the back of Laura's hand. She gave me a quick smile. I picked up Laura's hand. It was warm, the nails polished, perfectly manicured. I encircled the broad wrist with my fingers, and I held her.

"When I left, he drank rat poison," Terri said. She clasped her arms with her hands. "They took him to the hospital in Santa Fe. That's where we lived then, about ten miles out. They saved his life. But his gums went crazy from it. I mean they pulled away from his teeth. After that, his teeth stood out like fangs. My God," Terri said. She waited a minute, then let go of her arms and picked up her glass.

"What people won't do!" Laura said.

"He's out of the action now," Mel said. "He's dead."

Mel handed me the saucer of limes. I took a section, squeezed it over my drink, and stirred the ice cubes with my finger.

"It gets worse," Terri said. "He shot himself in the mouth. But he bungled that too. Poor Ed," she said. Terri shook her head.

"Poor Ed nothing," Mel said. "He was dangerous."

Mel was forty-five years old. He was tall and rangy with curly soft hair. His face and arms were brown from the tennis he played. When he was sober, his gestures, all his movements, were precise, very careful.

"He did love me though, Mel. Grant me that," Terri said. "That's all I'm asking. He didn't love me the way you love me. I'm not saying that. But he loved me. You can grant me that, can't you?"

"What do you mean, he bungled it?" I said.

Laura leaned forward with her glass. She put her elbows on the table and held her glass in both hands. She glanced from Mel to Terri and waited with a look of bewilderment on her open face, as if amazed that such things happened to people you were friendly with.

"How'd he bungle it when he killed himself?" I said.

"I'll tell you what happened," Mel said. "He took this twenty-two pistol he'd bought to threaten Terri and me with. Oh, I'm serious, the man was always threatening. You should have seen the way we lived in those days. Like fugitives. I even bought a gun myself. Can you believe it? A guy like me? But I did. I bought one for self-defense and carried it in the glove compartment. Sometimes I'd have to leave the apartment in the middle of the night. To go to the hospital, you know? Terri and I weren't married then, and my first wife had the house and kids, the dog, everything, and Terri and I were living in this apartment here. Sometimes, as I say, I'd get a call in the middle of the night and have to go in to the hospital at two or three in the morning. It'd be dark out there in the parking lot, and I'd break into a sweat before I could even get to my car. I never knew if he was going to come up out of the shrubbery or from behind a car and start shooting. I mean, the man was crazy. He was capable of wiring a bomb, anything. He used to call my service at all hours and say he needed to talk to the doctor, and when I'd return the call, he'd say, 'Son of a bitch, your days are numbered.' Little things like that. It was scary, I'm telling you."

"I still feel sorry for him," Terri said.

"It sounds like a nightmare," Laura said. "But what exactly happened after he shot himself?"

Laura is a legal secretary. We'd met in a professional capacity. Before we knew it, it was a courtship. She's thirty-five, three years younger than I am. In addition to being in love, we like each other and enjoy one another's company. She's easy to be with.

"What happened?" Laura said.

Mel said, "He shot himself in the mouth in his room. Someone heard the shot and told the manager. They came in with a passkey, saw what had happened, and called an ambulance. I happened to be there when they brought him in, alive but past recall. The man lived for three days. His head swelled up to twice the size of a normal head. I'd never seen anything like it, and I hope I never do again. Terri wanted to go in and sit with him when she found out about it. We had a fight over it. I didn't think she should see him like that. I didn't think she should see him, and I still don't."

"Who won the fight?" Laura said.

"I was in the room with him when he died," Terri said. "He never came up out of it. But I sat with him. He didn't have anyone else."

"He was dangerous," Mel said. "If you call that love, you can have it."

"It was love," Terri said. "Sure, it's abnormal in most people's eyes. But he was willing to die for it. He did die for it."

"I sure as hell wouldn't call it love," Mel said. "I mean, no one knows what he did it for. I've seen a lot of suicides, and I couldn't say anyone ever knew what they did it for."

Mel put his hands behind his neck and tilted his chair back. "I'm not interested in that kind of love," he said. "If that's love, you can have it."

Terri said, "We were afraid. Mel even made a will out and wrote to his brother in California who used to be a Green Beret. Mel told him who to look for if something happened to him."

Terri drank from her glass. She said, "But Mel's right—we lived like fugitives. We were afraid. Mel was, weren't you, honey? I even called the police at one point, but they were no help. They said they couldn't do anything until Ed actually did something. Isn't that a laugh?" Terri said.

She poured the last of the gin into her glass and waggled the bottle. Mel got up from the table and went to the cupboard. He took down another bottle.

"Well, Nick and I know what love is," Laura said. "For us, I mean," Laura said. She bumped my knee with her knee. "You're supposed to say something now," Laura said, and turned her smile on me.

For an answer, I took Laura's hand and raised it to my lips. I made a big production out of kissing her hand. Everyone was amused.

"We're lucky," I said.

"You guys," Terri said. "Stop that now. You're making me sick. You're still on the honeymoon, for God's sake. You're still gaga, for crying out loud. Just wait. How long have you been together now? How long has it been? A year? Longer than a year?"

"Going on a year and a half," Laura said, flushed and smiling.

"Oh, now," Terri said. "Wait awhile."

She held her drink and gazed at Laura.

"I'm only kidding," Terri said.

Mel opened the gin and went around the table with the bottle.

"Here, you guys," he said. "Let's have a toast. I want to propose a toast. A toast to love. To true love," Mel said.

We touched glasses.

"To love," we said.

Outside in the backyard, one of the dogs began to bark. The leaves of the aspen that leaned past the window ticked against the glass. The afternoon sun was like a presence in this room, the spacious light of ease and generosity. We could have been anywhere, somewhere enchanted. We raised our glasses again and grinned at each other like children who had agreed on something forbidden.

"I'll tell you what real love is," Mel said. "I mean, I'll give you a good example. And then you can draw your own conclusions." He poured more gin into his glass. He added an ice cube and a sliver of lime. We waited and sipped our drinks. Laura and I touched knees again. I put a hand on her warm thigh and left it there.

"What do any of us really know about love?" Mel said. "It seems to me we're just beginners at love. We say we love each other and we do, I don't doubt it. I love Terri and Terri loves me, and you guys love each other too. You know the kind of love I'm talking about now. Physical love, that impulse that drives you to someone special, as well as love of the other person's being, his or her essence, as it were. Carnal love and, well, call it sentimental love, the day-to-day caring about the other person. But sometimes I have a hard time accounting for the fact that I must have loved my first wife too. But I did, I know I did. So I suppose I am like Terri in that regard. Terri and Ed." He thought about it and then he went on. "There was a time when I thought I loved my first wife more than life itself. But now I hate her guts. I do. How do you explain that? What happened to that love? What happened to it, is what I'd like to know. I wish someone could tell me. Then there's Ed. Okay, we're back to Ed. He loves Terri so much he tries to kill her and he winds up killing himself." Mel stopped talking and swallowed from his glass. "You guys have been together eighteen months and you love each other. It shows all over you. You glow with it. But you both loved other people before you met each other. You've both been married before, just like us. And you probably loved other people before that too, even. Terri and I have been together five years, been married for four. And the terrible thing, the terrible thing is, but the good thing too, the saving grace, you might say, is that if something happened to one of us—excuse me for saying this—but if something happened to one of us tomorrow, I think the other one, the other person, would grieve for a while, you know, but then the surviving party would go out and love again, have someone else soon enough. All this, all of this love we're talking about, it would just be a memory. Maybe not even a memory. Am I wrong? Am I way off base? Because I want you to set me straight if you think I'm wrong. I want to know. I mean, I don't know anything, and I'm the first one to admit it."

"Mel, for God's sake," Terri said. She reached out and took hold of his wrist. "Are you getting drunk? Honey? Are you drunk?"

"Honey, I'm just talking," Mel said. "All right? I don't have to be drunk to say what I think. I mean, we're all just talking, right?" Mel said. He fixed his eyes on her.

"Sweetie, I'm not criticizing," Terri said.

She picked up her glass.

"I'm not on call today," Mel said. "Let me remind you of that. I am not on call," he said.

"Mel, we love you," Laura said.

Mel looked at Laura. He looked at her as if he could not place her, as if she was not the woman she was.

"Love you too, Laura," Mel said. "And you, Nick, love you too. You know something?" Mel said. "You guys are our pals," Mel said.

He picked up his glass.

Mel said, "I was going to tell you about something. I mean, I was going to prove a point. You see, this happened a few months ago, but it's still going on right now, and it ought to make us feel ashamed when we talk like we know what we're talking about when we talk about love."

"Come on now," Terri said. "Don't talk like you're drunk if you're not drunk."

"Just shut up for once in your life," Mel said very quietly. "Will you do me a favor and do that for a minute? So as I was saying, there's this old couple who had this car wreck out on the interstate. A kid hit them and they were all torn to shit and nobody was giving them much chance to pull through."

Terri looked at us and then back at Mel. She seemed anxious, or maybe that's too strong a word.

Mel was handing the bottle around the table.

"I was on call that night," Mel said. "It was May or maybe it was June. Terri and I had just sat down to dinner when the hospital called. There'd been this thing out on the interstate. Drunk kid, teenager, plowed his dad's pickup into this camper with this old couple in it. They were up in their mid-seventies, that couple. The kid—eighteen, nineteen, something—he was DOA. Taken the steering wheel through his sternum. The old couple, they were alive, you understand. I mean, just barely. But they had everything. Multiple fractures, internal injuries, hemorrhaging, contusions, lacerations, the works, and they each of them had themselves concussions. They were in a bad way, believe me. And, of course, their age was two strikes against them. I'd say she was worse off than he was. Ruptured spleen along with everything else. Both kneecaps broken. But they'd been wearing their seatbelts and, God knows, that's what saved them for the time being."

"Folks, this is an advertisement for the National Safety Council," Terri said. "This is your spokesman, Dr. Melvin R. McGinnis, talking." Terri laughed. "Mel," she said, "sometimes you're just too much. But I love you, hon," she said.

"Honey, I love you," Mel said.

He leaned across the table. Terri met him halfway. They kissed.

"Terri's right," Mel said as he settled himself again. "Get those seatbelts on. But seriously, they were in some shape, those oldsters. By the time I got down there, the kid was dead, as I said. He was off in a corner, laid out on a gurney. I took one look at the old couple and told the ER nurse to get me a neurologist and an orthopedic man and a couple of surgeons down there right away."

He drank from his glass. "I'll try to keep this short," he said. "So we took the two of them up to the OR and worked like fuck on them most of the night. They had these incredible reserves, those two. You see that once in a while. So we did everything that could be done, and toward morning we're giving them a fifty-fifty chance, maybe less than that for her. So here they are, still alive the next morning. So, okay, we move them into the ICU, which is where they both kept plugging away at it for two weeks, hitting it better and better on all the scopes. So we transfer them out to their own room."

Mel stopped talking. "Here," he said, "let's drink this cheapo gin the hell up. Then we're going to dinner, right? Terri and I know a new place. That's where we'll go, to this new place we know about. But we're not going until we finish up this cut-rate, lousy gin."

Terri said, "We haven't actually eaten there yet. But it looks good. From the outside, you know."

"I like food," Mel said. "If I had it to do all over again, I'd be a chef, you know? Right, Terri?" Mel said.

He laughed. He fingered the ice in his glass.

"Terri knows," he said. "Terri can tell you. But let me say this. If I could come back again in a different life, a different time and all, you know what? I'd like to come back as a knight. You were pretty safe wearing all that armor. It was all right being a knight until gunpowder and muskets and pistols came along."

"Mel would like to ride a horse and carry a lance," Terri said.

"Carry a woman's scarf with you everywhere," Laura said.

"Or just a woman," Mel said.

"Shame on you," Laura said.

Terri said, "Suppose you came back as a serf. The serfs didn't have it so good in those days," Terri said.

"The serfs never had it good," Mel said. "But I guess even the knights were vessels to someone. Isn't that the way it worked? But then everyone is always a vessel to someone. Isn't that right? Terri? But what I liked about knights, besides their ladies, was that they had that suit of armor, you know, and they couldn't get hurt very easy. No cars in those days, you know? No drunk teenagers to tear into your ass."

"Vassals," Terri said.

"What?" Mel said.

"Vassals," Terri said. "They were called vassals, not vessels."

"Vassals, vessels," Mel said, "what the fuck's the difference? You knew what I meant anyway. All right," Mel said. "So I'm not educated. I learned my stuff. I'm a heart surgeon, sure, but I'm just a mechanic. I go in and I fuck around and I fix things. Shit," Mel said.

"Modesty doesn't become you," Terri said.

"He's just a humble sawbones," I said. "But sometimes they suffocated in all that armor, Mel. They'd even have heart attacks if it got too hot and they were too tired and worn out. I read somewhere that they'd fall off their horses and not be able to get up because they were too tired to stand with all that armor on them. They got trampled by their own horses sometimes."

"That's terrible," Mel said. "That's a terrible thing, Nicky. I guess they'd just lay there and wait until somebody came along and made a shish kebab out of them."

"Some other vessel," Terri said.

"That's right," Mel said. "Some vassal would come along and spear the bastard in the name of love. Or whatever the fuck it was they fought over in those days."

"Same things we fight over these days," Terri said.

Laura said, "Nothing's changed."

The color was still high in Laura's cheeks. Her eyes were bright. She brought her glass to her lips.

Mel poured himself another drink. He looked at the label closely as if studying a long row of numbers. Then he slowly put the bottle down on the table and slowly reached for the tonic water.

"What about the old couple?" Laura said. "You didn't finish that story you started."

Laura was having a hard time lighting her cigarette. Her matches kept going out.

The sunshine inside the room was different now, changing, getting thinner. But the leaves outside the window were still shimmering, and I stared at the pattern they made on the panes and on the Formica counter. They weren't the same patterns, of course.

"What about the old couple?" I said.

"Older but wiser," Terri said.

Mel stared at her.

Terri said, "Go on with your story, hon. I was only kidding. Then what happened?"

"Terri, sometimes," Mel said.

"Please, Mel," Terri said. "Don't always be so serious, sweetie. Can't you take a joke?"

"Where's the joke?" Mel said.

He held his glass and gazed steadily at his wife.

"What happened?" Laura said.

Mel fastened his eyes on Laura. He said, "Laura, if I didn't have Terri and if I didn't love her so much, and if Nick wasn't my best friend, I'd fall in love with you. I'd carry you off, honey," he said.

"Tell your story," Terri said. "Then we'll go to that new place, okay?"

"Okay," Mel said. "Where was I?" he said. He stared at the table and then he began again.

"I dropped in to see each of them every day, sometimes twice a day if I was up doing other calls anyway. Casts and bandages, head to foot, the both of them. You know, you've seen it in the movies. That's just the way they looked, just like in the movies. Little eye-holes and nose-holes and mouth-holes. And she had to have her legs slung up on top of it. Well, the husband was very depressed for the longest while. Even after he found out that his wife was going to pull through, he was still very depressed. Not about the accident, though. I mean, the accident was one thing, but it wasn't everything. I'd get up to his mouth-hole, you know, and he'd say no, it wasn't the accident exactly but it was because he couldn't see her through his eye-holes. He said that was what was making him feel so bad. Can you imagine? I'm telling you, the man's heart was breaking because he couldn't turn his goddamn head and *see* his goddamn wife."

Mel looked around the table and shook his head at what he was going to say.

"I mean, it was killing the old fart just because he couldn't *look* at the fucking woman."

We all looked at Mel.

"Do you see what I'm saying?" he said.

Maybe we were a little drunk by then. I know it was hard keeping things in focus. The light was draining out of the room, going back through the window where it had come from. Yet nobody made a move to get up from the table to turn on the overhead light.

"Listen," Mel said. "Let's finish this fucking gin. There's about enough left here for one shooter all around. Then let's go eat. Let's go to the new place."

"He's depressed," Terri said. "Mel, why don't you take a pill?"

Mel shook his head. "I've taken everything there is."

"We all need a pill now and then," I said.

"Some people are born needing them," Terri said.

She was using her finger to rub at something on the table. Then she stopped rubbing.

"I think I want to call my kids," Mel said. "Is that all right with everybody? I'll call my kids," he said.

Terri said, "What if Marjorie answers the phone? You guys, you've heard us on the subject of Marjorie? Honey, you know you don't want to talk to Marjorie. It'll make you feel even worse."

"I don't want to talk to Marjorie," Mel said. "But I want to talk to my kids."

"There isn't a day goes by that Mel doesn't say he wishes she'd get married again. Or else die," Terri said. "For one thing," Terri said, "she's bankrupting us. Mel says it's just to spite him that she won't get married again. She has a boyfriend who lives with her and the kids, so Mel is supporting the boyfriend too."

"She's allergic to bees," Mel said. "If I'm not praying she'll get married again, I'm praying she'll get herself stung to death by a swarm of fucking bees."

"Shame on you," Laura said.

"Bzzzzzzz," Mel said, turning his fingers into bees and buzzing them at Terri's throat. Then he let his hands drop all the way to his sides.

"She's vicious," Mel said. "Sometimes I think I'll go up there dressed like a beekeeper. You know, that hat that's like a helmet with the plate that comes down over your face, the big gloves, and the padded coat? I'll knock on the door and let loose a hive of bees in the house. But first I'd make sure the kids were out, of course."

He crossed one leg over the other. It seemed to take him a lot of time to do it. Then he put both feet on the floor and leaned forward, elbows on the table, his chin cupped in his hands.

"Maybe I won't call the kids, after all. Maybe it isn't such a hot idea. Maybe we'll just go eat. How does that sound?"

"Sounds fine to me," I said. "Eat or not eat. Or keep drinking. I could head right on out into the sunset."

"What does that mean, honey?" Laura said.

"It just means what I said," I said. "It means I could just keep going. That's all it means."

"I could eat something myself," Laura said. "I don't think I've ever been so hungry in my life. Is there something to nibble on?"

"I'll put out some cheese and crackers," Terri said.

But Terri just sat there. She did not get up to get anything.

Mel turned his glass over. He spilled it out on the table.

"Gin's gone," Mel said.

Terri said, "Now what?"

I could hear my heart beating. I could hear everyone's heart. I could hear the human noise we sat there making, not one of us moving, not even when the room went dark.

JOURNAL WRITINGS

1. **Describe** in a paragraph a memory you have of someone you once loved but no longer do. Explain what attracted you to that person and what later may have made you "fall out of love." How do you now **define** the feeling you once had for this person?

2. In Carver's story, in spite of Ed's abuse, Terri keeps insisting that he loved her. Agree or disagree with Terri, and explain your reasons. (Consider: Is love a mental attitude, a feeling, a way of behaving, all or some of these, or none of these?)

BRAINSTORMING AND DRAFTING

3. Choosing one of the two couples—Nick and Laura or Mel and Terri—try to predict the direction in which their relationship is heading. Draft a paragraph discussing the features of their relationship that led you to this prediction.

4. In a small group, make a list of several places in the story where the word *love* is used. Each member of the group might then select one of these instances and **analyze** in a few sentences how the character **defines** love in that instance. After **comparing** the characters' definitions, the group can then evaluate whether any of them constitutes "true love." (Or, if you are working individually, choose any one instance to write about and add your own sentence evaluating whether "true love" is present.)

THE AUTHOR'S METHODS

5. Why is the story of the old couple so important to Mel? Explain how this "mini-story" fits into the story as a whole.
6. Throughout the story, the author repeatedly pictures the characters drinking gin and tonic. In a paragraph, develop some reasons why Carver might want us to see them drinking.
7. In this story, as in much modern fiction, the author does not explicitly tell us his view of the issue. Instead, he lets the characters do the talking. Yet the characters cannot seem to agree on what love is. Write a few sentences explaining why Carver might want to show us their disagreements.

FORMAL WRITING AND RESEARCH PAPERS

8. If Mel had a second life, he would like to come back as a knight in armor because he could be "pretty safe wearing all that armor." Write an **analysis** of Mel's character in which you discuss this **symbolic** wish to help explain his thinking.
9. Choose one or more of Robert Solomon's models or **metaphors** and demonstrate in depth how it applies to the characters and/or relationships in Carver's story.
10. Research some of the **causes** of divorce that sociologists or psychologists have suggested. (Consult, for example, *Psychological Abstracts*, the *Social Sciences Index*, and the card or computer catalog.) Write an extended paper in which you apply one or more of these causes to Carver's story and, if possible, to Plato's **myth**.

Simone de Beauvoir

The Woman in Love

(1952)

Born in Paris, France, Simone de Beauvoir (1908–1986) was raised by a
Catholic mother and an agnostic father. Rebelling against religious tradition
and social convention, she adopted an independent life-style that included a
fifty-one-year relationship with philosopher Jean-Paul Sartre, whom she
never married. Educated at the Sorbonne, University of Paris, she taught
philosophy in Marseilles, Rouen, and Paris, and published numerous
philosophical works, as well as several novels, short stories, essays, and
four autobiographies. Her works include *Existentialism and the Wisdom of
the Ages* and the novels *She Came to Stay* and *The Blood of Others*.

   She is probably best known for what has become the classic statement
of twentieth-century feminism, *The Second Sex,* from which the following
selection is taken. In this book she argues that women need to become
autonomous; that they should not automatically embrace marriage and
motherhood; and that they should achieve their own economic
independence through satisfying careers. In the following selection, de
Beauvoir examines what she views as the dependency of many women of
her time in love relationships. Her tone demands careful evaluation—often
she describes the situation as she sees it, leaving the reader to infer that
she regards much of what she sees as unacceptable.

PREVIEW

Do men experience love differently from women? Explain your answer.

The word *love* has by no means the same sense for both sexes, and this is one cause
of the serious misunderstandings that divide them. Byron well said: "Man's love
is of man's life a thing apart; 'Tis woman's whole existence." Nietzsche expresses
the same idea in *The Gay Science:*

> The single word love in fact signifies two different things for man and woman. What
> woman understands by love is clear enough: it is not only devotion, it is a total gift of
> body and soul, without reservation, without regard for anything whatever. This
> unconditional nature of her love is what makes it a *faith,** the only one she has. As for
> man, if he loves a woman, what he *wants** is that love from her; he is in consequence

---

* [Author's Note] Nietzsche's italics.

far from postulating the same sentiment for himself as for woman; if there should be men who also felt that desire for complete abandonment, upon my word, they would not be men.

Men have found it possible to be passionate lovers at certain times in their lives, but there is not one of them who could be called "a great lover"; in their most violent transports, they never abdicate completely; even on their knees before a mistress, what they still want is to take possession of her; at the very heart of their lives they remain sovereign subjects; the beloved woman is only one value among others; they wish to integrate her into their existence and not to squander it entirely on her. For woman, on the contrary, to love is to relinquish everything for the benefit of a master. As Cécile Sauvage puts it: "Woman must forget her own personality when she is in love. It is a law of nature. A woman is nonexistent without a master. Without a master, she is a scattered bouquet."

The fact is that we have nothing to do here with laws of nature. It is the difference in their situations that is reflected in the difference men and women show in their conceptions of love. The individual who is a subject, who is himself, if he has the courageous inclination toward transcendence, endeavors to extend his grasp on the world: he is ambitious, he acts. But an inessential creature is incapable of sensing the absolute at the heart of her subjectivity; a being doomed to immanence cannot find self-realization in acts. Shut up in the sphere of the relative, destined to the male from childhood, habituated to seeing in him a superb being whom she cannot possibly equal, the woman who has not repressed her claim to humanity will dream of transcending her being toward one of these superior beings, of amalgamating herself with the sovereign subject. There is no other way out for her than to lose herself, body and soul, in him who is represented to her as the absolute, as the essential. Since she is anyway doomed to dependence, she will prefer to serve a god rather than obey tyrants—parents, husband, or protector. She chooses to desire her enslavement so ardently that it will seem to her the expression of her liberty; she will try to rise above her situation as inessential object by fully accepting it; through her flesh, her feelings, her behavior, she will enthrone him as supreme value and reality: she will humble herself to nothingness before him. Love becomes for her a religion.

. . . the adolescent girl wishes at first to identify herself with males; when she gives that up, she then seeks to share in their masculinity by having one of them in love with her; it is not the individuality of this one or that one which attracts her; she is in love with man in general. "And you, the men I shall love, how I await you!" writes Irène Reweliotty. "How I rejoice to think I shall know you soon: especially You, the first." Of course the male is to belong to the same class and race as hers, for sexual privilege is in play only within this frame. If man is to be a demigod, he must first of all be a human being, and to the colonial officer's daughter the native is not a man. If the young girl gives herself to an "inferior," it is for the reason that she wishes to degrade herself because she believes she is unworthy of love; but normally she is looking for a man who represents male superiority. She is soon to ascertain that many individuals of the favored sex are sadly contingent and earthbound, but at first her presumption is favorable to them; they are called on less to prove their worth than to avoid too gross a disproof of it—which accounts for many mistakes, some of them serious. A naïve young girl is caught by the gleam of virility, and in her eyes male worth is shown, according to circumstances, by physical strength, distinction of manner, wealth, cultivation, intelligence, authority, social status, a military uniform; but what she always wants is for her lover to represent the essence of manhood.

Familiarity is often sufficient to destroy his prestige; it may collapse at the first kiss, or in daily association, or during the wedding night. Love at a distance, however, is only a fantasy, not a real experience. The desire for love becomes a passionate love only when it is carnally realized. Inversely, love can arise as a result of physical intercourse; in this case the sexually dominated woman acquires an exalted view of a man who at first seemed to her quite insignificant.

But it often happens that a woman succeeds in deifying none of the men she knows. Love has a smaller place in woman's life than has often been supposed. Husband, children, home, amusements, social duties, vanity, sexuality, career, are much more important. Most women dream of a *grand amour*, a soul-searing love. They have known substitutes, they have been close to it; it has come to them in partial, bruised, ridiculous, imperfect, mendacious forms; but very few have truly dedicated their lives to it. The *grandes amoureuses* are most often women who have not frittered themselves away in juvenile affairs; they have first accepted the traditional feminine destiny: husband, home, children; or they have known pitiless solitude; or they have banked on some enterprise that has been more or less of a failure. And when they glimpse the opportunity to salvage a disappointing life by dedicating it to some superior person, they desperately give themselves up to this hope. Mlle Aïssé, Juliette Drouet, and Mme d'Agoult were almost thirty when their love-life began, Julie de Lespinasse not far from forty. No other aim in life which seemed worth while was open to them, love was their only way out.

Even if they can choose independence, this road seems the most attractive to a majority of women: it is agonizing for a woman to assume responsibility for her life. Even the male, when adolescent, is quite willing to turn to older women for guidance, education, mothering; but customary attitudes, the boy's training, and his own inner imperatives forbid him to content himself in the end with the easy solution of abdication; to him such affairs with older women are only a stage through which he passes. It is man's good fortune—in adulthood as in early childhood—to be obliged to take the most arduous roads, but the surest; it is woman's misfortune to be surrounded by almost irresistible temptations; everything incites her to follow the easy slopes; instead of being invited to fight her own way up, she is told that she has only to let herself slide and she will attain paradises of enchantment. When she perceives that she has been duped by a mirage, it is too late; her strength has been exhausted in a losing venture.

The psychoanalysts are wont to assert that woman seeks the father image in her lover; but it is because he is a man, not because he is a father, that he dazzles the girl child, and every man shares in this magical power. Woman does not long to reincarnate one individual in another, but to reconstruct a situation: that which she experienced as a little girl, under adult protection. She was deeply integrated with home and family, she knew the peace of quasi-passivity. Love will give her back her mother as well as her father, it will give her back her childhood. What she wants to recover is a roof over her head, walls that prevent her from feeling her abandonment in the wide world, authority that protects her against her liberty. This childish drama haunts the love of many women; they are happy to be called "my little girl, my dear child"; men know that the words: "you're just like a little girl," are among those that most surely touch a woman's heart. We have seen that many women suffer in becoming adults; and so a great number remain obstinately "babyish," prolonging their childhood indefinitely in manner and dress. To become like a child again in a man's arms fills their cup with joy. The hackneyed theme: "To feel so little in your arms, my love," recurs again and again in amorous dialogue and in love letters. "Baby mine," croons the lover, the woman calls herself "your little one," and so on. A young woman will write: "When will he come, he who can dominate me?" And when he comes, she will love to sense his manly superiority. . . .

The supreme goal of human love, as of mystical love, is identification with the loved one. The measure of values, the truth of the world, are in his consciousness; hence it is not enough to serve him. The woman in love tries to see with his eyes; she reads the books he reads, prefers the pictures and the music he prefers; she is interested only in the landscapes she sees with him, in the ideas that come from him; she adopts his friendships, his enmities, his opinions; when she questions herself, it is his reply she tries to hear; she wants to have in her lungs the air he has already breathed; the fruits and flowers that do not come from his hands have no taste and no fragrance. Her idea of location in space, even, is upset: the center of the world is no longer the place where she is, but that occupied by her lover; all roads lead to his home, and from it. She uses his words, mimics his gestures, acquires his eccentricities and his tics. "I am Heathcliffe," says Catherine in *Wuthering Heights;* that is the cry of every woman in love; she is another incarnation of her loved one, his reflection, his double: she is *he.* She lets her own world collapse in contingence, for she really lives in his.

The supreme happiness of the woman in love is to be recognized by the loved man as a part of himself; when he says "we," she is associated and identified with him, she shares his prestige and reigns with him over the rest of the world; she never tires of repeating—even to excess—this delectable "we." As one necessary to a being who is absolute necessity, who stands forth in the world seeking necessary goals and who gives her back the world in necessary form, the woman in love acquires in her submission that magnificent possession, the absolute. It is this certitude that gives her lofty joys; she feels exalted to a place at the right hand of God. Small matter to her to have only second place if she has *her* place, forever, in a most wonderfully ordered world. So long as she is in love and is loved by and necessary to her loved one, she feels herself wholly justified: she knows peace and happiness. Such was perhaps the lot of Mlle Aïsse with the Chevalier d'Aydie before religious scruples troubled his soul, or that of Juliette Drouet in the mighty shadow of Victor Hugo.

But this glorious felicity rarely lasts. No man really is God. The relations sustained by the mystic with the divine Absence depend on her fervor alone; but the deified man, who is not God, is present. And from this fact are to come the torments of the woman in love. Her most common fate is summed up in the famous words of Julie de Lespinasse: "Always, my dear friend, I love you, I suffer and I await you." To be sure, suffering is linked with love for men also; but their pangs are either of short duration or not overly severe. Benjamin Constant wanted to die on account of Mme Récamier: he was cured in a twelvemonth. Stendhal regretted Métilde for years, but it was a regret that perfumed his life without destroying it. Whereas woman, in assuming her role as the inessential, accepting a total dependence, creates a hell for herself. Every woman in love recognizes herself in Hans Andersen's little mermaid who exchanged her fishtail for feminine legs through love and then found herself walking on needles and live coals. It is not true that the loved man is absolutely necessary, above chance and circumstance, and the woman is not necessary to him; he is not really in a position to justify the feminine being who is consecrated to his worship, and he does not permit himself to be possessed by her.

An authentic love should assume the contingence of the other; that is to say, his lacks, his limitations, and his basic gratuitousness. It would not pretend to be a mode of salvation, but a human interrelation. Idolatrous love attributes an absolute value to the loved one, a first falsity that is brilliantly apparent to all outsiders. "*He* isn't worth all that love,"is whispered around the woman in love, and posterity wears a pitying smile at the thought of certain pallid heroes, like Count Guibert. It is a searing disappointment to the woman to discover the faults, the mediocrity of her idol. Novelists, like Colette, have often depicted this bitter anguish. The disillusion is still more cruel than that of the child who sees the father's prestige crumble, because the woman has herself selected the one to whom she has given over her entire being.

Even if the chosen one is worthy of the profoundest affection, his truth is of the earth, earthy, and it is no longer this mere man whom the woman loves as she kneels before a supreme being; she is duped by that spirit of seriousness which declines to take values as incidental—that is to say, declines to recognize that they have their source in human existence. Her bad faith raises barriers between her and the man she adores. She offers him incense, she bows down, but she is not a friend to him since she does not realize that he is in danger in the world, that his projects and his aims are as fragile as he is; regarding him as the Faith, the Truth, she misunderstands his freedom—his hesitancy and anguish of spirit. This refusal to apply a human measuring scale to the lover explains many feminine paradoxes. The woman asks a favor from her lover. Is it granted? Then he is generous, rich, magnificent; he is kingly, he is divine. Is it refused? Then he is avaricious, mean, cruel; he is a devilish or a bestial creature. One might be tempted to object: if a "yes" is such an astounding and superb extravagance, should one be surprised at a "no"? If the "no" discloses such abject selfishness, why wonder so much at the "yes"? Between the superhuman and the inhuman is there no place for the human?

A fallen god is not a man: he is a fraud; the lover has no other alternative than to prove that he really is this king accepting adulation—or to confess himself a usurper. If he is no longer adored, he must be trampled on. In virtue of that glory with which she has haloed the brow of her beloved, the woman in love forbids him any weakness; she is disappointed and vexed if he does not live up to the image she has put in his place. If he gets tired or careless, if he gets hungry or thirsty at the wrong time, if he makes a mistake or contradicts himself, she asserts that he is "not himself" and she makes a grievance of it. In this indirect way she will go so far as to take him to task for any of his ventures that she disapproves; she judges her judge, and she denies him his liberty so that he may deserve to remain her master. Her worship sometimes finds better satisfaction in his absence than in his presence; as we have seen, there are women who devote themselves to dead or otherwise inaccessible heroes, so that they may never have to face them in person, for beings of flesh and blood would be fatally contrary to their dreams. Hence such disillusioned sayings as: "One must not believe in Prince Charming. Men are only poor creatures," and the like. They would not seem to be dwarfs if they had not been asked to be giants. . . .

Genuine love ought to be founded on the mutual recognition of two liberties; the lovers would then experience themselves both as self and as other: neither would give up transcendence, neither would be mutilated; together they would manifest values and aims in the world. For the one and the other, love would be revelation of self by the gift of self and enrichment of the world. In his work on self-knowledge* George Gusdorf sums up very exactly what *man* demands of love.

> Love reveals us to ourselves by making us come out of ourselves. We affirm ourselves by contact with what is foreign and complementary to us. . . . Love as a form of perception brings to light new skies and a new earth even in the landscape where we have always lived. Here is the great secret: the world is different, I myself *am different.* And I am no longer alone in knowing it. Even better: someone has apprised me of the fact. Woman therefore plays an indispensable and leading role in man's gaining knowledge of himself.

This accounts for the importance to the young man of his apprenticeship in love; we have seen how astonished Stendhal, Malraux, were at the miracle expressed in the phrase: "I myself, I am different." But Gusdorf is wrong when he writes: "And *similarly* man represents for woman an indispensable intermediary between herself and herself," for today her situation is not *similar;* man is revealed in a different aspect but he remains himself, and his new aspect is integrated with the sum total of his personality. It would be the same with woman only if she existed no less essentially than man as *pour-soi;* this would imply that she had economic independence, that she moved toward ends of her own and transcended herself, without using man as an agent, toward the social whole. Under these circumstances, love in equality is possible, as Malraux depicts it between Kyo and May in *Man's Fate.* Woman may even play the virile and dominating role, as did Mme de Warens with Rousseau, and, in Colette's *Chéri,* Léa with Chéri.

But most often woman knows herself only as different, relative; her *pour-*

---

* *La Découverte de soi* (Paris, 1948), pp. 421, 425. [Tr.]

autrui, relation to others, is confused with her very being; for her, love is not an intermediary "between herself and herself" because she does not attain her subjective existence; she remains engulfed in this loving woman whom man has not only revealed, but created. Her salvation depends on this despotic free being that has made her and can instantly destroy her. She lives in fear and trembling before this man who holds her destiny in his hands without quite knowing it, without quite wishing to. She is in danger through an other, an anguished and powerless onlooker at her own fate. Involuntary tyrant, involuntary executioner, this other wears a hostile visage in spite of her and of himself. And so, instead of the union sought for, the woman in love knows the most bitter solitude there is; instead of cooperation, she knows struggle and not seldom hate. For woman, love is a supreme effort to survive by accepting the dependence to which she is condemned; but even with consent a life of dependency can be lived only in fear and servility.

Men have vied with one another in proclaiming that love is woman's supreme accomplishment. "A woman who loves as a woman becomes only the more feminine," says Nietzsche; and Balzac: "Among the first-rate, man's life is fame, woman's life is love. Woman is man's equal only when she makes her life a perpetual offering, as that of man is perpetual action." But therein, again, is a cruel deception, since what she offers, men are in no wise anxious to accept. Man has no need of the unconditional devotion he claims, nor of the idolatrous love that flatters his vanity; he accepts them only on condition that he need not satisfy the reciprocal demands these attitudes imply. He preaches to woman that she should give—and her gifts bore him to distraction; she is left in embarrassment with her useless offerings, her empty life. On the day when it will be possible for woman to love not in her weakness but in her strength, not to escape herself but to find herself, not to abase herself but to assert herself—on that day love will become for her, as for man, a source of life and not of mortal danger. In the meantime, love represents in its most touching form the curse that lies heavily upon woman confined in the feminine universe, woman mutilated, insufficient unto herself. The innumerable martyrs to love bear witness against the injustice of a fate that offers a sterile hell as ultimate salvation.

JOURNAL WRITINGS

1. **Describe** in detail a relationship you have observed in which one person "deified" the other (that is, made the other into a godlike creature or placed him/her on a pedestal). What special characteristics did the person on the pedestal have, according to his/her partner? What evidence can you cite to show that the person on the pedestal actually did or did not have these characteristics? Why might someone want to "deify" another human being?

2. De Beauvoir distinguishes between male and female love by what she views as the more conditional nature of man's love versus the more *uncondi-*tional type of woman's love, which she calls a "total gift of body and soul." In a paragraph, **describe** the way in which you or someone you know behaves

in a love relationship. How does this behavior **compare** or **contrast** with de Beauvoir's view of the nature of male or female love? Now that you have read the article, what (if any) changes would you make in your response to the Preview question for this reading?

BRAINSTORMING AND DRAFTING

3.   Answer Journal Writing 1 if you have not already done so. Then **generalize** on the basis of the relationship you described: Draft a paragraph in which you speculate in detail on some possible advantages and/or disadvantages in being the person on a pedestal. Provide some real or imagined **examples** to substantiate your assertions.

4.   Identify a couple from literature (perhaps from Raymond Carver's story), film, or television in which one person is more dominant while the other behaves more submissively. Carefully **describe** the behaviors of each person that show dominance and submission. Explain whether you think these behaviors contribute to the relative success or failure of this relationship. What sort of "power" distribution do you think works best in a relationship?

THE AUTHOR'S METHODS

5.   What are some of de Beauvoir's reasons for using quotations from other authors? For instance, why does she include the words of Cécile Sauvage in the second paragraph? Does de Beauvoir agree with Sauvage? How can you tell? What does de Beauvoir think of the "bouquet" **symbol** in this passage? Try to pose and answer these kinds of questions to help explain the purpose of other quoted passages.

FORMAL WRITING AND RESEARCH PAPERS

6.   Using de Beauvoir's assertions on the ways males and females often experience love, **describe** and **analyze** the ways Cupid and Psyche approach love in Edith Hamilton's story in this unit. Include specific **examples** of the characters' behavior to show how they do or do not substantiate de Beauvoir's views.

7.   In the library or at home, find two or three traditional fairy tales (such as *Cinderella*) that involve a love relationship. **Analyze** these relationships in de Beauvoir's terms, and try to identify any patterns of similarities or differences among them. Include in the paper a **generalization** on what such patterns imply about the ways men and women love, according to the authors of these tales.

8.   De Beauvoir published this selection in 1952. Write a paper entitled "The 'Nineties' Woman in Love" or "The 'Nineties' Man in Love" in which you

compare and/or contrast the behaviors and attitudes of contemporary males or females in love with the behaviors and attitudes that de Beauvoir describes. Use one or more library sources on gender studies to help substantiate your views. (Try, for example, the *Social Sciences Index*, *Women's Studies Abstracts*, and the card or computer catalog.) You might conclude by evaluating the direction these behaviors and attitudes have taken or by speculating on their evolution in the future.

9.   De Beauvoir comments: "It is agonizing for a woman to assume responsibility for her life." Using a biographical, historical, or newspaper index, or the card or computer catalog, find some biographical data on a woman whom you believe has assumed responsibility for her life. In a paper, begin by stating what types of behavior might be expected from such women. Then explain in detail how the woman you have researched meets the criteria in your definition.

Edith Hamilton

Cupid and Psyche

(1942)

Born in Germany, Edith Hamilton (1867–1963) received a B.A. and M.A. from Bryn Mawr College, where she majored in Latin and Greek. She spent much of her career as headmistress of Bryn Mawr School in Maryland. In her teaching, she emphasized the learning and values of ancient Greece and Rome. Only after her retirement at age sixty-three did she begin to publish her books, many of which dealt with classical studies. She was honored with the National Achievement Award and the Constance Lindsay Skinner Award from the Women's National Book Association. Her works include *The Greek Way,* an exploration of Greek civilization written in a clear, accessible style, *The Roman Way,* and *The Prophets of Israel.* In *Mythology* (1942), which includes the story "Cupid and Psyche," she refashions many of the Greek, Roman, and Norse legends, attempting to capture the original authors' spirit and styles.

The tale of "Cupid and Psyche," she notes, was originally told by the Latin writer Apuleius. Like many classical myths, it may suggest to the reader certain contemporary psychological ideas about jealousy, communication, and male-female conflicts that the original author may or may not have consciously intended. Examining degrees of power and trust in a love relationship, the story also portrays incredible mythological ordeals to suggest the problems that many lovers encounter in their relationships.

PREVIEWS

A. What fears might prevent someone from loving a very attractive man or woman?
B. What fears might prevent someone from communicating openly with a loved one?

There was once a king who had three daughters, all lovely maidens, but the youngest, Psyche, excelled her sisters so greatly that beside them she seemed a very goddess consorting with mere mortals. The fame of her surpassing beauty spread over the earth, and everywhere men journeyed to gaze upon her with wonder and adoration and to do her homage as though she were in truth one of the immortals. They would even say that Venus herself could not equal this mortal. As they thronged in ever-growing numbers to worship her loveliness no one any more gave a thought to Venus herself. Her temples were neglected; her altars foul with cold ashes; her favorite towns deserted and falling in ruins. All the honors once hers were now given to a mere girl destined some day to die.

It may well be believed that the goddess would not put up with this treatment. As always when she was in trouble she turned for help to her son, that beautiful winged youth whom some call Cupid and others Love, against whose arrows there is no defense, neither in heaven nor on the earth. She told him her wrongs and as always he was ready to do her bidding. "Use your power," she said, "and make the hussy fall madly in love with the vilest and most despicable creature there is in the whole world." And so no doubt he would have done, if Venus had not first shown him Psyche, never thinking in her jealous rage what such beauty might do even to the God of Love himself. As he looked upon her it was as if he had shot one of his arrows into his own heart. He said nothing to his mother, indeed he had no power to utter a word, and Venus left him with the happy confidence that he would swiftly bring about Psyche's ruin.

What happened, however, was not what she had counted on. Psyche did not fall in love with a horrible wretch, she did not fall in love at all. Still more strange, no one fell in love with her. Men were content to look and wonder and worship— and then pass on to marry someone else. Both her sisters, inexpressibly inferior to her, were splendidly married, each to a king. Psyche, the all-beautiful, sat sad and solitary, only admired, never loved. It seemed that no man wanted her.

This was, of course, most disturbing to her parents. Her father finally traveled to an oracle of Apollo to ask his advice on how to get her a good husband. The god answered him, but his words were terrible. Cupid had told him the whole story and had begged for his help. Accordingly Apollo said that Psyche, dressed in deepest mourning, must be set on the summit of a rocky hill and left alone, and that there her destined husband, a fearful winged serpent, stronger than the gods themselves, would come to her and make her his wife.

The misery of all when Psyche's father brought back this lamentable news can be imagined. They dressed the maiden as though for her death and carried her to the hill with greater sorrowing than if it had been to her tomb. But Psyche herself kept her courage. "You should have wept for me before," she told them, "because of the beauty that has drawn down upon me the jealousy of Heaven. Now go, knowing that I am glad the end has come." They went in despairing grief, leaving the lovely helpless creature to meet her doom alone, and they shut themselves in their palace to mourn all their days for her.

On the high hilltop in the darkness Psyche sat, waiting for she knew not what terror. There, as she wept and trembled, a soft breath of air came through the stillness to her, the gentle breathing of Zephyr, sweetest and mildest of winds. She felt it lift her up. She was floating away from the rocky hill and down until she lay upon a grassy meadow soft as a bed and fragrant with flowers. It was so peaceful there, all her trouble left her and she slept. She woke beside a bright river; and on its bank was a mansion stately and beautiful as though built for a god, with pillars of gold and walls of silver and floors inlaid with precious stones. No sound was to be heard; the place seemed deserted and Psyche drew near, awestruck at the sight of such splendor. As she hesitated on the threshold, voices sounded in her ear. She could see no one, but the words they spoke came clearly to her. The house was for her, they told her. She must enter without fear and bathe and refresh herself. Then a banquet table would be spread for her. "We are your servants," the voices said, "ready to do whatever you desire."

The bath was the most delightful, the food the most delicious, she had ever enjoyed. While she dined, sweet music breathed around her: a great choir seemed to sing to a harp, but she could only hear, not see, them. Throughout the day, except for the strange companionship of the voices, she was alone, but in some inexplicable way she felt sure that with the coming of the night her husband would be with her. And so it happened. When she felt him beside her and heard his voice softly murmuring in her ear, all her fears left her. She knew without seeing him that here was no monster or shape of terror, but the lover and husband she had longed and waited for.

This half-and-half companionship could not fully content her; still she was happy and the time passed swiftly. One night, however, her dear though unseen husband spoke gravely to her and warned her that danger in the shape of her two sisters was approaching. "They are coming to the hill where you disappeared, to weep for you," he said; "but you must not let them see you or you will bring great sorrow upon me and ruin to yourself." She promised him she would not, but all the next day she passed in weeping, thinking of her sisters and herself unable to comfort them. She was still in tears when her husband came and even his caresses could not check them. At last he yielded sorrowfully to her great desire. "Do what you will," he said, "but you are seeking your own destruction." Then he warned her solemnly not to be persuaded by anyone to try to see him, on pain of being separated from him forever. Psyche cried out that she would never do so. She would die a hundred times over rather than live without him. "But give me this joy," she said: "to see my sisters." Sadly he promised her that it should be so.

The next morning the two came, brought down from the mountain by Zephyr. Happy and excited, Psyche was waiting for them. It was long before the three could speak to each other; their joy was too great to be expressed except by tears and embraces. But when at last they entered the palace and the elder sisters saw its surpassing treasures; when they sat at the rich banquet and heard the marvelous music, bitter envy took possession of them and a devouring curiosity as to who was the lord of all this magnificence and their sister's husband. But Psyche kept faith; she told them only that he was a young man, away now on a hunting expedition. Then filling their hands with gold and jewels, she had Zephyr bear them back to the hill. They went willingly enough, but their hearts were on fire with jealousy. All their own wealth and good fortune seemed to them as nothing compared with Psyche's, and their envious anger so worked in them that they came finally to plotting how to ruin her.

That very night Psyche's husband warned her once more. She would not listen when he begged her not to let them come again. She never could see him, she reminded him. Was she also to be forbidden to see all others, even her sisters so dear to her? He yielded as before, and very soon the two wicked women arrived, with their plot carefully worked out.

Already, because of Psyche's stumbling and contradictory answers when they asked her what her husband looked like, they had become convinced that she had never set eyes on him and did not really know what he was. They did not tell her this, but they reproached her for hiding her terrible state from them, her own sisters. They had learned, they said, and knew for a fact, that her husband was not a man, but the fearful serpent Apollo's oracle had declared he would be. He was kind now, no doubt, but he would certainly turn upon her some night and devour her.

Psyche, aghast, felt terror flooding her heart instead of love. She had wondered so often why he would never let her see him. There must be some dreadful reason. What did she really know about him? If he was not horrible to look at, then he was cruel to forbid her ever to behold him. In extreme misery, faltering and stammering, she gave her sisters to understand that she could not deny what they said, because she had been with him only in the dark. "There must be something very wrong," she sobbed, "for him so to shun the light of day." And she begged them to advise her.

They had their advice all prepared beforehand. That night she must hide a sharp knife and a lamp near her bed. When her husband was fast asleep she must leave the bed, light the lamp, and get the knife. She must steel herself to plunge it swiftly into the body of the frightful being the light would certainly show her. "We will be near," they said, "and carry you away with us when he is dead."

Then they left her torn by doubt and distracted what to do. She loved him; he was her dear husband. No; he was a horrible serpent and she loathed him. She would kill him—She would not. She must have certainty—She did not want certainty. So all day long her thoughts fought with each other. When evening came, however, she had given the struggle up. One thing she was determined to do: she would see him.

When at last he lay sleeping quietly, she summoned all her courage and lit the lamp. She tiptoed to the bed and holding the light high above her she gazed at what lay there. Oh, the relief and the rapture that filled her heart. No monster was revealed, but the sweetest and fairest of all creatures, at whose sight the very lamp seemed to shine brighter. In her first shame at her folly and lack of faith, Psyche fell on her knees and would have plunged the knife into her own breast if it had not fallen from her trembling hands. But those same unsteady hands that saved her betrayed her, too, for as she hung over him, ravished at the sight of him and unable to deny herself the bliss of filling her eyes with his beauty, some hot oil fell from the lamp upon his shoulder. He started awake: he saw the light and knew her faithlessness, and without a word he fled from her.

She rushed out after him into the night. She could not see him, but she heard his voice speaking to her. He told her who he was, and sadly bade her farewell. "Love cannot live where there is no trust," he said, and flew away. "The God of Love!" she thought. "He was my husband, and I, wretch that I am, could not keep faith with him. Is he gone from me forever? . . . At any rate," she told herself with rising courage, "I can spend the rest of my life searching for him. If he has no more love left for me, at least I can show him how much I love him." And she started on her journey. She had no idea where to go; she knew only that she would never give up looking for him.

He meanwhile had gone to his mother's chamber to have his wound cared for, but when Venus heard his story and learned that it was Psyche whom he had chosen, she left him angrily alone in his pain, and went forth to find the girl of whom he had made her still more jealous. Venus was determined to show Psyche what it meant to draw down the displeasure of a goddess.

Poor Psyche in her despairing wanderings was trying to win the gods over to her side. She offered ardent prayers to them perpetually, but not one of them would do anything to make Venus their enemy. At last she perceived that there was no hope for her, either in heaven or on earth, and she took a desperate resolve. She would go straight to Venus; she would offer herself humbly to her as her servant, and try to soften her anger. "And who knows," she thought, "if he himself is not there in his mother's house." So she set forth to find the goddess who was looking everywhere for her.

When she came into Venus' presence the goddess laughed aloud and asked her scornfully if she was seeking a husband since the one she had had would have nothing to do with her because he had almost died of the burning wound she had given him. "But really," she said, "you are so plain and ill-favored a girl that you will never be able to get you a lover except by the most diligent and painful service. I will therefore show my good will to you by training you in such ways." With that she took a great quantity of the smallest of the seeds, wheat and poppy and millet and so on, and mixed them all together in a heap. "By nightfall these must all be sorted," she said. "See to it for your own sake." And with that she departed.

Psyche, left alone, sat still and stared at the heap. Her mind was all in a maze because of the cruelty of the command; and, indeed, it was of no use to start a task so manifestly impossible. But at this direful moment she who had awakened no compassion in mortals or immortals was pitied by the tiniest creatures of the field, the little ants, the swift-runners. They cried to each other, "Come, have mercy on this poor maid and help her diligently." At once they came, waves of them, one after another, and they labored separating and dividing, until what had been a confused mass lay all ordered, every seed with its kind. This was what Venus found when she came back, and very angry she was to see it. "Your work is by no means over," she said. Then she gave Psyche a crust of bread and bade her sleep on the ground while she herself went off to her soft, fragrant couch. Surely if she could keep the girl at hard labor and half starve her, too, that hateful beauty of hers would soon be lost. Until then she must see that her son was securely guarded in his chamber where he was still suffering from his wound. Venus was pleased at the way matters were shaping.

The next morning she devised another task for Psyche, this time a dangerous one. "Down there near the riverbank," she said, "where the bushes grow thick, are sheep with fleeces of gold. Go fetch me some of their shining wool." When the worn girl reached the gently flowing stream, a great longing seized her to throw herself into it and end all her pain and despair. But as she was bending over the water she heard a little voice from near her feet, and looking down saw that it came from a green reed. She must not drown herself, it said. Things were not as bad as that. The sheep were indeed very fierce, but if Psyche would wait until they came out of the bushes toward evening to rest beside the river, she could go into the thicket and find plenty of the golden wool hanging on the sharp briars.

So spoke the kind and gentle reed, and Psyche, following the directions, was able to carry back to her cruel mistress a quantity of the shining fleece. Venus received it with an evil smile. "Someone helped you," she said sharply. "Never did you do this by yourself. However, I will give you an opportunity to prove that you really have the stout heart and the singular prudence you make such a show of. Do you see that black water which falls from the hill yonder? It is the source of the terrible river which is called hateful, the river Styx. You are to fill this flask from it." That was the worst task yet, as Psyche saw when she approached the waterfall. Only a winged creature could reach it, so steep and slimy were the rocks on all sides, and so fearful the onrush of the descending waters. But by this time it must be evident to all the readers of this story (as, perhaps, deep in her heart it had become evident to Psyche herself) that although each of her trials seemed impossibly hard, an excellent way out would always be provided for her. This time her savior was an eagle, who poised on his great wings beside her, seized the flask from her with his beak and brought it back to her full of the black water.

But Venus kept on. One cannot but accuse her of some stupidity. The only effect of all that had happened was to make her try again. She gave Psyche a box which she was to carry to the underworld and ask Proserpine to fill with some of her beauty. She was to tell her that Venus really needed it, she was so worn-out from nursing her sick son. Obediently as always Psyche went forth to look for the road to Hades. She found her guide in a tower she passed. It gave her careful directions how to get to Proserpine's palace, first through a great hole in the earth, then down to the river of death, where she must give the ferryman, Charon, a penny to take her across. From there the road led straight to the palace. Cerberus, the three-headed dog, guarded the doors, but if she gave him a cake he would be friendly and let her pass.

All happened, of course, as the tower had foretold. Proserpine was willing to do Venus a service, and Psyche, greatly encouraged, bore back the box, returning far more quickly than she had gone down.

Her next trial she brought upon herself through her curiosity and, still more, her vanity. She felt that she must see what that beauty-charm in the box was; and, perhaps, use a little of it herself. She knew quite as well as Venus did that her looks were not improved by what she had gone through, and always in her mind was the thought that she might suddenly meet Cupid. If only she could make herself more lovely for him! She was unable to resist the temptation; she opened the box. To her sharp disappointment she saw nothing there; it seemed empty. Immediately, however, a deadly languor took possession of her and she fell into a heavy sleep.

At this juncture the God of Love himself stepped forward. Cupid was healed of his wound by now and longing for Psyche. It is a difficult matter to keep Love imprisoned. Venus had locked the door, but there were the windows. All Cupid had to do was to fly out and start looking for his wife. She was lying almost beside the palace, and he found her at once. In a moment he had wiped the sleep from her eyes and put it back into the box. Then waking her with just a prick from one of his arrows, and scolding her a little for her curiosity, he bade her take Proserpine's box to his mother and he assured her that all thereafter would be well.

While the joyful Psyche hastened on her errand, the god flew up to Olympus. He wanted to make certain that Venus would give them no more trouble, so he went straight to Jupiter himself. The Father of Gods and Men consented at once to all that Cupid asked—"Even though," he said, "you have done me great harm in the past—seriously injured my good name and my dignity by making me change myself into a bull and a swan and so on. . . . However, I cannot refuse you."

Then he called a full assembly of the gods, and announced to all, including Venus, that Cupid and Psyche were formally married, and that he proposed to bestow immortality upon the bride. Mercury brought Psyche into the palace of the gods, and Jupiter himself gave her the ambrosia to taste which made her immortal. This, of course, completely changed the situation. Venus could not object to a goddess for her daughter-in-law; the alliance had become eminently suitable. No doubt she reflected also that Psyche, living up in heaven with a husband and children to care for, could not be much on the earth to turn men's heads and interfere with her own worship.

So all came to a most happy end. Love and the Soul (for that is what Psyche means) had sought and, after sore trials, found each other; and that union could never be broken.

JOURNAL WRITINGS

1. Briefly **describe** a relationship you have observed in which jealousy played a part. Then describe the role of jealousy in the story. Evaluate the effects of jealousy on each relationship.
2. When Psyche disobeys Cupid by shining the light on him, he tells her angrily, "Love cannot live where there is no trust." The **narrator** of the story seems to agree with this assertion; he calls Psyche's attempt to see her husband "folly" and "faithlessness." Explain why you agree or disagree with Cupid and the narrator; that is, discuss your own view of trust, indicating how far it should extend. Then use your view to evaluate their behavior.

BRAINSTORMING AND DRAFTING

3. How might Psyche **define** love? Would her definition differ from Cupid's? If so, how? **Compare** and/or **contrast** the elements in each definition with one of Robert Solomon's **metaphors** of love in his essay, "Models and Metaphors: 'The Game of Love.'"

4.   Draft a paragraph in which you **analyze** the importance of physical attractiveness to one of the major characters (Venus, Cupid, or Psyche). Use evidence from the story to support your assertions. What does the author imply about the role of attractiveness in relationships?

THE AUTHOR'S METHODS

5.   In traditional **symbolism,** light is often a positive presence, indicating knowledge, intelligence, insight, or spiritual virtue, while darkness typically portends mystery, ignorance, and perhaps evil. **Analyze** the various uses of light and darkness in the story, and indicate whether or how the author maintains the traditional meanings for these symbols.
6.   Literary writers will often use **conflict** to maintain suspense in a story. Find some sentences that create suspense through a conflict; then locate some corresponding sentences that show how the suspense is relieved. Write a paragraph detailing these problems and their resolutions; write a second paragraph in which you **generalize** about how problems are solved in this story. **Conclude** your second paragraph by indicating what these solutions imply about men and women.

CREATIVE PROJECT

7.   Write a condensed version of the story in a contemporary setting, using a realistic situation and emphasizing the **themes** (underlying ideas) and qualities of character that are most important to you. Optional commentary: Exchange papers with a partner. Read your partner's version and take notes on the themes and qualities he or she is trying to emphasize. After each person discusses the other's story, write a brief paper **comparing** and/or **contrasting** the partner's story with Hamilton's "Cupid and Psyche."

FORMAL WRITING AND RESEARCH PAPERS

8.   Write a paper **analyzing** Psyche's character. In particular, what sort of *woman* is she? You might consider, for example, whether she has any contradictory impulses; how she responds to Cupid, to her sisters, to Venus; how she would measure up to de Beauvoir's implied standards for a woman in love. Find instances in the story to support each quality you discuss. Evaluate the effect of each quality on her relationship with Cupid.
9.   Do some research on psychologists' views of communication or openness in a relationship. (Consult, for example, *Psychological Abstracts* and the card or computer catalog.) Using citations from your sources, explain the views and apply them to the relationship between Cupid and Psyche. You may also wish to apply them to the characters in David Leavitt's story, "Territory," in this unit.

Romaine Brooks

The Mummy

(1930)

Romaine Brooks (1874–1970) was born into a wealthy family, but after an unhappy childhood she embarked on an independent life, deliberately separating herself from her mother and brother. She studied art in Rome, lived for a while in Capri, which allowed her more freedom to express her lesbian identity, and then established a residence in Paris. Perhaps because of her inherited fortune, she painted only when she pleased. Often she would compose insightful portraits of her friends, revealing their inner traits. Renata Borgatti and Ida Rubinstein were a pianist and dancer, respectively, whose images she memorialized in portraits. She also painted images of androgynous women.

Her more abstract line drawings convey her themes symbolically. *The Mummy,* one such drawing, teases the viewer with its suggestion of an enigmatic relationship. The figures represented are entwined through Brooks's deft use of lines and curves.

JOURNAL WRITINGS

1. There are two figures in the pencil drawing on the following page. Look at the figure on the right, examining closely the facial expression and the bodily position. Pretend this figure is yourself. Write a paragraph about how you feel and **describe** the apparent situation in the drawing that makes you feel this way.
2. Now study the figure on the left, noticing especially the positions of its arms and legs, and the amount of space it occupies compared with the figure on the right. Pretend this left figure is yourself. Write a paragraph about what you are doing, why you are doing it, and how you feel during this action.

BRAINSTORMING AND DRAFTING

3. Reread de Beauvoir's essay or Hamilton's story in this unit. Draft a paragraph explaining how some of the ideas might be applied to Brooks's drawing.
4. Mummification was a process used by the ancient Egyptians to embalm (prevent decay and provide fragrance) and wrap dead bodies. Explain how each process (the embalming and the wrapping) might take on **symbolic**

significance and help to explain Brooks's ideas about the interaction between the two figures in the drawing.

THE ARTIST'S METHODS

5.   Write a paragraph in which you **describe** the various types of lines in the drawing and discuss their purpose in conveying the artist's **theme(s)**.
6.   Propose some reasons why Brooks chose to present her ideas in a pencil drawing rather than through another artistic medium, such as a painting.

FORMAL WRITING AND RESEARCH PAPERS

7.   Art critics who have studied Brooks's works often mention her interest in androgyny and hermaphroditism. Write a paper in which you **define** these terms and **argue** that they do or do not apply to *The Mummy*.

8. Find a painting or drawing (either exhibited or reproduced in a book) that you feel illustrates one or more of the ideas in this unit. Using the card or computer catalog, find some secondary sources that comment on the artist's work. Write a paper in which you explain in detail how some of the ideas from this unit apply to the painting or drawing. Identify and document the sources from the unit, as well as the secondary sources that you use to support your own ideas.

David Leavitt

Territory

(1983)

A young American short-story writer, David Leavitt was born in 1961, in Pittsburgh, Pennsylvania. He received a B.A. from Yale University, where he took a number of creative writing courses. Though his interest in writing started around the age of five, he began composing fiction seriously as a freshman at Yale. He received national attention when, at twenty-one, he published "Territory," his first short story, in *The New Yorker*. Since then, he has frequently contributed stories and essays to *The New Yorker, Harper's, Esquire,* and *The New York Times Book Review*. His novel, *The Lost Language of Cranes,* was published in 1986. The recipient of numerous honors for his fiction, he received the O. Henry Award for his story "Counting Months."

"Territory," now part of his short-story collection, *Family Dancing,* presents characters who participate in a nontraditional love relationship. Leavitt deals sympathetically with the problems of the son who wants his mother to accept him and his partner. The mother's views and feelings are also examined, both in their surface manifestations and in their more subtle innuendos.

PREVIEW

Your brother or sister tells you he/she is homosexual. Record your responses.

Neil's mother, Mrs. Campbell, sits on her lawn chair behind a card table outside the food co-op. Every few minutes, as the sun shifts, she moves the chair and table several inches back so as to remain in the shade. It is a hundred degrees outside, and bright white. Each time someone goes in or out of the co-op a gust of air-conditioning flies out of the automatic doors, raising dust from the cement.

Neil stands just inside, poised over a water fountain, and watches her. She has on a sun hat, and a sweatshirt over her tennis dress; her legs are bare, and shiny with cocoa butter. In front of her, propped against the table, a sign proclaims: MOTHERS, FIGHT FOR YOUR CHILDREN'S RIGHTS—SUPPORT A NON-NUCLEAR FUTURE. Women dressed exactly like her pass by, notice the sign, listen to her brief spiel, finger pamphlets, sign petitions or don't sign petitions, never give money. Her weary eyes are masked by dark glasses. In the age of Reagan, she has declared, keeping up the causes of peace and justice is a futile, tiresome, and unrewarding effort; it is therefore an effort fit only for mothers to keep up. The sun bounces off the window glass through which Neil watches her. His own reflection lines up with her profile.

Later that afternoon, Neil spreads himself out alongside the pool and imagines he is being watched by the shirtless Chicano gardener. But the gardener, concentrating on his pruning, is neither seductive nor seducible. On the lawn, his mother's large Airedales—Abigail, Lucille, Fern—amble, sniff, urinate. Occasionally, they accost the gardener, who yells at them in Spanish.

After two years' absence, Neil reasons, he should feel nostalgia, regret, gladness upon returning home. He closes his eyes and tries to muster the proper background music for the cinematic scene of return. His rhapsody, however, is interrupted by the noises of his mother's trio—the scratchy cello, whining violin, stumbling piano—as she and Lillian Havalard and Charlotte Feder plunge through Mozart. The tune is cheery, in a Germanic sort of way, and utterly inappropriate to what Neil is trying to feel. Yet it *is* the music of his adolescence; they have played it for years, bent over the notes, their heads bobbing in silent time to the metronome.

It is getting darker. Every few minutes, he must move his towel so as to remain within the narrowing patch of sunlight. In four hours, Wayne, his lover of ten months and the only person he has ever imagined he could spend his life with, will be in this house, where no lover of his has ever set foot. The thought fills him with a sense of grand terror and curiosity. He stretches, tries to feel seductive, desirable. The gardener's shears whack at the ferns; the music above him rushes to a loud, premature conclusion. The women laugh and applaud themselves as they give up for the day. He hears Charlotte Feder's full nasal twang, the voice of a fat woman in a pink pants suit—odd, since she is a scrawny, arthritic old bird, rarely clad in anything other than tennis shorts and a blouse. Lillian is the fat woman in the pink pants suit; her voice is thin and warped by too much crying. Drink in hand, she calls out from the porch, "Hot enough!" and waves. He lifts himself up and nods to her.

The women sit on the porch and chatter; their voices blend with the clink of ice in glasses. They belong to a small circle of ladies all of whom, with the exception of Neil's mother, are widows and divorcées. Lillian's husband left her twenty-two years ago, and sends her a check every month to live on; Charlotte has been divorced twice as long as she was married, and has a daughter serving a long sentence for terrorist acts committed when she was nineteen. Only Neil's mother has a husband, a distant sort of husband, away often on business. He is away on business now. All of them feel betrayed—by husbands, by children, by history.

Neil closes his eyes, tries to hear the words only as sounds. Soon, a new noise accosts him: his mother arguing with the gardener in Spanish. He leans on his elbows and watches them; the syllables are loud, heated, and compressed, and seem on the verge of explosion. But the argument ends happily; they shake hands. The gardener collects his check and walks out the gate without so much as looking at Neil.

He does not know the gardener's name; as his mother has reminded him, he does not know most of what has gone on since he moved away. Her life has gone on, unaffected by his absence. He flinches at his own egoism, the egoism of sons.

"Neil! Did you call the airport to make sure the plane's coming in on time?"

"Yes," he shouts to her. "It is."

"Good. Well, I'll have dinner ready when you get back."

"Mom—"

"What?" The word comes out in a weary wail that is more of an answer than a question.

"What's wrong?" he says, forgetting his original question.

"Nothing's wrong," she declares in a tone that indicates that everything is wrong. "The dogs have to be fed, dinner has to be made, and I've got people here. Nothing's wrong."

"I hope things will be as comfortable as possible when Wayne gets here."

"Is that a request or a threat?"

"Mom—"

Behind her sunglasses, her eyes are inscrutable. "I'm tired," she says. "It's been a long day. I . . . I'm anxious to meet Wayne. I'm sure he'll be wonderful, and we'll all have a wonderful, wonderful time. I'm sorry. I'm just tired."

She heads up the stairs. He suddenly feels an urge to cover himself; his body embarrasses him, as it has in her presence since the day she saw him shirtless and said with delight, "Neil! You're growing hair under your arms!"

Before he can get up, the dogs gather round him and begin to sniff and lick at him. He wriggles to get away from them, but Abigail, the largest and stupidest, straddles his stomach and nuzzles his mouth. He splutters and, laughing, throws her off. "Get away from me, you goddamn dogs," he shouts, and swats at them. They are new dogs, not the dog of his childhood, not dogs he trusts.

He stands, and the dogs circle him, looking up at his face expectantly. He feels renewed terror at the thought that Wayne will be here so soon: Will they sleep in the same room? Will they make love? He has never had sex in his parents' house. How can he be expected to be a lover here, in this place of his childhood, of his earliest shame, in this household of mothers and dogs?

"Dinnertime! Abbylucyferny, Abbylucyferny, dinnertime!" His mother's litany disperses the dogs, and they run for the door.

"Do you realize," he shouts to her, "that no matter how much those dogs love you they'd probably kill you for the leg of lamb in the freezer?"

Neil was twelve the first time he recognized in himself something like sexuality. He was lying outside, on the grass, when Rasputin—the dog, long dead, of his childhood—began licking his face. He felt a tingle he did not recognize, pulled off his shirt to give the dog access to more of him. Rasputin's tongue tickled coolly. A wet nose started to sniff down his body, toward his bathing suit. What he felt frightened him, but he couldn't bring himself to push the dog away. Then his mother called out, "Dinner," and Rasputin was gone, more interested in food than in him.

It was the day after Rasputin was put to sleep, years later, that Neil finally stood in the kitchen, his back turned to his parents, and said, with unexpected ease, "I'm a homosexual." The words seemed insufficient, reductive. For years, he had believed his sexuality to be detachable from the essential him, but now he realized that it was part of him. He had the sudden, despairing sensation that though the words had been easy to say, the fact of their having been aired was incurably damning. Only then, for the first time, did he admit that they were true, and he shook and wept in regret for what he would not be for his mother, for having failed her. His father hung back, silent; he was absent for that moment as he was mostly absent—a strong absence. Neil always thought of him sitting on the edge of the bed in his underwear, captivated by something on television. He said, "It's O. K., Neil." But his mother was resolute; her lower lip didn't quaver. She had enormous reserves of strength to which she only gained access at moments like this one. She hugged him from behind, wrapped him in the childhood smells of perfume and brownies, and whispered, "It's O. K., honey." For once, her words seemed as inadequate as his. Neil felt himself shrunk to an embarrassed adolescent, hating her sympathy, not wanting her to touch him. It was the way he would feel from then on whenever he was in her presence—even now, at twenty-three, bringing home his lover to meet her.

All through his childhood, she had packed only the most nutritious lunches, had served on the PTA, had volunteered at the children's library and at his school, had organized a successful campaign to ban a racist history textbook. The day after he told her, she located and got in touch with an organization called the Coalition of Parents of Lesbians and Gays. Within a year, she was president of it. On weekends, she and the other mothers drove their station wagons to San Francisco, set up their card tables in front of the Bulldog Baths, the Liberty Baths, passed out literature to men in leather and denim who were loath to admit they even had mothers. These men, who would habitually do violence to each other, were strangely cowed by the suburban ladies with their informational booklets, and bent their heads. Neil was a sophomore in college then, and lived in San Francisco. She brought him pamphlets detailing the dangers of bathhouses and back rooms, enemas and poppers, wordless sex in alleyways. His excursion into that world had been brief and lamentable, and was over. He winced at the thought that she knew all his sexual secrets, and vowed to move to the East Coast to escape her. It was not very different from the days when she had campaigned for a better playground, or tutored the Hispanic children in the audiovisual room. Those days, as well, he had run away from her concern. Even today, perched in front of the co-op, collecting signatures for nuclear disarmament, she was quintessentially a mother. And if the lot of mothers was to expect nothing in return, was the lot of sons to return nothing?

Driving across the Dumbarton Bridge on his way to the airport, Neil thinks, I have returned nothing; I have simply returned. He wonders if she would have given birth to him had she known what he would grow up to be.

Then he berates himself: Why should he assume himself to be the cause of her sorrow? She has told him that her life is full of secrets. She has changed since he left home—grown thinner, more rigid, harder to hug. She has given up baking, taken up tennis; her skin has browned and tightened. She is no longer the woman who hugged him and kissed him, who said, "As long as you're happy, that's all that's important to us."

The flats spread out around him; the bridge floats on purple and green silt, and spongy bay fill, not water at all. Only ten miles north, a whole city has been built on gunk dredged up from the bay.

He arrives at the airport ten minutes early, to discover that the plane has landed twenty minutes early. His first view of Wayne is from behind, by the baggage belt. Wayne looks as he always looks—slightly windblown—and is wearing the ratty leather jacket he was wearing the night they met. Neil sneaks up on him and puts his hands on his shoulders; when Wayne turns around, he looks relieved to see him.

They hug like brothers; only in the safety of Neil's mother's car do they dare to kiss. They recognize each other's smells, and grow comfortable again. "I never imagined I'd actually see you out here," Neil says, "but you're exactly the same here as there."

"It's only been a week."

They kiss again. Neil wants to go to a motel, but Wayne insists on being pragmatic. "We'll be there soon. Don't worry."

"We could go to one of the bathhouses in the city and take a room for a couple of aeons," Neil says. "Christ, I'm hard up. I don't even know if we're going to be in the same bedroom."

"Well, if we're not," Wayne says, "we'll sneak around. It'll be romantic."

They cling to each other for a few more minutes, until they realize that people are looking in the car window. Reluctantly, they pull apart. Neil reminds himself that he loves this man, that there is a reason for him to bring this man home.

He takes the scenic route on the way back. The car careers over foothills, through forests, along white four-lane highways high in the mountains. Wayne tells Neil that he sat next to a woman on the plane who was once Marilyn Monroe's psychiatrist's nurse. He slips his foot out of his shoe and nudges Neil's ankle, pulling Neil's sock down with his toe.

"I have to drive," Neil says. "I'm very glad you're here."

There is a comfort in the privacy of the car. They have a common fear of walking hand in hand, of publicly showing physical affection, even in the permissive West Seventies of New York—a fear that they have admitted only to one another. They slip through a pass between two hills, and are suddenly in residential Northern California, the land of expensive ranch-style houses.

As they pull into Neil's mother's driveway, the dogs run barking toward the car. When Wayne opens the door, they jump and lap at him, and he tries to close it again. "Don't worry. Abbylucyferny! Get in the house, damn it!"

His mother descends from the porch. She has changed into a blue flower-print dress, which Neil doesn't recognize. He gets out of the car and halfheartedly chastises the dogs. Crickets chirp in the trees. His mother looks radiant, even beautiful, illuminated by the headlights, surrounded by the now quiet dogs, like a Circe with her slaves. When she walks over to Wayne, offering her hand, and says, "Wayne, I'm Barbara," Neil forgets that she is his mother.

"Good to meet you, Barbara," Wayne says, and reaches out his hand. Craftier than she, he whirls her around to kiss her cheek.

Barbara! He is calling his mother Barbara! Then he remembers that Wayne is five years older than he is. They chat by the open car door, and Neil shrinks back—the embarrassed adolescent, uncomfortable, unwanted.

So the dreaded moment passes and he might as well not have been there. At dinner, Wayne keeps the conversation smooth, like a captivated courtier seeking Neil's mother's hand. A faggot son's sodomist—such words spit into Neil's head. She has prepared tiny meatballs with fresh coriander, fettucine with pesto. Wayne talks about the street people in New York; El Salvador is a tragedy; if only Sadat had lived; Phyllis Schlafly—what can you do?

"It's a losing battle," she tells him. "Every day I'm out there with my card table, me and the other mothers, but I tell you, Wayne, it's a losing battle. Sometimes I think us old ladies are the only ones with enough patience to fight."

Occasionally, Neil says something, but his comments seem stupid and clumsy. Wayne continues to call her Barbara. No one under forty has ever called her Barbara as long as Neil can remember. They drink wine; he does not.

Now is the time for drastic action. He contemplates taking Wayne's hand, then checks himself. He has never done anything in her presence to indicate that the sexuality he confessed to five years ago was a reality and not an invention. Even now, he and Wayne might as well be friends, college roommates. Then Wayne, his savior, with a single, sweeping gesture, reaches for his hand, and clasps it, in the midst of a joke he is telling about Saudi Arabians. By the time he is laughing, their hands are joined. Neil's throat contracts; his heart begins to beat violently. He notices his mother's eyes flicker, glance downward; she never breaks the stride of her sentence. The dinner goes on, and every taboo nurtured since childhood falls quietly away.

She removes the dishes. Their hands grow sticky; he cannot tell which fingers are his and which Wayne's. She clears the rest of the table and rounds up the dogs.

"Well, boys, I'm very tired, and I've got a long day ahead of me tomorrow, so I think I'll hit the sack. There are extra towels for you in Neil's bathroom, Wayne. Sleep well."

"Good night, Barbara," Wayne calls out. "It's been wonderful meeting you."

They are alone. Now they can disentangle their hands.

"No problem about where we sleep, is there?"

"No," Neil says. "I just can't imagine sleeping with someone in this house."

His leg shakes violently. Wayne takes Neil's hand in a firm grasp and hauls him up.

Later that night, they lie outside, under redwood trees, listening to the hysteria of the crickets, the hum of the pool cleaning itself. Redwood leaves prick their skin. They fell in love in bars and apartments, and this is the first time that they have made love outdoors. Neil is not sure he has enjoyed the experience. He kept sensing eyes, imagined that the neighborhood cats were staring at them from behind a fence of brambles. He remembers he once hid in this spot when he and some of the children from the neighborhood were playing sardines, remembers the intoxication of small bodies packed together, the warm breath of suppressed laughter on his neck. "The loser had to go through the spanking machine," he tells Wayne.

"Did you lose often?"

"Most of the time. The spanking machine never really hurt—just a whirl of hands. If you moved fast enough, no one could actually get you. Sometimes, though, late in the afternoon, we'd get naughty. We'd chase each other and pull each other's pants down. That was all. Boys and girls together!"

"Listen to the insects," Wayne says, and closes his eyes.

Neil turns to examine Wayne's face, notices a single, small pimple. Their lovemaking usually begins in a wrestle, a struggle for dominance, and ends with a somewhat confusing loss of identity—as now, when Neil sees a foot on the grass, resting against his leg, and tries to determine if it is his own or Wayne's.

From inside the house, the dogs begin to bark. Their yelps grow into alarmed falsettos. Neil lifts himself up. "I wonder if they smell something," he says.

"Probably just us," says Wayne.

"My mother will wake up. She hates getting waked up."

Lights go on in the house; the door to the porch opens.

"What's wrong, Abby? What's wrong?" his mother's voice calls softly.

Wayne clamps his hand over Neil's mouth. "Don't say anything," he whispers.

"I can't just—" Neil begins to say, but Wayne's hand closes over his mouth again. He bites it, and Wayne starts laughing.

"What was that?" Her voice projects into the garden. "Hello?" she says.

The dogs yelp louder. "Abbylucyferny, it's O.K., it's O.K." Her voice is soft and panicked. "Is anyone there?" she asks loudly.

The brambles shake. She takes a flashlight, shines it around the garden. Wayne and Neil duck down; the light lands on them and hovers for a few seconds. Then it clicks off and they are in the dark—a new dark, a darker dark, which their eyes must readjust to.

"Let's go to bed, Abbylucyferny," she says gently. Neil and Wayne hear her pad into the house. The dogs whimper as they follow her, and the lights go off.

Once before, Neil and his mother had stared at each other in the glare of bright lights. Four years ago, they stood in the arena created by the headlights of her car, waiting for the train. He was on his way back to San Francisco, where he was marching in a Gay Pride Parade the next day. The train station was next door to the food co-op and shared its parking lot. The co-op, familiar and boring by day, took on a certain mystery in the night. Neil recognized the spot where he had skidded on his bicycle and broken his leg. Through the glass doors, the brightly lit interior of the store glowed, its rows and rows of cans and boxes forming their own horizon, each can illuminated so that even from outside Neil could read the labels. All that was missing was the ladies in tennis dresses and sweatshirts, pushing their carts past bins of nuts and dried fruits.

"Your train is late," his mother said. Her hair fell loosely on her shoulders, and her legs were tanned. Neil looked at her and tried to imagine her in labor with him—bucking and struggling with his birth. He felt then the strange, sexless love for women which through his whole adolescence he had mistaken for heterosexual desire.

A single bright light approached them; it preceded the low, haunting sound of the whistle. Neil kissed his mother, and waved goodbye as he ran to meet the train. It was an old train, with windows tinted a sort of horrible lemon-lime. It stopped only long enough for him to hoist himself on board, and then it was moving again. He hurried to a window, hoping to see her drive off, but the tint of the window made it possible for him to make out only vague patches of light—street lamps, cars, the co-op.

He sank into the hard, green seat. The train was almost entirely empty; the only other passenger was a dark-skinned man wearing bluejeans and a leather jacket. He sat directly across the aisle from Neil, next to the window. He had rough skin and a thick mustache. Neil discovered that by pretending to look out the window he could study the man's reflection in the lemon-lime glass. It was only slightly hazy—the quality of a bad photograph. Neil felt his mouth open, felt sleep closing in on him. Hazy red and gold flashes through the glass pulsed in the face of the man in the window, giving the curious impression of muscle spasms. It took Neil a few minutes to realize that the man was staring at him, or, rather, staring at the back of his head—staring at his staring. The man smiled as though to say, I know exactly what you're staring at, and Neil felt the sickening sensation of desire rise in his throat.

Right before they reached the city, the man stood up and sat down in the seat next to Neil's. The man's thigh brushed deliberately against his own. Neil's eyes were watering; he felt sick to his stomach. Taking Neil's hand, the man said, "Why so nervous, honey? Relax."

Neil woke up the next morning with the taste of ashes in his mouth. He was lying on the floor, without blankets or sheets or pillows. Instinctively, he reached for his pants, and as he pulled them on came face to face with the man from the train. His name was Luis; he turned out to be a dog groomer. His apartment smelled of dog.

"Why such a hurry?" Luis said.

"The parade. The Gay Pride Parade. I'm meeting some friends to march."

"I'll come with you," Luis said. "I think I'm too old for these things, but why not?"

Neil did not want Luis to come with him, but he found it impossible to say so. Luis looked older by day, more likely to carry diseases. He dressed again in a torn T-shirt, leather jacket, bluejeans. "It's my everyday apparel," he said, and laughed. Neil buttoned his pants, aware that they had been washed by his mother the day before. Luis possessed the peculiar combination of hypermasculinity and effeminacy which exemplifies faggotry. Neil wanted to be rid of him, but Luis's mark was on him, he could see that much. They would become lovers whether Neil liked it or not.

They joined the parade midway. Neil hoped he wouldn't meet anyone he knew; he did not want to have to explain Luis, who clung to him. The parade was full of shirtless men with oiled, muscular shoulders. Neil's back ached. There were floats carrying garishly dressed prom queens and cheerleaders, some with beards, some actually looking like women. Luis said, "It makes me proud, makes me glad to be what I am." Neil supposed that by darting into the crowd ahead of him he might be able to lose Luis forever, but he found it difficult to let him go; the prospect of being alone seemed unbearable.

Neil was startled to see his mother watching the parade, holding up a sign. She was with the Coalition of Parents of Lesbians and Gays; they had posted a huge banner on the wall behind them proclaiming: OUR SONS AND DAUGHTERS, WE ARE PROUD OF YOU. She spotted him; she waved, and jumped up and down.

"Who's that woman?" Luis asked.

"My mother. I should go say hello to her."

"O.K.," Luis said. He followed Neil to the side of the parade. Neil kissed his mother. Luis took off his shirt, wiped his face with it, smiled.

"I'm glad you came," Neil said.

"I wouldn't have missed it, Neil. I wanted to show you I cared."

He smiled, and kissed her again. He showed no intention of introducing Luis, so Luis introduced himself.

"Hello, Luis," Mrs. Campbell said. Neil looked away. Luis shook her hand, and Neil wanted to warn his mother to wash it, warned himself to check with a V.D. clinic first thing Monday.

"Neil, this is Carmen Bologna, another one of the mothers," Mrs. Campbell said. She introduced him to a fat Italian woman with flushed cheeks, and hair arranged in the shape of a clamshell.

"Good to meet you, Neil, good to meet you," said Carmen Bologna. "You know my son, Michael? I'm so proud of Michael! He's doing so well now. I'm proud of him, proud to be his mother I am, and your mother's proud, too!"

The woman smiled at him, and Neil could think of nothing to say but "Thank you." He looked uncomfortably toward his mother, who stood listening to Luis. It occurred to him that the worst period of his life was probably about to begin and he had no way to stop it.

A group of drag queens ambled over to where the mothers were standing. "Michael! Michael!" shouted Carmen Bologna, and embraced a sticklike man wrapped in green satin. Michael's eyes were heavily dosed with green eyeshadow, and his lips were painted pink.

Neil turned and saw his mother staring, her mouth open. He marched over to where Luis was standing, and they moved back into the parade. He turned and waved to her. She waved back; he saw pain in her face, and then, briefly, regret. That day, he felt she would have traded him for any other son. Later, she said to him, "Carmen Bologna really was proud, and, speaking as a mother, let me tell you, you have to be brave to feel such pride."

Neil was never proud. It took him a year to dump Luis, another year to leave California. The sick taste of ashes was still in his mouth. On the plane, he envisioned his mother sitting alone in the dark, smoking. She did not leave his mind until he was circling New York, staring down at the dawn rising over Queens. The song playing in his earphones would remain hovering on the edges of his memory, always associated with her absence. After collecting his baggage, he took a bus into the city. Boys were selling newspapers in the middle of highways, through the windows of stopped cars. It was seven in the morning when he reached Manhattan. He stood for ten minutes on East Thirty-fourth Street, breathed the cold air, and felt bubbles rising in his blood.

Neil got a job as a paralegal—a temporary job, he told himself. When he met Wayne a year later, the sensations of that first morning returned to him. They'd been up all night, and at six they walked across the park to Wayne's apartment with the nervous, deliberate gait of people aching to make love for the first time. Joggers ran by with their dogs. None of them knew what Wayne and he were about to do, and the secrecy excited him. His mother came to mind, and the song, and the whirling vision of Queens coming alive below him. His breath solidified into clouds, and he felt happier than he had ever felt before in his life.

The second day of Wayne's visit, he and Neil go with Mrs. Campbell to pick up the dogs at the dog parlor. The grooming establishment is decorated with pink ribbons and photographs of the owner's champion pit bulls. A fat, middle-aged woman appears from the back, leading the newly trimmed and fluffed Abigail, Lucille, and Fern by three leashes. The dogs struggle frantically when they see Neil's mother, tangling the woman up in their leashes. "Ladies, behave!" Mrs. Campbell commands, and collects the dogs. She gives Fern to Neil and Abigail to Wayne. In the car on the way back, Abigail begins pawing to get on Wayne's lap.

"Just push her off," Mrs. Campbell says. "She knows she's not supposed to do that."

"You never groomed Rasputin," Neil complains.

"Rasputin was a mutt."

"Rasputin was a beautiful dog, even if he did smell."

"Do you remember when you were a little kid, Neil, you used to make Rasputin dance with you? Once you tried to dress him up in one of my blouses."

"I don't remember that," Neil says.

"Yes. I remember," says Mrs. Campbell. "Then you tried to organize a dog beauty contest in the neighborhood. You wanted to have runners-up—everything."

"A dog beauty contest?" Wayne says.

"Mother, do we have to—"

"I think it's a mother's privilege to embarrass her son," Mrs. Campbell says, and smiles.

When they are about to pull into the driveway, Wayne starts screaming, and pushes Abigail off his lap. "Oh, my God!" he says. "The dog just pissed all over me."

Neil turns around and sees a puddle seeping into Wayne's slacks. He suppresses his laughter, and Mrs. Campbell hands him a rag.

"I'm sorry, Wayne," she says. "It goes with the territory."

"This is really disgusting," Wayne says, swatting at himself with the rag.

Neil keeps his eyes on his own reflection in the rearview mirror and smiles.

At home, while Wayne cleans himself in the bathroom, Neil watches his mother cook lunch—Japanese noodles in soup. "When you went off to college," she says, "I went to the grocery store. I was going to buy you ramen noodles, and I suddenly realized you weren't going to be around to eat them. I started crying right then, blubbering like an idiot."

Neil clenches his fists inside his pockets. She has a way of telling him little sad stories when he doesn't want to hear them—stories of dolls broken by her brothers, lunches stolen by neighborhood boys on the way to school. Now he has joined the ranks of male children who have made her cry.

"Mama, I'm sorry," he says.

She is bent over the noodles, which steam in her face. "I didn't want to say anything in front of Wayne, but I wish you had answered me last night. I was very frightened—and worried."

"I'm sorry," he says, but it's not convincing. His fingers prickle. He senses a great sorrow about to be born.

"I lead a quiet life," she says. "I don't want to be a disciplinarian. I just don't have the energy for these—shenanigans. Please don't frighten me that way again."

"If you were so upset, why didn't you say something?"

"I'd rather not discuss it. I lead a quiet life. I'm not used to getting woken up late at night. I'm not used—"

"To my having a lover?"

"No, I'm not used to having other people around, that's all. Wayne is charming. A wonderful young man."

"He likes you, too."

"I'm sure we'll get along fine."

She scoops the steaming noodles into ceramic bowls. Wayne returns, wearing shorts. His white, hairy legs are a shocking contrast to hers, which are brown and sleek.

"I'll wash those pants, Wayne," Mrs. Campbell says. "I have a special detergent that'll take out the stain."

She gives Neil a look to indicate that the subject should be dropped. He looks at Wayne, looks at his mother; his initial embarrassment gives way to a fierce pride—the arrogance of mastery. He is glad his mother knows that he is desired, glad it makes her flinch.

Later, he steps into the back yard; the gardener is back, whacking at the bushes with his shears. Neil walks by him in his bathing suit, imagining he is on parade.

That afternoon, he finds his mother's daily list on the kitchen table:

TUESDAY

7:00—breakfast
Take dogs to groomer
Groceries (?)

Campaign against Draft—4–7

Buy underwear
Trios—2:00

Spaghetti
Fruit
Asparagus if sale
Peanuts
Milk

Doctor's Appointment (make)
Write Cranston/Hayakawa
re disarmament

Handi-Wraps
Mozart
Abigail
Top Ramen
Pedro

Her desk and trash can are full of such lists; he remembers them from the earliest days of his childhood. He had learned to read from them. In his own life, too, there have been endless lists—covered with check marks and arrows, at least one item always spilling over onto the next day's agenda. From September to November, "Buy plane ticket for Christmas" floated from list to list to list.

The last item puzzles him: Pedro. Pedro must be the gardener. He observes the accretion of names, the arbitrary specifics that give a sense of his mother's life. He could make a list of his own selves: the child, the adolescent, the promiscuous faggot son, and finally the good son, settled, relatively successful. But the divisions wouldn't work; he is today and will always be the child being licked by the dog, the boy on the floor with Luis; he will still be everything he is ashamed of. The other lists—the lists of things done and undone—tell their own truth: that his life is measured more properly in objects than in stages. He knows himself as "jump rope," "book," "sunglasses,""underwear."

"Tell me about your family, Wayne," Mrs. Campbell says that night, as they drive toward town. They are going to see an Esther Williams movie at the local revival house: an underwater musical, populated by mermaids, underwater Rockettes.

"My father was a lawyer," Wayne says. "He had an office in Queens, with a neon sign. I think he's probably the only lawyer in the world who had a neon sign. Anyway, he died when I was ten. My mother never remarried. She lives in Queens. Her great claim to fame is that when she was twenty-two she went on 'The $64,000 Question.' Her category was mystery novels. She made it to sixteen thousand before she got tripped up."

"When I was about ten, I wanted you to go on 'Jeopardy,'" Neil says to his mother. "You really should have, you know. You would have won."

"You certainly loved 'Jeopardy,'" Mrs. Campbell says. "You used to watch it during dinner. Wayne, does your mother work?"

"No," he says. "She lives off investments."

"You're both only children," Mrs. Campbell says. Neil wonders if she is ruminating on the possible connection between that coincidence and their "alternative life style."

The movie theater is nearly empty. Neil sits between Wayne and his mother.

There are pillows on the floor at the front of the theater, and a cat is prowling over them. It casts a monstrous shadow every now and then on the screen, disturbing the sedative effect of water ballet. Like a teen-ager, Neil cautiously reaches his arm around Wayne's shoulder. Wayne takes his hand immediately. Next to them, Neil's mother breathes in, out, in, out. Neil timorously moves his other arm and lifts it behind his mother's neck. He does not look at her, but he can tell from her breathing that she senses what he is doing. Slowly, carefully, he lets his hand drop on her shoulder; it twitches spasmodically, and he jumps, as if he had received an electric shock. His mother's quiet breathing is broken by a gasp; even Wayne notices. A sudden brightness on the screen illuminates the panic in her eyes, Neil's arm frozen above her, about to fall again. Slowly, he lowers his arm until his fingertips touch her skin, the fabric of her dress. He had gone too far to go back now; they are all too far.

Wayne and Mrs. Campbell sink into their seats, but Neil remains stiff, holding up his arms, which rest on nothing. The movie ends, and they go on sitting just like that.

"I'm old," Mrs. Campbell says later, as they drive back home. "I remember when those films were new. Your father and I went to one on our first date. I loved them, because I could pretend that those women underwater were flying—they were so graceful. They really took advantage of Technicolor in those days. Color was something to appreciate. You can't know what it was like to see a color movie for the first time, after years of black-and-white. It's like trying to explain the surprise of snow to an East Coaster. Very little is new anymore, I fear."

Neil would like to tell her about his own nostalgia, but how can he explain that all of it revolves around her? The idea of her life before he was born pleases him. "Tell Wayne how you used to look like Esther Williams," he asks her.

She blushes. "I was told I looked like Esther Williams, but really more like Gene Tierney," she says. "Not beautiful, but interesting. I like to think I had a certain magnetism."

"You still do," Wayne says, and instantly recognizes the wrongness of his comment. Silence and a nervous laugh indicate that he has not yet mastered the family vocabulary.

When they get home, the night is once again full of the sound of crickets. Mrs. Campbell picks up a flashlight and calls the dogs. "Abbylucyferny, Abbylucyferny," she shouts, and the dogs amble from their various corners. She pushes them out the door to the back yard and follows them. Neil follows her. Wayne follows Neil, but hovers on the porch. Neil walks behind her as she tramps through the garden. She holds out her flashlight, and snails slide from behind bushes, from under rocks, to where she stands. When the snails become visible, she crushes them underfoot. They make a wet cracking noise, like eggs being broken.

"Nights like this," she says, "I think of children without pants on, in hot South American countries. I have nightmares about tanks rolling down our street."

"The weather's never like this in New York," Neil says. "When it's hot, it's humid and sticky. You don't want to go outdoors."

"I could never live anywhere else but here. I think I'd die. I'm too used to the climate."

"Don't be silly."

"No, I mean it," she says. "I have adjusted too well to the weather."

The dogs bark and howl by the fence. "A cat, I suspect," she says. She aims her flashlight at a rock, and more snails emerge—uncountable numbers, too stupid to have learned not to trust light.

"I know what you were doing at the movie," she says.

"What?"

"I know what you were doing."

"What? I put my arm around you."

"I'm sorry, Neil," she says. "I can only take so much. Just so much."

"What do you mean?" he says. "I was only trying to show affection."

"Oh, affection—I know about affection."

He looks up at the porch, sees Wayne moving toward the door, trying not to listen.

"What do you mean?" Neil says to her.

She puts down the flashlight and wraps her arms around herself. "I remember when you were a little boy," she says. "I remember, and I have to stop remembering. I wanted you to grow up happy. And I'm very tolerant, very understanding. But I can only take so much."

His heart seems to have risen into his throat. "Mother," he says, "I think you know my life isn't your fault. But for God's sake, don't say that your life is my fault."

"It's not a question of fault," she says. She extracts a Kleenex from her pocket and blows her nose. "I'm sorry, Neil. I guess I'm just an old woman with too much on her mind and not enough to do." She laughs halfheartedly. "Don't worry. Don't say anything," she says. "Abbylucyferny, Abbylucyferny, time for bed!"

He watches her as she walks toward the porch, silent and regal. There is the pad of feet, the clinking of dog tags as the dogs run for the house.

He was twelve the first time she saw him march in a parade. He played the tuba, and as his elementary-school band lumbered down the streets of their then small town she stood on the sidelines and waved. Afterward, she had taken him out for ice cream. He spilled some on his red uniform, and she swiped at it with a napkin. She had been there for him that day, as well as years later, at that more memorable parade; she had been there for him every day.

Somewhere over Iowa, a week later, Neil remembers this scene, remembers other days, when he would find her sitting in the dark, crying. She had to take time out of her own private sorrow to appease his anxiety. "It was part of it," she told him later. "Part of being a mother."

"The scariest thing in the world is the thought that you could unknowingly ruin someone's life," Neil tells Wayne. "Or even change someone's life. I hate the thought of having such control. I'd make a rotten mother."

"You're crazy," Wayne says. "You have this great mother, and all you do is complain. I know people whose mothers have disowned them."

"Guilt goes with the territory," Neil says.

"Why?" Wayne asks, perfectly seriously.

Neil doesn't answer. He lies back in his seat, closes his eyes, imagines he grew up in a house in the mountains of Colorado, surrounded by snow—endless white snow on hills. No flat places, and no trees; just white hills. Every time he has flown away, she has come into his mind, usually sitting alone in the dark, smoking. Today she is outside at dusk, skimming leaves from the pool.

"I want to get a dog," Neil says.

Wayne laughs. "In the city? It'd suffocate."

The hum of the airplane is druglike, dazing. "I want to stay with you a long time," Neil says.

"I know." Imperceptibly, Wayne takes his hand.

"It's very hot there in the summer, too. You know, I'm not thinking about my mother now."

"It's O.K."

For a moment, Neil wonders what the stewardess or the old woman on the way to the bathroom will think, but then he laughs and relaxes.

Later, the plane makes a slow circle over New York City, and on it two men hold hands, eyes closed, and breathe in unison.

JOURNAL WRITINGS

1. Trace your feelings about Neil's homosexuality through several parts of the story. Explain why you do or do not sympathize with Neil. Identify **specific** incidents in the story that led you to these feelings. After reading the story, would you change your answer to the Preview question? If so, how?

2. The first words in the story are "Neil's mother," and much of Neil's anxiety seems related to thoughts about his mother. Their actual conversation, however, does little to relieve these anxieties. Pretend you are in Neil's place. Write a letter to Mrs. Campbell in which you carefully consider her feelings and tell her some of yours. Your purpose is to try to establish a more comfortable relationship between you and her.

BRAINSTORMING AND DRAFTING

3. Read the excerpt from Gordon Allport's *The Nature of Prejudice* in Unit One of this book. Using some of Allport's principles, draft a paragraph **arguing** that Mrs. Campbell is or is not prejudiced against homosexuals.

4. List some ways in which the **abstract** problem of prejudice against homosexuals would apply to **concrete** situations in American society today. (You may wish to discuss your list in a small group.) Draft a few sentences detailing one of the items on your list, and explain how it may or may not apply to Neil in Leavitt's story.

THE AUTHOR'S METHODS

5. Compare Leavitt's use of light with Hamilton's in "Cupid and Psyche." For each story, explain both the literal and **symbolic** purpose of the light and show how it illustrates character or helps to suggest the **theme**(s) in the story.

6. "'It goes with the territory,'" Mrs. Campbell tells Wayne after her dog urinates on him. Neil also **alludes** to the story's title as he tells Wayne, "'Guilt goes with the territory.'" Look up the word *territory* in a college dictionary and examine all of the meanings listed. Choose the most appropriate meaning for these two statements, giving reasons for your choice. Explain in one or two paragraphs why the word is useful as a title for the story.

CREATIVE PROJECT

7. Write a brief, short story about a lesbian who must deal with her father's feelings about her chosen life-style.

FORMAL WRITING AND RESEARCH PAPERS

8. Who controls whom in this story? Write a paper on the issue of control, demonstrating how it affects several of the characters and indicating what it implies. You may wish to include a discussion of (or **comparison** with) Simone de Beauvoir's views, in this unit, on the effects of "power" distribution in a relationship.

9. Locate some library sources on society's beliefs (realities or misconceptions) about homosexuality. Try, for example, *Sociological Abstracts*, *Psychological Abstracts*, and the card or computer catalog. Write a paper explaining and **analyzing** as many of these beliefs as you think appear in Leavitt's story. Speculate on one or more reasons why the author might want to include such beliefs.

10. The gay rights issue has become a compelling social controversy. Find several recent sources detailing arguments both for and against specific homosexual rights. (Try, for example, *The National Newspaper Index*, *The Social Sciences Index*, and the card or computer catalog.) Then write a paper **arguing** your own position on the issue. Use several sources to help you support your arguments with reasons and examples. You may also wish to include sources that you argue against. Refer to Leavitt's story in your paper in whatever way you deem appropriate.

Saint Augustine

On the Evil of Lust

(A.D. 413–426)

Augustine (A.D. 354–430) was born in Algeria, Africa. A mildly rebellious adolescent, he attended school but was not an enthusiastic student, though he did enjoy Latin and particularly liked reading Cicero. After furthering his education in Carthage, however, he became a teacher and, later, a dedicated scholar and effective orator in Milan, Italy. Meanwhile, pursuing his philosophical and theological interests, he at first embraced the cult of Manichaeism but later found its outlook to be unacceptable. In A.D. 387, he was baptized as a Christian. Returning to Africa in 389, he was later ordained a priest and then bishop of Hippo. Augustine wrote numerous scriptural explications and other religious treatises, among them *Christian Doctrine* and *The Trinity*. His *Confessions* is an autobiographical account of selected events in his life, including his sensual affairs before his conversion to Christianity.

In *The City of God Against the Pagans,* from which this selection is taken, Augustine disputes popular views of history and religion, asserting instead a need to recall the primacy of the one Christian God in the lives and thoughts of human beings. He further examines the implications of this view for human activities. In the following selection, he describes what he regards as the "fallen" state of human beings—a separation between body and mind when sexual feelings are aroused. For Augustine, the human sexual act is associated with shameful feelings that result from the biblical act of disobedience against God.

PREVIEW

Under what circumstances, if any, would you consider sexual *desire* (as different from a sexual *act*) to be immoral? Give your reasons.

. . . although there are lusts for many things, yet when the term lust is employed without the mention of any object, nothing comes to mind usually but the lust that excites the shameful parts of the body. Moreover, this lust asserts its power not only over the entire body, nor only externally, but also from within. It convulses all of a man when the emotion in his mind combines and mingles with the carnal drive to produce a pleasure unsurpassed among those of the body. The effect of this is that at the very moment of its climax there is an almost total eclipse of acumen and, as it were, sentinel alertness. But surely any friend of wisdom and holy joys, who lives in wedlock but knows, as the Apostle admonished, "how to possess his bodily vessel in holiness and honour, not in the disease of lust like the gentiles who do not know God," would prefer, if he could, to beget children without this kind of lust. For he would want his mind to be served, even in this function of engendering offspring, by the parts created for this kind of work, just as it is served by the other members, each assigned to its own kind of work. They would be set in motion when the will urged, not stirred to action when hot lust surged.

But not even those who are enamoured of this pleasure are aroused whether to marital intercourse or to the uncleanness of outrageous vice just when it is their will. At times the urge intrudes uninvited; at other times it deserts the panting lover, and although desire is ablaze in the mind, the body is frigid. In this strange fashion lust refuses service not only to the will to procreate but also to the lust for wantonness; and though for the most part it solidly opposes the mind's restraint, there are times when it is divided even against itself and, having aroused the mind, inconsistently fails to arouse the body.

On the Nakedness of the First Human Beings, Which Seemed to Them Base and Shameful After They Sinned.

It is reasonable then that we should feel very much ashamed of such lust, and reasonable too that those members which it moves or does not move by its own right, so to speak, and not in full subjection to our will, should be called pudenda or shameful parts as they were not before man sinned; for we read in Scripture: "They were naked, and not embarrassed." And the reason for this is not that they were unaware of their nakedness, but that their nakedness was not yet base because lust did not yet arouse those members apart from their will, and the flesh did not yet bear witness, so to speak, through its own disobedience against the disobedience of man.

For the first human beings had not been created blind, as the ignorant multitude think, since Adam saw the animals upon which he bestowed names, and of Eve we read: "The woman saw that the tree was good for food and that it was a delight for the eyes to behold." Accordingly, their eyes were not closed, but they were not open, that is, attentive so as to recognize what a boon the cloak of grace afforded them, in that their bodily members did not know how to oppose their will. When this grace was lost and punishment in kind for their disobedience was inflicted, there came to be in the action of the body a certain shameless novelty, and thereafter nudity was indecent. It drew their attention and made them embarrassed.

This is why Scripture says of them, after they had violated God's command in open transgression: "And the eyes of both were opened, and they discovered that they were naked, and they sewed fig leaves together and made themselves aprons." "The eyes of both," we are told, "were opened," yet not that they might see, since they could see already, but that they might distinguish between the good that they had lost and the evil into which they had fallen. This also explains why the tree itself, which was to enable them to make such a distinction if they laid hands on it to eat its fruit in spite of the prohibition, was named for that fact and called the tree of the knowledge of good and evil. For experience of discomfort in sickness gives a clearer insight into the joys of health as well.

Accordingly, "they realized that they were naked," stripped naked, that is, of the grace that kept nakedness of body from embarrassing them before the law of sin came into opposition with their minds. Thus they learned what they would more fortunately not have known if through belief in God and obedience to his word they had refrained from an act that would compel them to find out by experience what harm unbelief and disobedience could do. Therefore, embarrassed by their flesh's disobedience, a punishment that bore witness to their own disobedience, "they sewed fig leaves together and made themselves aprons (*campestria*)," that is, loin-cloths, a term employed by certain translators. (Moreover, though *campestria* is a Latin word, it derives its origin from the practice of young men who used to cover up their pudenda while they exercised in the nude on the so-called *campus* or field. Hence, those who are so girt are commonly designated as *campestrati*.) Thus modesty, prompted by a sense of shame, covered what was disobediently aroused by lust against a will condemned for disobedience.

Ever since that time, this habit of concealing the pudenda has been deeply ingrained in all peoples, descended, as they are, from the original stock. In fact, certain barbarians do not expose those parts of the body even in the bath but wash with their coverings on. In the dark retreats of India too certain men who practice philosophy in the nude (and hence are called gymnosophists) nevertheless use coverings for their genitals, though they have none for the other parts of the body.

On the Sense of Shame in Sexual Intercourse, Whether Promiscuous or Marital.

Let us consider the act itself that is accomplished by such lust, not only in every kind of licentious intercourse, for which hiding-places are prerequisite to avoid judgment before human tribunals, but also in the practice of harlotry, a base vice that has been legalized by the earthly city. Although in the latter case the practice is not under the ban of any law of this city, nevertheless even the lust that is allowed and free of penalty shuns the public gaze. Because of an innate sense of shame even brothels have made provision for privacy, and unchastity found it easier to do without the fetters of legal prohibition than shamelessness did to eliminate the secret nooks of that foul business.

But this harlotry is called a base matter even by those who are base themselves, and although they are enamoured of it, they dare not make public display of it. What of marital intercourse, which has for its purpose, according to the terms of the marriage contract, the procreation of children? Lawful and respectable though it is, does it not seek a chamber secluded from witnesses? Before the bridegroom begins even to caress his bride, does he not first send outside all servants and even his own groomsmen as well as any who had been permitted to enter for kinship's sake, whatever the tie? And since, as a certain "supreme master of Roman eloquence" also maintains, all right actions wish to be placed in the light of day, that is, are eager to become known, this right action also desires to become known, though it still blushes to be seen. For who does not know what goes on between husband and wife for the procreation of children? Indeed, it is for the achievement of this purpose that wives are married with such ceremony. And yet, when the act for the birth of children is being consummated, not even the children that may already have been born from the union are allowed to witness it. For this right action does indeed seek mental light for recognition of it, but it shrinks from visual light. What is the reason for this if not that something by nature fitting and proper is carried out in such a way as to be accompanied also by something of shame as punishment?

JOURNAL WRITINGS

1. Make a list of all the words or expressions you can think of that you have used to suggest sexual intercourse. Try to **classify** the words into categories. For instance, some ways of categorizing them might be: (a) Which of the words are positive? Negative? Neutral? Or: (b) Which imply moral acts? Immoral? Amoral (neither moral nor immoral)? Or: (c) Which can be found in a standard college dictionary? In a dictionary of slang terms? Or: (d) How many would you mention to your parents? To classmates? To close friends? To a lover? Set up a similar list of words that Augustine uses for *intercourse* and categorize his words in the same manner. Write a paragraph on the similarities and/or differences between your list of words and Augustine's.

2. In a college dictionary, find a **definition** of *shame*. Explain the meaning of shame in your own words in some detail, giving an **example** of it. Do you agree with Augustine that the sexual parts of our bodies are "shameful" and that sexual intercourse is morally good only when it is practiced for the purpose of procreation? If so, explain your reasons in a paragraph. If not, write an opposing **argument** to his view, and respond to his idea that we cover the sexual parts of our bodies because we are "prompted by a sense of shame." You may wish to consider your answer to Journal Writing 1 to help you establish your views.

BRAINSTORMING AND DRAFTING

3. In the second, third, and fourth paragraphs, Augustine discusses the relationship of lust and free will. Read the introduction to the Free Choice unit of this book and the selection from John Milton's *Paradise Lost*. Draft a paragraph explaining how Augustine's position on the question of free will **compares** with or **contrasts** to the position that God the Father takes in Milton's poem.

4. Agree or disagree: Some of Augustine's attitudes are still present in contem-

porary society in a variety of ways. If you agree, list some ways and jot down a specific **example** of each. If you disagree, list same examples to show how these attitudes have changed.

THE AUTHOR'S METHODS

5.   Make a list of the **examples** or **allusions** that Augustine uses to support his ideas. Write a paragraph or two indicating the purpose of each example and evaluating its effectiveness in support of his argument.
6.   The language of this translation contains a number of **metaphors** or metaphorical allusions about the relationship of sexual desire to the body and to the mind, such as "obscene heat" and "total eclipse of acumen and . . .sentinel alertness." Consult the glossary to refresh your memory on the meaning of metaphor. Find two or three additional metaphors in Augustine's essay. Draft a paragraph explaining the apparent purpose(s) of these metaphors, and evaluate the degree of their effectiveness.

FORMAL WRITING AND RESEARCH PAPERS

7.   Write a paper in which you explain and **compare** Augustine's attitude toward sexuality with your own. Be sure to support your **generalizations** with specific reasons and concrete **examples** which you can draw from film, television, or fiction. You may wish to revise a portion of your answer to Journal Writing 2 as part of your paper.
8.   Find some **biographical,** religious, or historical sources that recount the events of Augustine's life. Write an **essay** in which you first **describe** the important events of his life in your own words, and then explain the influences in his life that may have helped to shape his attitudes toward sexuality.

Reay Tannahill

Sexuality in Early China

(1980)

A native of Scotland, Reay Tannahill (born 1929) received an M.A. from the University of Glasgow. Early in her career, she served as reporter for the *Times* of London. Later, she became advertising manager for Thames & Hudson and advertising consultant for the Folio Society, both of London, where she now resides.

Pursuing her interest in historical writing, she published *Food in History* in 1973, *Flesh and Blood: A History of the Cannibal Complex* in 1975, and *Sex in History,* from which the following selection is taken. In this piece, Tannahill focuses on the paradox of liberal sexual practice (for the males) within a framework of stringent discipline. The practices she describes grew out of the religious philosophy of Taoism; they provide an interesting contrast to the attitudes of Augustine, because they seem to imply that the sexual practice becomes a sacred duty.

PREVIEW

List some of the reasons why people have sexual intercourse in our society.

While the Fathers of the early Christian church advocated sexual abstinence as the only sure route to heaven, other equally devout men in another part of the world took precisely the opposite view. "The more women with whom a man has intercourse, the greater will be the benefit he derives from the act," said one, and another added, "If in one night he can have intercourse with more than ten women it is best." This was one of the doctrines of Tao, "the Way," "the Supreme Path of Nature," a philosophy that permeated the whole structure of Chinese thought and society for more than 2,000 years.

The ideas on which China built one of history's most refined civilizations were ideas that had been discarded by almost all other peoples somewhere on the long march from the paleolithic to the postneolithic era. Only the Chinese, refusing to contract out of the old I-thou relationship with nature . . . began to develop a world view that owed nothing to gods created in the human image. To them, existence appeared as a dynamic movement of perpetual change, a space-time continuum of fluid energy in which man and beast, grass, trees, rocks, mountains, clouds, rain, wind, river, and sea were all indissolubly merged. Nothing *was* because everything was in the process of becoming. In effect, the reader who reads the end of this sentence is no longer the same being as the reader who began it.

For the non-abstract mind, perhaps the least unsatisfactory way of visualizing the Chinese concept of creation is as a kind of multidimensional weather map, with constantly varying channels of atmospheric pressure, air currents flowing, colliding, and recoiling, clouds teased out into wisps of cirrus, fluffed into slow-moving cumulus, or towering in thunderheads. And weaving an erratic vapor trail through them all, powered as if by a series of spectral gear wheels, the force known as *ch'i*—the vital essence, the breath of life—whose path is the Supreme Path, the Way, Tao.

The key feature of this Chinese perception of the world, as of the weather map, is movement, unevenness, undulation. All the elements are in a continuing state of advance or retreat. When one thrusts forward, another must fall back. When one contracts, another expands. There is no active without a corresponding passive, no positive without a compensating negative.

Until the middle of the first millennium B.C. these ideas remained vague, understood but unexpressed. Then the divination manual, the *I-ching* (the "Book of Changes"), named the passive force *yin* and the active *yang* and described how they meshed together to propel the *ch'i* along the Supreme Path. "The interaction of one *yin* and one *yang* is called Tao, and the resulting constant generative process is called 'change.'"

The philosophy that grew around the concept of the Way was known as Taoism, and its adherents believed (and still believe) that long life and happiness, immortality even, would result if instead of being subjected to the artificiality of tightly structured societies man could learn to live in perfect harmony with nature. To achieve this, it was necessary for each individual to aim, in his or her own existence, at the same harmonious interaction of *yin* and *yang* as was responsible, in nature, for energizing the *ch'i*, the breath of life, and to learn how to strengthen both elements as, in nature, they were strengthened by contact with, and absorption of, each other.

The opposing yet complementary forces of *yin* and *yang* could be observed in many natural phenomena. The moon and winter were both *yin*, the sun and summer *yang*. When the sexual parallels came to be drawn, woman—despite a common misapprehension not only in the West but sometimes in China itself—was classified not as pure *yin* but as "lesser *yin*," and man, similarly, as "lesser *yang*." It was a recognition of the psychological truth that there is an element of active *yang* in even the most passive woman and of negative *yin* in even the most positive man. The associated belief that, in both sexes, the subsidiary element fed and strengthened the principal one was to play a crucial role in the development of Taoist and indeed all Chinese views on sex.

Since it was the exercise of mind and will that had led humanity astray from the natural Path, the disciplines that led back to it were necessarily disciplines of the body. One of the most important of these was, of course, sex, whose relevance was easy enough to explain without recourse to too much obscure symbolism. It took little effort of the imagination to recognize that sexual intercourse was the human equivalent of interaction between the cosmic forces of *yin* and *yang*, even when the parallels were drawn not in the direct fleshly sense of vagina and penis, but more subtly as *yin* essence (the moisture lubricating a woman's sexual organs) and *yang* essence (man's semen).

The sexual disciplines of Taoism were easy to understand and, within limits, pleasurable to follow, but others required a more positive approach, a deliberate dedication. This was not because they were mysterious in themselves. Indeed, few modern doctors asked to prescribe a regimen for a long and healthy life would find much to argue with in the basic Taoist program—regular exercise, balanced diet, good breath control, sun therapy, and a full sex life—although for the final item on the list, the elixir of immortality, they would probably substitute its twentieth-century successor, the vitamin pill.* When the requirements of *yin-yang* harmony were grafted on to such a program, however, most of the disciplines ceased to be simple either to perform or to understand.

The whole philosophy of Tao, in fact, became at an early stage so abstruse, so inextricably linked with the mysteries of divination, that only the most committed student could hope to progress beyond first principles. The real problem was that although the basic concept could be perceived without very great difficulty by means of instinct or intuition, it was resistant to the constraint of language. Words, except for the true adept, only too often made nonsense of it. "Being is Non-Being and Non-Being is Being. . . . The Real is Empty and the Empty is Real. . . . " Partly as a result, diagrams, calligraphy, painting and sculpture— whose meaning did not have to be filtered through the rational mind—became a characteristic philosophical-religious device. Whereas a Renaissance painting of the Virgin and Child, or the Last Supper, or the Crucifixion, illustrates only a fragmentary part of the whole of Christian belief, a thirteenth-century Sung landscape conveys the entire philosophic harmony of *yin* and *yang*. That this same harmony could also be conveyed by frankly erotic representations of sexual intercourse was a bonus for Taoists who were low on artistic sensibility.

The Tao Masters lived and thought on a level too rarefied for the common man, their dissertations as unrelated to the mind of the "average" Chinese as those of modern theologians to the once-a-month Western churchgoer. On the level of ordinary life, as a result, the convoluted, sophisticated philosophy of Taoism was transformed into a magical creed whose followers abandoned reason in favor of faith. But just as the Fathers of the early Christian church helped to shape the attitude to sex of the whole Western world, so the Taoist Masters helped to shape that of the Chinese. Just as the European of early medieval times knew, without quite understanding why, that sex was sinful but occasionally permissible, so his contemporary in China knew, without quite understanding why, that sex was a sacred duty and one that he must perform frequently and

---

* [Author's Note] Wisely. The early elixirs usually brought mortality rather than immortality. Large numbers of royal personages and high officials joined their ancestors prematurely after consuming potions that frequently included lead and arsenic.

conscientiously if he was truly to achieve harmony with the Supreme Path, the Way, Tao.

THE CLOUDS AND THE RAIN

Since sexual intercourse was one of the main highways to heaven there was no reason to remain silent about it. Quite the opposite, even if normal Chinese reticence on personal matters often had the effect of excluding it from general conversation. This scarcely mattered, for it was the Chinese who produced the world's earliest known, most comprehensive, and most detailed sex manuals. Many Westerners even today would regard these as pornographic, but pornography is a matter of cultural conditioning. To the Chinese they were serious works, seriously designed to educate their readers in the manner of achieving *yin-yang*, woman-man, harmony. Since they were Taoist in conception and Taoism was a *yin* creed, calm, flexible, intuitive, they were intended as much for the woman as for the man, and indeed were frequently given to a bride before her wedding.

The official bibliography listing the most important books in circulation during the early Han dynasty (206 B.C.–A.D. 24) included eight such manuals, all but one of them running to 20 or more chapters. Although the texts of these no longer exist in their original form, scholars believe that they were rewritten, re-edited, reissued again and again over the centuries, so that the eight "new" Art of the Bedchamber books listed (together with thirteen "Taoist classics" on the subject) in the bibliography of the seventh-century Sui dynasty were not very different from their Han predecessors. Even the Sui books have vanished, but substantial fragments of them were preserved in a Japanese work compiled in the tenth century, the *l-shin-pō*. It was at about this time that Japan came under the spell of Chinese culture and began to build her own prosperous, worldly, tolerant civilization along very similar lines. The Japanese, in fact, were to preserve traditional Chinese appreciation of sexual activity long after it had been suppressed in China itself.

Most of the Chinese handbooks appear to have been divided into six sections. First, there were introductory remarks on the cosmic significance of the sexual encounter; then came recommendations about foreplay; then a description of the act of intercourse, including approved techniques and positions. The practical side having been dealt with, there followed sections on the therapeutic value of sex and on how to choose the right woman and how she should conduct herself during pregnancy. The final section contained useful recipes and prescriptions. Like all good instruction manuals, the sex handbooks were illustrated with pictures that were not purely decorative but designed for handy bedside reference. . . .

Yin-yang harmony was the primary concern of all the handbooks, and intercourse the first stage in its achievement, intercourse that was a human reflection of the mating of earth and heaven, when clouds rose mistily from the land to meet the rain descending from the skies. "Clouds and rain" is still, today, the standard literary expression for the act of intercourse, an echo of nature beliefs far more primitive than those of Taoist times.

Not inappropriately, perhaps, woman's *yin* essence was believed to be inexhaustible, while man's *yang* essence, or semen, was limited in quantity and correspondingly precious. Its quality was of supreme importance. It could be (and, the experts insisted, should be) regularly fed and strengthened by the *yin* essence that was its natural supplement. This was a process that was achieved during intercourse.

The ideal, according to the handbooks, was for man to prolong intercourse for as long as possible; the longer he remained inside the woman, the more *yin* essence he would absorb. He must also, without fail, rouse her to orgasm, when her essence reached maximum potency. To the Chinese, uniquely, a woman's orgasm was no less important to the man than to herself.

But there was an important qualification. There was little purpose in strengthening the man's *yang* essence if he promptly squandered it by himself reaching a climax.

The basic way of avoiding this, said the Master Tung-hsüan (who is believed to have been a seventh-century physician), was as follows. At the last moment, "the man closes his eyes and concentrates his thoughts; he presses his tongue against the roof of his mouth, bends his back, and stretches his neck. He opens his nostrils wide and squares his shoulders, closes his mouth, and sucks in his breath. Then [he will not ejaculate and] the semen will ascend inward on its own account." What the Master recommended, in effect, was a few moments' powerful self-discipline.

As well as this method of *coitus reservatus*, the Chinese used *coitus obstructus*. It was described in *Important Matters of the Jade Chamber.* "When, during the sexual act, the man feels he is about to ejaculate, he should quickly and firmly, using the fore and middle fingers of the left hand, put pressure on the spot between scrotum and anus, simultaneously inhaling deeply and gnashing his teeth scores of times, without holding his breath. Then the semen will be activated but not yet emitted; it returns from the Jade Stalk* and enters the brain." What this method achieved, in fact as distinct from theory, was diversion of the seminal fluid from the penis into the bladder, from which it would later be flushed away with the urine. It was a kind of internal *coitus interruptus* and had the same contraceptive effect; in fact, it was used for birth control purposes in later times by Turks, Armenians, the islanders of the Marquesas, and the sophisticated nineteenth-century commune founded by John Humphrey Noyes at Oneida, New York. . . .

The authors of the handbooks, well aware that *coitus reservatus* and *obstructus* were techniques that not all men could be expected to practice on a regular basis, also specified how much semen a man could afford to lose without damaging his system. As a general rule, said the *Principles of Nurturing Life,* "in

---

* [Author's Note] "Jade Stalk" was one of several Chinese synonyms for the penis, and the reference was not, of course, to green jade but to the more precious, creamy-colored "white" jade. Other synonyms were Red Bird, Coral Stem, Heavenly Dragon Pillar, and Swelling Mushroom. A woman's sexual organs might be The Open Peony Blossom, Golden Lotus, Receptive Vase, or The Cinnabar (or Vermilion) Gate.

spring man can allow himself to emit semen once every three days, in summer and autumn twice a month. During winter one should save it and not ejaculate at all." The loss of *yang* energy caused by one emission in winter was "a hundred times greater than one emission in spring."

Readers of the *Secret Instructions concerning the Jade Chamber* were vouchsafed more detail. "Strongly-built men of 15 years can afford to emit semen twice a day; thin ones once a day, and the same applies to men of twenty. Strongly-built men of 30 may ejaculate once a day, weaker men once in two days." At the ages of 40, 50, and 60 there was a diminishing frequency, from once in three days to once in 20 days, and the sturdy 70-year-old might still risk it once a month. But "weak ones should not ejaculate any more at that age."

One of the great Taoist physicians, Sun Szû-mo, who lived in the seventh century, had a cautionary tale to tell about the dangers of ignoring this advice. Some years earlier, he reported, a peasant of over 70 had come to consult him. "He said, 'For several days my *yang* essence has been most exuberant, so much so that I want to have intercourse with my wife even during daytime, and reach a climax every time. Now I do not know whether this is bad or good at my advanced age?' I replied, 'It is most unfortunate! You know what happens with an oil lamp? Just before it goes out, its wick first burns low and then suddenly flares up. *Then* it goes out. . . . I greatly fear for you and can only advise you to take great care of yourself.' Six weeks later the man fell ill and died." Sun chose to put the case on record as "a warning to future generations."

Taoist philosophy was fundamentally more interested in the cosmic than the human reproductive properties of a man's semen, but it recognized the desire to produce children as a fact of nature. In this, as in all else, there were *yin-yang* rules to be obeyed. For the child who would be conceived to be born sturdy and healthy, it was necessary for the father's *yang* essence to be at peak potency, which meant that it had to be built up over a number of sexual encounters without ejaculating until the final, crucial occasion. All the handbooks emphasized that the preliminary *yin* nourishment should come from a number of different women. "If a man continually changes the women with whom he has intercourse, the benefit will be great. If in one night he can have intercourse with more than ten women it is best." The reason for this was that "if he always couples with one and the same woman, her vital essence will gradually grow weaker, and in the end she will be in no fit condition to give the man benefit. Moreover, the woman herself will become emaciated."

Some discrimination was required in the choice of preliminary partners. There was no need for the girls to be beautiful, but they should be pleasant, well brought up, small, plump, and shapely, and, for preference, just reaching maturity. The *yin* essence of a woman who had "disheveled hair and coarse face, a long neck and a protruding Adam's apple, irregular teeth and a manly voice" would be more likely to ruin the man's *yang* potency than strengthen it.

Like the Greeks and many later generations in the West, the Chinese believed that a woman was most likely to conceive during the first few days after menstruation. Said the Master Tung-hsüan, "If [a man] mates with her on the first or third day thereafter, he will obtain a son. If on the fourth or fifth day, a girl will be conceived. All emissions of semen during intercourse after the fifth day are merely spilling one's seed without any purpose."

It was not only purposeless but extremely foolish to spill one's seed when the heavens were unfriendly. Children conceived during the day or at midnight, when there was thunder, an eclipse of the sun, a rainbow, or a waxing or waning moon, were all liable to meet unpleasant fates. Even if the father had made the understandable mistake of drinking too much just before the momentous occasion, he condemned his child to a life of epilepsy, boils, and ulcers.

There must have been times when even the most dedicated Taoist felt that celibacy would be easier. But it was a quite unacceptable escape route for the Chinese: improper, a betrayal of man's duty to his ancestors, and contrary to the rhythm of nature. Taoism held that a man's mind grew restive if he were deprived of sex and that his spirit suffered accordingly. However unwittingly, the physician Sun Szû-mo agreed with St. Paul that it would be excellent if the mind could be "always serene and entirely untroubled by thoughts of sex. . . . But among 10,000 men there is perhaps one who can achieve this." This guarded view of celibacy was to prove a serious obstacle to the spread in China of Christianity and Hinayana Buddhism, both of which denounced the sexual impulse.

JOURNAL WRITINGS

1. In a paragraph, discuss whether or not religion or a sense of morality affects your attitude toward sex or your decision to have, or refrain from, sexual intercourse. How does your response **compare** with the way religion affects the early Chinese attitudes toward sex?
2. Most of the rules on sexual practices in ancient China seem to pertain to males. **Describe** in detail the probable social role of the female under Taoism. How would you react if you were a woman living in that society? How do you think the Chinese women reacted?

BRAINSTORMING AND DRAFTING

3. Despite their obvious differences, the sexual attitudes of Augustine and of the Taoists nevertheless show interesting similarities. In a small group, discuss as many similarities as you can. Each member of the group should then draft a well-developed paragraph elaborating on one of the similarities, and read his or her paper to the group. (Or, you may choose to list your own similarities, selecting one to write about.)
4. Which aspects of the Taoist attitudes are also present in contemporary North American society? Describe each attitude and give an **example** of the form the attitude or belief now takes.

THE AUTHOR'S METHODS

5. In the first or introductory paragraph of this essay, Tannahill writes three sentences: The first sets up a **comparison** with an opposing view; the second offers two quotations that capture the reader's interest and encapsulate the Taoist attitude; the third places that attitude into the framework of philosophy and history. Imitate Tannahill's paragraph by writing the same kind of historical introduction for Augustine's essay. As far as possible, use similar sentence structures as well.

6. Tannahill sometimes uses a series of words (say, three or more items) to provide colorful, interesting, often concrete **examples** or even to manipulate **tone** and meaning. For instance, the second paragraph states: " . . . man and beast, grass, trees, rocks, mountains, clouds, rain, wind, river, and sea were all indissolubly merged." Find at least one other series in the reading and explain its purpose. Then write some sentences of your own in which you include a series of items as you **describe** the Taoist sexual practice.

CREATIVE PROJECT

7. List several areas in which the Taoists *differ from* Saint Augustine. Then write a debate between Augustine and a Taoist philosopher on the topic of sexuality. Your **tone** may be serious, comic, or a mixture of both. In any case, the debate should demonstrate that you clearly understand the views of each speaker.

FORMAL WRITING AND RESEARCH PAPERS

8. " . . . there is an element of active *yang* in even the most passive woman and of negative *yin* in even the most positive man." The word *androgyny* describes a similar combination of so-called "masculine" and "feminine" traits combined in one person. Write a paper **arguing** for or against such a solution to polar divisions between the sexes. Provide **examples** from literature, film, or television to support your views.

9. Read some sources on the history of sexuality that include commentary on sexual practices in early India (or another ancient civilization of your choice). Consult the card or computer catalog and your librarian for help. Using a historical perspective similar to Tannahill's, write an **essay** in which you **describe** these practices. You may wish to use some of Tannahill's subtopics, if they are appropriate to your ideas: reasons for sex; any disciplines commonly practiced; relation of males to females; number of partners; frequency of intercourse; use of manuals; use of sexual symbols. Of course, you may choose your own categories if you prefer. For the last section of your paper, explain fully whether you as a male or female would prefer to have lived in ancient India (or your chosen country).

John D'Emilio and Estelle B. Freedman

The Sexualized Society

(1988)

John D'Emilio (born 1948) received a B.A., M.A., and Ph.D. from Columbia University. Before completing his doctoral degree, he worked as a policy analyst on child-care issues, and studied prison reform for the New York State Council of Churches. He is currently teaching in the history department at the University of North Carolina at Greensboro. Interested in sexuality as an issue of power and politics, he became an active participant in the gay movement. In 1983, he published *Sexual Politics, Sexual Communities: The Making of a Homosexual Minority, 1940–1970,* which documents the growth of the gay subculture and the beginnings of the gay political movement.

Estelle Freedman (born 1947) received a B.A. from Barnard College and an M.A. and a Ph.D. in history from Columbia University. Currently professor of history at Stanford University, she has been honored with awards for distinguished teaching and outstanding service to undergraduate education. She has served as associate editor of *Signs: A Journal of Women in Culture and Society;* in 1981, she published *Their Sisters' Keepers: Women's Prison Reform in America, 1830–1930.* The following selection from *Intimate Matters: A History of Sexuality in America* documents changing patterns of sexual behavior over several decades of American life. From the economic aspects to less traditional living arrangements, the reading examines behavior and attitude shifts of "major proportions."

PREVIEW

Argue in support of one of the following:
(a)   Sex should be practiced only within marriage.
(b)   Sex should be practiced only when love is present.
(c)   Sex may be practiced whenever two adults give their consent.

Toward the end of the 1960s John Williamson, a successful engineer in southern California, purchased a fifteen-acre retreat in the Santa Monica mountains. Graced with a view of the ocean, the secluded site sported a two-story mansion, several smaller houses, and a building that contained an Olympic-sized pool. Williamson intended to make the property the setting in which to implement an experiment in sexual freedom. For years, a group of people "had met regularly at his house to discuss and explore ways of achieving greater fulfillment in marriage." They were all "middle-class people," many of them prosperous professionals like himself, "who held responsible jobs in the community [and] were integrated in the social system."[1] Over time, the discussions led to action, including the swapping of marital partners for sexual excitement and group sex. Williamson's newly acquired property, Sandstone, would give the venture institutional expression.

In the succeeding years, Sandstone became something of an underground tourist attraction, bringing through its doors upper-middle-class adventurers in search of new kinds of personal fulfillment and erotic delights. Those who made the trek could take off their clothes or leave them on. They could sip wine, smoke marijuana, and converse by the fireplace upstairs, or wander downstairs where they would find, in the words of one visitor, "a parlor for pleasure-seekers, providing sights and sounds that . . . [they] had never imagined they would ever encounter under one roof during a single evening." They would see

> shadows and faces and interlocking limbs, rounded breasts and reaching fingers, moving buttocks, glistening backs, shoulders, nipples, navels, long blond hair spread across pillows, thick dark arms holding soft white hips, a woman's head hovering over an erect penis. Sighs, cries of ecstasy could be heard, the slap and suction of copulating flesh, laughter, murmuring, music from the stereo, crackling black burning wood.

Perhaps the only thing more surprising than Sandstone itself was the fact that a prominent journalist would write about it. Gay Talese's *Thy Neighbor's Wife*, from which this description is taken, became a widely reviewed, much discussed best-seller.[2]

Although Sandstone was unusual, the attraction of successful professionals to it and the marketing of it by Talese suggest that the liberal consensus about sex had dissolved. Feminists and gay liberationists were not the only ones challenging its assumptions. By the late 1960s the belief in sex as the source of personal meaning had permeated American society. The expectation that marriage would fulfill the quest could no longer be sustained. Aided by the values of a consumer culture and encouraged by the growing visibility of sex in the public realm, many Americans came to accept sexual pleasure as a legitimate, necessary component of their lives, unbound by older ideals of marital fidelity and permanence. Society was indeed becoming sexualized. From the mid-1960s to the 1980s, as the liberal consensus disintegrated, the nation experienced perhaps the greatest transformation in sexuality it had ever witnessed. The marketing of sex, important shifts in attitudes, and major changes in the life cycle of Americans all encouraged alterations in patterns of sexual behavior.

THE BUSINESS OF SEX

One unmistakable sign of the reorganization of sexuality came through the large-scale invasion by entrepreneurs into the field of sex. The tension in sexual liberalism, between the celebration of the erotic as the peak experience in marriage and the effort to contain its expression elsewhere, made sex ripe for commercial exploitation. Since the mid-nineteenth century, the erotic had attracted entrepreneurs. But, as we have seen, it mostly remained a marginal, illicit industry. As the Supreme Court in the 1950s and 1960s shook the legal edifice that kept sexual imagery within certain limits, the capitalist impulse seized upon sexual desire as an unmet need that the marketplace could fill. Wherever Americans looked, it seemed, the erotic beckoned in the guise of a commodity.

Pornography provides one convenient measure of the dynamic that was underway. Long confined to a shadowy underground, and formerly taking the shape of a home industry, it became in the 1970s highly visible. Thousands of movie houses featuring triple-"X"-rated films dotted the country, ranging from drive-ins on the outskirts of towns, and theaters in the central city, to fancy establishments in modern shopping malls. North Carolina and South Carolina boasted the largest concentration of adult theaters, belying the notion that pornography was the product of big-city decadence. Some of the films, such as *Deep Throat* and *The Devil in Miss Jones*, achieved respectability of sorts, becoming cult favorites that attracted large audiences. In most cities, adult bookstores sold hard-core sex magazines and paperbacks without the literary pretensions or journalistic substance to which *Playboy* and its competitors aspired. A substantial portion of newsstand sales came from publications that the police would have seized a decade earlier. Technological advances offered new opportunities and new audiences for the distribution of pornography. The introduction of video-cassette recorders in the late 1970s opened the door to a booming business in sex films for home consumption. As one maker of pornographic videos remarked, "There are some people who would like to frequent sex theaters, but for various reasons they don't. They're either ashamed to be seen going in, they don't want to take their wives with them, or whatever. This way, they're able to see the X material in the privacy of their own home, and it doesn't seem so distasteful to them." Men brought their wives or girlfriends to help them select the evening's viewing fare. Soon, the rental of pornographic movies was providing the essential margin of profit for many video stores. The spread of cable television, meanwhile, allowed producers to avoid the constraints of the federally regulated networks. A subsidiary of Time, Inc., for instance, used cable television to distribute a weekly program, *Midnight Blue*, that featured couples having sex.[3]

By the 1980s, economic analysts were referring to the "sex industry." A multi-billion-dollar endeavor, it featured high-salaried executives, a large work force, brisk competition, board meetings, and sales conventions. Al Goldstein, the publisher of *Screw* who "diversified" in the 1970s, remarked on the contrast between the sleazy image of the industry and its more prosaic—and profitable—reality. "People come into my office," he said, "and they think there are supposed to be 12 women under my desk. If there is anybody under there, it's 12 tax accountants. Or 12 attorneys. I'm a capitalist. I'm good at what I do." Industry boosters promoted the field as they would any other. Dennis Sobin, who edited *The Adult Business Report*, the chief trade magazine of the industry, commented that "the sex business has the same potential for sales and profits as the food industry. It is a growth industry that cannot go backwards."[4]

One reason, perhaps, for the confidence of this new breed of entrepreneur was that they could arguably see themselves as simply the least hypocritical of an entire spectrum of marketers of sexuality. Not only had pornography moved into the light of day, but sexual imagery had become incorporated into the mainstream of American life. Advertisers broke new ground in their use of the erotic to excite consumers. In newspaper ads, clothing manufacturers and department stores featured pre-pubescent girls in flirtatious poses. Record companies enticed buyers with sexually suggestive album covers. Calvin Klein commissioned billboards with models naked from the waist up, their buttocks snugly fitted into his designer jeans. "The tighter they are, the better they sell," he commented.[5] By the 1980s, male bodies, too, were being used to promote sales. On television, commercials for any number of products projected the message that consumption promised the fulfillment of erotic fantasies and appetites.

The visual entertainment media also made sex a staple of their shows. An evening of television might begin with game shows in which attractive female models draped themselves over prizes representing a consumer's dreams, progress to situation comedies where the plot revolved around the titillating possibilities of sexual encounters, and end with steamy adult dramas. Instead of *I Love Lucy*, viewers laughed at the innuendo of *Three's Company*, in which a man and two women cohabited, or they might wonder when Sam and Diane, the main characters in *Cheers*, would make it into bed. Rather than the simple cops-and-robbers plots of *The Untouchables*, the award-winning *Hill Street Blues* closed many episodes in the bedroom of its chief protagonists. Popular nighttime soap operas combined the themes of money, power, and sex into high Nielsen ratings. Potboiler novels became mini-series, with titles such as *Sin*, or *Hollywood Wives*, in which the characters trotted around the globe in search of sexual adventure. Multi-million-dollar budgets and the absence of frontal nudity were about the only differences between these network specials and their prodigal pornographic cousins.

The permeation of sex throughout the culture made itself felt in other ways. In the morning newspapers, "Dear Abby" and Ann Landers found themselves addressing more and more explicit sexual scenarios. A series of articles in one midwestern daily advised single men and women that "there is nothing wrong with sharing physical pleasure with somebody else. Sure, old moralistic rules flash by, but for a growing number of us they can satisfactorily be put aside. For once, it's exhilarating to be the 'bad' kid. . . . By having a variety of partners we learn there are interesting variations on the theme."[6] In the early 1980s, Dr. Ruth Westheimer, a radio personality with a grandmotherly wholesomeness, became something of a national hero, as well as a highly paid lecturer, through her enthusiastic prescriptions for sexual happiness. Magazines made space for pages of personal ads where a "DWM" (divorced white male) might seek "SF" (single female) for walks, talks, and an afternoon affair. Cars sported bumper stickers ("firemen have long hoses," "elevator operators like to go down," "teachers do it with class") that jocularly associated occupational identity with sexual prowess.

So much openness about sexuality had an impact on the prescriptive literature to which Americans were so partial. By the 1970s, marital advice books were fast losing their audience to popular sex manuals. Many of them—*Everything You Always Wanted to Know about Sex, The Sensuous Man, The Sensuous Woman*—became runaway best-sellers. Dispensing with the genteel language and scientific descriptions characteristic of midcentury books for the married, they endorsed sexual experimentation in language that twenty years earlier had been the province of pornography. "Put your girl in a soft, upholstered chair," the author of *The Sensuous Man* advised, .

> and kneel in front of her so your head comes about to the level of her breasts. . . . Now slide her off the chair and right onto that beautiful erect shaft. The feeling is dizzying. She is wet and very, very hot; you are face to face and in about as deep as you can be. . . . [It's] an exciting way to come. . . . [7]

Alex Comfort's *The Joy of Sex* played on the theme of a popular cookbook by offering menus of its own for the sexual gourmet. Liberally illustrated with erotic drawings, it depicted naked men and women in an endless variety of sexual positions. Comfort's success propelled publishers to commission companion volumes for gay men and lesbians. Even books aimed at supposedly traditional Americans dispensed with reticence. Marabel Morgan's *The Total Woman* may have held that woman's place was in the home, but it also instructed housewives to greet their husbands at the end of the day dressed in a transparent nightgown. [8]

CHANGING LIFE CYCLES AND NEW SEXUAL PATTERNS

As entrepreneurs were weaving sexuality into the fabric of public life, Americans were simultaneously experiencing dramatic demographic changes. Between the 1960s and the 1980s, the life cycle of many Americans became considerably more complex and unpredictable. The timing of marriage and childbearing, control over fertility, the instability of the traditional nuclear family, and innovations in living arrangements all encouraged a reorganization of sexual standards.

The unusual demographic patterns of the baby-boom era reversed themselves with startling rapidity in the 1970s. Between 1960 and 1980, the marriage rate declined by a quarter. By 1985, the median age of marriage for men had risen to 25.5 years, while for women it jumped to 23.2. Along with later marriage came an overall decline in fertility. Beginning in the mid-1970s, the fertility of American women hovered at the replacement level, far below the peaks reached in the late 1950s. The accessibility of legal abortions, the accelerating trend toward sterilization, and the availability of reliable contraceptives put absolute control of fertility within reach for the married. Especially within the middle class, childlessness emerged as a serious option to consider. As one couple noted, "We are the only people we know who have a child, or at least the only people we know well. . . . Some [of our friends] are married, a few might as well be, others aren't totally opposed to the idea—and they have all either ruled out families entirely or postponed them until the very distant future." By the end of the 1970s more than a quarter of married women in their late twenties remained childless. [9]

Not only were Americans marrying later and having fewer children, but families were much less likely to remain intact. Aided by the liberalization of state laws, the divorce rate began a steep climb in the mid-1960s. Between 1960 and 1980, the number of divorced men and women rose by almost two hundred percent; the divorce rate itself jumped ninety percent. For blacks, the impact of divorce was even more widely felt. In 1980, over a quarter of black men and women between the ages of twenty-five and fifty-four were divorced, in comparison to less than ten percent of whites. Many of the divorced remarried eventually, yet second marriages had even less chance of surviving. Although the rush to divorce had slowed somewhat by 1980, marriages of the late seventies had only a one-in-two chance of surviving.

All of these shifts affected the size and structure of American households, which tended to grow smaller and become more diversified in composition. During the 1970s, over half of the new households created were nonfamily ones. The traditional two-parent family with children accounted for only three-fifths of all living arrangements by 1980. Even that figure tended to overstate its predominance, since many of those families would experience dissolution, and most Americans could expect to spend a portion of their childhood and adult years in "nontraditional" situations.

One widely touted demographic innovation of the 1970s was the rise of cohabitation among men and women. Hardly noted by 1960 census-takers, it became a highly visible phenomenon in the 1970s, tripling in frequency. Although cohabiting couples constituted only three percent of American households, the chances of an individual participating in such an arrangement were much higher. One study found that almost one in five American men had lived for at least six months with a woman other than their spouse. The phenomenon was more common among blacks than whites, and a majority of the men had been previously married. Surveying the changing nature of American lifestyles, the sociologists Philip Blumstein and Pepper Schwartz confidently predicted that cohabitation "will probably become more visible and more common."[10]

In the midst of this reorganization of household and family structure, one element of change elicited special comment—the rise of the working mother. White married women had been steadily entering the labor force since World War II, and for black wives work outside the home had always been a common experience. But the rapid movement of mothers into paid employment surprised most observers. By the early 1980s a majority of mothers, including those with children of preschool age, were working for wages. Some of this change owed its origin to feminism, which validated the choices of mothers who sought employment. Some of it was due to financial necessity. As inflation escalated in the 1970s, and the changing structure of economic and social life raised the consumption needs of many families, the pressure for mothers to work mounted. Among married couples in 1980, wives with family incomes between twenty-five thousand and fifty thousand dollars were most likely to be employed. The absence of female employment consigned many families to subsistence living. Moreover, as the divorce rate mounted and more women found themselves heading households, many mothers had no choice but to work.

Whatever the motives, the high proportion of women in the work force promised upheavals in the realm of personal life and heterosexual relations. Working women were both cause and effect of many demographic changes—the rising age of marriage, later childbearing, the decline in fertility, the spread of single-person households, and cohabitation. Unhappy marriages, in which spouses felt compelled out of duty or desperation to remain together, might more readily dissolve. As Paul Glick, a Census Bureau demographer who had studied marriage and divorce for a generation, commented, "Women who enter the marketplace gain greater confidence, expand their social circles independent of their husbands' friends, taste independence and are less easy to satisfy, and more likely to divorce." Or, as one Indiana wife put it, "Women don't have to put up with [men's] crap—they can support themselves."[11] Working women brought greater confidence and more power to their relationships with men. Although conflict might ensue as couples readjusted their expectations, surveys indicated nevertheless that younger males in particular preferred the more egalitarian results that came with the modification of traditional sex roles.

These demographic shifts hit the black community with special force. Although black-white differentials in family structure actually narrowed in the 1970s, nontraditional living arrangements still appeared with much greater frequency among blacks. Overall incidence rates of divorce, female-headed households, and out-of-wedlock births remained higher. By 1980 almost half of black households were female-headed, a majority of black infants were born to unmarried women, and only a minority of black children were being raised in two-parent households. Approximately half of black adults were not married and living with their spouse. In assessing these statistics, one sociologist was moved to comment that "all is not well between black men and women." In contrast to the mid-1960s, when the Moynihan report provoked so much controversy within the civil rights movement, black leaders in the eighties felt freer to air their own concerns. By the early 1980s, many were rating the issue of family life equally with jobs and education as a critical concern of the community. Eleanor Holmes Norton, who served in the Carter administration, called it "the most serious long-term crisis in the black community."[12]

When combined with the invasion of sexuality into so much of the public realm, these new demographic patterns among Americans presaged a major shift in sexual behavior and attitudes. The later age of marriage increased the likelihood that women as well as men would enter the institution sexually experienced. The rise in divorce meant that more and more Americans would be searching for new sexual partners as mature adults. Children and adolescents would know that their parents were having sex outside of marriage; the openness with which heterosexual cohabitation, lesbianism, and male homosexuality were discussed provided visible alternatives to marriage. Postponed childbearing and low fertility made obvious the distinction between sex for procreation and for pleasure. Women who worked and had more sexual experience were better placed to negotiate the terms of a sexual relationship with a partner. The new explicitness of so much popular literature about the erotic almost guaranteed that many Americans would have their sexual repertoires greatly enhanced. Perhaps most significantly, the growing complexity of the American life cycle substantially weakened the hegemony of marriage as the privileged site for sexual expression. As one longitudinal study of families in Detroit concluded, "The decision to marry or remain single is now considered a real and legitimate choice between acceptable alternatives, marking a distinct shift in attitude from that held by Americans in the past."[13]

Survey data from a variety of sources confirm a striking shift in sexual values toward approval of nonmarital sexuality. As late as the 1950s, for instance, polls suggested that fewer than a quarter of Americans endorsed premarital sex for men and women. By the 1970s, these figures had been reversed. Especially among the young, substantial majorities registered their approval. Although males, blacks, the college-educated and higher-income families were more likely to accept premarital sexuality, the differences between groups were disappearing. Only older Americans and religiously devout whites tended to maintain a stance of moral disapproval. The generation gap was especially pronounced over some of the more radical departures from past orthodoxy. One study found that three-quarters of Americans over sixty-five opposed the practice of cohabitation, while the figures were reversed for the under-thirty population. Similarly, when confronted with the contemporary openness of the gay community, younger Americans proved more than three times as likely as their seniors to display tolerance for homosexuality. In their study of American couples, Blumstein and Schwartz found that among married couples, cohabiting heterosexuals, gay men, and lesbians, majorities of everyone except wives expressed approval for sexual relationships devoid of love.[14]

One important ideological source for the revamping of sexual beliefs was feminism. Particularly among younger heterosexuals, traditional notions of male and female differences weakened in the 1970s. Most looked forward to marriages in which roles blurred. Many younger males abandoned the allegiance to a double standard of behavior for their female peers. For both men and women, expectations about sexuality and intimacy changed. As Sophie Freud Loewenstein, a Boston social worker, explained it,

> Women who have taken it for granted that their sexual satisfaction was unimportant are now reading about women having multiple orgasms. Many men realize that they've been ripped off by being programmed to deny their expressive aspects. It becomes a possibility to throw out some of the old sex roles and change drastically. That change can be very frightening, but the atmosphere makes it more permissible.[15]

As its critique of sex-role conditioning spread throughout the culture, feminism altered the attitudes of Americans about the proper behavior of men and women.

Demographic change, shifts in attitudes, and the eroticism that so much of the public realm displayed contributed to a major alteration in the sexual life of many Americans. Unmarried youth as well as conjugal pairs, urban male homosexuals as well as heterosexual couples, experienced important modifications in their patterns of sexual behavior. Among other things, sexual experience was beginning at a younger age, acts once considered deviant were more widely incorporated into heterosexual relations, and the gap between the sex lives of men and women was narrowing.

The behavior of the young and the unmarried dramatically illustrates the extent of change. From the mid-1960s onward the incidence of premarital intercourse among white females zoomed upward, narrowing substantially the disparity in experience between them and their male peers. Survey after survey of white college students in every part of the country confirmed this shift. By 1980 large majorities of female students were engaging in coitus, often in relationships that held no expectation of marriage. Among black women, too, there was evidence of change, though primarily in the age at which coitus began. Between 1971 and 1976, fifteen- and sixteen-year-olds were half again as likely to have engaged in intercourse. In the early 1970s, a much broader survey that included men and women of varying educational levels also documented the rise in premarital coitus among women. By then young women were as likely to have sex as were the men in Kinsey's study a generation earlier. Morton Hunt, the author, also confirmed a greater variety in practices. Where Kinsey had found few heterosexuals who had tried fellatio or cunnilingus, by the 1970s it was a commonplace experience among those in their twenties. The frequency of intercourse for young men and women was also substantially higher, while masturbation, especially among women, was starting earlier and had become more widespread. [16]

Evidence of other sorts substantiates these survey findings. On college campuses, health services routinely distributed contraceptive information and devices to students. For those who began having intercourse earlier, or who did not attend college, Planned Parenthood clinics offered an alternative source of assistance. In Muncie, Indiana, for example, a third of teenage girls used the services of Planned Parenthood in 1979. The rise in births to unmarried teenagers, as well as the large number who sought abortions, also suggest that a growing proportion of the young were sexually active. [17]

These changes in patterns of behavior took place in a social context different from that which had shaped the behavior of youth between the 1920s and the 1960s. For one, formal dating evinced a sharp decline. Teenage youth socialized casually in groups without pairing off; friendships between males and females were more common. As one high school boy described it, in drawing a contrast between himself and his father:

> Once he told me that he wasn't brought up to think about women the way guys like me do, and it was vice versa back then. "We were scared of each other; we didn't really have *friends* of the opposite sex" is the way he said it to me. Now that's changed! I can talk with girls I'm not dating—I mean, be real friendly with them. There's one girl at school who's the person I feel easiest with there. We're pals, but I've never wanted to make out with her!

This ease of interaction had implications for the progress of sexual experience. When the young did pair off, it tended to signal an already serious relationship. They were less likely to move gradually through the stages of kissing, necking, and petting before deciding to have intercourse. In fact, one observer of the young concluded that petting, so important in the sexual initiation of midcentury adolescents, "seems destined to take its place as a historical curiosity." [18]

The demographic patterns of the late 1960s and 1970s, as well as the less measurable effects of feminist ideology, also contributed to the shape of change. As women became sexually active earlier in life, as the age of marriage rose, and their participation in the labor force promised greater autonomy, more of them could approach sexual experience with different expectations. One twenty-eight-year-old blue-collar female, cohabiting with a male partner, firmly expressed her right to an erotic life. "I may have had an unusual upbringing, but it never occurred to me that a man wouldn't let me be sexy," she said. "I have the same needs and moods as a man, and I am not going to let some chauvinist pig stifle them." Another single woman, also in her twenties, justified nonmonogamy on the basis of her strong sexual desires. "I have a roving eye and sometimes I give in to it. . . . I consider myself a very sexual person and I need an adventure from time to time. And I think [my cohabiting partner] does too. But that's all it is—fun and a little bit of an ego thrill."[19] Their comments suggest that at least some women had moved a long distance from the 1950s, when sexual intercourse had to be justified as a sign of an abiding romantic attachment.

Not surprisingly, the erotic dimension of marriage also changed profoundly during these years. Although some elements of the past persisted, especially concerning gender differences in initiating sex, the conjugal relationship was moving rapidly in the direction of greater variety, higher levels of satisfaction, and more frequent intercourse. For instance, a study comparing the sexual practices of married couples in the early 1970s with those in the Kinsey reports found twice as many couples departing from the missionary position. Except among black couples, oral sex—both cunnilingus and fellatio—had been incorporated into the sexual repertoire of husbands and wives to such an extent that the author of the study, Morton Hunt, called the change an "increase . . . of major and historic proportions." Among whites, the move toward variety in technique and position extended across the social spectrum, narrowing considerably the class differences that Kinsey had noted. The frequency of intercourse had also risen, in a reverse of the trend displayed by Kinsey's respondents. As Hunt explained,

> Although in [Kinsey's] time the frequency of marital coitus was declining due to the wife's rising status and her growing right to have a voice in sexual matters, the regularity of her orgasm in marital intercourse was rising. . . . This increase in orgiastic reliability and overall sexual satisfaction eventually offset the forces that caused the initial drop in coital activity.

Only ten percent of the wives in Hunt's survey described their sexual relations of the preceding year as unpleasant or of no interest to them. Of the ninety percent claiming satisfaction, three-quarters were content with the frequency while one-quarter wished for more.[20]

The visibility of sex in the culture certainly contributed to these trends. Not only did it encourage an interest in the erotic, but it also made information much more readily available to adults. Particularly among working-class wives, who as late as the 1940s and 1950s were often dependent on their husbands to lead the way, the barriers to active sexual agency were dropping. A waitress in her mid-thirties described the initiative she took:

> What changed our sex life was that a bunch of us girls on the same block started reading books and passing them around—everything from how-to-do-it sex books to real porno paperbacks. Some of the men said that the stuff was garbage, but I can tell you that my husband was always ready to try out anything. . . . Some of it was great, some was awful . . . and some was just funny, like the honey business.

Another woman, married to a blue-collar worker, had him buy sex manuals to spice up their love life. "We found all different ways of caressing and different positions, and it was very nice because we realized that these things weren't dirty," she explained. "Like I could say to my husband 'Around the world in eighty days!' and he'd laugh and we'd really go at it." Moreover, much of the literature written in the 1970s, such as *The Hite Report* and Nancy Friday's *My Secret Garden*, presented sex from women's vantage point. The emphasis in these works shifted from simultaneous orgasm through intercourse to forms of pleasuring suitable for women, or what one commentator called "separate but equal orgasms." Thus, even the supposedly immutable "sex act" underwent redefinition in ways that weakened a male monopoly over the nature of sex.[21]

As couples experimented with different techniques of lovemaking, the erotic became a vehicle for exploring new realms of intimacy and power. Some men enjoyed the sensation that came from knowing they were satisfying their partners. "The whole process [of oral sex] makes me feel good about myself," said one husband. "I take serious pride in being a good lover and satisfying my partner, giving her pleasure." A businesswoman remarked that "I like oral sex very much because it is extremely intimate and I'm moved by it as an act of intimacy." For some women, oral sex evoked feelings of power. "I do feel powerful when he does it. I feel quite powerful," said one. "Sort of the Amazon mentality—all-powerful woman." Another experienced similar emotions when performing fellatio. "I'm exerting power. I'm rewarding him," she commented. "The giving of pleasure is a powerful position, and the giving of oral sex is a real, real gift of pleasure."[22]

The cultural validation of erotic pleasure also contributed to a historic shift in expectations. Among earlier generations, men and women had found themselves at odds about the frequency of sex in marriage. At the turn of the century, at least among the white middle class, many women submitted to their husbands' desires; by midcentury, many men felt themselves sexually deprived. But a survey of couples conducted in the late 1970s found virtual agreement among men and women about sexual satisfaction and frequency. Eighty-nine percent of married men and women who had sex three or more times a week expressed contentment with their sex life; among those who had sex once a week or less, the figure dropped to fifty-three percent for each gender. The responses of unmarried cohabiting couples provided roughly similar findings. Not only were most men and women indicating similar preferences, but they expected relatively high frequencies of sex. According to Blumstein and Schwartz, among all the couples they studied—heterosexual, gay male, and lesbian—"a good sex life is central to a good overall relationship," and infrequent sex provoked discontent with all aspects of the relationship. Even the readers of a mainstream women's magazine such as *Redbook* had incorporated high expectations about sex into their lives. After polling 100,000 women, the editors found that "women are becoming increasingly active sexually and are less likely to accept an unsatisfactory sex life as part of the price to be paid for marriage."[23]

One reason, undoubtedly, for the shifts in heterosexual relationships was the availability of birth control. The dramatic move in the 1960s toward effective contraception continued into the 1970s. By mid-decade three out of four married couples relied on the pill, the IUD, or sterilization.[24] Then, too, the legalization of first-trimester abortions provided a measure of last resort for wives whose contraceptive efforts failed. Though it is difficult to know how great an increase in the incidence of abortion took place in the seventies, the fact that it was medically safe and legal at least removed the dangers that formerly attached to it. The near universality of birth control practices had virtually eliminated the constraints that fears about pregnancy had imposed on the sex life of married women. It also highlighted the degree to which the erotic had been divorced from procreation.

The separation of sex from reproduction also emerged from another quarter. Not only could couples safely have sex without the expectation of conception, but technological innovations were making it possible to have babies without sex. Science was upsetting age-old certainties about the natural connection between sex and procreation. "Remember when there was only one way to make a baby?" an advertisement for a 1979 CBS special report asked. "That was yesterday. Today, nature's role is being challenged by science. Conception without sex. Egg fertilization outside the womb. 'Surrogate' mothers who can bear other couples' children. Frozen embryos stored in 'supermarkets' for future implantation."[25] Among other things, scientific change was allowing lesbian couples to have children, without choosing marriage, through the cooperation of male sperm donors. Public policy added another dimension to technological change, as welfare agencies allowed single women and single men to adopt children, thus emphasizing the distinction between biological and social parenting. Though the new technology would raise some vexing problems of its own, as the controversy over Baby M revealed, people were nonetheless making choices that seemed to confirm that making love and making babies were not the same.

The new visibility that gay life achieved in the 1970s also emphasized the weakened link between procreation and the erotic. Although it is difficult to measure change in this area with any degree of precision, certainly the social life of gay men and lesbians had altered considerably. The many organizations that existed throughout the country allowed greater ease in making friends and acquaintances, and in embarking upon relationships. Less police harassment made it safer for bars to open and stay in operation. Regional music festivals brought thousands of lesbians together for several days of companionship; annual rituals such as the gay pride marches each June became celebrations of community cohesiveness even as they made a political statement. Church attendance, political club membership, and professional caucuses all contributed to a broadening of an identity in which the erotic played a prominent role. But the historic invisibility of gay male and lesbian life makes it impossible to compare the erotic dimension of gay experience from one generation to another. Even in the 1970s there were few studies that moved beyond the impressionism of journalistic observations.

A study that did, the work of Philip Blumstein and Pepper Schwartz, is interesting in part because of the comparison it allows between men and women, and between heterosexuals and homosexuals. The researchers found that a good sexual adjustment was as important to a successful relationship among gay male and lesbian respondents as among heterosexuals, and that the higher the frequency of sex the greater the sense of satisfaction. But lesbians seemed content to have sex less often, and after two years in a relationship, the lesbian couples tended to see a significant decline in the frequency of sex. Young lesbians were more likely to engage in oral sex than were older women, and among all the couples, gay men placed the greatest stock in variety in sexual technique. Lesbians proved very similar to heterosexual men and women in the extent of nonmonogamy—twenty-eight percent of lesbians, twenty-five percent of husbands, and twenty-one percent of wives—whereas for gay men, nonmonogamy was a way of life. Furthermore, among couples that did not practice monogamy male homosexuals tended to have sex with a far larger number of partners. One percent of the lesbians, seven percent of the husbands, but more than two-fifths of the gay men, had sex with more than twenty partners while living with a mate.[26]

Even in an era that witnessed an expansion of erotic opportunities, the experience of some urban gay men appeared to stand outside the norm. When Kinsey undertook his study in the 1940s he found that although male homosexuals on average had sex less frequently than heterosexual men, some of them had far more partners in the course of a lifetime. In the 1970s, as the urban gay subculture became larger and more accessible, the chances for sexual encounters multiplied. Heterosexuals may have had their singles bars where they could meet a partner for an evening of sex, but in large cities, gay bathhouses, bars with back rooms, and stores showing pornographic films allowed gay male patrons to have sex with a series of men in rapid succession. For many, sexual promiscuity became part of the fabric of gay life, an essential element holding the community together. Yet the fact that such sex businesses could operate in the 1970s relatively free of police harassment and that the media could spotlight them in discussions of gay life says as much about heterosexual norms as about those of gay men. In the larger metropolitan areas, male homosexuals were no longer serving as symbols of sexual deviance; their eroticism no longer divided the good from the bad. Heterosexuals sustained a vigorous singles nightlife, and advertised in magazines for partners; suburban couples engaged in mate-swapping; sex clubs were featuring male strippers, with women in the role of voyeur. By the end of the decade, some "straight" men and women were even patronizing a heterosexual equivalent of the gay bathhouse, as the success of places like Plato's Retreat in New York demonstrated. The experience of the urban gay subculture stood as one point along a widened spectrum of sexual possibilities that modern America now offered.

Although it would be foolhardy to deny the depth and breadth of the changes that had occurred by the end of the 1970s, one must also acknowledge the continuities with the past. Blumstein and Schwartz, for instance, found that "there *are* new men and new women, among both heterosexual and homosexual couples, who are dealing with sexual responsibilities in new ways and trying to modify the traditions that their maleness and femaleness bring to their relationships." But they were fewer in number than the pair of sociologists expected to find, and the persistence of tradition was particularly hard for some heterosexual women whose partners proved "less 'liberated' than she—or he—thought he was."[27] Marriages were happier and more intimate than a generation earlier, but partly because so many unhappy ones ended in divorce. In a culture that was coming to identify frequent, pleasurable, varied, and ecstatically satisfying sex as a preeminent sign of personal happiness, the high rate of marital dissolution could easily mean that large numbers of Americans were failing to reach these standards. The differences in the patterns of behavior of gay men and lesbians also pointed to the continuing salience of gender in shaping sexual meanings. Moreover, while lesbians and male homosexuals had carved out some space for themselves in society, the frequency of physical assaults upon visibly gay men and women suggested that their form of nonprocreative sex still provoked outrage. Feminism, too, may have opened new realms of sexual expressiveness for women, but the extent of rape and other forms of male sexual violence still made sex an arena of danger for them. The much-vaunted "sexual revolution," though real in many ways, was hardly complete.

Two issues, in particular, were emerging by the end of the 1970s to suggest the contradictory emotions that still enshrouded sex. Since the advent of penicillin in the 1940s, the threat of venereal disease had, to a significant degree, faded as an inhibitor of nonmonogamous sexual expression. But, in the midst of Americans' recently acquired sexual "freedom," the media spotlighted a new venereal scourge. Herpes, which *Time* magazine labeled "today's scarlet letter" and the "new leprosy," was reaching epidemic proportions among young urban heterosexuals. Though the condition posed far less physical danger than syphilis, it provoked guilt and panic as well as a pulling back from erotic encounters for some. A medical professional reported that "we hear it over and over: I won't have sex again." Among victims, the disease elicited feelings of self-pollution—"you never think you're clean enough," said one. The *Soho Weekly News*, a New York paper popular among young professionals in the city, was moved to proclaim "current sexual practice" as "the real epidemic." For many, the spread of herpes came to symbolize the inherent flaws in an ethic of sexual permissiveness. Pleasure brought retribution; disease became a marker of weak moral character.[28]

Another "epidemic," that of teenage pregnancy, also highlighted ambivalence about the erotic. Although most Americans tended to look benignly upon sex between unmarried adults, the spread of sexual experience among teenagers troubled them. To a large extent, adolescents were pursing the erotic without the approval or the guidance of their elders. Despite the visibility of sex in the culture, the acquisition of knowledge by the young remained sporadic and haphazard, largely "a private, individually motivated and covert affair," in the opinion of one sex researcher. Some parents felt it was simply wrong, despite their own experience. As one middle-class mother in Muncie had phrased it, "Just because it was right for me doesn't make it okay for my kids." A survey of high school youth in the early 1980s found that almost half had learned nothing about sex from their parents. Nor were schools rushing to fill the gap. By the late 1970s only half a dozen states mandated sex education; in most places, curriculum remained up to the local school districts, which generally displayed the same caution or disregard that occurred in the home. In one New York City suburb, a high school principal refused to let the editor of the school paper print an article about birth control methods. A California school district provided sex instruction in conjunction with drivers education, indicating how marginal it was to the academic curriculum. "In order to avoid controversy," according to the authors of *Sex and the American Teenager*, "schools embrace boredom."[29]

The result of this abdication of responsibility by schools and parents was that the young were often left to drift into sexual activity without guidance and with little knowledge. Teenagers whose parents were unwilling to talk with them about sex, or who did not receive sex education in school, were more prone to engage in intercourse. Yet they were also likely to be ignorant of how conception occurred or how to prevent it. Even when schools did provide instruction, they often acted too late. One North Carolina fifteen-year-old learned about condoms in a junior high school class, after he had been having intercourse for two years. "And then I realized, man, I've been taking a lot of chances. Thirteen, fourteen, fifteen . . . Lord's been good to me," he said. Others were not so lucky, as the incidence of teenage pregnancy revealed. In 1976, among the premaritally sexually active, twenty-seven percent of white girls and forty-five percent of blacks had become pregnant by the age of eighteen. Ironically, in view of the laissez-faire stance that adults seemed to take, the young were looking for advice. As Robert Coles and Geoffrey Stokes concluded on the basis of their work with high school students,

> It seems clear from our interviews that some kids who are planning to enter sexual relationships *want* to be told to wait. But those who can't talk to their parents hear either nothing or a ritualized naysaying that has no bearing on their *immediate* situation—and those who can may find their parents unwilling to take the responsibility for saying anything more than "Be careful."[30]

Meanwhile, for those who had made their choice to have sex, accurate information about reproduction, conception, and birth control might at least save them from the tragedy of unwanted pregnancies.

That so many teenage girls were becoming pregnant in an age when reliable contraception was available says much about the contradictions within the sexually permissive culture of the 1960s and 1970s. From everywhere sex beckoned, inciting desire, yet rarely did one find reasoned presentations of the most elementary consequences and responsibilities that sexual activity entailed. Youth had more autonomy from adult supervision than ever before, allowing them to explore the erotic at a time of profound physiological changes, but adults seemed to respond by implicitly drawing a boundary at sexual activity during adolescence. Perhaps one could not stop the young from experimenting, but neither would society endorse their behavior. The result was a social problem of tragic dimensions, one that placed in bold relief the ambivalence of American society toward sex. And, the fact that young girls were left to pay a higher price for sexual activity served as a poignant commentary on the persistence of gender in the structuring of sexuality in the postliberal era.

The reshaping of sexuality in the 1960s and 1970s was of major proportions. The marketing of sex, new demographic patterns, and the movements of women and homosexuals for equality all fostered a substantial revision in attitudes and behavior. In some ways, the process of sexualization represented pushing the logic of sexual liberalism to its extreme: once sex had been identified as a critical aspect of happiness, how could one justify containing it in marriage? Even before the 1960s, the behavior of youth and the commercial manipulation of the erotic had suggested the vulnerability of the liberal consensus. By the end of the 1970s, it was obvious that the consensus had dissolved. As Americans married later, postponed childbearing, and divorced more often, and as feminists and gay liberationists questioned heterosexual orthodoxy, nonmarital sexuality became commonplace and open. And, all of this took place in a social environment in which erotic imagery was ubiquitous.

The collapse of sexual liberalism did not, however, lead to a new, stable consensus. By the end of the 1970s, conservative proponents of an older sexual order had appeared. Their efforts to stem the tide of change and, indeed, to restore sexuality to a reproductive marital context would demonstrate the continuing power of sex to generate controversy.

Notes

[1] Gay Talese, *Thy Neighbor's Wife* (Garden City, N.Y., 1980; paperback, 1981), p. 188.

[2] *Ibid.*, p. 398.

[3] New York *Times*, April 5, 1979, p. B15.

[4] New York *Times*, February 10, 1981, p. B6, and February 9, 1981, p. B6.

[5] New York *Times*, February 9, 1981, p. B6.

[6] Theodore Caplow et al., *Middletown Families* (Minneapolis, 1982), pp. 173–74.

[7] Quoted in Morton Hunt, *Sexual Behavior in the 1970s* (New York, 1974), p. 9.

[8] Alex Comfort, ed., *The Joy of Sex: A Gourmet Guide to Love Making* (New York, 1972); Marabel Morgan, *The Total Woman* (Old Tappan, N.J., 1975).

[9] *New York Times Sunday Magazine*, May 25, 1975, p. 10. Unless otherwise noted, the demographic information in this and the following paragraphs is from Andrew Hacker, ed., *U/S: A Statistical Portrait of the American People* (New York, 1983).

[10] Richard R. Clayton and Harwin L. Voss, "Shacking Up: Cohabitation in the 1970s," *Journal of Marriage and the Family* 39 (1977), pp. 273–83; Philip Blumstein and Pepper Schwartz, *American Couples: Money, Work, Sex* (New York, 1983; paperback, 1985), p. 36.

[11] New York *Times*, November 27, 1977, p. 74; Caplow et al., *Middletown Families*, p. 131.

[12] Robert Staples, *Black Masculinity* (San Francisco, 1982), p. 115; New York *Times*, August 13, 1984, p. B4.

[13] New York *Times*, December 23, 1982, p. C5.

[14] See Hunt, *Sexual Behavior in the 1970s*, p. 21; B. K. Singh, "Trends in Attitudes toward Premarital Sexual Relations," *Journal of Marriage and the Family* 42 (1980), pp. 387–93; New York *Times*, November 27, 1977, p. 75; Norval D. Glenn and Charles N. Weaver, "Attitudes Toward Premarital, Extramarital, and Homosexual Relations in the U.S. in the 1970s," *Journal of Sex Research* 15 (1978), pp. 108–18; Blumstein and Schwartz, *American Couples*, pp. 255, 272.

[15] New York *Times*, November 28, 1977, p. 36.

[16] Ira E. Robinson and Davor Jedlicka, "Change in Sexual Attitudes and Behavior of College Students from 1965 to 1980: A Research Note," *Journal of Marriage and the Family* 44 (1982), pp. 237–40; Robert R. Bell and Kathleen Coughey, "Premarital Sexual Experience Among College Females, 1958, 1968, and 1978," *Family Relations* 29 (1980), pp. 353–57; Melvin Zelnick, Young J. Kim, and John F. Kanter, "Probabilities of Intercourse and Conception Among Teenage Women, 1971 and 1976," *Family Planning Perspectives* 11 (1979), pp. 177–83; Hunt, *Sexual Behavior in the 1970s*, pp. 150, 166, 77, 87.

[17] Caplow et al., *Middletown Families*, pp. 169–70, 185.

[18] Robert Coles and Geoffrey Stokes, *Sex and the American Teenager* (New York, 1985), p. 7; Hunt, *Sexual Behavior in the 1970s*, p. 142.

[19] Blumstein and Schwartz, *American Couples*, pp. 208, 282.

[20] Hunt, *Sexual Behavior in the 1970s*, pp. 202, 198, 187, 192.

[21] *Ibid.*, pp. 183–84; Barbara Ehrenreich, Elizabeth Hess, and Gloria Jacobs, *Re-Making Love: The Feminization of Sex* (Garden City, N.Y., 1986), p. 100.

[22] Blumstein and Schwartz, *American Couples*, pp. 232, 236.

[23] *Ibid.*, pp. 201–3; Ehrenreich et al., *Re-Making Love*, p. 164.

[24] New York *Times*, July 22, 1977, p. 1.

[25] New York *Times*, October 31, 1979, p. C19.

[26] Blumstein and Schwartz, *American Couples*, pp. 202–3, 236, 273. For another study see Karla Jay and Allen Young, *The Gay Report: Lesbians and Gay Men Speak Out About Sexual Experiences and Life Styles* (New York, 1979).

[27] Blumstein and Schwartz, *American Couples*, p. 305.

[28] Allan M. Brandt, *No Magic Bullet: A Social History of Venereal Disease in the United States Since 1880* (New York, 1985), pp. 170–74, 179–82.

[29] Hunt, *Sexual Behavior in the 1970s*, p. 130; Caplow et al., *Middletown Families*, p. 171; Coles and Stokes, *Sex and the American Teenager*, p. 38.

[30] Coles and Stokes, *Sex and the American Teenager* pp. 37, 99.

JOURNAL WRITINGS

1. The reading comments that "cohabitation" has become "highly visible" in recent decades. Develop a paragraph or two discussing the possible advantages and disadvantages of living together without marriage; state your own view of this arrangement based on your discussion.

2. "As its critique of sex-role conditioning spread throughout the culture, feminism altered the attitudes of Americans about the proper behavior of men and women." Focusing on specific couples, **describe** any differences you have noticed between sex-role *behaviors* of your parents' generation and the behaviors of couples in your own age group. Or use Cupid and

Psyche as an example of older, more traditional sex-role behavior, and contrast their actions with a modern couple. If you do not perceive any differences, describe the similarities between the two sets of behaviors. Show how your observations do or do not support the comments in the reading about sex roles.

BRAINSTORMING AND DRAFTING

3.   D'Emilio and Freedman maintain that the media exploits sex to make money. What is the meaning of *exploit?* Choose a film released in the last six months or a current television program or a commercial that includes obvious or subtle sexuality. **Analyze** the film, program, or commercial, describing briefly how sex is used. Then explain why you believe such use does or does not constitute exploitation.

4.   Another phenomenon recorded by the authors is the higher incidence of divorce in contemporary society. Draft a paragraph sketching the possible negative as well as positive effects of divorce on the divorced partners themselves or on their children, or on potential love relationships. Which, if any, of these effects are reflected in the character of Mel McGinnis in Raymond Carver's story?

THE AUTHORS' METHODS

5.   D'Emilio and Freedman begin their essay by **narrating** a brief anecdote about Sandstone, an "experiment in sexual freedom." Why is this an effective opening? Draft an anecdotal opening for an essay on sex education.

6.   In paragraph eight, the authors begin with a **generalization** followed by several concrete **examples** to persuade us that the generalization is true. Develop a persuasive paragraph of your own by offering a general idea about unplanned pregnancies. Follow your generalization with specific examples or facts to support your generalization.

FORMAL WRITING AND RESEARCH PAPERS

7.   Pretend you are living in the year 2050. Write an imaginative paper in which you document the social changes in sexual attitudes and behavior that have taken place between the years 2000 and 2050. Provide hypothetical **examples,** anecdotes, and statistics to support your ideas.

8.   As a small-group project, each member should research the nature and extent of sex education in a secondary school where he or she lives, either by visiting the school or by a telephone interview. As a group, develop a set of criteria for evaluating the sex instruction. After sharing information, each member should write an individual paper **describing** each program in

detail and evaluating it according to the group's criteria, and ranking it among the programs considered. (Or, you can do this as an individual project by gathering your own information, setting your criteria, and evaluating the program you have studied.)

9. Do some research on "date rape." (Consult, for example, *The National Newspaper Index, Women's Studies Abstracts,* and *Sociological Abstracts.* Write an **argumentative** paper in which you attempt to persuade an audience of college students that the nature and extent of this type of rape make it particularly dangerous for them. Recommend some measures to help avoid this danger. Or, you may wish to argue that date rape is a pseudo-problem, perhaps created by feminists, hysterical women, and media hyperbole (exaggeration).

Joyce Carol Oates

Where the Shadow Is Darkest

(1970)

A contemporary American writer, Joyce Carol Oates (born 1938) began her life in a small town in New York State. As a child, she received her primary schooling in a one-room country schoolhouse, but she pursued her secondary education in the town. She went on to attain a Bachelor's degree in English from Syracuse University and an M.A. in English from the University of Wisconsin, where she met her husband. Although she wrote an average of a novel per semester, even as an undergraduate, she did not decide to become a professional writer until she happened to see one of her short stories mentioned in *Best American Short Stories.*

Since that decision, Oates has become one of America's most prolific writers, producing dozens of often lengthy novels, as well as numerous short stories, poems, plays, essays, and critical analyses. In 1970, she received the National Book Award for her novel entitled *them;* she has also received two O. Henry prizes. Currently, she is the Roger S. Berlind Distinguished Professor in the Humanities at Princeton University, a post that enables her to combine both teaching and writing.

While she is less well known for her poetry than for her fiction, many of her poems contain themes that are expanded upon in her stories. She often focuses on people's inner lives and the relationship of internal realities to social, moral, and political concerns. In the following poem, she explores the interior emotional processes of two individuals as they love. The poem also unites the themes of love and sexuality.

PREVIEW

What does the word *falling* in the expression "falling in love" imply about the nature of love? Why do you think the expression persists in our language?

-

swinging in
to love again—
dropping away again—

time does not move for us
except in strange
lazy loops
tying us together—
releasing us
to the air's surface—

Our lives are two shadows
by accident touching
and where the shadow is darkest
there
we are together forever—

what we would forget
in our multiple selves
the darkest shadow recalls for us
and swings us strongly
to love again
together—

JOURNAL WRITINGS

1. Oates begins the poem with the progressive **verb** "swinging" rather than
    the expected "falling." Try to remember from your childhood how you felt
    when you were on a swing; list some adjectives that **describe** that sensation.
    How do each of the words on your list relate to the idea of love? Why do you
    think Oates chose "swinging" instead of "falling"? How do the two words
    differ in their implications about love? (See your answer to the Preview
    question.)
2. Draw some pictures that visually represent the action of the poem's first
    stanza. Write a paragraph explaining what happens during "dropping
    away" and discuss whether or not you think "dropping away" is a problem in
    a continuing relationship.

BRAINSTORMING AND DRAFTING

3. Explain how Nick/Laura and Mel/Terri in Raymond Carver's story fit into
    the action of the first stanza of Oates's poem. Provide **examples** of their
    words or behavior that support your opinion.
4. The **narrator** of this poem seems mostly unaware of a world outside the two
    lovers' experience of each other. Write a **definition** of love implied by the
    narrator's assumption. Draft a paragraph explaining why you agree or
    disagree with this definition, specifying the role you think society (family,
    friends, coworkers, professionals, etc.) might play in relation to a loving
    couple.

THE AUTHOR'S METHODS

5. In a dictionary or encyclopedia of **symbolism,** look up the meanings of "shadow" and "darkness" adopted by both traditional and modern cultures. How do these meanings help to explain the psychological action of the poem? The physical action?

6. Oates uses **alliteration** and **assonance** in the poem. Consult the glossary for definitions of these terms. Find several **examples** of each technique in the poem, and write a paragraph suggesting ways in which the techniques enhance the poem's meaning.

FORMAL WRITING AND RESEARCH PAPERS

7. Ask several of your peers who have not read Oates's poem how they interpret her phrase "multiple selves." After carefully considering the **definitions** you gather, write a paper in which you construct your own definition of the concept, and apply it in depth to your own life. In your discussion, include a full explanation of its role and significance in any love relationships you are now experiencing or may experience in the future. Use specific **examples** to support your ideas.

8. Read the introduction to the Free Choice unit. With these issues in mind, write a paper in which you explore the questions of how much control and responsibility an individual can have during love and sex. In the paper, identify the level of control that the narrator implies in Oates's poem. Discuss the "clues" in the poem that lead you to this evaluation. Compare this level of control with that implied by Augustine's essay and Tannahill's selection. Finally, offer your own view on how much control and responsibility, if any, we should expect from young adults during love and sex.

Remedios Lissaraga Varo

The Lovers

(1963)

Maria de los Remedios Varo Y Uranga (1913–1963) was born in Spain, and spent much of her childhood traveling with her family until they settled in Madrid. Sent to school in a Catholic convent, Varo rebelled against the strict discipline. Instead of her catechism, she read adventure stories. Later, she studied art at the Academia de San Fernando. Attracted to surrealist ideas, Varo went to Paris but escaped to Mexico just prior to the Nazi invasion. Except for periodic travels, Varo remained in Mexico and married Walter Gruen. Gradually, she evolved a fantastical style of her own. Her paintings, though often seemingly humorous, generally suggest serious psychological issues, especially those pertaining to women.

Her paintings include *Woman Leaving the Psychoanalyst,* a surrealist portrait of a woman whose mask falls as her own head emerges, *Capillary Movement,* a comic reversal of the Rapunzel story in which Varo depicts gentlemen sporting long handlebar mustaches, and *The Vegetarian Vampires,* a dining scene picturing fantastic figures who grow wings on their hats and keep pet chickens as they consume their vegetables. *The Lovers* is a mixed–media/Masonite work that presents two lovers oblivious of everything except each other. Meanwhile, floodwaters rise around them.

JOURNAL WRITINGS

1. Write a paragraph **describing** the similarities and differences between the two figures in the painting on the following page. What seems to attract them more: likenesses or differences? In another paragraph, describe similarities and differences between yourself and a friend or romantic partner. What attracts you more: likenesses or differences? Which kind of attraction makes for a better relationship? Why?
2. Look at the lovers' faces. **Describe** their mood: Do they feel happy, sad, serious, playful, angry, calm, anxious? Imagine and describe a plausible situation that may have led them to feel this way.

BRAINSTORMING AND DRAFTING

3.   **Compare** the lovers in the painting with the lovers in Joyce Carol Oates's poem, especially in relation to their surroundings. Using this information, propose a definition of love that you think both Varo's lovers and Oates's lovers would approve. Evaluate this **definition** from your own point of view.
4.   Write two different captions for this painting: one for a booklet of paintings to be used in an eighth-grade art-appreciation class, and one for an exhibit in your college art gallery. Then draft a paragraph in which you **describe** the differences in your captions and also give reasons for your choice of writing strategies.

THE ARTIST'S METHODS

5.   Let your eyes follow the many lines and other movements in this painting. In a paragraph propose a **symbolic** significance for the directions you see, and show how these movements enhance the overall meaning of the painting.
6.   **Describe** some ways that Varo "limits" the lovers by proportioning their space. What does this spatial arrangement suggest about the artist's **theme?**

FORMAL WRITING AND RESEARCH PAPERS

7.   Write a paper explaining the problems you see when two lovers ignore their "surroundings." Begin by **defining** "surroundings" (see your answer to question 3 under Brainstorming and Drafting); then explain and give specific **examples** of the problems. In the second part of your paper, recommend specific ways that lovers might solve such problems. *Alternative:* Write a paper arguing against the need for lovers to take account of their surroundings.
8.   Research some of the sociological theories of interpersonal attraction or marital choice. (Consult the *Social Sciences Index,* the *Sociological Abstracts,* and the card or computer catalog.) What role does similarity play? How important are "complementary" needs? Use your findings to analyze Varo's painting and at least one of the couples in Raymond Carver's story.
9.   Do some research on the psychological implications of egotism or narcissism. (Consult *Psychological Abstracts* or a basic psychology textbook.) Write a paper in which you examine one of these terms. Explain its implications for a person's self-image, and discuss some possible effects this concept might have on a relationship. Then apply your findings to Varo's painting. Be sure to document your sources.

Anton Chekhov

Lady with Lapdog

(1899)

A Russian playwright and short-story writer, Anton Pavlovich Chekhov
(1860–1904) at first pursued a medical career, but as his comic sketches
became increasingly popular, he decided to devote most of his time to his
literary work. The early "sketches" began to develop into deeper, more
insightful stories. In 1898, his now famous play *The Seagull* was presented
at The Moscow Art Theater. During his career as a writer, he also did
charitable medical work, often giving free treatment in his spare time.
However, he was plagued by symptoms of tuberculosis (the disease that
killed him at the age of forty-four).

During his relatively short life, he managed to write several plays and
more than 150 short stories. Besides *The Seagull,* his dramas include *Uncle
Vanya* and *The Cherry Orchard.* To the short story as an art form, he
contributed a psychological acumen and often a comic touch. "Lady with
Lapdog" presents characters engaged in a timeless dilemma of forbidden
love. In the context of nineteenth-century Russian society, bound by
traditional conventions, such relationships must have seemed unresolvable.

PREVIEW

Do you think that an extramarital affair is ever justifiable? Give reasons for your answer.

I

The appearance on the front of a new arrival—a lady with a lapdog—became the
topic of general conversation. Dmitry Dmitrich Gurov, who had been a fortnight
in Yalta and got used to its ways, was also interested in new arrivals. One day,
sitting on the terrace of Vernet's restaurant, he saw a young woman walking along
the promenade; she was fair, not very tall, and wore a toque*; behind her trotted
a white pomeranian.†

---

* toque—a close-fitting hat without a brim. [Eds.]
† Pomeranian—a small dog with long thick straight hair. [Eds.]

Later he came across her in the park and in the square several times a day. She was always alone, always wearing the same toque, followed by the white pomeranian. No one knew who she was, and she became known simply as the lady with the lapdog.

"If she's here without her husband and without any friends," thought Gurov, "it wouldn't be a bad idea to strike up an acquaintance with her."

He was not yet forty, but he had a twelve-year-old daughter and two school-boy sons. He had been married off when he was still in his second year at the university, and his wife seemed to him now to be almost twice his age. She was a tall, black-browed woman, erect, dignified, austere, and, as she liked to describe herself, a "thinking person". She was a great reader, preferred the new "advanced" spelling, called her husband by the more formal "Dimitry" and not the familiar "Dmitry"; and though he secretly considered her not particularly intelligent, narrow-minded, and inelegant, he was afraid of her and disliked being at home. He had been unfaithful to her for a long time, he was often unfaithful to her, and that was why, perhaps, he almost always spoke ill of women, and when men discussed women in his presence, he described them as *the lower breed*.

He could not help feeling that he had had enough bitter experience to have the right to call them as he pleased, but all the same without *the lower breed* he could not have existed a couple of days. He was bored and ill at ease among men, with whom he was reticent and cold, but when he was among women he felt at ease, he knew what to talk about with them and how to behave; even when he was silent in their company he experienced no feeling of constraint. There was something attractive, something elusive in his appearance, in his character and his whole person, that women found interesting and irresistible; he was aware of it, and was himself drawn to them by some irresistible force.

Long and indeed bitter experience had taught him that every new affair, which at first relieved the monotony of life so pleasantly and appeared to be such a charming and light adventure, among decent people and especially among Muscovites,* who are so irresolute and so hard to rouse, inevitably developed into an extremely complicated problem and finally the whole situation became rather cumbersome. But at every new meeting with an attractive woman he forgot all about this experience, he wanted to enjoy life so badly and it all seemed so simple and amusing.

And so one afternoon, while he was having dinner at a restaurant in the park, the woman in the toque walked in unhurriedly and took a seat at the table next to him. The way she looked, walked, and dressed, wore her hair, told him that she was of good social standing, that she was married, that she was in Yalta for the first time, that she was alone and bored. . . . There was a great deal of exaggeration in the stories about the laxity of morals among the Yalta visitors, and he dismissed them with contempt, for he knew that such stories were mostly made up by people who would gladly have sinned themselves if they had had any idea how to go about it; but when the woman sat down at the table three yards away from him he remembered these stories of easy conquests and excursions to the mountains

---

* Muscovites—natives of Moscow. [Eds.]

and the tempting thought of a quick and fleeting affair, an affair with a strange woman whose very name he did not know, suddenly took possession of him.

He tried to attract the attention of the dog by calling softly to it, and when the pomeranian came up to him he shook a finger at it. The pomeranian growled. Gurov again shook a finger at it.

The woman looked up at him and immediately lowered her eyes.

"He doesn't bite," she said and blushed.

"May I give him a bone?" he asked, and when she nodded, he said amiably: "Have you been long in Yalta?"

"About five days."

"And I am just finishing my second week here."

They said nothing for the next few minutes.

"Time flies," she said without looking at him, "and yet it's so boring here."

"That's what one usually hears people saying here. A man may be living in Belev and Zhizdra or some other God-forsaken hole and he isn't bored, but the moment he comes here all you hear from him is 'Oh, it's so boring! Oh, the dust!' You'd think he'd come from Granada!"

She laughed. Then both went on eating in silence, like complete strangers; but after dinner they strolled off together, and they embarked on the light playful conversation of free and contented people who do not care where they go or what they talk about. They walked, and talked about the strange light that fell on the sea; the water was of such a soft and warm lilac, and the moon threw a shaft of gold across it. They talked about how close it was after a hot day. Gurov told her that he lived in Moscow, that he was a graduate in philology but worked in a bank, that he had at one time thought of singing in a private opera company but had given up the idea, that he owned two houses in Moscow. . . . From her he learnt that she had grown up in Petersburg, but had got married in the town of S—, where she had been living for the past two years, that she would stay another month in Yalta, and that her husband, who also needed a rest, might join her. She was quite unable to tell him what her husband's job was, whether he served in the offices of the provincial governor or the rural council, and she found this rather amusing herself. Gurov also found out that her name and patronymic* were Anna Sergeyevna.

Later, in his hotel room, he thought about her and felt sure that he would meet her again the next day. It had to be. As he went to bed he remembered that she had only recently left her boarding school, that she had been a schoolgirl like his own daughter; he recalled how much diffidence and angularity there was in her laughter and her conversation with a stranger—it was probably the first time in her life she had found herself alone, in a situation when men followed her, looked at her, and spoke to her with only one secret intention, an intention she could hardly fail to guess. He remembered her slender, weak neck, her beautiful grey eyes.

---

* patronymic—name derived from an ancestor. [Eds.]

"There's something pathetic about her, all the same," he thought as he fell asleep.

II

A week had passed since their first meeting. It was a holiday. It was close indoors, while in the streets a strong wind raised clouds of dust and tore off people's hats. All day long one felt thirsty, and Gurov kept going to the terrace of the restaurant, offering Anna Sergeyevna fruit drinks and ices. There was nowhere to go.

In the evening, when the wind had dropped a little, they went to the pier to watch the arrival of the steamer. There were a great many people taking a walk on the landing pier; some were meeting friends, they had bunches of flowers in their hands. It was there that two peculiarities of the Yalta smart set at once arrested attention: the middle-aged women dressed as if they were still young girls and there was a great number of generals.

Because of the rough sea the steamer arrived late, after the sun had set, and she had to swing backwards and forwards several times before getting alongside the pier. Anna Sergeyevna looked at the steamer and the passengers through her lorgnette,* as though trying to make out some friends, and when she turned to Gurov her eyes were sparkling. She talked a lot, asked many abrupt questions, and immediately forgot what it was she had wanted to know; then she lost her lorgnette in the crowd of people.

The smartly dressed crowd dispersed; soon they were all gone, the wind had dropped completely, but Gurov and Anna were still standing there as though waiting to see if someone else would come off the boat. Anna Sergeyevna was no longer talking. She was smelling her flowers without looking at Gurov.

"It's a nice evening," he said. "Where shall we go now? Shall we go for a drive?"

She made no answer.

Then he looked keenly at her and suddenly put his arms round her and kissed her on the mouth. He felt the fragrance and dampness of the flowers and immediately looked round him fearfully: had anyone seen them?

"Let's go to your room," he said softly.

And both walked off quickly.

It was very close in her hotel room, which was full of the smell of the scents she had bought in a Japanese shop. Looking at her now, Gurov thought: "Life is full of strange encounters!" From his past he preserved the memory of carefree, good-natured women, whom love had made gay and who were grateful to him for the happiness he gave them, however short-lived; and of women like his wife, who made love without sincerity, with unnecessary talk, affectedly, hysterically, with such an expression, as though it were not love or passion, but something

---

* lorgnette—eyeglasses on a handle. [Eds.]

much more significant; and of two or three very beautiful, frigid women, whose faces suddenly lit up with a predatory expression, an obstinate desire to take, to snatch from life more than it could give; these were women no longer in their first youth, capricious, unreasoning, despotic, unintelligent women, and when Gurov lost interest in them, their beauty merely aroused hatred in him and the lace trimmings on their négligés looked to him then like the scales of a snake.

But here there was still the same diffidence and angularity of inexperienced youth—an awkward feeling; and there was also the impression of embarrassment, as if someone had just knocked at the door. Anna Sergeyevna, this lady with the lapdog, apparently regarded what had happened in a peculiar sort of way, very seriously, as though she had become a fallen woman—so it seemed to him, and he found it odd and disconcerting. Her features lengthened and drooped, and her long hair hung mournfully on either side of her face; she sank into thought in a despondent pose, like a woman taken in adultery in an old painting.

"It's wrong," she said. "You'll be the first not to respect me now."

There was a water-melon on the table. Gurov cut himself a slice and began to eat it slowly. At least half an hour passed in silence.

Anna Sergeyevna was very touching; there was an air of a pure, decent, naïve woman about her, a woman who had very little experience of life; the solitary candle burning on the table scarcely lighted up her face, but it was obvious that she was unhappy.

"But, darling, why should I stop respecting you?" Gurov asked. "You don't know yourself what you're saying."

"May God forgive me," she said, and her eyes filled with tears. "It's terrible."

"You seem to wish to justify yourself."

"How can I justify myself? I am a bad, despicable creature. I despise myself and have no thought of justifying myself. I haven't deceived my husband, I've deceived myself. And not only now. I've been deceiving myself for a long time. My husband is, I'm sure, a good and honest man, but, you see, he is a flunkey. I don't know what he does at his office, all I know is that he is a flunkey. I was only twenty when I married him, I was eaten up by curiosity, I wanted something better. There surely must be a different kind of life, I said to myself. I wanted to live. To live, to live! I was burning with curiosity. I don't think you know what I am talking about, but I swear I could no longer control myself, something was happening to me, I could not be held back, I told my husband I was ill, and I came here. . . . Here too I was going about as though in a daze, as though I was mad, and now I've become a vulgar worthless woman whom everyone has a right to despise."

Gurov could not help feeling bored as he listened to her; he was irritated by her naïve tone of voice and her repentance, which was so unexpected and so out of place; but for the tears in her eyes, he might have thought that she was joking or play-acting.

"I don't understand," he said gently, "what it is you want."

She buried her face on his chest and clung close to him.

"Please, please believe me," she said, "I love a pure, honest life. I hate immorality. I don't know myself what I am doing. The common people say 'the devil led her astray'. I too can now say about myself that the devil has led me astray."

"There, there . . . " he murmured.

He gazed into her staring, frightened eyes, kissed her, spoke gently and affectionately to her, and gradually she calmed down and her cheerfulness returned; both of them were soon laughing.

Later, when they went out, there was not a soul on the promenade, the town with its cypresses looked quite dead, but the sea was still roaring and dashing itself against the shore; a single launch tossed on the waves, its lamp flickering sleepily.

They hailed a cab and drove to Oreanda.

"I've just found out your surname, downstairs in the lobby," said Gurov. "Von Diederitz. Is your husband a German?"

"No. I believe his grandfather was German. He is of the Orthodox faith himself."

In Oreanda they sat on a bench not far from the church, looked down on the sea, and were silent. Yalta could scarcely be seen through the morning mist. White clouds lay motionless on the mountain tops. Not a leaf stirred on the trees, the cicadas chirped, and the monotonous, hollow roar of the sea, coming up from below, spoke of rest, of eternal sleep awaiting us all. The sea had roared like that down below when there was no Yalta or Oreanda, it was roaring now, and it would go on roaring as indifferently and hollowly when we were here no more. And in this constancy, in this complete indifference to the life and death of each one of us, there is perhaps hidden the guarantee of our eternal salvation, the never-ceasing movement of life on earth, the never-ceasing movement towards perfection. Sitting beside a young woman who looked so beautiful at the break of day, soothed and enchanted by the sight of all that fairy-land scenery—the sea, the mountains, the clouds, the wide sky—Gurov reflected that, when you came to think of it, everything in the world was really beautiful, everything but our own thoughts and actions when we lose sight of the higher aims of existence and our dignity as human beings.

Someone walked up to them, a watchman probably, looked at them, and went away. And there seemed to be something mysterious and also beautiful in this fact, too. They could see the Theodosia boat coming towards the pier, lit up by the sunrise, and with no lights.

"There's dew on the grass," said Anna Sergeyevna, breaking the silence.

"Yes. Time to go home."

They went back to the town.

After that they met on the front every day at twelve o'clock, had lunch and dinner together, went for walks, admired the sea. She complained of sleeping badly and of her heart beating uneasily, asked the same questions, alternately worried by feelings of jealousy and by fear that he did not respect her sufficiently. And again and again in the park or in the square, when there was no one in sight, he would draw her to him and kiss her passionately. The complete idleness, these kisses in broad daylight, always having to look round for fear of someone watching them, the heat, the smell of the sea, and the constant looming into sight of idle, well-dressed, and well-fed people seemed to have made a new man of him; he told Anna Sergeyevna that she was beautiful, that she was desirable, made passionate love to her, never left her side, while she was often lost in thought and kept asking him to admit that he did not really respect her, that he was not in the least in love with her and only saw in her a vulgar woman. Almost every night they drove out of town, to Oreanda or to the waterfall; the excursion was always a success, and every time their impressions were invariably grand and beautiful.

They kept expecting her husband to arrive. But a letter came from him in which he wrote that he was having trouble with his eyes and implored his wife to return home as soon as possible. Anna Sergeyevna lost no time in getting ready for her journey home.

"It's a good thing I'm going," she said to Gurov. "It's fate."

She took a carriage to the railway station, and he saw her off. The drive took a whole day. When she got into the express train, after the second bell, she said:

"Let me have another look at you. . . . One last look. So."

She did not cry, but looked sad, just as if she were ill, and her face quivered.

"I'll be thinking of you, remembering you," she said. "Good-bye. You're staying, aren't you? Don't think badly of me. We are parting for ever. Yes, it must be so, for we should never have met. Well, good-bye. . . . "

The train moved rapidly out of the station; its lights soon disappeared, and a minute later it could not even be heard, just as though everything had conspired to put a quick end to this sweet trance, this madness. And standing alone on the platform gazing into the dark distance, Gurov listened to the churring of the grasshoppers and the humming of the telegraph wires with a feeling as though he had just woken up. He told himself that this had been just one more affair in his life, just one more adventure, and that it too was over, leaving nothing but a memory. He was moved and sad, and felt a little penitent that the young woman, whom he would never see again, had not been happy with him; he had been amiable and affectionate with her, but all the same in his behaviour to her, in the tone of his voice and in his caresses, there was a suspicion of light irony, the somewhat coarse arrogance of the successful male, who was, moreover, almost twice her age. All the time she called him good, wonderful, high-minded; evidently she must have taken him to be quite different from what he really was, which meant that he had involuntarily deceived her.

At the railway station there was already a whiff of autumn in the air; the evening was chilly.

"Time I went north too," thought Gurov, as he walked off the platform. "High time!"

III

At home in Moscow everything was already like winter: the stoves were heated, and it was still dark in the morning when the children were getting ready to go to school and having breakfast, so that the nurse had to light the lamp for a short time. The frosts had set in. When the first snow falls and the first day one goes out for a ride in a sleigh, one is glad to see the white ground, the white roofs, the air is so soft and wonderful to breathe, and one remembers the days of one's youth. The old lime trees and birches, white with rime, have such a benignant look, they are nearer to one's heart than cypresses and palms, and beside them one no longer wants to think of mountains and the sea.

Gurov had been born and bred in Moscow, and he returned to Moscow on a fine frosty day; and when he put on his fur coat and warm gloves and took a walk down Petrovka Street, and when on Saturday evening he heard the church bells ringing, his recent holiday trip and the places he had visited lost their charm for him. Gradually he became immersed in Moscow life, eagerly reading three newspapers a day and declaring that he never read Moscow papers on principle. Once more he could not resist the attraction of restaurants, clubs, banquets, and anniversary celebrations, and once more he felt flattered that well-known lawyers and actors came to see him and that in the Medical Club he played cards with a professor as his partner. Once again he was capable of eating a whole portion of the Moscow speciality of sour cabbage and meat served in a frying-pan. . . .

Another month and, he thought, nothing but a memory would remain of Anna Sergeyevna; he would remember her as through a haze and only occasionally dream of her with a wistful smile, as he did of the others before her. But over a month passed, winter was at its height, and he remembered her as clearly as though he had only parted from her the day before. His memories haunted him more and more persistently. Every time the voices of his children doing their homework reached him in his study in the stillness of the evening, every time he heard a popular song or some music in a restaurant, every time the wind howled in the chimney—it all came back to him: their walks on the pier, early morning with the mist on the mountains, the Theodosia boat, and the kisses. He kept pacing the room for hours remembering it all and smiling, and then his memories turned into daydreams and the past mingled in his imagination with what was going to happen. He did not dream of Anna Sergeyevna, she accompanied him everywhere like his shadow and followed him wherever he went. Closing his eyes, he saw her as clearly as if she were before him, and she seemed to him lovelier, younger, and tenderer than she had been; and he thought that he too was much better than he had been in Yalta. In the evenings she gazed at him from the bookcase, from the fireplace, from the corner—he heard her breathing, the sweet rustle of her dress. In the street he followed women with his eyes, looking for anyone who resembled her. . . .

He was beginning to be overcome by an overwhelming desire to share his memories with someone. But at home it was impossible to talk of his love, and outside his home there was no one he could talk to. Not the tenants who lived in his house, and certainly not his colleagues in the bank. And what was he to tell them? Had he been in love then? Had there been anything beautiful, poetic, edifying, or even anything interesting about his relations with Anna Sergeyevna? So he had to talk in general terms about love and women, and no one guessed what he was driving at, and his wife merely raised her black eyebrows and said:

"Really, Dimitry, the role of a coxcomb* doesn't suit you at all!"

One evening, as he left the Medical Club with his partner, a civil servant, he could not restrain himself, and said:

"If you knew what a fascinating woman I met in Yalta!"

The civil servant got into his sleigh and was about to be driven off, but suddenly he turned round and called out:

"I say!"

"Yes?"

"You were quite right: the sturgeon† *was* a bit off."

These words, so ordinary in themselves, for some reason hurt Gurov's feelings: they seemed to him humiliating and indecent. What savage manners! What faces! What stupid nights! What uninteresting, wasted days! Crazy gambling at cards, gluttony, drunkenness, endless talk about one and the same thing. Business that was of no use to anyone and talk about one and the same thing absorbed the greater part of one's time and energy, and what was left in the end was a sort of dock-tailed, barren life, a sort of nonsensical existence, and it was impossible to escape from it, just as though you were in a lunatic asylum or a convict chain-gang!

Gurov lay awake all night, fretting and fuming, and had a splitting headache the whole of the next day. The following nights too he slept badly, sitting up in bed thinking, or walking up and down his room. He was tired of his children, tired of the bank, he did not feel like going out anywhere or talking about anything.

In December, during the Christmas holidays, he packed his things, told his wife that he was going to Petersburg to get a job for a young man he knew, and set off for the town of S——. Why? He had no very clear idea himself. He wanted to see Anna Sergeyevna, to talk to her, to arrange a meeting, if possible.

He arrived in S——in the morning and took the best room in a hotel, with a fitted carpet of military grey cloth and an inkstand grey with dust on the table, surmounted by a horseman with raised hand and no head. The hall porter supplied him with all the necessary information: Von Diederitz lived in a house of his own in Old Potter's Street, not far from the hotel. He lived well, was rich, kept his own carriage horses, the whole town knew him. The hall-porter pronounced the name: Dridiritz.

Gurov took a leisurely walk down Old Potter's Street and found the house. In front of it was a long grey fence studded with upturned nails.

"A fence like that would make anyone wish to run away," thought Gurov, scanning the windows and the fence.

As it was a holiday, he thought, her husband was probably at home. It did not matter either way, though, for he could not very well embarrass her by calling at the house. If he were to send in a note it might fall into the hands of the husband and ruin everything. The best thing was to rely on chance. And he kept walking

---

* coxcomb—a conceited male, overly concerned with his appearance. [Eds.]

† sturgeon—a large fish found in fresh and salt waters. [Eds.]

up and down the street and along the fence, waiting for his chance. He watched a beggar enter the gate and the dogs attack him; then, an hour later, he heard the faint indistinct sounds of a piano. That must have been Anna Sergeyevna playing. Suddenly the front door opened and an old woman came out, followed by the familiar white pomeranian. Gurov was about to call to the dog, but his heart began to beat violently and in his excitement he could not remember its name.

He went on walking up and down the street, hating the grey fence more and more, and he was already saying to himself that Anna Sergeyevna had forgotten him and had perhaps been having a good time with someone else, which was indeed quite natural for a young woman who had to look at that damned fence from morning till night. He went back to his hotel room and sat on the sofa for a long time, not knowing what to do, then he had dinner and after dinner a long sleep.

'How stupid and disturbing it all is,' he thought, waking up and staring at the dark windows: it was already evening. 'Well, I've had a good sleep, so what now? What am I going to do tonight?'

He sat on a bed covered by a cheap grey blanket looking exactly like a hospital blanket, and taunted himself in vexation:

"A *lady* with a lapdog! Some adventure, I must say! Serves you right!"

At the railway station that morning he had noticed a poster announcing in huge letters the first performance of *The Geisha Girl* at the local theatre. He recalled it now, and decided to go to the theatre.

"Quite possibly she goes to first nights," he thought.

The theatre was full. As in all provincial theatres, there was a mist over the chandeliers and the people in the gallery kept up a noisy and excited conversation; in the first row of the stalls stood the local dandies with their hands crossed behind their backs; here, too, in the front seat of the Governor's box, sat the Governor's daughter, wearing a feather boa, while the Governor himself hid modestly behind the portière so that only his hands were visible; the curtain stirred, the orchestra took a long time tuning up. Gurov scanned the audience eagerly as they filed in and occupied their seats.

Anna Sergeyevna came in too. She took her seat in the third row, and when Gurov glanced at her his heart missed a beat and he realized clearly that there was no one in the world nearer and dearer or more important to him than that little woman with the stupid lorgnette in her hand, who was in no way remarkable. That woman lost in a provincial crowd now filled his whole life, was his misfortune, his joy, and the only happiness that he wished for himself. Listening to the bad orchestra and the wretched violins played by second-rate musicians, he thought how beautiful she was. He thought and dreamed.

A very tall, round-shouldered young man with small whiskers had come in with Anna Sergeyevna and sat down beside her; he nodded at every step he took and seemed to be continually bowing to someone. This was probably her husband, whom in a fit of bitterness at Yalta she had called a flunkey. And indeed there was something of a lackey's obsequiousness in his lank figure, his whiskers, and the little bald spot on the top of his head. He smiled sweetly, and the gleaming insignia of some scientific society which he wore in his buttonhole looked like the number on a waiter's coat.

In the first interval the husband went out to smoke and she was left in her seat. Gurov, who also had a seat in the stalls, went up to her and said in a trembling voice and with a forced smile:

"Good evening!"

She looked up at him and turned pale, then looked at him again in panic, unable to believe her eyes, clenching her fan and lorgnette in her hand and apparently trying hard not to fall into a dead faint. Both were silent. She sat and he stood, frightened by her embarrassment and not daring to sit down beside her. The violinists and the flautist began tuning their instruments, and they suddenly felt terrified, as though they were being watched from all the boxes. But a moment later she got up and walked rapidly towards one of the exits; he followed her, and both of them walked aimlessly along corridors and up and down stairs. Figures in all sorts of uniforms—lawyers, teachers, civil servants, all wearing badges—flashed by them; ladies, fur coats hanging on pegs, the cold draught bringing with it the odour of cigarette-ends. Gurov, whose heart was beating violently, thought:

"Oh Lord, what are all these people, that orchestra, doing here?"

At that moment he suddenly remembered how after seeing Anna Sergeyevna off he had told himself that evening at the station that all was over and that they would never meet again. But how far they still were from the end!

She stopped on a dark, narrow staircase with a notice over it: "To the Upper Circle."

"How you frightened me!" she said, breathing heavily, still looking pale and stunned. "Oh dear, how you frightened me! I'm scarcely alive. Why did you come? Why?"

"But, please, try to understand, Anna," he murmured hurriedly. "I beg you, please, try to understand. . . . "

She looked at him with fear, entreaty, love, looked at him intently, so as to fix his features firmly in her mind.

"I've suffered so much," she went on, without listening to him. "I've been thinking of you all the time. The thought of you kept me alive. And yet I tried so hard to forget you—why, oh why did you come?"

On the landing above two schoolboys were smoking and looking down, but Gurov did not care. He drew Anna Sergeyevna towards him and began kissing her face, her lips, her hands.

"What are you doing? What are you doing?" she said in horror, pushing him away. "We've both gone mad. You must go back tonight, this minute. I implore you, by all that's sacred . . . Somebody's coming!"

Somebody was coming up the stairs.

"You must go back," continued Anna Sergeyevna in a whisper. "Do you hear? I'll come to you in Moscow. I've never been happy, I'm unhappy now, and I shall never be happy, never! So please don't make me suffer still more. I swear I'll come to you in Moscow. But now we must part. Oh, my sweet, my darling, we must part!"

She pressed his hand and went quickly down the stairs, looking back at him all the time, and he could see from the expression in her eyes that she really was unhappy. Gurov stood listening for a short time, and when all was quiet he went to look for his coat and left the theatre.

IV

Anna Sergeyevna began going to Moscow to see him. Every two or three months she left the town of S—, telling her husband that she was going to consult a Moscow gynaecologist, and her husband believed and did not believe her. In Moscow she stayed at the Slav Bazaar and immediately sent a porter in a red cap to inform Gurov of her arrival. Gurov went to her hotel, and no one in Moscow knew about it.

One winter morning he went to her hotel as usual (the porter had called with his message at his house the evening before, but he had not been in). He had his daughter with him, and he was glad of the opportunity of taking her to school, which was on the way to the hotel. Snow was falling in thick wet flakes.

"It's three degrees above zero," Gurov was saying to his daughter, "and yet it's snowing. But then, you see, it's only warm on the earth's surface, in the upper layers of the atmosphere the temperature's quite different."

"Why isn't there any thunder in winter, Daddy?"

He explained that, too. As he was speaking, he kept thinking that he was going to meet his mistress and not a living soul knew about it. He led a double life: one for all who were interested to see, full of conventional truth and conventional deception, exactly like the lives of his friends and acquaintances; and another which went on in secret. And by a kind of strange concatenation of circumstances, possibly quite by accident, everything that was important, interesting, essential, everything about which he was sincere and did not deceive himself, everything that made up the quintessence of his life, went on in secret, while everything that was a lie, everything that was merely the husk in which he hid himself to conceal the truth, like his work at the bank, for instance, his discussions at the club, his ideas of the lower breed, his going to anniversary functions with his wife—all that happened in the sight of all. He judged others by himself, did not believe what he saw, and was always of the opinion that every man's real and most interesting life went on in secret, under cover of night. The personal, private life of an individual was kept a secret, and perhaps that was partly the reason why civilized man was so anxious that his personal secrets should be respected.

Having seen his daughter off to her school, Gurov went to the Slav Bazaar. He took off his fur coat in the cloakroom, went upstairs, and knocked softly on the door. Anna Sergeyevna, wearing the grey dress he liked most, tired out by her journey and by the suspense of waiting for him, had been expecting him since the evening before; she was pale, looked at him without smiling, but was in his arms the moment he went into the room. Their kiss was long and lingering, as if they had not seen each other for two years.

"Well," he asked, "how are you getting on there? Anything new?"

"Wait, I'll tell you in a moment. . . . I can't . . . "

She could not speak because she was crying. She turned away from him and pressed her handkerchief to her eyes.

"Well, let her have her cry," he thought, sitting down in an armchair. "I'll wait."

Then he rang the bell and ordered tea; while he was having his tea, she was still standing there with her face to the window. She wept because she could not control her emotions, because she was bitterly conscious of the fact that their life was so sad: they could only meet in secret, they had to hide from people, like thieves! Was not their life ruined?

"Please, stop crying!" he said.

It was quite clear to him that their love would not come to an end for a long time, if ever. Anna Sergeyevna was getting attached to him more and more strongly, she worshipped him, and it would have been absurd to tell her that all this would have to come to an end one day. She would not have believed it, anyway.

He went up to her and took her by the shoulders, wishing to be nice to her, to make her smile; and at that moment he caught sight of himself in the looking glass.

His hair was already beginning to turn grey. It struck him as strange that he should have aged so much, that he should have lost his good looks in the last few years. The shoulders on which his hands lay were warm and quivering. He felt so sorry for this life, still so warm and beautiful, but probably soon to fade and wilt like his own. Why did she love him so? To women he always seemed different from what he was, and they loved in him not himself, but the man their imagination conjured up and whom they had eagerly been looking for all their lives; and when they discovered their mistake they still loved him. And not one of them had ever been happy with him. Time had passed, he had met women, made love to them, parted from them, but not once had he been in love; there had been everything between them, but no love.

It was only now, when his hair was beginning to turn grey, that he had fallen in love properly, in good earnest—for the first time in his life.

He and Anna Sergeyevna loved each other as people do who are very dear and near, as man and wife or close friends love each other; they could not help feeling that fate itself had intended them for one another, and they were unable to understand why he should have a wife and she a husband; they were like two migrating birds, male and female, who had been caught and forced to live in separate cages. They had forgiven each other what they had been ashamed of in the past, and forgave each other everything in their present, and felt that this love of theirs had changed them both.

Before, when he felt depressed, he had comforted himself by all sorts of arguments that happened to occur to him on the spur of the moment, but now he had more serious things to think of, he felt profound compassion, he longed to be sincere, tender. . . .

"Don't cry, my sweet," he said. "That'll do, you've had your cry. . . . Let's talk now, let's think of something."

Then they had a long talk. They tried to think how they could get rid of the necessity of hiding, telling lies, living in different towns, not seeing one another for so long. How were they to free themselves from their intolerable chains?

"How? How?" he asked himself, clutching at his head. "How?"

And it seemed to them that in only a few more minutes a solution would be found and a new, beautiful life would begin; but both of them knew very well that the end was still a long, long way away and that the most complicated and difficult part was only just beginning.

JOURNAL WRITINGS

1.   List some of the elements you think each partner should contribute toward a happy or satisfying marriage. Write a paragraph or two applying these elements to the respective marriages of Gurov and Anna, giving some reasons why each marriage appears to be unhappy.

2.   While Anna and Gurov enjoy some fun together, painful aspects of their relationship seem almost continually present. Write a paragraph discussing the obvious as well as the more subtle **causes** of their suffering. Write a second paragraph detailing other kinds of suffering that may occur even in a "legitimate" love relationship.

BRAINSTORMING AND DRAFTING

3.   In the reading by Robert Solomon at the beginning of this unit, review his comments under his subheading "The Ontology of Loneliness." **Summarize** Solomon's model and discuss whether or not this model of "love" helps to explain the relationship between Anna and Gurov.

4.   Review Simone de Beauvoir's portrait of the traditional woman's dependency. To what extent does Anna conform to de Beauvoir's portrait? Draft a paragraph explaining your answer in detail.

THE AUTHOR'S METHODS

5.   Chekhov often uses oppositions to dramatize an idea. One such opposition appears in his "romantic" **allusions** (to love, physical or sensual features, beautiful nature images, fragrances, etc.), which are often paralleled by scenes depicting mundane, unattractive reality. Find some details in the text for each of these opposing visions. Then draft a paragraph indicating how these details help to explain both the characters and the **theme.**

6.   Write a paragraph explaining the moral issues raised by such **symbols** as the lapdog, the fence around Anna's house, her lorgnette, the headless horseman in Gurov's hotel room, or any other symbols that you feel are relevant.

How do these symbols fit into Chekhov's overall attitude toward the couple's plight?

CREATIVE PROJECT

7.   Write a sequel to the story, indicating the future development of Anna and Gurov's relationship, based on Chekhov's presentations of their characters thus far, and on the social-historical background of nineteenth-century Russia. (Consult some sources, such as *Historical Abstracts*, on the social history.)

FORMAL WRITING AND RESEARCH PAPERS

8.   In a formal paper, **analyze** the way Gurov acts in a relationship, including his relationship with his wife, with other women, and with Anna throughout the story. Discuss whether his attitudes and behavior are static (remain the same) or whether they develop (change) during the story.

9.   Using sources published in the last decade or so, find some information on adultery as a sociological or psychological phenomenon. (Consult, for example, *Psychological Abstracts* or *Sociological Abstracts* and the card or computer catalog.) In an extended paper, use some of these ideas to illuminate Chekhov's story. Some questions to help you think about the issues: (a) Can adultery ever be considered emotionally mature behavior? (b) What might be some of the motives—conscious or unconscious— behind an individual's decision to have an affair? (c) What social conditions enable affairs to flourish? (See also D'Emilio and Freedman's article.) (d) How would Augustine or modern religious officials regard adultery? You do not need to answer all of these questions or to answer them in order. You may even wish to substitute your own research question(s) instead.

Bertrand Russell

Marriage

(1929)

A man of diverse talents, Bertrand Russell (1872–1970) was born in England and educated at Trinity College in Cambridge. During his long life, he married four times and was divorced three; he had children with two of his wives. Russell held professorships at various colleges in England, China, and the United States. His published writings in philosophy, mathematics, history, and social and political science reflect his diverse intellectual interests.

Perhaps his most famous works are *A History of Western Philosophy* and *Principia Mathematica.* Among his many awards is the Nobel Prize for Literature (1950). Known as a great conversationalist, he often challenged popular assumptions and adopted controversial positions in his writings. The following selection, taken from his book *Marriage and Morals,* examines the "traditional" concept of monogamous marriage in the context of other societies' customs. Russell proposes what many would consider a radical change in our attitude toward marriage as an institution.

PREVIEW

Is it possible to find lifelong happiness with one partner? Why or why not?

. . . I propose to discuss marriage without reference to children, merely as a relation between men and women. Marriage differs, of course, from other sex relations by the fact that it is a legal institution. It is also in most communities a religious institution, but it is the legal aspect which is essential. The legal institution merely embodies a practice which exists not only among primitive men but among apes and various other animals. Animals practise what is virtually marriage, wherever the cooperation of the male is necessary to the rearing of the young. As a rule, animal marriages are monogamic, and according to some authorities this is the case in particular amongst the anthropoid apes. It seems, if these authorities are to be believed, that these fortunate animals are not faced with the problems that beset human communities, since the male, once married, ceases to be attracted to any other female, and the female, once married, ceases to be attractive to any other male. Among the anthropoid apes, therefore, although they do not have the assistance of religion, sin is unknown, since instinct suffices to produce virtue. There is some evidence that among the lowest races of savages a similar state of affairs exists. Bushmen are said to be strictly monoga- mous, and I understand that the Tasmanians (now extinct) were invariably faithful to their wives. Even in civilized mankind faint traces of a monogamic instinct can sometimes be perceived. Considering the influence of habit over behaviour, it is perhaps surprising that the hold of monogamy on instinct is not stronger than it is. This, however, is an example of the mental peculiarity of human beings, from which spring both their vices and their intelligence, namely the power of imagination to break up habits and initiate new lines of conduct.

It seems probable that what first broke up primitive monogamy was the intrusion of the economic motive. This motive, wherever it has any influence upon sexual behaviour, is invariably disastrous, since it substitutes relations of slavery or purchase for relations based upon instinct. In early agricultural and pastoral communities both wives and children were an economic asset to a man. The wives worked for him, and the children, after the age of five or six, began to be useful in the fields or in tending beasts. Consequently the most powerful men aimed at having as many wives as possible. Polygamy can seldom be the general practice of a community, since there is not as a rule a great excess of females; it is the prerogative of chiefs and rich men. Numerous wives and children form a valuable property, and will therefore enhance the already privileged position of their owners. Thus the primary function of a wife comes to be that of a lucrative domestic animal, and her sexual function becomes subordinated. At this level of civilization it is as a rule easy for a man to divorce his wife, though he must in that case restore to her family any dowry that she may have brought. It is, however, in general impossible for a wife to divorce her husband.

The attitude of most semi-civilized communities towards adultery is of a piece with this outlook. At a very low level of civilization adultery is sometimes tolerated. The Samoans, we are told, when they have to go upon a journey, fully expect their wives to console themselves for their absence.* At a slightly higher level, however, adultery in women is punished with death or at best with very severe penalties. Mungo Park's account of Mumbo Jumbo used to be well known when I was young, but I have been pained in recent years to find highbrow Americans alluding to Mumbo Jumbo as a god of the Congo. He was in fact neither a god nor connected with the Congo. He was a pretence demon invented by the men of the upper Niger to terrify women who had sinned. Mungo Park's account of him so inevitably suggests a Voltairean view as to the origins of religion that it has tended to be discreetly suppressed by modern anthropologists, who cannot bear the intrusion of rational scoundrelism into the doings of savages. A man who had intercourse with another man's wife was, of course, also a criminal, but a man who had intercourse with an unmarried woman did not incur any blame unless he diminished her value in the marriage market.

---

* [Author's Note] Margaret Mead, "Coming of Age in Samoa," 1928, p. 104 ff.

With the coming of Christianity this outlook was changed. The part of religion in marriage was very greatly augmented, and infractions of the marriage law came to be blamed on grounds of taboo rather than of property. To have intercourse with another man's wife remained, of course, an offence against that man, but to have any intercourse outside marriage was an offence against God, and this, in the view of the Church, was a far graver matter. For the same reason divorce, which had previously been granted to men on easy terms, was declared inadmissible. Marriage became a sacrament and therefore lifelong.

Was this a gain or a loss to human happiness? It is very hard to say. Among peasants the life of married women has always been a very hard one, and on the whole it has been hardest among the least civilized peasants. Among most barbarous peoples a woman is old at twenty-five, and cannot hope at that age to retain any traces of beauty. The view of woman as a domestic animal was no doubt very pleasant for men, but for women it meant a life of nothing but toil and hardship. Christianity, while in some ways it made the position of women worse, especially in the well-to-do classes, did at least recognize their theological equality with men, and refused to regard them as absolutely the property of their husbands. A married woman had not, of course, the right to leave her husband for another man, but she could leave him for a life of religion. And on the whole progress towards a better status for women was easier, in the great bulk of the population, from the Christian than from the pre-Christian standpoint.

When we look round the world at the present day and ask ourselves what conditions seem on the whole to make for happiness in marriage and what for unhappiness, we are driven to a somewhat curious conclusion, that the more civilized people become the less capable they seem of lifelong happiness with one partner. Irish peasants, although until recent times marriages were decided by the parents, were said by those who ought to know them to be on the whole happy and virtuous in their conjugal life. In general, marriage is easiest where people are least differentiated. When a man differs little from other men, and a woman differs little from other women, there is no particular reason to regret not having married some one else. But people with multifarious tastes and pursuits and interests will tend to desire congeniality in their partners, and to feel dissatisfied when they find that they have secured less of it than they might have obtained. The Church, which tends to view marriage solely from the point of view of sex, sees no reason why one partner should not do just as well as another, and can therefore uphold the indissolubility of marriage without realizing the hardship that this often involves.

Another condition which makes for happiness in marriage is paucity of unowned women and absence of social occasions when husbands meet other women. If there is no possibility of sexual relations with any woman other than one's wife, most men will make the best of the situation and, except in abnormally bad cases, will find it quite tolerable. The same thing applies to wives, especially if they never imagine that marriage should bring much happiness. That is to say, a marriage is likely to be what is called happy if neither party ever expected to get much happiness out of it.

Fixity of social custom, for the same reason, tends to prevent what are called unhappy marriages. If the bonds of marriage are recognized as final and irrevocable, there is no stimulus to the imagination to wander outside and consider that a more ecstatic happiness might have been possible. In order to secure domestic peace where this state of mind exists, it is only necessary that neither the husband nor the wife should fall outrageously below the commonly recognized standard of decent behaviour, whatever this may be.

Among civilized people in the modern world none of these conditions for what is called happiness exist, and accordingly one finds that very few marriages after the first few years are happy. Some of the causes of unhappiness are bound up with civilization, but others would disappear if men and women were more civilized than they are. Let us begin with the latter. Of these the most important is bad sexual education, which is a far commoner thing among the well-to-do than it can ever be among peasants. Peasant children early become accustomed to what are called the facts of life, which they can observe not only among human beings but among animals. They are thus saved from both ignorance and fastidiousness. The carefully educated children of the well-to-do, on the contrary, are shielded from all practical knowledge of sexual matters, and even the most modern parents, who teach children out of books, do not give them that sense of practical familiarity which the peasant child early acquires. The triumph of Christian teaching is when a man and woman marry without either having had previous sexual experience. In nine cases out of ten where this occurs, the results are unfortunate. Sexual behaviour among human beings is not instinctive, so that the inexperienced bride and bridegroom, who are probably quite unaware of this fact, find themselves overwhelmed with shame and discomfort. It is little better when the woman alone is innocent but the man has acquired his knowledge from prostitutes. Most men do not realize that a process of wooing is necessary after marriage, and many well-brought-up women do not realize what harm they do to marriage by remaining reserved and physically aloof. All this could be put right by better sexual education, and is in fact very much better with the generation now young than it was with their parents and grandparents. There used to be a widespread belief among women that they were morally superior to men on the ground that they had less pleasure in sex. This attitude made frank companionship between husbands and wives impossible. It was, of course, in itself quite unjustifiable, since failure to enjoy sex, so far from being virtuous, is a mere physiological or psychological deficiency, like a failure to enjoy food, which also a hundred years ago was expected of elegant females.

Other modern causes of unhappiness in marriage are, however, not so easily disposed of. I think that uninhibited civilized people, whether men or women, are generally polygamous in their instincts. They may fall deeply in love and be for some years entirely absorbed in one person, but sooner or later sexual familiarity dulls the edge of passion, and then they begin to look elsewhere for a revival of the old thrill. It is, of course, possible to control this impulse in the interests of morality, but it is very difficult to prevent the impulse from existing. With the growth of women's freedom there has come a much greater opportunity for conjugal infidelity than existed in former times. The opportunity gives rise to the thought, the thought gives rise to the desire, and in the absence of religious scruples the desire gives rise to the act.

Women's emancipation has in various ways made marriage more difficult. In old days the wife had to adapt herself to the husband, but the husband did not have to adapt himself to the wife. Nowadays many wives, on grounds of woman's right to her own individuality and her own career, are unwilling to adapt themselves to their husbands beyond a point, while men who still hanker after the old tradition of masculine domination see no reason why they should do all the adapting. This trouble arises especially in connection with infidelity. In old days the husband was occasionally unfaithful, but as a rule his wife did not know of it. If she did, he confessed that he had sinned and made her believe that he was penitent. She, on the other hand, was usually virtuous. If she was not, and the fact came to her husband's knowledge, the marriage broke up. Where, as happens in many modern marriages, mutual faithfulness is not demanded, the instinct of jealousy nevertheless survives, and often proves fatal to the persistence of any deeply rooted intimacy even where no overt quarrels occur.

There is another difficulty in the way of modern marriage, which is felt especially by those who are most conscious of the value of love. Love can flourish only as long as it is free and spontaneous; it tends to be killed by the thought that it is a duty. To say that it is your duty to love so-and-so is the surest way to cause you to hate him or her. Marriage as a combination of love with legal bonds thus falls between two stools. Shelley says:

> "I never was attached to that great sect
> Whose doctrine is, that each one should select
> Out of the crowd a mistress or a friend,
> And all the rest, though fair and wise, commend
> To cold oblivion, though it is in the code
> Of modern morals, and the beaten road
> Which those poor slaves with weary footsteps tread,
> Who travel to their home among the dead
> By the broad highway of the world, and so
> With one chained friend, perhaps a jealous foe,
> The dreariest and the longest journey go."

There can be no doubt that to close one's mind on marriage against all the approaches of love from elsewhere is to diminish receptivity and sympathy and the opportunities of valuable human contacts. It is to do violence to something which, from the most idealistic standpoint, is in itself desirable. And like every kind of restrictive morality it tends to promote what one may call a policeman's outlook upon the whole of human life—the outlook, that is to say, which is always looking for an opportunity to forbid something.

For all these reasons, many of which are bound up with things undoubtedly good, marriage has become difficult, and if it is not to be a barrier to happiness it must be conceived in a somewhat new way. One solution often suggested, and actually tried on a large scale in America, is easy divorce. I hold, of course, as every humane person must, that divorce should be granted on more grounds than are admitted in the English law, but I do not recognize in easy divorce a solution of the troubles of marriage. Where a marriage is childless, divorce may be often the right solution, even when both parties are doing their best to behave decently; but where there are children the stability of marriage is to my mind a matter of considerable importance. . . . I think that where a marriage is fruitful and both parties to it are reasonable and decent, the expectation ought to be that it will be lifelong, but not that it will exclude other sex relations. A marriage which begins with passionate love and leads to children who are desired and loved ought to produce so deep a tie between a man and woman that they will feel something infinitely precious in their companionship, even after sexual passion has decayed, and even if either or both feels sexual passion for some one else. This mellowing of marriage has been prevented by jealousy, but jealousy, though it is an instinctive emotion, is one which can be controlled if it is recognized as bad, and not supposed to be the expression of a just moral indignation. A companionship which has lasted for many years and through many deeply felt events has a richness of content which cannot belong to the first days of love, however delightful these may be. And any person who appreciates what time can do to enhance values will not lightly throw away such companionship for the sake of new love.

It is therefore possible for a civilized man and woman to be happy in marriage, although if this is to be the case a number of conditions must be fulfilled. There must be a feeling of complete equality on both sides; there must be no interference with mutual freedom; there must be the most complete physical and mental intimacy; and there must be a certain similarity in regard to standards of values. (It is fatal, for example, if one values only money while the other values only good work.) Given all these conditions, I believe marriage to be the best and most important relation that can exist between two human beings. If it has not often been realized hitherto, that is chiefly because husband and wife have regarded themselves as each other's policeman. If marriage is to achieve its possibilities, husbands and wives must learn to understand that whatever the law may say, in their private lives they must be free.

JOURNAL WRITINGS

1.   Construct your own criteria for a "happy" marriage. For example, should the partners continue to experience an ecstatic, body-tingling sensation? A feeling of contentment? Peace of mind? Should there be an absence of problems? Should the couple have a certain way of relating? What are some other signs of a happy marriage? How does your list compare or contrast with Russell's "conditions" for a happy marriage?

2.   **Define** polygamy. Could the concept work in American society today? Why or why not? Write a paragraph assessing its probable effect on personal relationships.

BRAINSTORMING AND DRAFTING

3. Russell **describes** the wives in some less civilized cultures as "economic assets" to their husbands. Propose some **specific** ways in which women in these cultures literally became economic assets. Can the modern wife also be a "lucrative domestic animal"? Explain how the modern woman's economic role in marriage is similar to and/or different from the role of women in earlier times. Provide some **examples** to support your ideas. Alternative: Can these same questions be posed about the husband's economic role in marriage? If so, you may choose to answer those questions instead.

4. "I think that where a marriage is fruitful and both parties to it are reasonable and decent, the expectation ought to be that it will be lifelong, but not that it will exclude other sex relations." Organize an exploratory debate: The class can divide randomly into two sections, with each side facing the other. All students on Side A (no matter what their own position) should list several reasons why one might *affirm* Russell's statement above, while students on Side B should list reasons why one might *deny* his contention. Then each side should alternately (a) offer one reason for its position, and (b) allow one person on the opposite side to rebut that reason. The instructor or a peer moderator should ensure that each side follows this procedure fairly. When the issues have been thoroughly explored, each student should draft a paragraph offering reasons for his or her own position.

THE AUTHOR'S METHODS

5. In the first paragraph, Russell spends several sentences telling us about animal monogamy. What is the purpose of this strategy? Does it enhance his **argument,** weaken it, or have no effect on it? Explain your answer in a paragraph.

6. List the features of a good **concluding** paragraph. Which of these features are present in Russell's last paragraph? What features does it contain that are not on your list? Write a paragraph evaluating the overall effectiveness of his conclusion.

FORMAL WRITING AND RESEARCH PAPERS

7. Write a paper in which you evaluate the problems of Gurov and Anna in Chekhov's story from Russell's point of view. Offer specific **examples** from both selections to support your ideas. (You need not agree with Russell to discuss his point of view.)

8. "The Church, which tends to view marriage solely from the point of view of sex, sees no reason why one partner should not do just as well as another, and can therefore uphold the indissolubility of marriage without realizing the hardship that this often involves." Does Russell provide any support for

this assertion in the reading? Write a paper assessing the validity of Russell's statement today. You may wish to explore whether one or more of the recent popes of the Catholic church (for example, John XXIII, Paul VI, John Paul II) have made any pronouncements or written encyclicals on marriage. Or, you could read the writings of contemporary theologians on the issue. In either case, use information from your research to substantiate your assertions.

9.   Russell objects to the English divorce laws of his time. List your own criteria for when divorce should be allowed; then do some research on divorce laws in your home state. (Ask your librarian to direct you to available sources.) Write a paper in which you explain the legal opportunities for divorce in that state, and evaluate the nature and extent of these opportunities in light of your own criteria. (You may want to revise your criteria after you have read several sources.) Try to provide a few case studies to support your ideas.

Herb Goldberg

Driving Each Other Crazy on the Way to Liberation

(1983)

A native of Berlin, Germany, Herb Goldberg (born 1937) received a B.A. from City College, New York, and a Ph.D. from Adelphi University in 1963. Currently professor of psychology at California State University, Los Angeles, he also maintains a private practice in psychotherapy and has written several books for a lay audience on psychological and sociological topics. Two of these books focus on the male experience: *The Hazards of Being Male* (1976) and *The New Male: From Self-Destruction to Self-Care* (1979).

In *The New Male-Female Relationship,* from which the following selection is taken, Goldberg explores the crises that can occur in love relationships when sex roles fluctuate in response to rising consciousness. Believing themselves liberated, both men and women may act in contradictory ways, which can spark confusion, anger, and resentment when the behavior is not sufficiently understood.

PREVIEW

How "liberated" are you from the traditional male or female sex role? Using a scale of one to ten (one being most traditional and ten being most liberated), give yourself a rating and provide reasons for your choice.

Ambivalence in the man-woman relationship in this era of women's and men's liberation seems commonplace. Intense passion, euphoria, and commitment are followed by withdrawal into oneself, intellectualizing, threatening, or severing the relationship; the pattern is one of coming close, then backing away. We emerge like wounded, self-protective children from our safe corners, just long enough to test our latest fantasy and to momentarily risk being open and vulnerable. More often than not we retreat feeling wounded again and disillusioned.

Those who are in a committed relationship fantasize leaving and being "free" again. They find their emotions and responses toward their partners swinging between extremes: they feel close then totally distant, loving then hateful, with warm attraction changing into cold detachment, insecure clinging becoming defensive autonomy. Those who are unattached find endless reasons not to get emotionally involved with the latest possible partner.

The ideologies of liberation are a major element in producing this "crazy-making" ambivalence. In a time of awakening to the issues, we come to see the problems and the theoretical solutions intellectually, but our intellectual vision is advanced far beyond our emotional development. As a result our intellectual awareness demands a form of relationship that is often in complete contradiction to our deeper cravings and capacities.

Thus, when one part of oneself is satisfied, another part feels deprived, threatened, or resentful. Nothing feels completely right or enough, so we drive each other and ourselves crazy with double messages and conflicting expectations. We ask for something, then react negatively when we get it. "Don't treat me like a child, but take care of me!" she says. "Be independent, but need me!" is his refrain.

Writer Phyllis Raphael disclosed, "I am tired of being a lonely, self-reliant adult. I am bored with liberation. I am fed up with sexual freedom and sick to death of a life without commitment. . . . I am no longer able to live by the old rules, but I cannot find any new ones that work either, and it is driving me crazy. What the answer is I do not know, but I am beginning to believe I am too frightened ever to love anyone again, and that scares me more than words can say. I am a lonely, self-reliant adult. Quite frankly, I despise it."[1]

An article recently published on the contemporary male's dilemma expressed a comparable mood: "These are dark days for love. . . . Today there is heat without adhesion. Men and women circle each other, wrestlers on guard, costumed and self-conscious. . . . [They] fall to the mat—in an embrace or a headlock, depending on whose side you're on. It is over in seconds. Next! . . . It used to happen some other way, didn't it?"

The male writer concludes, "He knows that if he waits much longer, that if he doesn't soon find this woman, his years will be filled with no more than a series of fast-fading images. . . . His life will be no life at all."[2]

This driving yourself and others crazy on the way to liberation is painful, yet natural in a period of transition. On the one hand, it seems inherent in the human experience to be constantly pulled between the poles of security and desire for growth, between intimacy needs and the lust for freedom. It is also in the nature of an intellectualized society such as ours that we are torn between our emotions and our expectations and attitudes. The many variations on the theme might include the "liberated" woman who still blames men for all her problems just like the traditional woman, or the "liberated" man who deludes himself into believing that he is giving up some control when he tells his lover to take the initiative sexually tonight. There is the woman who claims both the rights of liberation and the prerogative of being put first because she's a woman; and the man who discusses his feelings, but in an intellectual way. There is the "liberated" woman who creates and uses the aura of being assertive, independent, and sexual to make herself more attractive to men in order to more rapidly achieve the traditional goal of getting married to a successful man and being taken care of. She exposes her true motives and her facade of being liberated when, on failing to reach her goal of marriage or exclusivity, she angrily abandons a relationship she ostensibly was involved in for its own sake, and not to get a husband. Her counterpart is the "liberated, gentle" man who uses a facade of warmth, sensitivity, eye contact, and "understanding the woman's plight" to gain the traditional masculine goal of seduction more easily and less expensively than he could were he playing by traditional rules. He exposes his true motives when he quickly pulls away from the relationship after he has accomplished his goal or been denied it.

Contradictions and hypocrisies, conscious and otherwise, abound. In addition, what we believe is our visionary intellectual awareness may simply be a defensive denial of opposite feelings inside ourselves, rather than a genuinely humanistic impulse. Much of liberation rhetoric contains a protesting-too-much quality that deserves a skeptical response. It encloses and narrows, rather than opening and expanding.

True growth is largely a gradual, even imperceptible, nonintellectual process. Hence the gap between "enlightened" attitudes and less conscious emotional reactions is probably largest in those who make their leaps into "awareness" dramatically and rapidly—the result of a "click experience" coming as a powerful defensive reaction against the painful strictures of one's past, rather than developing out of an objective perspective and a slow, genuine growth process leading to wholeness. They develop counterdefenses to their original gender defenses. Genuine closeness becomes almost, if not totally, impossible, as every response is eventually found objectionable and every person of the opposite sex is found wanting.

Conflicting messages between the sexes, therefore, become the norm in this time of transition. We move rapidly between reaching out and pulling away, depending on whether our minds or our emotions are prevailing. Defensive protections against this confusion develop and they make our intimate man-woman encounters progressively more unstable and short-lived. If Los Angeles, where I live, is any indication, the total coupling sequence, from excitement to boredom to rage, which used to take years, is now often being played out in the span of one weekend.

THE WAYS *SHE* DRIVES *HIM* CRAZY

Torn between her old and new selves, the woman reviles and mocks the sexist macho, but then finds herself equally offended by the man who is consciously working to liberate himself in order to be what she claims to want. Repulsed by the "liberated" male, she may find, suddenly and confusingly to herself and others, that Mr. Macho begins to look good again. She protests the lack of emotional expressiveness and vulnerability in the male, but, as one woman in a moment of unadorned truth said, "I'm so sick of the bleeding-heart men who want to tell you how they feel all the time—to 'share themselves.' God, I start to miss the old-time guy who kept his feelings to himself."

Child care and the sharing of this responsibility is a major issue for the emerging woman. Here again, however, the man who buys into this demand for major involvement in the child-raising process might find himself receiving subtle or even direct communications of resentment. Feminist Robin Morgan articulated the basis for this sentiment: "Motherhood is the one area where *we're* raised to have some power, and sure, we're ambivalent about sharing it." Describing her own experience of letting her husband care for their infant son while she was on a lecture tour, she said, "You *do* regret that someone else was there when the baby took his first step."[3]

Well-known writer Jane Howard traveled cross-country to research her book on women. She was sometimes accompanied by her lover. On the trip, he was in the supportive role traditionally played by women who accompany their men on business trips. "While she interviews and leaps from place to place he sightsees, museum hops, waits in hotel rooms for her return. Mostly they do not get along well and the irony of role reversal escapes nobody. She is hypercritical; he cannot drive a car and she cannot stand it. She doesn't realize, however, that her own clashing needs and sensibilities are one of the more poignant themes of the book—the dilemma of the self-governing woman whose extreme competence only makes her more intolerant of her man's shortcomings. After all, the confusion wails, he's a man and he *should* be smarter, stronger, better than I. Autonomy vs. take-care-of-me. Surely a contemporary dilemma" was the way the female writer analyzed it.[4]

One forty-seven-year-old man, embittered by what he felt were the hypocritical responses of his own wife and other women he knew, wrote the following:

One of the things that I have learned about people over the years is that they lie a great deal. You can't go by what they say—only on what they do. You say that "women are eager to see men change." They might say this to you but I invite you to look at the reality. The macho man is still the man who gets the most pussy. Women—especially the feminists—talk and talk about the man who can cry, who is in touch with his emotions, etc., but the guy they climb into bed with is the guy with the fewest feminine characteristics. Actually, it would seem as if the arrow of evolution itself is inexorably pointed in the direction of macho. Since the macho man is going to get more pussy than the non-macho, his characteristics are more likely to be perpetuated since he is going to have more children. Also, whether he is around or not, his children will be raised by a mother who admires macho and will steer her sons in that direction.

Women want to mate with men who have power or the appearance of it. While it is rare that non-macho types have power, it is possible and has happened—largely through accidents of royal birth in the past and bureaucratic staying power in the present. I have the impression that these kinds of freaks are able to get few women in spite of their power. One reads of the effete nobleman whose conjugal duties are taken over by a gardener, etc.

Several weeks ago, my wife to whom I've been married for 21 years and I were in a restaurant late at night. Some young punk made some remarks to her. She never did tell me exactly what he said. She demanded that I take action. Well, yes, I scared the hell out of him and he ran away. Do you think I enjoyed my meal? I shook all the way through it. I expected a gang of guys to be waiting when we got out. All through the meal I fingered my pocket knife and planned street-fight strategy. Nothing happened. Do I like the macho role? Hell, no! But what else is there? I will play any role my wife wants me to play. This year she passed me in income. She can drive better than I can. She can operate any machinery I can operate. But I still am the one she looks to for protection.

Actually, when you talk about less macho, you are simply saying that young men should act more like old men. Do women really want this? Not on your life!

Perhaps the dilemma many men find themselves in today is most graphically reflected in a comment by a woman who was leaving her husband. In desperation, he asked her, "If I change the way I am, can we make it?" to which she replied, "My list of resentments would only grow in a new way."

Some women *seem* to transcend this time of confusion by making a leap into macho defenses. They rigidly deny their dependency, emotions, and fears. Then they pay the price that men do—loneliness, a driven goal-oriented life-style, and a lack of sensitivity to their impact on the men who flee from relationships with them.

As female machos, they experience the world much the same way as the masculine male. They protest that they have it as bad as the contemporary man, and indeed they do. Macho can exist in male or female. It is a set of defense mechanisms against experiencing and acknowledging needs, vulnerability, dependency, fear, passivity, emotion. The sum of these defenses is detached, dehumanized behavior. A woman, therefore, can be just as macho as a man, and, by the same token, a man can have feminine defenses. *It is the effect of these masculine and feminine defenses that produces interpersonal problems and distortions in awareness, not a person's gender.*

A group of men, at a communications lab for men and women interested in working toward a new man-woman relationship, confronted the women with the no-win situation they felt themselves to be in:

> You want to be related to as a separate, autonomous person and yet be taken care of at the same time. If we take you at face value and relate to you completely as an equal, you feel resentful and frustrated. If we cater to you in traditional ways, you say you feel demeaned and offended.
>
> You want us to be intimate and deeply connected to you in a relationship. If we get attached, you start feeling bored, unchallenged and engulfed, and tell us we're getting too dependent. If we resist, we are accused of being immature, narcissistic, and fearful of commitment.
>
> You want to be related to as a person, not a sex object, but then you're attracted to men according to their occupational status—their positions of power and their wealth. When we relate to you in kind, you pull away in resentment and disappointment, blaming us and labeling us chauvinists.
>
> You want us to show feelings, but, on a deeper level, you still associate our display of emotion with weakness. If we show emotion, you find us weak. If the emotions are ones you don't like, such as anger, jealousy, dependency, or neediness, you accuse us of being hostile or troubled. If we control our feelings, you say we're defensive and closed.
>
> You resent and reject any expectations that you take primary responsibility for domestic chores. Yet you still see us as the ones primarily responsible for financial

support. When we do make great efforts to share in domestic responsibilities, you get critical of our competence and tend to discourage us because you say that we're intruding. If we're not good and steady providers, you lose respect and attraction for us as "men."

If we make major decisions without consulting you, you feel controlled. If we don't make the decisions, or put the responsibility in your lap, you see us as indecisive and unsure of ourselves.

If we don't hang out with male friends, you say you want us to, and even complain that we're always underfoot. If we do have close friends and we invest time and emotion in these relationships, you complain of being neglected and suggest that our behavior is immature and even suggestive of latent homosexuality.

If we're sexually aggressive, you react negatively to our "demanding, pressuring behavior." If we aren't sexually aggressive or wait for you to do your share of the initiation of sex, you see us as ineffectual, passive, unmasculine lovers.

You want us to be more sexually relaxed and sensual and less goal driven and performance conscious. Yet you're upset and wonder what's wrong when we don't have an erection. You still expect us to be fine sexual performers.

You encourage us to work less, but you don't make concrete proposals on ways to spend less money. If we continue to work hard, you see us as obsessed with money, success and ambition, and avoiding the relationship. If we start to play more and work less, we get overwhelmed with the anxiety and responsibility of being the primary support for the family because you're not really taking up enough of the slack.

You complain about the lack of communication. When we say, "Okay, let's try. What do you want to talk about?" you say, "I don't know. You start."

You tell us you want to know when we're angry. If we do risk expressing strong angry reactions, you respond by withdrawing, crying, blaming, and accusing us of being hostile and insensitive.

If we're dominant in the relationship, you say we're being controlling. If we give up being dominant, often nothing happens because you don't fill the vacuum, and you see us as being weak.

If we say we want to be nurtured and taken care of, you see us as dependent and demanding. If we resist being vulnerable by not revealing our needs, you say we're afraid of exposing ourselves and getting close.

You say you want us to be spontaneous and real in interacting with you. If we are, however, and "being real" includes behavior and language that you don't like or you consider to be sexist, you become critical and judgmental of us. You're really telling us that you want us to be "real," but only in ways that please you.

You want us to be ambitious and successful, but still be relaxed, intimate and connected. You want us to be the "best of all possible worlds" in a way that it is impossible. You want a warm, intimate being and a world-beater all rolled up in one, and that doesn't exist.

THE WAYS *HE* DRIVES *HER* CRAZY

The history of men driving women crazy with double messages on their path to liberation is briefer and less well documented because the women's movement and changes have a twenty-year history, while men's consciousness raising has only begun recently. Even the awareness of any need for change is still being resisted by many men.

Whereas women's conflicts leading to crazymaking responses center on issues of taking control, being direct and assertive, owning their sexuality, and expressing aggression, men's conflicts are founded in the opposite issues. Men on the way to liberation are trying to discover *how to let go* of rigid tendencies to control and be autonomous, unemotional, unneeding, aggressive, sexually driven, and invulnerable, while at the same time retaining a sense of safety, of being appropriately masculine, attractive to women, and respected by men and women alike.

On a deeper level still, a man may want to free himself up, yet hold on to the excitement his masculine orientation provides him through continuous challenges and battles. Furthermore, his desire to see the woman change and become an equal partner conflicts with a reluctance to lose the power and control over her that he feels guarantees her attachment and continuing interest.

Unlike the contemporary women who feel that their growth takes precedence over their relationship with a man, most men fear changing in a way that will jeopardize their attractiveness to a woman. This, of course, is the key difference in the quality and quantity of women's and men's attempts at change today. Psychologically, he is significantly more isolated and less capable of forming meaningful relationships than she, and therefore significantly more dependent on her, in the deepest sense, than she is on him. Because *he needs her significantly more than she needs him, he fears changing in a way that might alienate her.*

As he struggles to change, he drives her crazy with his own contradictory messages. He conveys that he wants a woman to be strong, independent, and assertive, but then becomes romantically attracted to the woman who plays the traditionally feminine games of being adoring and submissive. This bind was expressed cogently by a woman who had worked hard and honestly to become everything a desirable yet autonomous person should be. She was self-reliant yet nurturing and caring, the kind of woman who could head a corporation and still love being at home with her children. She said "So, now he says I've become *too much* for him. When I'm passive, I'm boring. When I'm strong, I'm too threatening."

A twenty-eight-year-old, unmarried professional woman described the disappointment she felt with a man she was beginning to become fond of:

> On a recent trip I was on, an interesting incident happened. The first night that we went out to dinner we ate at a very expensive restaurant. Cliff picked up the tab for it. The second night, we also ate in a very expensive restaurant. When it came time to pay the bill I said, "I'd like to pay for dinner tonight." He made a very mild protest and then he let me pay. If he had really pushed the point, I wouldn't have gotten him into an embarrassing situation. I'd have let him pay for the dinner and talked to him about it later. But he didn't. I thought that it was really neat that somebody with a lot of traditional views could let this happen, and I was going to compliment him about it later.
>
> I got home and I opened up my cigarette case and there was the money for the dinner that he had slipped in. The first thought I had was that it was very much like

something my father would do to me when I was a little girl. He'd let me pay for something, and later I'd find the money somewhere. . . . It's something that you do that's nice for a little child, but it's not something that you do for an adult person that you respect. It's not just how men see women. It's how they are refusing to see women too that I think is equally as important.

A married woman in the process of investing considerable time and energy in her career found herself experiencing intense anger over the bind she found herself in. "I'm expected to be affectionate, devoted to my family, and at the same time I know that society doesn't put much value on that, though they pay some lip service to it. If I'm not constantly affectionate, close, and loving, then I'm a failure as a woman. If I do make that my primary thing, then I'm taken for granted and considered a failure as a person. Periodically, when I get in touch with what's happening, I can barely contain the rage I feel inside me over being trapped like this."

The dominant, excruciating threat to women involves the struggle to develop their autonomous strength and yet retain their lovability and attractiveness to men, and to themselves. They experience the hypocritical reactions of men who praise them yet hotly pursue the old-time *femme fatale*. Small wonder many become embittered, like the sensitive man who finds himself being ignored by women.

One woman writer called these "perilous times—women will have to stick it out, learn to survive the fear that independence and self-definition can only be had at the expense of love and warmth."[5]

Dr. Robert Tucker, associate professor of psychiatry at Yale University, who along with his psychologist wife, Dr. Leotta Tucker, developed "Black love" workshops to help close the gap between black men and women, described the double-bind the strong black woman finds herself in today: "Men often commend black women for their strength, but their admiration is not demonstrated in the ways they relate to women. They resent black women for not being soft and submissive. In a sense, they are asking women to be all things."[6]

Dr. A. Poussaint, a Harvard psychiatrist, also commented on the black man's attitude toward strong women: "Men get upset when women seem to be competitive with them in every day kinds of ways, by challenging them, by testing their personhood, their self-esteem, touching off insecurities, when there seems always to be some one-upmanship going on in the relationship."[7]

Women at the communications lab previously referred to in this chapter confronted the men with the no-win situation they were finding themselves placed in by them:

You tell us you want us to be directly, assertively, and openly sexual and then you become passive, intimidated, and rejecting when we do. If we're directly sexual, you're turned off or threatened by the absence of challenge and seduction, even though you tell us you like the honesty. If we're less sexually available, you accuse us of playing games.

You want us to take responsibility, pay for ourselves, and not lean on you for support. Yet you're threatened and resentful if that process takes us away from you in terms of time, emotional involvement, or our need for you. In other words, you want us to have our own means of support, but to treat our jobs as if they were avocations that did not take anything away from you. You don't want our independence to develop to the point where we're no longer dependent on you, because you're afraid we may come to realize that we don't need or even like you at all.

If we're available to you and cater to your needs, you take us for granted and even lose respect for us. If we don't attend to you, you accuse us of being selfish and rejecting.

You want us to handle our outside work without expressing frustrations or feelings about it. You lecture us about the ways of the world and on how to be more objective, pragmatic, and self-serving. If we listen to you and adopt that style and become ambitious and successful, you call us cold, "ballbreakers," and "unfeminine."

You want us to take responsibility for decisions and for structuring the time when we're together. When we do, and we tell you what we've planned, you react critically because our plans are different from what you would have planned, or you're just uninterested. If we don't make decisions or plans, you attack us for not taking responsibility, for being boring, and for lacking imagination.

You tell us you want us to know what makes us angry and to express that to you directly. When we do, you accuse us of being hostile, rejecting, judgmental, and castrating. If we withhold the anger, you accuse us of being phony and manipulative, and you don't really trust us.

You want us to be more objective and logical in our approach to the relationship. When we are, you call us unfeeling, uncaring, or too detached. If we don't, you get exasperated by our "irrationality" and accuse us of being "crazy."

You want to be the central person in our lives. When you are, you feel we're too demanding of your time and energy. When we don't center our lives around you, you accuse us of being unloving and rejecting.

You want us to take care of ourselves physically, to be active and in shape. At the same time, you don't like it if you think we're going to become "jocks" or athletically competitive. If we become more athletic, you begin to relate to us as a buddy and become less attracted to us sexually. You start to look at the passive, "frail" woman on the sidelines, with her makeup and high heels, who thinks you're Superman because she's so uncoordinated. If we don't stay in shape, you accuse us of being lazy and letting ourselves go.

You say you want the relationship to be more playful and interesting. When we get really playful and loosen up, you look really uncomfortable and try to shut us down.

PARTNERS DRIVING EACH OTHER CRAZY

Striving for a liberated, equal relationship ("close but free and equal") that, at the same time, guarantees all the benefits and security of the traditional relationship is at the root of volatile, fragile, crazymaking couple interactions. He says, "I meet a 'strong' woman. The moment we get emotionally involved, however, she turns into a little girl who gives up her identity and wants to be taken care of." She says, "I meet a 'liberated' man. The moment we get involved, he wants to possess and control me; and when I give him what he says he wants—someone to love him and still let him be—he backs off and disappears."

A classic arena for such conflicting messages is sexuality. He says he wants her to be more directly sexual, and she professes to want that too. Yet when she is, he feels put upon and she wonders whether she is making herself too easily available. Further, his casual response to her new sexuality makes her feel undesirable. Being directly sexual also means abandoning a traditional source of power for her. She becomes resentful if he seems to take sex with her for granted. She tells him he doesn't have to feel pressured to perform, yet reacts negatively to his lack of an erection or arousal. He also becomes threatened and feels pressured when she begins to *expect* orgasms and slow, sensual love-making, and it tends to tense him up. He tells her he wants her to be sexual but gets aroused more by her unavailability.

In their relationship in general, they tend to become increasingly self-conscious and consequently immobilized with each other, fearful of pressuring each other and resentful of anything that suggests a sexist expectation. Her defensiveness about sexism makes it increasingly more difficult for him to ask for what he wants, even though she may tell him to be direct. He fears she will see him as demanding or as putting her in a subservient role. Likewise, she wants to be more direct and open but fears that she will offend him. So each witholds needs and feelings, and deep-seated resentments over giving but not getting develop. In addition, each wants growth and change in the other, but with no threat to his or her own security.

Michael and Debby Richards are a contemporary couple, in a volatile relationship because of these endlessly conflicting messages and impulses. They live in a small, growing community in Colorado that is rooted traditionally, yet is very much a part of the stream of new awareness about the roles of men and women.

Debby is a competition-caliber skier and part-time carpenter. Michael is a computer salesman with a quiet, introspective, and sensitive manner. Torn between their traditional-rooted needs and their newly awakened desires for liberation, they were driving each other crazy, to the point of repeated major fights in which divorce was threatened, when they consulted a therapist to help them with their relationship.

Debby, now thirty, became the mother of two children in her early twenties and had to leave college, but since developed an independent lifestyle. After several years she returned to school, and spent many hours at skiing practice and exercising to stay in condition, coming home at erratic hours. This meant that, though her husband was providing their sole financial support, he often had to prepare meals for himself and the children. Debby was insistent that her husband not have traditional wifely expectations of her and that he be supportive of her educational and athletic endeavors. She would tell him, "You got me pregnant when I was young so I couldn't finish school."

Michael, a driven businessman, was searching for ways to lighten his schedule so he could spend more time with friends and also study music. And he felt deeply hurt that his wife was seldom there to greet him or make dinner when he returned home from work.

Arguments would break out regularly as she insisted Michael was trying to control her and force her into the role of old-fashioned wife. He countered that she didn't really care about him.

Heated exchanges would also take place regarding decision making. They were selling their home and building a new one, so they needed to find a place to live in the interim. Debby would resist assuming responsibility for relocating. Michael would fume that she expected him to do everything. She would counter that whenever she did make decisions, as he requested, he was always critical of her choices. When he took the matter of relocation in hand (Debby had said, "You take care of it. Just move us in"), she resented him for not consulting her before the final decision.

Both acknowledged their interest in others sexually, but denied having had affairs. Jealousy and suspicion built until they finally decided to reveal their sexual fantasies to each other. When Debby described hers about other men they both knew, Michael acted hurt and angry. When she became reluctant to continue the discussion, he accused her, "You're holding back stuff. I don't trust you. You don't level with me."

Equally painful fights would break out over the rearing of their hyperactive daughter. Michael would accuse Debby of ignoring the girl or overprotecting her, to which Debby would counter, "You take care of her, then," whereupon Michael would call her an irresponsible mother.

Therapy for this couple required over a year of work on taking responsibility and not blaming, recognizing the double-binds they put each other in, and separating out their deeper emotional responses from their more advanced intellectual ideas about what a liberated marriage should be.

Another variation on partners' driving each other crazy with inconsistent and contradictory expectations involved a recently married couple in their late thirties who had descended from a euphoric, "magical" courtship to near violence within six months of marriage. Both had already been divorced, in order to escape very traditional marriages, and vowed never to get tied into such a structure again. Within three hours of meeting at a singles vacation resort, Victoria told Matt that she was "hot for him" and wanted to make love. Matt reacted with delight at her directness and they had passionate sex for the rest of the day. Matt was in awe of Victoria's casual use of "vulgar language" and her aggressiveness combined with womanly charm. He also admired her casual attitude toward spending money. She was the "live life to the fullest" woman he'd been looking for after fifteen years of a very traditional marriage to an "uptight, conventional woman who didn't know how to have fun."

At the time of their meeting Matt was unemployed and not looking seriously for a job. Instead, he lived on his meager savings and spent his days practicing piano and writing in his journal. Victoria thought that his relaxed attitude toward work was wonderful.

A month later, they decided to marry, convinced that each had found a "magic" person in the other. However, within three months, Matt began reacting negatively to Victoria's frank language and her "ostentatious, sexy" clothing. These were the same things that had originally delighted him about this "far-out liberated lady," as he used to describe her. Now he was calling her a foul-mouthed slut, and accusing her of acting seductive toward every attractive man she saw. He tore up and threw away the bikini that he had loved so much the day they met. He also began to criticize her for her spendthrift habits. Though she had always prided herself on her independence, she deferred to his criticism and tried to change to please him.

Victoria meanwhile was becoming increasingly irritated at Matt's passive attitude toward finding a job and his always being underfoot at their apartment. She became enraged when he went clothes shopping with her credit card.

Prior to the marriage, Matt had had numerous friends and acquaintances. Victoria had admired him for having close male friends. After the wedding, she acted suspicious and hurt when he went off to spend a day with his buddies. She called him a "latent homo" and wondered why he'd still be interested in being with his bachelor friends.

Victoria would alternate between acting tough and independent, then crying like a hurt little girl. Matt would alternate between being the macho husband-master and acting like a dependent little boy. Whichever role either played, it eventually became a source of conflict, and the fights became progressively more explosive till they reached the point of violence. These people were hopelessly entangled in the conflict between their old traditional selves and their new selves, when they decided to divorce.

Having one foot in tradition and the other in a vision of a liberated relationship, "open, honest, free, and spontaneous," many couples drive each other crazy with these contradictory expectations. The major areas of such conflicts are:

Grow (Change)
BUT
Don't Threaten My Security

Feeling expansive, secure, and optimistic, partners provide mutual encouragement to develop and change. Feeling insecure and rejected, they fear the same changes as threats to the relationship, at which time attempts are made to undermine the other person's development. If one changes, the other is threatened. When changes stop, threat turns to boredom.

Be Open and Honest
BUT
Don't Be Insensitive and Hurtful

There is a desire in every liberation-minded couple to be totally honest, to avoid the hypocrisy of being intimate and deceitful at the same time. Truth and directness can be hurtful or threatening, however. If this weren't true, the information and feedback wouldn't have been withheld in the first place. When there is openness, the other person is likely to feel hurt. If openness is avoided, there are accusations of being dishonest.

Be Free
BUT
Be Close

The hunger to be close but free is one of the most powerful forms of liberation crazymaking. The fantasy such couples have is one of intense intimacy coupled with complete freedom. Double-bind messages become rampant in this atmosphere. Accusations of engulfment and desires for freedom are followed by screams of outraged pain over feeling rejected and abandoned whenever either partner behaves autonomously.

Be Yourself
BUT
Be Appropriate and Realistic

This is the conflict between the desire to have one's partner "be real" and the desire for him or her to accommodate any changes to one's own limitations. Either way, resentment builds. Being real may provoke feelings of rejection in one's partner. The accommodation of one's changes to the limits and anxieties of the partner leads to a sense of being controlled by the latter.

Express Your True Feelings
BUT
Express Only Those Feelings That Fit My Image of You

When women and men encourage each other to share real feelings, they often really mean only those feelings that are controllable and do not impair the romantic image. Women tell men to feel free to cry or express hurt or pain, but seem to forget that being honest about feelings includes the expression of unattractive emotions and responses, including boredom, rage, confusion, jealousy, and possessiveness. These negative emotions tend to be interpreted as neurotic and hostile when they are openly expressed. Likewise, when women are open about the full range of their impulses and feelings—including boredom, horniness, resistance to playing the womanly role, interest in other men—they're met with defensive hostility.

LIBERATION PHILOSOPHY AS DISGUISED RAGE

Single men who say that all liberated women are hypocrites wanting the best of both worlds; liberated single women who say there are no good men left; feminists who are defensive and suspicious of men no matter what they do (if he's macho, he's a sexist; if he's trying to liberate himself, he's a phony) and who cloak their hostility in the abstractions and polemics of liberation philosophy; people who passionately cherish their autonomy, not allowing anyone to intrude on their space—all may be rationalizing, channeling, and thereby controlling intense internal rage toward the opposite sex. Their liberation philosophies become the means by which they transform this rage into acceptable and "enlightened" philosophical positions. While maintaining that they desire intimacy under the right conditions, they never seem to find those conditions or to meet anyone who is perfect enough. Their underlying repressed rage creates the detachment and carping that put members of the opposite sex on the defensive and make it impossible for anybody to get close without being psychologically dissected and humiliated.

In an age of transition such as we are in today, the psychological challenge is to separate out what is articulated philosophically from the emotional intent underneath it. When is a philosophical position about liberation to be taken literally, and when is it an unconsciously disguised attempt at one-upmanship designed to bludgeon the opposite sex? In the latter case, others are repeatedly placed in a position where no matter what they do (except perhaps die or disappear), they're wrong, failing, or suspect. The desire for intimacy may be expressed, but the underlying motivation is to wall oneself in and keep relationships away. A posture of constantly blaming others and the injustices of society is taken.

This can be equally true for either men or women who are involved in their own "liberation changes." The "click experience" that feminists originally defined as the moment of sudden enlightenment about sexism, an experience that many men today are also having, while being initially exhilarating and freeing, may symbolically represent the clicking of the gate to forever bar that feared intimacy with the opposite sex. The liberation philosophy thus becomes a rigid, tight system that tolerates no new or dissonant information that could alter the "enlightened" point of view. It creates permanent insulation by putting the individual behind an intricate intellectual defense structure, even though a conscious desire for intimacy is expressed.

In this sense, the newly liberated person resembles the religious fanatics who believe they are trying to enlighten and help, but who succeed only in driving others away by confronting them with their "sinful," or in this case "sexist," ways. Isolating themselves is the unconscious and ultimate intent of such liberationists. The overt message they articulate may be humanistic but the emotional tone behind it is critical, righteous, judgmental, hostile, and distancing. They cut themselves off progressively from all those who resist becoming similarly enlightened. After a while, however, they find reasons to disagree even with those who seem to hold basically the same philosophies as they do, but whom they come to see as hypocrites or as not being dedicated enough. They are left isolated on top of their own liberation mountain. Their philosophies are revealed as disguises—as barriers used to keep intimate contact away, to deny and control their own dangerous rage, and to affirm their superiority.

Much of contemporary double-binding must be viewed in this light in order to be understood. Nothing you do is right because the underlying intent of the other person is to maintain an impenetrable wall. These are men and women who have been so wounded by intimate encounters in this time of transition that they have become suspicious, defensive, and enraged. In some cases they may also fear being cannibalized by intimacy, and other threatening fantasies projected onto the opposite sex. Consequently, trying to break through their wall is exhausting and usually futile.

A common illusion is that intimacy can be had between two people who share the same philosophy about liberation and nonsexist relationships. This is a fallacy based on the confusion of process (how two people relate) with content (the philosophy they share). It is an ultimate crazymaker because of the strong feeling each has that "we *should* be able to make this relationship work because we have the same values and attitudes about roles and relationships." Sharing similar abstract ideas about liberation, however, is rarely an adequate basis for intimacy if one is "falling in love" with a philosophy that emerges from the defenses against rage and resistances to intimacy of the other. Consequently, the relationship evolves into a cold, analytic, mutually judgmental standoff.

These two people circle, observe, analyze, and criticize each other to exhaustion. Each eventually becomes disillusioned because the other isn't what he or she "pretended" to be, and the relationship "doesn't feel good anymore." Both are left with a sense of betrayal and even greater anger, disillusionment, and self-protectiveness.

Relationships are lived and defined in process ("how we feel being together"), not in content ("we both cook and enjoy playing racquetball"). In the case of the "liberated" couple, the shared ideas about relationships are often attractive and abstractly perfect, but the process between the two on a moment-to-moment basis is intellectualized, controlled, cautious, and joyless. Trying to improve the relationship by tinkering with the content only intensifies the crazymaking.

How can one determine when a liberation philosophy is defensive, a displacement of disguised rage designed to isolate the person behind a wall of superiority? If the philosophy is a cover for disguised rage . . .

- There is a tendency to think in terms of "All men are . . . " or "All women are . . . " and the only exceptions made are for those of the opposite sex who hold a philosophy identical to one's own. Eventually, those people too are found to be ideologically flawed.
- There is a sense of hopelessness about ever making a relationship work because of the supposed absence of suitably liberated partners of the opposite sex.
- When a relationship begins to sour, the philosophy or values of the other person are blamed. Frequently, there is disillusionment over the fact that the other person didn't live up to the ideals he or she espoused and wasn't the person advertised.
- In discussing philosophical beliefs about liberation with someone who holds an opposing position, there is a tendency to become irritated and to rapidly reach the boiling point, bringing an end to the discussion.
- The liberation philosophy is basically impenetrable by those with opposing ideas or information. Nothing another says seems to ever change the way of thinking or alter philosophical convictions.
- There is an attraction to literature, drama, poetry, films, and art that support the favored point of view, while ignoring, depreciating, or condemning any contrary artistic expression.
- In moods of "clarity," there is a tendency to believe the absolute worst about the opposite sex, e.g., "All men are rapists," "All women are manipulators and exploiters."
- The slightest, mildly offensive remark or behavior by a person one is involved with can transform good feelings into anger, and produce a desire

to break off the relationship entirely. All bonds are fragile, tenuous, and marked by the absence of humor and flexibility. They can dissolve overnight.

AUTHENTIC LIBERATION

The completely nonsexist, gentle man and the strong but nurturing and nonmanipulative woman are probably defensive, crazymaking imposters. In the short period of time since people have become aware of sexist issues and begun the painful, complex work of breaking through deeply rooted patterns and responses, the growth progress in everyone is erratic at best, with regular periods of regression following any positive changes. *Genuine* growth is slow, threatening, and often resisted.

The authentic transitional person is inevitably inconsistent, wavering between traditional responses and genuine change. In the process, the surfacing of anger, fear, and distrust in regard to the opposite sex is natural and genuine. The man who pretends no such anger and is consistently sensitive and nonsexist, and the woman who denies any feelings of helplessness or dependency on men, have only added on another layer of crazymaking repression, or simply are skillful manipulators of liberation images.

Resistance and ambivalence are therefore signs of authenticity. Few of us have had the kind of healthy, nonsexist upbringing needed for a smooth transition into gender-free consciousness. In fact, those who are authentically least sexist are probably those who have made no great effort to be so and are not even aware of the issues involved. Their attitude has simply emerged from a healthy upbringing that kept gender strictures to a minimum.

The raging woman who makes a ceremonial display of her autonomy and the gentle man who loudly telegraphs his sensitivity are both to be distrusted. Genuine change is a struggle and acting as if one has been transformed has as much to do with reality as television doctoring has to do with medicine. Authentic transition to liberation is raw, confusing, and tentative, but does not result in a total lack of intimacy with the opposite sex.

Dealing with the ambivalence, confusion, inconsistencies, and discomfort of this change requires, first and foremost, an acknowledgment of resistances and contradictions and an acceptance of one's limitations. Women will continue to want to be taken care of somewhat for some time, while men will have difficulty with emotional expression and will fear giving up control. This is not a liberation crime.

Authentic liberation will be recognized by its *being*, not by the *doing* of controlled, "perfectly nonsexist" acts. That is, the genuinely liberated man will generate a human atmosphere, while the liberated female will create a dynamic one that invites a strong person-to-person response, without defensiveness or intimidation or intellectualization. They will create an atmosphere that is positive and supportive, not cautious, self-conscious, or fraught with fear over saying or doing something sexist. Real change will probably be as subtle and imperceptible as the growth of a plant, rather than resulting from an obsessive hammering away at issues. The flowering will be known through its impact, which will be human-izing and comfortably egalitarian.

Notes

[1] Phyllis Raphael, "So Sane—and Going Crazy," *The Village Voice*, Oct. 20, 1975, p. 55.

[2] Lee Eisenberg, "Looking for a Wife," *Esquire*, Dec. 1980, p. 30.

[3] "The Superwoman Squeeze," *Newsweek*, May 19, 1980, p. 74.

[4] Marcia Seligson, "Author and Her Subjects Bare Souls in 'A Different Woman,'" *Los Angeles Times Calendar*, Dec. 16, 1973, p. 82.

[5] Karen Durbin, "A Woman Talks About Her Identity," *Mademoiselle*, July 1972, p. 162.

[6] "The War Between the Sexes: Is It Manufactured or Real?", *Ebony*, June 1979, p. 38.

[7] Ibid., p. 39.

JOURNAL WRITINGS

1. Write a paragraph **describing** the extent to which members of your family participated in typical sex-role behaviors when you were a child. In another paragraph, explain how you might (or do) deal with sex roles when interact-ing with your own spouse and children.
2. **Narrate** an incident you have observed that reveals a sex-role tension in a love relationship. Suggest some ways that may help to alleviate this tension.

BRAINSTORMING AND DRAFTING

3. Throughout the reading, Goldberg examines ambivalences in male-female relationships. **Define** ambivalence, and draft a paragraph in which you apply the concept to the characters in David Leavitt's story or in Anton Chekhov's story.
4. In a small group, compile a list of the sex-role behaviors of Cupid and Psyche in Hamilton's story. Working from the list, the group should then discuss these behaviors by **describing** any problems caused by the behav-iors and evaluating whether or not the problems were resolved at the **conclusion** of the story. (Or, you can do the project individually: Compile your own list, then draft a paragraph or two describing the problems, and decide whether they are resolved at the end of the story.)

THE AUTHOR'S METHODS

5. Under the subheading "Partners Driving Each Other Crazy," Goldberg **narrates** two extended **examples** in which he **describes** the problems of Michael/Debby and Victoria/Matt. In the section that follows these anec-dotes, the author moves from these concrete examples to **generalizations**

about relationship problems. Write your own extended example of a sex-role relationship problem (or expand upon the one you wrote for Journal Writing 2); then, imitating Goldberg's method, write another paragraph that generalizes on the problem in this relationship.

6.   Examine the notes at the conclusion of this reading. Find a past or current issue of one of the magazines that Goldberg lists, and read several paragraphs from an article in it. Then do the same with an academic or professional psychology journal. Write a paragraph on the differences you find between the two articles. For example, examine the vocabulary, length and structure of sentences, use of footnotes or endnotes, amount of technical information, etc. **Conclude** by explaining why you think Goldberg **alludes** to these magazines rather than to the professional journals; note also which kind of sources you would choose for an English paper and a psychology paper.

FORMAL WRITING AND RESEARCH PAPERS

7.   Write a paper in which you explore the progress or lack of progress you have made in your own sex-role behavior. Use specific **examples** and anecdotes from your own life to support your **generalizations.** (You may wish to review your answer to the Preview question for this reading—have your ideas on the topic changed after reading the selection and thinking about the issues?)

8.   Research the words of some popular love songs from early to mid-twentieth century. (Consult, for example, the *Music Index,* the *Magazine Index,* and the card or computer catalog.) Write a paper in which you **compare** and **contrast** the sex-role assumptions behind these lyrics with the assumptions behind several current love songs. **Conclude** by **generalizing** about the degree of change, if any.

9.   In groups of three or four, assume you are collaborating as editors of an anthology (a collection of articles or readings such as those in this textbook) to be used in a composition class. Conduct a library search in which everyone in the group is responsible for finding two selections for a unit on sex-role behaviors in love relationships. (Consult the *Humanities Index, Psychological Abstracts,* the *Social Sciences Index, Sociological Abstracts,* and the card or computer catalog.) The selections may be **essays** or chapters from books in any field, short stories, or poems. As a group, construct a set of criteria for choosing selections appropriate to a college composition anthology. After reading all of the selections, members of the group should choose four for the anthology. Each member should then write an individual paper in which he or she **summarizes** each of the selections chosen and explains why it was selected. Then briefly explain why each of the other selections was not included. (The project can also be done individually. If you are doing your own research, find at least six articles, and choose three for the anthology. Other steps in the project would remain the same.)

Roy W. Menninger

Decisions in Sexuality: An Act of Impulse, Conscience, or Society?

(1971)

Roy W. Menninger, M.D. (born 1926), graduated from Swarthmore College, Pennsylvania, and received his medical degree from Cornell University Medical College, New York. A practicing psychiatrist in Topeka, Kansas, Menninger has also been chief of neuropsychiatry in an Austrian army hospital. He has held many executive positions in the Menninger Foundation, an organization that studies human behavior and offers workshops on psychological issues. He has served on numerous government, private, and community boards concerned with mental health and sexuality issues. A Fellow of the American Psychiatric Association and the American College of Physicians, he has also served as consulting editor in psychiatry for the *Journal on Medical Aspects of Human Sexuality.*

The following essay examines the complex, often unconscious motives that affect our freedom to make decisions about sexual behavior. The relationship of sex with love is explored, as well as the importance of dealing with the problem openly.

PREVIEW

List some of the possible influences that may prompt a college student's decision to begin a sexual relationship.

The revolution in sexual attitudes, with a concomitant increase in the freedom to talk about sex, think about it, and even experiment with it, confronts many of us with a need for personal decisions about sexual activity, the kind and the amount, that those who knew a simpler, earlier mode of living did not have to face. The pressure for action is enormous. Daily, those in our environment barrage us with sexual imagery in the service of selling everything from cars to deodorants, from books to a sure-fire method of becoming popular. This latent interest in things sexual is vigorously mobilized by appeals to one's sense of adequacy, capacity, importance, and even one's sense of worth. Sex becomes a means of persuading, demanding, exploiting, motivating. Such widespread consumption of sexual imagery and ideas has effectively promoted the more subtle, general view that sexual experimentation is now more acceptable and justifiable than ever before. Even more insidiously, however, it has begun to imply that those who do *not* participate in this sexual freedom are the deviants.

These pleasures, these invitations, blandishments, and opportunities, all have one element in common: they appear to arise in the environment, from some source external to the self. By offering, encouraging, and persuading, they nullify the questioning doubts that may arise from within and may seriously obscure other pressing personal concerns and anxieties by recasting them in the disguise of sexuality.

Particularly for the adolescent and young adult, sexual activity is available both to express and to escape from compelling personal problems. It becomes a means, for example, that enables the dissident or angry or unhappy individual to reject the "morality of the establishment" by a sexual act. He (or she) may consider that he is "searching for his real self" through sex. Or he may become convinced that sex is the true route to "authentic relationships," that it will disclose personal reality by literally stripping away the covers that conceal; or he may believe that only through a sexual relationship will he find at last a long-sought sense of worth. Sexual activity, rationalized as an end in itself, is thus easily corrupted by internal conflicts and becomes a means to other ends that may be painful, costly, and even self-destructive.

These internal and external forces are enormously complex and operate on us in ways we do not always recognize. Without consciously deciding to do so, we may nevertheless find ourselves involved in complicated and painful situations that include sexual activity; and these "nondecisions" are made by default in response to pressures we did not understand. Even a conscious plan to embark on a sexual affair may contain the seeds of destruction if it masks elements of unsettled internal conflict.

We can therefore profitably explore the field of forces in which a decision, or nondecision, about sexuality comes to be made. This kind of analysis can offer a broader perspective of our own behavior for the tough business of managing one's life.

The first force to which I will refer is that force or a combination of forces that arises from something we call the id. It is a mythical place, but as a word it effectively captures the notion of biologically based drives or pressures that seek discharge. These inborn forces are a part of the biological given of the individual; they seek expression in whatever ways and through whatever routes may be open. This sequence is, at one and the same time, a problem for the individual to manage and an opportunity, for these forces constitute basic energies the individual harnesses to accomplish his personal goals and objectives. What the individual utilizes from the id is the energy and its propensity to seek discharge. It constitutes the fire, the steam; it keeps the personality engine going.

We group these two id forces into dichotomies variously called "love and hate," "sex and aggression," "creation and destruction," "life and death." These are words intended merely to represent ideas, not things, but here we use them to characterize the polar qualities of the instinctual forces that drive the individual's behavior. Contained and properly channeled by the mature personality, they enable us to work, love, and live in effective and mutually satisfying ways.

When neurosis, circumstance, or stress weakens the mature controls of the personality, these forces threaten to break into consciousness and produce an internal experience of great discomfort to which we give the name "anxiety." In defense against this very unpleasant emotion, we are often driven to behave in ways that are in turn potentially destructive or self-defeating. A young man, made anxious by the closeness that an intimate affair has produced, may react with a devil-may-care denial and press impulsively into a sexual experience that leads to guilt, estrangement from the girl, and even more anxiety.

A second pressure that we must take into account is one derived from another part of the personality called the superego. This portion of the personality cannot be localized anatomically; it is not palpable, although it sometimes feels as real as if it were. Rather, the term is a helpful way of grouping together some functions and some forces that we observe to have powerful effects upon a person. In nonmedical terms, the superego is the conscience, or internal policeman. It is the still, small voice inside us that says "no" as we reach for something we should not have. It is also a repository for the values we have acquired from our parents and from the socialization processes of school and society.

The superego also contains the ego-ideal, that image of perfection that guides our behavior by espousing all the values and standards to which we aspire. Violation of these internal standards produces the pang of conscience we label "guilt." By its capacity to evoke guilty feelings, our superego insures compliance to certain preset standards that, like laws passed by an earlier generation, seem immutable and unavoidable. Since the standards and values that both guide and control us are incorporated at a very young age, they are in fact relatively unchangeable and operate in subtle but compelling ways that are often beneath our conscious awareness.

Environment is the third locus of forces that act upon the individual. From the moment of birth to this present moment, each one of us is continually required to take environmental demands into account. We are aware of the many forms that they may take, but two need mention here: productivity and conformity. These things our environment expects—indeed demands them of us—and in return gives us nurture, intimacy, support, approbation, and the opportunity for participation. There is promise of status and worth—values that are important to us—but only if we cooperate.

These three forces—the id, the superego, and the environment—combine and recombine to confront the individual with a continuing need to weigh this advantage against that cost, this opportunity against that consequence. Each individual personality has evolved an executive structure that weighs these risks, chooses, and thereby maintains a balance among these myriad forces. This executive body is called the ego. In common parlance, the word has selfish and narcissistic connotations, but its technical meaning refers to the "personality management" functions performed by the individual. Maintaining this vital balance is the ego's main task. To the extent that it is successful, what we see is growth, development, maturity, and a gradual mastery of the inner and outer environments. We see all the qualities of vigor and effectiveness that we call "health." Degrees of failure by the ego to manage the many demands upon it lead to the various disablements we call disease or malfunction: the neuroses and the psychoses. But short of such seriously imbalanced states, quite normal people all have days when their balancing functions are less than adequate. At those times they experience feelings indicative of ego failure: depression, anxiety, and uneasiness. These are common feelings and are characteristic of the situation that arises when pressures from within or without are more intense than one can manage.

From this brief survey of the world of personality, we should be left with a new appreciation of the incredible burdens of management that our personality executive, the ego, must carry, and perhaps even some amazement at the degree of success that most of us experience most of the time. But for each of us, the ego is less successful in its functions in certain areas and under certain circumstances than in others. The more stable and the more supportive our family background, the fewer are these areas of trouble and the less destructive are our bouts with imbalance. Even for the stable, and certainly for the less secure among us, growth itself, and the passage through adolescence into young adulthood, is rocky, and intensifications of the pressures on the executive ego are sharp. Several observations about the problems of decision-making during this period are in order.

First, no decision occurs in the absence of conflict, and, indeed, conflict is so elemental a part of the human condition that there can be no question of avoiding it, whether we actively make decisions about ourselves or try to ignore the need for them and allow circumstances to make "nondecisions" for us. The question is not the elimination of conflict within and around us, but its management. What strategies we develop, what allies, what sources of understanding, what kinds of external supports and strengths—these will determine how successful we are and thus how well adjusted we remain.

Second, conflict, whether internal or external, invariably carries an emotional quality with it: anguish, pain, anxiety—even fear and despair. Indeed, the presence of these feelings is *prima facie* evidence of the presence of conflict, recognized or not, and their persistence or deepening is unarguable evidence of conflict denied, avoided, disguised, and unresolved. They should signal—in ourselves and in those we are concerned about—a need for additional strategies for conflict resolution and, particularly, help from someone else.

Third, it should be clear that everything we do, think, say, or feel contains elements of each of these personality and environmental forces. *No* bit of behavior can be attributed solely to the conscience, or the id, or even the environment. This position will confound those of us who insist that they are (and therefore their behavior is) solely a product of the environment—and that is where the responsibility, the fault, and the cause all lie. They fail to see the parts of themselves that also contribute to the problem, they fail to see what they do that makes matters worse, and they fail to understand their part in finding a solution or a better compromise. These failures are an easy cop-out, a serious lapse of personal responsibility.

Fourth, effective decision-making by the executive ego depends in the last analysis on our capacity for thought. Man is a problem-solving animal, and this capability is expressed in his use of the mental activity called thought. Like many obvious statements, this one seems trivial and hardly worth mention, let alone emphasis. But the sad fact is that effective thought is often absent from the scene of conflict, and the means of resolving the pressures of the ego are thereby sorely reduced or even altogether lacking.

Under certain conditions of overwhelming anxiety or confusion, and in people whose style is to act first and think second (if at all), action itself may serve to short-circuit the thinking process. Impulsive behavior then becomes a device by which to escape, not simply to avoid thinking out a better plan, but to avoid the anxiety, the intense discomfort that would accompany a confrontation with the problem and a thoughtful search for the understanding that would solve it. In this context, action to evade thought seldom solves the underlying issue, because it represents a flight from it that leaves the conflict essentially unaltered and potentially able to re-create the problem again and again.

Fifth, as with any executive decision, the better the facts are understood, the better the decision is likely to be. Unfortunately for the ego, the "facts" it needs to understand are at best only dimly seen, for the ego is only barely conscious of many of the pressures from the id, from the superego, and even from the environment. Some of these forces are quite simply unconscious, but even others, which we may be able to perceive, are badly misrepresented by that mental process of self-deceit most of us know quite well: rationalization. It is an unfortunate fact that most people are exceptionally skillful in concealing important psychological facts from themselves—even frankly denying the existence of the obvious. Observers, even relatively unsophisticated ones, are seldom as easily fooled by us as we are by ourselves. This state of affairs points to the critical importance of using the intelligence and perceptions of others to help us better understand ourselves. I will refer to this strategy again later.

How then does all this bear upon issues of sex, our focus here? Primarily in that sexual behaviors are simultaneously much more highly motivated (by the id drive), much more socially loaded (producing severe environmental pressures), and much more prone to provoke internal conflict with one's conscience than almost any other kind of behavior. Consequently, many problems involving self-esteem and value, personal judgment and feelings of fear, guilt, or anxiety are brought into sharp relief by the prospect or experience of sexual behavior. In the white-hot focus of so many colliding forces from superego, id, and environment, the ego finds decisions about sexual activity considerably more difficult, and considerably more liable to defect, than most other usual daily decisions. The five characteristics of the executive ego's decisions are particularly apparent when the decisions are about sexual behavior. They are typically conflictual and emotion-laden, expressive of internal forces of personality as well as the environment, action-provoking and thought-avoiding, and full of self-deception. It is this latter point especially that requires emphasis, for the failure of the ego to discern clearly the forces of conscience and inner conflict will inevitably lead to potentially destructive decisions based on self-deceiving rationalizations, or equally destructive "nondecisions" based on denial and impulsive, thought-free action.

The very plasticity of the sexual drive contributes to the potential for failing to recognize the inner conflicts or anxieties that may be present and critically important. The impulse of which overt sexual activity is presumably an ultimate expression is capable of protean forms. It is generally appreciated that man may express sexual feelings through art, music, or literature, in forms that reveal nothing obviously sexual.

We seem much less aware of the converse fact: that sexual behavior is a ready vehicle for the expression of feelings or concerns that are not in any sense sexual, and it is very commonly used unwittingly as a means for managing (usually poorly) personal problems that are not the slightest bit sexual in nature. Thus used, sexual activity is in no way a constructive, creative expression of love, but a repetitious, destructive expression of unresolved conflict that makes the personal problems worse and irreparably distorts one's capacity for loving sexual relationships.

Sex sometimes masquerades as love. It is sometimes an antidote for loneliness, taken as evidence of personal worth and value, or proof of existence: "If I can engage in the sexual act I must be alive." For some it is a demonstration of potency and masculine adequacy. However, the issue is not that any sexual act does indeed do some of these things; in the context of a loving relationship, it does do all of them. Rather, the issue is recognizing that we are frequently quite unaware of the extent to which illegitimate or inappropriate needs may actually piggy-back their way to expression or solution through sexual activity.

Let us consider what some of these illegitimate needs may be. First, from the environment: There is a widespread belief, reinforced by the pseudo-philosophy of *Playboy* magazine, that the "Big Orgasm" is an adequate definition of potency and a mature relationship. Its presence is a kind of *summum bonum.** This absurd criterion of maturity has created a new guilt that throws consternation into all. We may now feel guilty if we do *not* experience orgasm. Indeed, it reflects a more general view that one needs to engage in sexual activity to maintain good health. Utter nonsense! This is part of a hedonistic mythology that creeps in upon us and applies social pressure to conform. For example, the pre-eminence of the intensely focused, self-indulgent, narcissistic pleasure, which the *Playboy* concept of sex epitomizes, produces an assumption in the young inexperienced person that this is the manner in which 97 percent of the people behave. In truth, the statistics are nothing of the sort, but the unsophisticated does not know that, for he reads *Playboy* and feels compelled to behave in that way too, if he is not to suffer the pains of poor health and social ostracism. The environment thus perpetuates the mythical view that the intensity of the sexual experience has everything to say about truth, existence, and reality.

Equally vigorously perpetuated is the myth that a successful marriage

---

* *summum bonum*—"the highest good."[Eds.]

depends on a successful sex life. People who are in love usually do not complain of sexual difficulties. Those who do complain about sexual difficulties do so because they lack the warm qualities that hold a marriage together, and the sexual relationship serves to focus attention on this deficiency.

These exemplify typical current environmental pressures; there are many others with which we are familiar: such beliefs as "everybody is doing it now" or "this is the way to become a man (or a woman)." These are malicious pressures because they are hard to recognize for what they are and even harder to defeat, since they may be actively advocated by the peer culture. They comprise an important part of the external forces pressing upon an individual.

Now let us consider some of the pressures from within. Contesting the biological urge are the forces of conscience, demanding continence and restraint. At times they are consciously identified with one's parents and enhance the conflict by making sex a test of one's liberation from the family and a measure of his or her independence. Aware of a sense of dependent needs left over from childhood, an individual may use sexual behavior as a route to throw off these longings for a simple, protected past—only to select a partner who mothers him!

Even as this example suggests, sexual relationships typically embody much of one's ideas about himself and what kind of person he thinks he is or is not. Close relationships may then express a wish for a manner of being, sought but not achieved; or they may be expressive of parts of himself that he regards as highly undesirable. It is in this way that personal concerns may sneak into expression through sexual decisions, confuse both the individual and his partner about the meaning of the experience, and provoke a whole spectrum of feelings and reactions that can complicate one's emotional life and health beyond measure. In particular, these reactions often develop a compelling momentum of their own and drive the individual deeper and deeper into a relationship or a state of mind that nothing short of radical intervention will interrupt.

The sexual act sometimes becomes an arena for the expression of a neurotic need to possess, to own, to keep, to control, to dominate. Again, these are infantile needs, unresolved hang-overs from one's childhood years, and pushed toward solution through the sexual experience. Unrecognized and unfaced, they may subvert the potential for a loving relationship and precipitate a series of unfortunate and destructive decisions. Jealousy, for example, is a reflection of an intense need to own, to possess, and to keep, and it may often be underscored by a demand for sexual experience as a form of proof.

Unrequited self-needs must be considered, too. People may use sexual attractiveness as an evidence of personal worth. "If somebody will love me, then I must be worth something." The tragedy in this piggy-backed solution to the problem is that it is an unreal, temporary respite from self-doubt that leaves the basic problems untouched and creates a secondary upsurge of self-hate after the fact; for the superego then extracts its price: one feels even more unworthy, irritable, and depressed. In an effort to mitigate these feelings of self-hate, one generates the hope that next time true love will triumph and those feelings of guilt and unworthiness will be washed away. This hope is a vain one, for the destructive cycle is only set off again. Unrecognized self-needs for identity often are apparent in young boys as they engage in impulsive sexual activity and boasting to disguise a diffused, fragmented, and immature masculinity. This behavior is again reinforced by the environment and amplified by the expectations of the group, and it produces potentially difficult consequences.

Let me give you a couple of cases to illustrate some of these points.

Eileen was an attractive, young college sophomore whose attitudes of bravado and certainty contrasted sharply with her haggard and anxious appearance. She made quite a point of her extensive sexual experience and rather aggressively argued that her attitudes about free love were evidence that she rejected her parents' traditional values as phony, superficial, and utterly middle class.

She sought psychiatric help the morning after her affair with the eighth different boy in eight months. She reported that she was not able to study and her school performance had fallen so far that she was on the point of leaving before she was thrown out. She denied any particular feelings of depression, self-preoccupation, or doubt and vociferously rejected any suggestion that her promiscuity was at all unusual. She was particularly vehement in her insistence that she enjoyed sex, that she had orgasm in every sexual encounter, and that each affair was more exciting than the last. All this insistence notwithstanding, her condition continued to deteriorate. She began to drink heavily, became obviously more depressed, and even began to voice thoughts of suicide.

Only after she slept with a boy whom she said she despised did her facade of sexual satisfaction and enjoyment crack. What emerged was a poignant history that had begun with an intense affair with the first boy who had ever asked her out more than twice. When he eventually broke off with her, she denied her devastating disappointment by initiating a series of promiscuous affairs, typically with boys whose social status was lower than hers and who frequently treated her with disdain and contempt. This sequence was endlessly repeated, sustained by her fantasies that the next affair would be like the first, but at a terrible cost to her self-esteem, her ability to work, and her mental health.

Her excessive need for a loving relationship as proof of her own worth not only drove her prematurely into an involvement she was not prepared for, but left her further unable to manage the rejection and its consequences of negative judgments about her value as a lovable person. Her inability to manage this loss to her self-esteem led her into a succession of decisions that were, paradoxically, progressively more destructive. Had she had some means by which to examine the meanings of her first decision to become involved, especially after the trauma of rejection, she might have been spared the long and personally expensive course of events that followed. All of her protestations to the contrary, her sexual behavior clearly had nothing at all to do with sex as a loving and creative act.

Esther came to a large state university from a small midwest town where she had been raised by a deeply religious and controlling—but benevolent—family. She had always looked forward to college as a moment of liberation. Although she insisted that she was never happier in her life, she spent a great deal of time writing long avowals of happiness to her parents. She was apparently unaware of how lonely and homesick she felt in the wake of departing from the close-knit family where she had been the only child. She met and became deeply involved with a college senior who seemed exceedingly mature and highly attractive. When he showed some interest in her, her sense of appreciation for his attentions gave way to infatuation and then to an intensely emotional affair. What for the boy was simply a last fling before leaving college came to be her very life. When she began to fear the possibility of losing him she became pregnant, although it was clear that this event was not a conscious intentional act on her part: she had "forgotten" when her safe period was.

This event forced them into a marriage that came to be grossly resented by both and ended in divorce before she was twenty. Although she eventually recovered a more mature perspective and developed a productive and satisfactory life, it was not without considerable pain to many people, great expense, and, perhaps most tragic of all, an unwanted child.

Her unrecognized and unmastered problems of separation from a close but dominating family life stimulated a series of personal decisions in which sexuality came to be the glue that would hold together a traumatized self. Since an experience as intense and ephemeral as the sexual one lacks continuity and provides no solid foundation for anything beyond biological discharge, her use of sex as a solution was foreordained to fail. It could not possibly resolve her unacknowledged conflict between her wish for independence and her wish to remain the deeply loved daughter of her parents.

In the two cases I have cited, the decision to engage in sexual behavior was powerfully influenced by conflicting but denied ideas about one's self and one's relation to other important people. The hidden nature of these persistently active conflicts led to their re-creation in the setting of an affair at school, which both reactivated and failed to solve pre-existing concerns. In turn, sexual behavior became a means for simultaneously expressing these conflicts and avoiding a conscious confrontation with them that might have led to a tempering of the disastrous consequences that followed.

Of course, any of fifty other examples could have been selected, for almost every sexual decision requires that the participants face issues and questions that are rarely fully perceived, sufficiently defined, or adequately confronted. At the critical point of passionate involvement, a thoughtful appreciation of all these parts of the decision must seem impossible, and perhaps it is—then. But one act need not lead thoughtlessly to the next with no pause for contemplation between. How is one to use these moments of reflection, if one can, in fact, catch hold of them?

Since it is our capacity for thought that enables us to work out such problems and eventually make good decisions, it is critical to consider by what means one can generate problem-solving thinking in the face of the many forces that seem to discourage it. My prescription is both simple and difficult: to find the means and the opportunity to talk—to talk with one's confidant, one's allies, one's friends, one's counselors, one's psychiatrist, and even perhaps, for some of us, one's parents. It is surprising that the universality of these problems has not led to a universal appreciation of the need to share them, discuss them, consider them, talk about them, and, finally, to think effectively about them.

Unfortunately, the opportunity for such specialized forms of talking as counseling or psychotherapy are available only to a very few, and typically only when such a serious crisis has developed that more is involved than the making of a decision. What is missing is an opportunity for all of us who are concerned about these problems, but still effectively struggling with them, to talk them out. Everyone, if his ego is to maintain that optimal balance, needs to be able to talk, to be listened to.

There is a means by which this can be done to suit the needs of ordinary people troubled with experiences and feelings and doubts about their abilities to resolve them. This means is the discussion group with one's peers—appropriately moderated by someone skilled in leading group discussions and simultaneously capable of empathy and objectivity. Such discussion groups are natural on college campuses where people of similar ages are struggling with similar problems. The gregarious nature of college life helps to break down the individualistic orientation that puts a high premium on the isolation that tends to discourage a collaborative approach to solving socio-psychological problems.

Such discussion groups cannot only provide the benefits of multiple perspectives on common problems, but also offer that special warmth and support that only a group can provide. In the course of sharing experiences and doubts, one not only discovers the unreality of the *Playboy* philosophy, but finds a different kind of genuineness and personal involvement that goes beyond the intimacy of the two-party relationship—and yet contributes a greater meaning to it. In the context of groups, the important qualities of empathy, openness, candor, and the capacity to listen to one's friends as well as one's self are rewarded, reinforced, and become a basis for more effective relationships with persons beyond the discussion group itself.

In such a context, one has the means and the opportunity for learning to use words as a way of testing alternatives, analyzing problems, and developing strategies—strategies that can help us deal more effectively with the issues of sexuality which confront us all. The group enables one to use the support a consensus can provide and adds to dimensions of self-knowledge that no amount of isolated introspection or even deep discussion with one's beloved can ever yield. In such a context one can learn to think more clearly about one's self and the world he is part of and thereby achieve a better balance in his decision-making among the ever-present forces of superego, id, and environment.

Out of such experiences can come the basis for more effective living, more mutually satisfying relationships with others, and a more accurate and comforting sense of one's self. The means to create such supportive and rewarding discussion groups are at hand: what is needed is a general recognition by students and administration alike that the needs of struggling, concerned youth in search of gratifying solutions to the problem of being human can be well met by the opportunity to talk together.

JOURNAL WRITINGS

1. List some of your values (things that are important to you) regarding love, sex, and marriage that you believe your parents would accept. In a second

list, identify the values of friends and classmates that you have accepted. Which, if any, of the values in one list contradict values in the other? Write a paragraph in which you: (a) explore why you have adopted values that differ from those of your parents, or (b) suggest some reasons why you have retained the same values as your parents, or (c) combine (a) and (b).

2. "Even a conscious plan to embark on a sexual affair may contain the seeds of destruction if it masks elements of unsettled internal conflict." In a paragraph, provide a detailed **example** of Menninger's "unsettled internal conflict" that you have observed in men or women of your own age. If possible, also **describe** an example of "destruction" (perhaps following upon one of the conflicts) that you have witnessed which illustrates Menninger's belief in the negative consequences of a sexual decision that is not truly free.

BRAINSTORMING AND DRAFTING

3. Menninger warns of the danger of self-deception in decisions about sexuality. Briefly **describe** a situation from a story, film, or television episode that illustrates the practice of self-deception (also known as "tunnel vision") in a romantic and/or sexual encounter. Draft a paragraph identifying one or more of the reasons the individual may have given for becoming involved in the encounter. Indicate the degree of freedom you believe the individual had when making his/her choice.

4. Draft a paragraph explaining how some of Menninger's ideas might apply to the type of woman de Beauvoir writes about in "The Woman in Love." Indicate the amount of freedom such a woman might feel in her intimate relationships, and provide reasons for your assertions.

THE AUTHOR'S METHODS

5. Menninger's writing is **argumentative** in that he attempts to convince us of the seriousness and complexity of the problem, and he wants us to consider his solution. A piece of writing is rarely "pure" argument, however. Write an **essay** in which you explain and give **examples** of several different writing strategies that Menninger uses to support his argument. For example, does he include **narration** (a "story"), **description** (concrete details), **exposition** (explanation), **definition**, or any other strategies? **Conclude** by evaluating the effectiveness of these writing strategies in helping him achieve his overall purpose of persuading the reader.

6. Imitate some of Menninger's strategies by writing an **argumentative** problem-solution paper on the role you think parents should have in their children's sex education. (You may already have written an introduction to this essay if you focused on the parents' role in your answer to question 5 following the D'Emilio/Freedman selection.) Remember that you need to choose writing strategies that will help convince us of the nature and complexity of the problem. As you **describe** your solution(s), make sure it/they are realistic and manageable.

CREATIVE PROJECT

7. Drawing on Menninger's ideas, write a dialogue between two unmarried people in which one is urging sexual intercourse, while the other expresses reluctance. Then write a paragraph in which you suggest the motives of each person in adhering to his or her position.

FORMAL WRITING AND RESEARCH PAPERS

8. Menninger refers to different types of guilt. Depending upon our value system, we may regard guilt as a rational and tolerable influence that guides our moral actions in sexual decisions, or as a negative, irrational, often painful force that inhibits our enjoyment—or perhaps a mixture of both. Write a paper **comparing** and/or **contrasting** the nature and effect of sexual guilt in Chekhov's "Lady with Lapdog" and Leavitt's "Territory." Use **specific** examples from the stories to support your assertions. Explain how some of Menninger's ideas could help the characters come to terms with their guilt.

9. Using a basic or developmental psychology textbook, or a specialized encyclopedia of psychology, do some background reading on the psychological concept of self-esteem. In a paper, explain the concept in detail, noting the difference between self-esteem and conceit; **describe** the methods psychologists use to measure self-esteem. In the next section of your paper, discuss some problems that might arise in a relationship when one or both parties have low self-esteem. Finally, suggest some ways of developing self-esteem, and evaluate the relative effectiveness of each method.

10. Do some research on the "encounter group," a psychological approach relying upon group interaction, which rose to popularity in the seventies but has since come under some criticism. (Consult *Psychological Abstracts,* the *Social Sciences Index,* and the card or computer catalog.) Write a paper on Menninger's proposed solution in which you incorporate your research on encounter groups. Begin by explaining the encounter method, including some of its variations. Demonstrate how Menninger's proposed solution—the formation of peer groups—is similar to or different from the encounter groups you have described. Then evaluate the effectiveness and practicality of Menninger's proposal in achieving his purpose.

William H. Masters, Virginia E. Johnson, and Robert C. Kolodny

The AIDS Virus and Sexuality

(1988)

William H. Masters (born 1915) is a well-known sex researcher, physician, and educator. After receiving a medical degree from the University of Rochester, he became a practicing obstetrician and gynecologist, as well as a professor in the same field at Washington University School of Medicine in St. Louis. The recipient of many awards, he has published numerous articles and several books. Probably his best-known work is *Human Sexual Response,* which he coauthored with Virginia Johnson; his more recent books (also in collaboration with Johnson) include *The Pleasure Bond* and *Homosexuality in Perspective.*

Virginia E. Johnson (born 1925) is a psychologist who attended Drury College, the University of Missouri, and the University of Louisville. In 1971, she married William Masters and worked with him as codirector of the Masters and Johnson Institute, a biology research foundation. In addition to the books she wrote with Masters, she has also coauthored several works with Robert Kolodny, including *Textbook of Human Sexuality for Nurses.*

Robert C. Kolodny is a physician and chairman of the board of the Behavioral Medicine Institute in Connecticut; he is also a member of the board of directors at the Masters and Johnson Institute. In addition to the books he wrote with Masters and Johnson, he is the author of other works, including *How to Survive Your Adolescent's Adolescence* (with Nancy J. Kolodny, Thomas E. Bratter, and Cheryl Deep).

The following selection, taken from *Crisis: Heterosexual Behavior in the Age of AIDS,* begins by defining the AIDS virus and explaining how several types of sexual contact enable the virus to invade the human body. Applying this physiological information to sexual behavior, the authors then explore different types of sexual choices, noting the potential consequences of each.

PREVIEW

List all the emotions you experience when you hear someone talk about AIDS or when you read a newspaper article about the disease. Why do you think you have these feelings?

AIDS is a deadly syndrome, or collection of clinical features, that is known to be caused by the human immunodeficiency virus (HIV, previously called HTLV-III or LAV). HIV damages the immune system—the system that ordinarily protects the body against infection—leaving a person especially susceptible to other infections and to a variety of malignancies. AIDS itself is actually the end stage of infection with HIV. In earlier stages of the infection, many people have no visible symptoms, whereas others experience various types of mild illness or more serious health problems that can be debilitating but do not fit the diagnostic criteria for a full-blown case of AIDS. . . . While there is some uncertainty about how many of those infected with HIV will ultimately develop AIDS, it is increasingly apparent that the majority will eventually die of this disorder.

In most cases, the AIDS virus is spread from one person to another either by sexual contact or by sharing intravenous drug needles and syringes. . . . Once inside the body, the virus vigorously attacks certain lymphocytes (a type of white blood cell), called T-helper cells, that ordinarily are the key coordinators of the immune system. The invasion is an intriguing one that is almost like a military operation. First, the AIDS virus seeks out and identifies the T-helper cells as targets. Next, it attaches itself to the outside of the cell, from which it will launch its actual attack. After penetrating the cell membrane, the virus sheds its outer protein coat, releasing a strand of genetic material called RNA (ribonucleic acid), which is transformed by a unique enzyme into several strands of DNA (deoxyribonucleic acid), another form of genetic material that carries important molecular coding for the production of amino acids and proteins within the cell. This DNA, acting something like a missile, then penetrates the nucleus of the T-helper cell, which is the heart of the cell's usual operations.

In the cell nucleus the DNA from the virus is combined with the host cell's own genetic code so that the host cell becomes, in effect, a mini-factory for producing copies of the virus. Every time the infected host cell divides, copies of the AIDS virus are produced along with more host cells, each of which contains the viral DNA code. Because the AIDS virus copying cycle is generally restricted until such time as the infected host cell is activated, the entire process can be compared to planting tens of thousands of time bombs in a territory that is being invaded in preparation for later destruction. While the activation process is not fully understood at present, it seems that other infections (including hepatitis B, herpes, and possibly syphilis) may trigger such an event, raising the possibility that other infections may trigger multiplication of previously dormant HIV infection. Once the T-helper cell is activated and the AIDS virus reproduces, the cell is killed. As a result, people with AIDS often have a low lymphocyte count. In fact, many people with HIV infection have a lowered lymphocyte count prior to getting AIDS. The drop in the number of lymphocytes may be a precursor of imminent malfunction in the immune system, since unusual infections that are often associated with AIDS are more likely to occur once the number of T-helper cells is depleted so much that the surviving cells cannot coordinate operations of the immune system very effectively.

The AIDS virus also selectively infects several other cells that are part of the immune system: B cells, monocytes, and macrophages. While these cells are not typically killed by HIV, even when it reproduces, their functioning as an integral part of the immune system is clearly disrupted. It is also thought that these cells may serve as an important reservoir for persistent viral infection in persons infected with HIV.

In addition, the AIDS virus selectively attacks, invades, and destroys cells in the brain. Though the exact mechanism of this attack is not certain at present, one line of reasoning suggests that HIV infects monocytes outside the central nervous system. The infected monocytes then serve as a sort of Trojan horse* for carrying the infection past the body's usually formidable line of defense for the brain itself, a protective filter known as the blood-brain barrier. Once inside the brain, the infected monocytes may release chemical substances that are toxic to brain cells, resulting in the various brain disorders frequently encountered in people with AIDS.

Despite uncertainties about some of the precise mechanisms involved in the biology of HIV infection, it is clear that this is a persistent infection. . . .

SEXUAL TRANSMISSION

While there is general agreement that any sexual contact involving the exchange of biological fluids from one partner to another results in a risk of HIV transmission (if one partner is infected), there is a great deal of uncertainty about the exact magnitude of risk attending various types of sexual activity. The greatest risk seems to be associated with anal intercourse, in both homosexuals and heterosexuals. This is partly because the tissue lining the rectum is relatively delicate and susceptible to tears, but it may also reflect other factors, including a difference in the pH of the rectum compared to that of the vagina, a different microbial environment, or a difference in tissue resistance to penetration by the invading virus particles.

Vaginal intercourse is also conclusively known to transmit the AIDS virus, both from man to woman and from woman to man. At present it appears that the risk of infection from vaginal intercourse is considerably lower than the risk

---

* Trojan horse—In the classical myth about the war between the Trojans and the Greeks, the Trojans took a large wooden horse into their city, unaware that Greek soldiers were hiding in its hollow body. During the night, the Greeks emerged and unlocked the protective gates of Troy, allowing the entire Greek army to enter and conquer the city. The expression is used here to suggest a force that insidiously destroys from a privileged internal position. [Eds.]

associated with anal intercourse, but this assessment is more guesswork than scientific certainty. In several studies of transmission of the AIDS virus from one spouse to the other, there has been no strong correlation with anal sex, suggesting that unprotected vaginal intercourse is also a frequent means of spreading the infection. On the other hand, it has been estimated that the risk of an infected man's transmitting HIV to a woman through a single act of unprotected vaginal intercourse is approximately 1 in 1,000, while the risk of an infected woman's transmitting HIV to a man in a single act of unprotected vaginal intercourse is about 1 in 2,000. We believe that these estimates are unduly optimistic, since we have preliminary evidence from our own research that the risk is about 1 in 400 for women and 1 in 600 for men.

It has been clearly shown that the AIDS virus is present in relatively high concentrations in the semen of infected men. It has also been shown that the AIDS virus is present in cervical and vaginal secretions, although the concentrations of the virus seem to be somewhat lower in these fluids than in semen. There doesn't seem to be any time during the menstrual cycle when the virus typically disappears, so from the viewpoint of potential infectivity, there is no such thing as a "safe" time in the woman's menstrual calendar. Because the menstrual flow carries the additional risk of blood mixing with cervical and vaginal secretions, there is a distinct possibility, as yet unconfirmed, that vaginal intercourse (or cunnilingus) during this time is more dangerous from the viewpoint of infectivity than when menstruation is not occurring.

There is much less certainty about whether HIV is spread by oral sex. The *Surgeon General's Report on Acquired Immune Deficiency Syndrome*, prepared in 1986, makes no mention of oral-genital transmission except for the following statement: "If you or your partner is at high risk, avoid mouth contact with the penis, vagina, or rectum." Various studies have found no evidence of an increased risk of HIV infection linked to oral sex. For instance, Winkelstein and his co-workers, reporting on a large prospective study of men in San Francisco (where they saw no evidence of HIV infection in heterosexual men), found that engaging in oral sex did not increase the risk of HIV infection among homosexual or bisexual men who had not engaged in anal sex.* Similarly, a study by Padian and her co-workers of 97 female sexual partners of men with HIV infection found no indication of a heightened risk of viral transmission associated with oral sex, although women who engaged in anal sex in addition to vaginal or oral sex were 2.3 times more likely to acquire HIV infection than those who did not. However, none of the women in this study participated exclusively in oral sex, so it is quite possible that fellatio with ejaculation may *transmit* HIV even though it doesn't *increase* the risk of transmission above the level found with vaginal intercourse.

---

* [Authors' Note] Unfortunately, because they quantified oral sex only in terms of "none" or "some" rather than doing a more detailed frequency analysis, their results may have masked a significant influence of oral sex. That is, it might have been revealing to look at the subgroup of men who engaged in oral sex with a relatively high frequency (e.g., 100 times per year or more) compared to those who never engaged in oral sex or those who engaged in oral sex infrequently (e.g., fewer than 12 times a year).

Despite these failures to find evidence suggesting that the AIDS virus can be transmitted by oral sex, other reports provide a different perspective. Possibly the most compelling is a 1987 study by Fischl and co-workers that found strong statistical support for a link between oral sex and transmission of the AIDS virus in a study of 45 AIDS patients and their spouses, both male and female (26 of the 45 spouses, or 58%, showed evidence of HIV infection, indicating a high rate of sexual transmission among heterosexuals).* We have also seen two cases of HIV infection in exclusively homosexual males (ages 21 and 33) who had never engaged in anal sex but participated in oral-genital sex with high degrees of frequency.

Though there is as yet no research conclusively proving that the AIDS virus can be transmitted by oral sex, we want to stress that it is a virtual certainty that this mode of spreading the infection is real. For one thing, there is no known viral or bacterial STD that is *not* spread, at least at times, by oral-genital contact. Furthermore, the difficulty of "proving" that oral-genital sex transmits the AIDS virus is largely an artifact: because it would be patently unethical to perform experiments on humans to try to prove the existence of this mode of transmission, we are forced to rely on somewhat oblique research strategies in which the actual effects of oral sex are generally masked due to other (confounding) sexual prac-tices. Finally, it is perhaps even more likely that the mucous membrane lining of the mouth will have minor cuts, scratches, blisters, or abrasions both from eating and from using a toothbrush or dental floss than it is that the mucosa of the rectum will be torn during anal sex; that such lesions would provide an easy portal of entry for the virus—carried in either semen or vaginal secretions—is essentially unarguable.

There is even more skepticism about the AIDS virus being transmitted by kissing. Here again, there is no question that this route of transmission is possible. The AIDS virus has been isolated repeatedly from saliva; other sexually transmitted diseases, including genital herpes and syphilis, can be spread in this manner; and the point just raised about the common existence of cuts, scratches, or abrasions on the lips or in the mouth is applicable, particularly in terms of "soul kissing" or "French kissing"—that is, deep, tongue-probing, saliva-mixing kisses.

Those who prefer to believe that the virus can't be spread by kissing cite two facts to make their case. The first is that the virus is present in lower concentra-tions in saliva than in semen or blood, which certainly appears to be true based on the relatively crude studies that have been done to date. However, there is probably enough live virus present to infect another person. The second fact, which is also true in a limited sense but of dubious comfort, is that so far no one has identified a case of AIDS in which kissing was the definite means of transmis-sion. Yet this is just another instance in which the inability to experiment in a

---

*[Authors' Note] Fischl and co-workers did, in fact, quantify the frequency of oral sex in their subjects, which may have allowed them to reach a more accurate conclusion. They defined "repeated oral sex" as "at least two contacts per month or 50% or more of total sexual activity."

carefully controlled way creates confusion. Despite the importance of knowing whether kissing can actually transmit the AIDS virus, it is clearly unethical to conduct such studies with humans, and it is nonsensical to require such "proof" from real-life circumstances that are unlikely to arise very frequently within view of researchers.

It seems strange to have to raise such an obvious point, but if there are lingering uncertainties about the transmission of a deadly infection, shouldn't we be adopting precautions against the worst-case possibility rather than making the most optimistic assumption? After all, this is quite literally a life-and-death matter, not an intellectual discussion with purely philosophical ramifications. And yet the medical/scientific community has given the public a rather reassuring assessment suggesting that kissing is not apt to be a means of spreading the AIDS virus. This raises the question of whether the intention behind such a posture is to inform people of the relevant risks or to take the path of least resistance, stressing only the proven dangers and virtually ignoring those that are possible but not yet thoroughly documented. . . .

SEXUAL CHOICES IN THE AGE OF AIDS

Unless there is a remarkable and currently unanticipated breakthrough such as the development of a vaccine to prevent infection with the AIDS virus or the discovery of a cure for AIDS, we must all face the realities that the AIDS epidemic brings to our world. More than anything, this calls for making responsible, informed choices about our sexual behavior. . . . We will discuss various aspects of sexual behavior in relation to the risk of contracting the AIDS virus.

Abstinence

Although the choice does not have much appeal to most adults, there is something to be said for a deliberate decision to abstain from sexual activity as a means of completely avoiding the risks of sexual exposure to the AIDS virus. To serve this purpose, though, abstinence can't be a part-time proposition: it must become, in effect, a way of life. Clearly, choosing abstinence (as a cognitive act) and being completely abstinent (as a behavioral act) are not the same: even among Catholic priests, whose clerical vows impose lifelong celibacy, there have been more than a few cases of AIDS.

Our experience over the years suggests that in general women seem to find abstinence an easier choice than do men. At least at this stage of the AIDS epidemic, this pattern continues to be borne out: our impression is that more single heterosexual women than unmarried heterosexual men are choosing abstinence. Without delving into the specific reasons behind this difference— which we believe are more culturally determined than biologically based—we will simply point out that the reasons for deciding to abstain from sex at a given time in one's life are apt to be particularly complex. When the decision is made in relation to AIDS, the common denominator for both genders seems to be fear, as shown by comments from several people we've interviewed who have chosen this option.

A 33-year-old recently divorced woman: All the news stories about AIDS still affecting mainly homosexuals, bisexuals, and addicts don't convince me. This disease is a killer, not just something you treat discreetly at your doctor's office with a shot of penicillin. Perhaps if I meet the right person I'll change my mind, but for now it's a relief to know that sex—except masturbation—is completely off limits.

A 21-year-old single male college student: I used to think that AIDS was some sort of rare, exotic illness that would never touch the people I know. I got a rude awakening when two classmates of mine found out that they're infected. To me, postponing sex for a few years sounds safe—like not going sailing in the middle of a storm. When the storm is over, then I'll be ready to sail.

A 26-year-old never-married woman: Let's face it—sex just isn't the most important thing in life. I'm certainly not opposed to sex, and I used to enjoy sex, but right now the sanest choice for me is no sex at all. No sex, no worries. No sex, no AIDS. It's really a very simple equation, isn't it?

A 23-year-old single nurse: I resisted jumping into bed with guys when I was a teenager and when I was in college. I suppose then I just wasn't ready. Now I'm ready, but I'm frightened too. So I'm not going to change my mind until I meet the man I'll marry. I guess there's something to be said for good old-fashioned virginity.

Abstinence is not an option being chosen exclusively by heterosexuals. A number of gay men have told us that they are reluctantly choosing abstinence rather than risk the high odds of exposure to AIDS during sex with other men. Here are two representative comments:

A 34-year-old gay male: I became alarmed by the news stories about AIDS in 1983 or 1984. It was clear to me that I was in the "official" highest risk group, and this was confirmed when a number of friends of mine came down with AIDS and died. Now, I may not be a genius, but I was smart enough to know that I don't want to trust my life to a condom. So the only sensible choices seemed to be: settle down in a one-on-one relationship with someone who's healthy, or give up sex. Giving up sex was simpler. It didn't really complicate my life. And I have no illusions about being celibate—it's a way of staying worry-free and staying alive.

A 27-year-old gay male: Gay pride is a great sentiment when there's something to be proud of, but being gay is nothing like that today. Not only is there that constant gnawing fear inside—"Was that guy really okay?"—and worries about losing your job, your apartment, and your sanity, but you have to wonder what it says about the intelligence of gays who keep going to bars, bathhouses, and parties with no particular precautions about sex. I'm no kamikaze. Being asexual for a while is better than the alternative.

We have also spoken with gay men who chose abstinence only after first trying to switch over to a heterosexual life. Most of these men, who had been exclusively or almost exclusively homosexual, were disappointed with the attempt to convert to heterosexual activity. (In contrast, we have seen many bisexual men who seem to have made a shift to exclusive heterosexual sex relatively easily.)

Safe Sex

There is one set of circumstances under which all forms of sexual activity can be considered totally and completely safe from the standpoint of exposure to the AIDS virus. This is, of course, a relationship—either heterosexual or homosexual—where both partners have had no prior sexual contacts with anyone else and have not been exposed to the AIDS virus by nonsexual means. Although couples whose sexual histories are so exclusive may have been relatively rare in the past few decades, it is very possible that the strong comfort and appeal of absolute certainty in terms of worries about AIDS will make this type of sexual biography more common in the future.

One of the pragmatic questions that arises in regard to such relationships, and that will recur repeatedly at later points in this discussion, is how to be certain that your partner is telling the truth about his or her sexual past. The issue is not as simple as it might first seem to be. For one thing, judging from our experience with couples both clinically and in research, people are more apt to engage in some form of deception about their sexual biographies than they are to tell all. This tendency is probably compounded when an issue as volatile as possible previous exposure to the AIDS virus comes into play. Indeed, it is not difficult to imagine circumstances in which revealing one's sexual history to a partner could precipitate the breakup of a relationship, or at least seriously undermine the trust of that relationship.

Consider, for example, a young man in his early twenties who has been dating a woman for more than three years and has now become engaged to her. They have not previously had sexual intercourse, and they are both, heterosexually speaking, virgins. The man, however, had a brief homosexual relationship in his freshman year of college, involving only a handful of sexual encounters. He is certainly at risk for being infected with the AIDS virus. After wrestling with his conscience on the matter, he decides with great difficulty to tell his fiancée of these past encounters. On learning this news, she becomes so distraught that she breaks off their engagement. This situation is certainly possible, though more often than not, in our experience, it would play out differently: the typical man with this sort of sexual history would keep the information to himself, leaving his fiancée to believe that he is as inexperienced as she is. In either case, the consequences are dismaying.

Not very long ago it was reasonably accepted and even expected etiquette in most social circles for the great majority of young adults to have been sexually active prior to meeting the person they would decide to marry. Today the accepted etiquette is changing drastically as concerns over AIDS mount. While this certainly doesn't mean that people who have already been sexually active wish they hadn't been—in fact, relatively few single, never-married adults seem to want to be sexually inexperienced—it does create a new set of pressures when they decide it's time to marry. Judging from interviews we've conducted with several hundred college students, a sizable number of males and females will lie to a prospective spouse about their past sex lives. Few of them will claim to be totally inexperienced sexually, but many will minimize the number of sexual partners they've had or misstate the extent of their sexual experience. Some who will tell a prospective spouse that they have had previous sexual experiences will nevertheless lie about the consistency of condom use in these encounters. Substantial numbers of women will—certainly understandably—refuse to tell a partner about having been raped or having been the victim of incest. Men will be particularly apt to hide information about past homosexual experiences and sex with prostitutes.

What this means is that it is difficult to be certain about the truthfulness of what someone else tells you about his or her sexual past. For this reason, even couples who are deeply in love, plan to marry, and have no reason to doubt each other's claims of no prior sexual contacts should probably consider being tested for antibodies to the AIDS virus. Though this sort of testing may provide only a low yield of positive results, it may be advisable because it can detect cases where infection with the virus has occurred through nonsexual as well as sexual means.

Testing for Safe Sex

While the risk of infection with the AIDS virus is greater among people who have had numerous sex partners than among those who have had few, *anyone* with prior sexual experience, however limited, must be regarded as a potential asymptomatic carrier of the virus. Likewise, anyone who has injected illicit drugs or received a transfusion in the preceding decade must be regarded as a potential carrier of the AIDS virus. Since there are now some 3 million HIV-infected Americans—most of whom, as we've said before, do not realize that they are infected and contagious to others—it should be a matter of utmost concern to anyone entering a new relationship to ascertain that a prospective partner is *not* infected before physical intimacy passes the stage of snuggling. Because infection with the AIDS virus cannot be detected from a person's appearance, and because personal disclaimers, no matter how seemingly heartfelt and sincere, cannot reliably indicate freedom from infection, a more objective means of evaluation is required.

As a practical matter (albeit a cumbersome one), the only way to achieve a high degree of certainty at present is for both persons in the relationship to jointly agree to antibody testing before beginning any sexual activity. For the most stringent and conclusive assessment currently available, each person should first have an antibody screening test (such as the ELISA), to be followed by a more definitive test (such as the Western blot) in the event that the first test is even weakly positive. This minimizes—but does not completely eliminate—the possibility of false positive results. Then the couple should abstain from sexual activity with each other or with any other partner for a six-month period, at which time they should again be tested for antibodies to the AIDS virus. (The purpose of retesting after six months is to exclude the small but real number of cases in which the initial test occurs too soon after infection for detectable quantities of antibody to be in circulation.) With negative antibody tests in both partners at both testing times, and with an absolute commitment to remaining sexually monogamous, the couple can have the highest possible degree of confidence that there is no risk of contracting sexually transmitted AIDS. (It is of course possible that even if a couple undergoes this sort of double testing and remains absolutely monogamous, one of them could still be infected with the AIDS virus by nonsexual means. In this event, the virus could certainly be transmitted sexually to the other partner.)

Most couples will probably not be willing to abstain from sexual activity for the six-month waiting period suggested above. It is, after all, an easy way to lose one's ardor—to replace passion with the cold, calculated precision of a scientific protocol. Furthermore, our sexual urges are not as likely to be ruled by temperate reason as, say, our willingness to wear a seatbelt in a car. And although wearing a seatbelt doesn't generally interfere with getting to our destination or using the car in almost any manner we choose, and certainly doesn't result in a six-month delay, many people deliberately disdain seatbelts even where it's a clear violation of the law (and of common sense about personal safety) not to use them. So the chances that large numbers of people will adopt the stringent double-testing conditions outlined above are slim indeed.

For this reason, we offer an alternative, slightly less reliable but still highly valid method of double-testing that permits sexual activity to commence promptly after the results of the initial antibody tests are received. If both partners' initial tests are negative, they can engage in sexual activity with the proviso that it involve absolutely consistent use of a condom during any episode of either vaginal intercourse or fellatio, as well as total abstinence from anal sex. Now, as we will discuss in more detail shortly, the use of a condom is not at all foolproof in preventing the transmission of the AIDS virus. But it will reduce the risk of exposure to the virus, not only when it is completely effective as a mechanical barrier, but even if it leaks—for in all probability the defective device still greatly reduces the number of virus particles to which the partner is exposed. Thus, in a situation that begins with one round of antibody testing—which may detect, based on current scientific estimates, approximately 98% of infected persons—the use of a condom makes the risk much lower than it would otherwise be. Needless to say, if condoms are not used consistently, the risk is somewhat higher.

There are two particular areas of vulnerability in the testing approaches just described. Both hinge on the issue of trust. First, assuming you and your partner have both agreed to be tested, how confident can you be that you are going to be accurately informed of your partner's test result? Second, even if both of you have negative tests, how certain can you be that your partner isn't having sexual contact with someone else, thus potentially becoming infected from an affair that you don't know about?

The need to be sure that your partner has in fact been tested and that you can verify the results is not just a theoretical one that can be lightly set aside. For one thing, there are malicious, greedy businesses already in operation selling people (mostly men) bogus "certified-AIDS-free" identification cards. (In some cases, the purchaser realizes he is getting a phony document; in other cases, the purchaser gives a blood sample and is charged a fee for a blood test that is never done, so that he or she is under the impression that the ID card or document is

accurate.) Such ventures are fundamentally different from companies that actually perform the testing they sell (sometimes with accuracy, sometimes not), but
it is quite difficult for the typical consumer to check out the operations and track
record of private businesses in this area. We also know of cases in which people,
including prostitutes, have forged official-looking letters from physicians or
laboratories stating that they were tested for AIDS and the results were negative.
Prostitutes have an obvious economic incentive for such a ploy; in several
instances we've encountered, men have used such letters in attempts at picking
women up in bars. Furthermore, there are thousands of people who know that
they're infected and are deliberately hiding this information from their sex
partners. Some of them, having already gone through testing procedures, may be
smart enough to know how to fake it (with regard to sham testing and "reporting")
convincingly enough that an unwary partner will be fooled.

Beyond these cases of more or less preplanned, deliberate deception looms a
much larger category. Here we include many ordinary, straightforward people
who are genuinely shocked to discover that they've tested positive for antibodies
to the AIDS virus. Some of them are so distraught that they completely deny the
accuracy of the report. ("It must've been a mistake in the lab; maybe they mixed
up my blood sample with someone else's.") Others simply deny the reality of the
situation. ("It just can't be. I feel perfectly well—I *know* nothing's wrong with
me.") Still others refuse to believe that they could be infectious to someone else.
("The antibodies in my blood mean that I was able to fight off the virus, not that
I'm infected or that I could make anyone sick.") And others, even after they've
been counseled and even realizing the implications of their infection, choose to
hide the truth from current or future sex partners. This may be the most
dangerous group of all. And it is in this group that we find some who will hide
their actual test results from their partners, claiming that "the test was okay"—
and creating a clear potential for further spread of the virus.

Without belaboring the darker side of the human soul that permits such
deception (and subsequent harm), it is useful to point out possible ways of
avoiding these problems. For instance, a couple—either heterosexual or homosexual—can go to a physician for HIV testing, as millions have in the past for
premarital testing, and instruct the physician that the test results are to be
discussed openly with both of them. In some instances the physician may request
that they sign a consent form authorizing such a discussion, since it involves, in
effect, a waiver of personal privacy, but this is a simple issue. Another possibility
is to use a clinic or public health facility that permits anonymous testing. In this
situation the partners exchange code numbers so that each can call the testing
office and receive the other's results. (Of course, this approach won't work if you
can't verify that the tested blood sample and the code number actually belonged
to your partner. Although this probably sounds somewhat farfetched, anyone
familiar with drug-testing programs knows that there have frequently been
attempts to substitute a "clean" urine specimen for one that will test positive for
illegal substances.) Finally, it is possible in some locations to go directly to a
university-run or hospital-based laboratory for confidential testing. If both partners instruct the laboratory to send their test results to them by certified mail in a

single envelope, they can open the document together to see the lab report on each test.

The second type of vulnerability in the testing strategy we've suggested involves the trust implicit in believing that your partner will be absolutely monogamous once the testing has been completed (or during the six-month interval between the first and second tests). Unfortunately, assumptions about sexual fidelity can be dangerous to your health. For example, in screening people for participation in . . . [a study of two heterosexual populations], we found that among 785 married men between the ages of 20 and 40, 44.3% had had at least one extramarital sexual partner in the preceding five years. Among 541 married women we screened, 32.3% had had extramarital sex in the same five-year period. These figures are similar to data from other investigations.

Kinsey and his co-workers estimated in 1948 that half of all married males in their sample had had extramarital coitus; in their 1953 report Kinsey's group noted that by age 40, 26% of married women had been extramaritally involved at least once. In 1975 a survey conducted by *Redbook* reported that 38% of married women aged 35 to 39 had extramarital sexual experience. In 1983 Blumstein and Schwartz found that 26% of husbands and 21% of wives in their sample had been nonmonogamous since the start of their relationship; among their sample group of unmarried people living together, 33% of the males and 30% of the females had not been monogamous. Blumstein and Schwartz note that marriage seems to make people more deceptive about their sexual behavior. They also observe, "*A couple can never be completely sure that their relationship will remain monogamous. Ten years of monogamy does not mean the eleventh is safe.*" (Among gay men in long-term relationships, 82% had outside sex, and for lesbians the corresponding figure was 28%, according to the same study.)

It is certainly correct to point out that these early data were collected, by and large, before the AIDS epidemic and may not be completely applicable today as awareness of the risk of AIDS increases. Nevertheless, government statistics on other sexually transmitted diseases such as syphilis, which show increased numbers in 1987 compared to prior periods, do not point to a drop in non-monogamous behavior among heterosexuals. Likewise, the findings on current patterns of sexual behavior . . . do not give much credence to the wishful notion that most heterosexuals have significantly modified their sex lives in response to the threat of AIDS. Indeed, although there has been much made of the distinct decrease in unsafe sex among gay men—including the practice of anonymous sex with multiple partners—at least some research suggests that this may have been a temporary change largely limited to a few metropolitan areas.

For these reasons it is important to realize that the promise of safe sex offered by the double-testing procedure outlined here is only as good as the behavioral commitment to that objective. Testing only gives a snapshot of evidence about your condition at a particular point in time. If you are uninfected and you jeopardize your health status by having sex outside the "safe" relationship, you also potentially jeopardize the health of your partner, who innocently trusts in your common sense and sense of fair play. But the reality is, sadly, that the forbidden fruit is often more appealing than what is readily accessible, so it is virtually certain that even as the numbers mount in the AIDS epidemic, millions of people will continue to follow libidinal urges that put them directly at risk of being infected with the AIDS virus.

There is no specific, foolproof solution we can offer here. While we are not suggesting that extrarelationship sex is always morally wrong, it seems reasonable to make the following points:

1. If you suspect that your partner has been sexually active with someone else, talk about your concern and find out what he or she has to say.
2. If your partner denies having extrarelationship sex and you aren't satisfied, consider asking your partner to be tested again.
3. Before embarking on any form of nonmonogamous sex, think carefully about the risks you're running—for your partner as well as yourself.
4. If the prospect of sex outside your primary relationship is so compelling that you can't put it out of your mind, consider having your prospective partner undergo testing to confirm that he or she isn't infected with the AIDS virus. If he or she refuses, our best advice is to head straight for the door.

There is one more cautionary note that we should add here. Recently, a number of entrepreneurs have hit upon an idea that sounds like an easy, straightforward way of simultaneously capitalizing on people's fears of AIDS and providing a useful public service. They have organized so-called AIDS-free singles groups that for a monthly or annual fee provide periodic HIV testing and expect members to have sexual contact solely with other group members (and avoid IV drug abuse). The theory behind this approach is simple: if you can prevent exposure to the virus by not doing drugs and by limiting your sexual contacts to people who are not infected, you can't come down with AIDS. In a sense this is an extension of the double-testing monogamous strategy we've recommended here, but instead of monogamy it calls for loyalty and sexual fidelity to a group. Unfortunately, there is apt to be a huge gap between theory and practice with such clubs and organizations. Referring to the diminishing probability that people in such clubs or groups will consistently conform to the rules, a physician at the AMA observes, "It's like people who go on diets: they're able to sustain it for a while, but then their commitment wanes."

The bottom line here is that testing programs aimed at fostering truly safe sex do not provide an ironclad, unassailable guarantee. What is required for assurance that no sexual exposure to the AIDS virus can occur is for two partners to be accurately tested on two occasions, at least six months apart, and then—assuming there has been laboratory confirmation of their seronegative status—to maintain absolute sexual monogamy. Good intentions will not suffice. Unwavering adherence to a code of honor and trust is necessary—including the uncomfortable but requisite step of notifying one's partner immediately if there has been any extrarelationship sexual activity, and abstaining from sex with that partner until such time as testing certifies that no infection has occurred.

One of the disconcerting problems in combating the spread of the AIDS virus is that many people who know they have been exposed to infection refuse to be tested to determine their antibody status. For instance, when the U.S. Centers for Disease Control conducted a national survey of the sex partners of hemophiliacs, they found that only one-third had undergone such testing. This situation is particularly worrisome since it shows in a rather explicit way that education and counseling efforts with this population have been far less effective than experts had hoped. And because people need to know their HIV status so they can avoid transmitting the virus to their sex partners or, in the case of women, to their babies, this is not just an academic issue.

We have encountered a similar reluctance to be tested among the sex partners of HIV-infected drug addicts. In attempting to gather data on the rate of transmission of HIV infection from an infected man to his sex partner (correlated with the frequency and types of sexual activity engaged in by the couple), we found that the majority of women we interviewed refused to be tested. The most common reason for avoiding the test was fear: fear of finding out they might be infected, fear of being told not to become pregnant, and fear of losing their partner. Intriguingly, many of these women were resigned to the probability that they were already infected but felt that by not being tested they didn't have to confront the issue psychologically. Some of them, in fact, felt that as long as the infection wasn't "proven" scientifically, it would remain dormant. To this group, one of the primary risks of being tested was that confirmation of HIV infection would make the condition more serious, somehow activating the virus in their bodies by providing sure knowledge of its presence.

The same type of fear operates in the broader population of those who know or suspect that they have been exposed to the AIDS virus. For example, in our study group of 400 men and women with large numbers of sex partners in the preceding five years, only 3 of the 45 people who thought they were at risk had previously undergone testing on their own. Conversely, the experience at a number of public testing programs, such as those in New York City, has been that many people who are not particularly at risk for the infection rush in to be tested.

People who consider themselves at risk for HIV infection often avoid testing because they feel that finding out they are infected won't be helpful. After all, many of them point out, there is no treatment available to eradicate the infection or even to slow its progression. Furthermore, they say, discovering you're infected will only complicate your life and cause a good deal of psychological anguish as well. This sort of resignation to fate presents one of the central public health problems of the AIDS epidemic. The hundreds of thousands of carriers of the virus who go on with life as usual, oblivious to the possibility of being infected, constitute a major vector in the continuing spread of the epidemic. They are not just numbers in an epidemiological maze: they are men and women who continue to lead sexually active lives, many of them exposing multiple partners to the AIDS virus each year. They are people who, irresponsibly clinging to their personal excuses for not being tested, silently spread slow death to those with whom they couple in erotic abandon.

The Trouble with Condoms

As part of the effort to combat the spread of AIDS, various experts and groups, including the U.S. Surgeon General, have strongly endorsed the use of condoms. In keeping with this recommendation, condoms have been distributed to homosexual men, on college campuses, and in other settings as part of "safe sex" kits, and a number of public education campaigns have also proclaimed that using a condom constitutes "safe sex." While it is true that condom use can effectively *reduce* the risks of unsafe sex, it is emphatically not true that condoms provide a foolproof means of avoiding exposure to the AIDS virus. Condoms can make for *safer* sex but do not guarantee safe sex.

The basic premise that a condom provides an effective mechanical barrier to the spread of the AIDS virus via semen or vaginal secretions is supported scientifically by several laboratory studies. The most relevant report involved tests of both latex and natural condoms. The condoms were filled with a fluid containing very high concentrations of the AIDS virus—about 5,000 times greater than the amounts found in semen—and were subjected to pressure, but there was no evidence that the virus leaked out of any of the condoms tested. Studies of the same type had previously shown that viruses similar in size to the AIDS virus, such as the herpes simplex virus, do not pass through condoms either. There is some uncertainty, however, as to whether condoms made of natural materials such as lamb's intestine are as effective in this regard as latex condoms. This point has not been discussed adequately in the media or in most educational materials intended for the general public, so consumers are somewhat undereducated on this matter. At present, at least, a cautious view suggests that all condoms are not created equal.

Unfortunately, condoms have never been known to be foolproof. As most people realize, they provide only a flimsy barrier, and they are subject to manufacturing or packaging defects that may cause them to leak. The scope of this problem is greater than most condom users probably realize. For example, in the spring of 1987 the U.S. Food and Drug Administration conducted detailed studies of the effectiveness of 204 sample lots of latex condoms. About 1 out of every 5 sample batches leaked. While the failure rate was highest among imported brands (30 of the 98 imported sample lots failed, compared to "only" 11 failures in the 106 domestically manufactured sample batches), such data show that defective condoms are far from rare. Besides defects that can occur in the manufacturing or packaging of condoms, the material the condom is made from can become brittle as it ages or dries out. Nevertheless, most brands of condoms don't have effective storage and use dates stamped on their packages (as is mandatory for spermicidal creams and jellies, as well as most medications), so consumers have no way of knowing how long a batch of condoms has been on the shelf. In addition, it is obvious that condoms can be torn or punctured during use. There are no precise statistics on the frequency of this problem, but it doesn't stretch the imagination very much to see how a fingernail can tear a condom while it is being put on.

Actual use statistics—compiled not in artificial laboratory studies but in field trials by humans—rather consistently show that condoms are far from 100% effective. Most reports we have seen indicate failure rates of 10% to 15% for condoms as birth control devices. While it is true that inconsistent or improper use of condoms (technically known as user failure) may be more of a problem than leaks in the condom (method failure), it is also pertinent to note that pregnancies don't occur every time a condom "fails." If we assume that pregnancy is only likely to occur during one week out of each menstrual cycle, and that a single act of unprotected intercourse during this fertile period only results in conception approximately 1 out of 8 times, the probability of pregnancy occurring from a single random failure of condom use is about 3% (that is, about 1 in 32). This means that a 10% to 15% failure rate (in terms of pregnancies) among couples using condoms consistently on each and every sexual contact during the year probably indicates an actual failure rate (in terms of "leaks") three to five times higher.

Two recent studies provide evidence that this is not just a theoretical problem. In one, Padian and her co-workers studied 97 female partners of 93 men infected with the AIDS virus. They found that 23% of the women were infected, and concluded, "Condom use was not significantly associated with protection from infection." In another study evaluating a group of AIDS patients and their spouses, it was found that 3 out of 18 who used condoms regularly became infected—a failure rate of 16.7%.

One other aspect of condom use should be mentioned. Although a condom without leaks may provide an effective mechanical barrier to the AIDS virus contained in semen (and will also protect the penis from virus particles in vaginal or cervical secretions), unless the condom is put on virtually at the beginning of a firm erection, there is a possibility that the male's sex partner will be exposed to preejaculatory fluid containing virus. Furthermore, unless the condom is removed soon after ejaculation occurs, there is a chance that semen will spill out of the condom onto the labia of the vagina or even into the vagina itself as the male's erection recedes and the condom no longer fits so tightly around the penis. Since many couples find the post-orgasmic glow a time of tenderness in which they want to lie quietly together with their genitals still in union, they run a distinct risk of having just such spillage occur. Finally, unless the penis is carefully washed to get rid of the residue of semen once a condom is removed, there may be live virus present on both the shaft and head of the penis that can certainly be contagious if rubbed against a cut or scratch or rash or blister—in fact, any abradement of the skin.

This is not to say that using condoms to reduce the risk of exposure to the AIDS virus is pointless. A good case can be made that consistent condom use will in fact provide a certain degree of protection. But to think that condom use is perfect, or even near perfect, in eliminating the risk of HIV transmission is foolishness of the highest order. Yet many medical experts, public health officials, and educators have jumped on the bandwagon proclaiming condoms are "life-saving" devices, giving the public the impression that using condoms is all that has to be done. Though this is understandable—endorsing condom use is better than taking no action at all, and for professionals committed to dealing with the public health impact of AIDS one of the major frustrations has been how very little they've been able to recommend to a concerned public short of abstinence from sex and illicit drugs—to suggest that condom use is a complete answer in the fight against AIDS is to oversimplify and mislead in an irresponsible fashion.

Making Unsafe Sex Safer

For those whose partners are unwilling to undergo voluntary testing in order to establish that they're free of infection with the AIDS virus, virtually any sex act carries with it a certain degree of risk. Even as seemingly innocuous an act as mutual manual stimulation of the genitals is not completely risk-free. If pre-ejaculatory fluid or semen comes in contact with a sore, a cut, or a rash on the partner's hand or body, there is a possibility of infection. Likewise, if a man stimulating his partner's genitals inserts a finger into her vagina, he will come in skin contact with vaginal secretions that may be infected. If there is a break in the skin of his finger or hand, or if he subsequently touches another part of his body where there is a break in the skin, he runs a small but distinct risk of infection.

One possible solution to this quandary would be for sex partners of uncertain testing status to wear disposable plastic gloves during all intimate moments. These gloves, after all, aren't too different from condoms. Yet we are unwilling to seriously entertain such an outlandish notion—right now, it seems so unnatural and artificial as to violate the essential dignity of humanity. A better (that is, less offensive-sounding) solution might be for partners to use nonoxynol-9–containing creams or jellies for genital stimulatory activities, since it has been shown that nonoxynol-9, which is the active chemical ingredient in a number of spermicides, effectively kills the AIDS virus.

Couples with unknown HIV status, or couples in which one partner is known to be infected, should absolutely avoid anal intercourse. Based on present evidence, there seems to be little doubt that anal intercourse is the riskiest form of sexual activity. To engage in anal coitus when there is a possibility that one partner is infected is to tempt fate—and biological reality—too strongly. In our judgment, relying on condom use for anal intercourse when one partner is infected or when one or both partners have unknown HIV status is still taking an unwarranted risk that is compounded over time if the activity is repeated.

Similarly, if we are to give credence to the data from Africa and to our own findings, it is unacceptably risky to engage in penile-vaginal intercourse when one or both partners' HIV status is unknown or when one partner is known to be infected. In the absence of studies showing that this risk is significantly reduced by the use of condoms, to rely on condoms for truly safe sex—or even a reasonable approximation of safe sex—is to blatantly disregard the facts. The condom industry, of course, will take grave exception to this statement. Readers can expect a rather vitriolic critique of our recommendations about condoms from this group, which has a vested economic interest in maintaining the illusion that condoms confer an adequate degree of protection against the AIDS virus.

Oral-genital sex presents a somewhat different problem. Here, at least as of late 1987, there is a lack of substantive research documenting the relative degree of risk associated with oral sex by itself. In one study of homosexual men in San Francisco, there did not seem to be any statistically significant increased risk of HIV infection among men who engaged in oral-genital sex compared to those who didn't—although 24% of the men who had any history of oral-genital contact were infected, compared to 18.2% of those who had not engaged in oral-genital sex. . . . This study did not make any attempt to quantify the frequency or number of oral-genital contacts, so that a man who reported performing fellatio once in the two years preceding the study was placed in the same group, for statistical purposes, as a man who performed fellatio dozens of times a month. This may explain why these researchers found no indication that oral-genital sex was associated with an increased risk of infection with the AIDS virus. However, in a study of 45 adults with AIDS and their spouses, 12 of 26 spouses who participated in repeated oral sex became infected during the study, whereas only 2 out of 19 uninfected spouses regularly engaged in oral sex.

In light of this uncertainty, until more definitive evidence is available, oral-genital sex should be avoided unless it is known that both partners are HIV-free. Using a condom while performing fellatio is not only aesthetically distasteful to most people, it also increases the likelihood of the condom's being torn by contact with teeth—a mechanical hazard that condoms were not manufactured to endure.

We should also add that any type of sexual activity posing a significant risk of exposure to a partner's blood should particularly be avoided when both partners are not known to be free of HIV infection. In this category we include not only the obvious, such as sadomasochistic sex that involves beatings, whipping, or the use of needles, pins, or other sharp objects, but also vigorous biting or scratching or any kind of sex play that can cause bleeding, since blood can certainly transmit the AIDS virus via nongenital erotic contact. In addition, although no reliable research has yet been done on this topic, it is probably wise to avoid coitus, cunnilingus, or finger insertion into the vagina during a woman's menstrual flow if her HIV status is uncertain.

In short, this is a time for considerable caution in sexual conduct. The need for caution is most pronounced in terms of choosing a partner. Prostitutes, male homosexuals, IV drug abusers, males with bisexual experiences, and people who have had large numbers of sexual partners are especially risky as sex partners until it can be shown by testing that they are free of HIV infection. Trusting attitudes should be tempered by the seriousness of the current situation: since you can't tell if people are infected with the AIDS virus by how they look, and since you can't really rely on their own recitation of their sexual history, you are just being prudent by insisting that someone who wants to get in bed with you accompany you to a clinic for testing first.

JOURNAL WRITINGS

1. How do you think the AIDS epidemic has affected sexual attitudes in your age group? Give reasons for your answer.
2. What information in the reading would most influence the sexual behavior of college students? Explain your answer in a paragraph.

BRAINSTORMING AND DRAFTING

3. In a small group, compile a list of false beliefs that people have about AIDS. Draft a paragraph summarizing these beliefs; in a second paragraph, refute these factual errors with correct information.
4. In "The Sexualized Society," D'Emilio and Freedman do not discuss the AIDS crisis (though they do explore its political implications later in their book). Pretend that you are D'Emilio or Freedman. Draft a substantial paragraph in which you bring readers up to date about current sexual behavior during the AIDS epidemic. To do this, you will need to generalize from some of the facts provided by Masters/Johnson/Kolodny. Write, as D'Emilio and Freedman do, from a historical perspective.
5. After considering the choices for sexual behavior that the authors present in the reading, select the choice that *least* appeals to you. Draft a paragraph in which you argue against this option, providing several reasons for your view.

THE AUTHORS' METHODS

6. In the two sections of this reading, the authors first present the topic from the perspective of a natural scientist, and then from a sociologist's point of view. What kind of information does each section emphasize? Is one section more objective (neutral) than the other? What evidence leads you to that conclusion?
7. How knowledgeable about science do the authors probably assume their audience is? For example, have the authors written this material for scientific specialists, for moderately educated lay readers, or for those who have not yet graduated from high school? Draft a paragraph in which you cite evidence from the article to support your answer.

FORMAL WRITING AND RESEARCH PAPERS

8. Using your knowledge about the AIDS crisis, your own moral judgment, and your perceptions about handling relationships, which you have gained from the other readings in this unit or from personal experience, write a

paper recommending an approach to sexual behavior for today's college students. Provide reasons, examples, or other substantive support to persuade an audience of your peers that your recommendations are reasonable and necessary.

9.   This reading was taken from a book published in 1988. Consult the *Social Sciences Index,* the *General Science Index,* and the card or computer catalog to find a minimum of six sources on AIDS published *in the 1990s.* Write a research paper in which you evaluate whether the more recent scientific "facts" about AIDS and the recommendations about sexual behavior are: (a) approximately similar to those in the 1988 piece, (b) somewhat different from the 1988 piece, (c) significantly different from the 1988 piece. If you detect differences, try to assess whether they are the result of a different author's viewpoint or a shift in the general consensus based on new information. Assume an academic audience of professors and students who have *not* read any of the articles. Organize your paper according to *ideas,* rather than by sources.

BROAD PERSPECTIVES ON PERSONAL RELATIONSHIPS

OverView of the Unit

While a personal relationship can be one of the most rewarding experiences of our lives, most of us have encountered at least some problems as we strive to establish and maintain our best relationships. From your readings in this unit, identify some of the problems occurring in romantic love, sex, or marriage that may undermine the satisfaction we can gain from a relationship. Referring to several authors, **describe** these problems in detail. Use your knowledge and experience to suggest one or more reasonable solutions for each problem.

ClusterWritings

1.   Choose any combination of at least five readings/illustrations from this unit and **summarize** some of the various **definitions** of love suggested by each selection. (Some readings may state or imply more than one definition; therefore, indicate the character or the portion of the selection that suggests each definition you choose.) Explain each definition fully, and provide evidence from the reading to support your explanation. Then construct your own best working definition—one that incorporates your view of love. Explain fully the implications of your definition.

2.   **Analyze** the differences between some of the earlier views of sexuality (for example, Plato, Hamilton, Augustine, Tannahill, Chekhov, Brooks) and some of the more recent ones (for example, D'Emilio and Freedman, Leavitt, Masters and Johnson and Kolodny, Oates, Russell). Organize your

essay according to *ideas*, rather than articles, as you fully **describe** what the views were and how they changed. In the last section of your paper, evaluate the changes, and explain in detail the reasons for your evaluation.

3. Identify and explain several different views of acceptable marital behavior that you have found in the readings. (In several selections, you can infer some types of marital behavior, even though marriage may not have been the author's primary emphasis. See, for example, Hamilton, Tannahill, Chekhov, D'Emilio and Freedman, Russell, Goldberg.) Organize your essay according to *ideas*, rather than articles. In the last section of your paper, explain and give reasons for your own view of acceptable marital behavior.

4. Choose any two readings that deal with sex-role behaviors of men or women during personal relationships. *Compare* and/or *contrast* the behaviors of the men or women in each reading. Evaluate this behavior according to your own standards.

5. Open communication about love or sex (or the absence of such communication) plays a role in the readings by Solomon, Carver, Leavitt, Hamilton, and Menninger. Explain and give **examples** of your own definition of real communication in a relationship. Then **classify** and **analyze** the types of communication (or absence of it) presented in some of the readings above.

6. Assess the importance that other social relationships (family, friends, "society" in general) should have for lovers. Refer to several selections in explaining your own view. (You might consider, for example, Solomon, Carver, Leavitt, Hamilton, Oates, Varo, Russell.) Though you will find contradictory views on this topic, you can agree or disagree with the material in ways appropriate to your paper.

7. Choose three selections in this unit that you think might appeal to three different audiences. Begin your paper by discussing the importance of audience to a writer. Then **classify** each reading according to the type of audience assumed and **describe** each audience in detail. (You might consider, for instance, its probable age group, educational level, background knowledge of the subject at hand, its ability to understand a type of vocabulary, the need for examples, etc.) **Conclude** by **describing** the audience you assumed as you wrote the paper, and explain the reasons for your assumption.

8. In what ways does the writing in the literary selections (short stories and poem) differ from the writing in the prose **essays**? For example, how are the rhetorical features, methods, or **conventions** of Hamilton's story different from the rhetorical features, methods, or **conventions** of Menninger's article? (You may wish to add or substitute other paired examples.) What rhetorical features do your paired authors share? Explain your answers fully and give specific **examples** from the selections to support your views. **Conclude** by **generalizing** about the role of purpose in writing.

9. Select one subtopic of this unit that has given you some valuable insights into your own life. Choose at least three readings that deal with the subtopic and write a personal **essay** demonstrating how this information has made or will make a difference in your life.

Three

FREE CHOICE

The Nature of Freedom and Responsibility

Despite hundreds of years of debate by many of the world's foremost thinkers, the thorny question of whether we choose and act freely still defies easy answers. The question, of course, is not merely whether we make choices; we all "choose," even if we are sometimes only choosing not to choose. The real question concerns whether we make our choices and perform our actions *freely*.

Philosophers often define a free action as one that could have been otherwise than it was. For example, we have chosen to pursue a college education, but we could have chosen to find a job instead. Some philosophers believe not only that we are at liberty to choose our occupations, but also that we are free to choose right or wrong actions and to form our own personalities. Those who take the position, at one end of the spectrum, that human beings are generally able to choose and act with complete freedom are sometimes called libertarians.

At the opposite end of the spectrum are those who assume that our choices and actions are always restricted or "determined" in some way. For example, some believe that a god-figure, in effect, plans our lives for us since he or she knows that we will go to college before we do it. Others may say that our behavior is caused by the roles we play unconsciously, by our parents' treatment of us, by society's discriminatory attitudes, or by its definition of physical attractiveness. Still others insist that our government, business, economic status, the authorities we respect, our peer groups, even our own bodies may insidiously determine our behavior. Philosophers who adopt this position—that we are absolutely limited or "determined" by one or more of these causal factors—are called hard determinists.

One important question that we must ask ourselves is whether these two polar positions are the only perspectives available to us. Another set of thinkers assumes that this is not the case. Instead, its adherents try to reconcile the two opposing positions. They assert that human actions are "caused" (as the hard determinists would say), but our actions are not necessarily "forced" or "compelled"; therefore, some of our actions are still free. Let's examine some of the varieties of freedom these philosophers accept.

For instance, they would judge us to be physically free if we are not chained to our desks or locked in our homes or dorms. Or, they would deem us to be intellectually free if we are consciously aware of the roles we've adopted and if we know what the choices are. Moreover, because we have not been blackmailed by someone threatening to harm us or by our parents' threat to stop feeding us if we do not attend college, we may, in these philosophers' judgment, be morally free as well. In addition, if our government makes no laws stipulating that we must attend college, then we possess political freedom too. Thus, while parental or peer pressure may have *caused* us to attend college, these pressures have not necessarily *compelled* us to do so. Of course, we may be imprisoned, unaware, coerced by a more compelling motive or by a law to make a particular choice. Therefore, sometimes we act freely, and other times we do not. Those who take this middle ground are often called soft determinists or compatibilists because they believe that the two opposing positions each bear some degree of truth and can thus exist compatibly with each other.

Are the soft determinists merely quibbling over definitions? Do the hard determinists fail to appreciate subtle differences? Are the libertarians clinging to naive and outdated belief systems? Clearly, these philosophical possibilities represent only the beginning of a deep and complicated intellectual controversy.

The readings in this unit will demonstrate that these and many other questions continue to perplex not only philosophers, but also psychologists, sociologists, theologians, poets and novelists, photographers, biologists, journalists, and others. For example, while Jean-Paul Sartre and Anaïs Nin argue that we are generally free to choose what we become, Charlotte Perkins Gilman, Ben Bagdikian, and Erich Fromm, among others, attempt to understand the internal and external controls upon us. Some writers, eager to make people aware of these limitations, suggest that we can exert our wills to overcome these controls. For example, Alice Walker, Jack Sawyer, Norman Cousins, and Rabindranath Tagore assume that recognizing the problem can lead to its solution.

Why have so many people cared so long and so much about this problem? One reason, we suspect, is that the problem is not merely academic. In fact, our power and dignity as human beings seem to be threatened by these issues. For example, if our destinies are fixed, then we have little or no control over our lives. We become like machines, passive receptors of an external power, acting without real thought. Another, perhaps equally compelling, reason is that the degree of moral and legal responsibility we must accept for our actions depends upon the amount of real control we have over them. If people never act freely, then are they truly responsible for their actions? If they could not have done otherwise than they did, can we justify punishing them for their misdeeds? Or if they can choose freely, how can we encourage human beings to develop their potential and to accept responsibility for their actions?

Who is best qualified to help us grapple with these questions? Are there any "right" or "wrong" answers? What does our own personal experience tell us about the amount and kind of freedom we have? Can we trust this experience or are we victims of illusion? As you read the selections in this unit, you will find examples of many different approaches to these questions. Some authors may seem ambiguous about their positions; some, if asked, would perhaps say they have no answers, only questions; several may not even have been conscious of dealing with this particular controversy when they wrote. As you read, you may be tempted to match selections with philosophical categories, but the readings are not intended to be precise examples of particular categories. Indeed, you will quickly discover that most of the works defy easy labeling. Instead, we offer them to help you reflect deeply and critically about the controversy—to encourage you to explore many types of arguments and imaginative renderings of the question. Although the conflicting voices you will hear may perplex you at first, they will, in the end, help you to appreciate and respect the complexity of the topic. As you analyze each work, decide for yourself whether each author or artist makes a persuasive case for his or her unique vision of the controversy.

John Milton

From *Paradise Lost*

(1667)

Born in London, John Milton (1608–1674) attended Christ's College in Cambridge, where he studied Latin and Greek. While in college, he began writing poetry in English. By 1652, he had become totally blind but continued his writing. Intensely interested in Protestant church politics, he wrote many pamphlets on such themes as the incompleteness of the Reformation and the necessity of divorce in failed marriages. His greatest achievement, however, is his poetry, including many sonnets as well as longer poems such as *Lycidas, L'Allegro* and *Il Penseroso, Paradise Lost,* and *Samson Agonistes.*

The following selection is from *Paradise Lost,* Milton's twelve-book epic poem in blank verse. As Book III opens, God the Father is sitting on His heavenly throne, with His Son (Christ) on His right. Gazing at the newly created earth, at Adam and Eve, at Hell, and at the raging, revengeful Satan, God the Father speaks to His Son, foretelling Satan's temptation of Adam and Eve and their choice to sin. God emphasizes the human freedom to choose good or evil, but He shows His awareness of Satan's influence and indicates humanity's opportunity for redemption.

PREVIEW

According to the biblical story, God knew that human beings would "choose" to sin before He created them. Do humans still have freedom of choice if a god already knows what they will do? Why or why not?

Only begotten Son, seest thou what rage
Transports our adversary, whom no bounds
Prescrib'd, no bars of Hell, nor all the chains
Heapt on him there, nor yet the main Abyss
Wide interrupt can hold; so bent he seems
On desperate revenge, that shall redound*
Upon his own rebellious head. And now

---

* redound—reflect.[Eds.]

Through all restraint broke loose he wings his way
Not far off Heav'n, in the Precincts of light,
Directly towards the new created World,
And Man there plac't, with purpose to assay†
If him by force he can destroy, or worse,
By some false guile pervert; and shall pervert;
For Man will heark'n‡ to his glozing§ lies,
And easily transgress the sole Command,
Sole pledge of his obedience: So will fall
Hee and his faithless Progeny: whose fault?
Whose but his own? ingrate, he had of mee
All he could have; I made him just and right,
Sufficient to have stood, though free to fall.

Such I created all th' Ethereal‖ Powers
And Spirits, both them who stood and them who fail'd;
Freely they stood who stood, and fell who fell.
Not free, what proof could they have giv'n sincere
Of true allegiance, constant Faith or Love,
Where only what they needs must do, appear'd,
Not what they would? what praise could they receive?
What pleasure I from such obedience paid,
When Will and Reason (Reason also is choice)
Useless and vain, of freedom both despoil'd,
Made passive both, had serv'd necessity,
Not mee. They therefore as to right belong'd,
So were created, nor can justly accuse
Thir maker, or thir making, or thir Fate;
As if Predestination# over-rul'd
Thir will, dispos'd by absolute Decree
Or high foreknowledge; they themselves decreed
Thir own revolt, not I: if I foreknew,
Foreknowledge had no influence on their fault,
Which had no less prov'd certain unforeknown.
So without least impulse or shadow of Fate,
Or aught by me immutably foreseen,
They trespass, Authors to themselves in all
Both what they judge and what they choose; for so
I form'd them free, and free they must remain,

---

† assay—test.[Eds.]

‡ heark'n—listen.[Eds.]

§ glozing—smooth-talking.[Eds.]

‖ ethereal—heavenly.[Eds.]

predestination—the belief that God preplans whatever comes to pass.[Eds.]

Till they enthrall themselves: I else must change
Thir nature, and revoke the high Decree
Unchangeable, Eternal, which ordain'd
Thir freedom: they themselves ordain'd thir fall.
The first sort by thir own suggestion fell,
Self-tempted, self-deprav'd: Man falls deceiv'd
By th' other first: Man therefore shall find grace,
The other none: in Mercy and Justice both,
Through Heav'n and Earth, so shall my glory excel,
But Mercy first and last shall brightest shine.

JOURNAL WRITINGS

1. Write a paragraph **describing** a choice you made between good and evil at some point in your past. In retrospect, how freely do you think you made this choice? Explain why you think so.
2. Explore some reasons why you as a parent, or future parent, might find it beneficial for yourself to allow your children some freedom of choice. Then find the lines in the poem explaining why God finds it better for Himself to grant humans freedom of choice. Would God's reason be applicable to your own list? Why or why not?

BRAINSTORMING AND DRAFTING

3. Read the introduction to this unit, noting especially the four types of freedom. Apply as many of these types as you can to Milton's poem, explaining how the characters in the poem illustrate each category.
4. In a small group or working individually, list the advantages and disadvantages of living a life completely ruled by fate. Then draft your own paragraph arguing that: (a) fate is preferable to free choice, or (b) free choice is preferable to fate.
5. Read Ben H. Bagdikian's article in this unit. How might God the Father's concept of free choice apply to journalists and television producers?

THE AUTHOR'S METHODS

6. Find at least five words in the poem that suggest a *lack* of free choice. Using a college dictionary, **define** each word in a sentence or two. After reviewing your definitions, write a paragraph in which you show how some of these words fit together to create or emphasize meaning in the poem.
7. **Skim** through the poem to find a series of lines that make up one full sentence. Read the lines aloud to a classmate or to yourself; pause only at punctuation marks. Discuss with your partner (or jot down some ideas on)

Milton's poetic technique of using punctuation to set off meaningful phrases or clauses. Draft a paragraph **paraphrasing** the lines in your sentence.

CREATIVE PROJECT

8. Pretend you are Adam or Eve, pondering the choice of whether or not to follow Satan's suggestion to disobey God. Write a journal entry **describing** the thoughts that will lead to your decision.

FORMAL WRITING AND RESEARCH PAPERS

9. In a formal paper, **analyze** the qualities of God the Father that arise from his position on the question of free will and its consequences for Adam and Eve. Provide **examples** from the reading to support your ideas.
10. To what extent should parents allow their college-age children the freedom to make their own moral choices? Interview two parents from different families and two college-age children, also from different families, on this question. Write a formal, **argumentative** paper in which you take your own position on this issue. Offer several reasons for your view, and give **examples** to illustrate your ideas. Incorporate some of the material from your interviews. You may also wish to review your answer to question 2 under Journal Writings as you think about ideas for the paper.

Jean-Paul Sartre

Existential Choice*

(1947)

Jean-Paul Sartre (1905–1980) was a French philosopher, novelist, dramatist, and critic, well known for his influence on twentieth-century intellectual life. After studying philosophy at the Ecole Normale Supérieure, he began his career by teaching, but was taken prisoner by the Germans while in military service during World War II. His captivity aroused him to a need for social action. After the war, he gave up teaching and devoted his time to writing, lecturing, and political action. In 1964, he refused to accept the Nobel Prize for literature.

Of the many works he published, some of the best known include *Nausea, The Wall and Other Stories, The Flies,* and *Existentialism and Humanism,* from which the following selection is taken. In this excerpt, Sartre begins by insisting upon the most complete human freedom. He then grapples with the implications of such freedom and the dilemma of being fully responsible in a godless world, where social action is nevertheless crucial to our survival.

PREVIEW

How responsible do you think you are for the kind of person you have become? Give reasons for your answer.

What is meant . . . by saying that existence precedes essence? It means that, first of all, man exists, turns up, appears on the scene, and, only afterwards, defines himself. If man, as the existentialist conceives him, is indefinable, it is because at first he is nothing. Only afterward will he be something, and he himself will have made what he will be. Thus, there is no human nature, since there is no God to conceive it. Not only is man what he conceives himself to be, but he is also only what he wills himself to be after this thrust toward existence.

Man is nothing else but what he makes of himself. Such is the first principle of existentialism. It is also what is called subjectivity, the name we are labeled

---

* Sartre's title is "Existentialism." [Eds.]

with when charges are brought against us. But what do we mean by this, if not that man has a greater dignity than a stone or table? For we mean that man first exists, that is, that man first of all is the being who hurls himself toward a future and who is conscious of imagining himself as being in the future. Man is at the start a plan which is aware of itself, rather than a patch of moss, a piece of garbage, or a cauliflower; nothing exists prior to this plan; there is nothing in heaven; man will be what he will have planned to be. Not what he will want to be. Because by the word "will" we generally mean a conscious decision, which is subsequent to what we have already made of ourselves. I may want to belong to a political party, write a book, get married; but all that is only a manifestation of an earlier, more spontaneous choice that is called "will." But if existence really does precede essence, man is responsible for what he is. Thus, existentialism's first move is to make every man aware of what he is and to make the full responsibility of his existence rest on him. And when we say that a man is responsible for himself, we do not only mean that he is responsible for his own individuality, but that he is responsible for all men.

The word subjectivism has two meanings, and our opponents play on the two. Subjectivism means, on the one hand, that an individual chooses and makes himself; and, on the other, that it is impossible for man to transcend human subjectivity. The second of these is the essential meaning of existentialism. When we say that man chooses his own self, we mean that every one of us does likewise; but we also mean by that that in making this choice he also chooses all men. In fact, in creating the man that we want to be, there is not a single one of our acts which does not at the same time create an image of man as we think he ought to be. To choose to be this or that is to affirm at the same time the value of what we choose, because we can never choose evil. We always choose the good, and nothing can be good for us without being good for all.

If, on the other hand, existence precedes essence, and if we grant that we exist and fashion our image at one and the same time, the image is valid for everybody and for our whole age. Thus, our responsibility is much greater than we might have supposed, because it involves all mankind. If I am a workingman and choose to join a Christian trade-union rather than be a communist, and if by being a member I want to show that the best thing for man is resignation, that the kingdom of man is not of this world, I am not only involving my own case—I want to be resigned for everyone. As a result, my action has involved all humanity. To take a more individual matter, if I want to marry, to have children; even if this marriage depends solely on my own circumstances or passion or wish, I am involving all humanity in monogamy and not merely myself. Therefore, I am responsible for myself and for everyone else. I am creating a certain image of man of my own choosing. In choosing myself, I choose man.

This helps us understand what the actual content is of such rather grandiloquent words as anguish, forlornness, despair. As you will see, it's all quite simple.

First, what is meant by anguish? The existentialists say at once that man is anguish. What that means is this: the man who involves himself and who realizes that he is not only the person he chooses to be, but also a law-maker who is, at the same time, choosing all mankind as well as himself, can not help escape the feeling of his total and deep responsibility. Of course, there are many people who are not anxious; but we claim that they are hiding their anxiety, that they are fleeing from it. Certainly, many people believe that when they do something, they themselves are the only ones involved, and when someone says to them, "What if everyone acted that way?" they shrug their shoulders and answer, "Everyone doesn't act that way." But really, one should always ask himself, "What would happen if everybody looked at things that way?" There is no escaping this disturbing thought except by a kind of double-dealing. A man who lies and makes excuses for himself by saying "not everybody does that," is someone with an uneasy conscience, because the act of lying implies that a universal value is conferred upon the lie.

Anguish is evident even when it conceals itself. This is the anguish that Kierkegaard called the anguish of Abraham. You know the story: an angel has ordered Abraham to sacrifice his son; if it really were an angel who has come and said, "You are Abraham, you shall sacrifice your son," everything would be all right. But everyone might first wonder, "Is it really an angel, and am I really Abraham? What proof do I have?"

There was a madwoman who had hallucinations; someone used to speak to her on the telephone and give her orders. Her doctor asked her, "Who is it who talks to you?" She answered, "He says it's God." What proof did she really have that it was God? If an angel comes to me, what proof is there that it's an angel? And if I hear voices, what proof is there that they come from heaven and not from hell, or from the subconscious, or a pathological condition? What proves that they are addressed to me? What proof is there that I have been appointed to impose my choice and my conception of man on humanity? I'll never find any proof or sign to convince me of that. If a voice addresses me, it is always for me to decide that this is the angel's voice; if I consider that such an act is a good one, it is I who will choose to say that it is good rather than bad.

Now, I'm not being singled out as an Abraham, and yet at every moment I'm obliged to perform exemplary acts. For every man, everything happens as if all mankind had its eyes fixed on him and were guiding itself by what he does. And every man ought to say to himself, "Am I really the kind of man who has the right to act in such a way that humanity might guide itself by my actions?" And if he does not say that to himself, he is masking his anguish.

There is no question here of the kind of anguish which would lead to quietism, to inaction. It is a matter of a simple sort of anguish that anybody who has had responsibilities is familiar with. For example, when a military officer takes the responsibility for an attack and sends a certain number of men to death, he chooses to do so, and in the main he alone makes the choice. Doubtless, orders come from above, but they are too broad; he interprets them, and on this interpretation depend the lives of ten or fourteen or twenty men. In making a decision he can not help having a certain anguish. All leaders know this anguish. That doesn't keep them from acting; on the contrary, it is the very condition of their action. For it implies that they envisage a number of possibilities, and when they choose one, they realize that it has value only because it is chosen. We shall see that this kind of anguish, which is the kind that existentialism describes, is explained, in addition, by a direct responsibility to the other men whom it involves. It is not a curtain separating us from action, but is part of action itself.

When we speak of forlornness, a term Heidegger was fond of, we mean only that God does not exist and that we have to face all the consequences of this. The existentialist is strongly opposed to a certain kind of secular ethics which would like to abolish God with the least possible expense. About 1880, some French teachers tried to set up a secular ethics which went something like this: God is a useless and costly hypothesis; we are discarding it; but, meanwhile, in order for there to be an ethics, a society, a civilization, it is essential that certain values be taken seriously and that they be considered as having an *a priori** existence. It must be obligatory, *a priori*, to be honest, not to lie, not to beat your wife, to have children, etc., etc. So we're going to try a little device which will make it possible to show that values exist all the same, inscribed in a heaven of ideas, though otherwise God does not exist. In other words—and this, I believe, is the tendency of everything called reformism in France—nothing will be changed if God does not exist. We shall find ourselves with the same norms of honesty, progress, and humanism, and we shall have made of God an outdated hypothesis which will peacefully die off by itself.

The existentialist, on the contrary, thinks it very distressing that God does not exist, because all possibility of finding values in a heaven of ideas disappears along with Him; there can no longer be an *a priori* Good, since there is no infinite and perfect consciousness to think it. Nowhere is it written that the Good exists, that we must be honest, that we must not lie; because the fact is we are on a plane where there are only men. Dostoievsky said, "If God didn't exist, everything would be possible." That is the very starting point of existentialism. Indeed, everything is permissible if God does not exist, and as a result man is forlorn, because neither within him nor without does he find anything to cling to. He can't start making excuses for himself.

If existence really does precede essence, there is no explaining things away by reference to a fixed and given human nature. In other words, there is no determinism, man is free, man is freedom. On the other hand, if God does not exist, we find no values or commands to turn to which legitimize our conduct. So, in the bright realm of values, we have no excuse behind us, nor justification before us. We are alone, with no excuses.

That is the idea I shall try to convey when I say that man is condemned to be free. Condemned, because he did not create himself, yet, in other respects is free; because, once thrown into the world, he is responsible for everything he does. The existentialist does not believe in the power of passion. He will never agree that a sweeping passion is a ravaging torrent which fatally leads a man to certain acts and is therefore an excuse. He thinks that man is responsible for his passion.

The existentialist does not think that man is going to help himself by finding in the world some omen by which to orient himself. Because he thinks that man

---

* *a priori*—accepted on the basis of theory rather than experience. [Eds.]

will interpret the omen to suit himself. Therefore, he thinks that man, with no support and no aid, is condemned every moment to invent man. Ponge, in a very fine article, has said, "Man is the future of man." That's exactly it. But if it is taken to mean that this future is recorded in heaven, that God sees it, then it is false, because it would really no longer be a future. If it is taken to mean that, whatever a man may be, there is a future to be forged, a virgin future before him, then this remark is sound. But then we are forlorn.

To give you an example which will enable you to understand forlornness better, I shall cite the case of one of my students who came to see me under the following circumstances: his father was on bad terms with his mother, and, moreover, was inclined to be a collaborationist; his older brother had been killed in the German offensive of 1940, and the young man, with somewhat immature but generous feelings, wanted to avenge him. His mother lived alone with him, very much upset by the half-treason of her husband and the death of her older son; the boy was her only consolation.

The boy was faced with the choice of leaving for England and joining the Free French Forces—that is, leaving his mother behind—or remaining with his mother and helping her to carry on. He was fully aware that the woman lived only for him and that his going-off—and perhaps his death—would plunge her into despair. He was also aware that every act that he did for his mother's sake was a sure thing, in the sense that it was helping her to carry on, whereas every effort he made toward going off and fighting was an uncertain move which might run aground and prove completely useless; for example, on his way to England he might, while passing through Spain, be detained indefinitely in a Spanish camp; he might reach England or Algiers and be stuck in an office at a desk job. As a result, he was faced with two very different kinds of action: one, concrete, immediate, but concerning only one individual; the other concerned an incomparably vaster group, a national collectivity, but for that very reason was dubious, and might be interrupted en route. And, at the same time, he was wavering between two kinds of ethics. On the one hand, an ethics of sympathy, of personal devotion; on the other, a broader ethics, but one whose efficacy was more dubious. He had to choose between the two.

Who could help him choose? Christian doctrine? No. Christian doctrine says, "Be charitable, love your neighbor, take the more rugged path, etc., etc." But which is the more rugged path? Whom should he love as a brother? The fighting man or his mother? Which does the greater good, the vague act of fighting in a group, or the concrete one of helping a particular human being to go on living? Who can decide *a priori*? Nobody. No book of ethics can tell him. The Kantian ethics says, "Never treat any person as a means, but as an end." Very well, if I stay with my mother, I'll treat her as an end and not as a means; but by virtue of this very fact, I'm running the risk of treating the people around me who are fighting, as means; and, conversely, if I go to join those who are fighting, I'll be treating them as an end, and, by doing that, I run the risk of treating my mother as a means.

If values are vague, and if they are always too broad for the concrete and specific case that we are considering, the only thing left for us is to trust our instincts. That's what this young man tried to do; and when I saw him, he said, "In the end, feeling is what counts. I ought to choose whichever pushes me in one direction. If I feel that I love my mother enough to sacrifice everything else for her—my desire for vengeance, for action, for adventure—then I'll stay with her. If, on the contrary, I feel that my love for my mother isn't enough, I'll leave."

But how is the value of a feeling determined? What gives his feeling for his mother value? Precisely the fact that he remained with her. I may say that I like so-and-so well enough to sacrifice a certain amount of money for him, but I may say so only if I've done it. I may say, "I love my mother well enough to remain with her" if I have remained with her. The only way to determine the value of this affection is, precisely, to perform an act which confirms and defines it. But, since I require this affection to justify my act, I find myself caught in a vicious circle.

On the other hand, Gide has well said that a mock feeling and a true feeling are almost indistinguishable; to decide that I love my mother and will remain with her, or to remain with her by putting on an act, amount somewhat to the same thing. In other words, the feeling is formed by the acts one performs; so, I can not refer to it in order to act upon it. Which means that I can neither seek within myself the true condition which will impel me to act, nor apply to a system of ethics for concepts which will permit me to act. You will say, "At least, he did go to a teacher for advice." But if you seek advice from a priest, for example, you have chosen this priest; you already knew, more or less, just about what advice he was going to give you. In other words, choosing your adviser is involving yourself. The proof of this is that if you are a Christian, you will say, "Consult a priest." But some priests are collaborating, some are just marking time, some are resisting. Which to choose? If the young man chooses a priest who is resisting or collaborating, he has already decided on the kind of advice he's going to get. Therefore, in coming to see me he knew the answer I was going to give him, and I had only one answer to give: "You're free, choose, that is, invent." No general ethics can show you what is to be done; there are no omens in the world. The Catholics will reply, "But there are." Granted—but, in any case, I myself choose the meaning they have.

When I was a prisoner, I knew a rather remarkable young man who was a Jesuit. He had entered the Jesuit order in the following way: he had had a number of very bad breaks; in childhood, his father died, leaving him in poverty, and he was a scholarship student at a religious institution where he was constantly made to feel that he was being kept out of charity; then, he failed to get any of the honors and distinctions that children like; later on, at about eighteen, he bungled a love affair; finally, at twenty-two, he failed in military training, a childish enough matter, but it was the last straw.

This young fellow might well have felt that he had botched everything. It was a sign of something, but of what? He might have taken refuge in bitterness or despair. But he very wisely looked upon all this as a sign that he was not made for secular triumphs, and that only the triumphs of religion, holiness, and faith were open to him. He saw the hand of God in all this, and so he entered the order. Who can help seeing that he alone decided what the sign meant?

Some other interpretation might have been drawn from this series of setbacks; for example, that he might have done better to turn carpenter or revolutionist. Therefore, he is fully responsible for the interpretation. Forlornness implies that we ourselves choose our being. Forlornness and anguish go together.

As for despair, the term has a very simple meaning. It means that we shall confine ourselves to reckoning only with what depends upon our will, or on the ensemble of probabilities which make our action possible. When we want something, we always have to reckon with probabilities. I may be counting on the arrival of a friend. The friend is coming by rail or street-car; this supposes that the train will arrive on schedule, or that the street-car will not jump the track. I am left in the realm of possibility; but possibilities are to be reckoned with only to the point where my action comports with the ensemble of these possibilities, and no further. The moment the possibilities I am considering are not rigorously involved by my action, I ought to disengage myself from them, because no God, no scheme, can adapt the world and its possibilities to my will. When Descartes said, "Conquer yourself rather than the world," he meant essentially the same thing.

The Marxists to whom I have spoken reply, "You can rely on the support of others in your action, which obviously has certain limits because you're not going to live forever. That means: rely on both what others are doing elsewhere to help you, in China, in Russia, and what they will do later on, after your death, to carry on the action and lead it to its fulfillment, which will be the revolution. You even *have* to rely upon that, otherwise you're immoral." I reply at once that I will always rely on fellow-fighters insofar as these comrades are involved with me in a common struggle, in the unity of a party or a group in which I can more or less make my weight felt; that is, one whose ranks I am in as a fighter and whose movements I am aware of at every moment. In such a situation, relying on the unity and will of the party is exactly like counting on the fact that the train will arrive on time or that the car won't jump the track. But, given that man is free and that there is no human nature for me to depend on, I can not count on men whom I do not know by relying on human goodness or man's concern for the good of society. I don't know what will become of the Russian revolution; I may make an example of it to the extent that at the present time it is apparent that the proletariat plays a part in Russia that it plays in no other nation. But I can't swear that this will inevitably lead to a triumph of the proletariat. I've got to limit myself to what I see.

Given that men are free and that tomorrow they will freely decide what man will be, I can not be sure that, after my death, fellow-fighters will carry on my work to bring it to its maximum perfection. Tomorrow, after my death, some men may decide to set up Fascism, and the others may be cowardly and muddled enough to let them do it. Fascism will then be the human reality, so much the worse for us.

Actually, things will be as man will have decided they are to be. Does that mean that I should abandon myself to quietism? No. First, I should involve myself; then, act on the old saw, "Nothing ventured, nothing gained." Nor does it mean that I shouldn't belong to a party, but rather that I shall have no illusions and shall do what I can. For example, suppose I ask myself, "Will socialization, as such, ever come about?" I know nothing about it. All I know is that I'm going to do everything in my power to bring it about. Beyond that, I can't count on anything. Quietism is the attitude of people who say, "Let others do what I can't do." The doctrine I am presenting is the very opposite of quietism, since it declares, "There is no reality except in action." Moreover, it goes further, since it adds, "Man is nothing else than his plan; he exists only to the extent that he fulfills himself; he is therefore nothing else than the ensemble of his acts, nothing else than his life."

According to this, we can understand why our doctrine horrifies certain people. Because often the only way they can bear their wretchedness is to think, "Circumstances have been against me. What I've been and done doesn't show my true worth. To be sure, I've had no great love, no great friendship, but that's because I haven't met a man or woman who was worthy. The books I've written haven't been very good because I haven't had the proper leisure. I haven't had children to devote myself to because I didn't find a man with whom I could have spent my life. So there remains within me, unused and quite viable, a host of propensities, inclinations, possibilities, that one wouldn't guess from the mere series of things I've done."

Now, for the existentialist there is really no love other than one which manifests itself in a person's being in love. There is no genius other than one which is expressed in works of art; the genius of Proust is the sum of Proust's works; the genius of Racine is his series of tragedies. Outside of that, there is nothing. Why say that Racine could have written another tragedy, when he didn't write it? A man is involved in life, leaves his impress on it, and outside of that there is nothing. To be sure, this may seem a harsh thought to someone whose life hasn't been a success. But, on the other hand, it prompts people to understand that reality alone is what counts, that dreams, expectations, and hopes warrant no more than to define a man as a disappointed dream, as miscarried hopes, as vain expectations. In other words, to define him negatively and not positively. However, when we say, "You are nothing else than your life," that does not imply that the artist will be judged solely on the basis of his works of art; a thousand other things will contribute toward summing him up. What we mean is that a man is nothing else than a series of undertakings, that he is the sum, the organization, the ensemble of the relationships which make up these undertakings.

When all is said and done, what we are accused of, at bottom, is not our pessimism, but an optimistic toughness. If people throw up to us our works of fiction in which we write about people who are soft, weak, cowardly, and sometimes even downright bad, it's not because these people are soft, weak, cowardly, or bad; because if we were to say, as Zola did, that they are that way because of heredity, the workings of environment, society, because of biological or psychological determinism, people would be reassured. They would say, "Well, that's what we're like, no one can do anything about it." But when the existentialist writes about a coward, he says that this coward is responsible for his cowardice. He's not like that because he has a cowardly heart or lung or brain; he's not like that on account of his physiological makeup; but he's like that because he has made himself a coward by his acts. There's no such thing as a cowardly constitution; there are nervous constitutions; there is poor blood, as the common people say, or strong constitutions. But the man whose blood is poor is not a coward on that account, for what makes cowardice is the act of renouncing or yielding. A constitution is not an act; the coward is defined on the basis of the acts he performs. People feel, in a vague sort of way, that this coward we're talking about is guilty of being a coward, and the thought frightens them. What people would like is that a coward or a hero be born that way.

One of the complaints most frequently made about *The Ways of Freedom* can be summed up as follows: "After all, these people are so spineless, how are you going to make heroes out of them?" This objection almost makes me laugh, for it assumes that people are born heroes. That's what people really want to think. If you're born cowardly, you may set your mind perfectly at rest; there's nothing you can do about it; you'll be cowardly all your life, whatever you may do. If you're born a hero, you may set your mind just as much at rest; you'll be a hero all your life; you'll drink like a hero and eat like a hero. What the existentialist says is that the coward makes himself cowardly, that the hero makes himself heroic. There's always a possibility for the coward not to be cowardly any more and for the hero to stop being heroic. What counts is total involvement; some one particular action or set of circumstances is not total involvement.

Thus, I think we have answered a number of the charges concerning existentialism. You see that it can not be taken for a philosophy of quietism, since it defines man in terms of action; nor for a pessimistic description of man—there is no doctrine more optimistic, since man's destiny is within himself; nor for an attempt to discourage man from acting, since it tells him that the only hope is in his acting and that action is the only thing that enables a man to live. Consequently, we are dealing here with an ethics of action and involvement.

JOURNAL WRITINGS

1.   According to Sartre, we are not born with any particular nature; rather, we begin our existence unshaped, and then we choose by our behavior to become whatever type of person we are. In a paragraph, **describe** the kind of person you are, indicating especially your moral standards. In another paragraph, speculate on what the world would be like if everyone lived by your standards.

2.   Sartre believes that people with a deep sense of responsibility suffer anguish while making their choices. **Narrate** a situation that required you to make a choice. Assess the degree of responsibility (if any) you felt for others and for yourself; explain whether you experienced the anguish Sartre talks about.

BRAINSTORMING AND DRAFTING

3.   Draft one paragraph on the similarities and a second paragraph on the differences between God the Father's position in Milton's poem and Sartre's

position in this selection regarding: (a) how free we are, and (b) how responsible we are for our choices. Explain why you agree or disagree with each author's position. You may wish to refer to your answer to the Preview question for this reading.

4. Sartre says we are "condemned" to be free. In a small group (or working alone), discuss or list the **connotations** of the word "condemned." Then draft your own paragraph explaining what Sartre's reasons might be for using the word.

5. Read Anaïs Nin's essay in this unit. In what sense does she offer an antidote to the anguish and despair found in Sartre's universe?

THE AUTHOR'S METHODS

6. Find at least two places in the text where Sartre **defines** a term and then gives an **example** of it in the context of free choice or responsibility. After detailing these instances in a paragraph, evaluate the usefulness of each. In another paragraph, imitate the author's method by defining the term *prejudice* and giving an example of it in the context of the question of free choice.

7. In the third paragraph of Sartre's essay, he uses a number of **transitional** words or phrases. Identify these and explain how these words help to reveal the author's meaning in the passage.

FORMAL WRITING AND RESEARCH PAPERS

8. Sartre asserts that we use excuses of various sorts (for example, our passion) to avoid taking responsibility for our choices. Write a formal paper in which you present and **analyze** some of the daily "excuses" people use to avoid responsibility for their actions. In your **thesis,** make an **argumentative** assertion about these excuses; your paper should also evaluate their validity in response to Sartre's assertion. Be sure to include one or more real or hypothetical **examples** for each excuse.

9. From a recent newspaper story or through library research (see the *National Newspaper Index*), find a **description** of a court case in which the accused person admits committing a crime but offers some reason why he/she should not be held responsible or punished. Write a paper **arguing** that the accused should or should not be held responsible for his/her act, depending on the degree of freedom the accused apparently had. At some appropriate point in your paper, allude to Sartre's concept of responsibility either to support your ideas or to show that, in this case, his concept will not work.

Anaïs Nin

Refusal to Despair

(1975)

Anaïs Nin (1903–1977) was born in Paris and spent her early life in France. When her father deserted the family, she came to New York City with her mother and brothers. Mainly self-educated, she developed an interest in writing, partly as a route to self-discovery. Her friendships and associations with such literary figures and thinkers as Henry Miller and psychiatrist Otto Rank influenced much of her work.

Nin is perhaps best known for her multivolume *Diary,* which dramatically traces her struggles toward personal and literary selfhood; the diaries also spotlight the singular cultural and historical issues of the twentieth century. Her fiction includes *The House of Incest, A Spy in the House of Love,* and a collection of short stories, *Under a Glass Bell.* The following selection, originally addressed to a live audience, contains Nin's characteristic refusal to passively accept what destiny threatens. Instead, she offers her listeners a way to use their freedom actively, a new, more dynamic approach to social and political problems.

PREVIEW

List some of the current events, situations, or problems in today's world that you feel you have no control over. Do these lessen the amount of freedom you have? Why or why not?

I think we are living now in a period which in some ways resembles the time of the plague. It sounds like a very exaggerated image, but we are confronted every day with despair and horror. There is the nightmare of the war and the fear of the bomb, but you know as well as I all the events that cause our universal anxiety. So the feeling I wanted to give you tonight is that during these events, during these happenings, it is as important for us to step out of history as it is for us to live within it. We have to step out of it in order to find the strength with which to participate in it, with which to live in it, and with which to achieve what I was finally able to achieve in the later diaries, which is a *refusal to despair.* This has meant creativity on the one hand and relationship on the other—the obsession with establishing intimate contact, with friendship, with every form of relationship to man, woman, child, to people close to us and to people in other countries.

It's not only the artist who talks about creativity. We can begin to create in a desert of life, we can begin to create with those that we live with, we can begin to create as children do—immediately writing poems or painting when they can hardly hold a brush or a pen. This creativity is a constant interaction between our life and the struggle with larger issues such as history, whose victim we can become. And in order not to be victimized by it we also have to learn to live apart from it. It's not escape, it's having a place that we return to in order to regain our strength, in order to regain our values, in order not to be shattered by events.

It's almost like the man who goes to the bottom of the ocean and takes with him some oxygen to equalize the pressure. I'm talking about equalizing the pressure between outer actions and events which are shattering and devastating to us and then the place where we recompose and reconstruct ourselves, where we finally achieve what Jung called the second birth. The second birth we are entirely responsible for; it's a self-creation. This second birth is the one that *you* can make, and the discovery of that to me was always a great relief. As long as we expect the changes to come only from the outside or from action outside or from political systems, then we are bound to feel helpless, to feel sometimes that reality is bigger and stronger than we are. But if suddenly we begin to feel that there is one person *we* can change, simultaneously we change many people around us. And as a writer I suddenly discovered the enormous radius of influence that one person can have.

So when we make this interior change we do affect the external world. Now everybody separated that and said: there is *either* rushing virtuously to live a collective life *or else* there is this selfish introspection and concern with your own development. But the two are completely interdependent, they are completely interactive; and the more you have this response to life, the more you have a source to respond with, then of course the more enrichment you pass around you. Why we made a dichotomy between those two—saying that the two wouldn't enrich each other—I don't know. Because whatever the individual does for himself and by himself is something that ultimately flows back again like a river into the collective unconscious.* So if we are disappointed today in the external changes it's because not enough of us have worked at raising a better quality of human being: one who is more aware, more able to evaluate, judge others, judge the characters of our leaders.

That is the kind of responsibility I think we have to take. For example, when I got hysterical over the assassination of Dr. King, what I felt was guilt, a kind of total guilt. Though I am incapable of such an act of hostility, still I felt it came from all our hostilities. I wrote at the end of one diary about war. When war came in '39, I said: "I have never been responsible for an act of war and yet I am now involved in this thing that has happened to the whole world." And even then I felt that this was an aggregate of all our hostilities, and that's why I fight hostility.

---

* collective unconscious—a portion of the unconscious that stems from our evolutionary development, and is the same for everyone. [Eds.]

We have to work upon ourselves because, as Loren Eisley said, every time we come to terms with hostility within ourselves we are creating the possibility of someday not having war. In other words, I'm putting back into the self the responsibility for the collective life. If each one of us took very seriously the fact that every little act, every little word we utter, every injury we do to another human being is really what is projected into larger issues; if we could once begin to think of it that way, then each one of us, like a small cell, would do the work of creating a human self, a kind of self who wouldn't have ghettos, a kind of self that wouldn't go to war. Then we could begin to have the cell which would influence an enormous amount of cells around you. I don't think we can measure the radius of the personal influence of one person, within the home, outside of the home, in the neighborhood, and finally in national affairs.

We never connected those two; we always thought we had to approach the larger issues directly; we never thought we could transform the larger issues by transforming ourselves. If first of all every individual had taught himself lucidity about character, the knowledge of psychological disturbances in depth, and had learned to go inside of himself, he could learn to perceive the workings of others, he would be able to choose better leaders. He would be able to do whatever it is that he does in his profession far better if he had this added lucidity, this clairvoyance that the recognition of other people's subtlety and complexity gives.

As recently as a few weeks ago, I was reading a book called *Future Shock*—which gave *me* a shock! Because it implied that because of technology and our world's accelerated rhythm, we were doomed not to relate to each other. Because things were happening so fast and we were moving from town to town and we were uprooted and we were transients, we didn't have time really for relation. What shocked me was the concept that technology should dictate to us what our human relations should be and decide that because our life has been accelerated we have no time for relationship. This is the unfortunate consequence of the false concept we had about *contact*. And what helped us to distort the sense of contact was the media, which gave us the illusion that we were in touch with all the world and everything that was happening in the world. The media fabricate personalities and offer as false a vision of the world as we can possibly have. Although sometimes it serves us, most of the time it deceives us. So, ultimately it comes back to the way we conceive of human beings or events or history or wars or other nations or other races; only from some kind of evaluation from within, not from the media, do we really come to an understanding of others. The media give us a false sense of communication and of contact.

We talk about media and we talk about new sensitive tapes and we think about all kinds of ways of recording, but we never think of our bodies and our mind and our hearts as receptors. And that can only happen when we develop a sensitivity, when we get rid of the defenses which I call the calluses of the soul. R. D. Laing has a beautiful long paragraph explaining that while we all have a hope of authentic encounters and relationships taking place, they will not take place until we unmask ourselves, until we get rid of the persona, until we get rid of the defenses, the projections and introjections. He mentions all the interferences; and the diary revealed to me, when I finally opened it up to you, what those interferences were. They were mostly fear, fear of other human beings—which I suddenly lost the moment that I published the diaries. So the gamble proved to me that if we gamble in depth, if we offer the deep and the genuine part of ourselves, then it's not destructible. We cannot be destroyed.

Alvin Toffler also says in *Future Shock* that the students who are turning toward astrology, toward mysticism, toward the East, toward anything of the spirit, are *dropping out* of technology. I say: "No, they are trying to find a source of strength and a center so that technology doesn't enslave us, so that we are the captains of our own lives." So I don't agree with him at all. The turning toward other things is really an attempt to create a self which can then survive in the air in which we live. He lays great stress on what he calls the acceleration of our lives, and he argues that this is ruining the possibility of contact, of friendships. But I was able to disprove that this year because I took an unusually heavy load of lectures. I couldn't say no; I said yes, yes, yes and I went all over the country. Finally it became very accelerated. I saw so many people, and they passed by so quickly. Yet in spite of that, seeing thousands of people, I was able to select friends and make friendships in those few minutes of passing. So it isn't necessary for us to be victims of accelerated living or of transience or of moving away. It is a question of how deep the contact is when the contact is made.

I always had the wish to commune with others, despite the fact that during childhood, what I call my bridge to the world was broken by the desertion of the father, a situation which usually instills a great deal of mistrust. Traumas create this mistrust of human beings, because a human being can hurt you, can desert you, can betray you. Yet I still say that it's a million times better to risk being deserted or betrayed than to withdraw into a fortress of alienation, shut the door and break the contact with others. Because then we really die. That is death. That is emotional death. It is mistrust that makes us do that, mistrust and fear of pain, which I expressed in the diary very often. As a child of eleven, I said I never wanted to love again because whatever you love you lose—I was thinking of my Spanish grandmother whom I would never see again. So I learned that mistrust was the root of the separation between human beings.

I struggled all my life—now with the women's studies, with the women's movement, with men—to involve everyone in this connection, this contact which comes out of feeling for others. For though I experienced mistrust, I did not let that make me insensitive. Yet what *Future Shock* says, specifically almost, is that we are bound to become insensitive; that since we receive too much information, are battered by too many events, and are confronted with the whole universe, the best thing to do and the thing we will ultimately do is to shut off the source of feeling. That's why it's a dangerous book, I think. It's a shocking book because it is accepting what technology might do to us instead of saying we have to struggle against this tendency, against the dehumanization and loss of contact occasioned by the acceleration of life or the fact that we move about so much.

I read a remarkable statement the other day about Aldous Huxley who, toward the end of his life when he was invited to speak at Berkeley, said: "I expect that you think I will talk about very scholarly things and give you the sum of all my life's knowledge." And he went on and on about what he knew people expected of him. But then he said: "Tonight I only feel like coming to ask you to be a little kinder to each other."

This warmth is something we all need, we need nourishment, we need encouragement. Our culture, however, made us ashamed of paying compliments, of saying beautiful things to other people. We were not supposed to. A compliment was a falsity in itself to the Puritan. You never said anything complimentary. Now the Latin races encourage compliments. They believe that if someone looks beautiful today one should say it. Why do we eliminate that? Why should we consider it false to give each other the nourishing encouragement which sustains us, which is the obverse of destructive criticism, of hostility?

Messages are conveyed by the eyes, sometimes by no words at all. It is no excuse to say that technology has accelerated our life to the point where we pass others without noticing them, without contacting, or without a real meeting. A real meeting can take place in one instant. But how does that come about? How do we reach a moment when in one instant we can communicate with another human being?

The most beautiful metaphor I know for this connecting with others I discovered when I was invited to Stanford by the electrical engineers to talk about the integrated circuits. I couldn't understand first of all why I was invited. I didn't know anything about integrated circuits. I tried to read the book by the professor who invited me and finally had to ask my friends for explanations. When I got there I was shown through the laboratory and finally talked with the fifteen electrical engineers who do electronic circuits. They showed me the drawings on the walls, the large drawings that they start with and which become smaller and smaller. And then I understood that as a metaphor this was really a wonderful thing. Of course when the artist is ignorant of science then he turns science into a metaphor. And I always said that the artist today will use the images of science, that he will use all the marvelous metaphors of science when he really begins to understand them. So I began to understand the integrated circuit, and I began to think of it as an image of our psychic problem, which was really to find all these fine, terribly delicate connections with other human beings.

Now these circuits are damaged very often in childhood and we don't receive anything. These circuits very often are damaged by the culture or they become insensitive to stimuli. There is also in *Future Shock* the theory that, as a result of technology, we are receiving too many messages, too much information which we cannot cope with, too much devastating news of everything that is happening in the world, and that the way human beings protect themselves from too much emotional receptivity is by trying not to feel at all. And Toffler points out the dangers, just as the psychologists have, of what corresponds to the physical shock in the face of an accident or a sudden death or a sudden tragedy: the body ceases in a sense to be really alive or conscious, and this condition, known as psychic shock, is the way we protect ourselves when we see, for instance, the war in Vietnam on television. The way we have learned to protect ourselves is *not to feel,* which is a terrible danger because then we really become sub-human or non-human and are as far away from our real connection with other human beings as we possibly can be. So we have to fight these dangerous elements in technology which come with an expanded universe and the illusion the media give us of being in touch with everything simply because we are given so much to *see*. You can only be in touch by feeling.

So the integrated circuit is really for the human being quite different from the scientific integrated circuit. It is really the channel of feeling that has to be kept open. Now how do we do that when we want to protect ourselves from feeling too much or from being devastated or being disintegrated by experience? Well, my suggestion was that you build up a sufficient inner spiritual resistance— what I call "the spirit house." We must not close off the circuits, the emotional circuits. That's not the way. Because then we become arid and we really die, psychically. So all those words we used so carelessly before, such as alienation, dropping out, all those words really had a very fatal meaning. Because it is really a kind of death to separate from others, to separate from what is happening in the world, to separate from feeling.

I think if we came back to the concept of a small and intimate universe and then realized that what we call the communal life or mass movements are really aggregates of individuals and that the more marvelous, the more developed, the more expanded, the deeper, the more poetic, the more free the individual is, then the mass, the larger movements, would take on a different character. We would not be subjected then to the will or to the distorted power-thoughts of other people. Somehow we felt that the best thing for the community was to abdicate our individuality, not to think for ourselves or to examine ourselves, never realizing that what we could bring to the group and what we brought to the communal life was really the summary of our own self-development, our own growth, and that the more we bring something that *we* have already worked out to the collective life, the more we bring to this mass movement. If we brought something besides our problems or our difficulties or the unsolved parts of our lives, then these tremendously large movements would have another character. They would not serve for war and they wouldn't serve for separations between races and they wouldn't divide us. We wouldn't have so much hostility as we have in our society, a frightening amount of hostility. It's almost a blind hostility that doesn't even know where it comes from, blind anger which strikes out at others and blames others always for whatever trouble we find ourselves in.

To me war is a multiplication of our own hostilities, and possibly we are beginning to realize that. For example, when I went to Germany, invited to the Book Fair, I went with a tight heart because so many of my friends are Jews, and I felt very full of hatred of Germany. But on the radio they had a philosopher, who is now the head of the government of the new Germany, saying that we had to combat hostility, individually, every one of us, if we didn't want a war again. *He was saying that, over the radio.* That was my first inkling that possibly there was a new Germany—this consciousness of what hostility or of what passivity toward the leader could lead to.

So we can't go on just marching and expecting the change to come always from outside. We tried and we saw that some external changes could be made: the abortion laws, women's rights. There are some changes that can be effected from the outside. But the greatest and most important change must be inner; we must change ourselves as human beings. Because we have really caused minor wars and minor types of violence right amongst ourselves, within our immediate and personal situations: in the family, in relationships, in school, and through our hostility towards the stranger. I experienced that very strongly when I first came to America. The foreigner was an outsider. This feeling belongs to the American culture, and until recently (now I've been adopted) they always used to say "Paris-born Anaïs Nin"—as they say "Russian-born Nabokov" or "Polish-born Kozinski." That is a way of saying that you are an outsider.

Then the anger about blaming society for the situation in which we find ourselves—blaming, say, man for the situation in which woman finds herself. I don't believe in that because I believe very much our double responsibility, that we engage ourselves in destructive relationships, that we have a part of the responsibility, unconsciously. When I engaged in a destructive relationship with Gonzalo, there was a part of me that was living through him—the rebel—which I refused to live out myself. I wasn't a victim of anything. There was something going on there which happened to be a destructive alliance. But there was also a positive thing; he was showing me how destructive explosions were, how destructive that kind of rebellion was, the kind of rebellion he manifested. So that I was learning, I was experiencing, I was testing that through another person.

I'll tell you one thing I do feel. I feel we do have a surplus of hostility, of undirected hostility, because we refuse to take part of the responsibility for the things we find ourselves caught in, and that we despair because we only live on the external part of history. If we are going to live in history then we are going to have despair; if we find absolutely no nourishing, no revitalizing, no recharging power in ourselves, then we're going to be bitter and we are always going to be shifting the blame either to society or to the other—or on man, as some women are doing at the moment. You see this makes us feel helpless. If we are helpless, we are angry and if we are angry, we're violent.

I came to realize that our need and hunger for closeness, after the terrible period of alienation, occurred because we always blamed alienation on every possible cause except the right one. We were alienated from *ourselves*. How could we love, how could we give, how could we trust, how could we share what we didn't have to give? If we did not spend some time in creating ourselves in depth and power, with what were we going to relate to others?

And of course when you're interested in growth, you're interested in the growth of those around you. They are absolutely interdependent. You grow only insofar as people around you are also growing and expanding and becoming freer. It is something that is interactive, something that you give to each other.

It isn't something that you accomplish alone. What you accomplish alone and what you have to do first of all is to *exist*, to *be*, so that you can be then a friend or a lover or a mother or a child. In other words, what our culture was saying was something so illogical, so impossible. It was saying: "Don't concern yourself with yourself. Be generous, be active in the world, give yourself to causes and all that *without a self!*" What can you give when there is no self, when you have no sensitivity, no receptivity, no warmth, nothing to contact others *with?* And this error grew and grew.

In our twenties we have conflicts. We think everything is either-or, black or white; we are caught between them and we lose all our energy in the conflicts. My answer, later on in maturity, was to do them all. Not to exclude any, not to make a choice. I wanted to be a woman, I wanted to be an artist, I wanted to be everything. And I took everything in, and the more you take in the more strength you find waiting to accomplish things and to expand your life, instead of the other (which is what we have been taught to do) which is to look for structure and to fear change, *above all to fear change.* Now I didn't fear change, and that is another thing I learned from psychology, that we evolve. We don't need revolutions provided we evolve, provided we are constantly open to new experience, provided we are constantly open to other human beings and what they have to give us.

There is a beautiful book, entitled *Out of Africa,* by Isak Dinesen, who had a coffee farm and lived a long time with the Africans. Natural disasters played a central role in the court of justice of the Africans and were used as evidence, whether in the case of an accident or a deliberate act like murder. This is a totally different idea of justice, absolutely different from ours, and she had a very difficult time trying to see things as the Africans saw them. But she conceded that it was part of their culture and it was sincere. It was their concept of justice, and it had to be carried out. She didn't try to impose white justice on the African village. The recognition of other cultures and other forms of thought, knowing when to yield, I think is part of our gift for relationship. There is a time when yielding is not conceding but acceptance of the other's existence and also of the motivation for what he does.

This is a good night to talk about the source of strength which we need when the outer changes fail us. Before, when I talked about that, people said I was referring to the Ivory Tower, to a great concern and obsession with art and a turning away from action. But I never meant that. I meant that they were interrelated and that when we can't act in the outside or the outside doesn't change and we want to break our heads against the things that we can't change, then it is time just simply to move back to the center of ourselves. I discovered this source of strength in the way all of us discover a source of strength, which is during the first traumatic experiences, the first handicaps, the first difficulties. Coming from what the social welfare calls the broken home, being uprooted, knowing what poverty is, coming to a country whose language I didn't know—all these things taught me simply to put my roots in the self. As I said, I became "a lady with transportable roots." This is very important to all of us because our culture gave us a false impression of the value of living completely in history, completely objectively, completely outside in what was happening—that there was something almost evil about subjectivity. . . . So I like to have this image of a place where you construct some source of strength, some way of resisting outer pressures. And I didn't mean the Ivory Tower. I often say if you write me a letter to the Ivory Tower, I won't answer.

I started with a conviction which I've never had to retract: that all of us can be hurt or in trouble. I had another conviction, which came from Baudelaire, that in all of us there is a man, a woman, and child—which solves all the question of militancy! In all of us there is a man, a woman, and a child, and the child is usually an orphan. So we have a tremendous task to do: we have to take care of this orphan in ourselves and in others; we have to act out our creativity in every moment of our life. And I remember doing something which was considered very silly at the time. When war was imminent in '39, I was living on a houseboat. I hadn't finished painting and fixing it and so I was still working on it while my friends were collapsing and saying: "The war is coming. Why are you painting and fixing the boat?" I said: "Well, I'm only doing it to sustain my own defiance of catastrophe." It was really a spiritual thing. I had to do that to maintain myself from collapsing—as they were collapsing *in my boat!* It was just a challenge. You see, I knew the war was coming. It wasn't lack of a sense of reality, it wasn't schizophrenia. I knew perfectly well what was coming. But I wanted to make a gesture which strengthened *me,* which strengthened this capacity to endure catastrophe.

This is why I have been able to speak, for instance at City College in Los Angeles, which is almost entirely Black. They are the most underprivileged students that you could possibly imagine, their backgrounds are so very difficult. But they understood when I spoke. They had a student paper, and all the paper said was: the world is falling apart. That was their image of the world—that it was hopeless. They had lost faith in any social change, and the only thing they did understand was that I asked them to put their stability in themselves. They understood that, the search, in an unstable world, for a place of stability and clarity and faith. Some place to recover their faith. Because they feel that the external is immovable.

Walter Lippmann said that "the discontent that is shocking the world cannot be dealt with by politics only, or on the periphery of life, but must touch the central and intimate places of personal life. What has been wrecked cannot be restored by some new political gadget." This has been the substance of all my talks this year.

JOURNAL WRITINGS

1. From your personal experience, **describe** a problem over which you feel you have little or no control. According to Nin's theory, how might you exert your own will to influence this situation?
2. What do you think Nin means by "creating a self"? That is, what do we think about and what specific actions do we undertake on our way to becoming real selves?
3. Using the answers you gave in question 2 above, write a **description** of yourself—not your physical self, but your inner self. Try to identify all your strengths and weaknesses.

BRAINSTORMING AND DRAFTING

4. Milton, Sartre, and Nin discuss the idea of responsibility. How are their ideas similar? How do their attitudes toward responsibility differ? Which (if any) of these attitudes do you think is more valid? Why?

5. Nin mentions that some women become angry when they blame their problems on men. In a small group (or working individually), list and discuss two or three kinds of unequal situations in which women find themselves caught. Note some **specific** ways in which Nin might say that the women themselves may be partially responsible for these problems. Or give reasons why you disagree with Nin, showing instead that the women are not responsible for the problems.

THE AUTHOR'S METHODS

6. Nin alludes to several "authorities" such as Baudelaire, Eiseley, Laing, and Lippmann. Consult a **biographical** source in your library to identify one of these people. Then write a brief paragraph explaining why this person's background or work reinforces Nin's ideas.

7. Nin refers to the scientific **metaphor** of integrated circuits to explain the necessity of connecting with others emotionally. Would this kind of metaphoric language be acceptable in a biology lab report? In what disciplines (subjects) might this kind of writing be valued? Why do you think different disciplines value different uses of language?

FORMAL WRITING AND RESEARCH PAPERS

8. Using your personal experience with one or more technological devices, write a paper in which you agree or disagree with the idea that technology can enslave us. If you have read any of the selections in the Technology unit, you may wish to incorporate some of that material in your paper.

9. Select one of the examples of inequality from your answer to Brainstorming question 5. Consult the card or computer catalog or the *Social Sciences Index* in your library to find several sources on this topic. Then write a formal problem-solving paper in which you explain the problem in detail and recommend some ways in which women might exert their own will to help solve the problem.

Jacqueline Jones

In Pursuit of Freedom

(1985)

A native of Wilmington, Delaware, Jacqueline Jones (born 1948) received a B.A. from the University of Delaware and an M.A. and Ph.D. from the University of Wisconsin at Madison. She is currently a scholar and professor of history at Wellesley College, Massachusetts. In her first book, *Soldiers of Light and Love: Northern Teachers and Georgia Blacks, 1865–1873,* Jones examined the efforts of Yankee teachers to educate former slaves after the Civil War.

    The following selection is taken from her second book, *Labor of Love, Labor of Sorrow: Black Women, Work, and the Family from Slavery to the Present,* for which she received the Bancroft Prize from Columbia University. Emphasizing the plight of allegedly "freed" black women, Jones dramatically chronicles the severe limitations these women continued to suffer after emancipation. Offered political freedom, many nevertheless remained literally as well as symbolically imprisoned because of their emotional commitments.

PREVIEW

In 1863, President Abraham Lincoln issued the Emancipation Proclamation, which officially freed the slaves in all states still in rebellion against the Union. Imagine yourself as a slave confronted with the opportunity to be free. Write a few sentences weighing the risks as well as the potential rewards of freedom.

The institution of slavery disintegrated gradually. It cracked under the weight of Confederate preparations for war soon after cannons fired on Fort Sumter in April 1861 and finally crumbled (in some parts of the South many years after the Confederate surrender) when the last slaves were free to decide whether to leave or remain on their master's plantation. The specific ways in which southern defense strategy affected blacks varied according to time and place; before the war's end a combination of factors based on circumstance and personal initiative opened the way to freedom for many, but often slowly, and only by degrees. In the words of historian Leon Litwack, most slaves "were neither 'rebellious' nor 'faithful' in the fullest sense of these terms, but rather ambivalent and observant, some of them frankly opportunistic, many of them anxious to preserve their anonymity, biding their time, searching for opportunities to break the dependency that bound them to their white families." For women, the welfare of their children was often the primary consideration in determining an appropriate course of action once they confronted—or created—a moment ripe with possibilities.[1]

Three individual cases suggest the varying states of awareness and choice that could shape the decisions of slave women during this period of upheaval. In 1862 a seventy-year-old Georgia bondswoman engineered a dramatic escape for herself and twenty-two children and grandchildren. The group floated forty miles down the Savannah River on a flatboat and finally found refuge on a federal vessel. In contrast, Hannah Davidson recalled many years later that she and the other slaves on a Kentucky plantation lived in such rural isolation—and under such tyranny—that they remained in servitude until the mid-1880s: "We didn't even know we were free," she said. Yet Rosaline Rogers, thirty-eight years old at the war's end and mother of fourteen children, kept her family together on her master's Tennessee plantation, even after she was free to leave: "I was given my choice of staying on the same plantation, working on shares, or taking my family away, letting them out [to work in return] for their food and clothes. I decided to stay on that way; I could have my children with me." But, she added, the arrangement was far from satisfactory, for her children "were not allowed to go to school, they were taught only to work."[2]

The logic of resistance proceeded apace on plantations all over the South as slaveholders became increasingly preoccupied with the Confederacy's declining military fortunes. On a Mississippi plantation, Dora Franks overheard her master and mistress discuss the horror of an impending Yankee victory. The very thought of it made the white woman "feel lak jumpin' in de well," but, Dora Franks declared, "from dat minute I started prayin' for freedom. All de res' of de women done de same." Slaves did not have to keep apprised of rebel maneuvers on the battleground to take advantage of novel situations produced by an absent master, a greenhorn overseer, or a nervous mistress uncertain how to maintain the upper hand. Under these conditions black women, men, and children slowed their workpace to a crawl. "Awkward," "inefficient," "lazy," "erratic," "ungovernable," and "slack" (according to exasperated whites), they left weeds in the cotton fields, burned the evening's supper to a crisp, and let the cows trample the corn.[3]

Eliza Andrews, daughter of a prominent Georgia judge and slaveholder, expressed disgust when, a few days before the Confederacy's surrender, the family cook Lizzie stated emphatically that she would not be willing to prepare a meal "fur Jesus Christ to-day," let alone for two of her mistress's special friends. Aunt Lizzie and other slave women seemed to be fully aware of the effect their "insolence" had on mistresses "who had not been taught to work and who thought it beneath their standing to soil their hands." Safely behind Union lines, a Tennessee refugee told of an apocryphal encounter between her mistress and General Ulysses S. Grant: "Den she went back to the general, an' begged an' cried, and hel' out her han's, and say, 'General dese han's never was in dough—I never made a cake o' bread in my life; please let me have my cook!' " On some plantations, the suddenly open recalcitrance of female slaves seemed to portend a greater evil, as white parents and children whispered in hushed tones about faithful old mammies who might spy for the Yankees and cooks who could "burn us out" or "slip up and stick any of us in the back."[4]

Their chains loosened by the distractions of war, many slaves challenged the physical and emotional resolve of whites in authority. For the vast majority, however, the war itself only intensified their hardships. As the Confederacy directed more of its resources and manpower toward the defense effort, food supplies became scarce throughout the region. Planters and local government officials, anxious in the midst of black (and even white) rebels on their own soil and uncertain about the future of their new nation, reacted violently to isolated cases of real and imagined insubordination. The owner of a Georgia coastal plantation was so infuriated by the number of his slaves who had fled to Union lines that he took special precautions to hold onto his prized cook; he bound her feet in iron stocks so that "she had to drag herself around her kitchen all day, and at night she was locked into the corn-house." Refugees arrived in Union camps with fresh scars on their backs and told of masters and mistresses unleashing their bitterness on "blobber-mouth niggers [who] done cause a war."[5]

During wartime the responsibility for the care of children, the ill, and the elderly devolved upon slave women to an even greater extent than had been the case during the antebellum period. Military mobilization wreaked havoc on the already fragile ties that held slave families together. Efforts to restrict slave mobility prevented husbands from visiting their "broad" wives on a regular basis and discouraged cross-plantation marriages in general. Confederate slave impressment policies primarily affected men, who were put to work on military construction projects and in armies, factories, and hospitals. The practice of "refugeeing" highly valued slaves to the interior or to another state also meant that the strongest, healthiest men were taken away from plantation wives and children. To provide for the safety of those dependent on her while she tested the limits of a newfound freedom formed the core of a slave-becoming-freedwoman's dilemma.[6]

During the conflict, at different times in different parts of the South, the approaching Union army provided slaves with both an opportunity and an incentive to flee from their masters. Soon after the Union forces took control of the South Carolina Sea Islands, Elizabeth Botume, a newly arrived northern teacher, observed a refugee mother and her three children hurrying toward a government steamer:

> A huge negress was seen striding along with her hominy pot, in which was a live chicken, poised on her head. One child was on her back with its arms tightly clasped around her neck, and its feet about her waist, and under each arm was a smaller child. Her apron was tucked up in front, evidently filled with articles of clothing. Her feet were bare, and in her mouth was a short clay pipe. A poor little yellow dog ran by her side, and a half-grown pig trotted on before.

From other parts of the South came similar descriptions of women travelers balancing bundles on their heads and children on their backs. These miniature caravans exemplified the difficulties faced by single mothers who ran away from their masters and sought protection behind Union lines.[7]

To women like the Louisiana mother who brought her dead child ("shot by her pursuing master") into a Yankee army camp "to be buried, as she said, *free*," Union territory symbolized the end of an old life and the beginning of a new one. But it was an inauspicious beginning. Crowded together, often lacking food, shelter, and medicine, these human "contraband of war" lived a wretched existence. Moreover, in 1863 the refugee settlements—and virtually any areas under federal control—became targets for military officials seeking black male conscripts. Black men wanted to defend their families and fight for freedom, and almost a quarter of a million served the Union war effort in some formal capacity—half as soldiers, the rest as laborers, teamsters, craftsmen, and servants. More than 93,000 black men from the Confederate states alone—14 percent of the black male population aged eighteen to forty-five—fought with the Union army. However, the violent wrenching of draftees from their wives and children caused great resentment among the refugees. The women of one camp, wrote Elizabeth Botume, "were proud of volunteers, but a draft was like an ignominious seizure." The scene in another one "raided" by Yankee soldiers hardly resembled a haven for the oppressed; wives "were crying bitterly, some looked angry and revengeful, but there was more grief than anything else."[8]

Whether southern black men volunteered for or were pressed into Union military service, the well-being of their families remained a constant source of anxiety for them. Wives and children who remained behind in Confederate territory on their masters' plantation, and even some of those who belonged to owners sympathetic to the northern cause, bore the brunt of white men's anger as a way of life quickly began to slip away. Frances Johnson, a Kentucky slave woman whose husband was a Union soldier, reported that in 1864 her master had told her, "all the 'niggers' did mighty wrong in joining the Army." One day the following spring, she recalled, "my masters son . . . whipped me severely on my refusing to do some work for him which I was not in a condition to perform. He beat me in the presence of his father who told him [the son] to 'buck me and give me a thousand' meaning thereby a thousand lashes." The next day this mother of three managed to flee with her children and find refuge with her sister in nearby Lexington. In another case a Missouri slave woman wrote to her soldier husband, "They are treating me worse and worse every day. Our child cries for you," but added, " . . . do not fret too much for me for it wont be long before I will be free and then all we make will be ours." Accounts like these caused black soldiers to demand that the federal government provide their loved ones with some form of protection.[9]

In an effort to stay together and escape the vengeance of southern whites, some families followed their menfolk to the front lines. But soldiers' wives, denounced as prostitutes and "idle, lazy vagrants" by military officials, found that the army camps offered little in the way of refuge from callousness and abuse. The payment of soldiers' wages was a notoriously slow and unpredictable process, leaving mothers with responsibility for the full support of their children. The elaborate application procedures discouraged even qualified women from seeking aid from the Army Quartermaster Department. A few wives found jobs as laundresses and cooks in and around the camps, but gainful employment was not easy to come by during such chaotic times. Meanwhile, not only did many families lack basic creature comforts in the form of adequate clothing and shelter, they were at times deprived of what little they did have by Union officers who felt that the presence of black wives impaired the military efficiency of their husbands. At Camp Nelson, Kentucky, in late 1864, white soldiers leveled the makeshift shantytown erected by black women to house their children and left four hundred persons homeless in bitterly cold weather. Such was the treatment accorded the kin of "soldiers who were even then in the field fighting for that Government which was causing all this suffering to their people."[10]

Although many women had no choice but to seek food and safety from northern troops, often with bitterly disappointing results, others managed to attain relative freedom from white interference and remain on or near their old homesites. In areas where whites had fled and large numbers of black men had marched—or been marched off—with the Union army, wives, mothers, daughters, and sisters often grew crops and cared for each other. For example, several hundred women from the Combahee River region of South Carolina made up a small colony unto themselves in a Sea Island settlement. They prided themselves on their special handicrafts sent to their men "wid Mon'gomery's boys in de regiment": gloves and stockings made from "coarse yarn spun in a tin basin and knitted on reed, cut in the swamps." Together with men and women from other areas, the "Combees" cultivated cotton and potato patches, gathered ground nuts, minded the children, and nursed the ill.[11]

The end of the war signaled the first chance for large numbers of blacks to leave their slave quarters as a demonstration of liberty. Asked why she wanted to move off her master's South Carolina plantation, the former slave Patience responded in a manner that belied her name: "I must go, if I stay here I'll never know I'm free." An elderly black woman abandoned the relative comfort of her mistress's home to live in a small village of freed people near Greensboro, Georgia, so that she could, in her words, *"Joy my freedom!"* These and other freedwomen acted decisively to escape from the confinement of the place where they had lived as slaves. In the process they deprived the white South of a large part of its black labor supply.[12]

Amid the dislocation of Civil War, then, black women's priorities and obligations coalesced into a single purpose: to escape from the oppression of slavery while keeping their families intact. Variations on this theme recurred throughout the South, as individual women, in concert with their kin, composed their own hymns to emancipation more or less unfettered by the vicissitudes of war. Though the black family suffered a series of disruptions provoked by Confederates and Yankees alike, it emerged as a strong and vital institution once the conflict had ended. The destiny of freedwomen in the postbellum period would be inextricably linked to that of their freed families.

Notes

[1] Leon F. Litwack, *Been in the Storm So Long: The Aftermath of Slavery* (New York: Alfred A. Knopf, 1979), p. 162. Although lacking an analytical framework, this work is an excellent compendium of anecdotes and examples (drawn from a wealth of primary sources) related to the blacks' responses to the Civil War and emancipation.

Several studies are particularly useful in their treatment of the deinstitutionalization of slavery at the regional, state, and local levels: Clarence Mohr, "Georgia Blacks during Secession and Civil War, 1859–1865" (Ph.D. diss., University of Georgia, 1975); C. Peter Ripley, *Slaves and Freedmen in Civil War Louisiana* (Baton Rouge, LA: Louisiana State University Press, 1976); Robert F. Engs, *Freedom's First Generation: Black Hampton, Virginia, 1861–1890* (Philadelphia, PA: University of Pennsylvania Press, 1979); Armstead L. Robinson, "In the Shadow of Old John Brown: Insurrection Anxiety and Confederate Mobilization, 1861–1863," *Journal of Negro History* 65 (Fall 1980):279–97; John Cimprich, "Slave Behavior During the Federal Occupation of Tennessee, 1862–1865," *Historian* 44 (May 1982):335–46. See also Dorothy Sterling, ed., *We Are Your Sisters: Black Women in the Nineteenth Century* (New York: W. W. Norton, 1984), pp. 237–61.

[2] Thomas Wentworth Higginson, *Army Life in a Black Regiment* (Boston, MA: Fields, Osgood and Co., 1870), p. 247. The quotations from former slaves are taken from George P. Rawick, ed., *The American Slave: A Composite Autobiography*, 19 vols., Series 1 (Westport, CT: Greenwood Press, 1972), *Ohio Narratives*, vol. 16, p. 29; *Indiana Narratives*, vol. 6, pp. 165–66. Hereafter all references to this collection (Series 1) will include only the name of the state and part, volume, and page numbers.

[3] *Mississippi Narratives*, vol. 7, p. 52; [Leon F.] Litwack, *Been in the Storm So Long*, pp. 3–63.

[4] Eliza F. Andrews, *The War-Time Journal of a Georgia Girl, 1864–1865* (New York: D. Appleton and Co., 1908), pp. 111, 127–28, 355; *Florida Narratives*, vol. 17, p. 74; Laura S. Haviland, *A Woman's Life-Work: Labors and Experiences of Laura S. Haviland* (Chicago, IL: C. V. Waite and Co., 1887), p. 266; Litwack, *Been in the Storm So Long*, p. 162.

[5] Elizabeth Hyde Botume, *First Days Amongst the Contrabands* (Boston, MA: Lee and Shepard, 1893), p. 140; *Texas Narratives*, Pt. IV, vol. 5, pp. 193–94. See also Haviland, *Woman's Life-Work*, pp. 254, 268; Laura M. Towne, *Letters and Diary of Laura M. Towne; Written from the Sea Islands of South Carolina, 1862–1884*, ed. Rupert Sargent Holland (Cambridge, MA: Riverside Press, 1912), p. 24; Litwack, *Been in the Storm So Long*, pp. 10–11, 13, 54, 58, 182–83. Mohr documents the effects of war-time food shortages and the escalation of racial violence in "Georgia Blacks."

[6] Robert F. Durden, *The Gray and the Black: The Confederate Debate on Emancipation* (Baton Rouge, LA: Louisiana State University Press, 1972); James H. Brewer, *The Confederate Negro: Virginia's Craftsmen and Military Laborers, 1861–1865* (Durham, NC: Duke University Press, 1969); Ripley, *Slaves and Freedmen*, pp. 9–16, 151–57; Mohr, "Georgia Blacks," pp. 115, 129, 137–38, 149, 157; Randolph B. Campbell and Donald K. Pickens, "Document: 'My Dear Husband': A Texas Slave's Love Letter, 1862," *Journal of Negro History* 65 (Fall 1980):361–64.

[7] [Elizabeth Hyde] Botume, *First Days [Amongst the Contrabands]*, p. 15. Compare the description of a black woman on her way to Columbia, South Carolina, in December 1865 by John Richard Dennett, *The South As It Is: 1865–1866*, ed. Henry M. Christman (New York: Viking Press, 1965), p. 233: "She was a middle-aged woman, and appeared to be accompanied on her pilgrimage by her family. A little boy was following her, a little girl she led by the hand, and on her back was an infant slung in a shawl. A heavy bundle was balanced on her head. They all seemed weary as they trudged along through the mud, and their clothing was too scanty for the winter weather."

See also Clarence Mohr, "Before Sherman: Georgia Blacks and the Union War Effort, 1861–1864," *Journal of Southern History* 45 (August 1979):338–41; Ripley, *Slaves and Freedmen*, p. 150; Herbert G. Gutman, *The Black Family in Slavery and Freedom, 1750–1925* (New York: Pantheon, 1976), pp. 268–69; Engs, *Freedom's First Generation*, p. 27.

[8] Haviland, *Woman's Life-Work*, p. 304; Botume, *First Days*, p. 55; Towne, *Letters and Dairy*, p. 45; Susie King Taylor, *Reminiscences of My Life in Camp With the 33D United States Colored Troops Late*

1st S. C. Volunteers (Boston, MA: Published by the author, 1902), pp. 16–21; Gutman, *Black Family,* pp. 22–24; *Virginia Narratives,* vol. 16, p. 43; Berlin, Reidy, and Rowland, eds., *Black Military Experience,* p. 12. On the willingness of black men to fight on behalf of their families, see also Gutman, *Black Family,* pp. 371–85; Mohr, "Before Sherman," pp. 339–41.

Recruitment policies and tactics are discussed in Willie Lee Rose, *Rehearsal for Reconstruction: The Port Royal Experiment* (Indianapolis, IN: Bobbs-Merrill, 1964), pp. 264–69; Ripley, *Slaves and Freedmen,* pp. 108–9, 153–55; Gerteis, *From Contraband to Freedman;* Berlin, Reidy, and Rowland, eds., *Black Military Experience,* pp. 37–299.

Mathew Brady, the Civil War photographer, was primarily interested in corpses, cannon, and Union officers, but his *Illustrated History of the Civil War* (New York: Fairfax Press, n.d., orig. pub. 1912) contains pictures of black refugees (pp. 24, 146) and black laundresses at the camp in Yorktown (p. 141). All the women in the picture on p. 146 are wearing kerchiefs; the two men are wearing different kinds of hats. The picture shows eight women, two men, and eight children.

[9] "302: Affadavit of a Kentucky Black Soldier's Wife"; "296: Missouri Slave Woman to Her Soldier Husband," in Berlin, Reidy, and Rowland, eds., *Black Military Experience,* pp. 87, 686–87, 694–95. See also "314 E: Anonymous Virginia Black Soldier . . . ," ibid., p. 725.

[10] "312A: Affadavit of a Northern Missionary"; "313: Commander of a Tennessee Black Regiment to the Headquarters of the Department of the Mississippi and a Report by the Superintendent of Freedmen in West Tennessee"; "312B: Superintendent of the 'Refugee Home' at Camp Nelson, Kentucky, to the Freedmen's Bureau Commissioner," in Berlin, Reidy, and Rowland, eds., *Black Military Experience,* pp. 715–19; Victor B. Howard, "The Civil War in Kentucky: The Slave Claims His Freedom," *Journal of Negro History* 67 (Fall 1982):250–52. See also Litwack, *Been in the Storm So Long,* pp. 64–103; Ripley, *Slaves and Freedmen,* p. 155; Taylor, *Reminiscences,* p. 16.

For other firsthand accounts of black soldiers' families and their living conditions, see Trowbridge, *The South,* p. 288; Elizabeth Ware Pearson, ed., *Letters from Port Royal: 1862–1868* (New York: Arno Press, 1969; orig. pub. 1906), p. 41; Higginson, *Army Life in a Black Regiment.*

Issues related to the health of refugees in particular and freed people in general are discussed in Alan Raphael, "Health and Social Welfare of Kentucky Black People, 1865–1870," *Societas* 2 (Spring 1972):143–57; Marshall Scott Legan, "Disease and the Freedmen in Mississippi During Reconstruction," *Journal of the History of Medicine and Allied Sciences* 28 (July 1973):257–67.

[11] [Elizabeth Hyde] Botume, *First Days,* pp. 53–63.

[12] Patience quoted in Orville Vernon Burton, "Ungrateful Servants? Edgefield's Black Reconstruction: Part I of the Total History of Edgefield County, South Carolina" (Ph.D. diss., Princeton University, 1976), p. 136; Sidney Andrews, *The South Since the War: As Shown by Fourteen Weeks of Travel and Observation in Georgia and the Carolinas* (Boston, MA: Ticknor and Fields, 1866), p. 353.

JOURNAL WRITINGS

1. **Narrate** a situation from your personal experience in which you felt that your free choice was limited by your love for, or consideration of, other people or your recognition of an external situation. In what sense (if any) is your experience similar to that of the black women whom Jones discusses in the reading?

2. Sometimes exerting our wills creates a backlash of resistance from those in authority over us. **Summarize** an **example** of this from the reading. Despite the obvious disadvantages that the backlash caused, what advantages might have resulted from the blacks' efforts to pursue freedom before the law guaranteed it?

BRAINSTORMING AND DRAFTING

3. Reread the introduction to this unit. Draft a paragraph suggesting how the different types of freedom (or lack of a particular type) might be applied to black women before, during, and after the Civil War.
4. Jones notes that technically "freed" black women and children still had to bear the anger of southern whites who resisted the changes in their way of life, and even the resentment of northern white Union officers. How different is the situation today for minority groups? In a small group (or working individually), discuss some **examples** from group members' personal knowledge in which anger or fear has motivated authorities or a dominating group to limit, however subtly, the free choice of subordinate persons. Draft your own paragraph proposing reasons for this behavior.
5. In what sense might the black women Jones **describes** be considered dramatic **examples** of Sartre's concept of responsibility? Do you think he would approve of their decisions? Why or why not?

THE AUTHOR'S METHODS

6. List all the active **verbs** in the first two sentences. How do they contribute to the effectiveness of these sentences? Write several sentences about the effect of slavery on free choice, using as many strong active verbs as you can.
7. Identify an instance in the text when Jones paraphrases a scholarly source, and an instance when she presents a direct quotation from a former slave-woman. Examine the context of each reference. Then write a paragraph explaining how each of these citations enhances the effectiveness of the reading.

FORMAL WRITING AND RESEARCH PAPERS

8. Facing a dilemma between what they saw as a broader freedom or keeping their families together, many black women chose the latter. Do a prewriting exercise in which you list the possible advantages and disadvantages of each choice. Then write a formal paper evaluating the black women's decision, developing several reasons for your position.
9. Search the card or computer catalog or use one of the history or education indexes in your library to find some information on how much choice a particular minority group currently has in pursuing an education. Narrow the topic to a particular level of education (preschool, elementary, secondary, college); then write a paper in which you take a stand on the amount of choice a minority group currently has in this respect. Provide several reasons and **examples** to support your position.
10. "A draft was like an ignominious seizure." Using the card or computer catalog and *Historical Abstracts* or the *Social Sciences Index,* find some

information on conscientious objectors. Then write a paper in which you: (a) play the role of a conscientious objector and demonstrate how conscription diminishes freedom of choice and may have other disadvantages as well; or, (b) oppose the concept of conscientious objection and demonstrate that the relationship of conscription to free choice is not a valid argument, and that conscription may have other advantages as well.

James Baldwin

Previous Condition

(1948)

James Baldwin (1924–1987) was born in New York and raised in Harlem. Pressured by his stepfather's strong religious convictions and the demands of caring for his younger brothers and sisters, he sought refuge in reading and writing. He served as a youth minister and worked at odd jobs before making writing his career. After moving to Paris, he was able to view the racism in his own country from a different perspective. Much of his writing explores the complex problems of blacks who live in a twentieth-century society still reluctant to accept diversity.

Among his nonfiction works are *Notes of a Native Son* and *The Fire Next Time.* His fiction includes the novels *Go Tell It on the Mountain, Giovanni's Room,* and the short-story collection *Going to Meet the Man,* from which the following story is taken. Here Baldwin deals with a **theme** close to his own life: the twin problems of defining a past and accepting a self in the midst of a hostile, constricting environment. Peter, the main character, feels the effects of prejudice economically, socially, and vocationally. But Baldwin also moves beyond the external effects to explore some of the deeper personal causes.

PREVIEW

Should blacks and other minorities "play the game" according to the majority's rules in order to get ahead? Give reasons for your answer.

I woke up shaking, alone in my room. I was clammy cold with sweat; under me the sheet and the mattress were soaked. The sheet was gray and twisted like a rope. I breathed like I had been running.

I couldn't move for the longest while. I just lay on my back, spread-eagled, looking up at the ceiling, listening to the sounds of people getting up in other parts of the house, alarm clocks ringing and water splashing and doors opening and shutting and feet on the stairs. I could tell when people left for work: the hall doorway downstairs whined and shuffled as it opened and gave a funny kind of double slam as it closed. One thud and then a louder thud and then a little final click. While the door was open I could hear the street sounds too, horses' hoofs and delivery wagons and people in the streets and big trucks and motor cars screaming on the asphalt.

I had been dreaming. At night I dreamt and woke up in the morning trembling, but not remembering the dream, except that in the dream I had been running. I could not remember when the dream—or dreams—had started; it had been long ago. For long periods maybe, I would have no dreams at all. And then they would come back, every night, I would try not to go to bed, I would go to sleep frightened and wake up frightened and have another day to get through with the nightmare at my shoulder. Now I was back from Chicago, busted, living off my friends in a dirty furnished room downtown. The show I had been with had folded in Chicago. It hadn't been much of a part—or much of a show either, to tell the truth. I played a kind of intellectual Uncle Tom, a young college student working for his race. The playwright had wanted to prove he was a liberal, I guess. But, as I say, the show had folded and here I was, back in New York and hating it. I knew that I should be getting another job, making the rounds, pounding the pavement. But I didn't. I couldn't face it. It was summer. I seemed to be fagged out. And every day I hated myself more. Acting's a rough life, even if you're white. I'm not tall and I'm not good looking and I can't sing or dance and I'm not white; so even at the best of times I wasn't in much demand.

The room I lived in was heavy ceilinged, perfectly square, with walls the color of chipped dry blood. Jules Weissman, a Jewboy, had got the room for me. It's a room to sleep in, he said, or maybe to die in but God knows it wasn't meant to live in. Perhaps because the room was so hideous it had a fantastic array of light fixtures: one on the ceiling, one on the left wall, two on the right wall, and a lamp on the table beside my bed. My bed was in front of the window through which nothing ever blew but dust. It was a furnished room and they'd thrown enough stuff in it to furnish three rooms its size. Two easy chairs and a desk, the bed, the table, a straight-backed chair, a bookcase, a cardboard wardrobe; and my books and my suitcase, both unpacked; and my dirty clothes flung in a corner. It was the kind of room that defeated you. It had a fireplace, too, and a heavy marble mantelpiece and a great gray mirror above the mantelpiece. It was hard to see anything in the mirror very clearly—which was perhaps just as well—and it would have been worth your life to have started a fire in the fireplace.

"Well, you won't have to stay here long," Jules told me the night I came. Jules smuggled me in, sort of, after dark, when everyone had gone to bed.

"Christ, I hope not."

"I'll be moving to a big place soon," Jules said. "You can move in with me." He turned all the lights on. "Think it'll be all right for a while?" He sounded apologetic, as though he had designed the room himself.

"Oh, sure. D'you think I'll have any trouble?"

"I don't think so. The rent's paid. She can't put you out."

I didn't say anything to that.

"Sort of stay undercover," Jules said. "You know."

"Roger," I said.

I had been living there for three days, timing it so I left after everyone else had gone, coming back late at night when everyone else was asleep. But I knew it wouldn't work. A couple of the tenants had seen me on the stairs, a woman had surprised me coming out of the john. Every morning I waited for the landlady to come banging on the door. I didn't know what would happen. It might be all right. It might not be. But the waiting was getting me.

The sweat on my body was turning cold. Downstairs a radio was tuned in to the Breakfast Symphony. They were playing Beethoven. I sat up and lit a cigarette. "Peter," I said, "don't let them scare you to death. You're a man, too." I listened to Ludwig and I watched the smoke rise to the dirty ceiling. Under Ludwig's drums and horns I listened to hear footsteps on the stairs.

I'd done a lot of traveling in my time. I'd knocked about through St. Louis, Frisco, Seattle, Detroit, New Orleans, worked at just about everything. I'd run away from my old lady when I was about sixteen. She'd never been able to handle me. You'll never be nothin' *but* a bum, she'd say. We lived in an old shack in a town in New Jersey in the nigger part of town, the kind of houses colored people live in all over the U.S. I hated my mother for living there. I hated all the people in my neighborhood. They went to church and they got drunk. They were nice to the white people. When the landlord came around they paid him and took his crap.

The first time I was ever called nigger I was seven years old. It was a little white girl with long black curls. I used to leave the front of my house and go wandering by myself through town. This little girl was playing ball alone and as I passed her the ball rolled out of her hands into the gutter.

I threw it back to her.

"Let's play catch," I said.

But she held the ball and made a face at me.

"My mother don't let me play with niggers," she told me.

I did not know what the word meant. But my skin grew warm. I stuck my tongue out at her.

"I don't care. Keep your old ball." I started down the street.

She screamed after me: "Nigger, nigger, nigger!"

I screamed back: "Your mother was a nigger!"

I asked my mother what a nigger was.

"Who called you that?"

"I heard somebody say it."

"Who?"

"Just somebody."

"Go wash your face," she said. "You dirty as sin. Your supper's on the table."

I went to the bathroom and splashed water on my face and wiped my face and hands on the towel.

"You call that clean?" my mother cried. "Come here, boy!"

She dragged me back to the bathroom and began to soap my face and neck.

"You run around dirty like you do all the time, everybody'll call you a little nigger, you hear?" She rinsed my face and looked at my hands and dried me. "Now, go on and eat your supper."

I didn't say anything. I went to the kitchen and sat down at the table. I remember I wanted to cry. My mother sat down across from me.

"Mama," I said. She looked at me. I started to cry.

She came around to my side of the table and took me in her arms.

"Baby, don't fret. Next time somebody calls you nigger you tell them you'd rather be your color than be lowdown and nasty like some white folks is."

We formed gangs when I was older, my friends and I. We met white boys and their friends on the opposite sides of fences and we threw rocks and tin cans at each other.

I'd come home bleeding. My mother would slap me and scold me and cry.

"Boy, you wanna get killed? You wanna end up like your father?"

My father was a bum and I had never seen him. I was named for him: Peter.

I was always in trouble: truant officers, welfare workers, everybody else in town.

"You ain't never gonna be nothin' *but* a bum," my mother said.

By and by older kids I knew finished school and got jobs and got married and settled down. They were going to settle down and bring more black babies into the world and pay the same rents for the same old shacks and it would go on and on—

When I was sixteen I ran away. I left a note and told Mama not to worry, I'd come back one day and I'd be all right. But when I was twenty-two she died. I came back and put my mother in the ground. Everything was like it had been. Our house had not been painted and the porch floor sagged and there was somebody's raincoat stuffed in the broken window. Another family was moving in.

Their furniture was stacked along the walls and their children were running through the house and laughing and somebody was frying pork chops in the kitchen. The oldest boy was tacking up a mirror.

Last year Ida took me driving in her big car and we passed through a couple of towns upstate. We passed some crumbling houses on the left. The clothes on the line were flying in the wind.

"Are people living there?" asked Ida.

"Just darkies," I said.

Ida passed the car ahead, banging angrily on the horn. "D'you know you're becoming paranoiac, Peter?"

"All right. All right. I know a lot of white people are starving too."

"You're damn right they are. I know a little about poverty myself."

Ida had come from the kind of family called shanty Irish. She was raised in Boston. She's a very beautiful woman who married young and married for money—so now I can afford to support attractive young men, she'd giggle. Her husband was a ballet dancer who was forever on the road. Ida suspected that he went with boys. Not that I give a damn, she said, as long as he leaves me alone. When we met last year she was thirty and I was twenty-five. We had a pretty stormy relationship but we stuck. Whenever I got to town I called her; whenever I was stranded out of town I'd let her know. We never let it get too serious. She went her way and I went mine.

In all this running around I'd learned a few things. Like a prizefighter learns to take a blow or a dancer learns to fall, I'd learned how to get by. I'd learned never to be belligerent with policemen, for instance. No matter who was right, I was certain to be wrong. What might be accepted as just good old American independence in someone else would be insufferable arrogance in me. After the first few times I realized that I had to play smart, to act out the role I was expected to play. I only had one head and it was too easy to get it broken. When I faced a policeman I acted like I didn't know a thing. I let my jaw drop and I let my eyes get big. I didn't give him any smart answers, none of the crap about my rights. I figured out what answers he wanted and I gave them to him. I never let him think he wasn't king. If it was more than routine, if I was picked up on suspicion of robbery or murder in the neighborhood, I looked as humble as I could and kept my mouth shut and prayed. I took a couple of beatings but I stayed out of prison and I stayed off chain gangs. That was also due to luck, Ida pointed out once. "Maybe it would've been better for you if you'd been a little less lucky. Worse things have happened than chain gangs. Some of them have happened to you."

There was something in her voice. "What are you talking about?" I asked.

"Don't lose your temper. I said maybe."

"You mean you think I'm a coward?"

"I didn't say that, Peter."

"But you meant that. Didn't you?"

"No. I didn't mean that. I didn't mean anything. Let's not fight."

There are times and places when a Negro can use his color like a shield. He can trade on the subterranean Anglo-Saxon guilt and get what he wants that way; or some of what he wants. He can trade on his nuisance value, his value as forbidden fruit; he can use it like a knife, he can twist it and get his vengeance that way. I knew these things long before I realized that I knew them and in the beginning I used them, not knowing what I was doing. Then when I began to see it, I felt betrayed. I felt beaten as a person. I had no honest place to stand.

This was the year before I met Ida. I'd been acting in stock companies and little theaters; sometimes fairly good parts. People were nice to me. They told me I had talent. They said it sadly, as though they were thinking, What a pity, he'll never get anywhere. I had got to the point where I resented praise and I resented pity and I wondered what people were thinking when they shook my hand. In New York I met some pretty fine people; easygoing, hard-drinking, flotsam and jetsam; and they liked me; and I wondered if I trusted them; if I was able any longer to trust anybody. Not on top, where all the world could see, but underneath where everybody lives.

Soon I would have to get up. I listened to Ludwig. He shook the little room like the footsteps of a giant marching miles away. On summer evenings (and maybe we would go this summer) Jules and Ida and I would go up to the Stadium and sit beneath the pillars on the cold stone steps. There it seemed to me the sky was far away; and I was not myself, I was high and lifted up. We never talked, the three of us. We sat and watched the blue smoke curl in the air and watched the orange tips of cigarettes. Every once in a while the boys who sold popcorn and soda pop and ice cream climbed the steep steps chattering; and Ida shifted slightly and touched her blue-black hair; and Jules scowled. I sat with my knee up, watching the lighted half-moon below, the black-coated, straining conductor, the faceless men beneath him moving together in a rhythm like the sea. There were pauses in the music for the rushing, calling, halting piano. Everything would stop except the climbing soloist; he would reach a height and everything would join him, the violins first and then the horns; and then the deep blue bass and the flute and the bitter trampling drums; beating, beating and mounting together and stopping with a crash like daybreak. When I first heard the *Messiah* I was alone; my blood bubbled like fire and wine; I cried; like an infant crying for its mother's milk; or a sinner running to meet Jesus.

Now below the music I heard footsteps on the stairs. I put out my cigarette. My heart was beating so hard I thought it would tear my chest apart. Someone knocked on the door.

I thought: Don't answer. Maybe she'll go away.

But the knocking came again, harder this time.

Just a minute, I said. I sat on the edge of the bed and put on my bathrobe. I was trembling like a fool. For Christ's sake, Peter, you've been through this before. What's the worst thing that can happen? You won't have a room. The world's full of rooms.

When I opened the door the landlady stood there, red-and-whitefaced and hysterical.

"Who are you? I didn't rent this room to you."

My mouth was dry. I started to say something.

"I can't have no colored people here," she said. "All my tenants are complainin'. Women afraid to come home nights."

"They ain't gotta be afraid of me," I said. I couldn't get my voice up; it rasped and rattled in my throat; and I began to be angry. I wanted to kill her. "My friend rented this room for me," I said.

"Well, I'm sorry, he didn't have no right to do that, I don't have nothin' against you, but you gotta get out."

Her glasses blinked, opaque in the light on the landing. She was frightened to death. She was afraid of me but she was more afraid of losing her tenants. Her face was mottled with rage and fear, her breath came rushed and little bits of spittle gathered at the edges of her mouth; her breath smelled bad, like rotting hamburger on a July day.

"You can't put me out," I said. "This room was rented in my name." I started to close the door, as though the matter was finished: "I live here, see, this is my room, you can't put me out."

"You get outa my house!" she screamed. "I got the right to know who's in my house! This is a white neighborhood, I don't rent to colored people. Why don't you go on uptown, like you belong?"

"I can't stand niggers," I told her. I started to close the door again but she moved and stuck her foot in the way. I wanted to kill her, I watched her stupid, wrinkled frightened white face and I wanted to take a club, a hatchet, and bring it down with all my weight, splitting her skull down the middle where she parted her iron-grey hair.

"Get out of the door," I said. "I want to get dressed."

But I knew that she had won, that I was already on my way. We stared at each other. Neither of us moved. From her came an emanation of fear and fury and something else. You maggot-eaten bitch, I thought. I said evilly, "You wanna come in and watch me?" Her face didn't change, she didn't take her foot away. My skin prickled, tiny hot needles punctured my flesh. I was aware of my body under the bathrobe; and it was as though I had done something wrong, something monstrous, years ago, which no one had forgotten and for which I would be killed.

"If you don't get out," she said, "I'll get a policeman to put you out."

I grabbed the door to keep from touching her. "All right. All right. You can have the goddamn room. Now get out and let me dress."

She turned away. I slammed the door. I heard her going down the stairs. I threw stuff into my suitcase. I tried to take as long as possible but I cut myself while shaving because I was afraid she would come back upstairs with a policeman.

Jules was making coffee when I walked in.

"Good morning, good morning! What happened to you?"

"No room at the inn," I said. "Pour a cup of coffee for the notorious son of man. I sat down and dropped my suitcase on the floor."

Jules looked at me. "Oh. Well. Coffee coming up."

He got out the coffee cups. I lit a cigarette and sat there. I couldn't think of anything to say. I knew that Jules felt bad and I wanted to tell him that it wasn't his fault.

He pushed coffee in front of me and sugar and cream.

"Cheer up, baby. The world's wide and life—life, she is very long."

"Shut up. I don't want to hear any of your bad philosophy."

"Sorry."

"I mean, let's not talk about the good, the true, and the beautiful."

"All right. But don't sit there holding onto your table manners. Scream if you want to."

"Screaming won't do any good. Besides I'm a big boy now."

I stirred my coffee. "Did you give her a fight?" Jules asked.

I shook my head. "No."

"Why the hell not?"

I shrugged; a little ashamed now. I couldn't have won it. What the hell.

"You might have won it. You might have given her a couple of bad moments."

"Goddamit to hell, I'm sick of it. Can't I get a place to sleep without dragging it through the courts? I'm goddamn tired of battling every Tom, Dick, and Harry for what everybody else takes for granted. I'm tired, man, tired! Have you ever been sick to death of something? Well, I'm sick to death. And I'm scared. I've been fighting so goddamn long I'm not a person any more. I'm not Booker T. Washington. I've got no vision of emancipating anybody. I want to emancipate myself. If this goes on much longer, they'll send me to Bellevue, I'll blow my top, I'll break somebody's head. I'm not worried about that miserable little room. I'm worried about what's happening to me, *to me*, inside. I don't walk the streets, I crawl. I've never been like this before. Now when I go to a strange place I wonder what will happen, will I be accepted, if I'm accepted, can I accept?—"

"Take it easy," Jules said.

"Jules, I'm beaten."

"I don't think you are. Drink your coffee."

"Oh," I cried, "I know you think I'm making it dramatic, that I'm paranoiac and just inventing trouble! Maybe I think so sometimes, how can I tell? You get so used to being hit you find you're always waiting for it. Oh, I know, you're Jewish, you get kicked around, too, but you can walk into a bar and nobody *knows* you're Jewish and if you go looking for a job you'll get a better job than mine! How can I say what it feels like? I don't know. I know everybody's in trouble and nothing is easy, but how can I explain to you what it feels like to be black when I don't understand it and don't want to and spend all my time trying to forget it? I don't want to hate anybody—but now maybe, I can't love anybody either—are we friends? Can we be really friends?"

"We're friends," Jules said, "don't worry about it." He scowled. "If I wasn't Jewish I'd ask you why you don't live in Harlem." I looked at him. He raised his hand and smiled—"But I'm Jewish, so I didn't ask you. Ah Peter," he said, "I can't help you—take a walk, get drunk, we're all in this together."

I stood up. "I'll be around later. I'm sorry."

"Don't be sorry. I'll leave my door open. Bunk here for awhile."

"Thanks," I said.

I felt that I was drowning; that hatred had corrupted me like cancer in the bone.

I saw Ida for dinner. We met in a restaurant in the Village, an Italian place in a gloomy cellar with candles on the tables.

It was not a busy night, for which I was grateful. When I came in there were only two other couples on the other side of the room. No one looked at me. I sat down in a corner booth and ordered a Scotch old-fashioned. Ida was late and I had three of them before she came.

She was very fine in black, a high-necked dress with a pearl choker; and her hair was combed page-boy style, falling just below her ears.

"You look real sweet, baby."

"Thank you. It took fifteen extra minutes but I hoped it would be worth it."

"It was worth it. What're you drinking?"

"Oh—what're you drinking?"

"Old-fashioneds."

She sniffed and looked at me. "How many?"

I laughed. "Three."

"Well," she said, "I suppose you had to do something." The waiter came over. We decided on one Manhattan and one lasagna and one spaghetti with clam sauce and another old-fashioned for me.

"Did you have a constructive day, sweetheart? Find a job?"

"Not today," I said. I lit her cigarette. "Metro offered me a fortune to come to the coast and do the lead in *Native Son* but I turned it down. Type casting, you know. It's so difficult to find a decent part."

"Well, if they don't come up with a decent offer soon tell them you'll go back to Selznick. *He'll* find you a part with guts—the very *idea* of offering you *Native Son!* I wouldn't stand for it."

"You ain't gotta tell me. I told them if they didn't find me a decent script in two weeks I was through, that's all."

"Now that's talking, Peter my lad."

The drinks came and we sat in silence for a minute or two. I finished half of my drink at a swallow and played with the toothpicks on the table. I felt Ida watching me.

"Peter, you're going to be awfully drunk."

"Honeychile, the first thing a southern gentleman learns is how to hold his liquor."

"That myth is older than the rock of ages. And anyway you come from Jersey."

I finished my drink and snarled at her: "That's just as good as the South."

Across the table from me I could see that she was readying herself for trouble: her mouth tightened slightly, setting her chin so that the faint cleft showed: "What happened to you today?"

I resented her concern; I resented my need. "Nothing worth talking about," I muttered, "just a mood."

And I tried to smile at her, to wipe away the bitterness.

"Now I know something's the matter. Please tell me."

It sounded trivial as hell: "You know the room Jules found for me? Well, the landlady kicked me out of it today."

"God save the American republic," Ida said. "D'you want to waste some of my husband's money? We can sue her."

"Forget it. I'll end up with lawsuits in every state in the union."

"Still, as a gesture—"

"The devil with the gesture. I'll get by."

The food came. I didn't want to eat. The first mouthful hit my belly like a gong. Ida began cutting up lasagna.

"Peter," she said, "try not to feel so badly. We're all in this together the whole world. Don't let it throw you. What can't be helped you have to learn to live with."

"That's easy for you to say," I told her.

She looked at me quickly and looked away. "I'm not pretending that it's easy to do," she said.

I didn't believe that she could really understand it; and there was nothing I could say. I sat like a child being scolded, looking down at my plate, not eating, not saying anything. I wanted her to stop talking, to stop being intelligent about it, to stop being calm and grown-up about it; good Lord, none of us has ever grown up, we never will.

"It's no better anywhere else," she was saying. "In all of Europe there's famine and disease, in France and England they hate the Jews—nothing's going to change, baby, people are too empty-headed, too empty-hearted—it's always been like that, people always try to destroy what they don't understand—and they hate almost everything because they understand so little—"

I began to sweat in my side of the booth. I wanted to stop her voice. I wanted her to eat and be quiet and leave me alone. I looked around for the waiter so I could order another drink. But he was on the far side of the restaurant, waiting on some people who had just come in; a lot of people had come in since we had been sitting there.

"Peter," Ida said, "Peter please don't look like that."

I grinned: the painted grin of the professional clown. "Don't worry, baby, I'm all right. I know what I'm going to do. I'm gonna go back to my people where I belong and find me a nice, black nigger wench and raise me a flock of babies."

Ida had an old maternal trick; the grin tricked her into using it now. She raised her fork and rapped me with it across the knuckles. "Now, stop that. You're too old for that."

I screamed and stood up screaming and knocked the candle over: "Don't *do* that, you bitch, don't *ever* do that!"

She grabbed the candle and set it up and glared at me. Her face had turned perfectly white: "Sit down! Sit *down!*"

I fell back into my seat. My stomach felt like water. Everyone was looking at us. I turned cold, seeing what they were seeing: a black boy and a white woman, alone together. I knew it would take nothing to have them at my throat.

"I'm sorry," I muttered, "I'm sorry, I'm sorry."

The waiter was at my elbow. "Is everything all right, miss?"

"Yes, quite, thank you." She sounded like a princess dismissing a slave. I didn't look up. The shadow of the waiter moved away from me.

"Baby," Ida said, "forgive me, please forgive me."

I stared at the tablecloth. She put her hand on mine, brightness and blackness.

"Let's go," I said, "I'm terribly sorry."

She motioned for the check. When it came she handed the waiter a ten dollar bill without looking. She picked up her bag.

"Shall we go to a nightclub or a movie or something?"

"No, honey, not tonight." I looked at her. "I'm tired, I think I'll go on over to Jules's place. I'm gonna sleep on his floor for a while. Don't worry about me. I'm all right."

She looked at me steadily. She said: "I'll come see you tomorrow?"

"Yes, baby, please."

The waiter brought the change and she tipped him. We stood up; as we passed the tables (not looking at the people) the ground under me seemed falling, the doorway seemed impossibly far away. All my muscles tensed; I seemed ready to spring; I was waiting for the blow.

I put my hands in my pockets and we walked to the end of the block. The lights were green and red, the lights from the theater across the street exploded blue and yellow, off and on.

"Peter?"

"Yes?"

"I'll see you tomorrow?"

"Yeah. Come by Jules's. I'll wait for you."

"Goodnight, darling."

"Goodnight."

I started to walk away. I felt her eyes on my back. I kicked a bottle-top on the sidewalk.

God save the American republic.

I dropped into the subway and got on an uptown train, not knowing where it was going and not caring. Anonymous, islanded people surrounded me, behind newspapers, behind make-up, fat, fleshy masks and flat eyes. I watched the empty faces. (No one looked at me.) I looked at the ads, unreal women and pink-cheeked men selling cigarettes, candy, shaving cream, nightgowns, chewing gum, movies, sex; sex without organs, drier than sand and more secret than death. The train stopped. A white boy and a white girl got on. She was nice, short, svelte. Nice legs. She was hanging on his arm. He was the football type, blond, ruddy. They were dressed in summer clothes. The wind from the doors blew her print dress. She squealed, holding the dress at the knees and giggled and looked at him. He said something I didn't catch and she looked at me and the smile died. She stood so that she faced him and had her back to me. I looked back at the ads. Then I hated them. I wanted to do something to make them hurt, something that would crack the pink-cheeked mask. The white boy and I did not look at each other again. They got off at the next stop.

I wanted to keep on drinking. I got off in Harlem and went to a rundown bar on Seventh Avenue. My people, my people. Sharpies stood on the corner, waiting. Women in summer dresses pranced by on wavering heels. Click clack. Click clack. There were white mounted policemen in the streets. On every block there was another policeman on foot. I saw a black cop.

God save the American republic.

The juke box was letting loose with "Hamps' Boogie." The place was jumping, I walked over to the man.

"Rye," I said.

I was standing next to somebody's grandmother. "Hello, papa. What you puttin' down?"

"Baby, you can't pick it up," I told her. My rye came and I drank.

"Nigger," she said, "you must think you's somebody."

I didn't answer. She turned away, back to her beer, keeping time to the juke box, her face sullen and heavy and aggrieved. I watched her out of the side of my eye. She had been good looking once, pretty even, before she hit the bottle and started crawling into too many beds. She was flabby now, flesh heaved all over in her thin dress. I wondered what she'd be like in bed; then I realized that I was a little excited by her; I laughed and set my glass down.

"The same," I said. "And a beer chaser."

The juke box was playing something else now, something brassy and commercial which I didn't like. I kept on drinking, listening to the voices of my people, watching the faces of my people. (God pity us, the terrified republic.) Now I was sorry to have angered the woman who still sat next to me, now deep in conversation with another, younger woman. I longed for some opening, some sign, something to make me part of the life around me. But there was nothing except my color. A white outsider coming in would have seen a young Negro drinking in a Negro bar, perfectly in his element, in his place, as the saying goes. But the people here knew differently, as I did. I didn't seem to have a place.

So I kept on drinking by myself, saying to myself after each drink, Now I'll go. But I was afraid; I didn't want to sleep on Jules's floor; I didn't want to go to sleep. I kept on drinking and listening to the juke box. They were playing Ella Fitzgerald, "Cow-Cow Boogie."

"Let me buy you a drink," I said to the woman.

She looked at me, startled, suspicious, ready to blow her top.

"On the level," I said. I tried to smile. "Both of you."

"I'll take a beer," the young one said.

I was shaking like a baby. I finished my drink.

"Fine," I said. I turned to the bar.

"Baby," said the old one, "what's your story?"

The man put three beers on the counter.

"I got no story, Ma," I said.

JOURNAL WRITINGS

1. **Describe** some expectations that your parents have of you. **Compare** or **contrast** these to the expectations Peter's mother has of him. What effect do these parental expectations have on you? On Peter?

2. What kind of music do you like? What kind does Peter like? What groups of people do your taste and that of Peter identify each of you with? **Compare** or **contrast** the way Peter relates to his group with the way you relate to yours.

BRAINSTORMING AND DRAFTING

3. Look up **metaphor** in the glossary. In what sense does Peter's acting become a metaphor of how he deals with life? Write a paragraph in which you evaluate whether his way of dealing with life allows him more freedom or confirms his limitations. You may wish to consult your response to the Preview question.

4. In Jacqueline Jones's historical account, many freed slaves chose to remain in their "previous condition." **Compare** and/or **contrast** their motives for this choice with Peter's motives for returning to Harlem. How effective is their behavior in each case?

THE AUTHOR'S METHODS

5. "It was the kind of room that defeated you." This topic sentence, placed about three-fourths of the way through the fourth paragraph, captures the main point of the paragraph. What earlier details in the paragraph support Peter's feeling of defeat? Why does Baldwin place the topic sentence closer to the end of the paragraph? Complete Peter's sentence with a **generalization** about your bedroom or dorm room: "It was the kind of room that . . . " Then write a paragraph with **descriptive** details to support your idea. Place your topic sentence wherever you think it works best.
6. The story ends with the words, " 'I got no story, Ma,' I said." Write a paragraph in which you explain how this sentence changes or reinforces your understanding of the story.

CREATIVE PROJECT

7. Ida tells Peter: "Maybe it would've been better for you if you'd been a little less lucky. Worse things have happened than chain gangs. Some of them have happened to you." Pretend you are Ida, Peter's older, white, married friend. Write a diary entry about your words to Peter, an entry that Peter will never see. Reveal what you meant by these words, and explain why you didn't want to confront Peter with your meaning.

FORMAL WRITING AND RESEARCH PAPERS

8. Write an essay **analyzing** one or more of the "previous conditions" that affect Peter's behavior. Consider also Peter's reactions to these conditions. Construct a **thesis** that indicates what degree of responsibility Peter has for his problems.
9. Read "Notes of a Native Son" in the Prejudice unit. **Compare** and/or **contrast** the character of Peter in "Previous Condition" with the **narrator** of "Notes." For instance, what problems do they each have? How does each character react to his problems? (Add your own questions and answers.) Explain what conclusions about freedom you reached through this **analysis.**
10. Peter tells Jules, "Oh, I know, you're Jewish, you get kicked around, too, but you can walk into a bar and nobody *knows* you're Jewish and if you go looking for a job you'll get a better job than mine!" Is Peter right in implying that prejudice against Jews is somehow less restricting? Find a short story, short novel, poem, or film that illustrates prejudice against Jews. Consult the *Library of Congress Subject Headings* (LCSH) for some keywords to use in a subject search of the card or computer catalog of your library. Write a paper **comparing** and/or **contrasting** the effects of prejudice on the character presented in your work with the limitations on Peter in Baldwin's story. Then, evaluate Peter's statement to Jules.

Mort Walker

Beetle Bailey

(1989)

Addison Morton Walker (born 1922) grew up in Kansas City, Kansas. As a boy, he was often seen at the public library reading comics from all over the country. He decided to become a cartoonist one day as he watched his father double over with laughter while reading the comic strip "Moon Mullins." When Walker was fifteen, his first strip, "Lime Juicers," was published in the Kansas City *Journal*. In 1943, he was drafted by the U.S. Army; he became an intelligence officer in Italy during World War II. Later, he graduated from the University of Missouri, and began pursuing his career as a cartoonist in earnest.

Walker is the author of "Hi and Lois," with collaborator Dik Browne, and of "Boner's Ark." "Beetle Bailey" began in 1950 as "Joe College"; Walker changed the strip's format to a satire of the military during the Korean War, and the new format has remained ever since. Blending realism with nonrealism in the strip, Walker suggests the universal feelings of failure, anger, stupidity, cleverness, and triumph through such memorable characters as the apparently lazy yet sometimes ingenious Private Beetle and the authoritative, often furious Sergeant Snorkle who, ironically, can be easily conquered via his stomach. In the following strip, the Sergeant tries to demonstrate his authority by philosophizing. Typically, Walker undercuts the serious and potentially frightening philosophy of determinism through his humorous presentation of it.

JOURNAL WRITINGS

1. From your own life or the life of a family member or friend, **narrate** an incident in which you chose nonaction, and explain your reasons for doing so. **Compare** and/or **contrast** your reasons with what you believe to be Beetle's reasons—especially his deeper reasons—for choosing not to act.

2. Write a paragraph in which you use your own experience to agree or disagree with Sergeant Snorkle's opinion that each move in our lives determines our next move. Comment also on whether you think it is possible to "overcome" past moves.

Mort Walker, "Beetle Bailey." Reprinted with special permission of King Features Syndicate.

BRAINSTORMING AND DRAFTING

3.   Working in a small group or individually, find and read several other **examples** of the Beetle Bailey comic strip in which Beetle, a low-ranking soldier or "private," comes into conflict with Sergeant Snorkle, his superior. Try to reach a consensus (if you are working in a group) as to how Beetle reacts to authority. Then each person should draft a paragraph of his or her own, explaining how authority affects choice in Mort Walker's comic strips. Use **examples** to support your **generalizations.**

4.   **Describe** Walker's intended audience for "Beetle Bailey." Draft a paragraph explaining some ways in which Walker shows awareness of his audience in this particular strip.

THE ARTIST'S METHODS

5.   One of the traditional **conventions** of the comic strip is its division into blocks or panels. This method, which functions as a way of organizing material, might be compared with the use of headings in a science report or

topic sentences in a philosophy article. What other conventions can you find in the "Beetle Bailey" strip? Write a paragraph or two explaining the functions of each convention and **comparing/contrasting** it with a similar convention in an **essay** or literary work in this unit.

6.   Write a few sentences explaining how Walker makes the serious topic of determinism seem comic.

FORMAL WRITING AND RESEARCH PAPERS

7.   While Beetle's refusal to act appears comic, such an abdication of choice can have serious or even tragic consequences. Write a formal paper in which you explain and give specific **examples** of several situations wherein refusal to make an active choice leads to problems. (You may want to consider the narrator's problems in Charlotte Gilman's story as one situation; Peter's "escapes" in James Baldwin's story could be another.)

8.   Using the *Social Sciences Index* or the card or computer catalog, find some information on criminals who become "repeat offenders." Write a paper in which you use this information as you **analyze** Sergeant Snorkel's implication that past "moves" influence current choices. (See also your response to question 2 of Journal Writing.)

Charlotte Perkins Gilman

The Yellow Wallpaper

(1892)

Charlotte Perkins Gilman (1860–1935) was born in Hartford, Connecticut. Her childhood was plagued by poverty and frequent relocations after her father abandoned the family. Gilman married but suffered from severe emotional problems throughout her marriage. After undergoing a rigid treatment for "nervous disorders," she divorced her first husband, leaving her daughter with him. In 1900, she remarried and was able to find some satisfaction in her writing, speaking, and political activities. However, she committed suicide in 1935.

Gilman devoted her energies to women's issues, especially the choice that women of her time were forced to make between marriage and career. Her works include *Women and Economics, Concerning Children, Human Work,* and *Man-Made World.* The following short story, though fictional, clearly reflects Gilman's own rebellion against a limited social role for women, and her own struggle to find fulfillment as a creative artist. The story's narrator, less conscious than Gilman of the stereotypical role she fights against, becomes more obsessive as the story progresses to its dramatic climax.

PREVIEWS

A. Complete the following sentence at least five different ways: Society expects a woman to . . .
B. Write down all the feelings and ideas you associate with the color yellow.

It is very seldom that mere ordinary people like John and myself secure ancestral halls for the summer.

A colonial mansion, a hereditary estate, I would say a haunted house and reach the height of romantic felicity—but that would be asking too much of fate!

Still I will proudly declare that there is something queer about it.

Else, why should it be let so cheaply? And why have stood so long untenanted?

John laughs at me, of course, but one expects that.

John is practical in the extreme. He has no patience with faith, an intense horror of superstition, and he scoffs openly at any talk of things not to be felt and seen and put down in figures.

John is a physician, and *perhaps*—(I would not say it to a living soul, of course, but this is dead paper and a great relief to my mind)—*perhaps* that is one reason I do not get well faster.

You see, he does not believe I am sick! And what can one do?

If a physician of high standing, and one's own husband, assures friends and relatives that there is really nothing the matter with one but temporary nervous depression—a slight hysterical tendency—what is one to do?

My brother is also a physician, and also of high standing, and he says the same thing.

So I take phosphates or phosphites—whichever it is—and tonics, and air and exercise, and journeys, and am absolutely forbidden to "work" until I am well again.

Personally, I disagree with their ideas.

Personally, I believe that congenial work, with excitement and change, would do me good.

But what is one to do?

I did write for a while in spite of them; but it *does* exhaust me a good deal—having to be so sly about it, or else meet with heavy opposition.

I sometimes fancy that in my condition, if I had less opposition and more society and stimulus—but John says the very worst thing I can do is to think about my condition, and I confess it always makes me feel bad.

So I will let it alone and talk about the house.

The most beautiful place! It is quite alone, standing well back from the road, quite three miles from the village. It makes me think of English places that you read about, for there are hedges and walls and gates that lock, and lots of separate little houses for the gardeners and people.

There is a *delicious* garden! I never saw such a garden—large and shady, full of box-bordered paths, and lined with long grape-covered arbors with seats under them.

There were greenhouses, but they are all broken now.

There was some legal trouble, I believe, something about the heirs and co-heirs; anyhow, the place has been empty for years.

That spoils my ghostliness, I am afraid, but I don't care—there is something strange about the house—I can feel it.

I even said so to John one moonlight evening, but he said what I felt was a draught, and shut the window.

I get unreasonably angry with John sometimes. I'm sure I never used to be so sensitive. I think it is due to this nervous condition.

But John says if I feel so I shall neglect proper self-control; so I take pains to control myself—before him, at least, and that makes me very tired.

I don't like our room a bit. I wanted one downstairs that opened onto the piazza and had roses all over the window, and such pretty old-fashioned chintz hangings! But John would not hear of it.

He said there was only one window and not room for two beds, and no near room for him if he took another.

He is very careful and loving, and hardly lets me stir without special direction.

I have a schedule prescription for each hour in the day; he takes all care from me, and so I feel basely ungrateful not to value it more.

He said he came here solely on my account, that I was to have perfect rest and all the air I could get. "Your exercise depends on your strength, my dear," said he, "and your food somewhat on your appetite; but air you can absorb all the time." So we took the nursery at the top of the house.

It is a big, airy room, the whole floor nearly, with windows that look all ways, and air and sunshine galore. It was nursery first, and then playroom and gymnasium, I should judge, for the windows are barred for little children, and there are rings and things in the walls.

The paint and paper look as if a boys' school had used it. It is stripped off—the paper—in great patches all around the head of my bed, about as far as I can reach, and in a great place on the other side of the room low down. I never saw a worse paper in my life. One of those sprawling, flamboyant patterns committing every artistic sin.

It is dull enough to confuse the eye in following, pronounced enough constantly to irritate and provoke study, and when you follow the lame uncertain curves for a little distance they suddenly commit suicide—plunge off at outrageous angles, destroy themselves in unheard-of contradictions.

The color is repellent, almost revolting: a smouldering unclean yellow, strangely faded by the slow-turning sunlight. It is a dull yet lurid orange in some places, a sickly sulphur tint in others.

No wonder the children hated it! I should hate it myself if I had to live in this room long.

There comes John, and I must put this away—he hates to have me write a word.

We have been here two weeks, and I haven't felt like writing before, since that first day.

I am sitting by the window now, up in this atrocious nursery, and there is nothing to hinder my writing as much as I please, save lack of strength.

John is away all day, and even some nights when his cases are serious.

I am glad my case is not serious!

But these nervous troubles are dreadfully depressing.

John does not know how much I really suffer. He knows there is no reason to suffer, and that satisfies him.

Of course it is only nervousness. It does weigh on me so not to do my duty in any way!

I meant to be such a help to John, such a real rest and comfort, and here I am a comparative burden already!

Nobody would believe what an effort it is to do what little I am able—to dress and entertain, and order things.

It is fortunate Mary is so good with the baby. Such a dear baby!

And yet I *cannot* be with him, it makes me so nervous.

I suppose John never was nervous in his life. He laughs at me so about this wallpaper!

At first he meant to repaper the room, but afterward he said that I was letting it get the better of me, and that nothing was worse for a nervous patient than to give way to such fancies.

He said that after the wallpaper was changed it would be the heavy bedstead, and then the barred windows, and then that gate at the head of the stairs, and so on.

"You know the place is doing you good," he said, "and really, dear, I don't care to renovate the house just for a three months' rental."

"Then do let us go downstairs," I said. "There are such pretty rooms there."

Then he took me in his arms and called me a blessed little goose, and said he would go down cellar, if I wished, and have it whitewashed into the bargain.

But he is right enough about the beds and windows and things.

It is as airy and comfortable a room as anyone need wish, and, of course, I would not be so silly as to make him uncomfortable just for a whim.

I'm really getting quite fond of the big room, all but that horrid paper.

Out of one window I can see the garden—those mysterious deep-shaded arbors, the riotous old-fashioned flowers, and bushes and gnarly trees.

Out of another I get a lovely view of the bay and a little private wharf belonging to the estate. There is a beautiful shaded lane that runs down there from the house. I always fancy I see people walking in these numerous paths and arbors, but John has cautioned me not to give way to fancy in the least. He says that with my imaginative power and habit of story-making, a nervous weakness like mine is sure to lead to all manner of excited fancies, and that I ought to use my will and good sense to check the tendency. So I try.

I think sometimes that if I were only well enough to write a little it would relieve the press of ideas and rest me.

But I find I get pretty tired when I try.

It is so discouraging not to have any advice and companionship about my work. When I get really well, John says we will ask Cousin Henry and Julia down for a long visit, but he says he would as soon put fireworks in my pillow-case as to let me have those stimulating people about now.

I wish I could get well faster.

But I must not think about that. This paper looks to me as if it *knew* what a vicious influence it had!

There is a recurrent spot where the pattern lolls like a broken neck and two bulbous eyes stare at you upside down.

I get positively angry with the impertinence of it and the everlastingness. Up and down and sideways they crawl, and those absurd unblinking eyes are everywhere. There is one place where two breadths didn't match, and the eyes go all up and down the line, one a little higher than the other.

I never saw so much expression in an inanimate thing before, and we all know how much expression they have! I used to lie awake as a child and get more entertainment and terror out of blank walls and plain furniture than most children could find in a toy-store.

I remember what a kindly wink the knobs of our big old bureau used to have, and there was one chair that always seemed like a strong friend.

I used to feel that if any of the other things looked too fierce I could always hop into that chair and be safe.

The furniture in this room is no worse than inharmonious, however, for we had to bring it all from downstairs. I suppose when this was used as a playroom they had to take the nursery things out, and no wonder! I never saw such ravages as the children have made here.

The wallpaper, as I said before, is torn off in spots, and it sticketh closer than a brother—they must have had perseverance as well as hatred.

Then the floor is scratched and gouged and splintered, the plaster itself is dug out here and there, and this great heavy bed, which is all we found in the room, looks as if it had been through the wars.

But I don't mind it a bit—only the paper.

There comes John's sister. Such a dear girl as she is, and so careful of me! I must not let her find me writing.

She is a perfect and enthusiastic housekeeper, and hopes for no better profession. I verily believe she thinks it is the writing which made me sick!

But I can write when she is out, and see her a long way off from these windows.

There is one that commands the road, a lovely shaded winding road, and one that just looks off over the country. A lovely country, too, full of great elms and velvet meadows.

This wallpaper has a kind of sub-pattern in a different shade, a particularly irritating one, for you can only see it in certain lights, and not clearly then.

But in the places where it isn't faded and where the sun is just so—I can see a strange, provoking, formless sort of figure that seems to skulk about behind that silly and conspicuous front design.

There's sister on the stairs!

Well, the Fourth of July is over! The people are all gone, and I am tired out. John thought it might do me good to see a little company, so we just had Mother and Nellie and the children down for a week.

Of course I didn't do a thing. Jennie sees to everything now.

But it tired me all the same.

John says if I don't pick up faster he shall send me to Weir Mitchell* in the fall.

But I don't want to go there at all. I had a friend who was in his hands once, and she says he is just like John and my brother, only more so!

Besides, it is such an undertaking to go so far.

---

* Weir Mitchell—Silas Weir Mitchell (1829–1914), neurologist who introduced the "rest cure" for psychoneurotics. [Eds.]

I don't feel as if it was worthwhile to turn my hand over for anything, and I'm getting dreadfully fretful and querulous.

I cry at nothing, and cry most of the time.

Of course I don't when John is here, or anybody else, but when I am alone.

And I am alone a good deal just now. John is kept in town very often by serious cases, and Jennie is good and lets me alone when I want her to.

So I walk a little in the garden or down that lovely lane, sit on the porch under the roses, and lie down up here a good deal.

I'm getting really fond of the room in spite of the wallpaper. Perhaps *because* of the wallpaper.

It dwells in my mind so!

I lie here on this great immovable bed—it is nailed down, I believe—and follow that pattern about by the hour. It is as good as gymnastics, I assure you. I start, we'll say, at the bottom, down in the corner over there where it has not been touched, and I determine for the thousandth time that I *will* follow that pointless pattern to some sort of a conclusion.

I know a little of the principle of design, and I know this thing was not arranged on any laws of radiation, or alternation, or repetition, or symmetry, or anything else that I ever heard of.

It is repeated, of course, by the breadths, but not otherwise.

Looked at in one way, each breadth stands alone; the bloated curves and flourishes—a kind of "debased Romanesque"* with delirium tremens† go waddling up and down in isolated columns of fatuity.

But, on the other hand, they connect diagonally, and the sprawling outlines run off in great slanting waves of optic horror, like a lot of wallowing sea-weeds in full chase.

The whole thing goes horizontally, too, at least it seems so, and I exhaust myself trying to distinguish the order of its going in that direction.

They have used a horizontal breadth for a frieze, and that adds wonderfully to the confusion.

There is one end of the room where it is almost intact, and there, when the crosslights fade and the low sun shines directly upon it, I can almost fancy radiation after all—the interminable grotesque seems to form around a common center and rush off in headlong plunges of equal distraction.

It makes me tired to follow it. I will take a nap, I guess.

I don't know why I should write this.

I don't want to.

I don't feel able.

And I know John would think it absurd. But I *must* say what I feel and think in some way—it is such a relief!

But the effort is getting to be greater than the relief.

---

* Romanesque—an ancient style of architecture featuring heavy masonry construction with rounded arches. [Eds.]

† delirium tremens—restless trembling, which may include hallucinations; may follow alcoholic ingestion. [Eds.]

Half the time now I am awfully lazy, and lie down ever so much. John says I mustn't lose my strength, and has me take cod liver oil and lots of tonics and things, to say nothing of ale and wine and rare meat.

Dear John! He loves me very dearly, and hates to have me sick. I tried to have a real earnest reasonable talk with him the other day, and tell him how I wish he would let me go and make a visit to Cousin Henry and Julia.

But he said I wasn't able to go, nor able to stand it after I got there; and I did not make out a very good case for myself, for I was crying before I had finished.

It is getting to be a great effort for me to think straight. Just this nervous weakness, I suppose.

And dear John gathered me up in his arms, and just carried me upstairs and laid me on the bed, and sat by me and read to me till it tired my head.

He said I was his darling and his comfort and all he had, and that I must take care of myself for his sake, and keep well.

He says no one but myself can help me out of it, that I must use my will and self-control and not let any silly fancies run away with me.

There's one comfort—the baby is well and happy, and does not have to occupy this nursery with the horrid wallpaper.

If we had not used it, that blessed child would have! What a fortunate escape! Why, I wouldn't have a child of mine, an impressionable little thing, live in such a room for worlds.

I never thought of it before, but it is lucky that John kept me here after all; I can stand it so much easier than a baby, you see.

Of course I never mention it to them any more—I am too wise—but I keep watch for it all the same.

There are things in that wallpaper that nobody knows about but me, or ever will.

Behind that outside pattern the dim shapes get clearer every day.

It is always the same shape, only very numerous.

And it is like a woman stooping down and creeping about behind that pattern. I don't like it a bit. I wonder—I begin to think—I wish John would take me away from here!

It is so hard to talk with John about my case, because he is so wise, and because he loves me so.

But I tried it last night.

It was moonlight. The moon shines in all around just as the sun does.

I hate to see it sometimes, it creeps so slowly, and always comes in by one window or another.

John was asleep and I hated to waken him, so I kept still and watched the moonlight on that undulating wallpaper till I felt creepy.

The faint figure behind seemed to shake the pattern, just as if she wanted to get out.

I got up softly and went to feel and see if the paper *did* move, and when I came back John was awake.

"What is it, little girl?" he said. "Don't go walking about like that—you'll get cold."

I thought it was a good time to talk, so I told him that I really was not gaining here, and that I wished he would take me away.

"Why, darling!" said he. "Our lease will be up in three weeks, and I can't see how to leave before.

"The repairs are not done at home, and I cannot possibly leave town just now. Of course, if you were in any danger, I could and would, but you really are better, dear, whether you can see it or not. I am a doctor, dear, and I know. You are gaining flesh and color, your appetite is better, I feel really much easier about you."

"I don't weigh a bit more," said I, "nor as much; and my appetite may be better in the evening when you are here but it is worse in the morning when you are away!"

"Bless her little heart!" said he with a big hug. "She shall be as sick as she pleases! But now let's improve the shining hours by going to sleep, and talk about it in the morning!"

"And you won't go away?" I asked gloomily.

"Why, how can I, dear? It is only three weeks more and then we will take a nice little trip of a few days while Jennie is getting the house ready. Really, dear, you are better!"

"Better in body perhaps—" I began, and stopped short, for he sat up straight and looked at me with such a stern, reproachful look that I could not say another word.

"My darling," said he, "I beg of you, for my sake and for our child's sake, as well as for your own, that you will never for one instant let that idea enter your mind! There is nothing so dangerous, so fascinating, to a temperament like yours. It is a false and foolish fancy. Can you not trust me as a physician when I tell you so?"

So of course I said no more on that score, and we went to sleep before long. He thought I was asleep first, but I wasn't, and lay there for hours trying to decide whether that front pattern and the back pattern really did move together or separately.

On a pattern like this, by daylight, there is a lack of sequence, a defiance of law, that is a constant irritant to a normal mind.

The color is hideous enough, and unreliable enough, and infuriating enough, but the pattern is torturing.

You think you have mastered it, but just as you get well under way in following, it turns a back-somersault and there you are. It slaps you in the face, knocks you down, and tramples upon you. It is like a bad dream.

The outside pattern is a florid arabesque, reminding one of a fungus. If you can imagine a toadstool in joints, an interminable string of toadstools, budding and sprouting in endless convolutions—why, that is something like it.

That is, sometimes!

There is one marked peculiarity about this paper, a thing nobody seems to notice but myself, and that is that it changes as the light changes.

When the sun shoots in through the east window—I always watch for that first long, straight ray—it changes so quickly that I never can quite believe it.

That is why I watch it always.

By moonlight—the moon shines in all night when there is a moon—I wouldn't know it was the same paper.

At night in any kind of light, in twilight, candlelight, lamplight, and worst of all by moonlight, it becomes bars! The outside pattern, I mean, and the woman behind it is as plain as can be.

I didn't realize for a long time what the thing was that showed behind, that dim sub-pattern, but now I am quite sure it is a woman.

By daylight she is subdued, quiet. I fancy it is the pattern that keeps her so still. It is so puzzling. It keeps me quiet by the hour.

I lie down ever so much now. John says it is good for me, and to sleep all I can.

Indeed he started the habit by making me lie down for an hour after each meal.

It is a very bad habit, I am convinced, for you see, I don't sleep.

And that cultivates deceit, for I don't tell them I'm awake—oh, no!

The fact is I am getting a little afraid of John.

He seems very queer sometimes, and even Jennie has an inexplicable look.

It strikes me occasionally, just as a scientific hypothesis, that perhaps it is the paper!

I have watched John when he did not know I was looking, and come into the room suddenly on the most innocent excuses, and I've caught him several times *looking at the paper!* And Jennie too. I caught Jennie with her hand on it once.

She didn't know I was in the room, and when I asked her in a quiet, a very quiet voice, with the most restrained manner possible, what she was doing with the paper, she turned around as if she had been caught stealing, and looked quite angry—asked me why I should frighten her so!

Then she said that the paper stained everything it touched, that she had found yellow smooches on all my clothes and John's and she wished we would be more careful!

Did not that sound innocent? But I know she was studying that pattern, and I am determined that nobody shall find it out but myself!

Life is very much more exciting now than it used to be. You see, I have something more to expect, to look forward to, to watch. I really do eat better, and am more quiet than I was.

John is so pleased to see me improve! He laughed a little the other day, and said I seemed to be flourishing in spite of my wallpaper.

I turned it off with a laugh. I had no intention of telling him it was *because* of the wallpaper—he would make fun of me. He might even want to take me away.

I don't want to leave now until I have found it out. There is a week more, and I think that will be enough.

I'm feeling so much better!

I don't sleep much at night, for it is so interesting to watch developments; but I sleep a good deal during the daytime.

In the daytime it is tiresome and perplexing.

There are always new shoots on the fungus, and new shades of yellow all over it. I cannot keep count of them, though I have tried conscientiously.

It is the strangest yellow, that wallpaper! It makes me think of all the yellow things I ever saw—not beautiful ones like buttercups, but old, foul, bad yellow things.

But there is something else about that paper—the smell! I noticed it the moment we came into the room, but with so much air and sun it was not bad. Now we have had a week of fog and rain, and whether the windows are open or not, the smell is here.

It creeps all over the house.

I find it hovering in the dining-room, skulking in the parlor, hiding in the hall, lying in wait for me on the stairs.

It gets into my hair.

Even when I go to ride, if I turn my head suddenly and surprise it—there is that smell!

Such a peculiar odor, too! I have spent hours in trying to analyze it, to find what it smelled like.

It is not bad—at first—and very gentle, but quite the subtlest, most enduring odor I ever met.

In this damp weather it is awful. I wake up in the night and find it hanging over me.

It used to disturb me at first. I thought seriously of burning the house—to reach the smell.

But now I am used to it. The only thing I can think of that it is like is the *color* of the paper! A yellow smell.

There is a very funny mark on this wall, low down, near the mopboard. A streak that runs round the room. It goes behind every piece of furniture, except the bed, a long, straight, even *smooch,* as if it had been rubbed over and over.

I wonder how it was done and who did it, and what they did it for. Round and round and round—round and round and round—it makes me dizzy!

I really have discovered something at last.

Through watching so much at night, when it changes so, I have finally found out.

The front pattern *does* move—and no wonder! The woman behind shakes it!

Sometimes I think there are a great many women behind, and sometimes only one, and she crawls around fast, and her crawling shakes it all over.

Then in the very bright spots she keeps still, and in the very shady spots she just takes hold of the bars and shakes them hard.

And she is all the time trying to climb through. But nobody could climb through that pattern—it strangles so; I think that is why it has so many heads.

They get through and then the pattern strangles them off and turns them upside down, and makes their eyes white!

If those heads were covered or taken off it would not be half so bad.

I think that woman gets out in the daytime!

And I'll tell you why—privately—I've seen her!

I can see her out of every one of my windows!

It is the same woman, I know, for she is always creeping, and most women do not creep by daylight.

I see her in that long shaded lane, creeping up and down. I see her in those dark grape arbors, creeping all around the garden.

I see her on that long road under the trees, creeping along, and when a carriage comes she hides under the blackberry vines.

I don't blame her a bit. It must be very humilating to be caught creeping by daylight!

I always lock the door when I creep by daylight. I can't do it at night, for I know John would suspect something at once.

And John is so queer now that I don't want to irritate him. I wish he would take another room! Besides, I don't want anybody to get that woman out at night but myself.

I often wonder if I could see her out of all the windows at once.

But, turn as fast as I can, I can only see out of one at one time.

And though I always see her, she *may* be able to creep faster than I can turn! I have watched her sometimes away off in the open country, creeping as fast as a cloud shadow in a wind.

If only that top pattern could be gotten off from the under one! I mean to try it, little by little.

I have found out another funny thing, but I shan't tell it this time! It does not do to trust people too much.

There are only two more days to get this paper off, and I believe John is beginning to notice. I don't like the look in his eyes.

And I heard him ask Jennie a lot of professional questions about me. She had a very good report to give.

She said I slept a good deal in the daytime.

John knows I don't sleep very well at night, for all I'm so quiet!

He asked me all sorts of questions, too, and pretended to be very loving and kind.

As if I couldn't see through him!

Still, I don't wonder he acts so, sleeping under this paper for three months.

It only interests me, but I feel sure John and Jennie are affected by it.

Hurrah! This is the last day, but it is enough. John is to stay in town over night, and won't be out until this evening.

Jennie wanted to sleep with me—the sly thing; but I told her I should undoubtedly rest better for a night all alone.

That was clever, for really I wasn't alone a bit! As soon as it was moonlight and that poor thing began to crawl and shake the pattern, I got up and ran to help her.

I pulled and she shook. I shook and she pulled, and before morning we had peeled off yards of that paper.

A strip about as high as my head and half around the room.

And then when the sun came and that awful pattern began to laugh at me, I declared I would finish it today!

We go away tomorrow, and they are moving all my furniture down again to leave things as they were before.

Jennie looked at the wall in amazement, but I told her merrily that I did it out of pure spite at the vicious thing.

She laughed and said she wouldn't mind doing it herself, but I must not get tired.

How she betrayed herself that time!

But I am here, and no person touches this paper but Me—not *alive!*

She tried to get me out of the room—it was too patent! But I said it was so quiet and empty and clean now that I believed I would lie down again and sleep all I could, and not to wake me even for dinner—I would call when I woke.

So now she is gone, and the servants are gone, and the things are gone, and there is nothing left but that great bedstead nailed down, with the canvas mattress we found on it.

We shall sleep downstairs tonight, and take the boat home tomorrow.

I quite enjoy the room, now it is bare again.

How those children did tear about here!

This bedstead is fairly gnawed!

But I must get to work.

I have locked the door and thrown the key down into the front path.

I don't want to go out, and I don't want to have anybody come in, till John comes.

I want to astonish him.

I've got a rope up here that even Jennie did not find. If that woman does get out, and tries to get away, I can tie her!

But I forgot I could not reach far without anything to stand on!

This bed will *not* move!

I tried to lift and push it until I was lame, and then I got so angry I bit off a little piece at one corner—but it hurt my teeth.

Then I peeled off all the paper I could reach standing on the floor. It sticks horribly and the pattern just enjoys it! All those strangled heads and bulbous eyes and waddling fungus growths just shriek with derision!

I am getting angry enough to do something desperate. To jump out of the window would be admirable exercise, but the bars are too strong even to try.

Besides I wouldn't do it. Of course not. I know well enough that a step like that is improper and might be misconstrued.

I don't like to *look* out of the windows even—there are so many of those creeping women, and they creep so fast.

I wonder if they all come out of that wallpaper as I did?

But I am securely fastened now by my well-hidden rope—you don't get *me* out in the road there!

I suppose I shall have to get back behind the pattern when it comes night, and that is hard!

It is so pleasant to be out in this great room and creep around as I please!

I don't want to go outside. I won't, even if Jennie asks me to.

For outside you have to creep on the ground, and everything is green instead of yellow.

But here I can creep smoothly on the floor, and my shoulder just fits in that long smooch around the wall, so I cannot lose my way.

Why, there's John at the door!

It is no use, young man, you can't open it!

How he does call and pound!

Now he's crying to Jennie for an axe.

It would be a shame to break down that beautiful door!

"John, dear!" said I in the gentlest voice. "The key is down by the front steps, under a plantain leaf!"

That silenced him for a few moments.

Then he said, very quietly indeed, "Open the door, my darling!"

"I can't," said I. "The key is down by the front door under a plantain leaf!" And then I said it again, several times, very gently and slowly, and said it so often that he had to go and see, and he got it of course, and came in. He stopped short by the door.

"What is the matter?" he cried. "For God's sake, what are you doing!"

I kept on creeping just the same, but I looked at him over my shoulder.

"I've got out at last," said I, "in spite of you and Jane. And I've pulled off most of the paper, so you can't put me back!"

Now why should that man have fainted? But he did, and right across my path by the wall, so that I had to creep over him every time!

JOURNAL WRITINGS

1. Write a paragraph explaining some of the career or personal goals that you want to pursue, **describing** in detail how you would feel and what you would do if a family member or a spouse opposed your pursuit of those goals. In a second paragraph, state the **narrator's** desired goals in Gilman's story, and describe how she reacts when these goals are frustrated.

2. **Describe** some ways in which your family background affects you. In the story, how does the **narrator's** family background affect her?

BRAINSTORMING AND DRAFTING

3. In the story, John wields power over his wife. In a small group (or working individually), list some of John's actions, as well as several images of confinement, that suggest ways in which John limits his wife's freedom. Draft a topic sentence that **describes** John's power; follow with evidence from the story to support your assertion.

4. Trace the progress of the **narrator's** mental state through the story, noting especially her reaction to her limited freedom.

5.   "I wish I could get well faster" and "I ought to use my will . . . " Do these phrases indicate a lack of will? **Contrast** the first one with "I am determined to get better." What does the **narrator** really want? Draft a paragraph explaining what you think she wants, supporting your assertion with evidence from the story.

THE AUTHOR'S METHODS

6.   Choose any of the following words and write a paragraph explaining how the word suggests or confirms important ideas in the story: ancestral, patterns, yellow (see your answer to Preview question B), prescription, little goose, creeping, wallpaper.
7.   Examine Gilman's method of paragraphing. How does it differ from the type of paragraphing in the selections by Jones or Sartre? How does it **compare** with your own paragraphing in one of your academic papers? Write a brief paragraph **describing** Gilman's method and explaining its effect upon the meaning of the story.

FORMAL WRITING AND RESEARCH PAPERS

8.   Reread Anaïs Nin's article in this unit. Write a paper in which you **argue** that Nin's ideas on double responsibility and on self-definition would or would not help the narrator of Gilman's story to achieve free choice.
9.   Consult the *Social Sciences Index* or the card or computer catalog in your library to find information on how adherence to social roles can affect women's choices. In a formal paper addressed to an audience of college women, take a position on whether adherence to such roles is limiting or liberating, neither of these, or perhaps a combination of both. Use some of the information from your research to develop your own ideas and ways to convince your audience.

Jack Sawyer

On Male Liberation

(1970)

Jack Sawyer (born 1931) is a social psychologist from Nebraska. After receiving a Ph.D. from Purdue University in 1955, he served as research psychologist for the United States Army. He has taught psychology at the University of Chicago and Northwestern University, and has been a research fellow at Harvard University and at Wright Institute. Currently, he is vice-chairman of EFT Management Systems, Inc., in San Diego, California. He has contributed many articles to professional journals, and is the author (with Joseph Pleck) of *Men and Masculinity.*

In the following selection, originally published in *Liberation* magazine, Sawyer describes the stereotype of masculinity that has dominated our society for so long. Such preset roles, he argues, imprison us by dictating our attitudes and actions and thereby preventing the type of thinking and behavior that reflects real freedom.

PREVIEW

List the qualities that you and your peers associate with being "manly."

Male liberation calls for men to free themselves of the sex role stereotypes that limit their ability to be human. Sex role stereotypes say that men should be dominant; achieving and enacting a dominant role in relations with others is often taken as an indicator of success. "Success," for a man, often involves influence over the lives of other persons. But success in achieving positions of dominance and influence is necessarily not open to every man, as dominance is relative and hence scarce by definition. Most men in fact fail to achieve the positions of dominance that sex role stereotypes ideally call for. Stereotypes tend to identify such men as greater or lesser failures, and in extreme cases, men who fail to be dominant are the object of jokes, scorn, and sympathy from wives, peers, and society generally.

One avenue of dominance is potentially open to any man, however—dominance over a woman. As society generally teaches men they should dominate, it teaches women they should be submissive, and so men have the opportunity to dominate women. More and more, women, however, are reacting against the ill effects of being dominated. But the battle of women to be free need not be a battle against men as oppressors. The choice about whether men are the enemy is up to men themselves.

Male liberation seeks to aid in destroying the sex role stereotypes that regard "being a man" and "being a woman" as statuses that must be achieved through proper behavior. People need not take on restrictive roles to establish their sexual identity.

A major male sex role restriction occurs through the acceptance of a stereo-typic view of men's sexual relation to women. Whether or not men consciously admire the Playboy image, they are still influenced by the implicit sex role demands to be thoroughly competent and self-assured—in short, to be "manly." But since self-assurance is part of the stereotype, men who believe they fall short don't admit it, and each can think he is the only one. Stereotypes limit men's perception of women as well as of themselves. Men learn to be highly aware of a woman's body, face, clothes—and this interferes with their ability to relate to her as a whole person. Advertising and consumer orientations are among the societal forces that both reflect and encourage these sex stereotypes. Women spend to make themselves more "feminine," and men are exhorted to buy cigarettes, clothes, and cars to show their manliness.

The popular image of a successful man combines dominance both over women, in social relations, and over other men, in the occupational world. But being a master has its burdens. It is not really possible for two persons to have a free relation when one holds the balance of power over the other. The more powerful person can never be sure of full candor from the other, though he may receive the kind of respect that comes from dependence. Moreover, people who have been dependent are coming to recognize more clearly the potentials of freedom, and it is becoming harder for those who have enjoyed dominance to maintain this position. Persons bent on maintaining dominance are inhibited from developing themselves. Part of the price most men pay for being dominant in one situation is subscribing to a system in which they themselves are subordi-nated in another situation. The alternative is a system where men share, among themselves, and with women, rather than strive for a dominant role.

In addition to the dehumanization of being (or trying to be) a master, there is another severe, if less noticed, restriction from conventional male sex roles in the area of affect, play, and expressivity. Essentially, men are forbidden to play and show affect. This restriction is often not even recognized as a limitation, because affective behavior is so far outside the usual range of male activity.

Men are breadwinners, and are defined first and foremost by their perfor-mance in this area. This is a serious business and results in an end product—bringing home the bacon. The process area of life—activities that are enjoyed for the immediate satisfaction they bring—are not part of the central definition of men's role. Yet the failure of men to be aware of this potential part of their lives leads them to be alienated from themselves and from others. Because men are not permitted to play freely, or show affect, they are prevented from really coming in touch with their own emotions.

If men cannot play freely, neither can they freely cry, be gentle, nor show weakness—because these are "feminine," not "masculine." But a fuller concept of humanity recognizes that all men and women are potentially both strong and weak, both active and passive, and that these and other human characteristics are not the province of one sex.

The acceptance of sex role stereotypes not only limits the individual but has bad effects on society generally. The apparent attractions of a male sex role are strong, and many males are necessarily caught up with this image. Education from early years calls upon boys to be brave, not to cry, and to fight for what is theirs. The day when these were virtues, if it ever existed, is long past. The main effect now is to help sustain a system in which private "virtues" become public vices. Competitiveness helps promote exploitation of people all over the world, as men strive to achieve "success." If success requires competitive achievement, then an unlimited drive to acquire money, possessions, power, and prestige, is only seeking to be successful.

The affairs of the world have always been run nearly exclusively by men, at all levels. It is not accidental that the ways that elements of society have related to each other has been disastrously competitive, to the point of oppressing large segments of the world's population. Most societies operate on authoritarian bases—in government, industry, education, religion, the family, and other institutions. It has been generally assumed that these are the only bases on which to operate, because those who have run the world have been reared to know no other. But women, being deprived of power, have also been more free of the role of dominator and oppressor; women have been denied the opportunity to become as competitive and ruthless as men.

In the increasing recognition of the right of women to participate equally in the affairs of the world, then, there is both a danger and a promise. The danger is that women might end up simply with an equal share of the action in the competitive, dehumanizing, exploitative system that men have created. The promise is that women and men might work together to create a system that provides equality to all and dominates no one. The women's liberation movement has stressed that women are looking for a better model for human behavior than has so far been created. Women are trying to become human, and men can do the same. This implies that sex should not be limited by role stereotypes that define "appropriate" behavior. The present models of neither men nor women furnish adequate opportunities for human development. That one half of the human race should be dominant and the other half submissive is incompatible with a notion of freedom. Freedom requires that there not be dominance and submission, but that all individuals be free to determine their own lives as equals.

JOURNAL WRITINGS

1.   **Compare** and/or **contrast** Sawyer's description of being "manly" (first published in 1970) with the qualities you listed in the Preview question. Judging from your comparison, has society's image of "the male" changed over the past two decades? If you think so, write a paragraph **describing** the

changes. If not, give some reasons why you think changes have been slow or nonexistent.

2.   In a paragraph, **describe** the degree of dominance in a male over thirty whom you know. To what degree does this person conform to Sawyer's stereotype?

BRAINSTORMING AND DRAFTING

3.   Apply some of Sawyer's ideas to the males in Gilman's story, "The Yellow Wallpaper." Consider, especially, the effects of male-role stereotyping on individual personality and behavior, as evidenced by events in the story.

4.   In the last few paragraphs of his article, Sawyer objects to what he views as a "male" insistence on competitive dominance in world affairs. Choosing a historical event that happened in the last ten years, draft a paragraph explaining how the event illustrates or challenges Sawyer's theory of competition and resulting oppression.

THE AUTHOR'S METHODS

5.   In this brief article, Sawyer primarily offers us a series of **generalizations,** such as the following: "The popular image of a successful man combines dominance both over women, in social relations, and over other men, in the occupational world." Why does he not provide concrete **examples** of such statements? Write a few sentences that give a hypothetical or real-life example of one of his generalizations. If you were writing a research paper for a psychology class, would you include such examples? Why or why not? What does your answer imply about purpose and audience in writing?

6.   Sawyer uses several kinds of **transitional** devices to move his readers logically from one paragraph to another. For example, the opening paragraph ends with his assertion on "positions of dominance." The topic sentence of the second paragraph repeats the word "dominance" to establish a connection with the first paragraph, and specifies the idea by indicating "one avenue" of dominance. Thus, repetition and specification can function as **transitions.** Draft a paragraph in which you discuss some of Sawyer's other transitional devices between paragraphs.

FORMAL WRITING AND RESEARCH PAPERS

7.   Choose a film or television program with a male character who is partially or fully "liberated" from the restrictive masculine stereotype. How realistic or credible is this character? Write a full **analysis** of the character, including a discussion of his realism; provide specific **examples** from the film or program to support your **analysis.**

8. Using the card or computer catalog at your college or neighboring library, find a minimum of eight to ten books on the topic of male liberation. (You may wish to work in a small group on this project, with each member providing some of the books.) After **skimming** the overall content of each, write an **annotated bibliography** of the books. Include a **descriptive** commentary of the contents of each book and, where possible, an evaluation of the book's usefulness or accessibility for a student wishing to learn about the field of men's studies.

Rita Freedman

Props and Paint

(1986)

Rita Freedman (born 1940) is a psychologist from Brooklyn, New York. She received a Ph.D. from the State University of New York at Albany. She has taught in the psychology department at Ulster County Community College, State University of New York at New Paltz, and the College of New Rochelle. She currently has a private clinical practice in Scarsdale, New York. Approaching psychology from a feminist perspective, she studies how women are viewed by society as well as how they view themselves.

Her most recent book, *Bodylove: Learning to Like Our Looks and Ourselves* (1989), is a practical guide that offers specific exercises to help people accept their bodies. In the following selection from *Beauty Bound,* Freedman examines women's assumptions about the need for physical attractiveness. She demonstrates how the "props and paint" that women use help them conform to the desired female role model, but may also reinforce their imprisonment in society's preconceived image of the "ideal" female body.

PREVIEW

Should women wear makeup? Should men? Explain your answer.

Women are not really fairer than men. Their special beauty is not innate but an acquired disguise. To act out a myth is to impersonate a caricature. And so the ladies' room becomes the powder room, where the costumes of femininity are applied.

Props and paint are essential elements of the female role, as basic to the culture as to the economy. Though a woman may feel powerless in many ways, her body is an arena she can try to control. Cosmetic rituals serve as a source of salvation. Involving technology that would astound a fairy godmother, they combat appearance anxiety and provide an avenue of self-expression. They change the person as well as her image. As Jean Cocteau once observed, "A defect of the soul cannot be corrected on the face, but a defect of the face, if you can correct it, may correct a soul."[1]

And so women visit the "repair shops" for overhaul and fine tuning. Fabricating flesh into fantasy is not easy. What does feminized beauty currently entail? Faces are toned, moisturized, massaged, masked, peeled, lifted, and plastered with foundation, powder, base, and blush. Ears are pierced, pinned back. Brows are tweezed, penciled, dyed. Lashes are curled, and dressed with mascara. Lids are lined, shadowed, and surgically "done." Lips are glossed, frosted, plumped. Nose and chin are implanted, reduced, turned up or down. Hair is permed, rinsed, straightened, curled, dyed, teased, sprayed, wigged, greased, gelled. Teeth are capped, and removed to accent cheekbones. Nails are manicured, polished, wrapped. Body hair is removed by depilatories, waxing, tweezing, shaving of the upper lip, chin, brows, underarms, and legs. Breasts are augmented, reduced, lifted, padded. Torsos are corseted and girdled. Rumps are plumped. Tummies are tucked. Hips and thighs are firmed, reduced. Cellulite is "dissolved." Feet are reshaped by high-heeled, pointed shoes, and toes are amputated to fit them. To this partial list add a plethora of diet and exercise programs and a variety of fashions that constrict flesh or inhibit movement.

While make-overs are practiced by both sexes, men in Western cultures engage in them less often, less universally, and less frantically. Although few women indulge in all of the above rituals, virtually every woman interviewed felt that at least a few of them were imperative to her basic beauty routine.

What motivates females to transform themselves? The answer is a strong human need to conform to social norms. A personal decision—to have a perm or a face-lift for example—is dictated partly by group pressure. Women enact the popular image for the pleasure of being like others and of being liked by others. Beauty transformations produce the security of group acceptance while they reduce the fear of social rejection.

Cosmetic rituals are also valuable in legitimizing the purchase of human touch. Chimps groom each other for hours for the simple pleasure of physical contact. We have few rituals that encourage body contact in American culture, but manicurists, hairdressers, and body groomers are permitted to lay their hands on us. They know the workings of our flesh as well as the secrets of our heart. And they are not easily replaced. A few days after Nancy Reagan moved into the White House, her favorite manicurist was flown in from California for an emergency nail repair (a cross-continental manicure that reportedly cost $1,500 in travel expenses).

Beauty rituals often become "functionally autonomous." This means that the process takes on more importance than the end product. Like other daily habits, these rituals prove satisfying through mere repetition. "If it's Thursday, I must be having my nails done." The daily beauty fix can be as addictive, compelling, and expensive as some drug habits, and the withdrawal process just as painful.

For ladies of leisure, the pursuit of beauty has historically served as a kind of career, a central focus of existence quite as demanding as any full-time job. Busy making appointments and keeping them, having facials, pedicures, and body waxings, such women have been compared to the heroines of Russian plays who are really mourning their lives but try to conceal the mourning by devotion to their images.[2]

Commitment to beauty can continue even beyond the grave. Funeral outfits are sometimes prepared in advance of dying and instructions left with hair-dressers. After taking the sacrament, Madame de Pompadour's final act before death was to rouge her face. In a clever essay, Nancy Henley compares beauty parlors to funeral parlors and the work of beauticians to that of morticians. Both promise (if you pay enough) to produce a totally natural look; both carefully guard the secrets of their trade; and both use cosmetics to turn people into "unreal images and inhuman spectacles."[3] While funeral parlors mask death with the look of life, beauty parlors mask women with the look of loveliness. After the funeral of Princess Grace of Monaco, reporters were quick to reassure us that she looked as magnificent in death as in life ("perhaps even more so"). Do a fair face and a dead face really have so much in common? Is a sleeping princess, frozen in passive splendor, the ultimate model of femininity?

The symptoms of a comatose state are all too common among depressed women. Barbara, for example, was withdrawn and silent when she returned to therapy after her sophomore year at college. She spent much of the day either sleeping or weeping, waiting for something to shake her out of her depression. The shyness that had plagued her since childhood became much worse during college, and she was feeling extremely isolated.

Barbara had been my patient several years earlier, but I hardly recognized her. The awkward, unattractive teenager that I remembered had grown into a very pretty young woman. When I commented about the change in her appearance, she explained that her nose and chin had been remodeled right after high school graduation.

> I had expected to have my nose fixed for years. It's almost a ritual in our family. My mom and aunt had the same ethnic nose—my grandfather's. We always joked about it. Everyone just assumed that I'd have mine redone someday like they had. And so I did. Besides, Mom would never have left me alone until I got rid of that bump. She's so concerned about mixing with the right crowd and constantly talked about "The Nose" like some huge liability.

Since childhood, Barbara had felt overshadowed by an elegant and extroverted mother. This socially ambitious mother found her quiet and plain-looking daughter both a disappointment and a cosmetic challenge. Barbara described her own feelings after the surgery:

> In a way, I "came out" that summer after high school—sort of like a ceremony where I presented my new face to the world. Mom was very excited. I guess we both thought I'd be suddenly happier. But the shy part of me was still there. I felt proud but also ashamed. I didn't know what to say to people. And I still don't know whether to tell friends at school about my nose job. I look much better now, and I'm more confident about my appearance. But still so terribly self-conscious in new situations.

At the next therapy session I suggested that Barbara bring in a picture of herself before and after the surgery. We looked at the two photos and I asked if she ever wanted her old self back. Definitely not, she replied.

> It's not that I want to go back to that other person. She doesn't exist anymore. But I just can't figure out which parts of me are acceptable. I don't have to hide my face, but

the rest of me doesn't feel pretty enough. I don't know whether I can safely reveal myself to others without being rejected.

Barbara's depression was not caused directly by her cosmetic make-over, nor was her personality dramatically altered by it. Yet the psychodynamics of her depression changed as the problem of feeling unacceptable shifted from the outside to the inside.

People play out social scripts by sending subtle messages that conceal as much as they reveal. Like Barbara, we all try to defend "the territory of the self" from unwanted scrutiny. Like her, we discreetly guard secrets of our nose jobs and our electrolysis treatments. Gray hair is quietly washed away and body parts are veiled away. (The agoraphobic completely screens herself from public view.) While primitive people paint their faces to ward off evil spirits, Western women feel exposed without at least a dash of lipstick to protect them from the social forces that threaten. Few dare to venture out even to the corner grocery without putting on a touch of makeup as defensive fabrication. The more important the event, the more elaborate the defense.

Why must the territory of a woman's body be so carefully guarded? What is there about her that requires so much concealment and fabrication? Why must she use her body to tell so many social lies? . . .

Adornment serves as a kind of coded dialogue spoken through hair styles, jewelry, or body painting. Its vocabulary conveys subtle messages. In *The Decorated Body,* Robert Brain presents a fascinating review of cross-cultural cosmetic rituals. He explains that body decorating is concerned with questions both of self-identity and group identity: "Who am I and who are we together?" Cosmetics are more than simply a decorative mask, he writes; they imprint on body and mind the traditions and philosophy of the social group.[4]

Props and paint are used by both sexes to create a greater contrast between feminine and masculine characteristics. Brain concludes that in most societies males and females decorate differently but equally, whereas in Western cultures women adorn "to a far greater extent and in a greater variety of ways than men. . . . Body decoration has become primarily associated with female vanity." According to his analysis, the current Western preoccupation with female beauty grows from fundamental cultural values and reflects a strange denial of female sexuality. Beauty rituals are used primarily to make women "socially acceptable," he concludes. "A woman turns herself into a lady and her strongest motivation is to pursue social, not sexual, satisfaction." For example, Brain suggests that cosmetics call attention to the face as a way of distracting the eye from other erogenous areas.[5]

Our Western tradition linking body adornment with female vanity is long but by no means consistent. The Greek conception of beauty encompassed the total person, outer form as well as inner qualities. The male body was revered and considered more attractive than the female body. Early Christian teachings challenged the idea of beauty as mind-body unity, and "set beauty adrift—as an alienated, arbitrary, superficial enchantment."[6] The mind was associated with the higher values of culture and of men, while the body was relegated to the lower realms of nature and of women. Separated from the inner spirit, flesh was rejected as a narcissistic object, the proper concern of women but a dangerous temptation for men.

Fear of female beauty became part of religious asceticism. Tertullian, a second-century theologian, warned women never to enhance their appearance and to "neglect, conceal and veil their natural beauty," lest men be tempted to sin by seeing it. Consequently, female beauty took on exaggerated meaning and power. The British Parliament joined the Church in trying to restrain women from beautifying themselves. A bill passed in 1650, entitled "The Vice of Painting and Wearing Black Patches and Immodest Dresses of Women," was designed to protect men against "the false adornments of the painted, patched, plumped out, marriage hungry female."[7]

Religious injunctions against sexuality connected the female body with sorcery, so that beauty became linked with power and with evil. Part of the power of beauty stems from fear of the supernatural. A glamourized woman combines charm with enchantment. She bewitches, bothers, and bewilders. One drinks her in like a visual potion that captures and corrupts the soul. The Malleus Maleficarum, an infamous church document of 1486 that officially condoned the burning of witches, described woman as:

> Beautiful to look on, contaminating to the touch and deadly to keep. . . . A natural temptation, a desirable calamity, a delectable detriment, an evil of nature . . . painted with fair colors.[8]

Hundreds of thousands who were sacrificed as witches over several centuries were considered deviant in some way—too smart, too old, too bold, too long unwed. And some were condemned to burn merely for their faces alone—judged either too beautiful or too ugly to be endured. Erica Jong reflects on the faces of witches and ponders:

> What does a witch look like? . . . She is either exceedingly beautiful or horribly ugly, bewitching in her physical graces or terrifyingly hideous. In either case she menaces men, for her beauty both blinds and binds, and her ugliness assaults and astounds the senses. Whether he meets an ugly witch or a beautiful one, man is victimized by female power.[9]

Legends like those of Eve and Pandora connect woman with contamination and sin. Eve corrupts a perfect Eden by opening her mouth to the apple; Pandora pollutes the world by opening her "box" and exposing its contents. The bodies of these women go out of control, threatening the very downfall of "mankind." Therefore, they must be constrained for man's protection, and God takes the lead by punishing Eve with the travails of childbirth. The suffering of womankind becomes an extension of Eve's punishment, and an inherent part of womanhood. Cosmetic traditions that require female suffering, subordination, and self-sacrifice are justified through myths that portray women as threatening creatures who need constraint.

Beauty safely conceals woman's frightening dimensions, while compensating for her deficiencies. The adornments of feminine fashion—the painted ubiquitous smile, the dainty sandaled foot—are ingratiating symbols. They reassure a man that this particular woman is not Pandora's sister, not a devilish witch or a castrating bitch. Even as a glamourous vamp she at least does not resemble his dominating Mom. The trivia of lipstick and lace reassure him of her impotence. By donning the disguise of a doll, she signals her willingness to be "his little woman." And her mythical beauty serves as a survival tactic for them both.

Whenever sex was considered a weakness to which men succumbed, women were feared as seductive and corrupting. Consequently, codes of dress and veiling were enacted to hold their power in check. St. Thomas decreed self-adornment of females a mortal sin because it evoked lust. Yet he encouraged married women to look pretty purely to please their husbands "lest through despising her he fall into adultery." A contemporary update on this advice is found in such books as Helen Andelin's *Fascinating Womanhood*, and Marabel Morgan's *The Total Woman*, which urge a good Christian wife "to spruce up in order to keep your man."[10] (The exhortation to be both provocative and pure at the same time remains a central paradox of the beauty myth.)

Medieval chivalry was built on the adoration of female beauty as the symbol of chastity, purity, truth, and all else that was virtuous. Italian and Western European art depicted very little beauty bias until the time of the Renaissance, when females started to predominate in the work of Botticelli and Rubens. With Raphael, woman's body became glorified as the "essence of human beauty." An eighteenth-century painter suggested that a curved line was more naturally interesting than a straight one; hence, women's curves represented the true "line of beauty." The smallness, smoothness, and delicacy of the female nude were considered inherently lovely. Female models still far outnumber male models in contemporary figure-drawing classes.

For most of the eighteenth century, Western European men vied with women in adorning and displaying their bodies. Noblemen, as heavily turned out as the ladies, paraded in powdered wigs and satin pumps, showing off their shapely legs. Men's fashions were like women's: constantly changing and used to signal sex and status. Then came the French Revolution, which not only changed the social roles of men but dramatically altered men's appearance. This shift has been called "The Great Masculine Renunciation," during which males rejected most cosmetic rituals as effeminate.[11]

Along with the new ideals of the French republic came the belief that a man's most important function was not in the salon but in the office or factory. Tight breeches and codpieces were abandoned, silk stockings were replaced by loose trousers, and wigs were discarded for close-cropped hair. For the past two centuries, men in Western cultures generally have dressed modestly, shunned cosmetics, and worn utilitarian clothes. They have stopped displaying wealth overtly on their own bodies, adorning their wives instead with jewels or fur, making beauty woman's birthright and her burden.

In the United States, adornment became increasingly associated with women's lives and women's bodies in the early nineteenth century. Historian Lois Banner concludes in her book *American Beauty* that the social and work roles of men and women became more differentiated with the industrial revolution. Americans began to view the cultivation of beauty, along with the preservation of religious and spiritual values, as the special concern of women. Banner cites nineteenth-century poems, sermons, and manuals which assert that "it is woman's business to be beautiful," "woman *is* the beauty principle," and "beauty is unquestionably the mastercharm of that sex."[12]

Pictures of pinups, nymphs, and Gibson girls began to appear on streetcar posters, in barrooms, on packs of cards—a phenomenon that was later described as "the cult of women." By the turn of this century, the commercialism of female beauty was evident in the burgeoning fashion industry, the growing numbers of salons, the increasing use of cosmetics, and the marketing efforts that accompanied all of these.

A "Cinderella Mythology" developed for women in the nineteenth century as a counterpart to the "self-made-man" image, reports Banner. Young women in the antebellum years worked to turn themselves into elegant ladies while their mates worked to become men of property. Together they represented the essence of capitalist values. To "be a belle" was nothing other than a profession, wrote Harriet Beecher Stowe.[13] When a wife could spend her day pursuing beauty, it indicated leisure and thereby proclaimed her husband's success. Fashion represented fun and self-indulgence—the way elite life was meant to be.

Ironically, the Protestant work ethic, so basic to our American value system, indirectly promoted the pursuit of beauty as woman's work by preaching that diligence pays off and that no sacrifice is too great to achieve a worthy goal. For women who had few achievement arenas open to them, the work ethic easily translated into a mandate for personal make-over. Ambitious ladies poured their energy into beautification (which did not violate the traditional feminine role). And so the road to success took a detour through the beauty salon, making narcissism and Puritanism rather peculiar partners.

Meanwhile, nineteenth-century Darwinists predicted that all women eventually would be attractive, because men were selecting good-looking wives and passing this trait on to their children. The idea that beauty could (and therefore should) belong to every woman was soon adapted to commercial ends. Good looks were promoted as a "natural right" of all ladies. Since cosmetics can be sold to anyone who can afford them, they serve to democratize beauty by spreading it around. Buying and selling attractiveness fits nicely with the American values of egalitarianism, materialism, and rugged individualism, notes Banner.[14]

Ever since the turn of the century, women's magazines have featured "before and after" shots. The testimonials of ordinary housewives prove that nature needs only a gentle prod. Responsible women are told they owe it to themselves and to their families to make the effort. Those who ignore their potential have only themselves to blame. Once unattractiveness is equated with laziness, guilt is added to the stigma of looking plain or fat or old. As Zsa Zsa Gabor once quipped, "There are no ugly women, just lazy ones." When Barbara considers her before and after photos, she voices no regrets. Like most women, she is pleased with the results and feels a sense of accomplishment in her remade image.

It is only a short step from deceiving others to deceiving oneself. Beauty rituals, initially used to disguise a defect, eventually screen us from self-scrutiny. When constantly masked by make-over, one's own naked face can seem alien. This is why beauty products are marketed as if the changes they create are quite natural. The myth asserts that female beauty is innate, needing only to be brought to the surface and displayed. So-called pure products made of lemon balm, fresh milk or honey, pure wheat germ oil, with balanced pH maintain the illusion that nature remains in command. In the 1970s women responded to a decade of the "natural look" by buying more cosmetics than ever before to achieve an unmade-up image. As the real face becomes fused with fantasy and myth gives the illusion of truth, women end up feeling ashamed when caught unadorned. They learn their parts so well that they forget they are impersonating the role of fairy princess. . . .

When Barbara initially came for therapy at age fifteen, she was insecure and self-deprecating. I asked if there was anything she really liked about herself. Glancing down and extending her pretty sandal, she replied, "One thing I do have is a beautiful tiny foot." "Yes, but what else is special about you?" I prompted, knowing her many talents and trying to expand her feelings of worth. A long silence followed. Looking down once more, she finally added, "I guess I also have a nice high arch." Sadly, I wondered how often Barbara had heard the happily-ever-after ending of Cinderella, whose equally tiny foot had reshaped her destiny.

The story of Cinderella has much to teach about beauty transformations: how they incite envy, how they can be magically acquired, and how they attract and deceive men. Perhaps this tale has survived for over a thousand years in hundreds of versions because it socializes children so well to the special meaning of female beauty. Cinderella is a tale of rivalry. Women use deception, body mutilation, and witchcraft to compete for male attention. Bonds between women are strained while men are pursued, and the competition is fierce because there are not enough princes to go around.

In the beginning of his book on the role of fairy tales, Bruno Bettelheim writes that a child's greatest need is to find meaning in life above and beyond the events of the moment.[15] Piaget describes this search for meaning as a continuous adaptation to reality. Knowledge grows in small steps, says Piaget, as children try to construct a mental conception of events by asking over and over, "What is the world really like and how can I live in it?" Fairy-tale fantasy serves to fill the gaps in children's concepts. As simplified models, these stories and their characters reinforce the ways in which men and women relate to each other. They convey our social heritage, including cultural myths about gender roles.

All fairy tales are stories of personal transformation. In many of them, a part of the body is used to resolve some difficulty. Rapunzel's strong hair, Snow White's blood-red lips, Cinderella's unique foot, reassure children that even when they feel isolated or rejected by others, they can turn to their own bodies for strength and solace. In fact, fairy-tale figures—such as Goldilocks, Snow White, and Red Riding Hood—are often named for their appearance.

Fairy-tale characters are polarized as either good or evil, thus making identification easier for children, who view the world through primitive concepts. (Research shows that 80 percent of female fairy-tale characters are evil and ugly, and the remaining 20 percent are beautiful young girls.) Good = beauty =

clean = love on the one side; while on the other, bad = ugly = dirty = rejection. Cinderella was "as good as she was beautiful," we are told, and thus the two qualities become fused. When the stepsisters rename Ella "Cinderella," they "dirty" her name to correspond with her looks. (In some versions she is called Cinderslut, associating loss of virtue with loss of beauty.)

Once goodness and beauty are fused, virtue becomes harder to recognize under a soiled face. Eventually Cinderella must be made over, transformed so that goodness and beauty are reunited. According to Bettelheim, one moral of this tale is that virtue will be rewarded regardless of appearance. But even the most naive child knows intuitively that Cinderella could never have been loved by the Prince while dressed in rags. The hidden message, which children clearly hear, is that packaging counts, no matter how worthy the inner woman.

Cinderella has two mothers, a common fairy-tale device that appeals to our ambivalence about our own mothers. The dead natural mother is the good and loving one, who later returns in the form of a godmother. She is allied with men and with nature; she bestows beauty as a reward for purity. The bad mother (safely placed one step removed) is a cruel and jealous one who strips Cinderella of her finery and her father's love. She is insecure and dominating with men, and destroys the beauty of other women to reduce competition.

A closer look at these two mothers shows they both have a common goal that mothers have shared for centuries: marketing their daughters as brides. As in real life, fairy-tale mothers encourage the beauty rituals, model the fashions, and provide the motivation and means that turn their girls into marriage material. It is Barbara's mother who translates the acceptable images of femininity, pointing out the defects of Barbara's body and helping her to "correct" them. It was Victorian mothers who laced corsets ever tighter, Chinese mothers who initiated the rituals of foot-binding, African mothers who even today watch a tiny clitoris* being excised, black mothers who burn hair while ironing it straight, white mothers who arrange for nose jobs and lift five-year-olds onto the runways of beauty pageants. I remember my own mother taking me to the electrologist when I was twelve. It was a secret we shared with no one else, a mother-daughter conspiracy to "normalize" my face. I recall a young patient, barely fifteen, whose breasts were surgically reduced with her mother's consent.

When Cinderella's stepsisters struggle unsuccessfully to fit into the shoe, their mother holds out a knife, urging them to cut off a toe or slice down a heel. (Bettelheim notes that this is one of the few instances of self-mutilation in fairy tales.) The mother provides the means, gives the instructions, and ignores the pain and the crippling consequences. "Cut off your toes," she cries. "Once you are Queen you won't have to walk anymore"—an all too familiar refrain, echoed by our culture. "Cut off your education; once you are wed you won't need to work anymore." Or, more universally, "Cut off your name; once you are his you won't need your identity anymore."

---

* clitoris—the sensitive portion of the female external sex organ. [Eds.]

Beauty transformations are not passed down by mothers to victimize their daughters. Most mothers, whether good ones or bad ones, are simply fulfilling their role as socializers. They sense only too well that good looks may be the most important legacy they can pass on to a young girl. It is the mother's magic wand, an insurance policy to guarantee happiness ever after.

In conveying beauty rituals to their daughters, mothers also teach conformity to the feminine role. This process further strains the ambivalent love-hate relationship between mother and daughter. As a mother tries to coerce compliance to traditional beauty standards, tensions are increased. When a daughter rejects her mother's ideas about proper feminine appearance, she rejects her mother as well. For this very reason, girls may consciously choose beauty or body issues as a symbol of their struggle for independence (as tragically exemplified in young anorectic* women, for instance). At age thirteen, Barbara pleaded to have a second hole put in her already pierced ears. When her mother firmly denied permission, Barbara took a needle and in a difficult and defiant act, pierced the earlobes herself, thereby using a conflict over a beauty issue to proclaim her adolescent independence.

On the surface, one message of *Cinderella* is that cosmetic transformations fail. The stepsisters in their contrived finery are ridiculous figures, mocked and humiliated. Not so for the heroine, however. Cinderella's artifice is as great as her sisters', but she has been made over by the "good mother." Her transformation comes unsolicited, a reward for virtue and servitude. And she is beautified in secrecy, reminding us of the contemporary assurance that "only her hairdresser knows for sure." Often the private nature of beauty rituals further isolates a woman, who believes that she alone has a false bosom or a lifted face.

Rituals of cosmetic transformation create rivalry among women. When the palace ball in *Cinderella* is first announced, there is a flurry of activity, diets, dressmakers, and lessons in elocution and curtsying as contestants struggle to put on their disguises. Remember, however, that beauty is an exclusionary concept, attainable only by the few. The stepsisters (along with the waitresses and secretaries) who flock hopefully to the ball leave empty-handed, their self-esteem diminished along with their resources. This is the fairy-tale version of a beauty pageant, where young bodies are displayed, paraded, then divided into winners and losers.

The witchcraft provided by a godmother makes Cinderella not just pretty but spectacular. "The-Most-Beautiful-Girl-in-the-Land," we are told; "100 times, nay 1,000 times more beautiful than her sisters"; so beautiful that even those who know her best fail to recognize her. A hush falls as she enters the palace, followed by murmurs of astonishment. The prince finds her irresistible (and so does his father!); "even the fiddlers are amazed at her beauty."

Here, in fairy-tale form, is the magical power of female beauty: the power to attract crowds and control kings; the power of Miss America, of Marilyn M.,

---

* anorectic—one who continually lacks appetite for food. [Eds.]

Jackie O., and Princess Di—a power that women can rarely match in any other way. Hard at work in her clogs, Cinderella was ignored; transformed by her satins and slippers, she conquered the world.

There is a potent message here for the children who listen, the little ones who Piaget and Bettelheim tell us are testing reality in stories and searching for meaning in life. What do they learn? That without beauty, virtue goes unnoticed; that a girl's looks can be quickly and miraculously made over; that cosmetic transformation is the key to love and attention. Children also learn that power and happiness do not come to women through active pursuit and assertive engagement with life, but rather through obedience, servitude, patience, and, ultimately, through the magic of cosmetic make-over.

Cinderella's conquest at the ball is paradoxically a product of her passivity. Compliant and uncomplaining, she has denied anger, lived virtuously, been a good girl. Yet she seems incapable of meeting her own needs. When the messenger comes searching for the owner of the slipper, she stands mute, not daring to whisper "Here I am, my foot will fit." True to her nature, she waits to be discovered.

In the end, it is not her efforts but her unique body that resolves the conflict. Unable to act intentionally, she accidentally stumbles while fleeing in the dark, with the Prince in hot pursuit. Has she become a fallen woman, losing that "tiny receptacle into which some part of the body can slip and fit tightly?" asks Bettelheim.[16] With such marvelous erotic imagery, it is not surprising that this tale has survived for 1,000 years! As a vaginal symbol, the shoe is always made of glass or gold so that it cannot "stretch to fit another." (Glass also shatters, like a virgin's hymen.) Cinderella's childlike foot symbolizes purity and uniqueness. No other woman has one quite like it, the perfect size for this prince. Notice how one part of the female body becomes symbolic of the entire woman. Cinderella's beauty, innocence, and destiny are embodied in her tiny foot (in the same way that Barbara measured her value in terms of that one special trait).

Objectification and preoccupation with isolated body parts dehumanizes women, but it also degrades men when they become so obsessed with ankles or breasts they forget the person within. Bettelheim suggests that Cinderella would be loved no matter what she looked like. However the story's resolution rests on her foot size. This prince has developed a fetish. So preoccupied is he with finding the right foot that the stepsisters are able to trick him. By slicing down a heel or toe (in Grimm's account), they squeeze into the slipper and therefore into his life. He starts to carry off first one then the other to be wed, but blood is seen through the glass, exposing the sisters as imposters, as bleeding "nonvirgins." Their mutilations are symbolic of castration, for these aggressive women will stop at nothing, even cutting off flesh, to trap a man. In contrast, when Cinderella puts on the slipper (like a wedding ring), no blood flows. She remains virginal. Sexually passive, she does not threaten a man but waits to be taken by him.

The sexual symbolism of a tiny foot with its elegant slipper reflects the Far Eastern origins of this ancient tale. Crystal or embroidered shoes were often given to Chinese girls in reward for the agony of foot-binding, and to display their most precious body part. A bound foot in its elegant shoe is of course *the* classic example of the high price demanded by the myth of female beauty.

Fairy tales always end happily. Though we never know whether Cinderella loves the Prince (or whether he is even lovable), we believe in happiness ever after. The perfect fit of the shoe symbolizes her willingness to shape her life around his. However, the slipper can also be seen as a symbol of bondage. By conforming to the tiny dimensions of the feminine role, she is no longer free to grow. A pathetically stunted foot, the smallest in the land, is really only fit for a doll's life.

We are all fed a gourmet diet of Cinderella sagas and Miss America pageants, in which passivity is richly rewarded and beauty transformations buy security and love. As women now strive toward independence, there lingers the longing for a prince whose life can be slipped into and who can lift the burden of shaping one's own destiny. Colette Dowling calls this dilemma the "Cinderella Complex." Those of us suffering from this syndrome, she says, vacillate between the wish to achieve an authentic identity and the temptation to hold back and let a man confer one on us. Dowling believes that the unconscious wish to remain dependent prevents us from moving ahead in life. "We have been taught to believe that as females we cannot stand alone, that we are too fragile, too delicate, and too needful of protection," writes Dowling.[17] Like Cinderella, we wait for something external to change our lives. In effect, our feet feel too small to fill the shoes of a full-grown person. Like Cinderella, we stumble in our efforts to step out into the world, and like her, we turn to beauty transformations as a defense against unhappiness.

But the Cinderella Complex is not only reflected in ambivalence over independence. It is etched in a woman's flesh as well, from her reshaped nose to her frosted smile and platformed feet. Dowling describes the cosmetic disguise as a "counter phobic facade." Dressed up in an exterior of assertive self-confidence, many women remain internally vulnerable and self-doubting. Though looking powerfully beautiful, they feel essentially powerless. They are like Barbara who, at age fifteen, offered her pretty little foot and her nice high arch as the things she valued most in herself.

Women yearn for recognition. Uncertain of their place in the world, they struggle to determine what they want and more basically who they are. Attempts to attract attention through props and paint are part of this longing for confirmation of worth. Women are shouting, "Look at me, not through me. Acknowledge my presence." The Cinderella Complex translates into a mandate for beauty transformations. These further increase dependency by diverting a woman's energy, depleting her resources, and diminishing her self-esteem.

Notes

[1] Perutz, K. (1970). *Beyond the Looking Glass* (New York: William Morrow), p. 137.

[2] *Ibid.*

[3] Henley, N. "The American Way of Beauty: Of Parlors, Beauty and/or Funeral," in *The Paper*, vol. I, no. 15 (reprinted by KNOW Press, P.O. Box 10197, Pittsburgh, PA 15232).

[4] Brain, R. (1979). *The Decorated Body* (New York: Harper & Row), p. 184.

[5] *Ibid.*, pp. 136–7.

[6] Susan Sontag quoted in Pierre, C. (1976). *Looking Good* (New York: Reader's Digest Press), p. 106.

[7] Brain, p. 12.

[8] Hays, H. R. (1964). *The Dangerous Sex* (New York: Putnam), p. 142.

[9] Jong, E. (1981). *Witches* (New York: H. Abrams), p. 66.

[10] Andelin, H. (1965). *Fascinating Womanhood* (New York: Bantam); and Morgan, M. (1973). *The Total Woman* (Old Tappan, N.J.: Fleming H. Revell).

[11] Flügel, J. C. (1930). *The Psychology of Clothes* (New York: International University Press).

[12] Banner, Lois. (1983). *American Beauty* (New York: Knopf), pp. 9–10.

[13] Harriet Beecher Stowe quoted in *ibid.*, p. 23.

[14] *Ibid.*, p. 205.

[15] Bettelheim, B. (1976). *The Uses of Enchantment: The Meaning and Importance of Fairy Tales* (New York: Alfred Knopf).

[16] *Ibid.*, p. 265.

[17] Dowling, C. (1981). *The Cinderella Complex* (New York: Simon and Schuster), p. 20.

JOURNAL WRITINGS

1. How does the way you groom or adorn your body compare with the practices that Freedman **describes?** Do you think your grooming habits limit you to traditional male or female role-playing? Explain your answer.
2. Find an **example** of a newspaper, magazine, or television advertisement that pressures women to use "props" or "paint." **Describe** the ad in detail, and explain why you think it will or will not influence a particular woman you know.

BRAINSTORMING AND DRAFTING

3. How might Miss America pageant officials **define** beauty? How might weight lifters define physical attractiveness? Draft a paragraph in which you include these definitions, demonstrate what they have in common, and explain how such definitions could prove limiting.
4. In what sense does Freedman wrestle with the same issue as Gilman and Sawyer? Explain the similarities among the **themes** of these three selections, and indicate the different perspective that each writer chooses in order to arrive at his/her theme or **thesis.**

THE AUTHOR'S METHODS

5. In the third paragraph, most of Freedman's sentences include lists of **descriptive** words. How does this repetitive strategy reveal her meaning in the paragraph? Try the same strategy in your own paragraph in which you **describe** the emphasis placed on the male or female body in television advertisements. You may wish to consult your answer to question 2 of Journal Writings above.

6. Freedman often uses historical data to develop an idea. Find three instances of such data, and describe the **specific** purpose of each in the paragraph where it appears.

FORMAL WRITING AND RESEARCH PAPERS

7. "As women now strive toward independence, there lingers the longing for a prince whose life can be slipped into and who can lift the burden of shaping one's own destiny." Do you agree with Freedman that modern women still tend to limit their own freedom by allowing others (especially males) to shape their futures? Write a paper in which you **analyze** Freedman's assertion; use **examples** and anecdotes of people you know to support your assertions.

8. Freedman uses the Cinderella tale to illustrate how the female character can be limited by an exaggerated regard for physical beauty. Read another fairy tale that includes beauty as a consideration. Also find and read some secondary sources that deal with role-playing in fairy tales. (Try, for example, the *MLA Bibliography*, the *Humanities Index*, and the card or computer catalog.) Write a paper **arguing** that the emphasis on physical characteristics does or does not limit the characters (male or female) in the story.

Alice Walker

Beauty: When the Other Dancer Is the Self

(1983)

Alice Walker (born 1944) received a B.A. from Sarah Lawrence College in 1965. While maintaining positions as a writer-in-residence and professor of literature at several American colleges such as Wellesley and Brandeis, she published collections of poetry, short stories, essays, and novels. Though most of her literary works deal with the special problems of black women, her images of suffering humanity have universal appeal. She is perhaps best known for her novel *The Color Purple,* for which she received the Pulitzer Prize and the American Book Award in 1983. The novel was later made into a very successful film. A more recent novel is *The Temple of My Familiar.*

The following selection is from her collection of prose writings, *In Search of Our Mothers' Gardens: A Collection of Womanist Prose.* In this essay, Walker not only recounts a childhood profoundly changed and sadly limited by the perception of a physical deformity, but she also presents the potential for growth and freedom. Walker's account might also be considered a dramatic illustration of the women whom Rita Freedman describes in "Props and Paint."

PREVIEW

Think of someone whom you think is beautiful. What makes him or her beautiful? How do you **define** beauty?

It is a bright summer day in 1947. My father, a fat, funny man with beautiful eyes and a subversive wit, is trying to decide which of his eight children he will take with him to the county fair. My mother, of course, will not go. She is knocked out from getting most of us ready: I hold my neck stiff against the pressure of her knuckles as she hastily completes the braiding and then beribboning of my hair.

My father is the driver for the rich old white lady up the road. Her name is Miss Mey. She owns all the land for miles around, as well as the house in which we live. All I remember about her is that she once offered to pay my mother thirty-five cents for cleaning her house, raking up piles of her magnolia leaves, and washing her family's clothes, and that my mother—she of no money, eight children, and a chronic earache—refused it. But I do not think of this in 1947. I am two and a half years old. I want to go everywhere my daddy goes. I am excited at the prospect of riding in a car. Someone has told me fairs are fun. That there is room in the car for only three of us doesn't faze me at all. Whirling happily in my starchy frock, showing off my biscuit-polished patent-leather shoes and lavender socks, tossing my head in a way that makes my ribbons bounce, I stand, hands on hips, before my father. "Take me, Daddy," I say with assurance, "I'm the prettiest!"

Later, it does not surprise me to find myself in Miss Mey's shiny black car, sharing the back seat with the other lucky ones. Does not surprise me that I thoroughly enjoy the fair. At home that night I tell the unlucky ones all I can remember about the merry-go-round, the man who eats live chickens, and the teddy bears, until they say: that's enough, baby Alice. Shut up now, and go to sleep.

It is Easter Sunday, 1950. I am dressed in a green, flocked, scalloped-hem dress (handmade by my adoring sister, Ruth) that has its own smooth satin petticoat and tiny hot-pink roses tucked into each scallop. My shoes, new T-strap patent leather, again highly biscuit-polished. I am six years old and have learned one of the longest Easter speeches to be heard that day, totally unlike the speech I said when I was two: "Easter lilies / pure and white / blossom in / the morning light." When I rise to give my speech I do so on a great wave of love and pride and expectation. People in the church stop rustling their new crinolines. They seem to hold their breath. I can tell they admire my dress, but it is my spirit, bordering on sassiness (womanishness), they secretly applaud.

"That girl's a little *mess*," they whisper to each other, pleased.

Naturally I say my speech without stammer or pause, unlike those who stutter, stammer, or, worst of all, forget. This is before the word "beautiful" exists in people's vocabulary, but "Oh, isn't she the *cutest* thing!" frequently floats my way. "And got so much sense!" they gratefully add . . . for which thoughtful addition I thank them to this day.

It was great fun being cute. But then, one day, it ended.

I am eight years old and a tomboy. I have a cowboy hat, cowboy boots, checkered shirt and pants, all red. My playmates are my brothers, two and four years older than I. Their colors are black and green, the only difference in the way we are dressed. On Saturday nights we all go to the picture show, even my mother. Westerns are her favorite kind of movie. Back home, "on the ranch," we pretend we are Tom Mix, Hopalong Cassidy, Lash LaRue (we've even named one of our dogs Lash LaRue), we chase each other for hours rustling cattle, being outlaws, delivering damsels from distress. Then my parents decide to buy my brothers guns. These are not "real" guns. They shoot "BBs," copper pellets my brothers say will kill birds. Because I am a girl, I do not get a gun. Instantly I am relegated to the position of Indian. Now there appears a great distance between us. They shoot and shoot at everything with their new guns. I try to keep up with my bow and arrows.

One day while I am standing on top of our makeshift "garage"—pieces of tin nailed across some poles—holding my bow and arrow and looking out toward the fields, I feel an incredible blow in my right eye. I look down just in time to see my brother lower his gun.

Both brothers rush to my side. My eye stings, and I cover it with my hand. "If you tell," they say, "we will get a whipping. You don't want that to happen, do you?" I do not. "Here is a piece of wire," says the older brother, picking it up from the roof; "say you stepped on one end of it and the other flew up and hit you." The pain is beginning to start. "Yes," I say. "Yes, I will say that is what happened." If I do not say this is what happened, I know my brothers will find ways to make me wish I had. But now I will say anything that gets me to my mother.

Confronted by our parents we stick to the lie agreed upon. They place me on a bench on the porch and I close my left eye while they examine the right. There is a tree growing from underneath the porch that climbs past the railing to the roof. It is the last thing my right eye sees. I watch as its trunk, its branches, and then its leaves are blotted out by the rising blood.

I am in shock. First there is intense fever, which my father tries to break using lily leaves bound around my head. Then there are chills: my mother tries to get me to eat soup. Eventually, I do not know how, my parents learn what has happened. A week after the "accident" they take me to see a doctor. "Why did you wait so long to come?" he asks, looking into my eye and shaking his head. "Eyes are sympathetic," he says. "If one is blind, the other will likely become blind too."

This comment of the doctor's terrifies me. But it is really how I look that bothers me most. Where the BB pellet struck there is a glob of whitish scar tissue, a hideous cataract, on my eye. Now when I stare at people—a favorite pastime, up to now—they will stare back. Not at the "cute" little girl, but at her scar. For six years I do not stare at anyone, because I do not raise my head.

Years later, in the throes of a mid-life crisis, I ask my mother and sister whether I changed after the "accident." "No," they say, puzzled. "What do you mean?"

What do I mean?

I am eight, and, for the first time, doing poorly in school, where I have been something of a whiz since I was four. We have just moved to the place where the "accident" occurred. We do not know any of the people around us because this is a different county. The only time I see the friends I knew is when we go back to our old church. The new school is the former state penitentiary. It is a large stone building, cold and drafty, crammed to overflowing with boisterous, ill-disciplined children. On the third floor there is a huge circular imprint of some partition that has been torn out.

"What used to be here?" I ask a sullen girl next to me on our way past it to lunch.

"The electric chair," says she.

At night I have nightmares about the electric chair, and about all the people reputedly "fried" in it. I am afraid of the school, where all the students seem to be budding criminals.

"What's the matter with your eye?" they ask, critically.

When I don't answer (I cannot decide whether it was an "accident" or not), they shove me, insist on a fight.

My brother, the one who created the story about the wire, comes to my rescue. But then brags so much about "protecting" me, I become sick.

After months of torture at the school, my parents decide to send me back to our old community, to my old school. I live with my grandparents and the teacher they board. But there is no room for Phoebe, my cat. By the time my grand-parents decide there *is* room, and I ask for my cat, she cannot be found. Miss Yarborough, the boarding teacher, takes me under her wing, and begins to teach me to play the piano. But soon she marries an African—a "prince," she says—and is whisked away to his continent.

At my old school there is at least one teacher who loves me. She is the teacher who "knew me before I was born" and bought my first baby clothes. It is she who makes life bearable. It is her presence that finally helps me turn on the one child at the school who continually calls me "one-eyed bitch." One day I simply grab him by his coat and beat him until I am satisfied. It is my teacher who tells me my mother is ill.

My mother is lying in bed in the middle of the day, something I have never seen. She is in too much pain to speak. She has an abscess in her ear. I stand looking down on her, knowing that if she dies, I cannot live. She is being treated with warm oils and hot bricks held against her cheek. Finally a doctor comes. But I must go back to my grandparents' house. The weeks pass but I am hardly aware of it. All I know is that my mother might die, my father is not so jolly, my brothers still have their guns, and I am the one sent away from home.

"You did not change," they say.

Did I imagine the anguish of never looking up?

I am twelve. When relatives come to visit I hide in my room. My cousin Brenda, just my age, whose father works in the post office and whose mother is a nurse, comes to find me. "Hello," she says. And then she asks, looking at my recent school picture, which I did not want taken, and on which the "glob," as I think of it, is clearly visible, "You still can't see out of that eye?"

"No," I say, and flop back on the bed over my book.

That night, as I do almost every night, I abuse my eye. I rant and rave at it, in front of the mirror. I plead with it to clear up before morning. I tell it I hate and despise it. I do not pray for sight. I pray for beauty.

"You did not change," they say.

I am fourteen and baby-sitting for my brother Bill, who lives in Boston. He is my favorite brother and there is a strong bond between us. Understanding my feelings of shame and ugliness he and his wife take me to a local hospital, where the "glob" is removed by a doctor named O. Henry. There is still a small bluish crater where the scar tissue was, but the ugly white stuff is gone. Almost immediately I become a different person from the girl who does not raise her head. Or so I think. Now that I've raised my head I win the boyfriend of my dreams. Now that I've raised my head I have plenty of friends. Now that I've raised my head classwork comes from my lips as faultlessly as Easter speeches did, and I leave high school as valedictorian, most popular student, and *queen,* hardly believing my luck. Ironically, the girl who was voted most beautiful in our class (and was) was later shot twice through the chest by a male companion, using a "real" gun, while she was pregnant. But that's another story in itself. Or is it?

"You did not change," they say.

It is now thirty years since the "accident." A beautiful journalist comes to visit and to interview me. She is going to write a cover story for her magazine that focuses on my latest book. "Decide how you want to look on the cover," she says. "Glamorous, or whatever."

Never mind "glamorous," it is the "whatever" that I hear. Suddenly all I can think of is whether I will get enough sleep the night before the photography session: if I don't, my eye will be tired and wander, as blind eyes will.

At night in bed with my lover I think up reasons why I should not appear on the cover of a magazine. "My meanest critics will say I've sold out," I say. "My family will now realize I write scandalous books."

"But what's the real reason you don't want to do this?" he asks.

"Because in all probability," I say in a rush, "my eye won't be straight."

"It will be straight enough," he says. Then, "Besides, I thought you'd made your peace with that."

And I suddenly remember that I have.

I remember:

I am talking to my brother Jimmy, asking if he remembers anything unusual about the day I was shot. He does not know I consider that day the last time my father, with his sweet home remedy of cool lily leaves, chose me, and that I suffered and raged inside because of this. "Well," he says, "all I remember is standing by the side of the highway with Daddy, trying to flag down a car. A white man stopped, but when Daddy said he needed somebody to take his little girl to the doctor, he drove off."

I remember:

I am in the desert for the first time. I fall totally in love with it. I am so overwhelmed by its beauty, I confront for the first time, consciously, the meaning of the doctor's words years ago: "Eyes are sympathetic. If one is blind, the other will likely become blind too." I realize I have dashed about the world madly, looking at this, looking at that, storing up images against the fading of the light. *But I might have missed seeing the desert!* The shock of that possibility—and gratitude for over twenty-five years of sight—sends me literally to my knees. Poem after poem comes—which is perhaps how poets pray.

On Sight

I am so thankful I have seen
The Desert
And the creatures in the desert
And the desert Itself.

The desert has its own moon
Which I have seen
With my own eye.
There is no flag on it.

Trees of the desert have arms
All of which are always up
That is because the moon is up
The sun is up
Also the sky
The stars
Clouds
None with flags.

If there *were* flags, I doubt
the trees would point.
Would you?

But mostly, I remember this:

I am twenty-seven, and my baby daughter is almost three. Since her birth I have worried about her discovery that her mother's eyes are different from other people's. Will she be embarrassed? I think. What will she say? Every day she watches a television program called "Big Blue Marble." It begins with a picture of the earth as it appears from the moon. It is bluish, a little battered-looking, but full of light, with whitish clouds swirling around it. Every time I see it I weep with love, as if it is a picture of Grandma's house. One day when I am putting Rebecca down for her nap, she suddenly focuses on my eye. Something inside me cringes, gets ready to try to protect myself. All children are cruel about physical differences, I know from experience, and that they don't always mean to be is another matter. I assume Rebecca will be the same.

But no-o-o-o. She studies my face intently as we stand, her inside and me outside her crib. She even holds my face maternally between her dimpled little hands. Then, looking every bit as serious and lawyerlike as her father, she says, as if it may just possibly have slipped my attention: "Mommy, there's a *world* in your eye." (As in, "Don't be alarmed, or do anything crazy.") And then, gently, but with great interest: "Mommy, where did you *get* that world in your eye?"

For the most part, the pain left then. (So what, if my brothers grew up to buy even more powerful pellet guns for their sons and to carry real guns themselves. So what, if a young "Morehouse man" once nearly fell off the steps of Trevor Arnett Library because he thought my eyes were blue.) Crying and laughing I ran to the bathroom, while Rebecca mumbled and sang herself off to sleep. Yes indeed, I realized, looking into the mirror. There *was* a world in my eye. And I saw that it was possible to love it: that in fact, for all it had taught me of shame and anger and inner vision, I *did* love it. Even to see it drifting out of orbit in boredom, or rolling up out of fatigue, not to mention floating back at attention in excitement (bearing witness, a friend has called it), deeply suitable to my personality, and even characteristic of me.

That night I dream I am dancing to Stevie Wonder's song "Always" (the name of the song is really "As," but I hear it as "Always"). As I dance, whirling and joyous, happier than I've ever been in my life, another bright-faced dancer joins me. We dance and kiss each other and hold each other through the night. The other dancer has obviously come through all right, as I have done. She is beautiful, whole and free. And she is also me.

JOURNAL WRITINGS

1. In a paragraph, **describe** how your image of your body has affected your life. In a second paragraph, **compare** or **contrast** your physical self-image with the **narrator's** self-image as a child and adolescent.
2. What influence does the **narrator's** family have on her attitude toward beauty? What influence does your own family have on your attitude toward beauty? How do other college students affect your attitude? In each case, provide details or an **example** that demonstrates this influence or lack of it.

BRAINSTORMING AND DRAFTING

3. In a small group or working individually, compile a list of the problems the narrator has because of her damaged eye. **Classify** these problems into "internal" problems generated by her own mind or emotions and "external" problems caused mostly by society or other people. Then each person should choose one category, and draft a paragraph speculating on reasons or root causes for these problems and on ways to prevent them from occurring in the lives of college students.
4. How does the title help to reveal Walker's **theme?** Consider especially what the image of dancing suggests and in what sense an "other" exists.
5. How might Jean-Paul Sartre respond to Walker's essay? Explain your answer.

THE AUTHOR'S METHODS

6. In a paragraph, explore some features of Walker's writing that make her story sound dramatic. For instance, you might **describe** and give **examples** of her **verb** tenses, the length and patterns of her sentences, her paragraphing, etc.

7.   How does the poem "On Sight" show the narrator's growth in the **essay?** Consider especially the meaning of her **metaphor** "The desert has its own moon," as well as the images of upward pointing and the absence of a flag.

FORMAL WRITING AND RESEARCH PAPERS

8.   Walker's **narrator** has come to appreciate the value of "the world" in her eye: life's painful experiences of "shame and anger and inner vision." She therefore considers herself free from the pain and limitations caused by her earlier **definition** of beauty. Write a paper in which you: (a) discuss society's current concept of attractiveness for your peer group; and (b) evaluate to what degree (if any) someone in your peer group can challenge this concept without suffering from the pain that Walker's narrator experienced. Use evidence from Walker's and/or Freedman's articles and your personal experience to support your ideas.

9.   Using *Psychological Abstracts*, the *Social Sciences Index*, and the card or computer catalog, research the emotional problems of burn victims who experience scarring. Write a paper in which you explain these difficult problems in light of Walker's implied ideas. **Conclude** by recommending realistic, manageable ways that both society and the affected individual can try to alleviate some of the suffering; again use Walker's ideas as part of your solution.

Stanley Milgram

Some Conditions of Obedience and Disobedience to Authority

(1965)

Stanley Milgram (1933–1984) was a well-known social psychologist. He received his Ph.D. from Harvard University, and taught at Yale, Harvard, and the City University of New York. His writings include *Television and Anti-Social Behavior* and *The Individual in a Social World: Essays and Experiments.* His most famous and controversial work concerns his experiments on obedience, which he documents fully in *Obedience to Authority: An Experimental View.*

The following report of his original experiment first appeared in *Human Relations.* The report explains how the experiment was conducted and demonstrates what can happen when an authority figure orders people to inflict pain on others. Milgram also reports on results obtained when the conditions of the experiment were changed.

PREVIEW

Do you think that someone in authority could persuade you to perform an action that (a) you feel is wrong, and (b) you do not want to perform? Give reasons for your answer.

The situation in which one agent commands another to hurt a third turns up time and again as a significant theme in human relations.* It is powerfully expressed in the story of Abraham, who is commanded by God to kill his son. It is no accident

---

* [Author's Note] This research was supported by two grants from the National Science Foundation: NSF G-17916 and NSF G-24152. Exploratory studies carried out in 1960 were financed by a grant from the Higgins Funds of Yale University. I am grateful to John T. Williams, James J. McDonough, and Emil Elges for the important part they played in the project. Thanks are due also to Alan Elms, James Miller, Taketo Murata, and Stephen Stier for their aid as graduate assistants. My wife, Sasha, performed many valuable services. Finally, I owe a profound debt to the many persons in New Haven and Bridgeport who served as subjects. [Milgram's notes throughout, unless cited as the editors'.]

that Kierkegaard, seeking to orient his thought to the central themes of human experience, chose Abraham's conflict as the springboard to his philosophy.[1]

War too moves forward on the triad of an authority which commands a person to destroy the enemy, and perhaps all organized hostility may be viewed as a theme and variation on the three elements of authority, executant, and victim.[†] We describe an experimental program, recently concluded at Yale University, in which a particular expression of this conflict is studied by experimental means.

In its most general form the problem may be defined thus: if X tells Y to hurt Z, under what conditions will Y carry out the command of X and under what conditions will he refuse. In the more limited form possible in laboratory research, the question becomes: if an experimenter tells a subject to hurt another person, under what conditions will the subject go along with this instruction, and under what conditions will he refuse to obey. The laboratory problem is not so much a dilution of the general statement as one concrete expression of the many particular forms this question may assume.

One aim of the research was to study behavior in a strong situation of deep consequence to the participants, for the psychological forces operative in powerful and life-like forms of the conflict may not be brought into play under diluted conditions.

This approach meant, first, that we had a special obligation to protect the welfare and dignity of the persons who took part in the study; subjects were, of necessity, placed in a difficult predicament, and steps had to be taken to ensure their wellbeing before they were discharged from the laboratory. Toward this end, a careful, post-experimental treatment was devised and has been carried through for subjects in all conditions.[‡]

---

† [Author's Note] Consider, for example, J. P. Scott's analysis of war in his monograph on aggression:
"... while the actions of key individuals in a war may be explained in terms of direct stimulation to aggression, vast numbers of other people are involved simply by being part of an organized society.
... For example, at the beginning of World War I an Austrian archduke was assassinated in Sarajevo. A few days later soldiers from all over Europe were marching toward each other, not because they were stimulated by the archduke's misfortune, but because they had been trained to obey orders." (Slightly rearranged from Scott (1958), *Aggression*, p. 103.)[2]

‡ [Author's Note] It consisted of an extended discussion with the experimenter and, of equal importance, a friendly reconciliation with the victim. It made clear that the victim did *not* receive painful electric shocks. After the completion of the experimental series, subjects were sent a detailed report of the results and full purposes of the experimental program. A formal assessment of this procedure points to its overall effectiveness. Of the subjects, 83.7 percent indicated that they were glad to have taken part in the study; 15.1 percent reported neutral feelings; and 1.3 percent stated that they were sorry to have participated. A large number of subjects spontaneously requested that they be used in further experimentation. Four-fifths of the subjects felt that more experiments of this sort should be carried out, and 74 percent indicated that they had learned something of personal importance as a result of being in the study. Furthermore, a university psychiatrist, experienced in outpatient treatment, interviewed a sample of experimental subjects with the aim of uncovering possible injurious effects resulting from participation. No such effects were in evidence. Indeed, subjects typically felt that their participation was instructive and enriching. A more detailed discussion of this question can be found in Milgram (1964).[3]

TERMINOLOGY

If Y follows the command of X we shall say that he has obeyed X; if he fails to carry out the command of X, we shall say that he has disobeyed X. The terms to *obey* and to *disobey*, as used here, refer to the subject's overt action only, and carry no implication for the motive or experiential states accompanying the action.*

To be sure, the everyday use of the word *obedience* is not entirely free from complexities. It refers to action within widely varying situations, and connotes diverse motives within those situations: a child's obedience differs from a soldier's obedience, or the love, honor, and *obey* of the marriage vow. However, a consistent behavioral relationship is indicated in most uses of the term: in the act of obeying, a person does what another person tells him to do. Y obeys X if he carries out the prescription for action which X has addressed to him; the term suggests, moreover, that some form of dominance-subordination, or hierarchical element, is part of the situation in which the transaction between X and Y occurs.

A subject who complies with the entire series of experimental commands will be termed an *obedient* subject; one who at any point in the command series defies the experimenter will be called a *disobedient* or *defiant* subject. As used in this report the terms refer only to the subject's performance in the experiment, and do not necessarily imply a general personality disposition to submit to or reject authority.

---

* [Author's Note] To *obey* and to *disobey* are not the only terms one could use in describing the critical action of Y. One could say that Y is cooperating with X, or displays conformity with regard to X's commands. However, *cooperation* suggests that X agrees with Y's ends, and understands the relationship between his own behavior and the attainment of those ends. (But the experimental procedure, and, in particular, the experimenter's command that the subject shock the victim even in the absence of a response from the victim, preclude such understanding.) Moreover, cooperation implies status parity for the co-acting agents, and neglects the asymmetrical, dominance-subordination element prominent in the laboratory relationship between experimenter and subject. *Conformity* has been used in other important contexts in social psychology, and most frequently refers to imitating the judgments or actions of others when no explicit requirement for imitation has been made. Furthermore, in the present study there are two sources of social pressure; pressure from the experimenter issuing the commands, and pressure from the victim to stop the punishment. It is the pitting of a common man (the victim) against an authority (the experimenter) that is the distinctive feature of the conflict. At a point in the experiment the victim demands that he be let free. The experimenter insists that the subject continue to administer shocks. Which act of the subject can be interpreted as conformity? The subject may conform to the wishes of his peer or to the wishes of the experimenter, and conformity in one direction means the absence of conformity in the other. Thus the word has no useful reference in this setting, for the dual and conflicting social pressures cancel out its meaning.

In the final analysis, the linguistic symbol representing the subject's action must take its meaning from the concrete context in which that action occurs; and there is probably no word in everyday language that covers the experimental situation exactly, without omissions or irrelevant connotations. it is partly for convenience, therefore, that the terms *obey* and *disobey* are used to describe the subject's actions. At the same time, our use of the words is highly congruent with dictionary meaning.

SUBJECT POPULATION

The subjects used in all experimental conditions were male adults, residing in the greater New Haven and Bridgeport areas, aged 20 to 50 years, and engaged in a wide variety of occupations. Each experimental condition described in this report employed 40 fresh subjects and was carefully balanced for age and occupational types. The occupational composition for each experiment was: workers, skilled and unskilled: 40 percent; white collar, sales, business: 40 percent; professionals: 20 percent. The occupations were intersected with three age categories (subjects in 20's, 30's, and 40's, assigned to each condition in the proportions of 20, 40, and 40 percent, respectively).

THE GENERAL LABORATORY PROCEDURE*

The focus of the study concerns the amount of electric shock a subject is willing to administer to another person when ordered by an experimenter to give the "victim" increasingly more severe punishment. The act of administering shock is set in the context of a learning experiment, ostensibly designed to study the effect of punishment on memory. Aside from the experimenter, one naïve subject and one accomplice perform in each session. On arrival each subject is paid $4.50. After a general talk by the experimenter, telling how little scientists know about the effect of punishment on memory, subjects are informed that one member of the pair will serve as teacher and one as learner. A rigged drawing is held so that the naïve subject is always the teacher, and the accomplice becomes the learner. The learner is taken to an adjacent room and strapped into an "electric chair."

The naïve subject is told that it is his task to teach the learner a list of paired associates, to test him on the list, and to administer punishment whenever the learner errs in the test. Punishment takes the form of electric shock, delivered to the learner by means of a shock generator controlled by the naïve subject. The teacher is instructed to increase the intensity of electric shock one step on the generator on each error. The learner, according to plan, provides many wrong answers, so that before long the naïve subject must give him the strongest shock on the generator. Increases in shock level are met by increasingly insistent demands from the learner that the experiment be stopped because of the growing discomfort to him. However, in clear terms the experimenter orders the teacher to continue with the procedure in disregard of the learner's protests. *Thus, the naïve subject must resolve a conflict between two mutually incompatible de-*

---

* [Author's Note] A more detailed account of the laboratory procedure can be found in Milgram (1963).[4] A similar and independently evolved experimental procedure, employing a shock generator, victim, and learning task, was reported by Buss (1961). Buss used the technique for studying aggression, not obedience, and did not make use of the fundamental measure employed in the present study: breakoff points.[5]

*mands from the social field. He may continue to follow the orders of the experi-
menter and shock the learner with increasing severity, or he may refuse to follow
the orders of the experimenter and heed the learner's pleas. The experimenter's
authority operates not in a free field, but against ever-mounting countervailing
pressure from the person being punished.*

A few technical points need to be considered before the findings of the study
are described. For the purpose of delivering shock, a simulated shock generator
is used, with 30 clearly marked voltage levels that range from 15 to 450 volts.
(Each level is activated by one of 30 individual lever switches set in a horizontal
line.) The naïve subject is given a sample shock of 45 volts to convince him of the
authenticity of the instrument. The generator bears verbal designations that
range from "Slight Shock" to "Danger: Severe Shock."

The responses of the victim are standardized on tape, and each protest is
coordinated to a particular voltage level on the shock generator. Starting with 75
volts the learner begins to grunt and moan. At 150 volts he demands to be let out
of the experiment. At 180 volts he cries out that he can no longer stand the pain.
At 300 volts he refuses to provide any more answers to the memory test, insisting
that he is no longer a participant in the experiment and must be freed. In
response to this last tactic, the experimenter instructs the naïve subject to treat
the absence of an answer as equivalent to a wrong answer, and to follow the usual
shock procedure. The experimenter reinforces his demand with the statement:
"You have no other choice, you must go on!" (This imperative is used whenever
the naïve subject tries to break off the experiment.) If the subject refuses to give
the next higher level of shock, the experiment is considered at an end. A
quantitative value is assigned to the subject's performance based on the maxi-
mum-intensity shock he administered before breaking off. Thus any subject's
score may range from zero (for a subject unwilling to administer the first shock
level) to 30 (for a subject who proceeds to the highest voltage level on the board).
For any particular subject and for any particular experimental condition, the
degree to which participants have followed the experimenter's orders may be
specified with a numerical value, corresponding to the metric on the shock
generator.

This laboratory situation gives us a framework in which to study the subject's
reactions to the principal conflict of the experiment. Again, this conflict is
between the experimenter's demands that he continue to administer the electric
shock, and the learner's demands, which become increasingly more insistent,
that the experiment be stopped. The crux of the study is to vary systematically
the factors believed to alter the degree of obedience to the experimental commands, to learn under what conditions submission to authority is most probable
and under what conditions defiance is brought to the fore.

PILOT STUDIES

Pilot studies for the present research were completed in the winter of 1960; they
differed from the regular experiments in a few details: for one, the victim was

placed behind a silvered glass, with the light balance on the glass such that the victim could be dimly perceived by the subject (Milgram, 1961).[6]

Though essentially qualitative in treatment, these studies pointed to several significant features of the experimental situation. At first no vocal feedback was used from the victim. It was thought that the verbal and voltage designations on the control panel would create sufficient pressure to curtail the subject's obedience. However, this was not the case. In the absence of protests from the learner, virtually all subjects, once commanded, went blithely to the end of the board, seemingly indifferent to the verbal designations ("Extreme Shock" and "Danger: Severe Shock"). This deprived us of an adequate basis for scaling obedient tendencies. A force had to be introduced that would strengthen the subject's resistance to the experimenter's commands, and reveal individual differences in terms of a distribution of break-off points.

This force took the form of protests from the victim. Initially, mild protests were used, but proved inadequate. Subsequently, more vehement protests were inserted into the experimental procedure. To our consternation, even the strongest protests from the victim did not prevent all subjects from administering the harshest punishment ordered by the experimenter; but the protests did lower the mean maximum shock somewhat and created some spread in the subject's performance; therefore, the victim's cries were standardized on tape and incorporated into the regular experimental procedure.

The situation did more than highlight the technical difficulties of finding a workable experimental procedure: It indicated that subjects would obey authority to a greater extent than we had supposed. It also pointed to the importance of feedback from the victim in controlling the subject's behavior.

One further aspect of the pilot study was that subjects frequently averted their eyes from the person they were shocking, often turning their heads in an awkward and conspicuous manner. One subject explained: "I didn't want to see the consequences of what I had done." Observers wrote:

> . . . subjects showed a reluctance to look at the victim, whom they could see through the glass in front of them. When this fact was brought to their attention they indicated that it caused them discomfort to see the victim in agony. We note, however, that although the subject refuses to look at the victim, he continues to administer shocks.

This suggested that the salience of the victim may have, in some degree, regulated the subject's performance. If, in obeying the experimenter, the subject found it necessary to avoid scrutiny of the victim, would the converse be true? If the victim were rendered increasingly more salient to the subject, would obedience diminish? The first set of regular experiments was designed to answer this question.

IMMEDIACY OF THE VICTIM

This series consisted of four experimental conditions. In each condition the victim was brought "psychologically" closer to the subject giving him shocks.

In the first condition (Remote Feedback) the victim was placed in another room and could not be heard or seen by the subject, except that, at 300 volts, he pounded on the wall in protest. After 315 volts he no longer answered or was heard from.

The second condition (Voice Feedback) was identical to the first except that voice protests were introduced. As in the first condition the victim was placed in an adjacent room, but his complaints could be heard clearly through a door left slightly ajar and through the walls of the laboratory.*

The third experimental condition (Proximity) was similar to the second, except that the victim was now placed in the same room as the subject, and 1½ feet from him. Thus he was visible as well as audible, and voice cues were provided.

The fourth, and final, condition of this series (Touch-Proximity) was identical to the third, with this exception: The victim received a shock only when his hand rested on a shockplate. At the 150-volt level the victim again demanded to be let free and, in this condition, refused to place his hand on the shockplate. The experimenter ordered the naïve subject to force the victim's hand onto the plate. Thus obedience in this condition required that the subject have physical contact with the victim in order to give him punishment beyond the 150-volt level.

Forty adult subjects were studied in each condition. The data revealed that

---

* [Author's Note] It is difficult to convey on the printed page the full tenor of the victim's responses, for we have no adequate notation for vocal intensity, timing, and general qualities of delivery. Yet these features are crucial to producing the effect of an increasingly severe reaction to mounting voltage levels. (They can be communicated fully only by sending interested parties the recorded tapes.) In general terms, however, the victim indicates no discomfort until the 75-volt shock is administered, at which time there is a light grunt in response to the punishment. Similar reactions follow the 90- and 105-volt shocks, and at 120 volts the victim shouts to the experimenter that the shocks are becoming painful. Painful groans are heard on administration of the 135-volt shock, and at 150 volts the victim cries out, 'Experimenter, get me out of here! I won't be in the experiment any more! I refuse to go on!' Cries of this type continue with generally rising intensity, so that at 180 volts the victim cries out, 'I can't stand the pain,' and by 270 volts his response to the shock is definitely an agonized scream. Throughout, he insists that he be let out of the experiment. At 300 volts the victim shouts in desperation that he will no longer provide answers to the memory test; and at 315 volts, after a violent scream, he reaffirms with vehemence that he is no longer a participant. From this point on, he provides no answers, but shrieks in agony whenever a shock is administered; this continues through 450 volts. Of course, many subjects will have broken off before this point.

A revised and stronger set of protests was used in all experiments outside the Proximity series. Naturally, new baseline measures were established for all comparisons using the new set of protests.

There is overwhelming evidence that the great majority of subjects, both obedient and defiant, accepted the victims' reactions as genuine. The evidence takes the form of: (a) tension created in the subjects (see discussion of tension); (b) scores on "estimated-pain" scales filled out by the subjects immediately after the experiment; (c) subjects' accounts of their feelings in post-experimental interviews; and (d) quantifiable responses to questionnaires distributed to subjects several months after their participation in the experiments. This matter will be treated fully in a forthcoming monograph.

(The procedure in all experimental conditions was to have the naïve subject announce the voltage level before administering each shock, so that—independently of the victim's responses—he was continually reminded of delivering punishment of ever-increasing severity.)

obedience was significantly reduced as the victim was rendered more immediate to the subject. The mean maximum shock for the conditions is shown in Figure 1.

Expressed in terms of the proportion of obedient to defiant subjects, the findings are that 34 percent of the subjects defied the experimenter in the Remote condition, 37.5 percent in Voice Feedback, 60 percent in Proximity, and 70 percent in Touch-Proximity.

How are we to account for this effect? A first conjecture might be that as the victim was brought closer the subject became more aware of the intensity of his suffering and regulated his behavior accordingly. This makes sense, but our evidence does not support the interpretation. There are no consistent differences in the attributed level of pain across the four conditions (i.e., the amount of pain experienced by the victim as estimated by the subject and expressed on a 14-point scale). But it is easy to speculate about alternative mechanisms:

Empathic cues. In the Remote and to a lesser extent the Voice Feedback conditions, the victim's suffering possesses an abstract, remote quality for the subject. He is aware, but only in a conceptual sense, that his actions cause pain to another person; the fact is apprehended, but not felt. The phenomenon is common enough. The bombardier can reasonably suppose that his weapons will inflict suffering and death, yet this knowledge is divested of affect and does not move him to a felt, emotional response to the suffering resulting from his actions. Similar observations have been made in wartime. It is possible that the visual cues associated with the victim's suffering trigger empathic responses in the subject and provide him with a more complete grasp of the victim's experience. Or it is possible that the empathic responses are themselves unpleasant, possessing drive properties which cause the

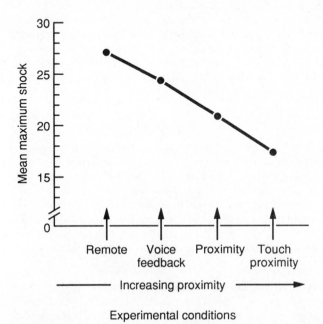

Figure 1. Mean maxima in proximity series.

subject to terminate the arousal situation. Diminishing obedience, then, would be explained by the enrichment of empathic cues in the successive experimental conditions.

Denial and narrowing of the cognitive field. The Remote condition allows a narrowing of the cognitive field so that the victim is put out of mind. The subject no longer considers the act of depressing a lever relevant to moral judgement, for it is no longer associated with the victim's suffering. When the victim is close it is more difficult to exclude him phenomenologically. He necessarily intrudes on the subject's awareness since he is continuously visible. In the Remote condition his existence and reactions are made known only after the shock has been administered. The auditory feedback is sporadic and discontinuous. In the Proximity conditions his inclusion in the immediate visual field renders him a continuously salient element for the subject. The mechanism of denial can no longer be brought into play. One subject in the Remote condition said: "It's funny how you really begin to forget that there's a guy out there, even though you can hear him. For a long time I just concentrated on pressing the switches and reading the words."

Reciprocal fields. If in the Proximity condition the subject is in an improved position to observe the victim, the reverse is also true. The actions of the subject now come under proximal scrutiny by the victim. Possibly, it is easier to harm a person when he is unable to observe our actions than when he can see what we are doing. His surveillance of the action directed against him may give rise to shame, or guilt, which may then serve to curtail the action. Many expressions of language refer to the discomfort or inhibitions that arise in face-to-face confrontation. It is often said that it is easier to criticize a man "behind his back" than to "attack him to his face." If we are in the process of lying to a person it is reputedly difficult to "stare him in the eye." We "turn away from others in shame" or in "embarrassment" and this action serves to reduce our discomfort. The manifest function of allowing the victim of a firing squad to be blindfolded is to make the occasion less stressful for him, but it may also serve a latent function of reducing the stress of the executioner. In short, in the Proximity conditions, the subject may sense that he has become more salient in the victim's field of awareness. Possibly he becomes more self-conscious, embarrassed, and inhibited in his punishment of the victim.

Phenomenal unity of act. In the Remote condition it is more difficult for the subject to gain a sense of *relatedness* between his own actions and the consequences of these actions for the victim. There is a physical and spatial separation of the act and its consequences. The subject depresses a lever in one room, and protests and cries are heard from another. The two events are in correlation, yet they lack a compelling phenomenological unity. The structure of a meaningful act—*I am hurting a man*—breaks down because of the spatial arrangements, in a manner somewhat analogous to the disappearance of phi phenomena when the blinking lights are spaced too far apart. The unity is more fully achieved in the Proximity condition as the victim is brought closer to the action that causes him pain. It is rendered complete in Touch-Proximity.

Incipient group formation. Placing the victim in another room not only takes him further from the subject, but the subject and the experimenter are drawn relatively closer. There is incipient group formation between the experimenter and the subject, from which the victim is excluded. The wall between the victim and the others deprives him of an intimacy which the experimenter and subject feel. In the Remote condition, the victim is truly an outsider, who stands alone, physically and psychologically.

When the victim is placed close to the subject, it becomes easier to form an alliance with him against the experimenter. Subjects no longer have to face the experimenter alone. They have an ally who is close at hand and eager to collaborate in a revolt against the experimenter. Thus, the changing set of spatial relations leads to a potentially shifting set of alliances over the several experimental conditions.

Acquired behavior dispositions. It is commonly observed that laboratory mice will rarely fight with their litter mates. Scott (1958) explains this in terms of passive inhibition. He writes: "By doing nothing under . . . circumstances [the animal] learns to do nothing, and this may be spoken of as passive inhibition . . . this principle has great importance in teaching an individual to be peaceful, for it means that he can learn not to fight simply by not fighting." Similarly, we may learn not to harm others simply by not harming them in everyday life. Yet this learning occurs in a context of proximal relations with others, and may not be generalized to that situation in which the person is physically removed from us. Or possibly, in the past, aggressive actions against others who were physically close resulted in retaliatory punishment which extinguished the original form of response. In contrast, aggression against others at a distance may have only sporadically led to retaliation. Thus the organism learns that it is safer to be aggressive toward others at a distance, and precarious to be so when the parties are within arm's reach. Through a pattern of rewards and punishments, he acquires a disposition to avoid aggression at close quarters, a disposition which does not extend to harming others at a distance. And this may account for experimental findings in the remote and proximal experiments.

Proximity as a variable in psychological research has received far less attention than it deserves. If men were sessile it would be easy to understand this neglect. But we move about; our spatial relations shift from one situation to the next, and the fact that we are near or remote may have a powerful effect on the psychological processes that mediate our behavior toward others. In the present situation, as the victim is brought closer to the subject ordered to give him shocks, increasing numbers of subjects break off the experiment, refusing to obey. The concrete, visible, and proximal presence of the victim acts in an important way to counteract the experimenter's power to generate disobedience.*

CLOSENESS OF AUTHORITY

If the spatial relationship of the subject and victim is relevant to the degree of obedience, would not the relationship of subject to experimenter also play a part?

There are reasons to feel that, on arrival, the subject is oriented primarily to

---

* [Author's Note] Admittedly, the terms *proximity, immediacy, closeness,* and *salience-of-the-victim* are used in a loose sense, and the experiments themselves represent a very coarse treatment of the variable. Further experiments are needed to refine the notion and tease out such diverse factors as spatial distance, visibility, audibility, barrier interposition, etc.

The Proximity and Touch-Proximity experiments were the only conditions where we were unable to use taped feedback from the victim. Instead, the victim was trained to respond in these conditions as he had in Experiment 2 (which employed taped feedback). Some improvement is possible here, for it should be technically feasible to do a proximity series using taped feedback.

the experimenter rather than to the victim. He has come to the laboratory to fit into the structure that the experimenter—not the victim—would provide. He has come less to understand his behavior than to *reveal* that behavior to a competent scientist, and he is willing to display himself as the scientist's purposes require. Most subjects seem quite concerned about the appearance they are making before the experimenter, and one could argue that this preoccupation in a relatively new and strange setting makes the subject somewhat insensitive to the triadic nature of the social situation. In other words, the subject is so concerned about the show he is putting on for the experimenter that influences from other parts of the social field do not receive as much weight as they ordinarily would. This overdetermined orientation to the experimenter would account for the relative insensitivity of the subject to the victim, and would also lead us to believe that alterations in the relationship between subject and experimenter would have important consequences for obedience.

In a series of experiments we varied the physical closeness and degree of surveillance of the experimenter. In one condition the experimenter sat just a few feet away from the subject. In a second condition, after giving initial instructions, the experimenter left the laboratory and gave his orders by telephone. In still a third condition the experimenter was never seen, providing instructions by means of a tape recording activated when the subjects entered the laboratory.

Obedience dropped sharply as the experimenter was physically removed from the laboratory. The number of obedient subjects in the first condition (Experimenter Present) was almost three times as great as in the second, where the experimenter gave his orders by telephone. Twenty-six subjects were fully obedient in the first condition, and only nine in the second (Chi square obedient *vs.* defiant in the two conditions, df = 14.7; $p < 0.001$). Subjects seemed able to take a far stronger stand against the experimenter when they did not have to encounter him face to face, and the experimenter's power over the subject was severely curtailed.*

Moreover, when the experimenter was absent, subjects displayed an interesting form of behavior that had not occurred under his surveillance. Though continuing with the experiment, several subjects administered lower shocks than were required and never informed the experimenter of their deviation from the correct procedure. (Unknown to the subjects, shock levels were automatically recorded by an Esterline-Angus event recorder wired directly into the shock generator; the instrument provided us with an objective record of the subjects' performance.) Indeed, in telephone conversations some subjects specifically assured the experimenter that they were raising the shock level according to instruction, whereas in fact they were repeatedly using the lowest shock on the board. This form of behavior is particularly interesting: although these subjects acted in a way that clearly undermined the avowed purposes of the experiment,

---

* [Author's Note] The third condition also led to significantly lower obedience than this first situation in which the experimenter was present, but it contains technical difficulties that require extensive discussion.

they found it easier to handle the conflict in this manner than to precipitate an open break with authority.

Other conditions were completed in which the experimenter was absent during the first segment of the experiment, but reappeared at the point that the subject definitely refused to give higher shocks when commanded by telephone. Although he had exhausted his power via telephone, the experimenter could frequently force further obedience when he reappeared in the laboratory.

Experiments in this series show that the *physical presence* of an authority is an important force contributing to the subject's obedience or defiance. Taken together with the first experimental series on the proximity of the victim, it would appear that something akin to fields of force, diminishing in effectiveness with increasing psychological distance from their source, have a controlling effect on the subject's performance. As the victim is brought closer, the subject finds it harder to administer shocks to him. When the victim's position is held constant relative to the subject, and the authority is made more remote, the subject finds it easier to break off the experiment. This effect is substantial in both cases, but manipulation of the experimenter's position yielded the more powerful results. Obedience to destructive commands is highly dependent on the proximal relations between authority and subject.

TENSIONS

The description of final scores does not fully convey the character of the subjects' performance, and it would be useful to interrupt our reporting of quantitative relationships to remark on the subjects' general reaction to the situation.

One might suppose that a subject would simply break off or continue as his conscience and temperament dictated. Yet this is very far from what happened. There were powerful reactions of tension and emotional strain in a substantial proportion of the participants. Persons were observed to sweat, tremble, stutter, bite their lips, and groan as they found themselves increasingly implicated in the experimental conflict. Some sense of the subjects' mood can be found in a transcript of their remarks at break-off point. Here are the remarks of two defiant subjects:

> Is he banging? . . . Is he hurt out there? Well, I don't want to be responsible for anything that happens to him. No, I can't go on with it. I don't know whether he's all right or not. I mean he may have a heart condition or something; I wouldn't feel right doing it. He's banging for help. He's evidently in trouble or he wouldn't bang . . . I don't see any sense to this—to knocking him out or something. I just can't see it. [*Subject refuses to administer shocks*]   [*Subject 0108*]

> The man is banging. He wants to get out . . . I'm sorry. If the man wants to get out I'd just as soon stop . . . I don't want to administer any more [extremely excited] . . . I will gladly refund the check, but I will not harm this man . . . I'm sorry, I will not give him any more if he obviously wants to get out. There is no money in the world that will make me hurt another individual.   [*Subject 010X*]

And here is a transcript from an obedient subject. He began the experiment calmly, but became increasingly tense as the experiment proceeded. After administering the 150-volt shock, he began to address the experimenter in agitated tones:

> *150 volts delivered.* You want me to keep going?
> *165 volts delivered.* That guy is hollering in there. There's a lot of them here. He's liable to have heart condition. You want me to go?
> *180 volts delivered.* He can't stand it! I'm not going to kill that man in there! You hear him hollering? He's hollering. He can't stand it. What if something happens to him? . . . I'm not going to get that man sick in there. He's hollering in there. You know what I mean? I mean I refuse to take responsibility. He's getting hurt in there. He's in there hollering. Too many left here. Geez, if he gets them wrong. There's too many of them left. I mean who is going to take responsibility if anything happens to that gentleman?
> *[The experimenter accepts responsibility.]* All right.
> *195 volts delivered.* You see he's hollering. Hear that. Gee, I don't know.
> *[The experimenter says: "The experiment requires that you go on."]*—I know it does, sir, but I mean—hugh—he don't know what he's in for. He's up to 195 volts.
> *210 volts delivered.*
> *225 volts delivered.*
> *240 volts delivered.* Aw, no. You mean I've got to keep going up with the scale? No sir. I'm not going to kill that man! I'm not going to give him 450 volts!
> *[The experimenter says: "The experiment requires that you go on."]*—I know it does, but that man is hollering there, sir . . .

Despite his numerous, agitated objections, which were constant accompaniments to his actions, the subject unfailingly obeyed the experimenter, proceeding to the highest shock level on the generator. He displayed a curious dissociation between word and action. Although at the verbal level he had resolved not to go on, his actions were fully in accord with the experimenter's commands. This subject did not want to shock the victim, and he found it an extremely disagreeable task, but he was unable to invent a response that would free him from *E*'s authority. Many subjects cannot find the specific verbal formula that would enable them to reject the role assigned to them by the experimenter. Perhaps our culture does not provide adequate models for disobedience.

One puzzling sign of tension was the regular occurrence of nervous laughing fits. In the first four conditions 71 of the 160 subjects showed definite signs of nervous laughter and smiling. The laughter seemed entirely out of place, even bizarre. Full-blown, uncontrollable seizures were observed for 15 of these subjects. On one occasion we observed a seizure so violently convulsive that it was necessary to call a halt to the experiment. In the post-experimental interviews subjects took pains to point out that they were not sadistic types and that the laughter did not mean they enjoyed shocking the victim.

In the interview following the experiment subjects were asked to indicate on a 14-point scale just how nervous or tense they felt at the point of maximum tension (Figure 2). The scale ranged from "not at all tense and nervous" to "extremely tense and nervous." Self-reports of this sort are of limited precision

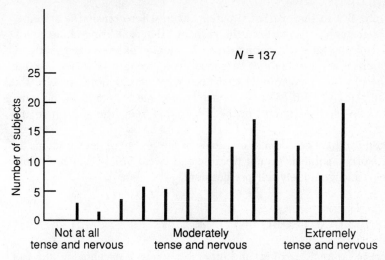

Figure 2. Level of tension and nervousness: The self-reports on "tension and nervousness" for 137 subjects in the Proximity experiments. Subjects were given a scale with 14 values ranging from "not at all tense and nervous" to "extremely tense and nervous." They were instructed: "Thinking back to that point in the experiment when you felt the most tense and nervous, indicate just how you felt by placing an X at the appropriate point on the scale." The results are shown in terms of midpoint values.

and at best provide only a rough indication of the subject's emotional response. Still, taking the reports for what they are worth, it can be seen that the distribution of responses spans the entire range of the scale, with the majority of subjects concentrated at the center and upper extreme. A further breakdown showed that obedient subjects reported themselves as having been slightly more tense and nervous than the defiant subjects at the point of maximum tension.

How is the occurrence of tension to be interpreted? First, it points to the presence of conflict. If a tendency to comply with authority were the only psychological force operating in the situation, all subjects would have continued to the end and there would have been no tension. Tension, it is assumed, results from the simultaneous presence of two or more incompatible response tendencies (Miller, 1944).[7] If sympathetic concern for the victim were the exclusive force, all subjects would have calmly defied the experimenter. Instead, there were both obedient and defiant outcomes, frequently accompanied by extreme tension. A conflict develops between the deeply ingrained disposition not to harm others and the equally compelling tendency to obey others who are in authority. The subject is quickly drawn into a dilemma of a deeply dynamic character, and the presence of high tension points to the considerable strength of each of the antagonistic vectors.

Moreover, tension defines the strength of the aversive state from which the subject is unable to escape through disobedience. When a person is uncomfortable, tense, or stressed, he tries to take some action that will allow him to terminate this unpleasant state. Thus tension may serve as a drive that leads to escape behavior. But in the present situation, even where tension is extreme, many subjects are unable to perform the response that will bring about relief. Therefore there must be a competing drive, tendency, or inhibition that precludes activation of the disobedient response. The strength of this inhibiting factor must be of greater magnitude than the stress experienced, or else the terminating act would occur. Every evidence of extreme tension is at the same time an indication of the strength of the forces that keep the subject in the situation.

Finally, tension may be taken as evidence of the reality of the situations for the subjects. Normal subjects do not tremble and sweat unless they are implicated in a deep and genuinely felt predicament.

BACKGROUND AUTHORITY

In psychophysics, animal learning, and other branches of psychology, the fact that measures are obtained at one institution rather than another is irrelevant to the interpretation of the findings, so long as the technical facilities for measurement are adequate and the operations are carried out with competence.

But it cannot be assumed that this holds true for the present study. The effectiveness of the experimenter's commands may depend in an important way on the larger institutional context in which they are issued. The experiments described thus far were conducted at Yale University, an organization which most subjects regarded with respect and sometimes awe. In post-experimental interviews several participants remarked that the locale and sponsorship of the study gave them confidence in the integrity, competence, and benign purposes of the personnel; many indicated that they would not have shocked the learner if the experiments had been done elsewhere.

This issue of background authority seemed to us important for an interpretation of the results that had been obtained thus far; moreover it is highly relevant to any comprehensive theory of human obedience. Consider, for example, how closely our compliance with the imperatives of others is tied to particular institutions and locales in our day-to-day activities. On request, we expose our throats to a man with a razor blade in the barber shop, but would not do so in a shoe store; in the latter setting we willingly follow the clerk's request to stand in our stockinged feet, but resist the command in a bank. In the laboratory of a great university, subjects may comply with a set of commands that would be resisted if given elsewhere. *One must always question the relationship of obedience to a person's sense of the context in which he is operating.*

To explore the problem we moved our apparatus to an office building in industrial Bridgeport and replicated experimental conditions, without any visible tie to the university.

Bridgeport subjects were invited to the experiment through a mail circular similar to the one used in the Yale study, with appropriate changes in letterhead, etc. As in the earlier study, subjects were paid $4.50 for coming to the laboratory. The same age and occupational distributions used at Yale and the identical personnel were employed.

The purpose in relocating in Bridgeport was to assure a complete dissociation from Yale, and in this regard we were fully successful. On the surface, the study appeared to be conducted by Research Associates of Bridgeport, an organization of unknown character (the title had been concocted exclusively for use in this study).

The experiments were conducted in a three-room office suite in a somewhat run-down commercial building located in the downtown shopping area. The laboratory was sparsely furnished, though clean, and marginally respectable in appearance. When subjects inquired about professional affiliations, they were informed only that we were a private firm conducting research for industry.

Some subjects displayed skepticism concerning the motives of the Bridgeport experimenter. One gentleman gave us a written account of the thoughts he experienced at the control board:

> . . . Should I quit this damn test? Maybe he passed out? What dopes we were not to check up on this deal. How do we know that these guys are legit? No furniture, bare walls, no telephone. We could of called the Police up or the Better Business Bureau. I learned a lesson tonight. How do I know that Mr. Williams [the experimenter] is telling the truth . . . I wish I knew how many volts a person could take before lapsing into unconsciousness . . .
>
> [*Subject 2414*]

Another subject stated:

> I questioned on my arrival my own judgment [about coming]. I had doubts as to the legitimacy of the operation and the consequences of participation. I felt it was a heartless way to conduct memory or learning processes on human beings and certainly dangerous without the presence of a medical doctor.
>
> [*Subject 2440V*]

There was no noticeable reduction in tension for the Bridgeport subjects. And the subjects' estimation of the amount of pain felt by the victim was slightly, though not significantly, higher than in the Yale study.

A failure to obtain complete obedience in Bridgeport would indicate that the extreme compliance found in New Haven subjects was tied closely to the background authority of Yale University; if a large proportion of the subjects remained fully obedient, very different conclusions would be called for.

As it turned out, the level of obedience in Bridgeport, although somewhat reduced, was not significantly lower than that obtained at Yale. A large proportion of the Bridgeport subjects were fully obedient to the experimenter's commands (48 percent of the Bridgeport subjects delivered the maximum shock versus 65 percent in the corresponding condition at Yale).

How are these findings to be interpreted? It is possible that if commands of a potentially harmful or destructive sort are to be perceived as legitimate they must occur within some sort of institutional structure. But it is clear from the study that it need not be a particularly reputable or distinguished institution. The Bridgeport experiments were conducted by an unimpressive firm lacking any credentials; the laboratory was set up in a respectable office building with title listed in the building directory. Beyond that, there was no evidence of benevolence or competence. It is possible that the *category* of institution, judged according to its professed function, rather than its qualitative position within that category, wins our compliance. Persons deposit money in elegant, but also in seedy-looking banks, without giving much thought to the differences in security they offer. Similarly, our subjects may consider one laboratory to be as competent as another, so long as it is a scientific laboratory.

It would be valuable to study the subjects' performance in other contexts which go even further than the Bridgeport study in denying institutional support to the experimenter. It is possible that, beyond a certain point, obedience disappears completely. But that point had not been reached in the Bridgeport office: almost half the subjects obeyed the experimenter fully.

FURTHER EXPERIMENTS

We may mention briefly some additional experiments undertaken in the Yale series. A considerable amount of obedience and defiance in everyday life occurs in connection with groups. And we had reason to feel in light of the many group studies already done in psychology that group forces would have a profound effect on reactions to authority. A series of experiments was run to examine these effects. In all cases only one naïve subject was studied per hour, but he performed in the midst of actors who, unknown to him, were employed by the experimenter. In one experiment (Groups for Disobedience) two actors broke off in the middle of the experiment. When this happened 90 percent of the subjects followed suit and defied the experimenter. In another condition the actors followed the orders obediently; this strengthened the experimenter's power only slightly. In still a third experiment the job of pushing the switch to shock the learner was given to one of the actors, while the naïve subject performed a subsidiary act. We wanted to see how the teacher would respond if he were involved in the situation but did not actually give the shocks. In this situation only three subjects out of forty broke off. In a final group experiment the subjects themselves determined the shock level they were going to use. Two actors suggested higher and higher shock levels; some subjects insisted, despite group pressure, that the shock level be kept low; others followed along with the group.

Further experiments were completed using women as subjects, as well as a set dealing with the effects of dual, unsanctioned, and conflicting authority. A final experiment concerned the personal relationship between victim and subject. These will have to be described elsewhere, lest the present report be extended to monographic length.

It goes without saying that future research can proceed in many different directions. What kinds of response from the victim are most effective in causing disobedience in the subject? Perhaps passive resistance is more effective than vehement protest. What conditions of entry into an authority system lead to greater or lesser obedience? What is the effect of anonymity and masking on the subject's behavior? What conditions lead to the subject's perception of responsibility for his own actions? Each of these could be a major research topic in itself, and can readily be incorporated into the general experimental procedure described here.

LEVELS OF OBEDIENCE AND DEFIANCE

One general finding that merits attention is the high level of obedience manifested in the experimental situation. Subjects often expressed deep disapproval of shocking a man in the face of his objections, and others denounced it as senseless and stupid. Yet many subjects complied even while they protested. The proportion of obedient subjects greatly exceeded the expectations of the experimenter and his colleagues. At the outset, we had conjectured that subjects would not, in general, go above the level of "Strong Shock." In practice, many subjects were willing to administer the most extreme shocks available when commanded by the experimenter. For some subjects the experiment provided an occasion for aggressive release. And for others it demonstrated the extent to which obedient dispositions are deeply ingrained and engaged, irrespective of their consequences for others. Yet this is not the whole story. Somehow, the subject becomes implicated in a situation from which he cannot disengage himself.

The departure of the experimental results from intelligent expectation, to some extent, has been formalized. The procedure was to describe the experimental situation in concrete detail to a group of competent persons, and to ask them to predict the performance of 100 hypothetical subjects. For purposes of indicating the distribution of break-off points, judges were provided with a diagram of the shock generator and recorded their predictions before being informed of the actual results. Judges typically underestimated the amount of obedience demonstrated by subjects.

In Figure 3, we compare the predictions of forty psychiatrists at a leading

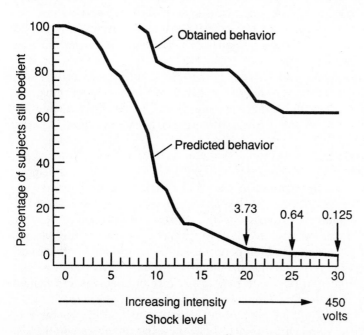

Figure 3. Predicted and obtained behavior in voice feedback.

medical school with the actual performance of subjects in the experiment. The psychiatrists predicted that most subjects would not go beyond the tenth shock level (150 volts; at this point the victim makes his first explicit demand to be freed). They further predicted that by the twentieth shock level (300 volts; the victim refuses to answer) 3.73 percent of the subjects would still be obedient; and that only a little over one-tenth of one percent of the subjects would administer the highest shock on the board. But, as the graph indicates, the obtained behavior was very different. Sixty-two percent of the subjects obeyed the experimenter's commands fully. Between expectation and occurrence there is a whopping discrepancy.

Why did the psychiatrists underestimate the level of obedience? Possibly, because their predictions were based on an inadequate conception of the determinants of human action, a conception that focuses on motives in *vacuo*. This orientation may be entirely adequate for the repair of bruised impulses as revealed on the psychiatrist's couch, but as soon as our interest turns to action in larger settings, attention must be paid to the situations in which motives are expressed. A situation exerts an important press on the individual. It exercises constraints and may provide push. In certain circumstances it is not so much the kind of person a man is, as the kind of situation in which he is placed, that determines his actions.

Many people, not knowing much about the experiment, claim that subjects who go to the end of the board are sadistic. Nothing could be more foolish than an overall characterization of these persons. It is like saying that a person thrown into a swift-flowing stream is necessarily a fast swimmer, or that he has great stamina because he moves so rapidly relative to the bank. The context of action must always be considered. The individual, upon entering the laboratory, becomes integrated into a situation that carries its own momentum. The subject's problem then is how to become disengaged from a situation which is moving in an altogether ugly direction.

The fact that disengagement is so difficult testifies to the potency of the forces that keep the subject at the control board. Are these forces to be conceptualized as individual motives and expressed in the language of personality dynamics, or are they to be seen as the effects of social structure and pressures arising from the situational field?

A full understanding of the subject's action will, I feel, require that both perspectives be adopted. The person brings to the laboratory enduring dispositions toward authority and aggression, and at the same time he becomes enmeshed in a social structure that is no less an objective fact of the case. From the standpoint of personality theory one may ask: What mechanisms of personality enable a person to transfer responsibility to authority? What are the motives underlying obedient and disobedient performance? Does orientation to authority lead to a short-circuiting of the shame-guilt system? What cognitive and emotional defenses are brought into play in the case of obedient and defiant subjects?

The present experiments are not, however, directed toward an exploration of the motives engaged when the subject obeys the experimenter's commands.

Instead, they examine the situational variables responsible for the elicitation of obedience. Elsewhere, we have attempted to spell out some of the structural properties of the experimental situation that account for high obedience, and this analysis need not be repeated here (Milgram, 1963). The experimental variations themselves represent our attempt to probe that structure, by systematically changing it and noting the consequences for behavior. It is clear that some situations produce greater compliance with the experimenter's commands than others. However, this does not necessarily imply an increase or decrease in the strength of any single definable motive. Situations producing the greatest obedience could do so by triggering the most powerful, yet perhaps the most idiosyncratic, of motives in each subject confronted by the setting. Or they may simply recruit a greater number and variety of motives in their service. But whatever the motives involved—and it is far from certain that they can ever be known—action may be studied as a direct function of the situation in which it occurs. This has been the approach of the present study, where we sought to plot behavioral regularities against manipulated properties of the social field. Ultimately, social psychology would like to have a compelling *theory of situations* which will, first, present a language in terms of which situations can be defined; proceed to a typology of situations; and then point to the manner in which definable properties of situations are transformed into psychological forces in the individual.*

POSTSCRIPT

Almost a thousand adults were individually studied in the obedience research, and there were many specific conclusions regarding the variables that control obedience and disobedience to authority. Some of these have been discussed briefly in the preceding sections, and more detailed reports will be released subsequently.

There are now some other generalizations I should like to make, which do not derive in any strictly logical fashion from the experiments as carried out, but which, I feel, ought to be made. They are formulations of an intuitive sort that have been forced on me by observation of many subjects responding to the pressures of authority. The assertions represent a painful alteration in my own thinking; and since they were acquired only under the repeated impact of direct observation, I have no illusion that they will be generally accepted by persons who have not had the same experience.

With numbing regularity good people were seen to knuckle under the demands of authority and perform actions that were callous and severe. Men who are in everyday life responsible and decent were seduced by the trappings of authority, by the control of their perceptions, and by the uncritical acceptance of the experimenter's definition of the situation, into performing harsh acts.

---

*[Author's Note] My thanks to Professor Howard Leventhal of Yale for strengthening the writing in this paragraph.

What is the limit of such obedience? At many points we attempted to establish a boundary. Cries from the victim were inserted; not good enough. The victim claimed heart trouble; subjects still shocked him on command. The victim pleaded that he be let free, and his answers no longer registered on the signal box; subjects continued to shock him. At the outset we had not conceived that such drastic procedures would be needed to generate disobedience, and each step was added only as the ineffectiveness of the earlier techniques became clear. The final effort to establish a limit was the Touch-Proximity condition. But the very first subject in this condition subdued the victim on command, and proceeded to the highest shock level. A quarter of the subjects in this condition performed similarly.

The results, as seen and felt in the laboratory, are to this author disturbing. They raise the possibility that human nature or, more specifically, the kind of character produced in American democratic society cannot be counted on to insulate its citizens from brutality and inhumane treatment at the direction of malevolent authority. A substantial proportion of people do what they are told to do, irrespective of the content of the act and without limitations of conscience, so long as they perceive that the command comes from a legitimate authority. If in this study an anonymous experimenter could successfully command adults to subdue a fifty-year-old man and force on him painful electric shocks against his protests, one can only wonder what government, with its vastly greater authority and prestige, can command of its subjects. There is, of course, the extremely important question of whether malevolent political institutions could or would arise in American society. The present research contributes nothing to this issue.

In an article titled "The Danger of Obedience," Harold J. Laski wrote:

> . . . civilization means, above all, an unwillingness to inflict unnecessary pain. Within the ambit of that definition, those of us who heedlessly accept the commands of authority cannot yet claim to be civilized men.
>
> . . . Our business, if we desire to live a life, not utterly devoid of meaning and significance, is to accept nothing which contradicts our basic experience merely because it comes to us from tradition or convention or authority. It may well be that we shall be wrong; but our self-expression is thwarted at the root unless the certainties we are asked to accept coincide with the certainties we experience. That is why the condition of freedom in any state is always a widespread and consistent skepticism of the canons upon which power insists.[8]

Notes

[1] Kierkegaard, S. 1843. *Fear and Trembling*. English edition, Princeton: Princeton University Press, 1941.

[2] Scott, J. P. 1958. *Aggression*. Chicago: University of Chicago Press.

[3] Milgram, S. 1964. "Issues in the study of obedience: a reply to Baumrind." *Amer. Psychol.* 1. 848–852.

[4] ———. 1963. "Behavioral study of obedience." *J. Abnorm. Soc. Psychol.* 67, 371–378.

[5] Buss, Arnold. 1961. *The Psychology of Aggression*. New York and London: John Wiley.

[6] Milgram, S. 1961. "Dynamics of obedience: experiments in social psychology." Mimeographed report, *National Science Foundation*, January 25.

[7] Miller, N. E. 1944. "Experimental studies of conflict." In J. McV. Hunt (ed.), *Personality and the Behavior Disorders*. New York: Ronald Press.

[8] Laski, Harold J. 1929. "The danger of obedience." *Harper's Monthly Magazine*, 15 June 1–10.

JOURNAL WRITINGS

1. **Describe** your initial reaction to the subjects' behavior in this experiment. How far do you think you would go if you were a subject? Why? Is your answer to the Preview question any different now that you have read the article? Why or why not?
2. In a paragraph or two, give some **examples** of how you usually react to authorities such as parents or guardians, employers, church officials, school authorities. Explain why you are or are not satisfied with your typical mode of reacting.

BRAINSTORMING AND DRAFTING

3. What competing pressures were the subjects under? What competing pressures were Adam and Eve under in Milton's poem? According to God the Father in the poem, how much free choice did Adam and Eve have? What do you suppose Milton's God character would say about the amount of free choice Milgram's subjects had? Draft a paragraph offering reasons why you agree or disagree with God the Father's probable opinion of Milgram's subjects.
4. According to Milgram, under what conditions did the amount of obedience change? In a small group (or working individually), list some possible reasons for the subjects' responses to these conditions. Then each person should draft two paragraphs: The first paragraph should incorporate the most compelling reasons from the list; the second should suggest some ways that parents might prepare their children to stand up to external pressures against their value system.
5. Review Mort Walker's "Beetle Bailey" comic strip. While Milgram's subjects accepted authority, Beetle seems to rebel against it. Is Beetle's choice any freer than the choice made by Milgram's subjects? Give reasons for your answer.

THE AUTHOR'S METHODS

6. In this article, Milgram organizes his material according to subject headings such as "Terminology," "Subject Population," etc. Find a selection in

this book (preferably one you have read) that is *not* organized by subject headings. Write a paragraph in which you **describe** the differences in organization between the two readings; include reasons why their respective authors might choose the types of organization they did.

7. Reread the section under the heading "The General Laboratory Procedure." What sort of audience do you think Milgram had in mind when he wrote this? What clues in the writing lead you to this conclusion? Rewrite the section in **summary** form for an audience of high school freshmen. What changes did you make to accommodate your audience?

CREATIVE PROJECT

8. Pretend you are one of Milgram's subjects, returning home just after the experiment. Write a diary entry exploring what degree of moral responsibility you feel that you have for your role in the experiment.

FORMAL WRITING AND RESEARCH PAPERS

9. The subjects in Milgram's experiment apparently assumed that disobedience is a negative rather than a positive concept. Write a paper in which you **analyze** how "society" engraves on the individual consciousness the idea of disobedience as undesirable. **Conclude** by suggesting ways that society might modify its emphasis on the undesirability of disobedience in certain situations.

10. Write a paper in which you apply Milgram's general **conclusions** to a historical situation such as the Holocaust, in which the Nazis destroyed six million European Jews; or the My Lai massacre during the Vietnam War; or the Watergate scandal during the Nixon administration. For helpful information, consult the *Historical Abstracts*, the *Public Affairs Information Service* (PAIS), and the card or computer catalog, among other sources.

Erich Fromm

Automaton Conformity

(1941)

Born in Frankfurt, Germany, Erich Fromm (1900–1980) became an American citizen in 1940. He received a Ph.D. from the University of Heidelberg. A psychoanalyst and social philosopher, he lectured extensively and taught at several colleges such as Bennington, New York University, Yale, and Michigan State. Approaching modern social problems from a psychoanalytic and often a moral perspective, Fromm examined the complex roots of twentieth-century alienation. Among his many books are *The Sane Society, Psychoanalysis and Religion, The Revolution of Hope: Toward a Humanized Technology,* and *The Art of Loving.*

The following selection comes from his best-known work, *Escape from Freedom,* in which Fromm asserts that people may accept a totalitarian government rather than suffer the isolation and responsibility that come with individualism and true freedom. In this excerpt, he describes a potentially dangerous scenario in which people lose their human qualities as they unconsciously relinquish the freedom of thinking, feeling, and willing.

PREVIEW

Do you believe that you generally think, feel, and act freely? Give reasons for your answer.

[. . . I shall discuss a . . .] mechanism of escape which is of the greatest social significance.

This particular mechanism is the solution that the majority of normal individuals find in modern society. To put it briefly, the individual ceases to be himself; he adopts entirely the kind of personality offered to him by cultural patterns; and he therefore becomes exactly as all others are and as they expect him to be. The discrepancy between "I" and the world disappears and with it the conscious fear of aloneness and powerlessness. This mechanism can be compared with the protective coloring some animals assume. They look so similar to their surroundings that they are hardly distinguishable from them. The person who gives up his individual self and becomes an automaton, identical with millions of other automatons around him, need not feel alone and anxious any more. But the price he pays, however, is high; it is the loss of his self.

The assumption that the "normal" way of overcoming aloneness is to become an automaton contradicts one of the most widespread ideas concerning man in our culture. The majority of us are supposed to be individuals who are free to think, feel, act as they please. To be sure this is not only the general opinion on the subject of modern individualism, but also each individual sincerely believes that he is "he" and that his thoughts, feelings, wishes are "his." Yet, although there are true individuals among us, this belief is an illusion in most cases and a dangerous one for that matter, as it blocks the removal of those conditions that are responsible for this state of affairs.

We are dealing here with one of the most fundamental problems of psychology which can most quickly be opened up by a series of questions. What is the self? What is the nature of those acts that give only the illusion of being the person's own acts? What is spontaneity? What is an original mental act? Finally, what has all this to do with freedom? . . . We shall try to show how feelings and thoughts can be induced from the outside and yet be subjectively experienced as one's own, and how one's own feelings and thoughts can be repressed and thus cease to be part of one's self. . . .

Let us start the discussion by analyzing the meaning of the experience which if put into words is, "I feel," "I think," "I will." When we say "I think," this seems to be a clear and unambiguous statement. The only question seems to be whether what I think is right or wrong, not whether or not *I* think it. Yet, one concrete experimental situation shows at once that the answer to this question is not necessarily what we suppose it to be. Let us attend an hypnotic experiment. Here is the subject A whom the hypnotist B puts into hypnotic sleep and suggests to him that after awaking from the hypnotic sleep he will want to read a manuscript which he will believe he has brought with him, that he will seek it and not find it, that he will then believe that another person, C, has stolen it, that he will get very angry at C. He is also told that he will forget that all this was a suggestion given him during the hypnotic sleep. It must be added that C is a person toward whom the subject has never felt any anger and according to the circumstances has no reason to feel angry; furthermore, that he actually has not brought any manuscript with him.

What happens? A awakes and, after a short conversation about some topic, says, "Incidentally, this reminds me of something I have written in my manuscript. I shall read it to you." He looks around, does not find it, and then turns to C, suggesting that he may have taken it; getting more and more excited when C repudiates the suggestion, he eventually bursts into open anger and directly accuses C of having stolen the manuscript. He goes even further. He puts forward reasons which should make it plausible that C is the thief. He has heard from others, he says, that C needs the manuscript very badly, that he had a good opportunity to take it, and so on. We hear him not only accusing C, but making up numerous "rationalizations" which should make his accusation appear plausible. (None of these, of course, are true and A would never have thought of them before.)

Let us assume that another person enters the room at this point. He would not have any doubt that A says what he thinks and feels; the only question in his mind would be whether or not his accusation is right, that is, whether or not the contents of A's thoughts conform to the real facts. We, however, who have witnessed the whole procedure from the start, do not care to ask whether the accusation is true. We know that this is not the problem, since we are certain that what A feels and thinks now are not *his* thoughts and feelings but are alien elements put into his head by another person.

The conclusion to which the person entering in the middle of the experiment comes might be something like this. "Here is A, who clearly indicates that he has all these thoughts. He is the one to know best what he thinks and there is no better proof than his own statement about what he feels. There are those other persons who say that his thoughts are superimposed upon him and are alien elements which come from without. In all fairness, I cannot decide who is right; any one of them may be mistaken. Perhaps, since there are two against one, the greater chance is that the majority is right." We, however, who have witnessed the whole experiment would not be doubtful, nor would the newcomer be if he attended other hypnotic experiments. He would then see that this type of experiment can be repeated innumerable times with different persons and different contents. The hypnotist can suggest that a raw potato is a delicious pineapple, and the subject will eat the potato with all the gusto associated with eating a pineapple. Or that the subject cannot see anything, and the subject will be blind. Or again, that he thinks that the world is flat and not round, and the subject will argue heatedly that the world is flat.

What does the hypnotic—and especially the post-hypnotic—experiment prove? It proves that we can have thoughts, feelings, wishes, and even sensual sensations which we subjectively feel to be *ours,* and yet that, although we experience these thoughts and feelings, they have been put into us from the outside, are basically alien, and are not what we think, feel, and so on.

What does the specific hypnotic experiment with which we started show? (1) The subject *wills* something, namely, to read his manuscript, (2) he *thinks* something, namely, that C has taken it, and (3) he *feels* something, namely, anger against C. We have seen that all three mental acts—his will impulse, his thought, his feeling—are not his own in the sense of being the result of his own mental activity; that they have not originated in him, but are put into him from the outside and are subjectively felt *as if* they were his own. He gives expression to a number of thoughts which have not been put into him during the hypnosis, namely, those "rationalizations" by which he "explains" his assumption that C has stolen the manuscript. But nevertheless these thoughts are his own only in a formal sense. Although they appear to explain the suspicion, we know that the suspicion is there first and that the rationalizing thoughts are only invented to make the feeling plausible; they are not really explanatory but come *post factum.**

---

* *post factum*—after the deed. [Eds.]

We started with the hypnotic experiment because it shows in the most unmistakable manner that, although one may be convinced of the spontaneity of one's mental acts, they actually result from the influence of a person other than oneself under the conditions of a particular situation. The phenomenon, however, is by no means to be found only in the hypnotic situation. The fact that the contents of our thinking, feeling, willing, are induced from the outside and are not genuine, exists to an extent that gives the impression that these pseudo acts are the rule, while the genuine or indigenous mental acts are the exceptions.

The pseudo character which *thinking* can assume is better known than the same phenomenon in the sphere of willing and feeling. It is best, therefore, to start with the discussion of the difference between genuine thinking and pseudo thinking. Let us suppose we are on an island where there are fishermen and summer guests from the city. We want to know what kind of weather we are to expect and ask a fisherman and two of the city people, who we know have all listened to the weather forecast on the radio. The fisherman, with his long experience and concern with this problem of weather, will start thinking, assuming that he had not as yet made up his mind before we asked him. Knowing what the direction of the wind, temperature, humidity, and so on mean as a basis for weather forecast, he will weigh the different factors according to their respective significance and come to a more or less definite judgment. He will probably remember the radio forecast and quote it as supporting or contradicting his own opinion; if it is contradictory, he may be particularly careful in weighing the reasons for his opinion; but, and this is the essential point, it is *his* opinion, the result of *his* thinking, which he tells us.

The first of the two city summer guests is a man who, when we ask him his opinion, knows that he does not understand much about the weather nor does he feel any compulsion to understand anything about it. He merely replies, "I cannot judge. All I know is that the radio forecast is thus and thus." The other man whom we ask is of a different type. He believes that he knows a great deal about the weather, although actually he knows little about it. He is the kind of person who feels that he must be able to answer every question. He thinks for a minute and then tells us "his" opinion, which in fact is identical with the radio forecast. We ask him for his reasons and he tells us that on account of wind direction, temperature, and so on, he has come to his conclusion.

This man's behavior as seen from the outside is the same as the fisherman's. Yet, if we analyze it more closely, it becomes evident that he has heard the radio forecast and has accepted it. Feeling compelled, however, to have his *own* opinion about it, he forgets that he is simply repeating somebody else's authoritative opinion, and believes that this opinion is one that he arrived at through his own thinking. He imagines that the reasons he gives us preceded his opinion, but if we examine these reasons we see that they could not possibly have led him to any conclusion about the weather if he had not formed an opinion beforehand. They are actually only pseudo reasons which have the function of making his opinion appear to be the result of his own thinking. He has the illusion of having arrived at an opinion of his own, but in reality he has merely adopted an authority's opinion without being aware of this process. It could very well be that he is right about the weather and the fisherman wrong, but in that event it would not be "his" opinion which would be right, although the fisherman would be really mistaken in "his own" opinion.

The same phenomenon can be observed if we study people's opinions about certain subjects, for instance, politics. Ask an average newspaper reader what he thinks about a certain political question. He will give you as "his" opinion a more or less exact account of what he has read, and yet—and this is the essential point—he believes that what he is saying is the result of his own thinking. If he lives in a small community where political opinions are handed down from father to son, "his own" opinion may be governed far more than he would for a moment believe by the lingering authority of a strict parent. Another reader's opinion may be the outcome of a moment's embarrassment, the fear of being thought unin-formed, and hence the "thought" is essentially a front and not the result of a natural combination of experience, desire, and knowledge. The same phenome-non is to be found in aesthetic judgments. The average person who goes to a museum and looks at a picture by a famous painter, say Rembrandt, judges it to be a beautiful and impressive picture. If we analyze his judgment, we find that he does not have any particular inner response to the picture but thinks it is beautiful because he knows that he is supposed to think it is beautiful. The same phenomenon is evident with regard to people's judgment of music and also with regard to the act of perception itself. Many persons looking at a famous bit of scenery actually reproduce the pictures they have seen of it numerous times, say on postal cards, and while believing "they" see the scenery, they have these pictures before their eyes. Or, in experiencing an accident which occurs in their presence, they see or hear the situation in terms of the newspaper report they anticipate. As a matter of fact, for many people an experience which they have had, an artistic performance or a political meeting they have attended, becomes real to them only after they have read about it in the newspaper.

The suppression of critical thinking usually starts early. A five-year-old girl, for instance, may recognize the insincerity of her mother, either by subtly realizing that, while the mother is always talking of love and friendliness, she is actually cold and egotistical, or in a cruder way by noticing that her mother is having an affair with another man while constantly emphasizing her high moral standards. The child feels the discrepancy. Her sense of justice and truth is hurt, and yet, being dependent on the mother who would not allow any kind of criticism and, let us say, having a weak father on whom she cannot rely, the child is forced to suppress her critical insight. Very soon she will no longer notice the mother's insincerity or unfaithfulness. She will lose the ability to think critically since it seems to be both hopeless and dangerous to keep it alive. On the other hand, the child is impressed by the pattern of having to believe that her mother is sincere and decent and that the marriage of the parents is a happy one, and she will be ready to accept this idea as if it were her own.

In all these illustrations of pseudo thinking, the problem is whether the thought is the result of one's own thinking, that is, of one's own activity; the problem is not whether or not the contents of the thought are right. As has been already suggested in the case of the fisherman making a weather forecast, "his" thought may even be wrong, and that of the man who only repeats the thought put into him may be right. The pseudo thinking may also be perfectly logical and rational. Its pseudo character does not necessarily appear in illogical elements. This can be studied in rationalizations which tend to explain an action or a feeling on rational and realistic grounds, although it is actually determined by irrational and subjective factors. The rationalization may be in contradiction to facts or to the rules of logical thinking. But frequently it will be logical and rational in itself; then its irrationality lies only in the fact that it is not the real motive of the action which it pretends to have caused.

An example of irrational rationalization is brought forward in a well-known joke. A person who had borrowed a glass jar from a neighbor had broken it, and on being asked to return it, answered, "In the first place, I have already returned it to you; in the second place, I never borrowed it from you; and in the third place, it was already broken when you gave it to me." We have an example of "rational" rationalization when a person, A, who finds himself in a situation of economic distress, asks a relative of his, B, to lend him a sum of money. B declines and says that he does so because by lending money he could only support A's inclinations to be irresponsible and to lean on others for support. Now this reasoning may be perfectly sound, but it would nevertheless be a rationalization because B had not wanted to let A have the money in any event, and although he believes himself to be motivated by concern for A's welfare he is actually motivated by his own stinginess.

We cannot learn, therefore, whether we are dealing with a rationalization merely by determining the logicality of a person's statement as such, but we must also take into account the psychological motivations operating in a person. The decisive point is not *what* is thought but *how* it is thought. The thought that is the result of active thinking is always new and original; original, not necessarily in the sense that others have not thought it before, but always in the sense that the person who thinks, has used thinking as a tool to discover something new in the world outside or inside of himself. Rationalizations are essentially lacking this quality of discovering and uncovering; they only confirm the emotional prejudice existing in oneself. Rationalizing is not a tool for penetration of reality but a *post-factum* attempt to harmonize one's own wishes with existing reality.

With feeling as with thinking, one must distinguish between a genuine feeling, which originates in ourselves, and a pseudo feeling, which is really not our own although we believe it to be. Let us choose an example from everyday life which is typical of the pseudo character of our feelings in contact with others. We observe a man who is attending a party. He is gay, he laughs, makes friendly conversation, and all in all seems to be quite happy and contented. On taking his leave, he has a friendly smile while saying how much he enjoyed the evening. The door closes behind him—and this is the moment when we watch him carefully. A sudden change is noticed in his face. The smile has disappeared; of course, that is to be expected since he is now alone and has nothing or nobody with him to evoke a smile. But the change I am speaking of is more than just the disappearance of the smile. There appears on his face an expression of deep sadness, almost of desperation. This expression probably stays only for a few seconds, and then the face assumes the usual masklike expression; the man gets into his car, thinks about the evening, wonders whether or not he made a good impression, and feels that he did. But was "he" happy and gay during the party? Was the brief expression of sadness and desperation we observed on his face only a momentary reaction of no great significance? It is almost impossible to decide the question without knowing more of this man. There is one incident, however, which may provide the clue for understanding what his gaiety meant.

That night he dreams that he is back with the A.E.F. in the war. He has received orders to get through the opposite lines into enemy headquarters. He dons an officer's uniform, which seems to be German, and suddenly finds himself among a group of German officers. He is surprised that the headquarters are so comfortable and that everyone is so friendly to him, but he gets more and more frightened that they will find out that he is a spy. One of the younger officers for whom he feels a particular liking approaches him and says, "I know who you are. There is only one way for you to escape. Start telling jokes, laugh and make them laugh so much that they are diverted by your jokes from paying any attention to you." He is very grateful for this advice and starts making jokes and laughing. Eventually his joking increases to such an extent that the other officers get suspicious, and the greater their suspicions the more forced his jokes appear to be. At last such a feeling of terror fills him that he cannot bear to stay any longer; he suddenly jumps up from his chair and they all run after him. Then the scene changes, and he is sitting in a streetcar which stops just in front of his house. He wears a business suit and has a feeling of relief at the thought that the war is over.

Let us assume that we are in a position to ask him the next day what occurs to him in connection with the individual elements of the dream. We record here only a few associations which are particularly significant for understanding the main point we are interested in. The German uniform reminds him that there was one guest at the party on the previous evening who spoke with a heavy German accent. He remembered having been annoyed by this man because he had not paid much attention to him, although he (our dreamer) had gone out of his way to make a good impression. While rambling along with these thoughts he recalls that for a moment at the party he had had the feeling that this man with the German accent had actually made fun of him and smiled impertinently at some statement he had made. Thinking about the comfortable room in which the headquarters were, it occurs to him that it looked like the room in which he had sat during the party last night, but that the windows looked like the windows of a room in which he had once failed in an examination. Surprised at this association, he went on to recall that before going to the party he was somewhat concerned about the impression he would make, partly because one of the guests was the brother of a girl whose interest he wanted to win, and partly because the host had much influence with a superior on whose opinion about him much depended for his professional success. Speaking about this superior he says how much he dislikes him, how humiliated he feels in having to show a friendly front toward him, and that he had felt some dislike for his host too, although he was not aware of it at all. Another of his associations is that he had told a funny incident about a bald man and then was slightly apprehensive lest he might have hurt his host who happened to be almost bald too. The streetcar struck him as strange since there did not seem to be any tracks. While talking about it, he remembers the streetcar he was riding on as a boy on his way to school, and a further detail occurs to him, namely, that he had taken the place of the streetcar driver and had thought that driving a streetcar was astonishingly little different from driving an automobile. It is evident that the streetcar stands for his own car in which he had driven home, and that his returning home reminded him of going home from school.

To anyone accustomed to understand the meaning of dreams, the implication of the dream and the accompanying associations will be clear by now, although only part of his associations have been mentioned and practically nothing has been said about the personality structure, the past and the present situation of the man. The dream reveals what his real feeling was at the previous night's party. He was anxious, afraid of failing to make the impression he wanted to make, angry at several persons by whom he felt ridiculed and not sufficiently liked. The dream shows that his gaiety was a means of concealing his anxiety and his anger, and at the same time of pacifying those at whom he was angry. All his gaiety was a mask; it did not originate in himself, but covered what "he" really felt: fear and anger. This also made his whole position insecure, so that he felt like a spy in an enemy camp who might be found out any moment. The fleeting expression of sadness and desperation we noticed on him just when he was leaving, now finds its affirmation and also its explanation: at that moment his face expressed what "he" really felt, although it was something "he" was not really aware of feeling. In the dream, the feeling is described in a dramatic and explicit way, although it does not overtly refer to the people toward whom his feelings were directed.

This man is not neurotic, nor was he under a hypnotic spell; he is a rather normal individual with the same anxiety and need for approval as are customary in modern man. He was not aware of the fact that his gaiety was not "his," since he is so accustomed to feel what he is supposed to feel in a particular situation, that it would be the exception rather than the rule which would make him aware of anything being "strange."

What holds true of thinking and feeling holds also true of willing. Most people are convinced that as long as they are not overtly forced to do something by an outside power, their decisions are theirs, and that if they want something, it is they who want it. But this is one of the great illusions we have about ourselves. A great number of our decisions are not really our own but are suggested to us from the outside; we have succeeded in persuading ourselves that it is we who have made the decision, whereas we have actually conformed with expectations of others, driven by the fear of isolation and by more direct threats to our life, freedom, and comfort.

When children are asked whether they want to go to school every day, and their answer is, "Of course, I do," is the answer true? In many cases certainly not. The child may want to go to school quite frequently, yet very often would like to play or do something else instead. If he feels, "I want to go to school every day," he may repress his disinclination for the regularity of schoolwork. He feels that he is expected to want to go to school every day, and this pressure is strong enough to submerge the feeling that he goes so often only because he has to. The child might feel happier if he could be aware of the fact that sometimes he wants to go and sometimes he only goes because he has to go. Yet the pressure of the sense of duty is great enough to give him the feeling that "he" wants what he is supposed to want.

It is a general assumption that most men marry voluntarily. Certainly there are those cases of men consciously marrying on the basis of a feeling of duty or obligation. There are cases in which a man marries because "he" really wants to. But there are also not a few cases in which a man (or a woman for that matter) consciously believes that he *wants* to marry a certain person while actually he finds himself caught in a sequence of events which leads to marriage and seems to block every escape. All the months leading up to his marriage he is firmly convinced that "he" wants to marry, and the first and rather belated indication that this may not be so is the fact that on the day of his marriage he suddenly gets panicky and feels an impulse to run away. If he is "sensible" this feeling lasts only for a few minutes, and he will answer the question whether it is his intention to marry with the unshakable conviction that it is.

We could go on quoting many more instances in daily life in which people seem to make decisions, seem to want something, but actually follow the internal or external pressure of "having" to want the thing they are going to do. As a matter of fact, in watching the phenomenon of human decisions, one is struck by the extent to which people are mistaken in taking as "their" decision what in effect is submission to convention, duty, or simple pressure. It almost seems that "original" decision is a comparatively rare phenomenon in a society which supposedly makes individual decision the cornerstone of its existence.

I wish to add one detailed example of a case of pseudo willing which can frequently be observed in the analysis of people who do not have any neurotic symptoms. One reason for doing so is the fact that, although this individual case has little to do with the broad cultural issues with which we are mainly concerned . . . [here], it gives the reader who is not familiar with the operation of unconscious forces an additional opportunity to become acquainted with this phenomenon. Moreover, this example stresses one point which, though being implicitly made already, should be brought forward explicitly: the connection of repression* with the problem of pseudo acts. Although one looks at repression mostly from the standpoint of the operation of the repressed forces in neurotic behavior, dreams, and so on, it seems important to stress the fact that every repression eliminates parts of one's real self and enforces the substitution of a pseudo feeling for the one which has been repressed.

The case I want to present now is one of a twenty-two-year-old medical student. He is interested in his work and gets along with people pretty normally. He is not particularly unhappy, although he often feels slightly tired and has no particular zest for life. The reason why he wants to be analyzed is a theoretical one since he wants to become a psychiatrist. His only complaint is some sort of blockage in his medical work. He frequently cannot remember things he has

---

* repression—the act of forcing ideas or feelings into the unconscious. [Eds.]

read, gets inordinately tired during lectures, and makes a comparatively poor showing in examinations. He is puzzled by this since in other subjects he seems to have a much better memory. He has no doubts about wanting to study medicine, but often has very strong doubts as to whether he has the ability to do it.

After a few weeks of analysis he relates a dream in which he is on the top floor of a skyscraper he had built and looks out over the other buildings with a slight feeling of triumph. Suddenly the skyscraper collapses and he finds himself buried under the ruins. He is aware of efforts being made to remove the debris in order to free him, and can hear someone say that he is badly injured and that the doctor will come very soon. But he has to wait what seems to be an endless length of time before the doctor arrives. When he eventually gets there the doctor discovers that he has forgotten to bring his instruments and can therefore do nothing to help him. An intense rage wells up in him against the doctor and he suddenly finds himself standing up, realizing that he is not hurt at all. He sneers at the doctor, and at that moment he awakes.

He does not have many associations in connection with the dream, but these are some of the more relevant ones. Thinking of the skyscraper he has built, he mentions in a casual way how much he was always interested in architecture. As a child his favorite pastime for many years consisted of playing with construction blocks, and when he was seventeen, he had considered becoming an architect. When he mentioned this to his father, the latter had responded in a friendly fashion that of course he was free to choose his career, but that he (the father) was sure that the idea was a residue of his childish wishes, that he really preferred to study medicine. The young man thought that his father was right and since then had never mentioned the problem to his father again, but had started to study medicine as a matter of course. His associations about the doctor being late and then forgetting his instruments were rather vague and scant. However, while talking about this part of the dream, it occurred to him that his analytic hour had been changed from its regular time and that while he had agreed to the change without any objection he had really felt quite angry. He can feel his anger rising now while he is talking. He accuses the analyst of being arbitrary and eventually says, "Well, after all, I cannot do what I want anyway." He is quite surprised at his anger and at this sentence, because so far he had never felt any antagonism toward the analyst or the analytic work.

Some time afterwards he has another dream of which he only remembers a fragment: his father is wounded in an automobile accident. He himself is a doctor and is supposed to take care of the father. While he is trying to examine him, he feels completely paralyzed and cannot do anything. He is terror-stricken and wakes up.

In his associations he reluctantly mentions that in the last few years he has had thoughts that his father might die suddenly, and these thoughts have frightened him. Sometimes he had even thought of the estate which would be left to him and of what he would do with the money. He had not proceeded very far with these phantasies, as he suppressed them as soon as they began to appear. In comparing this dream with the one mentioned before, it strikes him that in both cases the doctor is unable to render any efficient help. He realizes more clearly than ever before that he feels that he can never be of any use as a doctor. When it is pointed out to him that in the first dream there is a definite feeling of anger and derision at the impotence of the doctor, he remembers that often when he hears or reads about cases in which a doctor has been unable to help the patient, he has a certain feeling of triumph of which he was not aware at the time.

In the further course of the analysis other material which had been repressed comes up. He discovers to his own surprise a strong feeling of rage against his father, and furthermore that his feeling of impotence as a doctor is part of a more general feeling of powerlessness which pervades his whole life. Although on the surface he thought that he had arranged his life according to his own plans, he can feel now that deeper down he was filled with a sense of resignation. He realizes that he was convinced that he could not do what he wanted but had to conform with what was expected of him. He sees more and more clearly that he had never really wanted to become a physician and that the things which had impressed him as a lack of ability were nothing but the expression of passive resistance.

This case is a typical example of the repression of a person's real wishes and the adoption of expectations of others in a way that makes them appear to be his own wishes. We might say that the original wish is replaced by a pseudo wish.

This substitution of pseudo acts for original acts of thinking, feeling, and willing, leads eventually to the replacement of the original self by a pseudo self. The original self is the self which *is* the originator of mental activities. The pseudo self is only an agent who actually represents the role a person is supposed to play but who does so under the name of the self. It is true that a person can play many roles and subjectively be convinced that he is "he" in each role. Actually he is in all these roles what he believes he is expected to be, and for many people, if not most, the original self is completely suffocated by the pseudo self. Sometimes in a dream, in phantasies, or when a person is drunk, some of the original self may appear, feelings and thoughts which the person has not experienced for years. Often they are bad ones which he has repressed because he is afraid or ashamed of them. Sometimes, however, they are the very best things in him, which he has repressed because of his fear of being ridiculed or attacked for having such feelings.*

The loss of the self and its substitution by a pseudo self leave the individual in an intense state of insecurity. He is obsessed by doubt since, being essentially a reflex of other people's expectation of him, he has in a measure lost his identity. In order to overcome the panic resulting from such loss of identity, he is compelled to conform, to seek his identity by continuous approval and recognition by others. Since he does not know who he is, at least the others will know—if he acts

---

* [Author's Note] The psychoanalytic procedure is essentially a process in which a person tries to uncover this original self. "Free association" means to express one's original feelings and thoughts, telling the truth; but truth in this sense does not refer to the fact that one says what one thinks, but the thinking itself is original and not an adaptation to an expected thought. Freud has emphasized the repression of "bad" things; it seems that he has not sufficiently seen the extent to which the "good" things are subjected to repression also.

according to their expectation; if they know, he will know too, if he only takes their word for it.

The automatization of the individual in modern society has increased the helplessness and insecurity of the average individual. Thus, he is ready to submit to new authorities which offer him security and relief from doubt. . . .

JOURNAL WRITINGS

1. What is Fromm's **thesis?** What do you think he would say about each of the reasons that you listed in the Preview Question?
2. Fromm talks about "submission to convention, duty, or simple pressure." **Narrate** an incident from your own life when you did something for one of these reasons. Add a sentence or two commenting on how Fromm's **thesis** might apply to your incident.

BRAINSTORMING AND DRAFTING

3. Fromm postulates that those of us who engage in pseudo thinking, feeling, and willing have lost much of our "true selves." Why is he so concerned about this loss? In a small group (or working individually), compile a list of real dangers arising from the loss of self. Then each person should select one danger from the list and draft a paragraph explaining it in depth.
4. Reread the selection by Jean-Paul Sartre in this unit. Draft a paragraph in which you demonstrate in detail how the people whom Fromm describes fail to achieve Sartre's ideal of freedom.
5. Apply Milgram's concept of obedience to authority to this reading. According to Fromm, who or what acts as the implied authority? **Compare** or **contrast** the motives for obedience in each reading. What might motivate people to "disobey" the authoritative body in Fromm?

THE AUTHOR'S METHODS

6. In the second paragraph, Fromm uses an **analogy** to suggest the disappearance of the "I," noting that it can be **compared** "with the protective coloring some animals assume" so that "they are hardly distinguishable" from their surroundings. What is Fromm's purpose in using this analogy? Create your own analogy for an automaton. That is, complete the sentence: An automaton is like . . . Then write a paragraph demonstrating how your analogy illustrates the concept.
7. Many of Fromm's paragraphs begin with a **generalization** that leads to a concrete **example.** As a reader, how valuable are these examples for you? What would be the effect of leaving them out? Write a paragraph in which you begin with a generalization about how much free choice an automaton

has. Follow your topic sentence with an extended example of automaton behavior that you have observed in someone you know.

FORMAL WRITING AND RESEARCH PAPERS

8. Write a paper in which you **argue** for or against Fromm's **thesis** as it applies to you. That is, **analyze** to what extent your decisions have been affected by general cultural patterns, parental expectations, peer attitudes or practices, etc. Provide several extended **examples** like Fromm's to support your ideas. (Your answer to question 2 of Journal Writings may be useful here.) **Conclude** by evaluating whether you are comfortable with your own mode of decision making or whether you plan to make any changes in your behavior.

9. Find some information on mob or crowd psychology by consulting *Psychological Abstracts, Sociological Abstracts,* the *Social Sciences Index,* and the card or computer catalog. In addition to **general** ideas about this topic, collect several specific **examples** of the phenomenon. Using both kinds of information (the general as well as the specific), write a paper in which you apply Fromm's principles to the phenomenon of mob or crowd activity.

Ben H. Bagdikian

Dr. Brandreth Has Gone to Harvard

(1990)

Born in 1920 in Maras, Turkey, Ben Haig Bagdikian was brought to the United States as an infant and became a naturalized citizen in 1926. He received an A.B. from Clark University in 1941. Beginning his career as a reporter for the *Springfield Morning Union,* he later became associate editor for the magazine *Periodical House* and chief Washington correspondent for the *Providence Journal.* He has been a reporter as well as an editor for the *Saturday Evening Post* and the *Washington Post.* He has also taught at Syracuse, and is currently a professor at the Graduate School of Journalism at the University of California at Berkeley. Noted for his interest in social problems and his forthright, analytical criticism of the mass media, Bagdikian has been honored with such prestigious awards as the George Foster Peabody Award, a Guggenheim Fellowship, and a Pulitzer Prize. Besides several pamphlets and essays in anthologies, Bagdikian's writings include *In the Midst of Plenty: The Poor in America* and *The Information Machines: Their Impact on Men and the Media.*

The following selection is taken from the third edition of *The Media Monopoly,* which was originally published in 1983. Examining both subtle and explicit attempts to control media productions through advertising, Bagdikian presents a frightening scenario in which giant corporations shape the thinking of millions of Americans. He claims that advertisers not only influence the selection of content in a program or news article—they may even manipulate the type of images we see 'n particular occupations. Bagdikian includes specific cases and statistics to persuade us that advertisers are subtly eroding our freedom to make informed decisions.

PREVIEW

Do you think advertisers who support newspapers, radio, and television programs should have any control over what is written, spoken, or produced? Give reasons for your answer.

James Gordon Bennett, founder of the *New York Herald,* is one of American journalism's rambunctious bad boys. In August of 1835 his Ann Street plant suffered a disastrous fire, but the *Herald* was back on the street nineteen days later with the pronouncement:

> We are again in the field . . . more independent than ever. The Ann Street conflagration consumed types, presses, manuscripts, paper, some bad poetry, subscription books—all the outward appearance of the *Herald,* but its soul was saved.[1]

The *Herald* was "again in the field" but not "more independent than ever." After the fire Bennett was saved by a large advertising contract from a "Doctor Brandreth," a quack who sold phony cure-all pills. After the *Herald* was back in circulation, the Brandreth ads appeared in profusion. But so did a steady diet of "news" stories, presuming to be straight reporting, "more independent than ever," recounting heroic cures effected by none other than Dr. Brandreth's pills. While other pill makers complained that Brandreth was getting front-page news accounts as well as ads, Bennett replied in his news columns:

> Send us more advertisements than Dr. Brandreth does—give us higher prices—we'll cut Dr. Brandreth dead—or at least curtail his space. Business is business—money is money—and Dr. Brandreth is no more to us than "Mr. Money Broker."[2]

Nine months later, when Brandreth canceled his advertising contract, Bennett, in print, called the good doctor a "most impudent charlatan" who "deceived and cheated," something any moderately honest reporter could have written from the start.

In the new dignity of modern American journalism, this kind of corruption in the news is a thing of the past, having occurred only in the bad old days before the turn of the century. Modern media, it is said, are immunized by professional ethics from letting advertising influence editorial content.

Contemporary news and entertainment are, to use Bennett's phrase, "more independent than ever." Newspapers make 75 percent of their revenues from ads and devote about 65 percent of their daily space to them. Magazines, similarly clothed in virtue, make roughly half their money from ads, though they used to make more, and they, too, generally insist that their advertising departments never shape the articles, stories, and columns produced by professional editors and writers. Radio and television, the most pervasive media in American life, have varied nonadvertising content like game shows, situation comedies, cops-and-robbers serials, news, talk shows, documentaries, and musical recordings. These, broadcasters usually insist, are independent of the thirty-second and sixty-second commercials dropped into normal programming. In short, nineteenth-century money changers of advertising have been chased out of the twentieth-century temple of editorial purity.

It's a pretty picture. Unfortunately, it isn't true.

Present-day Brandreths have changed their technique. So have the contemporary Bennetts. The advertiser does not barge through the front door announcing, "I am Dr. Brandreth. I pay money to this network (newspaper, magazine, radio station) and I am pleased to introduce to you the producer (reporter, editor, writer) who, with all the powers vested by society in independent journalism, will proclaim the wonder of my pills." Except for a few clumsy operators, such a tactic is much too crude for the late twentieth century.

Today Dr. Brandreth makes his proper appearance in his ads. He then leaves politely by the front door, goes to the back of the television station (radio studio, newspaper newsroom, magazine editorial offices), puts on the costume of a professional producer (editor, reporter), and in his new guise declares, "I am an ethical professional producer (reporter, editor, writer) whom you have been told to trust. Through professional research and critical analysis it is my independent judgment that Dr. Brandreth's pills, politics, ideology, and industry are the salvation of our national soul."

Modern corruption is more subtle. At one time or another, advertisers have *successfully* demanded that the following ideas appear in programs around their ads.

All businessmen are good or, if not, are always condemned by other businessmen. All wars are humane. The status quo is wonderful. Also wonderful are all grocery stores, bakeries, drug companies, restaurants, and laundries. Religionists, especially clergy, are perfect. All users of cigarettes are gentle, graceful, healthy, youthful people. In fact, anyone who uses a tobacco product is a hero. People who commit suicide never do it with pills. All financial institutions are always in good shape. The American way of life is beyond criticism.

The above messages, to cite only a few, are not vague inferences. Major advertisers insisted, successfully, that these specific ideas be expressed not in the ads but in the ostensibly "independent" news reporting, editorial content, or entertainment programs of newspapers, magazines, radio, and television. The readers, listeners, and viewers do not know that these messages are planted by advertisers. They are not supposed to know. They are supposed to think that these ideas are the independent work of professional journalists and playwrights detached from anything commercial. If the audiences were told that the ideas represented explicit demands of corporations who advertised, the messages would lose their impact.

This is not saying that all journalists and screenwriters are forced to follow ideological lines. There is considerable latitude for description of events and ideas in the news, in magazine articles, and in broadcast programs. But there is a limit to this latitude, established by conventional wisdom in journalism and broadcasting. The most obvious limit is criticism of the idea of free enterprise or of other basic business systems. Some reporters often criticize specific corporate acts, to the rage of corporate leaders. But the taboo against criticism of the system of contemporary enterprise is, in its unspoken way, almost as complete within mainstream journalism and broadcast programming in the United States as criticism of communism is explicitly forbidden in the Soviet Union.[3]

The entry of pro-corporate ideas into news and entertainment is more specific and discernible than the convention against systemic criticism.

Procter & Gamble is the largest advertiser in television. For years it has been a leader in creating promotions in all media, including commercials inserted in television programs. It has always appreciated the power of advertising. The company was created in 1837 with a soap called, simply, White Soap.[4] But in 1879 Harley Procter, a descendant of the founder, read in the Forty-fifth Psalm, "All thy garments smell of myrrh and aloes and cassia out of the ivory palaces . . . " Ivory Soap was born and with it the first of the full-page ads for the product. Within a decade Procter & Gamble was selling thirty million cakes of the soap a day. Since then, the company has been spectacularly successful, combining soap, detergent, Christian religion, patriotism, and profit making. After World War II it projected its ideas to television programs in the form of advertising.

They, like most major advertisers, do not merely buy a certain number of commercials, deliver the tapes to the networks and local stations, and let the commercials fall where they may. Some television and radio ads are bought on that basis but not, usually, those of major advertisers. Big advertisers in particular want to know what time of day their commercials will be shown, since that helps define the makeup and size of the audience they are buying. And they want to know the nature of the program into which their commercial will be inserted.

In the early years of television, advertisers sponsored and produced entire news and entertainment programs. This gave them direct control over the nonadvertising part of the program and they inserted or deleted whatever suited their commercial and ideological purposes. NBC's news program in the early 1950s was called "Camel News Caravan" after its sponsor, Camel cigarettes, which banned all film of news that happened to take place where a No Smoking sign could be seen in the background.[5]

After the 1950s, networks produced their own shows and advertisers bought commercials of varying lengths for insertion during the networks' programming. Advertising was allotted six minutes per hour of prime-time evening hours and longer periods at other times of day. But no network produces a program without considering whether sponsors will like it. Prospective shows usually are discussed with major advertisers, who look at plans or tentative scenes and reject, approve or suggest changes.

Major advertisers like Procter & Gamble do not leave their desires in doubt.

The Federal Communications Commission held hearings in 1965 to determine how much influence advertisers had on noncommercial content of television and radio.[6] Albert N. Halverstadt, general advertising manager of Procter & Gamble, testified that the company established directives for programs in which Procter & Gamble would advertise. These policies were to create standards of "decency and common sense . . . I do not think it constitutes control." He then gave the FCC the formal requirements for television programs, as established by the medium's largest advertiser in their memorandums of instruction to their advertising agency:

> Where it seems fitting, the characters in Procter & Gamble dramas should reflect recognition and acceptance of the world situation in their thoughts and actions, although in dealing with war, our writers should minimize the "horror" aspects. The writers should be guided by the fact that any scene that contributes negatively to public morale is not acceptable. Men in uniform shall not be cast as heavy villains or portrayed as engaging in any criminal activity.[7]

Procter & Gamble was particularly interested in the image of business and business people on television programs:[8]

> There will be no material on any of our programs which could in any way further the concept of business as cold, ruthless, and lacking all sentiment or spiritual motivation.
>
> If a businessman is cast in the role of villain, it must be made clear that he is not typical but is as much despised by his fellow businessmen as he is by other members of society.
>
> Special attention shall be given to *any* mention, however innocuous, of the grocery and drug business as well as any other group of customers of the company. This includes industrial users of the company's products, such as bakeries, restaurants, and laundries.

The company view of religion and patriotism is built into programs. If, in a drama or documentary, a character attacks what the memo called "some basic conception of the American way of life" then a rejoinder "must be completely and convincingly made someplace in the same broadcast."

The same is true of what Procter & Gamble called "positive social forces": "Ministers, priests and similar representatives of positive social forces shall not be cast as villains or represented as committing a crime or be placed in any unsympathetic anti-social role."

The memo specifies, "If there is any question whatever about such material, it should be deleted."

Halverstadt testified that these policies were applied both to entertainment programs in which Procter & Gamble commercials appeared and to news and public affairs documentaries.

Thus, corporate ideology is built into entertainment and documentary programming that the audience believes is presented independent of thirty-second and sixty-second commercials that happen to appear in the program. It is sobering that these demands are made of a medium reaching eighty million homes for six and a half hours every day.

But insertion of corporate ideology and commercial themes in the nonadvertising portion of television programming is not limited to Procter & Gamble. An executive of Brown & Williamson Tobacco Corporation placed into evidence before the FCC the company's policy on programs carrying cigarette commercials, directives that prevailed until the end of televised cigarette commercials in 1970:

> Tobacco products should not be used in a derogatory or harmful way. And no reference or gesture of disgust, dissatisfaction or distaste be made in connection with them. Example: cigarettes should not be ground out violently in an ashtray or stamped out underfoot.
>
> Whenever cigarettes are used by antagonists or questionable characters, they should be regular size, plain ends and unidentifiable.
>
> But no cigarette should be used as a prop to depict an undesirable character. Cigarettes used by meritorious characters should be Brown & Williamson brands and they may be identifiable or not.

A vice-president of an advertiser of headache tablets, Whitehall Laboratories, told the FCC that the company demanded of networks that "if a scene depicted somebody committing suicide by taking a bottle of tablets, we would not want this to be on the air."

A vice-president of Prudential Insurance Company, sponsor of public affairs programs, said that a positive image of business and finance was important to sustain on the air. The company rejected the idea for a program on the Bank Holiday during the Depression because "it cast a little doubt on all financial institutions."

All major advertisers, it seems, would concur with a statement made by a Procter & Gamble vice-president for advertising in 1979: "We're in programming first to assure a good environment for our advertising."[9]

Corporate demands on television programs underlie what many consider the most grievous weakness of American television—superficiality, materialism, blandness, and escapism. The television industry invariably responds that the networks are only giving people what the people demand. But it is not what the public says it wants: It is what the advertisers demand.

At one time Bell & Howell Company attempted to break the pattern of escapist, superficial prime-time programs by sponsoring news documentaries.[10] The president of the company told the FCC that this was tried to help counter the standards applied by most advertisers, which he described, disapprovingly, as consisting of the following requirements:

> One should not associate with controversy; one should always reach for the highest ratings; one should never forget that there is safety in numbers; one should always remember that comedy, adventure and escapism provide the best atmosphere for selling.

Even if a nonescapist program becomes a commercial success, it is likely to be canceled by the networks or major local stations. In the early days of television there were outstanding serious programs, including live, original drama: "Kraft Television Theatre," "Goodyear Playhouse," "Studio One," "Robert Montgomery Presents," "U.S. Steel Hour," "Revlon Theater," "Omnibus," "Motorola TV Hour," "The Elgin Hour," "Matinee Theater," and "Playhouse 90." It was the era of striking television plays by playwrights such as Paddy Chayefsky, who said he had discovered "the marvelous world" of drama in the lives of ordinary people. Erik Barnouw in his definitive history of American broadcasting writes:

> That this "marvelous world" fascinated millions is abundantly clear from statistics. These plays—akin to genre paintings—held consistently high ratings. But one group hated them: the advertising profession . . . Most advertisers were selling magic. Their commercials posed the same problems that Chayefsky drama dealt with: people who feared failure in love and in business. But in the commercials there was always a solution as clear-cut as the snap of a finger: the problem could be solved by a new pill, deodorant, toothpaste, shampoo, shaving lotion, hair tonic, car, girdle, coffee, muffin recipe, or floor wax.[11]

Serious programs remind the audience that complex human problems are not solved by switching to a new deodorant. Contrary to the network characterization of audiences, a more sophisticated presentation of human affairs was accepted enthusiastically by television audiences during the 1950s, if the work was done with skill and sensitivity. If, in the midst of this, a commercial resolved serious human conflicts with a new brand of coffee, the commercial appeared for what it was—silly. A skillful documentary on assassinations in American politics is not an ideal "environment" for a commercial arguing that a new toothpaste with a secret ingredient will give long life, wealth, and sexual fulfillment.

Even "serious" commercials, like corporate image advertisements, are carefully placed in the most suitable programming. The manager of corporate communications for General Electric has said, "We insist on a program environment that reinforces our corporate messages."[12]

There is another reason networks and advertising agencies resist serious or nonescapist programs. Networks make most of their money between the hours of 8:00 and 11:00 P.M.—prime time. They wish to keep the audience tuned from one half-hour segment to the next and they prefer the "buying mood" sustained as well. A serious half-hour program in that period that has high ratings may, nevertheless, be questioned because it will interrupt the evening's flow of lightness and fantasy. In that sense, the whole evening is a single block of atmosphere—a selling atmosphere.

A major advertiser, Du Pont, told the FCC that the corporation finds its commercials more effective on "lighter, happier" programs.[13] Television is particularly suited to fantasy, imagery, and multidimensional effects. Commercials are brief, measured in split seconds. They disappear quickly, permitting no reflection after one image has been implanted before the next appears. The nonadvertising program is designed to leave undisturbed these emotional associations of commercials.

The printed media have not escaped the pressure, or the desire, to shape their nonadvertising content to support the mood and sometimes the explicit ideas of advertisers. Magazines were the first medium to carry sophisticated, artistic advertisements.[14] Magazines had graphic capabilities superior to newspapers, with better printing and color illustrations (the first successful national magazine, *Godey's Lady Book,* begun in 1830, hired 150 women to tint the magazine's illustrations by hand). Until late in the 1800s ads were a minor part of magazine publishing, but once national merchandising organizations grew, this national medium responded. By 1900 *Harper's,* for example, was carrying more ads in one year than it had in its previous twenty-two years.

Before television emerged in the 1950s, successful magazines were 65 percent ads. By that time, most magazines were fundamentally designed for advertising rather than editorial matter. The philosophy of Condé Nast had triumphed. Nast, who had created *Vogue, Vanity Fair, Glamour, Mademoiselle,* and *House and Garden,* regarded his mission "to bait the editorial pages in such a way to lift out of all the millions of Americans just the hundred thousand cultivated persons who can buy these quality goods."[15]

The role of most magazines, as seen by their owners, was to act as a broker in bringing together the buyers and sellers of goods. There was, and still is, a significant difference among magazines in how far they go to sell their readers to advertisers. But the influence of advertisers on magazine content continues.

A 1940 *Esquire* article declared that the guitar is a better accompaniment to singing than a piano. A few months later the magazine ran an apology, "We lost all our piano ads . . . We can and do beg the pardon of the piano manufacturers." By then the fiery owners of the magazine had already been tamed. Two years earlier they had started *Ken,* a magazine of liberal idealism that seemed to start with great promise.[16] Advertisers disliked the liberal ideas in its articles and not only refused to advertise in the new publication but threatened to pull out their ads from *Esquire* as well. So the owners of *Esquire* killed *Ken,* even though it met its circulation plans.

In 1962 Paul Willis, president of the Grocery Manufacturers Association, warned television operators that they had better run more programs boosting the food industry. He boasted that a similar warning had worked with national magazines.

> We suggested to the publishers that the day was here when their editorial department and business department might better understand their interdependent relationships . . . as their operations may affect the advertiser—their bread and butter.[17]

The periodical *Advertising Age* said Willis "pointed with pride" to favorable food articles printed thereafter by "Look, Reader's Digest, American Weekly, This Week, Saturday Evening Post, Good Housekeeping, Ladies' Home Journal, Family Circle, and Woman's Day, among others."

If, like Bennett's *Herald,* this was merely the bad old days, there has been little evidence to give comfort in recent years. Condé Nast could create *Vogue* in 1909 with his philosophy of using his articles to get "the cultivated persons who can buy these quality goods." In 1972, with *Vogue* under a new owner (S.I. Newhouse, the newspaper chain, which bought the Condé Nast magazines in 1959), it seemed to make no difference. Richard Shortway, publisher of *Vogue,* sixty-three years after Nast's candid statement, made his own candid statement: "The cold, hard facts of magazine publishing mean that those who advertise get editorial coverage."[18]

Magazines have been the Achilles' heel of corporations who also own book houses. The New York Times Company is a conglomerate involved in magazines, books, and broadcasting, as well as newspapers. In 1976 the *New York Times* published a series of articles on medical malpractice.[19] The news series angered the medical industry, including pharmaceutical firms. They could not retaliate effectively against the *New York Times,* which does not carry much medical advertising. But medicine-related advertisers were crucial to magazines published by the New York Times Company, including a periodical called *Modern Medicine.* Pharmaceutical firms threatened to withdraw 260 pages of their ads from *Modern Medicine,* a loss of half a million dollars, and the Times Company sold its medical magazines to Harcourt Brace Jovanovich.

The sale by the Times raises two interesting questions. How many papers, rather than sell profitable subsidiaries like the Times's medical magazines, would instead have decided not to print the malpractice series or have told their editors not to report such stories again? And what would happen, after the Times sold the magazines, if an author submitted a book manuscript on medical malpractice to the new owner of the magazines, the book publisher Harcourt Brace Jovanovich? Perhaps the more troublesome question is: Without anyone ever saying anything explicit, what would go through the mind of a decision maker at a book company, knowing what had happened at the New York Times?

Reader's Digest Association owns the magazine *Reader's Digest* and Funk & Wagnalls book publishing.[20] In 1968 Funk & Wagnalls prepared to publish a book, *The Permissible Lie*, which criticized the advertising industry. A month before publication date, Reader's Digest ordered its book subsidiary to cancel the book. Reader's Digest advertising revenues in its magazine, at that date, were $50 million a year and the association presumably felt threatened by loss of advertising from its magazine if its book subsidiary offended the advertising industry.

Newspapers are considered the most scrupulous of all the media subsidized by advertising. It has been a sacred edict in official newspaper ethics that church and state—news and advertising—are separate and that when there is any doubt each is clearly labeled. This is a relatively recent change. Thirty years ago it was common for newspapers to resist news that offended a major advertiser. Department store fires, safety violations in stores, public health actions against restaurants that advertised, and lawsuits against car dealers seldom made their way into print. The average paper printed stories about some advertiser or prospective advertiser that were solely promotional propaganda. A standard fixture in almost every newspaper was the memorandum from the business office—B.O.M., or "business office must," meaning that the news department was ordered to run a story for purposes of pleasing an advertiser.

Over the years on most newspapers—but not all—those blatant corruptions of news have diminished or disappeared. But censoring of information offensive to advertisers continues. News that might damage an advertiser generally must pass a higher threshold of drama and documentation than other kinds of news. More common in contemporary papers is the large quantity of "fluff"—material that is not news in any real sense but is nonadvertising material supporting of advertisers.

A 1978 study by the Housing Research Group of the Center for Responsive Law found that

> most newspaper real estate sections serve the real estate industry far better than they serve consumers and general readers . . . Articles that appear as "news" frequently are promotional pieces for developers, real estate agents, or industry associations.[21]

Examples in the study included the following: the *Birmingham* (Alabama) *News* printed four industry press releases without more than cosmetic rewriting on the front page of its real estate section; one issue of the *Sacramento Union* had more than a dozen articles promoting new subdivisions; press releases were substituted for news articles in the *Baltimore Sun, Birmingham News, Boston Herald American, New York Post, Philadelphia Evening Bulletin,* and *Washington Star.*

Bigger papers, including some of the country's most prestigious, often printed more real estate propaganda than did some smaller papers. The report said:

We were surprised to discover half a dozen smaller newspapers . . . that had a small but respectable real estate section. Their success in presenting real estate news in an objective, informative fashion compared quite favorably with some much larger newspapers.

These smaller papers were *Indianapolis Star, New Orleans Times-Picayune, Memphis Commercial Appeal,* and *St. Petersburg* (Fla.) *Times.*

The study seemed to have little impact. A year later a number of newspapers not only kept up the flood of industry promotional material masquerading as news but actually took real estate reporting out of the hands of reporters and gave it directly to the advertising department. These papers include the *Van Nuys* (Calif.) *Valley News, Los Angeles Herald Examiner, Houston Chronicle,* and *Dallas Morning News.*

The bulk of "news" in the newspaper is contained in similar special sections. The fashion section, for example, is almost always either taken from press releases submitted by designers and fashion houses or written by fashion editors who attend the fashion shows with all expenses paid by the fashion houses. The result is an annual flood of gushy promotion of exotic garments, all in a "news" section. The contamination becomes more blatant with time. In 1980 John Brooks, director of communications for the *Toronto Star,* said that when the paper created a new fashion section,

> all market research data was turned over to the editorial department so that planning of editorial content would be consistent with the wants and needs of readers and prospective readers. The Family Editor, under whose jurisdiction Fashion/80 would fall, spent a lot of time with advertising department personnel in meetings with advertisers.[22]

The same is true of travel and usually food sections. A survey in 1977 showed that 94 percent of food editors use food company releases for recipes and 38 percent attend food events at the expense of food companies.[23]

The growing trend among newspapers to turn over sections of the "news" to the advertising department usually produces copy that is not marked "advertising" but is full of promotional material under the guise of news. The advertising department of the *Houston Chronicle,* for example, provides all the "news" for the following sections of the paper: home, townhouse, apartments, travel, technology, livestock, and swimming pools. The vice-president of sales and marketing of the *Chronicle* said: "We do nothing controversial. We're not in the investigative business. Our only concern is giving editorial support to our ad projects."[24]

One of the most compelling needs for readers in the 1980s was reliable information about comparative shopping, yet it is one of the weakest elements in American newspapers. The consumer information most needed by families concerns industries with control over the advertising income of newspapers—food, transportation, and clothing. A feature that has always been extremely popular with readers during its spasmodic and brief appearances is the market basket survey. A reporter periodically buys the items on a typical family shopping list and writes a story about price changes in major supermarkets. It is not a story that grocery store advertisers like, so it has practically disappeared in American papers precisely when it is most needed. Even when the market basket surveys are conducted by university researchers, as at Purdue University, most papers refuse to carry the reports, one admitting it bent to advertisers' pressure.[25]

In 1980 the *Washington Star* announced a five-part series on the pros and cons of shopping coupons that have become common in newspapers, but the series was killed after the first story for fear of discouraging advertisers who bought space in the *Star* for shopping coupons.[26]

When small advertisers hurt big ones, the big ones almost always win. A company called Car/Puter International for $10 provides a consumer with a computer printout giving the list prices and dealers' prices of a car and its options. For another $10 the company will order the car from the manufacturer at $125 above dealers' cost, a large savings over ordinary dealer prices. Car dealers are a major newspaper advertiser. More than forty newspapers and magazines refused to run Car/Puter ads, one publisher admitting that the ad's problem was "its direct competitiveness with automobile dealers."[27]

Given the eagerness with which newspapers protect major advertisers, it is understandable that by now advertisers expect that when the interests of readers are in competition with the interests of advertisers, the newspapers will protect the advertisers.

A senior vice-president of MGM told newspaper executives in 1981 that he had seen too many negative reviews of movies and warned newspapers that the $500 million worth of movie ads

> cannot be taken for granted and you've got to get this word to your editorial counterparts . . . Today the daily newspaper does not always create a climate that is supportive and favorable to the motion picture industry . . . gratuitous and hateful reviews threaten to cause the romance between newspapers and the motion picture industry to wither on the vine.[28]

Camel cigarettes presumably was not surprised in 1981 when 300 daily newspapers accepted its astonishing offer to run the large Monday morning sports scores not as independent news but embedded in an advertising display called "Camel Scoreboard."[29] It was the first time a major category of printed news became the property of an advertiser.

Another ingenious method of controlling news was used by Air Canada. In 1978 it notified newspaper advertising managers that its ads would be canceled as long as any news story of an Air Canada crash or hijacking ran in the paper and if its ads were carried within two pages of a news story of any crash or hijacking on any airline.[30]

Daily journalism in the last twenty years has shown more initiative in probing social forces that affect people's lives, reported in the "hard news" sections of papers. But the influence of advertisers and publishers' fears of offending advertisers have created a no man's land of subject matter that few newspapers, or magazines or broadcasters, will enter. These taboo subjects include some of the most critical developments to American life—abuse of land planning in cities, harmful real estate developments, the auto lobby's crippling of public transportation. But perhaps the most shameful money-induced censorship of American news media, a corruption of news that has contributed to millions of deaths, is the decades-long handling of the link between tobacco and heart-lung diseases.

Tobacco first entered human experience sometime in the sixteenth century, as a cure for numerous ailments, an illusion encouraged and sometimes believed by tobacco growers and merchants. But over the centuries doubt grew about the wondrous claims for the weed.

The scientific method applied to medicine has for a long time used circumstantial evidence to end some of the traditional scourges of humanity. Long before the organism of bubonic plague was isolated, that frightening destroyer of whole societies was tamed by systematic observation: People exposed to fleas from sick rats died of the plague while those not exposed did not die. Before any specific agent was identified, the back of typhoid fever was broken by the conclusion that people exposed to contaminated water and milk more often contracted the disease than those who were not exposed. Throughout modern history, killer diseases have been tamed by an analysis of the common experience of those who got sick compared with those who stayed healthy—methods of the science of epidemiology.

Over time, observers using the same methods associated some diseases with smoking. By the 1920s and 1930s medical research in England pointed clearly to tobacco as a danger to humans. In 1933 a team under Dr. Raymond Pearl at Johns Hopkins University began a three-year study of all deaths of patients thirty-five years and older, listing them in categories as nonsmokers, light smokers, and heavy smokers. The study involved 6,813 cases and the results were clear: Smokers became sick and died much earlier than nonsmokers, and on the average the more people smoked the quicker they got sick and died. The report was carried by a standard science service to newspapers and magazines. But, strangely, newspapers, magazines, and radio, which seized upon less conclusive research on the causes of polio, influenza, and tuberculosis, often with over-dramatization of evidence, remained silent on the scientifically indicated causes of heart disease and cancer.

On February 24, 1936, Dr. Pearl delivered a paper to the New York Academy of Medicine. His paper concluded that tobacco shortens the life of all users, a piece of genuinely spectacular news affecting millions of readers and listeners. The session was covered by the press, but they either remained silent about the news or buried it. At the time there were eight daily papers in New York City. Six of them carried nothing of the report. The other two, including the *New York Times*, carried only a few paragraphs buried at the bottom of an inside page.[31]

In 1953, the American Medical Association announced that it would no longer accept tobacco advertising in its journals, including the most authoritative medical publication in the country, the *Journal of the AMA*. In 1954, the American Cancer Society released results of a study of 187,000 men. Cigarette smokers had a death rate from all diseases 75 percent higher than nonsmokers. Their death rate from lung cancer was as high as sixteen times greater than that for nonsmokers. It was the start of overwhelming evidence of an epidemic that took more lives than the disease that regularly hit front pages of newspapers and double-page spreads of magazines. It was increasingly clear that tobacco-linked disease is the biggest single killer in the United States, accounting for more than 300,000 deaths a year, the cause of one in every seven deaths in the country, killing six times more people annually than automobile accidents. But though the statistics are conclusive to medical authorities, to this day they are treated as controversial or non-existent by the news media.

If there is a date beyond which there is no justification for media silence or burial of the link between tobacco and widespread death, it is 1954. In 1953, the year the AMA banned tobacco ads from its journals, the *New York Times Index*, reflecting probably the best newspaper reporting on the tobacco-cancer link, had 248 entries under "Cancer" and "Smoking" and "Tobacco." Ninety-two percent said nothing about the link; of the 8 percent that did, only 2 percent were articles mainly about the tobacco-disease connection, the other 6 percent mostly denials of this from the tobacco industry. In 1954, the year of the American Cancer Society's study, the *New York Times Index* had 302 entries under the same titles. Of the stories dealing mainly with tobacco's link to disease, 32 percent were about the tobacco industry's denials and only 20 percent dealt with medical evidence.

In 1980, sixteen years later, there were still more stories in the daily press about the causes of influenza, polio, and tuberculosis than about the cause of one of every seven deaths in the United States.

There began to be suspicions of a strictly media disease: a strange paralysis whenever solid news pointed at tobacco as a definitive cause of disease and death. For years up to the present, medical evidence on tobacco and disease has been treated differently from any other information on carriers of disease that do not advertise. The print and broadcast media might make page 1 drama of a junior researcher's paper about a rare disease. But if it involved the 300,000 annual deaths from tobacco-related disease, the media either do not report it or they report it as a controversial item subject to rebuttal by the tobacco industry.

It is a history filled with curious events. In 1963, for example, Hudson Vitamin Products produced Smokurb, a substitute for cigarettes. The company had trouble getting its ads in newspapers and magazines and on the air. Eli Schonberger, president of Hudson's ad agency, said, "We didn't create this campaign to get into a fight with anyone, but some media just stall and put us off in the hope that we'll go away."[32]

This is, of course, strange behavior for media who are anxious for as much advertising as they can get. One major magazine told the company its product was "unacceptable."

The tobacco industry spends $4 a year for every American man, woman, and child for its cigarette advertising. The government's primary agency for educating the public about the dangers of cigarettes, the Department of Health and Human Services, spends one-third of a cent a year for every citizen.

National publications, especially the news magazines, are notorious for publishing dramatic stories about health and disease. *Time* and *Newsweek* have both had cover stories on cancer. *Newsweek*, for example, had a cover story January 26, 1978, entitled "What Causes Cancer?" The article was six pages long. On the third page it whispered about the leading cause—in a phrase it said that tobacco is the least disputed "carcinogen of all." The article said no more about the statistics or the medical findings of the tobacco-cancer link, except in a table, which listed the ten most suspected carcinogens—alphabetically, putting tobacco in next-to-last place. A week later, *Time,* in a common competitive duplication between the two magazines, ran a two-column article on the causes of cancer. The only reference it made to tobacco was that "smoking and drinking alcohol have been linked to cancer." A few weeks earlier, a *Time* essay urged smokers to organize to defeat antismoking legislation.

When R. C. Smith of *Columbia Journalism Review* studied seven years of magazine content after 1970, when cigarette ads were banned from television, he found:

> In magazines that accept cigarette advertising I was unable to find a single article, in several years of publication, that would have given readers any clear notion of the nature and extent of the medical and social havoc wreaked by the cigarette-smoking habit.[33]

The few magazines that refuse cigarette ads did much better at their reporting, he said. (The most prominent magazines that refuse cigarette ads are *Reader's Digest* and *The New Yorker.*)

The magazines that carried accurate articles on the tobacco-disease link suffered for it. In July 1957 *Reader's Digest* ran a strong article on medical evidence against tobacco. Later that month, the advertising agency the magazine had used for twenty-eight years said it no longer wanted the *Digest* as a client. The agency, Batten, Barton, Durstine and Osborn, had $1.3 million in business a year from the magazine. But another client, the American Tobacco Company, which spent $22 million a year with the agency, had asked the agency to choose between it and the *Reader's Digest.*

In 1980 a liberal-left magazine, *Mother Jones,* ran a series of articles on the link between tobacco and cancer and heart disease, after which tobacco companies canceled their ads with the magazine.[34]

Elizabeth Whelan reported, "I frequently wrote on health topics for women's magazines, and have been told repeatedly by editors to stay away from the subject of tobacco."[35] Whelan, on a campaign to counter the silence, worked with the American Council on Science and Health to ask the ten leading women's magazines to run articles on the growing incidence of smoking-induced disease among women, as these same magazines had done to promote the Equal Rights Amendment. None of the ten magazines—*Cosmopolitan, Harper's Bazaar, Ladies' Home Journal, Mademoiselle, Ms., McCall's, Redbook, Seventeen, Vogue,* or *Working Woman*—would run such an article.

Television, confronted with FCC moves to make it run anti-smoking commercials to counter what the FCC considered misleading cigarette ads, aired a few documentaries, most of them emphasizing the uncertainty of the tobacco link. The best of them was by CBS, in 1965. But Howard K. Smith, of ABC, speaking on a public-television panel, expressed what many have seen as the media's treatment of tobacco and disease:

To me that documentary was a casebook example of balance that drained a hot issue of its meaning. On that program there were doctors who had every reason to be objective, who maintained that cigarettes have a causal relation to cancer. On the other side, there were representatives of the tobacco industry, who have no reason to be objective, who stated persuasively the opposite. The public was left with a blurred impression that the truth lay between whereas, as far as I am concerned, we have everything but a signed confession from a cigarette that smoking has a causal relation to cancer.[36]

If magazines and broadcasting have been muffled on the national plague, newspapers have been no better. According to medical and other researchers, as well as the editors who produced it, the only lengthy in-depth special feature on tobacco and disease in a standard American daily newspaper was published by the *Charlotte* (North Carolina) *Observer* on March 25, 1979.

The answer lies in a simple statistic: Tobacco is the most heavily advertised product in America, and for a good reason. As the publishing trade journal *Printer's Ink* reported in 1937, "The growth of cigarette consumption has . . . been due largely to heavy advertising expenditure . . . " In 1954—the year beyond which any reasonable doubt of the link should have disappeared among the media—the trade journal of newspapers, *Editor & Publisher,* criticizing the American Cancer Society and the Surgeon General's reports as "scare news," complained that it had cost newspapers "much lineage and many dollars to some whose business it is to promote the sale of cigarettes through advertising— newspaper and advertising agencies."[37]

It is not surprising that surveys in 1980 by Gallup, Roper, and Chilton found that 30 percent of the public is unaware of the relationship between smoking and heart disease, 50 percent of women do not know that smoking during pregnancy increases the risk of stillbirth and miscarriage, 40 percent of men and women had no idea that smoking causes 80 percent of the 98,000 lung cancer deaths per year, and 50 percent of teenagers do not know that smoking may be addictive.[38]

If there was ever any question that in the bad old days of James Gordon Bennett or in the media of the 1980s advertising influences news and other information given to the public, tobacco makes it unmistakably clear. The tobacco industry since 1954 has spent more than $9 billion on advertising, most of it in newspapers, magazines, radio, and television. Newspapers, magazines, radio, and television have effectively censored news and entertainment to obscure the link between tobacco and death. During that period more than eight million Americans have died from tobacco-linked disease.

Ten years after the crucial findings of 1954, the *New York Daily News*, then the largest daily paper in the United States, carried a headline that read:

CIGGIES ASSAILED AGAIN—HO HUM

The paper commented:

Sure the *News* takes cigarette advertising and likes it and so what?[39]

Unfortunately, the spirit of Dr. Brandreth is alive, though eight million Americans who died prematurely from tobacco are not.

Notes

[1] In August of 1835. Frank Luther Mott, *American Journalism* (New York: Macmillan, 1972), 231.

[2] "Send us more advertisements." Alfred McClung Lee, *The Daily Newspaper in America* (New York: Macmillan, 1937), 317.

[3] This is not saying. For a description of the line between reporting corporate misdeeds and analysis of faults in the system, see Ben H. Bagdikian, "A Case of Split Personality at the *Wall Street Journal*," *Washington Journalism Review*, July/August 1981, 35–39.

[4] The company was created. Frank Presbery, *The History and Development of Advertising* (New York: Doubleday, Doran, 1929), 396.

[5] NBC's news program. Erik Barnouw, *Tube of Plenty* (New York: Oxford University Press, 1975), 170.

[6] The Federal Communications Commission held hearings. Federal Communications Commission, *Second Interim Report by the Office of Network Study, Television Network Program Procurement* (Washington, D.C., 1965).

[7] "Where it seems fitting." Senate Committee on Interstate and Foreign Commerce, *Report* (Washington, D.C., 1963), 446–53.

[8] Individual verbatim testimony in FCC hearing is from *New York Times*, 27 September 1961, 28 September 1961, 29 September 1961, 30 September 1961, 3 October 1961, 4 October 1961, 5 October 1961, 7 October 1961, 8 October 1961.

[9] "We're in programming." *Fortune*, 31 December 1979, 70.

[10] At one time Bell & Howell. *New York Times*, 28 September 1961, 83.

[11] "That this 'marvelous world.'" Barnouw, *Tube of Plenty*, 163.

[12] "We insist on a program environment." *Broadcasting*, 5 November 1979, 52.

[13] "Lighter, happier" programs. *New York Times*, 27 September 1961.

[14] Magazines were the first medium. Theodore Peterson, *Magazines in the Twentieth Century* (Urbana: University of Illinois Press, 1975), 5.

[15] "To bait the editorial pages." *Time*, 28 September 1942, 51–52.

[16] A 1940 *Esquire* article. Two years earlier. Peterson, *Magazines in the Twentieth Century*, 279.

[17] "We suggested." "Look, Reader's Digest." *Advertising Age*, 19 November 1962, 1.

[18] "The cold, hard facts." *Advertising Age*, 17 April 1972, 85.

[19] In 1976 the *New York Times*. Ben H. Bagdikian, "Newspaper Mergers," *Columbia Journalism Review*, March/April 1977, 19–20.

[20] Reader's Digest Association. *Publishers Weekly*, 17 June 1968, 49.

[21] "Most newspaper real estate." "We were surprised." Housing Research Group, *For Sale or for Rent* (Washington, D.C.: Center for Responsive Law, 1978).

[22] In 1980 John Brooks. *Editor & Publisher*, 18 October 1980, 20.

[23] A survey in 1977. "Food Section Survey," Food Editors Conference, Chicago, October 1977.

[24] "We do nothing controversial." *Editor & Publisher*, 31 March 1979, 11.

[25] Even when the market basket surveys. *Editor & Publisher*, 29 March 1980, 15. Joseph N. Uhl, director of the project, said that papers stopped carrying the reports after complaints from grocers.

[26] In 1980 the *Washington Star*. *Washington Journalism Review*, October 1980, 46–47.

[27] More than forty newspapers and magazines. *Los Angeles Times*, 24 October 1977, 1.

[28] "Cannot be taken." *Editor & Publisher*, 31 January 1981, 7, 44.

[29] Camel cigarettes. *Editor & Publisher*, 15 August 1981, 7; *Columbia Journalism Review*, November/December 1981, 26.

[30] Another ingenious method. *Editor & Publisher*, 11 November 1978, 4.

[31] Six of them carried nothing. George Seldes, *Never Tire of Protesting* (New York: Lyle Stuart, 1968), 62.

[32] In 1963, for example. *New York Times*, 22 July 1963, 35.

[33] When R. C. Smith. R. C. Smith, "The Magazines' Smoking Habit," *Columbia Journalism Review*, January/February 1978, 29–31.

[34] In 1980. *Mother Jones* carried articles on smoking hazards in its issues of April 1979 and January 1980, after which all its advertisements from tobacco companies were canceled. From interviews with publisher of *Mother Jones*.

[35] Elizabeth Whelan reported. Press release of American Council on Science and Health, San Francisco, 29 January 1980.

[36] "To me that documentary." "The Deadly Balance," *Columbia Journalism Review*, Fall 1965, 13.

[37] "Much lineage." *Editor & Publisher*, 24 July 1954.

[38] It is not surprising. Meyers, Iscoe, Jennings, Lenox, Minsky, and Sacks, *Staff Report of the Cigarette Advertising Investigation* (Washington, D.C.: Federal Trade Commission, May 1981), 5.

[39] "Sure the *News*." *Consumer Reports*, May 1964, 247.

JOURNAL WRITINGS

1. **Narrate** an **example** that you know about (perhaps from your own life) in which someone's freedom of speech or action was inhibited to avoid offending someone else. Was the restriction morally acceptable to you? Why or why not? Is the financial control by big business described in the reading similar to or different from the type of pressure exerted in your incident? Explain.

2. **Describe** a television program you are familiar with that illustrates one of the "good" images Bagdikian mentions (such as the businessman, grocers, pharmacists, religionists, etc.). In what sense does a profusion of such images limit our thinking?

BRAINSTORMING AND DRAFTING

3. What does Bagdikian mean by "serious" programming? Watch a "serious" television program. Then draft a paragraph or two in which you **analyze** the differences between this type of program and the more "superficial" type (such as you described in question 2 of Journal Writings). In what sense does the "serious" program allow us more freedom?

4. How is the **theme** of Erich Fromm's piece similar to the theme of Bagdikian's? How do the forms of control in each reading differ? Which form of control do you think might be easier to overcome? Why?

5. In what sense might this selection be considered the fulfillment of Anaïs

Nin's fears as well as her hopes? Draft a paragraph explaining how her ethical considerations might apply to the media.

THE AUTHOR'S METHODS

6. In the relatively long fifth paragraph (beginning "Contemporary news . . . "), the author **describes** several ways in which the media appear to be independent. He then inserts two very short sentences contradicting all of the proceding information in the paragraph. What effect does this strategy have on you as a reader? Imitate this method by drafting a paragraph about a television program; find a way of refuting your information with a brief sentence or two.
7. In a paragraph, explain how the full title of the piece helps to clarify its **thesis**.

CREATIVE PROJECT

8. Write a brief skit in which you present a business executive, pharmacist, religionist, etc., in a way that Bagdikian (rather than an advertiser) would approve.

FORMAL WRITING AND RESEARCH PAPERS

9. Pretend you are an executive in a company that manufactures some of its products in aerosol spray cans. You are preparing to buy a substantial amount of advertising time from a national television network. Suddenly you learn that one of the network's upcoming programs features a panel of environmental experts discussing the dangers of using aerosol sprays and recommending laws against them. How much freedom will you, as an advertiser, allow to a network that you support? Write a paper addressed to other executives in your company in which you recommend specific company policy in this and similar situations. Be sure to offer several good reasons for your position.
10. How much freedom does your college or high school publication have from the control of faculty sponsors or school administrators? How much *should* it have? Obtain several newspaper issues from your own or another school. **Analyze** the types of articles and their typical content. Write a paper in which you assess the overall degree of freedom. Use **examples** to support your assessment and include reasons why you think the amount of freedom is appropriate or inappropriate for a school newspaper or magazine.

Tillie Olsen

I Stand Here Ironing

(1956)

Born in 1913 in Omaha, Nebraska, Tillie Olsen worked in various office and industry jobs while she raised her children. Though her formal education ended with high school, she continued to educate herself through extensive reading. Her creative talent has earned her positions at such colleges as Amherst, Stanford, Massachusetts Institute of Technology, and the University of California at San Diego. Particularly interested in women and working people, she is known for her emotional writing and appealing prose style.

Her publications include *Yonnondio: From the Thirties* (a novel), *Silences* (nonfiction), and *Tell Me a Riddle* (a short-story collection). The following short story, now part of this collection, originally appeared in the *Pacific Spectator* as "Help Her to Believe." Olsen's own experience of the depression era of the 1930s is reflected in the story's narrator, who tortuously debates the degree of responsibility she might have for the problems of her first-born child. As the story opens, the mother, though speaking to herself, responds to the school counselor who has evidently contacted her about her daughter Emily.

PREVIEW

Explain why you do or do not believe that parents or guardians can have a strong influence on their children's personalities or behavior.

I stand here ironing, and what you asked me moves tormented back and forth with the iron.

"I wish you would manage the time to come in and talk with me about your daughter. I'm sure you can help me understand her. She's a youngster who needs help and whom I'm deeply interested in helping."

"Who needs help." Even if I came, what good would it do? You think because I am her mother I have a key, or that in some way you could use me as a key? She has lived for nineteen years. There is all that life that has happened outside of me, beyond me.

And when is there time to remember, to sift, to weigh, to estimate, to total? I will start and there will be an interruption and I will have to gather it all together again. Or I will become engulfed with all I did or did not do, with what should have been and what cannot be helped.

She was a beautiful baby. The first and only one of our five that was beautiful at birth. You do not guess how new and uneasy her tenancy in her now-loveliness. You did not know her all those years she was thought homely, or see her poring over her baby pictures, making me tell her over and over how beautiful she had been—and would be, I would tell her—and was now, to the seeing eye. But the seeing eyes were few or non-existent. Including mine.

I nursed her. They feel that's important nowadays. I nursed all the children, but with her, with all the fierce rigidity of first motherhood, I did like the books then said. Though her cries battered me to trembling and my breasts ached with swollenness, I waited till the clock decreed.

Why do I put that first? I do not even know if it matters, or if it explains anything.

She was a beautiful baby. She blew shining bubbles of sound. She loved motion, loved light, loved colour and music and textures. She would lie on the floor in her blue overalls patting the surface so hard in ecstasy her hands and feet would blur. She was a miracle to me, but when she was eight months old I had to leave her daytimes with the woman downstairs to whom she was no miracle at all, for I worked or looked for work and for Emily's father, who "could no longer endure" (he wrote in his good-bye note) "sharing want with us."

I was nineteen. It was the pre-relief, pre-WPA world of the depression. I would start running as soon as I got off the streetcar, running up the stairs, the place smelling sour, and awake or asleep to startle awake, when she saw me she would break into a clogged weeping that could not be comforted, a weeping I can yet hear.

After a while I found a job hashing at night so I could be with her days, and it was better. But it came to where I had to bring her to his family and leave her.

It took a long time to raise the money for her fare back. Then she got chicken pox and I had to wait longer. When she finally came, I hardly knew her, walking quick and nervous like her father, looking like her father, thin, and dressed in a shoddy red that yellowed her skin and glared at the pock marks. All the baby loveliness gone.

She was two. Old enough for nursery school they said, and I did not know then what I know now—the fatigue of the long day, and the lacerations of group life in nurseries that are only parking places for children.

Except that it would have made no difference if I had known. It was the only place there was. It was the only way we could be together, the only way I could hold a job.

And even without knowing, I knew. I knew the teacher that was evil because all these years it has curdled into my memory, the little boy hunched in the corner, her rasp, "why aren't you outside, because Alvin hits you? that's no reason, go out, scaredy." I knew Emily hated it even if she did not clutch and implore "don't go Mommy" like the other children, mornings.

She always had a reason why we should stay home. Momma, you look sick.

Momma, I feel sick. Momma, the teachers aren't there today, they're sick. Momma, we can't go, there was a fire there last night. Momma, it's a holiday today, no school, they told me.

But never a direct protest, never rebellion. I think of our others in their three-, four-year-oldness—the explosions, the tempers, the denunciations, the demands—and I feel suddenly ill. I put the iron down. What in me demanded that goodness in her? And what was the cost, the cost to her of such goodness?

The old man living in the back once said in his gentle way: "You should smile at Emily more when you look at her." What *was* in my face when I looked at her? I loved her. There were all the acts of love.

It was only with the others I remembered what he said, and it was the face of joy, and not of care or tightness or worry I turned to them—too late for Emily. She does not smile easily, let alone almost always as her brothers and sisters do. Her face is closed and sombre, but when she wants, how fluid. You must have seen it in her pantomimes, you spoke of her rare gift for comedy on the stage that rouses a laughter out of the audience so dear they applaud and applaud and do not want to let her go.

Where does it come from, that comedy? There was none of it in her when she came back to me that second time, after I had had to send her away again. She had a new daddy now to learn to love, and I think perhaps it was a better time. Except when we left her alone nights, telling ourselves she was old enough.

"Can't you go some other time, Mommy, like tomorrow?" she would ask. "Will it be just a little while you'll be gone? Do you promise?"

The time we came back, the front door open, the clock on the floor in the hall. She rigid awake. "It wasn't just a little while. I didn't cry. Three times I called you, just three times, and then I ran downstairs to open the door so you could come faster. The clock talked loud. I threw it away, it scared me what it talked."

She said the clock talked loud again that night I went to the hospital to have Susan. She was delirious with the fever that comes before red measles, but she was fully conscious all the week I was gone and the week after we were home when she could not come near the new baby or me.

She did not get well. She stayed skeleton thin, not wanting to eat, and night after night she had nightmares. She would call for me, and I would rouse from exhaustion to sleepily call back: "You're all right, darling, go to sleep, it's just a dream," and if she still called, in a sterner voice, "now go to sleep, Emily, there's nothing to hurt you." Twice, only twice, when I had to get up for Susan anyhow, I went in to sit with her.

Now when it is too late (as if she would let me hold and comfort her like I do the others) I get up and go to her at once at her moan or restless stirring. "Are you awake, Emily? Can I get you something, dear?" And the answer is always the same: "No, I'm all right, go back to sleep, Mother."

They persuaded me at the clinic to send her away to a convalescent home in the country where "she can have the kind of food and care you can't manage for her, and you'll be free to concentrate on the new baby." They still send children to that place. I see pictures on the society page of sleek young women planning affairs to raise money for it, or dancing at the affairs, or decorating Easter eggs or filling Christmas stockings for the children.

They never have a picture of the children so I do not know if the girls still wear those gigantic red bows and the ravaged looks on the every other Sunday when parents can come to visit "unless otherwise notified"—as we were notified the first six weeks.

Oh it is a handsome place, green lawns and tall trees and fluted flower beds. High up on the balconies of each cottage the children stand, the girls in their red bows and white dresses, the boys in white suits and giant red ties. The parents stand below shrieking up to be heard and the children shriek down to be heard, and between them the invisible wall "Not To Be Contaminated by Parental Germs or Physical Affection."

There was a tiny girl who always stood hand in hand with Emily. Her parents never came. One visit she was gone. "They moved her to Rose Cottage," Emily shouted in explanation. "They don't like you to love anybody here."

She wrote once a week, the laboured writing of a seven-year-old. "I am fine. How is the baby. If I write my leter nicely I will have a star. Love." There never was a star. We wrote every other day, letters she could never hold or keep but only hear read—once. "We simply do not have room for children to keep any personal possessions," they patiently explained when we pieced one Sunday's shrieking together to plead how much it would mean to Emily, who loved so to keep things, to be allowed to keep her letters and cards.

Each visit she looked frailer. "She isn't eating," they told us.

(They had runny eggs for breakfast or mush with lumps, Emily said later, I'd hold it in my mouth and not swallow. Nothing ever tasted good, just when they had chicken.)

It took us eight months to get her released home, and only the fact that she gained back so little of her seven lost pounds convinced the social worker.

I used to try to hold and love her after she came back, but her body would stay stiff, and after a while she'd push away. She ate little. Food sickened her, and I think much of life too. Oh she had physical lightness and brightness, twinkling by on skates, bouncing like a ball up and down up and down over the jump rope, skimming over the hill; but these were momentary.

She fretted about her appearance, thin and dark and foreign-looking at a time when every little girl was supposed to look or thought she should look a chubby blonde replica of Shirley Temple. The door-bell sometimes rang for her, but no one seemed to come and play in the house or be a best friend. Maybe because we moved so much.

There was a boy she loved painfully through two school semesters. Months later she told me how she had taken pennies from my purse to buy him candy. "Liquorice was his favourite and I brought him some every day, but he still liked Jennifer better'n me. Why, Mommy?" The kind of question for which there is no answer.

School was a worry to her. She was not glib or quick in a world where glibness and quickness were easily confused with ability to learn. To her overworked and exasperated teachers she was an overconscientious "slow learner" who kept trying to catch up and was absent entirely too often.

I let her be absent, though sometimes the illness was imaginary. How different from my now-strictness about attendance with the others. I wasn't working. We had a new baby, I was home anyhow. Sometimes, after Susan grew old enough, I would keep her home from school, too, to have them all together.

Mostly Emily had asthma, and her breathing, harsh and laboured, would fill the house with a curiously tranquil sound. I would bring the two old dresser mirrors and her boxes of collections to her bed. She would select beads and single ear-rings, bottle tops and shells, dried flowers and pebbles, old postcards and scraps, all sorts of oddments; then she and Susan would play Kingdom, setting up landscapes and furniture, peopling them with action.

Those were the only times of peaceful companionship between her and Susan. I have edged away from it, that poisonous feeling between them, that terrible balancing of hurts and needs I had to do between the two, and did so badly, those earlier years.

Oh there are conflicts between the others too, each one human, needing, demanding, hurting, taking—but only between Emily and Susan, no, Emily toward Susan that corroding resentment. It seems so obvious on the surface, yet it is not obvious. Susan, the second child, Susan, golden- and curly-haired and chubby, quick and articulate and assured, everything in appearance and manner Emily was not; Susan, not able to resist Emily's precious things, losing or sometimes clumsily breaking them; Susan telling jokes and riddles to company for applause while Emily sat silent (to say to me later: that was *my* riddle, Mother, I told it to Susan); Susan, who for all the five years' difference in age was just a year behind Emily in developing physically.

I am glad for that slow physical development that widened the difference between her and her contemporaries, though she suffered over it. She was too vulnerable for that terrible world of youthful competition, of preening and parading, of constant measuring of yourself against every other, of envy, "If I had that copper hair," or "If I had that skin. . . . " She tormented herself enough about not looking like the others, there was enough of the unsureness, the having to be conscious of words before you speak, the constant caring—what are they thinking of me? What kind of an impression am I making?—there was enough without having it all magnified by the merciless physical drives.

Ronnie is calling. He is wet and I change him. It is rare there is such a cry now. That time of motherhood is almost behind me when the ear is not one's own but must always be racked and listening for the child cry, the child call. We sit for a while and I hold him, looking out over the city spread in charcoal with its soft aisles of light. "*Shoogily*," he breathes and curls closer. I carry him back to bed, asleep. *Shoogily*. A funny word, a family word, inherited from Emily, invented by her to say: *comfort*.

In this and other ways she leaves her seal, I say aloud. And startle at my saying it. What do I mean? What did I start to gather together, to try and make coherent? I was at the terrible, growing years. War years. I do not remember them well. I was working, there were four smaller ones now, there was not time for her. She had to help be a mother, and housekeeper, and shopper. She had to set her seal. Mornings of crisis and near hysteria trying to get lunches packed, hair combed, coats and shoes found, everyone to school or Child Care on time, the baby ready for transportation. And always the paper scribbled on by a smaller one, the book looked at by Susan then mislaid, the homework not done. Running out to that huge school where she was one, she was lost, she was a drop; suffering over the unpreparedness, stammering and unsure in her classes.

There was so little time left at night after the kids were bedded down. She would struggle over books, always eating (it was in those years she developed her enormous appetite that is legendary in our family) and I would be ironing, or preparing food for the next day, or writing V-mail to Bill, or tending the baby. Sometimes, to make me laugh, or out of her despair, she would imitate happenings or types at school.

I think I said once: "Why don't you do something like this in the school amateur show?" One morning she phoned me at work, hardly understandable through the weeping: "Mother, I did it. I won, I won; they gave me first prize; they clapped and clapped and wouldn't let me go."

Now suddenly she was Somebody, and as imprisoned in her difference as she had been in anonymity.

She began to be asked to perform at other high schools, even in colleges, then at city and state-wide affairs. The first one we went to, I only recognized her that first moment when thin, shy, she almost drowned herself into the curtains. Then: Was this Emily? The control, the command, the convulsing and deadly clowning, the spell, then the roaring, stamping audience, unwilling to let this rare and precious laughter out of their lives.

Afterwards: You ought to do something about her with a gift like that—but without money or knowing how, what does one do? We have left it all to her, and the gift has as often eddied inside, clogged and clotted, as been used and growing.

She is coming. She runs up the stairs two at a time with her light graceful step, and I know she is happy tonight. Whatever it was that occasioned your call did not happen today.

"Aren't you ever going to finish the ironing, Mother? Whistler painted his mother in a rocker. I'd have to paint mine standing over an ironing-board." This is one of her communicative nights and she tells me everything and nothing as she fixes herself a plate of food out of the icebox.

She is so lovely. Why did you want me to come in at all? Why were you concerned? She will find her way.

She starts up the stairs to bed. "Don't get me up with the rest in the morning." "But I thought you were having midterms." "Oh, those," she comes back in, kisses me, and says quite lightly, "in a couple of years when we'll all be atom-dead they won't matter a bit."

She has said it before. She *believes* it. But because I have been dredging the past, and all that compounds a human being is so heavy and meaningful in me, I cannot endure it tonight.

I will never total it all. I will never come in to say: She was a child seldom smiled at. Her father left me before she was a year old. I had to work her first six years when there was work, or I sent her home and to his relatives. There were years she had care she hated. She was dark and thin and foreign-looking in a world where the prestige went to blondeness and curly hair and dimples, she was slow where glibness was prized. She was a child of anxious, not proud, love. We were poor and could not afford for her the soil of easy growth. I was a young mother, I was a distracted mother. There were the other children pushing up, demanding. Her younger sister seemed all that she was not. There were years she did not want me to touch her. She kept too much in herself, her life was such she had to keep too much in herself. My wisdom came too late. She has much to her and probably nothing will come of it. She is a child of her age, of depression, of war, of fear.

Let her be. So all that is in her will not bloom—but in how many does it? There is still enough left to live by. Only help her to know—help make it so there is cause for her to know that she is more than this dress on the ironing-board, helpless before the iron.

JOURNAL WRITINGS

1. List several of the events in Emily's childhood and background. Do you think they affected her? Why? Then **narrate** an incident or situation from your own childhood that had the *potential* to influence your personality, attitude toward life, or later behavior. Explain why you think this incident or situation did or did not have a determining influence on your life.
2. Why does the mother speak to herself instead of addressing the school counselor directly? Should the mother meet with this person to discuss Emily's problems? Why or why not?

BRAINSTORMING AND DRAFTING

3. Recalling Emily's comedy act in the school show, her mother tells us: "Now suddenly she was Somebody, and as imprisoned in her difference as she had been in anonymity." Draft a paragraph discussing several ways in which Emily was "imprisoned" during her childhood and adolescence. In a second paragraph, explain whether you agree with the mother that the comedy performance is simply a different kind of imprisonment, or whether you feel her acting is a move toward freedom.
4. How free were the mother's choices in the story? List reasons for your answer. To what degree, if any, is she responsible for Emily's personality and behavior?

THE AUTHOR'S METHODS

5. What is the significance of the title, particularly in the context of the last sentence of the story? Consider any possible **symbolic** overtones suggested by the iron, its movement, the dress, the mother's action of standing, etc.
6. In the last two paragraphs, the **narrator summarizes** and then **concludes**

the story. In what sense is her conclusion different from her summary? Examine your own ending paragraphs for a paper that you have written recently. What is the purpose of these paragraphs? Would you describe them as summaries or conclusions? **Revise** or **edit** them so that they serve you better as conclusions.

FORMAL WRITING AND RESEARCH PAPERS

7.   Write a paper **comparing** and/or **contrasting** the way Emily responds to her "imprisonment" with the way Peter, in Baldwin's story, responds to his limitations. (You may wish to consult your answer to Brainstorming question 3 above.) In preparing to write, you might think about how each character would **define** freedom, the ways in which each tries to solve problems, how successful each one is, and reasons for successes or failures. One way to **conclude** the paper might be to decide whether one character would be more likely than the other to progress toward freedom.

8.   Olsen's **description** of Emily's institutional care is strongly negative, and the mother seems to imply that such harsh, impersonal care may have had a determining effect on her life. Identify an educational or health-care institution in your area that specializes in young children's care (perhaps a nursery school, kindergarten, or children's hospital). Do some field research on the kind of care the children receive there. That is, observe and record the actions of personnel and children for several hours or perhaps on several occasions. Then write a paper in which you **describe** the kind of care the children receive and assess its probable effect on their lives. In a second section of your paper, **compare/contrast** this care and its effect with Emily's treatment and its negative effect on her life.

Dorothea Lange

Migrant Mother

(1936)

Born in Hoboken, New Jersey, Dorothea Lange (1895–1965) studied education at the New York Training School for Teachers but later turned to photography, which had interested her from her adolescent years. Beginning with a portrait business, she became concerned with the pressing and basic needs of people she saw in the streets during the depression. Hired by the federal government to document these concerns, she worked for photography editor Roy Stryker of the Farm Security Administration. Through her photos, she demonstrated how the lives of landowners and migrant workers were tragically shaped by economics, weather, and technology. Her works are housed in the Oakland Museum and in the Library of Congress.

Migrant Mother, her most famous photograph, was taken when she couldn't resist stopping at a pea-pickers camp in Nipomo, California, one rainy night, though she was weary from an already completed assignment and anxious to return to her own family. She found a "hungry and desperate mother" who, asking no questions, allowed Lange to take five exposures. Suggesting several complex and subtle types of bondage, the haunting, now classic photograph pictures a careworn, thirty-two-year-old woman and her children, forced by circumstances to survive by searching for vegetables in the freezing fields nearby.

JOURNAL WRITINGS

1. Write a paragraph in which you imagine the thoughts and feelings of the woman in the photograph. How do you feel watching her? Why might the photographer be interested in your feelings?
2. What freedoms, present and future, do the woman and children lack that many of us take for granted? Would their situation be different today? Explain your answer in a paragraph or two.

BRAINSTORMING AND DRAFTING

3. Draft a paragraph **describing** some of the personality traits you think the mother might have. Discuss **specific** details in the photograph (perhaps her face and hands, and the children's hair) that might suggest these traits. Which of these traits might help her overcome some of her limitations in the future? Explain.

4. **Compare** the woman in Lange's photograph with the woman in Olsen's short story, "I Stand Here Ironing." What concerns might they share about their children? Which woman has less reason to worry? Explain why you think so.

THE PHOTOGRAPHER'S METHODS

5. How does the black and white color affect your view of the picture? What does it suggest about the meaning? How would the effect be different if the photo were in color?

6. Examine all the *lines* you can find in the photo. Write a paragraph explaining how they help to suggest meaning.

FORMAL WRITING AND RESEARCH PAPERS

7. Consult a specialized encyclopedia for a definition of "economic determinism." Also consult some social science indexes such as *Poverty and Human Services Abstracts, P.A.I.S.,* and *Social Sciences Index,* as well as the card or computer catalog, to find some recent information on how poverty influences our choices. Choosing one social group (for example, inner-city residents, white westerners, blacks, native Americans, etc.), write a paper in which you demonstrate some of the ways in which poverty affects people's lives or behavior. Provide specific **examples** to support your assertions. **Conclude** by suggesting some realistic ways that this group can be helped.

Norman Cousins

Anatomy of an Illness as Perceived by the Patient

(1979)

Norman Cousins (1915–1990) attended Teachers College, Columbia University. The highly respected, award-winning editor of the *Saturday Review,* Cousins was also a presidential diplomat and professor of medical humanities at the University of California at Los Angeles. Interested in the arts, politics, and science, he often combined insights from many fields in his writings. His books include *Modern Man is Obsolete, The Last Defense in a Nuclear Age,* and *The Physician in Literature.*

The following selection is taken from *Anatomy of an Illness as Perceived by the Patient: Reflections on Healing and Regeneration.* In this opening chapter, he describes with scientific precision the degenerative, life-threatening disease that nearly overpowered him. Cousins maintains that by tapping the strength of our own wills, we can exert real control over our physical well-being.

PREVIEW

How do you think we might use our minds to exert control over our bodies? Explain your answer.

This . . . is about a serious illness that occurred in 1964. I was reluctant to write about it for many years because I was fearful of creating false hopes in others who were similarly afflicted. Moreover, I knew that a single case has small standing in the annals of medical research, having little more than "anecdotal" or "testimonial" value. However, references to the illness surfaced from time to time in the general and medical press. People wrote to ask whether it was true that I "laughed" my way out of a crippling disease that doctors believed to be irreversible. In view of those questions, I thought it useful to provide a fuller account than appeared in those early reports.

In August 1964, I flew home from a trip abroad with a slight fever. The malaise, which took the form of a general feeling of achiness, rapidly deepened. Within a week it became difficult to move my neck, arms, hands, fingers, and legs. My sedimentation rate was over 80. Of all the diagnostic tests, the "sed" rate is one of the most useful to the physician. The way it works is beautifully simple. The speed with which red blood cells settle in a test tube—measured in millimeters per hour—is generally proportionate to the severity of an inflammation or infection. A normal illness, such as grippe, might produce a sedimentation reading of, say, 30 or even 40. When the rate goes well beyond 60 or 70, however, the physician knows that he is dealing with more than a casual health problem. I was hospitalized when the sed rate hit 88. Within a week it was up to 115, generally considered to be a sign of a critical condition.

There were other tests, some of which seemed to me to be more an assertion of the clinical capability of the hospital than of concern for the well-being of the patient. I was astounded when four technicians from four different departments took four separate and substantial blood samples on the same day. That the hospital didn't take the trouble to coordinate the tests, using one blood specimen, seemed to me inexplicable and irresponsible. Taking four large slugs of blood the same day even from a healthy person is hardly to be recommended. When the technicians came the second day to fill their containers with blood for processing in separate laboratories, I turned them away and had a sign posted on my door saying that I would give just one specimen every three days and that I expected the different departments to draw from one vial for their individual needs.

I had a fast-growing conviction that a hospital is no place for a person who is seriously ill. The surprising lack of respect for basic sanitation; the rapidity with which staphylococci and other pathogenic organisms can run through an entire hospital; the extensive and sometimes promiscuous use of X-ray equipment; the seemingly indiscriminate administration of tranquilizers and powerful pain-killers, sometimes more for the convenience of hospital staff in managing patients than for therapeutic needs; and the regularity with which hospital routine takes precedence over the rest requirements of the patient (slumber, when it comes for an ill person, is an uncommon blessing and is not to be wantonly interrupted)—all these and other practices seemed to me to be critical shortcomings of the modern hospital.

Perhaps the hospital's most serious failure was in the area of nutrition. It was not just that the meals were poorly balanced; what seemed inexcusable to me was the profusion of processed foods, some of which contained preservatives or harmful dyes. White bread, with its chemical softeners and bleached flour, was offered with every meal. Vegetables were often overcooked and thus deprived of much of their nutritional value. No wonder the 1969 White House Conference on Food, Nutrition, and Health made the melancholy observation that a great failure of medical schools is that they pay so little attention to the science of nutrition.

My doctor did not quarrel with my reservations about hospital procedures. I was fortunate to have as a physician a man who was able to put himself in the position of the patient. Dr. William Hitzig supported me in the measures I took to fend off the random sanguinary assaults of the hospital laboratory attendants.

We had been close friends for more than twenty years, and he knew of my own deep interest in medical matters. We had often discussed articles in the medical press, including the *New England Journal of Medicine (NEJM)*, and *Lancet*. He was candid with me about my case. He reviewed the reports of the various specialists he had called in as consultants. He said there was no agreement on a precise diagnosis. There was, however, a consensus that I was suffering from a serious collagen illness—a disease of the connective tissue. All arthritic and rheumatic diseases are in this category. Collagen is the fibrous substance that binds the cells together. In a sense, then, I was coming unstuck. I had considerable difficulty in moving my limbs and even in turning over in bed. Nodules appeared on my body, gravel-like substances under the skin, indicating the systemic nature of the disease. At the low point of my illness, my jaws were almost locked.

Dr. Hitzig called in experts from Dr. Howard Rusk's rehabilitation clinic in New York. They confirmed the general opinion, adding the more particularized diagnosis of ankylosing spondylitis, which would mean that the connective tissue in the spine was disintegrating.

I asked Dr. Hitzig about my chances for full recovery. He leveled with me, admitting that one of the specialists had told him I had one chance in five hundred. The specialist had also stated that he had not personally witnessed a recovery from this comprehensive condition.

All this gave me a great deal to think about. Up to that time, I had been more or less disposed to let the doctors worry about my condition. But now I felt a compulsion to get into the act. It seemed clear to me that if I was to be that one in five hundred I had better be something more than a passive observer.

I asked Dr. Hitzig about the possible origin of my condition. He said that it could have come from any one of a number of causes. It could have come, for example, from heavy-metal poisoning, or it could have been the aftereffect of a streptococcal infection.

I thought as hard as I could about the sequence of events immediately preceding the illness. I had gone to the Soviet Union in July 1964 as chairman of an American delegation to consider the problems of cultural exchange. The conference had been held in Leningrad, after which we went to Moscow for supplementary meetings. Our hotel was in a residential area. My room was on the second floor. Each night a procession of diesel trucks plied back and forth to a nearby housing project in the process of round-the-clock construction. It was summer, and our windows were wide open. I slept uneasily each night and felt somewhat nauseated on arising. On our last day in Moscow, at the airport, I caught the exhaust spew of a large jet at point-blank range as it swung around on the tarmac.

As I thought back on that Moscow experience, I wondered whether the exposure to the hydrocarbons from the diesel exhaust at the hotel and at the airport had anything to do with the underlying cause of the illness. If so, that might account for the speculations of the doctors concerning heavy-metal poisoning. The trouble with this theory, however, was that my wife, who had been with me on the trip, had no ill effects from the same exposure. How likely was it that only one of us would have reacted adversely?

It seemed to me, as I thought about it, that there were two possible explanations for the different reactions. One had to do with individual allergy. The second was that I could have been in a condition of adrenal exhaustion and less apt to tolerate a toxic experience than someone whose immunologic system was fully functional.

Was adrenal exhaustion a factor in my own illness?

Again, I thought carefully. The meetings in Leningrad and Moscow had not been casual. Paper work had kept me up late nights. I had ceremonial responsibilities. Our last evening in Moscow had been, at least for me, an exercise in almost total frustration. A reception had been arranged by the chairman of the Soviet delegation at his dacha, located thirty-five to forty miles outside the city. I had been asked if I could arrive an hour early so that I might tell the Soviet delegates something about the individual Americans who were coming to dinner. The Russians were eager to make the Americans feel at home, and they had thought such information would help them with the social amenities.

I was told that a car and driver from the government automobile pool in Moscow would pick me up at the hotel at 3:30 P.M. This would allow ample time for me to drive to the dacha by 5:00, when all our Russian conference colleagues would be gathered for the social briefing. The rest of the American delegation would arrive at the dacha at 6:00 P.M.

At 6:00, however, I found myself in open country on the wrong side of Moscow. There had been a misunderstanding in the transmission of directions to the driver, the result being that we were some eighty miles off course. We finally got our bearings and headed back to Moscow. Our chauffeur had been schooled in cautious driving; he was not disposed to make up lost time. I kept wishing for a driver with a compulsion to prove that auto racing, like baseball, originally came from the U.S.S.R.

We didn't arrive at the dacha until 9:00 P.M. My host's wife looked desolate. The soup had been heated and reheated. The veal was dried out. I felt pretty wrung out myself. It was a long flight back to the States the next day. The plane was overcrowded. By the time we arrived in New York, cleared through the packed customs counters, and got rolling back to Connecticut, I could feel an uneasiness deep in my bones. A week later I was hospitalized.

As I thought back on my experience abroad, I knew that I was probably on the right track in my search for a cause of the illness. I found myself increasingly convinced, as I said a moment ago, that the reason I was hit hard by the diesel and jet pollutants, whereas my wife was not, was that I had had a case of adrenal exhaustion, lowering my resistance.

Assuming this hypothesis was true, I had to get my adrenal glands functioning properly again and to restore what Walter B. Cannon, in his famous book, *The Wisdom of the Body,* called homeostasis.

I knew that the full functioning of my endocrine system—in particular the adrenal glands—was essential for combating severe arthritis or, for that matter, any other illness. A study I had read in the medical press reported that pregnant women frequently have remissions of arthritic or other rheumatic symptoms. The reason is that the endocrine system is fully activated during pregnancy.

How was I to get my adrenal glands and my endocrine system, in general, working well again?

I remembered having read, ten years or so earlier, Hans Selye's classic book, *The Stress of Life*. With great clarity, Selye showed that adrenal exhaustion could be caused by emotional tension, such as frustration or suppressed rage. He detailed the negative effects of the negative emotions on body chemistry.

The inevitable question arose in my mind: what about the positive emotions? If negative emotions produce negative chemical changes in the body, wouldn't the positive emotions produce positive chemical changes? It is possible that love, hope, faith, laughter, confidence, and the will to live have therapeutic value? Do chemical changes occur only on the downside?

Obviously, putting the positive emotions to work was nothing so simple as turning on a garden hose. But even a reasonable degree of control over my emotions might have a salutary physiologic effect. Just replacing anxiety with a fair degree of confidence might be helpful.

A plan began to form in my mind for systematic pursuit of the salutary emotions, and I knew that I would want to discuss it with my doctor. Two preconditions, however, seemed obvious for the experiment. The first concerned my medication. If that medication were toxic to any degree, it was doubtful whether the plan would work. The second precondition concerned the hospital. I knew I would have to find a place somewhat more conducive to a positive outlook on life.

Let's consider these preconditions separately.

First, the medication. The emphasis had been on pain-killing drugs—aspirin, phenylbutazone (butazolidine), codeine, colchicine, sleeping pills. The aspirin and phenylbutazone were antiinflammatory and thus were therapeutically justifiable. But I wasn't sure they weren't also toxic. It developed that I was hypersensitive to virtually all the medication I was receiving. The hospital had been giving me maximum dosages: twenty-six aspirin tablets and twelve phenylbutazone tablets a day. No wonder I had hives all over my body and felt as though my skin were being chewed up by millions of red ants.

It was unreasonable to expect positive chemical changes to take place so long as my body was being saturated with, and toxified by, pain-killing medications. I had one of my research assistants at the *Saturday Review* look up the pertinent references in the medical journals and found that drugs like phenylbutazone and even aspirin levy a heavy tax on the adrenal glands. I also learned that phenylbutazone is one of the most powerful drugs being manufactured. It can produce bloody stools, the result of its antagonism to fibrinogen. It can cause intolerable itching and sleeplessness. It can depress bone marrow.

Aspirin, of course, enjoys a more auspicious reputation, at least with the general public. The prevailing impression of aspirin is that it is not only the most harmless drug available but also one of the most effective. When I looked into research in the medical journals, however, I found that aspirin is quite powerful in its own right and warrants considerable care in its use. The fact that it can be bought in unlimited quantities without prescription or doctor's guidance seemed indefensible. Even in small amounts, it can cause internal bleeding. Articles in the medical press reported that the chemical composition of aspirin, like that of phenylbutazone, impairs the clotting function of platelets, disc-shaped substances in the blood.

It was a mind-boggling train of thought. Could it be, I asked myself, that aspirin, so universally accepted for so many years, was actually harmful in the treatment of collagen illnesses such as arthritis?

The history of medicine is replete with accounts of drugs and modes of treatment that were in use for many years before it was recognized that they did more harm than good. For centuries, for example, doctors believed that drawing blood from patients was essential for rapid recovery from virtually every illness. Then, midway through the nineteenth century, it was discovered that bleeding served only to weaken the patient. King Charles II's death is believed to have been caused in part by administered bleedings. George Washington's death was also hastened by the severe loss of blood resulting from this treatment.

Living in the second half of the twentieth century, I realized, confers no automatic protection against unwise or even dangerous drugs and methods. Each age has had to undergo its own special nostrums. Fortunately, the human body is a remarkably durable instrument and has been able to withstand all sorts of prescribed assaults over the centuries, from freezing to animal dung.

Suppose I stopped taking aspirin and phenylbutazone? What about the pain? The bones in my spine and practically every joint in my body felt as though I had been run over by a truck.

I knew that pain could be affected by attitudes. Most people become panicky about almost any pain. On all sides they have been so bombarded by advertisements about pain that they take this or that analgesic at the slightest sign of an ache. We are largely illiterate about pain and so are seldom able to deal with it rationally. Pain is part of the body's magic. It is the way the body transmits a sign to the brain that something is wrong. Leprous patients pray for the sensation of pain. What makes leprosy such a terrible disease is that the victim usually feels no pain when his extremities are being injured. He loses his fingers or toes because he receives no warning signal.

I could stand pain so long as I knew that progress was being made in meeting the basic need. That need, I felt, was to restore the body's capacity to halt the continuing breakdown of connective tissue.

There was also the problem of the severe inflammation. If we dispensed with the aspirin, how would we combat the inflammation? I recalled having read in the medical journals about the usefulness of ascorbic acid in combating a wide number of illnesses—all the way from bronchitis to some types of heart disease. Could it also combat inflammation? Did vitamin C act directly, or did it serve as a starter for the body's endocrine system—in particular, the adrenal glands? Was it possible, I asked myself, that ascorbic acid had a vital role to play in "feeding" the adrenal glands?

I had read in the medical press that vitamin C helps to oxygenate the blood. If inadequate or impaired oxygenation was a factor in collagen breakdown, couldn't this circumstance have been another argument for ascorbic acid? Also, according to some medical reports, people suffering from collagen diseases are deficient in vitamin C. Did this lack mean that the body uses up large amounts of vitamin C in the process of combating collagen breakdown?

I wanted to discuss some of these ruminations with Dr. Hitzig. He listened carefully as I told him of my speculations concerning the cause of the illness, as well as my layman's ideas for a course of action that might give me a chance to reduce the odds against my recovery.

Dr. Hitzig said it was clear to him that there was nothing undersized about my will to live. He said that what was most important was that I continue to believe in everything I had said. He shared my excitement about the possibilities of recovery and liked the idea of a partnership.

Even before we had completed arrangements for moving out of the hospital we began the part of the program calling for the full exercise of the affirmative emotions as a factor in enhancing body chemistry. It was easy enough to hope and love and have faith, but what about laughter? Nothing is less funny than being flat on your back with all the bones in your spine and joints hurting. A systematic program was indicated. A good place to begin, I thought, was with amusing movies. Allen Funt, producer of the spoofing television program "Candid Camera," sent films of some of his CC classics, along with a motion-picture projector. The nurse was instructed in its use. We were even able to get our hands on some old Marx Brothers films. We pulled down the blinds and turned on the machine.

It worked. I made the joyous discovery that ten minutes of genuine belly laughter had an anesthetic effect and would give me at least two hours of pain-free sleep. When the pain-killing effect of the laughter wore off, we would switch on the motion-picture projector again, and, not infrequently, it would lead to another pain-free sleep interval. Sometimes, the nurse read to me out of a trove of humor books. Especially useful were E. B. and Katharine White's *Subtreasury of American Humor* and Max Eastman's *The Enjoyment of Laughter.*

How scientific was it to believe that laughter—as well as the positive emotions in general—was affecting my body chemistry for the better? If laughter did in fact have a salutary effect on the body's chemistry, it seemed at least theoretically likely that it would enhance the system's ability to fight the inflammation. So we took sedimentation rate reading just before as well as several hours after the laughter episodes. Each time, there was a drop of at least five points. The drop by itself was not substantial, but it held and was cumulative. I was greatly elated by the discovery that there is a physiologic basis for the ancient theory that laughter is good medicine.

There was, however, one negative side-effect of the laughter from the standpoint of the hospital. I was disturbing other patients. But that objection didn't last very long, for the arrangements were now complete for me to move my act to a hotel room.

One of the incidental advantages of the hotel room, I was delighted to find, was that it cost only about one-third as much as the hospital. The other benefits were incalculable. I would not be awakened for a bed bath or for meals or for medication or for a change of bed sheets or for tests or for examinations by hospital interns. The sense of serenity was delicious and would, I felt certain, contribute to a general improvement.

What about ascorbic acid and its place in the general program for recovery? In discussing my speculations about vitamin C with Dr. Hitzig, I found him completely open-minded on the subject, although he told me of serious questions that had been raised by scientific studies. He also cautioned me that heavy doses of ascorbic acid carried some risk of renal damage. The main problem right then, however, was not my kidneys; it seemed to me that, on balance, the risk was worth taking. I asked Dr. Hitzig about previous recorded experience with massive doses of vitamin C. He ascertained that at the hospital there had been cases in which patients had received up to 3 grams by intramuscular injection.

As I thought about the injection procedure, some questions came to mind. Introducing the ascorbic acid directly into the bloodstream might make more effective use of the vitamin, but I wondered about the body's ability to utilize a sudden, massive infusion. I knew that one of the great advantages of vitamin C is that the body takes only the amount necessary for its purposes and excretes the rest. Again, there came to mind Cannon's phrase—the wisdom of the body.

Was there a coefficient of time in the utilization of ascorbic acid? The more I thought about it, the more likely it seemed to me that the body would excrete a large quantity of the vitamin because it couldn't metabolize it fast enough. I wondered whether a better procedure than injection would be to administer the ascorbic acid through slow intravenous drip over a period of three or four hours. In this way we could go far beyond 3 grams. My hope was to start at 10 grams and then increase the dose daily until we reached 25 grams.

Dr. Hitzig's eyes widened when I mentioned 25 grams. This amount was far beyond any recorded dose. He said he had to caution me about the possible effect not just on the kidneys but on the veins in the arms. Moreover, he said he knew of no data to support the assumption that the body could handle 25 grams over a four-hour period, other than by excreting it rapidly through the urine.

As before, however, it seemed to me we were playing for bigger stakes: losing some veins was not of major importance alongside the need to combat whatever was eating at my connective tissue.

To know whether we were on the right track we took a sedimentation test before the first intravenous administration of 10 grams of ascorbic acid. Four hours later, we took another sedimentation test. There was a drop of nine full points.

Seldom had I known such elation. The ascorbic acid was working. So was laughter. The combination was cutting heavily into whatever poison was attacking the connective tissue. The fever was receding, and the pulse was no longer racing.

We stepped up the dosage. On the second day we went to 12.5 grams of ascorbic acid, on the third day, 15 grams, and so on until the end of the week, when we reached 25 grams. Meanwhile, the laughter routine was in full force. I was completely off drugs and sleeping pills. Sleep—blessed, natural sleep without pain—was becoming increasingly prolonged.

At the end of the eighth day I was able to move my thumbs without pain. By this time, the sedimentation rate was somewhere in the 80s and dropping fast. I couldn't be sure, but it seemed to me that the gravel-like nodules on my neck and the backs of my hands were beginning to shrink. There was no doubt in my mind that I was going to make it back all the way. I could function, and the feeling was indescribably beautiful.

I must not make it appear that all my infirmities disappeared overnight. For many months I couldn't get my arms up far enough to reach for a book on a high shelf. My fingers weren't agile enough to do what I wanted them to do on the organ keyboard. My neck had a limited turning radius. My knees were somewhat wobbly, and off and on, I have had to wear a metal brace.

Even so, I was sufficiently recovered to go back to my job at the *Saturday Review* full time again, and this was miracle enough for me.

Is the recovery a total one? Year by year the mobility has improved. I have become pain-free, except for one shoulder and my knees, although I have been able to discard the metal braces. I no longer feel a sharp twinge in my wrists when I hit a tennis ball or golf ball, as I did for such a long time. I can ride a horse flat out and hold a camera with a steady hand. And I have recaptured my ambition to play the Toccata and Fugue in D Minor, though I find the going slower and tougher than I had hoped. My neck has a full turning radius again, despite the statement of specialists as recently as 1971 that the condition was degenerative and that I would have to adjust to a quarter turn.

It was seven years after the onset of the illness before I had scientific confirmation about the dangers of using aspirin in the treatment of collagen diseases. In its May 8, 1971 issue, *Lancet* published a study by Drs. M. A. Sahud and R. J. Cohen showing that aspirin can be antagonistic to the retention of vitamin C in the body. The authors said that patients with rheumatoid arthritis should take vitamin C supplements, since it has often been noted that they have low levels of the vitamin in their blood. It was no surprise, then, that I had been able to absorb such massive amounts of ascorbic acid without kidney or other complications.

What conclusions do I draw from the entire experience?

The first is that the will to live is not a theoretical abstraction, but a physiologic reality with therapeutic characteristics. The second is that I was incredibly fortunate to have as my doctor a man who knew that his biggest job was to encourage to the fullest the patient's will to live and to mobilize all the natural resources of body and mind to combat disease. Dr. Hitzig was willing to set aside the large and often hazardous armamentarium of powerful drugs available to the modern physician when he became convinced that his patient might have something better to offer. He was also wise enough to know that the art of healing is still a frontier profession. And, though I can't be sure of this point, I have a hunch he believed that my own total involvement was a major factor in my recovery.

People have asked what I thought when I was told by the specialists that my disease was progressive and incurable.

The answer is simple. Since I didn't accept the verdict, I wasn't trapped in the cycle of fear, depression, and panic that frequently accompanies a supposedly incurable illness. I must not make it seem, however, that I was unmindful of the seriousness of the problem or that I was in a festive mood throughout. Being unable to move my body was all the evidence I needed that the specialists were dealing with real concerns. But deep down, I knew I had a good chance and relished the idea of bucking the odds.

Adam Smith, in his book, *Powers of the Mind,* says he discussed my recovery with some of his doctor friends, asking them to explain why the combination of laughter and ascorbic acid worked so well. The answer he got was that neither laughter nor ascorbic acid had anything to do with it and that I probably would have recovered if nothing had been done.

Maybe so, but that was not the opinion of the specialists at the time.

Two or three doctors, reflecting on the Adam Smith account, have commented that I was probably the beneficiary of a mammoth venture in self-administered placebos.*

Such a hypothesis bothers me not at all. Respectable names in the history of medicine, like Paracelsus, Holmes, and Osler, have suggested that the history of medication is far more the history of the placebo effect than of intrinsically valuable and relevant drugs. Such modalities as bleeding (in a single year, 1827, France imported 33 million leeches after its domestic supplies had been depleted); purging through emetics;** physical contact with unicorn† horns, bezoar stones,‡ mandrakes,§ or powdered mummies—all such treatments were no doubt regarded by physicians at the time as specifics with empirical sanction. But today's medical science recognizes that whatever efficacy these treatments may have had—and the records indicate that the results were often surprisingly in line with expectations—was probably related to the power of the placebo.

Until comparatively recently, medical literature on the phenomenon of the placebo has been rather sparse. But the past two decades have seen a pronounced interest in the subject. Indeed, three medical researchers at the University of California, Los Angeles, have compiled an entire volume on a bibliography of the placebo. (J. Turner, R. Gallimore, C. Fox, *Placebo: An Annotated Bibliography.* The Neuropsychiatric Institute, University of California, Los Angeles, 1974.) Among the medical researchers who have been prominently engaged in such studies are Arthur K. Shapiro, Stewart Wolf, Henry K. Beecher, and Louis Lasagna. . . . In connection with my own experience, I was fascinated by a report citing a study by Dr. Thomas C. Chalmers, of the Mount Sinai Medical

---

* placebo—a chemical substance having no effect but administered to someone who expects it to have a medicinal effect. [Eds.]

** emetic—a substance that induces vomiting. [Eds.]

† unicorn—in mythology, a horselike creature with a single horn in the middle of its forehead. [Eds.]

‡ bezoar stones—stones from the stomach or intestines of animals, formerly used as an antidote to poisons. [Eds.]

± mandrakes—European herbs with narcotic properties. [Eds.]

Center in New York, which compared two groups that were being used to test the theory that ascorbic acid is a cold preventative. "The group on placebo who thought they were on ascorbic acid," says Dr. Chalmers, "had fewer colds than the group on ascorbic acid who thought they were on placebo."

I was absolutely convinced, at the time I was deep in my illness, that intravenous doses of ascorbic acid could be beneficial—and they were. It is quite possible that this treatment—like everything else I did—was a demonstration of the placebo effect.

At this point, of course, we are opening a very wide door, perhaps even a Pandora's box. The vaunted "miracle cures" that abound in the literature of all the great religions all say something about the ability of the patient, properly motivated or stimulated, to participate actively in extraordinary reversals of disease and disability. It is all too easy, of course, to raise these possibilities and speculations to a monopoly status—in which case the entire edifice of modern medicine would be reduced to little more than the hut of an African witch doctor. But we can at least reflect on William Halse Rivers's statement, as quoted by Shapiro, that "the salient feature of the medicine of today is that these psychical factors are no longer allowed to play their part unwittingly, but are themselves becoming the subject of study, so that the present age is serving the growth of a rational system of psychotherapeutics."

What we are talking about essentially, I suppose, is the chemistry of the will to live. In Bucharest in 1972, I visited the clinic of Ana Aslan, described to me as one of Romania's leading endocrinologists. She spoke of her belief that there is a direct connection between a robust will to live and the chemical balances in the brain. She is convinced that creativity—one aspect of the will to live—produces the vital brain impulses that stimulate the pituitary gland, triggering effects on the pineal gland and the whole of the endocrine system. Is it possible that placebos have a key role in this process? Shouldn't this entire area be worth serious and sustained attention?

If I had to guess, I would say that the principal contribution made by my doctor to the taming, and possibly the conquest, of my illness was that he encouraged me to believe I was a respected partner with him in the total undertaking. He fully engaged my subjective energies. He may not have been able to define or diagnose the process through which self-confidence (wild hunches securely believed) was somehow picked up by the body's immunologic mechanisms and translated into antimorbid effects, but he was acting, I believe, in the best tradition of medicine in recognizing that he had to reach out in my case beyond the usual verifiable modalities. In so doing, he was faithful to the first dictum in his medical education: above all, do not harm.

Something else I have learned. I have learned never to underestimate the capacity of the human mind and body to regenerate—even when the prospects seem most wretched. The life-force may be the least understood force on earth. William James said that human beings tend to live too far within self-imposed limits. It is possible that these limits will recede when we respect more fully the natural drive of the human mind and body toward perfectibility and regeneration. Protecting and cherishing that natural drive may well represent the finest exercise of human freedom.

JOURNAL WRITINGS

1. In a paragraph, **describe** your own behavior or that of a person you know during the course of an illness. What decisions did you or that person make to influence the progress of the illness? What decisions were made for you or that person? Now that you've read Cousins's article, how much control do you think you or that person had over the progress of the illness?
2. How does Cousins demonstrate the ability to control his body? What similarities exist between his attitude and religious faith?

BRAINSTORMING AND DRAFTING

3. In a college dictionary, look up the difference between *determinism* and *determination*. How does each of these words apply to the situation that Cousins describes? Use evidence from the article to support your answer.
4. Through his attitude and actions, Cousins sometimes chose to assert his own will in opposition to medical authorities. Draft a paragraph in which you speculate on the dangers he could have encountered by making this choice. In a second paragraph, **analyze** the way that he managed his "rebellion" so as to lessen the probability of these dangers.
5. In what sense might Cousins's **thesis** be considered a solution to the problems of Peter, in Baldwin's story, or of the **narrator** in Gilman's story? What makes these two characters less likely to adopt Cousins's type of solution?

THE AUTHOR'S METHODS

6. Cousins uses several types of evidence to persuade us of the validity of his experience. Find an **example** of each type in the reading: (a) personal anecdote; (b) scientific study; (c) explanation; (d) statistics; (e) logical reasoning; (f) **allusion** to an authority. Then write a paragraph explaining which types are *most* and *least* likely to persuade you. Give reasons for your answer.
7. Is Cousins writing for an audience of scientists, nonscientists, or both? Cite **specific** features of the writing that lead you to this conclusion. Re-examine one of your own paragraphs written in response to any of the preceding questions for this reading. Who did you assume was your audience for this paragraph? What features of your writing are directed toward that audience?

FORMAL WRITING AND RESEARCH PAPERS

8. Write a paper in which you recommend several ways by which we can assume responsibility over our bodies. (Your answer to the Preview question may be helpful here.) Explain each of your recommendations in detail, and be sure to present each in the context of our ability to influence the health or well-being of our bodies.

9. Find several sources dealing with the will or lack of will demonstrated by patients in nursing homes or rehabilitation programs. (Try the *General Science Index*, the *Social Sciences Index*, *Sociological Abstracts*, and the card or computer catalog. You might also interview an administrator or nurse in these health-care facilities.) Write a paper in which you demonstrate that the exertion of willpower does or does not affect these patients' health. Recommend ways to enhance the effect of willpower, or suggest reasons why no such effect seems evident.

Rabindranath Tagore

Freedom

(1921)

Rabindranath Tagore (1861–1941) was born in Calcutta, West Bengal, India. Although he considered himself primarily a poet, he was famous not only for his outstanding poetry but also for an incredible output of plays, short stories, novels, and essays on history, religion, philosophy, politics, and other subjects; he was also a musician, painter, actor, and teacher. In his childhood, he had rebelled against formal schooling, preferring to educate himself through life experience, but he did attend University College in London. Writing in his native Bengali, he expressed humanistic, sometimes mystical interests and tried to achieve a fusion of ideas between East and West. He was a major influence on modern Indian culture, but his works have also been translated into many languages.

He received the Nobel Prize for Literature in 1913 for his poem *Gitanjali,* an attempt to find spiritual peace after the deaths of several family members. The following poem is from *The Fugitive and Other Poems.* Written in free verse, it does not take the form of more traditional poetry. Nevertheless, the poem uses several traditional poetic devices to emphasize the subtle complexities that threaten our freedom.

PREVIEW

Now that you have read many of the selections in this unit, make a list of the things from which you want to be free.

Freedom from fear is the freedom I claim for you, my Motherland!
—fear, the phantom demon, shaped by your own distorted dreams;
Freedom from the burden of ages, bending your head, breaking your back, blinding your eyes to the beckoning call of the future;
Freedom from shackles of slumber wherewith you fasten yourself to night's stillness, mistrusting the star that speaks of truth's adventurous path;
Freedom from the anarchy of a destiny, whose sails are weakly yielded to blind uncertain winds, and the helm to a hand ever rigid and cold as Death;
Freedom from the insult of dwelling in a puppet's world, where movements are started through brainless wires, repeated through mindless habits; where

figures wait with patient obedience for a master of show to be stirred into a moment's mimicry of life.

JOURNAL WRITINGS

1. Tagore calls fear "the phantom demon." In what sense is fear like a demon in the life of a country? In your own life? How is fear like a phantom?
2. Write a paragraph on "the burden of ages" in your own life. For example, you might discuss any past habits, patterns, customs, attitudes, personality traits, or actions of your ancestors, etc., that have burdened or limited you. Speculate on what you might do to free yourself.

BRAINSTORMING AND DRAFTING

3. In a small group (or working individually), list several different kinds of limitations that Tagore mentions in the poem (for example, fear). Then match each limitation with one or more **readings** in this unit that discuss or imply the same kind of limitation. Finally, each person should choose one limitation. After considering Tagore's comments on it as well as the ideas in the corresponding readings, draft a paragraph **arguing** the importance of achieving freedom from this particular limitation.
4. By referring to his Motherland in the opening line, Tagore seems to place his ideas into a political context. How would you **define** political freedom? How would you **classify** the other types he mentions? In what sense are they related to political freedom?

THE AUTHOR'S METHODS

5. List the different types of repetition in the poem. Write a paragraph explaining how repetition helps reveal the author's meaning. Use **examples** from the poem to support your ideas.
6. Tagore chose a nontraditional form for the poem. That is, it has no set **stanza**, regular **rhythm**, or **rhyme** pattern. Instead, the author uses an "open" form, which can have any number of lines, any length for a line, etc. How does Tagore's choice of form reinforce his words and meaning?

CREATIVE PROJECT

7. Write an original poem about the particular freedoms you discussed in the Preview question.

FORMAL WRITING AND RESEARCH PAPERS

8. Tagore writes about freedoms that he regards as most important to his country. What freedom(s) do you still need to achieve in your own country? Write a paper in which you explain and illustrate one of these freedoms, using specific **examples** to prove your points. Recommend and fully **describe** some realistic steps that will help your country progress toward this freedom.

9. The "burden of ages" in a third-world country may sometimes blind its people's eyes to future change and development. Consult a specialized encyclopedia to define "third-world country." Then find some information on one or more cultural practices or beliefs that you feel limit the people in some way in a particular third-world country. (Try, for example, the *Historical Abstracts* and the *Humanities Index,* as well as the card or computer catalog.) Write a paper in which you explain the problem and recommend some realistic ways by which these people can grow and change.

BROAD PERSPECTIVES ON FREE CHOICE

OverView of the Unit

In the introduction to the Free Choice unit, we mentioned that much disagreement exists on the amount of free choice that human beings can exercise. Think about the positions taken by the authors whom you have read in this unit. Without trying to assign philosophical labels to them, decide how you might group them according to how much (or how little) self-determination they grant to the people or groups of people whom they describe. Write a paper in which you explain their positions in some logical order (say, from least amount of self-determination to the most amount, or from most to least, or whatever order you find most appropriate). For each author, cite **specific** evidence from the reading or illustration to support your interpretation.

ClusterWritings

1. To what degree do you have free choice in your own life? Consider carefully the different aspects of human experience that you have studied in this unit. Use some of the information you have gained from these readings to support your ideas in a personal experience paper.

2. Using several readings as evidence, write a paper indicating whether—or to what degree—you think we can exert control over our *moral* selves. You may wish to review the selections by Milton, Sartre, Nin, Bagdikian, Olsen, and Milgram as possible evidence for your **argument**.

3. Are people's choices limited by their gender? If you think so, identify and

give **examples** of some areas of limitation and explain in detail a few ways to resolve the problem. If you think not, give several reasons and **examples** that illustrate your position. In either case, use several sources from the unit to support your **thesis**. (Consider, for example, the selections by Gilman, Sawyer, Freedman, A. Walker, Jones, Nin, and Olsen.)

4.   At times we may feel pressured to behave in a certain way because, in our minds, we have established a group or an individual as our "authority." Write an **essay** with a **thesis** about the general pattern of your own behavior in such situations. Refer to several types of "authorities" who exert pressure on your choices by alluding to selections from this unit. Possible sources might include Bagdikian, Milgram, Fromm, Gilman, Sawyer, Freedman, A. Walker, M. Walker.

5.   Some of the readings in this unit may seem more difficult than others. What makes a reading difficult? What makes it easier? Write an **essay** in which you establish criteria for difficult and easier readings. Use a variety of **examples** from the readings in this unit to illustrate each of your criteria.

6.   Economics affects (or can affect) choice in the selections by Olsen, Bagdikian, and Lange. **Describe** several different types of economic pressure suggested by these authors, indicating clearly how each one affects choice. Use **specific** details from the readings to illustrate your ideas. For each type of pressure you discuss, propose a manageable way to begin reducing such pressure in the future.

7.   The poet Tagore speaks of "fear, the phantom demon." Write a paper in which you explain how fear limits our freedom. Refer to selections in the unit to support your ideas. (Note that although many of the authors do not necessarily mention fear explicitly, the emotion may be subtly embedded in the selection.) **Conclude** by suggesting ways that human beings can begin to overcome these fears.

8.   Physical problems may seem even more formidable than other limitations as shapers of our choices. Using several selections from the unit, as well as your own knowledge and experience, assess the degree to which physical problems affect human freedom. (Possible sources from the unit include the readings by Cousins, A. Walker, Olsen, Lange.)

UNIT
Four

TECHNOLOGY
External Reality and the Human Person

*T*oolmaking has been a specifically human activity at least since neolithic times. Some anthropologists believe that this toolmaking ability is the crucial factor distinguishing human beings from the great apes. Whether or not that is true, certainly the ability to make and use tools enabled early humans to attain a level of environmental mastery that their predecessors could not. Yet those same early people, the makers of flint arrowheads, obsidian knives, and tightly woven baskets, were also moved to draw pictures of the animals they hunted, to fashion small figures in stone, and to bury flowers with their dead. We are very similar to those early humans, manifesting a desire to explore and understand both the inner dimension (the psychological, emotional, and spiritual parts of ourselves) and the outer dimension (our bodies and the material world in which we live). We continuously develop ways to master our environment, and we consistently assert the distinction between ourselves and that environment.

In this unit you are asked to examine the relationship between these two very different, yet very human, impulses.

On the one hand we experience an outward urge. Build something! Build it to last forever! From the relative simplicity of the stone knife we have advanced to the pyramids and developed the communications satellite. We have moved out of the cave, constructing progressively larger and more sophisticated buildings: the Parthenon, the Eiffel Tower, and the World Trade Center. This outward urge seeks to dominate, to control the world—to make it serve human material needs in every way possible.

Technology is the chief instrument of the outward urge. Do not confuse it with science, which is more recent and more abstract. Science is also an outward-looking process, but it strives merely to understand. Technology is the means by which humans manipulate things. Some examples may help you understand the difference between science and technology. Scientific study of the habits of salmon reveals that these fish return to the same streams at the same time year after year in order to spawn. Thousands of years ago the primitive technology of native-American tribes produced the nets (with a specific mesh size) to catch the returning fish most efficiently. This example illustrates how technology can exist before any formal science. But the opposite can also be true. The theoretical formulations about the nature of the atom were a necessary prerequisite to building the first atomic pile (the predecessor of nuclear power plants). This example demonstrates the more recent (and now more typical) situation in which scientific advancement produces technology of one sort or another.

Even as we listen to the voice of technology with its outward urge, we simultaneously experience an inward urge. Call it psyche, soul, spirit, or mind, men and women intuit within themselves a set of powers unrelated to the physical world. Among these powers are memory, reason, judgment, and feeling. From them arise the questions that we are constantly asking about the essential nature of things, about ourselves, and the world: Who am I? Why am I here? What's it all mean? This inward urge seeks to understand the inner nature of things—the self, other people, the world around us—and to find meaningful relationships among these things.

At the risk of oversimplifying, one might equate these two urges with characteristic human occupations. The engineer, the designer, the builder epitomize the outward urge: the desire to understand the world and to use technology to control the environment. The artist, the mystic, the philosopher epitomize the inward urge: the desire to explore and to comprehend the individual's personal response to reality. In some sense the two groups have divergent purposes, exploring in different directions. Yet in another sense they are convergent, striving to benefit all of humanity. There is a paradox here.

This unit asks you to struggle to resolve this paradox, as thinking individuals have tried to do since neolithic times. This struggle involves understanding not only yourself, but your world as well. Neither of these understandings has ever come easily. Today more than ever, because of accelerating technological change, it has become more difficult (and at the same time more important) to resolve this paradox, to achieve understanding of ourselves and our world.

Enormous technological changes have taken place during the past two centuries. Consider only a few examples. In transportation, the change progresses from the horse-drawn carriage to the space shuttle. In weapons, from the musket to the atom bomb. In communication, from the hand-written letter to the fax machine. These are not merely quantitative changes, they are qualitative ones as well. The amount and pace of change have profoundly affected our lives, sometimes in ways that we are hardly aware of. Henry Adams, writing in 1900, was trying to come to grips with these changes.

The impact of these changes only emphasizes the paradox. We know so much more about the world; we control so much more. Yet that complicates, rather than clarifies, our understanding of the world and of ourselves. Our actions become fraught with difficulties. We seek to be good and do good, but often our own actions seem to turn against us. The tractor, which most efficiently increases food production, may also destroy the soil on which that production depends. Our social institutions, designed to serve the physical needs of the people, often seem to corrupt them spiritually. In this unit, Joseph Wood Krutch and Loren Eiseley, in quite different ways, both talk about this spiritual dimension.

The essays, poems, and stories in this unit have been selected to help you think about this paradox, about the relation between our inward and outward urges. They show some of the ways technology influences our lives, and raise questions about our nature and our relation to technology. Let's look at some of these questions: What is human nature really like? Krutch, Whitman, and Zelazny explore the nature of humanity. Benét, Berman, and Minsky raise the question of whether we really run the machines or whether they may, someday, run—or replace—us. Dyson, Wilson, Gilkey, and McCaffrey raise various questions about the ways in which we may be changed by our relationships with machines.

The questions raised by each of the authors in this section are interesting and important because they explore some of the various ways in which technology is changing the way we live and think. Trying to answer their questions should lead you to scrutinize aspects of science and technology that most of us simply take for granted. Once you have begun this scrutiny, you should find yourself discovering many additional questions that you will want to answer.

Joseph Wood Krutch

A Meaning for "Humanism"

(1959)

Joseph Wood Krutch (1893–1970) was born in Knoxville, Tennessee. He received a degree in science at the University of Tennessee in 1915, and went on to receive his master's and doctoral degrees from Columbia University. An author who wrote both scientific works and literary criticism, he is remembered for *The Modern Temper* and for works on Poe, Johnson, and Thoreau, as well as numerous books about specific types of environments and animals.

Because the word *humanism* is used in vague and general ways, Krutch undertakes to define it. But he is also interested in justifying its importance in an age that takes science for granted but regards human values as less significant. His contrast between man as moralist and as "geometer" accentuates the theme of this unit—the divergent, yet related, human concern about the inner and outer dimensions of reality.

PREVIEW

Make a list of no more than ten qualities that you associate with being human. Select the two qualities on your list that you regard as most important (most humanizing). Are they inner or outer qualities? Is that important? Write a sentence about each of these two, giving your reason for selecting them.

"Humanism" has been used to mean too many things to be a very satisfactory term. Nevertheless, and in the absence of a better word, I shall use it here to stand for the complex of attitudes which this discussion has undertaken to defend.

In this sense a humanist is anyone who rejects the attempt to describe or account for man wholly on the basis of physics, chemistry, and animal behavior. He is anyone who believes that will, reason, and purpose are real and significant; that value and justice are aspects of a reality called good and evil and rest upon some foundation other than custom; that consciousness is so far from being a mere epiphenomenon that it is the most tremendous of actualities; that the unmeasurable may be significant; or, to sum it all up, that those human realities which sometimes seem to exist only in the human mind are the perceptions, rather than merely the creations, of that mind. He is, in other words, anyone who says that there are more things in heaven and earth than are dreamed of in the positivist philosophy.

Originally, to be sure, the term humanist meant simply anyone who made the study of ancient literature his chief concern. Obviously it means, as I use it, very much more. But there remains nevertheless a certain connection between the aboriginal meaning and that which I am attempting to give it, because those whom I describe as humanists usually recognize that literature and the arts have been pretty consistently "on their side" and because it is often to literature that they turn to renew their faith in the whole class of truths which the modern world has so consistently tended to dismiss as the mere figments of a wishfully thinking imagination.

In so far as this modern world gives less and less attention to its literary past, in so far as it dismisses that past as something outgrown and to be discarded much as the imperfect technology contemporary with it has been discarded, just to that extent does it facilitate the surrender of humanism to technology. In literature is to be found, directly expressed or, more often, indirectly implied, the most effective correction to the views now most prevalent among the thinking and unthinking alike.

The great imaginative writers present a picture of human nature and of human life which carries conviction and thus gives the lie to all attempts to reduce man to a mechanism. Novels, and poems, and dramas are so persistently concerned with the values which relativism rejects that one might even define literature as the attempt to pass value judgments upon representations of human life. More often than not those of its imagined persons who fail to achieve power and wealth are more successful than those who do not—by standards which the imaginative writer persuades us to accept as valid. And because we do recognize in their re-creations our own sense of what life is like but do not recognize it in the best documented accounts of most biologists, sociologists, political scientists, or psychologists, those of us who are humanists believe the accounts of the poets, novelists, and playwrights to be truer. Literature has been chiefly concerned with the good life as something not identical with the high standard of living and with man as the maker of his destiny rather than as a creature wholly made rather than making. Literature, more than anything else, has kept alive whatever resistance still exists to the various dismal sciences which have come so near to complete triumph everywhere else.

It is no doubt because many people dimly recognize this fact that some "defense of the humanities" has become an expected part of the college commencement address and other formal discussions of the state of the world. But it is because the recognition is wavering and dim that such defenses are commonly so weak and so often take the form of a mere parenthetical remark likely to come down to something like this: "And of course the humanities are important too but I have not time to say more on that subject now." Most of even those who undertake to "defend the humanities" at some length seem often embarrassed by what strikes them as the weakness of their case and to be expressing a sentimental nostalgia for a lost cause rather than faith in a living reality.

What they most usually seem to be saying is that though, of course, it is by science and technology that men *live,* the arts can be expected to furnish certain graces and to provide an opportunity for refined relaxation. Letters and the other arts are, therefore, merely the ornaments of civilized life. But are they not rather, for an age which has little contact with either theology or philosophy, almost the only preservers of what Mr. Oppenheimer* calls man's "humanity"?

Listen for a moment to a voice from another age:
"The truth is that knowledge of external nature, and the sciences which that knowledge requires or includes, are not the great or the frequent business of the human mind. Whether we provide for action or conversation, whether we wish to be useful or pleasing, the first requisite is the religious and moral knowledge of right and wrong, the next is an acquaintance with the history of mankind, and with those examples which may be said to embody truth, and prove by events the reasonableness of opinions. Prudence and Justice are virtues and excellences of all times and of all places; we are perpetually moralists, but we are geometricians only by chance."

When Samuel Johnson† wrote that passage he was defending what was already beginning to look like a lost cause. To a certain small number of his contemporaries it was, perhaps, still only a powerfully clear statement of an obvious truth. To many others it was a reminder of something men were beginning to forget. But I doubt if there were any to whom it seemed the mere paradox it has by now become. Today the vast majority of thinking men assume without argument that "knowledge of external nature" *is* the great, the frequent, and almost the only legitimate business of men. It is, they think, upon such knowledge of external nature that both our safety and that prosperity by which we set so much store depend. We are not perpetually moralists, and geometricians only by chance. We have become geometricians perpetually and moralists only by chance—if at all.

Moreover, to have become geometricians perpetually we have been led to deny most of Johnson's other fundamental assertions. We may, to be sure, occasionally remember that an acquaintance with the history of mankind is sometimes useful. But even that is useful chiefly to remind us of the follies we should avoid. And even partial agreement stops there. The dominant schools of psychology and sociology are so far from believing that Prudence and Justice are virtues of all times and of all places that they call upon the dominant school of anthropology to support their contention that *nothing* is true of all times and all places and that Prudence and Justice are so far from being the same everywhere that they do not exist except as abstractions derived from the local and temporary customs prevailing at some time and place. Morals are merely mores. There are cultures but no such thing as culture. There are justices, but no such thing as

---

* Oppenheimer, Robert—(1904–1967) directed the Manhattan Project, which developed the first atomic bomb. [Eds.]

† Johnson, Samuel—(1709–1784) eighteenth-century novelist and lexicographer. [Eds.]

Justice. We are not merely geometers; we are non-Euclidean geometers to whom one premise is as valid as another and there is no truth except what is logically deducible from one arbitrary premise or another.

The most obvious result of the decision made some two centuries or more ago to consider the knowledge of external nature the greatest, the most frequent, and perhaps the exclusive business of the human mind is the physical world in which we live. Had we not made that decision, we should not produce such an abundance of goods, travel so fast, be able to speak across so many miles to such vast hordes of listeners, or, of course, be in a position to destroy so quickly and so easily whole cities full of our fellow human beings.

The second most obvious result is that loss of which I have just spoken, the loss of confidence in any criteria by which the right and the wrong or even the ugly and the beautiful may be distinguished. That we are the better for this loss of what they insist was a misplaced confidence, many positivists are ready to assert. But it is not certain that a good many of the perplexities, the uncertainties, the anxieties, and the dangers which do perplex this present world—despite the fact that it is so much more abundant and powerful than any previous world—are not related to just this loss.

If man has no true nature as distinguished from what his condition at a given time creates; if no persisting needs, tastes, preferences, and capacities are either met or frustrated by that condition; then there is no reason why he should not be as contentedly "adjusted" to the condition of what Johnson calls a "geometrician" exclusively. But if there *is* such a thing as human nature, and if both man's history and his literature give some clue as to what that nature is; if, indeed, they reveal it more surely than all the polls, questionnaires and tests which "geometry" has been able to devise; then Johnson may be right when he suggests that it is in man's nature to be moral and, perhaps, even religious; that it is, as a matter of fact, in accord with his nature to be a moralist perpetually and a geometer only by chance. And if you do believe this to be true, then it may also seem that the deepest cause of the anxiety which has given its name to our age; that the deepest cause of the fact that man is not so secure, so happy, and so content in his age of power and abundance as it would seem that he should be; that he is, indeed, so frequently forced to seek the aid of psychiatrists or those who can minister to a mind diseased that we are told it is impossible to train as many such ministers as are now needed—if all this is true then, it may be, I say, that the deepest reason is simply this: Man's condition as geometer and as the child of geometry is not harmonious with his nature.

However that may be, we are at least coming to realize more and more vividly something which the earliest proponents of salvation by geometry never suspected, namely, that science is not only the solver of problems but also, at the same time, the creator of other problems. That this is to some extent true, we began to realize a long time ago. We realized, for instance, that the invention of the steam engine created the problem of child slavery in factories. We are also beginning to realize that science creates both abundance and the new problem created by the necessity for endlessly increasing consumption—indeed, for increasing sheer waste—if we are not to be buried and smothered under the load of abundance. And, of course, no other such realization ever came with the dramatic suddenness and the terrifying urgency of the realization that when the secret of atomic fission was discovered we were faced with a problem incomparably more threatening than any which science or technology had previously created.

How is that problem to be solved or even to be approached? The usual answer to such a question when it is asked of relatively minor problems has been: With a hair of the dog that bit you. The answer to the problems created by science is more science.

But does past history suggest that this is how the problems have been solved—when they have been solved at all? In so far as, say, the problem of child slavery was solved, it was not solved by science but by the conscience of mankind. It was man the moralist, not man the geometer, who solved it. It seems indubitably evident that the problem created by atomic fission cannot be solved by more knowledge of the kind which makes atomic fission possible. We come up against the fact, so often asserted and so often unconvincingly denied, that science can tell us *how to do* many different things but not whether any specific thing which *can be done, ought to be done.* It can tell us how to make a uranium bomb and how to make a hydrogen bomb. It can tell how a city full of people may most efficiently, and even most cheaply, be destroyed. But it cannot tell us what city, if any, *ought* to be so destroyed.

Some answer to that question will have to be given. It was given once, more than a decade ago, over Hiroshima. It seems likely enough that we shall have to give an answer again in the possibly not distant future. Whether we did and whether we will again answer it wisely, I will not attempt to say. But one thing is certain. The answer we did give and the answer we will give is not a scientific answer. It was and it will be an answer which depends, not on how man is functioning as a geometer, but on how he is functioning as a moralist.

If morals are nothing but mores, then the answer we will give will depend simply on what deductions are made from the prevailing mores and it will be wise or foolish only to the extent that it is logically consistent with those prevailing mores. But if morals are more than mores; if they are, as Johnson assumed, permanent; and if good morals are defined in terms of what is harmonious with something enduring in man's nature—then the wisdom or folly, the righteousness or the wickedness of the answer will depend upon the extent to which we have a true understanding of man's nature and upon our ability and willingness to act in accordance with it.

Most of even those relativists who are quite convinced that morals are, indeed, nothing but mores, that there is no justice but only conceptions of justice, are ready to grant that the songs and sayings, the folkways and the literature of any people are among the great crystallizers and transmitters of mores and of conceptions of justice. In other words and to be quite specific, it is not science but humanism which will give the answer to the question, "Upon whom and under what conditions shall a city full of human beings be wiped out?"

Probably those who finally formulate and implement the decision will be dimly if at all aware of the ultimate determinants of that decision. Consciously they may well be geometers only, but unconsciously they will be moralists also, because though men may philosophize and moralize well or ill, consciously or unconsciously, philosophize and moralize they must and do. In a civilization like ours, in which only geometry is much regarded, in which the answers that every man must give to moral and aesthetic and metaphysical questions are usually given thoughtlessly and impromptu, most people philosophize badly.

Under these circumstances it is exceedingly odd that those who set out at college commencements and elsewhere to "defend the humanities" should so often seem hard put to find anything very convincing to say; are so prone to speak of mere graces, and to speak in such merely nostalgic—sometimes indeed merely sentimental—terms. "The humanities" are *not* the ornaments of civilization; they are its salvation—if indeed it is to be saved. They are the best embodiments of the most important aspect of that history of mankind which, as Johnson proclaimed, provides us with "those examples which may be said to embody truth and prove by events the reasonableness of opinions." And even if there is no Truth, no Right, no Wrong, and no Justice, then, at least, arts and letters are in any society the principal source of those illusions concerning Truth, Right, Wrong, and Justice which guide its conduct.

Is there any sign, any hope that we will realize in time that we are perpetually compelled to make moral choices as well as to perform certain acts, and that neither technology nor the relativist philosophy can help us to make those choices except at random and without realizing that they are inescapable?

Many of our leading scientists are saying that we are devoting too little time to "fundamental research." We are, they say, using up in technological development our present stock of potentially useful knowledge and are not learning enough of that pure science which is pursued for its own sake though it so often turns out to be unexpectedly useful. No doubt they are right. But we ought to be doing more "fundamental thinking" as well as more fundamental research, devoting more time to those large general questions which the boastfully practical generally regard as mere cobweb spinning. In the long run nothing which any pure scientist can add to our knowledge of the atom might have as much effect upon our future as what some philosopher or even some poet may say. We have used up or cast aside our fundamental thinking.

The delusion of power is like the delusion of wealth. The individual thinks that if only he had more money, all would be well. Nations—indeed, mankind as a whole—believe that they lack nothing except more power. If we could only travel faster, build larger machines, and create more destructive explosions we should achieve an even higher standard of living—and no other good is definable. Throughout the ages moralists have—with little effect, however—attempted at least to expose the delusions associated with the desire for individual wealth. Even today some continue to do so. But few are aware that the pursuit of power is also a kind of folly, and many hail even the atom bomb as merely an unfortunate preliminary to those "peaceful uses of atomic power" which will, at last, usher in that Golden Age* which none of our other assumptions of power were quite sufficient to create.

In Samuel Johnson's *Rasselas*† the inventor of a flying machine refuses to demonstrate his invention because, so he says, men should not be allowed to fly until they have become virtuous. However unassailable his logic may seem, it is hardly worthwhile to suggest that we should simply agree not to develop any new instruments of power until we know just how good use could be made of them. Neither scientists nor inventors would be likely to accept any such general principle. Neither can mere laws or "plans" bring technology under control. If anything could control it, that would be some change in man himself, who will continue to pursue power rather than wisdom just so long as it is in power that he takes the greatest pride. If his heart were elsewhere then he might—just possibly—accomplish things more worth accomplishing than those with which he is now so busy. He might then follow the logic of his own evolving nature rather than the logic of evolving technology. The tail might then stop wagging the dog.

In a recent book, J. Robert Oppenheimer said: "In some sort of crude sense which no vulgarity, no humor, no overstatement can quite extinguish the physicists have known sin; and this is a knowledge they cannot lose." But what is this sin? Most of those who acknowledge it would answer correctly enough that it has something to do with the invention of the bomb and its use. But is it obviously wrong to beat to the draw an enemy who is trying to destroy you? Only the most uncompromising preachers of nonresistance as an unqualified obligation will say so.

Even more assuredly it is no sin to be a physicist. But if there is a sin of which the physicists were guilty, it was a sin they share with all who follow the faith of our times. It is the sin of believing that *the nature of the atom* is more important than *the nature of man;* that knowledge of matter is more useful, more important, and more significant than knowledge of another kind; that the most valid of injunctions is not "Know thyself"‡ but "Know the Not-Self"; that the key to wisdom is not self-mastery but the mastery of the powers which lie outside of man.

We cannot now "control the machine" because we are hypnotized by it; because we do not really want to control it. And we do not want to control it because in our hearts we believe it more interesting, more wonderful, more admirable, and more rich in potentialities than we ourselves are. We cannot break the hypnosis, cannot wake from our submissive dream, without retracing one by one the steps which brought us more and more completely under its spell.

Those steps were not taken yesterday and they cannot be retraced unless we

---

* Golden Age—a mythological period of nearly perfect earthly existence. [Eds.]

† *Rasselas*—a novel by Samuel Johnson about an Abyssinian prince who seeks the proper way to live. [Eds.]

‡ "Know Thyself"—Socrates's famous dictum. [Eds.]

are both willing and able to reassess the values which the hypnosis has imposed upon us. That would involve a willingness to ask how many of the "advantages" which power has conferred upon us really are advantageous. It would mean also getting rid of all our love of the machine for its own sake, of our delight in the small gadget as well as in the great. But if we did do all that these things imply, then we might begin to recover from our hypnosis.

If there are any signs of such an awakening they are faint and dubious. The main current tends to run in the long-familiar direction. To the average citizen knowledge means science, science means technology, and (a last debasement) the meaning of technology is reduced to "know-how." It took a Russian satellite in the sky to shake our complacency and it was shaken only because it suggested that the Russians had more "know-how" than we. And the lesson most commonly drawn has been that education should put even greater stress upon the development of such know-how, leaving even less time for "fundamental thinking."

Someday we may again discover that "the humanities" are something more than ornaments and graces. Sociology and psychology may again find man's consciousness more interesting than the mechanically determined aspects of his behavior and we may again be more concerned with what man *is* than with *what he has* and *what he can do*. We might again take more pride in his intellect than in his tools; might again think of him as pre-eminently *Homo sapiens* rather than *Homo faber*—man the thinker rather than man the maker. We might—at some distant day—come to realize again that the proper study of mankind is man.

But that time is certainly not yet. We have forgotten that know-how is a dubious endowment unless it is accompanied by other "knows"—by "know what," "know why," and—most important of all at the present moment—"know whether." Quite blandly and as a matter of course we still ask what are the needs of industry, not what are the needs of man.

In the Sanskrit Panchatantra,* that collection of romantic tales written down in an early century A.D., there is a fable which might have been devised for today. Three great magicians who have been friends since boyhood have continued to admit to their fellowship a simple fellow who was also a companion of their youth. When the three set out on a journey to demonstrate to a wider world the greatness of their art they reluctantly permit their humble friend to accompany them, and before they have gone very far, they come upon a pile of bones under a tree. Upon this opportunity to practice their art they eagerly seize. "I," says the first, "can cause these dead bones to reassemble themselves into a skeleton." And at his command they do so. "I," says the second, "can clothe that skeleton with flesh." And his miracle, also, is performed. Then, "I," says the third, "can now endow the whole with life."

At this moment the simpleton interposes. "Don't you realize," he asks, "that this is a tiger?" But the wise men are scornful. Their science is "pure"; it has no concern with such vulgar facts. "Well then," says the simpleton, "wait a moment." And he climbs a tree. A few moments later the tiger is indeed brought to

---

* Panchatantra—a collection (ca. A.D. 500) of animal stories in Sanskrit. [Eds.]

life. He devours the three wise men and departs. Thereupon the simpleton comes down from his tree and goes home.

There is no more perfect parable to illustrate what happens when know-how becomes more important than common sense—and common sense is at least the beginning of wisdom.

The ancients had a wise motto: *"Quo Urania ducit"*—Wherever Wisdom leads. We have somehow mistranslated or perverted it. Our motto has become *"Quo Uranium ducit."* And that, of course, is the antithesis of humanism.

JOURNAL WRITINGS

1. Determine what Krutch means by "humanity" and "humanism" by reading his essay very carefully. Write a sentence **defining** each term as Krutch uses it.
2. By using an encyclopedia or dictionary of philosophy, find out what a "positivist philosophy" is. Write the **definition** in your journal. Give a few reasons why you find this philosophy acceptable or unacceptable.
3. Krutch says that in order to control the machine we need to get rid "of all our love of the machine for its own sake." In your journal, write a few **examples,** perhaps from your own personal experiences, that illustrate this love of machines.

BRAINSTORMING AND DRAFTING

4. Discuss a problem that technology has helped to create. Invent a solution from the perspective of a moralist (as Krutch defines moralist), and write a paragraph describing this solution.
5. In a small group, compare the human qualities you have listed in the Preview exercise. Try to reach a consensus within the group on a short list of qualities (perhaps four or five) essential to the concept of humanity. Use this list to write a paragraph about what it means to be human.

THE AUTHOR'S METHODS

6. Krutch says, "Literature, more than anything else, has kept alive whatever resistance still exists to the various dismal sciences which have come so near to complete triumph everywhere else." Which words in this sentence define the attitude the author wants to communicate? Explain how these words affect you.
7. Krutch rejects the thinking of those who say "Morals are merely mores." Look up the meanings of "morals" and "mores" in a dictionary. Write an essay of no more than three paragraphs in which you distinguish between the two, and comment briefly on the significance of that distinction.

8. List the parts of Krutch's **argument.** The paragraph that begins "If man has no true . . . " (page 513) may help you to identify the main trend of his argument. **Paraphrase** his conclusion in a sentence or two and, in another sentence or two, **explain** why you agree or disagree with this conclusion.

FORMAL WRITING AND RESEARCH PAPERS

9. "The answer to the problems created by science is more science." Find some **examples** of problems created by science. Ask yourself whether science can solve any or all of these problems. Write a paper in which you use the examples to **argue** for or against the quotation.

10. Krutch mentions the emergence of "child slavery" in factories as a result of the invention of the steam engine. Find some information about working conditions for children in English factories during the period 1800–1850. (*The New Cambridge Modern History* would be a good starting point.) Write a paper in which you use the information from your research to show that Krutch's assertions are justified or unjustified.

Loren Eiseley

Science and the Sense of the Holy

(1978)

Loren Eiseley (1907–1977) was born and reared in Lincoln, Nebraska. He received his bachelor's degree from the University of Nebraska in 1933, and continued his studies at the University of Pennsylvania, where he earned his master's and doctoral degrees. Trained as an anthropologist, he also worked as a sociologist and an historian of science. But perhaps he was most famous for his essays about science. The recipient of numerous science awards, he was curator of the University of Pennsylvania Museum. Two of his better-known works are *Francis Bacon and the Modern Dilemma* (1963) and *The Night Country* (1971).

According to Eiseley, scientists can be categorized by their attitude toward the universe. Some take a reverent attitude, seeing not only an outer but an inner aspect to nature. Others, whom he calls "reductionists," regard nature as a purely material series of causes and effects. He supports his assertion with a rich series of examples, drawn not only from his own life, but from history, art, and literature.

PREVIEW

Write some notes to yourself defining what "holy" means to you personally—holy persons, places, things, ideas.

I

When I was a young man engaged in fossil hunting in the Nebraska badlands I was frequently reminded that the ravines, washes, and gullies over which we wandered resembled the fissures in a giant exposed brain. The human brain contains the fossil memories of its past—buried but not extinguished moments—just as this more formidable replica contained deep in its inner stratigraphic convolutions earth's past in the shape of horned titanotheres and stalking, dirk-toothed cats. Man's memory erodes away in the short space of a lifetime. Jutting from the coils of the earth brain over which I clambered were the buried remnants, the changing history, of the entire age of mammals—millions of years of vanished daylight with their accompanying traces of volcanic outbursts and upheavals. It may well be asked why this analogy of earth's memory should so preoccupy the mind of a scientist as to have affected his entire outlook upon nature and upon his kinship with—even his concern for—the plant and animal world about him.

Perhaps the problem can best be formulated by pointing out that there are two extreme approaches to the interpretation of the living world. One was expressed by Charles Darwin* at the age of twenty-eight; one by Sigmund Freud† in his mature years. Other men of science have been arrayed on opposite sides of the question, but the eminence of these two scholars will serve to point up a controversy that has been going on since science arose, sometimes quietly, sometimes marked by vitriolic behavior, as when a certain specialist wedded to his own view of the universe hurled his opponent's book into his wastebasket only to have it retrieved and cherished by a graduate student who became a lifelong advocate of the opinions reviled by his mentor. Thus it is evident that, in the supposed objective world of science, emotion and temperament may play a role in our selection of the mental tools with which we choose to investigate nature.

Charles Darwin, at a time when the majority of learned men looked upon animals as either automatons or creatures created merely for human exploitation, jotted thoughtfully into one of his early journals upon evolution the following observation:

"If we choose to let conjecture run wild, then animals, our fellow brethren in pain, disease, suffering and famine—our slaves in the most laborious works, our companions in our amusements—they may partake of our origin in one common ancestor—we may be all netted together."

What, we may now inquire, is the world view here implied, one way in which a great scientist looked upon the subject matter that was to preoccupy his entire working life? In spite of the fact that Darwin was, in his later years, an agnostic, in spite of confessing he was "in thick mud" so far as metaphysics was concerned, the remark I have quoted gives every sign of that feeling of awe, of dread of the holy playing upon nature, which characterizes the work of a number of naturalists and physicists down even to the present day. Darwin's remark reveals an intuitive sensitivity to the life of other creatures about him, an attitude quite distinct from that of the laboratory experimentalist who is hardened to the infliction of pain. In addition, Darwin's final comment that we may be all netted together in one gigantic mode of experience, that we are in a mystic sense one single diffuse animal, subject to joy and suffering beyond what we endure as individuals, reveals a youth drawn to the world of nature by far more than just the curiosity to be readily satisfied by the knife or the scalpel.

---

* Darwin, Charles—(1809–1882) English naturalist who developed the theory of evolution; author of *The Origin of Species*. [Eds.]

† Freud, Sigmund—(1856–1939) Austrian psychoanalyst who developed the idea of the subconscious. [Eds.]

If we turn to Sigmund Freud by way of contrast we find an oddly inhibited reaction. Freud, though obviously influenced by the elegant medical experimenters of his college days, groped his way alone, and by methods not subject to quantification or absolute verification, into the dark realms of the subconscious. His reaction to the natural world, or at least his feelings and intuitions about it, are basically cold, clinical, and reserved. He of all men recognized what one poet has termed "the terrible archaeology of the brain." Freud states that "nothing once constructed has perished, and all the earlier stages of development have survived alongside the latest." But for Freud, convinced that childhood made the man, adult reactions were apt to fall under the suspicion of being childhood ghosts raised up in a disguised fashion. Thus, insightful though he could be, the very nature of his study of man tended to generate distrust of that outgoing empathy we observed in the young Darwin. "I find it very difficult to work with these intangible qualities," confessed Freud. He was suspicious of their representing some lingering monster of childhood, even if reduced in size. Since Freud regarded any type of religious feeling—even the illuminative quality of the universe—as an illusion, feelings of awe before natural phenomena such as that manifested by Darwin were to him basically remnants of childhood and to be dismissed accordingly.

In *Civilization and Its Discontents* Freud speaks with slight condescension of a friend who claimed a sensation of eternity, something limitless, unbounded— "oceanic," to use the friend's expression. The feeling had no sectarian origin, no assurance of immortality, but implied just such a sense of awe as might lie at the root of the religious impulse. "I cannot," maintained Freud, "discover this 'oceanic' impulse in myself." Instead he promptly psychoanalyzes the feeling of oneness with the universe in the child's pleasure ego which holds to itself all that is comforting; in short, the original ego, the infant's ego, included everything. Later, by experience, contended Freud, our adult ego becomes only a shrunken vestige of that far more extensive feeling which "expressed an inseparable connection . . . with the external world."

In essence, then, Freud is explaining away one of the great feelings characteristic of the best in man by relegating it to a childhood atavistic survival in adult life. The most highly developed animals, he observes, have arisen from the lowest. Although the great saurians are gone, the dwarfed crocodile remains. Presumably if Freud had completed the analogy he would have been forced to say that crocodilian adults without awe and with egos shrunken safely into their petty concerns represented a higher, more practical evolutionary level than the aberrant adult who persists in feelings of wonder before which Freud recoiled with a nineteenth-century mechanist's distaste, although not without acknowledging that this lurking childlike corruption might be widespread. He chose to regard it, however, as just another manifestation of the irrational aspect of man's divided psyche.

Over six decades before the present, a German theologian, Rudolf Otto, had chosen for his examination what he termed *The Idea of the Holy (Das Heilige)*. Appearing in 1917 in a time of bitterness and disillusionment, his book was and is still widely read. It cut across denominational divisions and spoke to all those concerned with that *mysterium tremendum*,* that very awe before the universe which Freud had sighed over and dismissed as irrational. I think it safe to affirm that Freud left adult man somewhat shrunken and misjudged—misjudged because some of the world's scientists and artists have been deeply affected by the great mystery, less so the child at one's knee who frequently has to be disciplined to what in India has been called the "opening of the heavenly eye."

Ever since man first painted animals in the dark of caves he has been responding to the holy, to the numinous, to the mystery of being and becoming, to what Goethe† very aptly called "the weird portentous." Something inexpressible was felt to lie behind nature. The bear cult, circumpolar in distribution and known archaeologically to extend into Neanderthal times, is a further and most ancient example. The widespread beliefs in descent from a totemic animal, guardian helpers in the shapes of animals, the concept of the game lords who released or held back game to man are all part of a variety of a sanctified, reverent experience that extends from the beautiful rock paintings of South Africa to the men of the Labradorean forests or the Plains Indian seeking by starvation and isolation to bring the sacred spirits to his assistance. All this is part of the human inheritance, the wonder of the world, and nowhere does that wonder press closer to us than in the guise of animals which, whether supernaturally as in the caves of our origins or, as in Darwin's sudden illumination, perceived to be, at heart, one form, one awe-inspiring mystery, seemingly diverse and apart but derived from the same genetic source. Thus the *mysterium* arose not by primitive campfires alone. Skins may still prickle in a modern classroom.

In the end, science as we know it has two basic types of practitioners. One is the educated man who still has a controlled sense of wonder before the universal mystery, whether it hides in a snail's eye or within the light that impinges on that delicate organ. The second kind of observer is the extreme reductionist who is so busy stripping things apart that the tremendous mystery has been reduced to a trifle, to intangibles not worth troubling one's head about. The world of the secondary qualities—color, sound, thought—is reduced to illusion. The *only* true reality becomes the chill void of ever-streaming particles.

If one is a biologist this approach can result in behavior so remarkably cruel that it ceases to be objective but rather suggests a deep grain of sadism that is not science. To list but one example, a recent newspaper article reported that a great urban museum of national reputation had spent over a half-million dollars on mutilating experiments with cats. The experiments are too revolting to chronicle here and the museum has not seen fit to enlighten the public on the knowledge gained at so frightful a cost in pain. The cost, it would appear, lies not alone in animal suffering but in the dehumanization of those willing to engage in such blind, random cruelty. The practice was defended by museum officials, who in a muted show of scientific defense maintained the right to study what they chose "without regard to its demonstrable practical value."

---

* *mysterium tremendum*—Latin for "tremendous mystery." [Eds.]

† Goethe, Johann—(1749–1832) German poet, novelist, and dramatist; author of *Faust*. [Eds.]

This is a scientific precept hard to override since the days of Galileo,* as the official well knew. Nevertheless, behind its seamless façade of probity many terrible things are and will be done. Blaise Pascal, as far back as the seventeenth century, foresaw our two opposed methods.† Of them he said: "There are two equally dangerous extremes, to shut reason out, and to let nothing else in." It is the reductionist who, too frequently, would claim that the end justifies the means, who would assert reason as his defense and let that *mysterium* which guards man's moral nature fall away in indifference, a phantom without reality.

"The whole of existence frightens me," protested the philosopher Søren Kierkegaard;‡ "from the smallest fly to the mystery of the Incarnation, everything is unintelligible to me, most of all myself." By contrast, the evolutionary reductionist Ernst Haeckel,§ writing in 1877, commented that "the cell consists of matter . . . composed chiefly of carbon with an admixture of hydrogen, nitrogen and sulphur. These component parts, properly united, produce the soul and body of the animated world, and suitably nourished become man. With this single argument the mystery of the universe is explained, the Deity annulled and a new era of infinite knowledge ushered in." Since these remarks of Haeckel's, uttered a hundred years ago, the genetic alphabet has scarcely substantiated in its essential intricacy Haeckel's carefree dismissal of the complexity of life. If anything, it has given weight to Kierkegaard's wary statement or at least heightened the compassionate wonder with which we are led to look upon our kind.

"A conviction akin to religious feeling of the rationality or intelligibility of the world lies behind all scientific work of a high order," says Albert Einstein. Here once more the eternal dichotomy manifests itself. Thoreau, the man of literature, writes compassionately, "Shall I not have intelligence with the earth? Am I not partly leaves and vegetable mould myself?" Or Walt Whitman, the poet, protests in his *Song of Myself:* "whoever walks a furlong without sympathy walks to his own funeral drest in a shroud."

"Magnifying and applying come I"—he thunders—
"Outbidding at the start the old cautious hucksters . . .
Not objecting to special revelations, considering a curl of smoke or a hair on the back of my hand just as curious as any revelation."

Strange, is it not, that so many of these voices are not those of children, but those of great men—Newton playing on the vast shores of the universe, or Whitman touched with pity or Darwin infused with wonder over the clambering tree of life. Strange, that all these many voices should be dismissed as the atavistic yearnings of an unreduced childlike ego seeking in "oceanic" fashion to absorb its

---

* Galileo [Galilei]—(1564–1642) Italian mathematician and astronomer; proposed the heliocentric theory of the solar system. [Eds.]

† Pascal, Blaise—(1623–1662) French mathematician and theologian. [Eds.]

‡ Kierkegaard, Søren—(1813–1855) Danish existential philosopher. [Eds.]

§ Haeckel, Ernst—(1834–1919) German zoologist; coined term *ecology.* [Eds.]

entire surroundings, as though in revolt against the counting house, the laboratory, and the computer.

II

Not long ago in a Manhattan art gallery there were exhibited paintings by Irwin
Fleminger, a modernist whose vast lawless Martianlike landscapes contain cryp-
tic human artifacts. One of these paintings attracted my eye by its title: "Laws of
Nature." Here in a jumbled desert waste without visible life two thin laths had
been erected a little distance apart. Strung across the top of the laths was an
insubstantial string with even more insubstantial filaments depending from the
connecting cord. The effect was terrifying. In the huge inhuman universe that
constituted the background, man, who was even more diminished by his absence, had attempted to delineate and bring under natural law an area too big for
his comprehension. His effort, his "law," whatever it was, denoted a tiny measure
in the midst of an ominous landscape looming away to the horizon. The frail slats
and dangling string would not have sufficed to fence a chicken run.

The message grew as one looked. With all the great powers of the human
intellect we were safe, we understood, in degree, a space between some slats and
string, a little gate into the world of infinitude. The effect was crushing and it
brought before one that sense of the "other" of which Rudolf Otto spoke, the
sense beyond our senses, unspoken awe, or, as the reductionist would have it,
nothing but waste. There the slats stood and the string drooped hopelessly. It was
the natural law imposed by man, but outside its compass, again to use the words
of Thoreau, was something terrific, not bound to be kind to man. Not man's at all
really—a star's substance totally indifferent to life or what laws life might concoct.
No man would greatly extend that trifling toy. The line sagged hopelessly. Man's
attempt had failed, leaving but an artifact in the wilderness. Perhaps, I thought,
this is man's own measure. Perhaps he has already gone. The crepitation at my
spine increased. I felt the mood of the paleolithic artists, lost in the mysteries of
birth and coming, as they carved pregnant beasts in the dark of caves and tried by
crayons to secure the food necessarily wrung from similar vast landscapes. Their
art had the same holy quality that shows in the ivory figurines, the worship before
the sacred mother who brought man mysteriously into the limited world of the
cave mouth.

The numinous then is touched with superstition, the reductionist would say,
but all the rituals suggest even toward hunted animals a respect and sympathy
leading to ceremonial treatment of hunted souls; whereas by contrast in the
modern world the degradation of animals in experiments of little, or vile, meaning, were easily turned to the experimental human torture practiced at Dachau
and Buchenwald* by men dignified with medical degrees. So the extremes of
temperament stand today: the man with reverence and compassion in his heart

---

* Dachau/Buchenwald—concentration camps run by Hitler's regime.

whose eye ranges farther than the two slats in the wilderness, and the modern vandal totally lacking in empathy for life beyond his own, his sense of wonder reduced to a crushing series of gears and quantitative formula, the educated vandal without mercy or tolerance, the collecting man that I once tried to prevent from killing an endangered falcon, who raised his rifle, fired, and laughed as the bird tumbled at my feet. I suppose Freud might have argued that this was a man of normal ego, but I, extending my childlike mind into the composite life of the world, bled accordingly.

Perhaps Freud was right, but let us look once more at this brain that in many distinguished minds has agonized over life and the mysterious road by which it has come. Certainly, as Darwin recognized, it was not the tough-minded, logical inductionists of the early nineteenth century who in a deliberate distortion of Baconian philosophy solved the problem of evolution. Rather, it was what Darwin chose to call "speculative" men, men, in other words, with just a touch of the numinous in their eye, a sense of marvel, a glimpse of what was happening behind the visible, who saw the whole of the living world as though turning in a child's kaleidoscope.

Among the purely human marvels of the world is the way the human brain after birth, when its cranial capacity is scarcely larger than that of a gorilla or other big anthropoid, spurts onward to treble its size during the first year of life. The human infant's skull will soar to a cranial capacity of 950 cubic centimeters while the gorilla has reached only 380 cubic centimeters. In other words, the human brain grows at an exponential rate, a spurt which carries it almost to adult capacity at the age of fourteen.

This clever and specifically human adaptation enables the human offspring successfully to pass the birth canal like a reasonably small-headed animal, but in a more larval and helpless condition than its giant relatives. The brain burgeons after birth, not before, and it is this fact which enables the child, with proper care, to assimilate all that larger world which will be forever denied to its relative the gorilla. The big anthropoids enjoy no such expansion. Their brains grow without exponential quickening into maturity. Somewhere in the far past of man something strange happened in his evolutionary development. His skill has enhanced its youthful globularity; he has lost most of his body hair and what remains grows strangely. He demands, because of his immature emergence into the world, a lengthened and protected childhood. Without prolonged familial attendance he would not survive, yet in him reposes the capacity for great art, inventiveness, and his first mental tool, speech, which creates his humanity. He is without doubt the oddest and most unusual evolutionary product that this planet has yet seen.

The term applied to this condition is neoteny, or pedomorphism. Basically the evolutionary forces, and here "forces" stands for complete ignorance, seem to have taken a roughhewn ordinary primate and softened and eliminated the adult state in order to allow for a fantastic leap in brain growth. In fact, there is a growing suspicion that some, at least, of the African fossils found and ascribed to the direct line of human ascent in eastern Africa may never, except for bipedalism and some incipient tool-using capacities, have taken the human road at all.

Some with brains that seem to have remained at the same level through long ages have what amounts quantitatively to no more than an anthropoid brain. Allowing for upright posture and free use of the hand, there is no assurance that they spoke or in any effective way were more than well-adapted bipedal apes. Collateral relatives, in short, but scarcely to be termed men. All this is the more remarkable because their history can now be traced over roughly five if not six million years—a singularly unprogressive period for a creature destined later to break upon the world with such remarkable results after so long a period of gestation.

Has something about our calculations gone wrong? Are we studying, however necessarily, some bipedal cousins but not ancestral men? The human phylogeny which we seemed well on the way to arranging satisfactorily is now confused by a multiplicity of material contended over by an almost equal number of scholars. Just as a superfluity of flying particles is embarrassing the physicist, so man's evolution, once thought to be so clearly delineated, is showing signs of similar strain. A skull from Lake Rudolf with an estimated capacity of 775 cubic centimeters or even 800 and an antiquity ranging into the three-million-year range is at the human Rubicon,* yet much younger fossils are nowhere out of the anthropoid range.

Are these all parts of a single variable subhumanity from which we arose, or are some parts of this assemblage neotenous of brain and others not? The scientific exchanges are as stiff with politeness as exchanges between enemies on the floor of the Senate. "Professor so-and-so forgets the difficult task of restoring to its proper position a frontal bone trampled by cattle." A million years may be covertly jumped because there is nothing to be found in it. We must never lose sight of one fact, however: it is by neotenous brain growth that we came to be men, and certain of the South African hominids to which we have given such careful attention seem to have been remarkably slow in revealing such development. Some of them, in fact, during more years than present mankind has been alive seem to have flourished quite well as simple grassland apes.

Why indeed should they all have become men? Because they occupied the same ecological niche, contend those who would lump this variable assemblage. But surely paleontology does not always so bind its deliberations. We are here dealing with a gleam, a whisper, a thing of awe in the mind itself, that oceanic feeling which even the hardheaded Freud did not deny existed though he tried to assign it to childhood.

With animals whose precise environment through time may overlap, extinction may result among contending forms; it can and did happen among men. But with the first stirrings of the neotenous brain and its superinduced transformation of the family system a new type of ecological niche had incipiently appeared—a speaking niche, a wondering niche which need not have been first manifested in tools but in family organization, in wonder over what lay over the next hill or what

---

* Rubicon—river in northern Italy marking the border of the Roman Republic, which Caesar crossed without permission; by analogy any decisive step. [Eds.]

became of the dead. Whether man preferred seeds or flesh, how he regarded his silent collateral relatives, may not at first have induced great competition. Only those gifted with the pedomorphic brain would in some degree have fallen out of competition with the real. It would have been their danger and at the same time their beginning triumph. They were starting to occupy, not a niche in nature, but an invisible niche carved into thought which in time would bring them suffering, superstition, and great power.

It cannot, in the beginning, be recognized clearly because it is not a matter of molar teeth and seeds, or killer instincts and ill-interpreted pebbles. Rather it was something happening in the brain, some blinding, irradiating thing. Until the quantity of that gray matter reached the threshold of human proportions no one could be sure whether the creature saw with a human eye or looked upon life with even the faint stirrings of some kind of religious compassion.

The new niche in its beginnings is invisible; it has to be inferred. It does not lie waiting to be discovered in a pebble or a massive molar. These things are important in the human dawn but so is the mystery that ordained that mind should pass the channel of birth and then grow like a fungus in the night—grow and convolute and overlap its older buried strata, while a 600-pound gorilla retains by contrast the cranial content of a very small child. When man cast off his fur and placed his trust in that remarkable brain linked by neural pathways to his tongue he had potentially abandoned niches for dreams. Henceforth the world was man's niche. All else would live by his toleration—even the earth from which he sprang. Perhaps this is the hardest, most expensive lesson the layers of the fungus brain have yet to learn: that man is not as other creatures and that without the sense of the holy, without compassion, his brain can become a gray stalking horror—the deviser of Belsen.*

Its beginning is not the only curious thing about that brain. There are some finds in South Africa dating into immediately post-glacial times that reveal a face and calvaria more "modern" in appearance, more pedomorphic, than that of the average European. The skull is marked by cranial capacities in excess of 1700 cubic centimeters—big brained by any standards. The mastoids are childlike, the teeth reduced, the cranial base foreshortened. These people, variously termed Boskopoid or Strandlooper, have, in the words of one anthropologist, "the amazing cranium to face ratio of almost five to one. In Europeans it is about three to one. Face size has been modernized and subordinated to brain growth." In a culture still relying on coarse fare and primitive implements, the face and brain had been subtly altered in the direction science fiction writers like to imagine as the direction in which mankind is progressing. Yet here the curious foetalization of the human body seems to have outrun man's cultural status, though in the process giving warning that man's brain could still pass the straitened threshold of its birth.

How did these people look upon the primitive world into which they found themselves precipitated? History gives back no answer save that here there

---

* Belsen—concentration camp run by Hitler's regime. [Eds.]

flourished striking three-dimensional art—the art of the brother animal seen in beauty. Childlike, Freud might have muttered, with childlike dreams, rushed into conflict with the strong, the adult and shrunken ego, the ego that gets what it wants. Yet how strangely we linger over this lost episode of the human story, its pathos, its possible meaning. From whence did these people come? We are not sure. We are not even sure that they derive from one of the groups among the ruck of bipedal wandering apes long ago in Kenya that reveal some relationship to ourselves. Their development was slow, if indeed some of them took that road, the strange road to the foetalized brain that was to carry man outside of the little niche that fed him his tuberous, sandy diet.

We thought we were on the verge of solving the human story, but now we hold in our hands gross jaws and delicate, and are unsure of our direction save that the trail is longer than we had imagined twenty years ago. Yet still the question haunts us, the numinous, the holy in man's mind. Early man laid gifts beside the dead, but then in the modern unbelieving world, Ernst Haeckel's world, a renowned philosopher says, "The whole of existence frightens me," or another humbler thinker says, "In the world there is nothing to explain the world" but remembers the gold eyes of the falcon thrown brutally at his feet. He shivers while Freud says, "As for me I have never had such feelings." They are a part of childhood, Freud argues, though there are some who counter that in childhood—yes, even Freud might grant it—the man is made, the awe persists or is turned off by blows or the dullness of unthinking parents. One can only assert that in science, as in religion, when one has destroyed human wonder and compassion, one has killed man, even if the man in question continues to go about his laboratory tasks.

III

Perhaps there is one great book out of all American literature which best expresses the clash between the man who has genuine perception and the one who pursues nature as ruthlessly as a hunted animal. I refer to *Moby Dick,* whose narrator, Ishmael, is the namesake of a Biblical wanderer. Every literate person knows the story of Moby Dick and his pursuit by the crazed Captain Ahab who had yielded a leg to the great albino whale. It is the whale and Ahab who dominate the story. What does the whale represent? A symbol of evil, as some critics have contended? Fate, destiny, the universe personified, as other scholars have protested?

Moby Dick is "all a magnet," remarks Ahab cryptically at one moment. "And be he agent or be he principal I will wreak my hate upon him." Here, reduced to the deck of a whaler out of Nantucket, the old immortal questions resound, the questions labeled science in our era. Nothing is to go unchallenged. Thrice, by different vessels, Ahab is warned away from his contemplated conquest. The whale does not pursue Ahab, Ahab pursues the whale. If there is evil represented in the white whale it cannot be personalized. The evils of self-murder, of megalomania, are at work in a single soul calling up its foreordained destruction. Ahab heartlessly brushes aside the supplications of a brother captain to aid in the search for his son, lost somewhere in a boat in the trail of the white whale's passing. Such a search would only impede the headlong fury of the pursuit.

In Ahab's anxiety to "strike through the mask," to confront "the principal," whether god or destiny, he is denuding himself of all humanity. He has forgotten his owners, his responsibility to his crew. His single obsession, the hidden obsession that lies at the root of much Faustian overdrive in science, totally possesses him. Like Faust he must know, if the knowing kills him, if naught lies beyond. "All my means are sane," he writes, like Haeckel and many another since. "My motive and my object mad."

So it must have been in the laboratories of the atom breakers in their first heady days of success. Yet again on the third day Starbuck, the doomed mate, cries out to Ahab, "Desist. See. Moby Dick seeks thee not. It is thou, thou, that madly seekest him." This then is not the pursuit of evil. It is man in his pride that the almighty gods will challenge soon enough. Not for nothing is Moby Dick a white snow hill rushing through Pacific nights. He carries upon his brow the inscrutability of fate. Agent or principal, Moby Dick presents to Ahab the mystery he may confront but never conquer. There is no harpoon tempered that will strike successfully the heart of the great enigma.

So much for the seeking peg-legged man without heart. We know he launched his boats and struck his blows and in the fury of returning vengeance lost his ship, his comrades, and his own life. If, indeed, he pierced momentarily the mask of the "agent," it was not long enough to tell the tale. But what of the sometimes silent narrator, the man who begins the book with the nonchalant announcement, "Call me Ishmael," the man whose Biblical namesake had every man's hand lifted against him? What did he tell? After all, Moby Dick is his book.

Ishmael, in contrast to Ahab, is the wondering man, the acceptor of all races and their gods. In contrast to the obsessed Ahab he paints a magnificent picture of the peace that reigned in the giant whale schools of the 1840s, the snuffling and grunting about the boats like dogs, loving and being loved, huge mothers gazing in bliss upon their offspring. After hours of staring in those peaceful depths, "Deep down," says Ishmael, "there I still bathe in eternal mildness of joy." The weird, the holy, hangs undisturbed over the whales' huge cradle. Ishmael knows it, others do not.

At the end, when Ahab has done his worst and the *Pequod* with the wounded whale is dragged into the depths amidst shrieking seafowl, it is Ishmael, buoyed up on the calked coffin of his cannibal friend Queequeg, who survives to tell the tale. Like Whitman, like W. H. Hudson, like Thoreau, Ishmael, the wanderer, has noted more of nature and his fellow men than has the headstrong pursuer of the white whale, whether "agent" or "principal," within the universe. The tale is not of science, but it symbolizes on a gigantic canvas the struggle between two ways of looking at the universe: the magnification by the poet's mind attempting to see all, while disturbing as little as possible, as opposed to the plunging fury of Ahab with his cry, "Strike, strike through the mask, whatever it may cost in lives and suffering." Within our generation we have seen the one view plead for endangered species and reject the despoliation of the earth; the other has left us lingering in the shadow of atomic disaster. Actually, the division is not so abrupt as this would imply, but we are conscious as never before in history that there is an invisible line of demarcation, an ethic that science must sooner or later devise for itself if mankind is to survive. Herman Melville glimpsed in his huge mythology of the white beast that was nature's agent something that only the twentieth century can fully grasp.

It may be that those childlike big-brained skulls from Africa are not of the past but of the future, man, not, in Freud's words, retaining an atavistic child's ego, but pushing onward in an evolutionary attempt to become truly at peace with the universe, to know and enjoy the sperm-whale nursery as did Ishmael, to paint in three dimensions the beauty of the world while not to harm it.

Yesterday, wandering along a railroad spur line, I glimpsed a surprising sight. All summer long, nourished by a few clods of earth on a boxcar roof, a sunflower had been growing. At last, the car had been remembered. A train was being made up. The box car with its swaying rooftop inhabitant was coupled in. The engine tooted and slowly, with nodding dignity, my plant began to travel.

Throughout the summer I had watched it grow but never troubled it. Now it lingered and bowed a trifle toward me as the winds began to touch it. A light not quite the sunlight of this earth was touching the flower, or perhaps it was the watering of my aging eye—who knows? The plant would not long survive its journey but the flower seeds were autumn-brown. At every jolt for miles they would drop along the embankment. They were travelers—travelers like Ishmael and myself, outlasting all fierce pursuits and destined to re-emerge into future autumns. Like Ishmael, I thought, they will speak with the voice of the one true agent. "I only am escaped to tell thee."

JOURNAL WRITINGS

1. **Narrate** a personal experience in which you felt in awe of nature. Relate this experience to your idea of the holy.

BRAINSTORMING AND DRAFTING

2. In a group, discuss Eiseley's idea of the holy—try to **describe** it as precisely as possible. Each group should then present its description to the whole class.

3. Discuss the **contrast** between Darwin's view and that of Freud. Try to clarify the nature of each. Write an essay of three paragraphs: one describing each view and a third explaining why Eiseley agrees with one or the other.

THE AUTHOR'S METHODS

4.   Eiseley has divided his essay into three parts. Examine each of these parts and determine its content and function. Write a paragraph in which you discuss the relationship(s) among the parts of the essay.
5.   Look for **images** in this essay. Pick three that appeal to you. Write a paragraph that **analyzes** the effect of each image.

FORMAL WRITING AND RESEARCH PAPERS

6.   What, in Eiseley's view, is essential to the nature of humanity? Compare his view to the view of Krutch. Write an essay in which you explain how their views are similar or different.
7.   Gather information about animal experiments. What types of experiments are performed? How are they conducted? What purpose(s) do they serve? Write a documented paper in which you attack or defend such experiments.
8.   Eiseley mentions Dachau, Buchenwald, and Belsen. By consulting some historical sources (you might begin with *Twentieth Century Abstracts 1914–*), find out what sort of "experiments" medical doctors conducted in these places. What justification did they offer for these experiments? Write a paper that reports on these experiments and evaluates the experimenters' reasons for performing them.

Walt Whitman

Song of Myself, Section 44
(From *Leaves of Grass)*

(1855, 1881–1882)

Born in Huntington, Long Island, New York, Walt Whitman (1819–1892), had little formal education. At the age of eleven he began to work as an office boy for a lawyer, the first of a long series of miscellaneous jobs he held throughout his life. Eventually he became a printer and an editor; thereafter, he earned his living chiefly by writing. He published the first edition of *Leaves of Grass* in 1855, but he continued to revise and extend it throughout the rest of his life. During the Civil War he moved to Washington, D.C., in order to tend the wounded. While living there he supported himself by copying documents.

    Leaves of Grass is an enormous poetic work—more like a large collection of individual poems than a single, tightly knit poem. It was Whitman's life work in which he attempted a comprehensive poetic treatment of the American experience, which he regarded as representative of the best human achievement. In this short section, the narrator, who speaks for all humanity, asserts that we hold the highest place in the universe—almost as if the forces of nature were designed to support us.

PREVIEW

Think about yourself for a moment. What makes you, as a "self," distinct from the rest of the universe? Is your "self" an inner being or is it outer (like your body)? What sort of relationship do you think that your "self" has to the rest of the universe? Jot down some of your thoughts in response to these questions.

44

It is time to explain myself—let us stand up.

What is known I strip away,
I launch all men and women forward with me into the Unknown.

The clock indicates the moment—but what does eternity indicate?

We have thus far exhausted trillions of winters and summers,
There are trillions ahead, and trillions ahead of them.

Births have brought us richness and variety,
And other births will bring us richness and variety.

I do not call one greater and one smaller,
That which fills its period and place is equal to any.

Were mankind murderous or jealous upon you, my brother, my sister?
I am sorry for you, they are not murderous or jealous upon me,
All has been gentle with me, I keep no account with lamentation,
(What have I to do with lamentation?)

I am an acme of things accomplish'd, and an encloser of things to be,
My feet strike an apex of the apices of the stairs,
On every step bunches of ages, and larger bunches between the steps,
All below duly travel'd, and still I mount and mount.

Rise after rise bow the phantoms behind me,
Afar down I see the huge first Nothing, I know I was even there,
I waited unseen and always, and slept through the lethargic mist,
And took my time, and took no hurt from the fetid carbon.

Long I was hugg'd close—long and long.

Immense have been the preparations for me,
Faithful and friendly the arms that have help'd me.

Cycles ferried my cradle, rowing and rowing like cheerful boatmen,
For room to me stars kept aside in their own rings,
They sent influences to look after what was to hold me.

Before I was born out of my mother generations guided me,
My embryo has never been torpid, nothing could overlay it.

For it the nebula cohered to an orb,
The long slow strata piled to rest it on,
Vast vegetables gave it sustenance,
Monstrous sauroids transported it in their mouths and deposited it with care.

All forces have been steadily employ'd to complete and delight me,
Now on this spot I stand with my robust soul.

JOURNAL WRITINGS

1. Write a **paraphrase** of this poem. Briefly **describe** the feelings that you experienced while reading it.
2. Clearly the author of this poem feels good about himself. Write a paragraph that explains the basis of his self-esteem. Write a second paragraph about

qualities of your own personality that you really like and that form the basis for your own self-esteem.

BRAINSTORMING AND DRAFTING

3. By yourself or in a group, list the qualities Whitman enunciates for himself as the representative man. **Compare** this list with the list of qualities that you made while considering Krutch's essay on humanism. Write a paragraph about the differences between the two lists.

THE AUTHOR'S METHODS

4. How does the poem suggest that life is a sort of vast adventure? Use specific evidence from the poem to present your conclusions.
5. What feelings does this poem convey? How does it communicate these feelings? Again, look for **specific** details (words, **images, figures of speech**) in the poem that communicate feelings.

CREATIVE PROJECT

6. Write a poem imitating Whitman's style. Choose a topic about which you have deep feelings. Allen Ginsberg's poem "A Supermarket in California" is an example of such an imitative poem.

FORMAL WRITING AND RESEARCH PAPERS

7. "Man is the measure of all things." Decide whether you agree or disagree with this epigram and how it relates to the poem. Write an essay in which you explain the epigram and the poem; then explain your own ideas of humanity by responding to the ideas in both the epigram and poem.

Henry Adams

The Dynamo
and the Virgin (1900)

(1905)

A member of the only family to produce two American presidents, Henry
Adams (1838–1918) grew up in Quincy, Massachusetts, and received a
bachelor's degree from Harvard University in 1858. He served as secretary
to his father, Charles Francis Adams, the American ambassador to England,
from 1860 to 1870. During this time he lived in Washington, D.C., and
London. He then returned to Boston and served as a member of the history
faculty at Harvard University for seven years. His chief historical work,
*History of the United States during the Administrations of Thomas Jefferson
and James Madison* (9 volumes), was published between 1884 and 1891. In
1894, Adams was elected president of the American Historical Society. No
doubt his most famous writings are *Mont-Saint-Michel and Chartres* (1912)
and *The Education of Henry Adams* (1906), for which he received the
Pulitzer Prize posthumously.

For Adams everything is changing faster than he can comprehend. As
he attends the Great Exposition at Paris he ponders the technological
change that has taken place since a similar exposition in Chicago in 1893.
He wants to place the change in some sort of context, but finds himself
unable to do so. Fascinated by the new electrical generators (dynamos), he
compares their power to the spiritual power symbolized by the Virgin of
Chartres.

PREVIEW

Is the development of technology a nightmare? Do you sometimes feel threatened by
it?

Until the Great Exposition of 1900 closed its doors in November, Adams haunted
it, aching to absorb knowledge, and helpless to find it. He would have liked to
know how much of it could have been grasped by the best-informed man in the

world. While he was thus meditating chaos, Langley* came by, and showed it to him. At Langley's behest, the Exhibition dropped its superfluous rags and stripped itself to the skin, for Langley knew what to study, and why, and how; while Adams might as well have stood outside in the night, staring at the Milky Way. Yet Langley said nothing new, and taught nothing that one might not have learned from Lord Bacon,† three hundred years before; but though one should have known the "Advancement of Science" as well as one knew the "Comedy of Errors," the literary knowledge counted for nothing until some teacher should show how to apply it. Bacon took a vast deal of trouble in teaching King James I and his subjects, American or other, towards the year 1620, that true science was the development or economy of forces; yet an elderly American in 1900 knew neither the formula nor the forces; or even so much as to say to himself that his historical business in the Exposition concerned only the economies or developments of force since 1893, when he began the study at Chicago.

Nothing in education is so astonishing as the amount of ignorance it accumulates in the form of inert facts. Adams had looked at most of the accumulations of art in the storehouses called Art Museums; yet he did not know how to look at the art exhibits of 1900. He had studied Karl Marx‡ and his doctrines of history with profound attention, yet he could not apply them at Paris. Langley, with the ease of a great master of experiment, threw out of the field every exhibit that did not reveal a new application of force, and naturally threw out, to begin with, almost the whole art exhibit. Equally, he ignored almost the whole industrial exhibit. He led his pupil directly to the forces. His chief interest was in new motors to make his airship feasible, and he taught Adams the astonishing complexities of the new Daimler§ motor, and of the automobile, which, since 1893, had become a nightmare at a hundred kilometres an hour, almost as destructive as the electric tram which was only ten years older; and threatening to become as terrible as the locomotive steam-engine itself, which was almost exactly Adams's own age.

Then he showed his scholar the great hall of dynamos, and explained how little he knew about electricity or force of any kind, even of his own special sun, which spouted heat in inconceivable volume, but which, as far as he knew, might spout less or more, at any time, for all the certainty he felt in it. To him, the dynamo itself was but an ingenious channel for conveying somewhere the heat latent in a few tons of poor coal hidden in a dirty engine-house carefully kept out of sight; but to Adams the dynamo became a symbol of infinity. As he grew accustomed to the great gallery of machines, he began to feel the forty-foot dynamos as a moral force, much as the early Christians felt the Cross. The planet itself seemed less impressive, in its old-fashioned, deliberate, annual or daily revolution, than this huge wheel, revolving within arm's-length at some ver-

---

* Langley, Samuel—(1834–1906) American astronomer and airplane developer. [Eds.]

† Bacon, Francis—(1561–1626) English statesman, philosopher, and essayist; author of *Novum Organum*. [Eds.]

‡ Marx, Karl—(1818–1883) German socialist philosopher; author of *Communist Manifesto*. [Eds.]

§ Daimler, Gottlieb—(1834–1900) developer of internal combustion engine and automobile. [Eds.]

tiginous speed, and barely murmuring—scarcely humming an audible warning to stand a hair's-breadth further for respect of power—while it would not wake the baby lying close against its frame. Before the end, one began to pray to it; inherited instinct taught the natural expression of man before silent and infinite force. Among the thousand symbols of ultimate energy, the dynamo was not so human as some, but it was the most expressive.

Yet the dynamo, next to the steam-engine, was the most familiar of exhibits. For Adams's objects its value lay chiefly in its occult mechanism. Between the dynamo in the gallery of machines and the engine-house outside, the break of continuity amounted to abysmal fracture for a historian's objects. No more relation could he discover between the steam and the electric current than between the Cross and the cathedral. The forces were interchangeable if not reversible, but he could see only an absolute *fiat* in electricity as in faith. Langley could not help him. Indeed, Langley seemed to be worried by the same trouble, for he constantly repeated that the new forces were anarchical, and especially that he was not responsible for the new rays, that were little short of parricidal in their wicked spirit towards science. His own rays, with which he had doubled the solar spectrum, were altogether harmless and beneficent; but Radium denied its God—or, what was to Langley the same thing, denied the truths of his Science. The force was wholly new.

A historian who asked only to learn enough to be as futile as Langley or Kelvin,* made rapid progress under this teaching, and mixed himself up in the tangle of ideas until he achieved a sort of Paradise of ignorance vastly consoling to his fatigued senses. He wrapped himself in vibrations and rays which were new, and he would have hugged Marconi† and Branly‡ had he met them, as he hugged the dynamo; while he lost his arithmetic in trying to figure out the equation between the discoveries and the economies of force. The economies, like the discoveries, were absolute, supersensual, occult; incapable of expression in horse-power. What mathematical equivalent could he suggest as the value of a Branly coherer? Frozen air, or the electric furnace, had some scale of measurement, no doubt, if somebody could invent a thermometer adequate to the purpose; but X-rays had played no part whatever in man's consciousness, and the atom itself had figured only as a fiction of thought. In these seven years man had translated himself into a new universe which had no common scale of measurement with the old. He had entered a supersensual world, in which he could measure nothing except by chance collisions of movements imperceptible to his senses, perhaps even imperceptible to his instruments, but perceptible to each other, and so to some known ray at the end of the scale. Langley seemed prepared

---

* Kelvin, William Thomson—(1824–1907) British mathematician and physicist who worked on thermodynamics. [Eds.]

† Marconi, Guglielmo—(1874–1937) inventor of radio. [Eds.]

‡ Branly, Edouard—(1844–1940) French physicist and inventor. His "coherer" made Marconi's work on wireless telegraphy and radio possible. [Eds.]

for anything, even for an indeterminable number of universes interfused—physics stark mad in metaphysics.

Historians undertake to arrange sequences,—called stories, or histories—assuming in silence a relation of cause and effect. These assumptions, hidden in the depths of dusty libraries, have been astounding, but commonly unconscious and childlike; so much so, that if any captious critic were to drag them to light, historians would probably reply, with one voice, that they had never supposed themselves required to know what they were talking about. Adams, for one, had toiled in vain to find out what he meant. He had even published a dozen volumes of American history for no other purpose than to satisfy himself whether, by the severest process of stating, with the least possible comment, such facts as seemed sure, in such order as seemed rigorously consequent, he could fix for a familiar moment a necessary sequence of human movement. The result had satisfied him as little as at Harvard College. Where he saw sequence, other men saw something quite different, and no one saw the same unit of measure. He cared little about his experiments and less about his statesmen, who seemed to him quite as ignorant as himself and, as a rule, no more honest; but he insisted on a relation of sequence, and if he could not reach it by one method, he would try as many methods as science knew. Satisfied that the sequence of men led to nothing and that the sequence of their society could lead no further, while the mere sequence of time was artificial, and the sequence of thought was chaos, he turned at last to the sequence of force; and thus it happened that, after ten years' pursuit, he found himself lying in the Gallery of Machines at the Great Exposition of 1900, his historical neck broken by the sudden irruption of forces totally new.

Since no one else showed much concern, an elderly person without other cares had no need to betray alarm. The year 1900 was not the first to upset schoolmasters. Copernicus* and Galileo† had broken many professorial necks about 1600; Columbus had stood the world on its head towards 1500; but the nearest approach to the revolution of 1900 was that of 310, when Constantine set up the Cross. The rays that Langley disowned, as well as those which he fathered, were occult, supersensual, irrational; they were a revelation of mysterious energy like that of the Cross; they were what, in terms of mediéval science, were called immediate modes of the divine substance.

The historian was thus reduced to his last resources. Clearly if he was bound to reduce all these forces to a common value, this common value could have no measure but that of their attraction on his own mind. He must treat them as they had been felt; as convertible, reversible, interchangeable attractions on thought. He made up his mind to venture it; he would risk translating rays into faith. Such a reversible process would vastly amuse a chemist, but the chemist could not

---

* Copernicus, Nicolaus—(1473–1543) Polish astronomer who established the heliocentric theory of the solar system. [Eds.]

† Galileo [Galilei]—(1564–1642) Italian mathematician and astronomer; proposed the heliocentric theory. [Eds.]

deny that he, or some of his fellow physicists, could feel the force of both. When Adams was a boy in Boston, the best chemist in the place had probably never heard of Venus except by way of scandal, or of the Virgin except as idolatry; neither had he heard of dynamos or automobiles or radium; yet his mind was ready to feel the force of all, though the rays were unborn and the women were dead.

Here opened another totally new education, which promised to be by far the most hazardous of all. The knife-edge along which he must crawl, like Sir Lancelot in the twelfth century, divided two kingdoms of force which had nothing in common but attraction. They were as different as a magnet is from gravitation, supposing one knew what a magnet was, or gravitation, or love. The force of the Virgin was still felt at Lourdes, and seemed to be as potent as X-rays; but in America neither Venus nor Virgin ever had value as force—at most as sentiment. No American had ever been truly afraid of either.

This problem in dynamics gravely perplexed an American historian. The Woman had once been supreme; in France she still seemed potent, not merely as a sentiment, but as a force. Why was she unknown in America? For evidently America was ashamed of her, and she was ashamed of herself, otherwise they would not have strewn fig-leaves so profusely all over her. When she was a true force, she was ignorant of fig-leaves, but the monthly-magazine-made American female had not a feature that would have been recognized by Adam. The trait was notorious, and often humorous, but any one brought up among Puritans knew that sex was sin. In any previous age, sex was strength. Neither art nor beauty was needed. Every one, even among Puritans, knew that neither Diana of the Ephesians nor any of the Oriental goddesses was worshipped for her beauty. She was goddess because of her force; she was the animated dynamo; she was reproduction—the greatest and most mysterious of all energies; all she needed was to be fecund. Singularly enough, not one of Adams's many schools of education had ever drawn his attention to the opening lines of Lucretius, though they were perhaps the finest in all Latin literature, where the poet invoked Venus exactly as Dante* invoked the Virgin:—

"Quae quoniam rerum naturam *sola* gubernas."

The Venus of Epicurean philosophy survived in the Virgin of the Schools:—

"Donna, sei tanto grande, e tanto vali,
Che qual vuol grazia, e a te non ricorre,
Sua disianza vuol volar senz' ali."

All this was to American thought as though it had never existed. The true American knew something of the facts, but nothing of the feelings; he read the letter, but he never felt the law. Before this historical chasm, a mind like that of Adams felt itself helpless; he turned from the Virgin to the Dynamo as though he were a Branly coherer. On one side, at the Louvre and at Chartres, as he knew by

---

* Dante [Alighieri]—(1265–1321) Italian epic poet; author of *The Divine Comedy*. [Eds.]

the record of work actually done and still before his eyes, was the highest energy ever known to man, the creator of four-fifths of his noblest art, exercising vastly more attraction over the human mind than all the steam-engines and dynamos ever dreamed of; and yet this energy was unknown to the American mind. An American Virgin would never dare command; an American Venus would never dare exist.

The question, which to any plain American of the nineteenth century seemed as remote as it did to Adams, drew him almost violently to study, once it was posed; and on this point Langleys were as useless as though they were Herbert Spencers* or dynamos. The idea survived only as art. There one turned as naturally as though the artist were himself a woman. Adams began to ponder, asking himself whether he knew of any American artist who had ever insisted on the power of sex, as every classic had always done; but he could think only of Walt Whitman;† Bret Harte,‡ as far as the magazines would let him venture; and one or two painters, for the flesh-tones. All the rest had used sex for sentiment, never for force; to them, Eve was a tender flower, and Herodias§ an unfeminine horror. American art, like the American language and American education, was as far as possible sexless. Society regarded this victory over sex as its greatest triumph, and the historian readily admitted it, since the moral issue, for the moment, did not concern one who was studying the relations of unmoral force. He cared nothing for the sex of the dynamo until he could measure its energy.

Vaguely seeking a clue, he wandered through the art exhibit, and, in his stroll, stopped almost every day before St. Gaudens's General Sherman, which had been given the central post of honor. St. Gaudens‖ himself was in Paris, putting on the work his usual interminable last touches, and listening to the usual contradictory suggestions of brother sculptors. Of all the American artists who gave to American art whatever life it breathed in the seventies, St. Gaudens was perhaps the most sympathetic, but certainly the most inarticulate. General Grant or Don Cameron had scarcely less instinct of rhetoric than he. All the others—the Hunts, Richardson, John La Farge, Stanford White—were exuberant; only St. Gaudens could never discuss or dilate on an emotion, or suggest artistic arguments for giving to his work the forms that he felt. He never laid down the law, or affected the despot, or became brutalized like Whistler** by the brutalities of his world. He required no incense; he was no egoist; his simplicity of thought was excessive; he could not imitate, or give any form but his own to the creations of his hand. No one felt more strongly than he the strength of other men, but the idea that they could affect him never stirred an image in his mind.

---

* Spencer, Herbert—(1820–1903) English philosopher. [Eds.]

† Whitman—see biographical profile on page 533. [Eds.]

‡ Harte, Bret—(1836–1902) American humorous writer. [Eds.]

§ Herodias—(ca. 14 B.C.–ca. A.D. 40) second wife of Herod Antipas; mother of Salome. [Eds.]

‖ St. Gaudens, Augustus—(1848–1907) American sculptor. [Eds.]

** Whistler, James Abbott McNeill—(1834–1903) American painter. [Eds.]

This summer his health was poor and his spirits were low. For such a temper, Adams was not the best companion, since his own gaiety was not *folle;* but he risked going now and then to the studio on Mont Parnasse to draw him out for a stroll in the Bois de Boulogne, or dinner as pleased his moods, and in return St. Gaudens sometimes let Adams go about in his company.

Once St. Gaudens took him down to Amiens, with a party of Frenchmen, to see the cathedral. Not until they found themselves actually studying the sculpture of the western portal, did it dawn on Adams's mind that, for his purposes, St. Gaudens on that spot had more interest to him than the cathedral itself. Great men before great monuments express great truths, provided they are not taken too solemnly. Adams never tired of quoting the supreme phrase of his idol Gibbon,* before the Gothic cathedrals: "I darted a contemptuous look on the stately monuments of superstition." Even in the footnotes of his history, Gibbon had never inserted a bit of humor more human than this, and one would have paid largely for a photograph of the fat little historian, on the background of Notre Dame of Amiens, trying to persuade his readers—perhaps himself—that he was darting a contemptuous look on the stately monument, for which he felt in fact the respect which every man of his vast study and active mind always feels before objects worthy of it; but besides the humor, one felt also the relation. Gibbon ignored the Virgin, because in 1789 religious monuments were out of fashion. In 1900 his remark sounded fresh and simple as the green fields to ears that had heard a hundred years of other remarks, mostly no more fresh and certainly less simple. Without malice, one might find it more instructive than a whole lecture of Ruskin.† One sees what one brings, and at that moment Gibbon brought the French Revolution. Ruskin brought reaction against the Revolution. St. Gaudens had passed beyond all. He liked the stately monuments much more than he liked Gibbon or Ruskin; he loved their dignity; their unity; their scale; their lines; their lights and shadows; their decorative sculpture; but he was even less conscious than they of the force that created it all—the Virgin, the Woman—by whose genius "the stately monuments of superstition" were built, through which she was expressed. He would have seen more meaning in Isis‡ with the cow's horns, at Edfoo, who expressed the same thought. The art remained, but the energy was lost even upon the artist.

Yet in mind and person St. Gaudens was a survival of the 1500; he bore the stamp of the Renaissance, and should have carried an image of the Virgin round his neck, or stuck in his hat, like Louis XI.§ In mere time he was a lost soul that had strayed by chance into the twentieth century, and forgotten where it came from. He writhed and cursed at his ignorance, much as Adams did at his own, but

---

* Gibbon, Edward—(1737–1794) English historian; author of *The Decline and Fall of the Roman Empire.* [Eds.]

† Ruskin, John—(1819–1900) English art and social critic. [Eds.]

‡ Isis—Egyptian fertility goddess. [Eds.]

§ Louis XI—(1423–1483) king who established absolute monarchy in France. [Eds.]

in the opposite sense. St. Gaudens was a child of Benvenuto Cellini,* smothered in an American cradle. Adams was a quintessence of Boston, devoured by curiosity to think like Benvenuto. St. Gaudens's art was starved from birth, and Adams's instinct was blighted from babyhood. Each had but half of a nature, and when they came together before the Virgin of Amiens they ought both to have felt in her the force that made them one; but it was not so. To Adams she became more than ever a channel of force; to St. Gaudens she remained as before a channel of taste.

For a symbol of power, St. Gaudens instinctively preferred the horse, as was plain in his horse and Victory of the Sherman monument. Doubtless Sherman also felt it so. The attitude was so American that, for at least forty years, Adams had never realized that any other could be in sound taste. How many years had he taken to admit a notion of what Michael Angelo† and Rubens‡ were driving at? He could not say; but he knew that only since 1895 had he begun to feel the Virgin or Venus as force, and not everywhere even so. At Chartres—perhaps at Lourdes—possibly at Cnidos if one could still find there the divinely naked Aphrodite of Praxiteles§—but otherwise one must look for force to the goddesses of Indian mythology. The idea died out long ago in the German and English stock. St. Gaudens at Amiens was hardly less sensitive to the force of the female energy than Matthew Arnold|| at the Grande Chartreuse.** Neither of them felt goddesses as power—only as reflected emotion, human expression, beauty, purity, taste, scarcely even as sympathy. They felt a railway train as power; yet they, and all other artists, constantly complained that the power embodied in a railway train could never be embodied in art. All the steam in the world could not, like the Virgin, build Chartres.

Yet in mechanics, whatever the mechanicians might think, both energies acted as interchangeable forces on man, and by action on man all known force may be measured. Indeed, few men of science measured force in any other way. After once admitting that a straight line was the shortest distance between two points, no serious mathematician cared to deny anything that suited his convenience, and rejected no symbol, unproved or unprovable, that helped him to accomplish work. The symbol was force, as a compass-needle or a triangle was force, as the mechanist might prove by losing it, and nothing could be gained by ignoring their value. Symbol or energy, the Virgin had acted as the greatest force the Western world ever felt, and had drawn man's activities to herself more strongly than any other power, natural or supernatural, had ever done; the historian's

---

* Cellini, Benvenuto—(1500–1571) Italian goldsmith and sculptor. [Eds.]

† Michelangelo—(1475–1564) Italian painter, sculptor, and architect. [Eds.]

‡ Rubens, Peter Paul—(1577–1640) Flemish painter. [Eds.]

§ Praxiteles—(4th century B.C.) Athenian sculptor; famous for a statue of Aphrodite at Cnidos. [Eds.]

|| Arnold, Matthew—(1822–1888) English poet and critic; author of "Dover Beach" and *Culture and Anarchy.* [Eds.]

** Grande Chartreuse—main monastery of the Carthusians, a very strict order of monks. [Eds.]

business was to follow the track of the energy; to find where it came from and where it went to; its complex source and shifting channels; its values, equivalents, conversions. It could scarcely be more complex than radium; it could hardly be deflected, diverted, polarized, absorbed more perplexingly than other radiant matter. Adams knew nothing about any of them, but as a mathematical problem of influence on human progress, though all were occult, all reacted on his mind, and he rather inclined to think the Virgin easiest to handle.

The pursuit turned out to be long and tortuous, leading at last into the vast forests of scholastic science. From Zeno* to Descartes,† hand in hand with Thomas Aquinas,‡ Montaigne,§ and Pascal,‖ one stumbled as stupidly as though one were still a German student of 1860. Only with the instinct of despair could one force one's self into this old thicket of ignorance after having been repulsed at a score of entrances more promising and more popular. Thus far, no path had led anywhere, unless perhaps to an exceedingly modest living. Forty-five years of study had proved to be quite futile for the pursuit of power; one controlled no more force in 1900 than in 1850, although the amount of force controlled by society had enormously increased. The secret of education still hid itself somewhere behind ignorance, and one fumbled over it as feebly as ever. In such labyrinths, the staff is a force almost more necessary than the legs; the pen becomes a sort of blind-man's dog, to keep him from falling into the gutters. The pen works for itself, and acts like a hand, modelling the plastic material over and over again to the form that suits it best. The form is never arbitrary, but is a sort of growth like crystallization, as any artist knows too well; for often the pencil or pen runs into side-paths and shapelessness, loses its relations, stops or is bogged. Then it has to return on its trail, and recover, if it can, its line of force. The result of a year's work depends more on what is struck out than on what is left in; on the sequence of the main lines of thought, than on their play or variety. Compelled once more to lean heavily on this support, Adams covered more thousands of pages with figures as formal as though they were algebra, laboriously striking out, altering, burning, experimenting, until the year had expired, the Exposition had long been closed, and winter drawing to its end, before he sailed from Cherbourg, on January 19, 1901, for home.

JOURNAL WRITINGS

1.   Recall a situation in which you felt helpless in the face of technology—when you thought you ought to understand something but didn't. **Describe** the situation, explaining why you felt helpless.

---

* Zeno—(5th century B.C.) Greek philosopher famous for his paradoxes. [Eds.]

† Descartes, René—(1596–1650) French mathematician and philosopher. [Eds.]

‡ Aquinas, Saint Thomas—(1225?–1274) Italian philosopher and theologian. [Eds.]

§ Montaigne, Michel de—(1533–1592) French essayist. [Eds.]

‖ Pascal, Blaise—(1623–1662) French mathematician and theologian. [Eds.]

BRAINSTORMING AND DRAFTING

2. **Compare** and **contrast** the view of power (force) presented by Adams and Krutch. To do so, you will need to **define** each view as precisely and carefully as possible. Ask yourself which view seems more useful. You might arrange a debate between two groups, focusing on the utility of the two views. After thinking about or debating this issue, present your own conclusion in a short essay.

THE AUTHOR'S METHODS

3. Why do you imagine that Adams writes about himself in the third person? In a sentence or two describe the effect that this technique has on you as a reader.

FORMAL WRITING AND RESEARCH PAPERS

4. Select a year in your own life that you regard as a crisis or turning point. Write an **autobiographical** essay dealing with that year and its events. Try to achieve the sort of objectivity that is characteristic of Adams's chapter.
5. Get a copy of a major newspaper for the date of your own birth. Look through it for a report on an important technological or scientific development. Using other sources, gather more information about that development. Write a paper in which you explain the nature and importance of the development.

Tennessee Valley Authority

Pickwick Dam, Tennessee

This photograph, from the records of the Tennessee Valley Authority, was taken by an unknown photographer on an unknown date.

JOURNAL WRITINGS

1. Given the scant information available about this photograph, it exists almost without a context. Look at the photograph and write down whatever comes to mind. Analyze what you have written—what sort of response has the photograph evoked?

BRAINSTORMING AND DRAFTING

2. Focus on the human figure in the photograph. Discuss the relationship of the person to the machines. What does the photograph suggest about this relationship?
3. Think of the human figure in the photograph as Henry Adams. Write a few sentences that connect the photograph to the excerpt from Adams's autobiography.

CREATIVE PROJECT

4. Consider this as a setting for a science fiction story. What has happened? What is about to happen? Write a short story in which this setting plays an important part.

FORMAL WRITING AND RESEARCH PAPERS

5. What is the Tennessee Valley Authority (TVA)? What is its purpose, and how has it fulfilled that purpose? Is it controversial or was it once controversial? Find answers for these questions and write a documented paper based on the information you have gathered. Organize your paper either as a report (facts about TVA) or as an **argument** (opinion about TVA).
6. In a paragraph or two, **compare** the feelings evoked by this photograph and by Henry Adams's "The Dynamo and the Virgin (1900)."

Langdon Gilkey

The Religious Dilemmas of a Scientific Culture: The Interface of Technology, History and Religion

(1979)

Langdon Gilkey (born 1919) has published numerous books on religion and culture. Brought up in Chicago, he attended Harvard University, where he received his A.B. in 1940. He then went to teach at Yenching University, near Peking. When World War II began he was imprisoned by the Japanese. After the war he continued his education at Columbia University, earning his Ph.D. in 1954. He teaches philosophy of religion at Union Theological Seminary. He has been the recipient of both Fulbright and Guggenheim Fellowships.

PREVIEW

Think about some possible conflicts between science and religion. In a few sentences, describe two or three such conflicts.

Our title may well seem puzzling. We can certainly understand that a scientific culture poses dilemmas for traditional religion of any sort. This has been assumed ever since our culture became scientific in the sixteenth and seventeenth centuries, and it became a virtual certainty in the nineteenth. But can a scientific culture as it develops raise its own religious dilemmas and show itself to be in need of religion in the way agricultural and nomadic societies were? This is the question I would like to investigate. We shall begin by exploring a middle term, history, and our understanding of history. For science has greatly influenced our sense of history, of where we are all going—and wishes to do so. And with the question of the meaning of history, religion inevitably enters the scene.

THE SCIENTIFIC/TECHNOLOGICAL PHILOSOPHY OF HISTORY

Generally speaking, scientists and technologists have not been directly concerned with philosophical questions about history and its meaning. In fact the general effect of a scientific culture has been to regard speculative philosophy, and especially philosophy of history, as about as "mythical" and full of fancy as religion and theology—and both as quite unnecessary for intelligent understanding. Nevertheless, the scientific and technological communities, despite their best intentions, so to speak, have generated out of their own abilities, commitments and hopes, a new understanding of history both reflectively and existentially, both in our thoughts and in our feelings. Indeed, almost any book by a scientist, when it speaks of the importance of science or of its role in society, reflects a particular understanding of history common to the scientific community. A philosophy of history, therefore, has been and continues to be created by science not as a result of its direct inquiries, not as a scientific hypothesis experimentally tested and as such a part of the body of scientific knowledge. Rather it is created when the scientific community thinks of its own role in history, reflects on itself and its knowledge, and sees itself through that knowledge as a creative force in history. Such a philosophy of history—and a very hopeful one—has been a presupposition, an important spiritual foundation, of the modern scientific community since its beginnings in the sixteenth century. The shattering of that spiritual base in our day has been, therefore, a crisis for the scientific community itself and for the technological culture it helped to create.

As Francis Bacon,* the father of this understanding of science and of history, reiterated: greater knowledge (empirical not speculative knowledge) leads to greater control. When men and women know the way things around them work, then they can make those things work for them. Since science leads to far greater understanding of the dynamic causes of things, science is the secret of human control over the world. Thus with the advent of the scientific method—the deliberate, organized and successful effort to *know*—a new day will dawn for mankind: a day of new power, the power to control and direct, and so the power to remake the world, the power at last to realize human purposes through intelligent inquiry and the technical control which intelligence brings. Bacon's simple empiricistic understanding of the method of science has long since been superseded; but his vision of the role of science in human society and so in history has remained as the fundamental belief and hope of the modern scientific and technological world. Through this method we now know how to know, and through that knowledge to control. And as Dewey† was to point out, the two— knowing and controlling—are in the end one and the same thing, the same power of organized intelligence, as he put it, to remake its world. Science functions as the means to human power, power over nature, society, and men and women

---

* Francis Bacon—(1561–1626) English statesman, philosopher, and essayist; author of *Novum Organum*. [Eds.]

† John Dewey—(1859–1952) American pragmatist philosopher and educational theorist. [Eds.]

alike. Thus both old and developing nations have seen scientific and technological knowledge as the keys to their military power and to their economic and social well-being—and each capital becomes fearful for its security if its "lead" in pure science is threatened.

There are many evils from which we humans suffer, and almost as many interpretations of those ills: which ones are basic and which peripheral. Generally most profound religions have interpreted the fundamental ills as coming from the inside of the self and from its finitude: from desire, pride, disloyalty, lust, mortality and death. Not so modernity. For most moderns our ills have come not from inside ourselves but from external threats: from our subjection to external forces beyond our present control and so from our inability, in being ignorant of these forces and how they work, to control them. The disasters of nature: floods and drought; the problems of heat and cold; the vast spaces of nature to traverse; the difficulties of communication; the diseases of the body; the paucity of essential goods: clothing, houses, heating, lighting and so on—these have been for modern technological man the basic "problems" that beset us in life. Since these are the main evils we face, then, if through our knowledge we can develop tools or instruments with which to deal with them, if we can control these "fates" of disaster, hunger, disease and want that afflict us from the outside, will we not be happy? Not only then can more of us survive, but through the technologizing of industry, we can survive securely, full and well—and a new kind of human life will be possible. *Homo faber*, the tool maker, transformed through science into technological and industrial man, is the "authentic" man because he alone can eradicate evil and bring in a new authentic world. Of course I have left out here those two other great issues of modernity relevant to human well-being: the distribution and control of political power and the distribution of economic goods and property. My point is, however, that whatever political or economic system we choose, this trust in science, technology and industrialism, this confidence in verified knowledge, technical know-how and organizational techniques, to cure human ills has dominated the scene, whether we look at Europe and North America, at Russia or Rumania, at India, China or Japan. The ultimate, long-term faith of this modern culture which began in Europe was in the scientist and his knowledge; but its immediate and practical hope, one may say, lay in the engineer: the builder of roads and factories, cars, tractors and planes, apartments and cities, sanitation, detergents and improved fertilizers. Through technological and industrial expansion jobs are created, wants appeased, politics made stable, food production increased, economic life rendered solvent, and so the power and self-determination of a people guaranteed. We all know this to be in large part true, and, when we are honest, we admit that we too welcome its results. Human life on our planet can hardly survive, let alone be pleasant, without these three: science, technology and industrialism.

Modern science and technology, then, brought with them, both reflectively and in our feelings, a message of promise for the future. A new and better world was now possible. Thus in the seventeenth and eighteenth centuries the theory of progress arose—slowly among philosophers and intellectuals generally and as a cultural mood slowly shared by all—out of the role science and technology were beginning to play and promised to play in society. The "future" eventually appears on a wide scale as an important category of thought, as the "place" where this "new" will appear, as the place where the ills of the past and of the present will dissolve. Science and technology produced that understanding of history which has dominated our entire present—capitalist and Marxist alike—and has spread like fire across the globe wherever this culture has gone: the sense of an open future, of a future that will be better.

Out of this confidence in progress has emerged the new historical consciousness characteristic of modern culture: a sense of man's freedom in history to remake his world, of the possibility of the conquest of fate and evil, of human potentiality to fulfill itself and its life without either divine hope or a relation to eternity. No wonder modernity has to a new generation excited with this new knowledge and new techniques seemed to make traditional religion irrelevant and unnecessary in East and West alike. Science seemed to show that religion was incredible, a result of man's childish ignorance when he did not yet understand his world or his own powers in it. But perhaps more important, science made religious salvation irrelevant now that the weakness of man in achieving his desires had through knowledge been changed into power, the power to control whatever he wills to control.

Within the new historical consciousness a new sense of change appeared. Men and women have always been aware of changes in nature and in themselves: the cycle of the seasons around them, and the pattern of birth, growth, and death in all that lives. Also, they have often been aware of confusion, chaos, and the loss of all stability in their social world—as at the end of the Roman Empire or in the feudal disorder before the Tokugawa period in Japan.* But they had not been explicitly aware of a changing social world, of a transformation of the forms of life leading to something new, until modern times. Such awareness arose partly through the cataclysmic political events that overturned a seemingly changeless order: like the French Revolution in Europe† and the Meiji restoration in Japan.‡ But the deep modern awareness of steady and cumulative historical change has arisen, I believe, through the accelerated changes that technology and industrialism have effected in all our lands. Each of us sees, and feels deeply, the inexorable disappearance of the old and the appearance of the new in our social environment. Almost as if we were peering out of a speeding locomotive, the world we grew up in and felt at home in flashes by at lightning speed to be replaced by new scenery, by a new world. And with that transformation of the environment by expanding cities, exploding factories and new roads have come equally drastic changes in modes of life, in social relations, in the roles we each play in our world. We know in a new way that we live in a historical process, a process of the steady

---

* Tokugawa period—the era (1603–1867) when the shoguns of the Tokugawa family ruled Japan. [Eds.]

† French Revolution—the popular revolution that overthrew the Bourbon monarchy in 1789. [Eds.]

‡ Meiji restoration—in 1868, the emperor of Japan was restored as the active head of government, ending 1000 years of rule by military and civil governors. [Eds.]

change of the forms of our social environment and so of ourselves. We are conscious in a quite new way of being immersed in history, and thus of facing with tomorrow a world we may not expect or even want. It is no surprise that modern philosophy—of almost all sorts, naturalistic, idealistic, existential—has emphasized process, change and the temporality of being as opposed to the eternity and changelessness of being. This has been the modern experience of whatever being we have known, and our philosophies have expressed this sense of the historicity of all that is.

For most people—except for those given privileges by the old order—it was with relief, joy and expectation that the world of yesterday was disappearing and a new world of tomorrow was coming. Thus when this sense of change first appeared, it felt good: change was promise, the promise of a new that would be better. To be in process feels good if process equals growth and progress. Change has a different feel, however, if we are not too sure whether the new will be better or not; and it is terrifying if the new appears as menacing. In any case, it is evident once again how science, technology, and industrialism as the main agents of change in our social world have generated feelings and reflections about history. They have together helped to create our historical consciousness, our awareness of our historicity and temporality: that we are what we are in historical process, that we are immersed in social change, and that we can through intelligence and will refashion, shape, and direct that change. Despite all its positivism and empiricism, its impatience with speculative philosophy and theology, modernity at the deepest level has been founded on a new philosophy of history: a philosophy built on faith in knowledge and its power to control, on the triumph through knowledge of human purposes over blind fate, and so on the confidence that change—if guided by intelligence informed by inquiry—can realize human fulfillment in this life. Such a view of history as guided by science and shaped by technology was the implicit "religion" of the West until yesterday.

THE ANXIETY AND AMBIGUITY
ATTENDING SCIENCE/TECHNOLOGY

A change both in mood and in reflection, in feelings and in explicit thought, has occurred in the last decades with regard to this fundamental confidence in science and technology, and all that they imply about freedom, history and the future—like a sudden cover of storm clouds shutting out the bright sun. A chill, thematized in art, drama, novels and films and felt, if not thematized by most people, has settled over much of the West. The scientific community in particular is uncertain in an unprecedented way about its role and worried about its future and the future of the society it helped to create. Such anxiety appears whenever a "religious" confidence becomes shaky. The center of this new *Angst* is, I believe, a new intuition of the *ambiguity* of science and technology as forces in history. This is not primarily an uncertainty about the validity of scientific knowledge or about the reliability of technological skills. About these there are few new doubts—except among small (but growing) mystical and religious communities in the counterculture. It is rather a radical doubt about their "saving" character and an anxious feeling that they create as many new problems and dilemmas for human life as they resolve, and even that they compound our ills rather than dissolve them.

Beneath this anxiety, but rarely explicitly expressed, lie deeper and more devastating questions. If a valid science and a reliable technology can really compound our problems rather than dissolve them, what does *that* mean about man and about the history he helps to create? Do we really increase our dilemmas by using our intelligence, our inquiry, our techniques? What does *that* mean about us? When these questions are asked, it becomes evident that the *user* of knowledge and technology, and so man himself, is the cause of this ambiguity. Possibly knowledge, informed intelligence and the freedom to enact human purposes that they give are not enough. Something seems to be radically wrong with the ways we use our intelligence, our knowledge, and with the ways we enact our control. Can it be true that human creativity, in which we have so deeply believed, is in some strange way self-destructive, that there is in human freedom an element of the "demonic," and that intelligence and informed freedom, far from exorcising the fates of history, can create their own forms of fate over which they also have no control? As is evident, all the great philosophical and especially religious problems about human life are implicitly raised here, problems unanswerable by science and unresolvable by technology, and yet raised by both of them the moment the future they seem to create becomes apparently oppressive and menacing rather than bright and promising.

As we all know, these deeper questions about scientific knowledge and control have been brewing for some time. They began with the development and use of the terrible new weapons and the threat to human life itself which the technological power evidenced in those weapons represented. These questions continued with the realization that technology provides the political authorities and a potential scientific elite with new and dangerous powers over ordinary people: political powers based not only on weapons and communications systems unavailable to the people, but also on the possibility of psychological and even genetic control of entire populations. Technology seemed now not so much to guarantee freedom and self-determination, individuality of life-style and privacy of personal existence, freedom from *natural* fates and freedom for becoming human, but rather it seemed to open up the possibility of an all-encompassing totalitarianism that could crush individuality and humanity, a possibility in which the human would be subordinated to a new kind of *social* and *historical* fate. These fears have been expressed for some decades in the Western consciousness—for example by Huxley* and Orwell.† However, two new factors have recently become visible that have widely increased this uneasiness about a technological culture: one of them since World War II and the other in the last decade.

---

*Aldous Huxley—(1894–1963) English novelist and essayist; author of *Brave New World*. [Eds.]

† George Orwell—pseudonym of Eric Arthur Blair (1903–1950), English author who wrote *Animal Farm* and *1984*. [Eds.]

THE DEHUMANIZATION ATTENDING
A TECHNOLOGICAL CULTURE

The first can be referred to as the dehumanizing effects of a technological culture. As Jacques Ellul* has pointed out, technology is not only a matter of tools, instruments, machines and computers. It also characterizes a society in so far as it is organized, systematized or rationalized into an efficient organization: as in an army, an efficient business or a bureaucracy. Here all the human parts are integrated with each other into a practical, efficient, smooth-running organization where no time, effort or materials are wasted, where the product or the service is quickly, correctly and inexpensively created, and where a minimum of loss, error and cross-purpose is achieved. Thus are homes put up all alike by a single company and according to a single plan—for efficiency's sake. Thus is local government submerged in national bureaucracy. Thus do individual farms give way to farming combines. Thus is every small industry swallowed up by large, unified business or state concerns. The beneficial results of this technologizing or rationalizing of society are obvious: the rising standards of living of America, Europe and Japan have directly depended on the development of this sort of efficient, centralized administration of industry, distribution, services and government. And every developing country seeks to increase as rapidly as possible its rationalization of production and organization in order to feed, clothe, house and defend its people.

In the midst of these benefits, however, there have appeared other, negative consequences. As every advanced technological society has discovered, human beings are now not so much masters as the servants of the organizations they have created, servants in the sense that they find themselves "caught" and rendered inwardly helpless within the system in so far as they participate in it at all. By this I mean that they experience their personness, their individuality, their unique gifts, creativity and joy, their sense of their own being and worth sacrificed to the common systematic effort—an effort in which all that their own thought and ingenuity can contribute is to devise more practical means to an uncriticized end. Any considerations they might raise concerning creativity, aesthetics or the moral meaning of what is being done, any suggestions that might compromise the efficiency, the smooth-running of the whole team, are ipso facto "impracticable" and so by these standards irrational. Thus does the individuality of each lose its transcendence over the system; individual minds and consciences cease to be masters and become servants, devoted only to the harmony and success of the system. Human beings are present and are creative, but only as parts of a system; their worth is judged only with regard to their contribution as an efficient part; they are lured into being merely *parts* of a machine.

Society as a unified system has, moreover, proved ruthlessly destructive of many of the other, less public grounds of our identity as persons. It uproots us from that in which much of our identity, or sense of it, is founded, namely, our

---

*Jacques Ellul—(1912–) French theologian and social critic; author of *The Technological Society*. [Eds.]

identification with a particular place and with a particular community. For it gathers us into ever larger groups of people similarly organized, and then it moves us about from here to there, from these people to those, within the larger society. It rewards and satisfies us only externally by giving us things to consume or to watch. After all, such things are all that efficient organization can produce. Having dampened our creative activity in the world into the rote work expected of a mere part of a system, it now smothers the intensity of our private enjoyments by offering us the passive pleasures of mere consumption. Thus does it stifle our inwardness.

Ironically the West had in its spiritual career discovered and emphasized, as had no other culture, the reality, uniqueness and value of the inwardness of each human being, of what was once called the "soul." But a concurrent theme, its affirmation of the goodness of life, the intelligibility of the world and the possibility through knowledge of the latter's manipulation and control, has gradually achieved an almost exclusive dominance. The combination of these two themes had promised to reshape human existence in relation both to nature and to the forms of social life, culminating in technology, democracy and socialism. Thus in comparison with the Eastern world, the West had creatively learned to manipulate the external, objective world and done much to humanize and rationalize the objective social order. But it has in the process endangered its own inward soul, the reality and creativity of the spirit. Thus having through science, technology, democracy and socialism helped to rescue the Orient's social orders, it now must turn back to the Orient in order to rediscover its own inwardness. And it is doing so in great numbers—ironically just when the Orient is itself grasping after the lures of Western technology and external progress!

Technological society promised to free the individual from crushing work, from scarcity, disease and want, to free him to become himself by dispensing with these external fates. In many ways, on the contrary, it has emptied (or threatens to do so) rather than freed the self by placing each person in a homogeneous environment, setting him as a replaceable part within an organized system, and satisfying his external wants rather than energizing his creative powers. Thus appears the first paradox: the organization of modern society necessary to the survival and well-being of the race seems now to menace the humanity, the inwardness and the creativity, of the race. In seeking to live by means of a surplus of goods unknown before and for the sake of such goods, we have found that men and women are in danger of losing themselves inwardly and so of dying in the process. What had been seen clearly with regard to individual life by the wisdom of almost every religious tradition, has been proved objectively on a vast scale by modern consumer culture: men and women cannot live by bread alone.

THE ECOLOGICAL CRISIS ATTENDING ADVANCED TECHNOLOGY

Consciousness of the second menacing face of technology is astoundingly recent, within the last half-decade. This may be termed the "ecology" crisis in its widest connotations. It refers not only to the problems of technological and industrial pollution of the water, air and earth and the despoilation of whatever natural beauties are left—though these are serious enough problems, and with energy and resources short will only get worse! It refers centrally to the exhaustion through expanded industrial production of the earth's available resources, in the end a far more serious problem. Medicine and greater production of food have increased the population; technology in both agriculture and industry has at an accelerating pace increased our use of nature's resources of fuels, metals and chemicals. In order to feed and care for that mounting population, such agricultural and industrial growth must itself expand almost exponentially. And yet if it does, an absolute limit or term will soon be reached; these resources will come to an end, if not in two or three generations, then surely in four or five. The seemingly infinite expansion of civilization and its needs is in collision course with the obstinate finitude of available nature and threatens to engulf both civilization and nature. For the first time man's freedom in history menaces not only his fellow humans but nature as well. In the past, with the development of the techniques of civilization, history was freed from the overwhelming power of nature and its cycles and submitted nature to her own control. Now civilization and history have become so dominant in their power that they threaten to engulf nature in their own ambiguity.

In this case that ambiguity is very great. A world economy, whether its domestic forms be socialist or capitalist, facing the combination of expanded populations and both depleted and diminishing resources, is a world facing even more bitter rivalries and conflicts than the past has known. It is also, ironically, a world facing in new forms precisely those "fates" from which technology had promised to save us: scarcity, crowding, want and undue authority. If there are to be rational solutions to these problems impinging on us from the future, and there are, they will require an immense increase in corporate planning and control on a world scale: control of technological developments, of the industrial use of natural resources, of distribution, of the wide disparities in the use and consumption of resources. Freedom of experiment, freedom for new and radical thoughts and techniques, freedom for individual life-styles, may well be unaffordable luxuries in that age. Perhaps most important, such rational and peaceful solutions will require from the nations with power an extraordinary self-restraint in the use of their power, a willingness to sacrifice their affluence lest they be tempted to use their power to grab all that is left for the sake of that affluence. All of this bespeaks an increase of authority in our future undreamed of in the technological utopias of the recent past. Whether we desire it or not, we seem headed for a less free, less affluent, less individualistic, less dynamic and less innovative world. The long-term results of science and technology seem ironically to be bringing about anything but the individualistic, creative, secure world they originally promised. In fact this progressive, dynamic, innovative civilization seems to be in the process of generating its own antithesis: a stable, even stagnant society with an iron structure of rationality and authority, with a minimum of goods, of self-determination, of intellectual and personal freedom. Such a new and grim world is by no means a certainty, for nothing in history is fated. But unless our public life—technological, political, and economic—is directed by more reason and more self-sacrifice than in the past, such a future has a disturbingly high probability.

THE AMBIGUITIES OF TECHNOLOGY
AND THE AMBIGUITIES OF FREEDOM

As the hopes latent in science and technology gave birth despite themselves to a new understanding of history, so the new sense of their ambiguity raises for us a host of unavoidable questions about history and the relation of human freedom—of human intelligence, will and creativity—to history. Along with language, technology is in itself one of the most vivid manifestations of human freedom over its immediate environment. And, as we have seen, its growth in modernity has sparked the consciousness of that freedom in history, the ability of man to remake his world. And yet paradoxically, technology seems not so much creative of the freedom it represents as destructive of it—for it seems to be creating conditions which will of necessity absorb freedom into authority. Here the exercise of technological freedom, in order to remove the fates that determine freedom from the outside, has *itself* become a fate that menaces freedom—a strange ending.

This most vivid manifestation of freedom has exacerbated and not resolved the ambiguity of freedom, or of our use of it. In fact, technology, the creature of our freedom, has revealed the continual presence of what we can only call the demonic in history, the way our freedom is itself estranged and strangely bound—an old religious concept. For what clearly is amiss here, what reintroduces the ills we had thought almost banished, is not our intelligence, inquiry and technology per se; our creativity in itself is not at fault. Rather it is the demonic use to which it is put. At fault, as our religious traditions have emphasized, are the infinite desire and concupiscence, the greed and selfishness which motivate our use of scientific intelligence and technological power, which drive the infinity of industrial expansion that in turn ravishes and desecrates nature, and spurs us all to rivalry, conflict and doom. Under and behind the creativity of man, recently so clear to the modern West as the principle of historical salvation, lies the estrangement and so the demonic principle within man—whatever may be his ideals, his loyalties, his courage and ingenuity. Finally, and most ironically of all, man as the tool maker, as inquirer and technologist, has by modern savants been regarded as the paradigm of survival. He, not religious, mystical or mythical man, was the "practical" one who alone could handle "reality." Strangely now *homo faber*, as technologist supreme, seems himself to be alienated from "reality," bringing about through his technology his own self-destruction and showing himself to be the primary danger to the survival of his race. No more startling contradiction to the spirit of modernity from the Enlightenment to the present could be conceived.

Thus anew has what we can only call the *mystery* of history and of temporal being revealed itself to us, along with the potentiality of meaninglessness in the human story, as well as in individual life. Human creativity—yes, even informed intelligence and good purposes—is not simply "god" bringing to us unadulterated blessings, the answers to our every wish. With our creativity freeing us from old fates comes fate in a new form; with our creativity the demonic seems to be continually reintroduced into history. We live in a far stranger and more disturbing history than we thought, where even our apparent victories, our most cherished mastery, our greatest intellectual and practical triumphs, help to seal our doom!

THE AMBIGUITIES OF TECHNOLOGY AND RELIGIOUS RESPONSE

I need not in conclusion underline that these paradoxes arising out of the role of science and technology in modern life raise religious issues. It is obvious that all these questions make direct contact with the themes, meanings, questions and answers of speculative philosophy and high religion. If it is the way we use our creativity, our intelligence and freedom—not our lack of them—that is at fault, then is there any recourse for us from this estrangement of our own most treasured and precious powers, from this bondage of our wills to self-destruction? We seem to need rescue not so much from our ignorance and our weakness as from our own creative strength—not so that either our creativity or intelligence is lost, but so that their self-destructive power is gone. Thus the religious question of a transcendent *ground* of renewal, not from ourselves but from beyond ourselves, is raised by the most impressive of modernity's achievements—its scientific intelligence and its technological capacities. The creative role of religion is not to replace intelligence and technology with something else, but to enable us to be more intelligent, more rational, more self-controlled, and more just in our use of them. Further, if it is our use of creativity which threatens the meaning of our history—because it renders ambiguous our common future—then again the question of a meaning in *history* which is more than meaning which we can create or give to history appears. In the face of the fate with which our own creativity seems able to dominate us, the religious question arises whether there is any other providence that can rule the fates that seem to rule over us. Our history and our future are not threatened by the stars or the blind gods—by forces beyond us. Ironically they are threatened by a fate which our own freedom and ingenuity have themselves created. Here too, therefore, for us to be able to face our future with confidence—for we can no more live without technology than we can apparently live humanely with it—we must trust in a power that tempers and transmutes the evil that is in our every good and the unreason that is in our highest intelligence.

Such issues as these, raised not against science and technology but precisely by them, cannot be understood or even discussed without religious categories. Moreover, on the existential as well as on the reflective level, they cannot be handled without a confidence and a trust born of religion. The anxieties involved in facing such a potentially menacing future require the serenity, the courage and the willingness to sacrifice which only touch with the transcendent can bring. Modern culture in the development of its science and technology has not made religion irrelevant. It has made religious understanding and the religious spirit more necessary than ever if we are to be human and even if we are to survive. Technology by itself, technical-manipulative reason, if made the exclusive form of reason and of creativity, has been clearly shown to possess a built-in element that leads to its own destruction and the destruction of all it manipulates. It must be complemented by the religious dimension of man and by the participating, uniting function of reason if it, and we, are to survive at all.

Specifically, science, technology and the society they constitute must be tempered and shaped by the religious dimension of man, not with regard to their own modes of inquiry, their conclusions or even their specific programs—though the latter do need ethical as well as "practical" assessment; rather this tempering and shaping has to do with the humans who use them and on whom they are used. From religion alone has traditionally come the concern with the human that can prevent the manipulation of men and the dehumanization of society; and from religion alone can come the vision or conception of the human that can creatively guide social policy. From religious confidence alone has come the courage in the face of fate and despair—especially when these two arise from the distortion of *our own* creativity—concerning a future that will by no means be easier than the past. For humanism can count on only our own deepest creativity; when that too reveals itself as ambiguous, then despair and cynicism rather than humanistic confidence appear. From religion alone can come the healing of desire and concupiscence, that demonic driving force behind our use of technology that ravishes the world. And from religion alone can come a new understanding of the unity of nature, history and mankind—not in human subservience to nature and her cycles, but in an attitude which, recognizing the unique spiritual creativity of mankind, can still find human life a dependent part of a larger spiritual whole that includes the natural world on which we depend. Such a unity with nature has been expressed in much traditional religion, especially in the Orient. It must be re-expressed and reintegrated in the light of the modern consciousness of human freedom, technology and of history. Naturalistic humanism cannot achieve such a unity with nature through spirit. Without the category of the ultimate, the transcendent, or the divine beyond and yet inclusive of both nature and human being, man is either subordinated to nature or, recognizing his transcendence, uses her for his own "superior" ends. Thus religion is necessary in a technological society if such a society and the nature on which it depends are to survive.

But—and religion both East and West should take note—it is only a religion related to history, to social existence and to the human in its social and historical context that can complement, shape and temper technology. A religion that lifts us out of time or gives us only individual peace, that vacates society and history in favor of transcendence alone, will only encourage an irresponsible and so a demonic technology and will foster and not conquer a sense of fate within history. We are, whether we will or not, *in* history, immersed in historical and social process; and here our lives for good or ill are led. On our response to the social and historical destiny of our time—in this case a technological destiny of vast ambiguity—rests the validity and meaning of our inward spiritual life, of our religion. Only a religion that responds to a transcendence beyond our own self-destructive powers and yet that finds its task centered in our common historical and social future can become a genuine means of grace to us.

JOURNAL WRITINGS

1.   Gilkey asks whether a scientific culture needs religion. How does he answer this question? List the reasons he offers in support of his assertion.
2.   In your journal make some notes about the way that science affects your religious beliefs. Evaluate the impact of science on these beliefs; for instance, is its influence serious or only of minor importance?
3.   Select three or four quotations from this essay that deal with the philosophy of history; copy these quotations into your journal. Use **paraphrases** of these quotations to write a paragraph that **summarizes** the philosophy of history that Gilkey believes most scientists have held.

BRAINSTORMING AND DRAFTING

4.   Discuss the notion of evil. What is it? (Do not ignore the possibility that there may be more than one type of evil.) What is its source(s)? Use the discussion of these questions as the basis for a paragraph about how our concept of evil relates to science.
5.   Gilkey describes Bacon's view of the result of the scientific method when he says: "a new day will dawn for mankind: a day of new power, the power to control and direct, and so the power to remake the world, the power at last to realize human purposes through intelligent inquiry and the technical control which intelligence brings."
      Go back to Krutch's essay. On pages 515–516, you will find his comments on power. Discuss these two views, considering some of the following points: What strengths and/or weaknesses does each have? Is one or the other clearly wrong? Can the two be reconciled in any way? Write a brief statement that **summarizes** the discussion.

THE AUTHOR'S METHODS

6.   Gilkey often speaks of "religion," but he never mentions any specific religion. Why does he do this? How does this affect you as a reader?
7.   Write a **definition** of the "demonic" as Gilkey uses it. Compare what you have written with a dictionary definition. How do they differ? Are the differences significant?

FORMAL WRITING AND RESEARCH PAPERS

8.   Investigate the Meiji restoration in Japan. Write a documented argument showing whether it has had a profound impact upon shaping contemporary Japanese society.
9.   Gilkey regards exhaustion of resources as the primary ecological problem. Choose a resource (for example, oil) and research its use and availability. Write a documented report about our dependence on the particular resource and what impact its exhaustion might have on society.

O. B. Hardison

Disappearing Through the Skylight

(1989)

An outstanding scholar and literary critic, O. B. Hardison (1928–1990) received his A.B. and M.A. from the University of North Carolina. He went on to earn his Ph.D. at the University of Wisconsin. After teaching at the University of Tennessee at Knoxville and at Princeton, he joined the English faculty of the University of North Carolina in 1957, where he taught until 1969. He then became director of the Folger Shakespeare Library in Washington, D.C., a position that he held for the next fourteen years. In addition to scholarly works dealing with Medieval and Renaissance drama, he published *Toward Freedom and Dignity: The Humanities and the Idea of Humanity* (1974), *Entering the Maze: Identity and Change in Modern Culture* (1981), and *Upon the Shoulders of Giants: The Shaping of the Modern World* (1988).

This piece is a chapter from his most recent book, *Disappearing Through the Skylight: Culture and Technology in the Twentieth Century,* in which he argues that technology has produced a fundamental discontinuity in the way that human beings view the universe. Our past, with its sense of sequence and cause/effect relationships, is being replaced by a future in which order has little importance—or people impose whatever order they desire upon the world.

PREVIEW

Think about music videos. What sort of "reality" (if any) do they present? What is their appeal?

Science is committed to the universal. A sign of this is that the more successful a science becomes, the broader the agreement about its basic concepts: there is not a separate Chinese or American or Soviet thermodynamics, for example; there is simply thermodynamics. For several decades of the twentieth century there was a Western and a Soviet genetics, the latter associated with Lysenko's* theory that environmental stress *can* produce genetic mutations. Today Lysenko's theory is discredited, and there is now only one genetics.

---

* Lysenko, Trofim—(1898–1976) Russian biologist and agronomist. [Eds.]

As the corollary of science, technology also exhibits the universalizing tendency. This is why the spread of technology makes the world look ever more homogeneous. Architectural styles, dress styles, musical styles—even eating styles—tend increasingly to be world styles. The world looks more homogeneous because it *is* more homogeneous. Children who grow up in this world therefore experience it as a sameness rather than a diversity, and because their identities are shaped by this sameness, their sense of differences among cultures and individuals diminishes. As buildings become more alike, the people who inhabit the buildings become more alike. The result is described precisely in a phrase that is already familiar: the disappearance of history.

The automobile illustrates the point with great clarity. A technological innovation like streamlining or all-welded body construction may be rejected initially, but if it is important to the efficiency or economics of automobiles, it will reappear in different ways until it is not only accepted but universally regarded as an asset. Today's automobile is no longer unique to a given company or even to a given national culture. Its basic features are found, with variations, in automobiles in general, no matter who makes them.

A few years ago the Ford Motor Company came up with the Fiesta, which it called the "World Car." Advertisements showed it surrounded by the flags of all nations. Ford explained that the cylinder block was made in England, the carburetor in Ireland, the transmission in France, the wheels in Belgium, and so forth.

The Fiesta appears to have sunk without a trace. But the idea of a world car was inevitable. It was the automotive equivalent of the International Style. Ten years after the Fiesta, all of the large automakers were international. Americans had plants in Europe, Asia, and South America, and Europeans and Japanese had plants in America and South America, and in the Soviet Union (Fiat workers refreshed themselves with Pepsi-Cola). In the fullness of time international automakers will have plants in Egypt and India and the People's Republic of China.

As in architecture, so in automaking. In a given cost range, the same technology tends to produce the same solutions. The visual evidence for this is as obvious for cars as for buildings. Today, if you choose models in the same price range, you will be hard put at 500 paces to tell one make from another. In other words, the specifically American traits that lingered in American automobiles in the 1960s—traits that linked American cars to American history—are disappearing. Even the Volkswagen Beetle has disappeared and has taken with it the visible evidence of the history of streamlining that extends from D'Arcy Thompson* to Carl Breer† to Ferdinand Porsche.‡

---

* Thompson, D'Arcy—(1860–1948) American biologist who invented the word *streamline;* author of *On Growth and Form.* [Eds.]

† Breer, Carl—designed the Chrysler Airflow in 1934. [Eds.]

‡ Porsche, Ferdinand—(1909–) designed the Volkswagen. [Eds.]

If man creates machines, machines in turn shape their creators. As the automobile is universalized, it universalizes those who use it. Like the World Car he drives, modern man is becoming universal. No longer quite an individual, no longer quite the product of a unique geography and culture, he moves from one climate-controlled shopping mall to another, from one airport to the next, from one Holiday Inn to its successor three hundred miles down the road; but somehow his location never changes. He is cosmopolitan. The price he pays is that he no longer has a home in the traditional sense of the word. The benefit is that he begins to suspect home in the traditional sense is another name for limitations, and that home in the modern sense is everywhere and always surrounded by neighbors.

The universalizing imperative of technology is irresistible. Barring the catastrophe of nuclear war, it will continue to shape both modern culture and the consciousness of those who inhabit that culture.

This brings us to art and history again. Reminiscing on the early work of Francis Picabia and Marcel Duchamp,* Madame Gabrielle Buffet-Picabia wrote of the discovery of the machine aesthetic in 1949: "I remember a time . . . when every artist thought he owed it to himself to turn his back on the Eiffel Tower, as a protest against the architectural blasphemy with which it filled the sky. . . . The discovery and rehabilitation of . . . machines soon generated propositions which evaded all tradition, above all, a mobile, *extra* human plasticity which was absolutely new. . . ."

Art is, in one definition, simply an effort to name the real world. Are machines "the real world" or only its surface? Is the real world that easy to find? Science has shown the insubstantiality of the world. It has thus undermined an article of faith: the thingliness of things. At the same time, it has produced images of orders of reality underlying the thingliness of things. Are images of cells or of molecules or of galaxies more or less real than images of machines? Science has also produced images that are pure artifacts. Are images of self-squared dragons† more or less real than images of molecules?

The skepticism of modern science about the thingliness of things implies a new appreciation of the humanity of art entirely consistent with Kandinsky's‡ observation in *On the Spiritual in Art* that beautiful art "springs from inner need, which springs from the soul."* Modern art opens on a world whose reality is not "out there" in nature defined as things seen from a middle distance but "in here" in the soul or the mind. It is a world radically emptied of history because it is a form of perception rather than a content.

---

* Picabia, Francis (1879–1953), and Duchamp, Marcel (1887–1968)—French painters associated with beginning of Dadaism, an early twentieth-century art movement that rejected all conventions. [Eds.]

† self-squared dragons—phrase used to describe certain features of Mandelbrot fractal equations. [Eds.]

‡ Kandinsky, Wassily—(1866–1944) Russian post-impressionist painter, associated with the Bauhaus group. [Eds.]

The disappearance of history is thus a liberation—what Madame Buffet-Picabia refers to as the discovery of "a mobile extra-human plasticity which [is] absolutely new." Like science, modern art often expresses this feeling of liberation through play—in painting in the playfulness of Picasso and Joan Miró* and in poetry in the nonsense of Dada and the mock heroics of a poem like Wallace Stevens's† "The Comedian as the Letter C."

The playfulness of the modern aesthetic is, finally, its most striking—and also its most serious and, by corollary, its most disturbing—feature. The playfulness imitates the playfulness of science that produces game theory and virtual particles and black holes and that, by introducing human growth genes into cows, forces students of ethics to reexamine the definition of cannibalism. The importance of play in the modern aesthetic should not come as a surprise. It is announced in every city in the developed world by the fantastic and playful buildings of postmodernism and neomodernism and by the fantastic juxtapositions of architectural styles that typify collage city and urban adhocism.

Today modern culture includes the geometries of the International Style, the fantasies of façadism, and the gamesmanship of theme parks and museum villages. It pretends at times to be static but it is really dynamic. Its buildings move and sway and reflect dreamy visions of everything that is going on around them. It surrounds its citizens with the linear sculpture of pipelines and interstate highways and high-tension lines and the delicate virtuosities of the surfaces of the Chrysler Airflow and the Boeing 747 and the lacy weavings of circuits etched on silicon, as well as with the brutal assertiveness of oil tankers and bulldozers and the Tinkertoy complications of trusses and geodesic domes and lunar landers. It abounds in images and sounds and values utterly different from those of the world of natural things seen from a middle distance.

It is a human world, but one that is human in ways no one expected. The image it reveals is not the worn and battered face that stares from Leonardo's self-portrait, much less the one that stares, bleary and uninspired, every morning from the bathroom mirror. These are the faces of history. It is, rather, the image of an eternally playful and eternally youthful power that makes order whether order is there or not and that having made one order is quite capable of putting it aside and creating an entirely different one the way a child might build one structure from a set of blocks and then without malice and purely in the spirit of play demolish it and begin again. It is an image of the power that made humanity possible in the first place.

The banks of the nineteenth century tended to be neoclassic structures of marble or granite faced with ponderous rows of columns. They made a statement: "We are solid. We are permanent. We are as reliable as history. Your money is safe in our vaults."

---

* Picasso, Pablo—(1881–1973) Spanish painter and sculptor who developed cubism; Miró, Joan—(1893–1984) Spanish painter and sculptor who developed surrealism. [Eds.]

† Stevens, Wallace—(1879–1955) American poet. [Eds.]

Today's banks are airy structures of steel and glass, or they are storefronts with slot-machinelike terminals, or trailers parked on the lots of suburban shopping malls.

The vaults have been replaced by magnetic tapes. In a computer, money is sequences of digital signals endlessly recorded, erased, processed, and reprocessed, and endlessly modified by other computers. The statement of modern banks is "We are abstract like art and almost invisible like the Crystal Palace. If we exist at all, we exist as an airy medium in which your transactions are completed and your wealth increased."

That, perhaps, establishes the logical limit of the modern aesthetic. If so, the limit is a long way ahead, but it can be made out, just barely, through the haze over the road. As surely as nature is being swallowed up by the mind, the banks, you might say, are disappearing through their own skylights.

JOURNAL WRITINGS

1.   As briefly and concisely as possible, tell what this reading is about.
2.   Jot down several examples of the universalizing effect of technology. Ask yourself how you might use these for a paper.

BRAINSTORMING AND DRAFTING

3.   Hardison quotes Kandinsky as saying that art "springs from inner need, which springs from the soul." Is it possible to see science as having the same source? Consider R. R. Wilson's comments on the humanness of science in this connection. Write an outline of the main points for an **argument** about the sources of science and art.
4.   In a group, discuss the universalizing effects of technology. You may want to use the examples you jotted down in your journal writing. Are these effects positive or negative (or some combination of the two)? Exchange ideas about how you would use the various examples to deal with the positive or negative nature of these effects. List all the writing possibilities that the group has suggested.

THE AUTHOR'S METHODS

5.   Identify the central **metaphor** in this essay. Write a paragraph in which you discuss the function and effectiveness of this metaphor.
6.   Carefully examine the **image** of banks, which he introduces near the end of the essay. Explain why you think it is (or is not) an appropriate image for modern culture.

FORMAL WRITING AND RESEARCH PAPERS

7.   In this reading, Hardison refers to several people. Select one of these people (you will find some basic information in the footnotes). Find and read a biography or biographical article about the person. Write a report in which you explain what contribution this person has made to contemporary culture.

8.   Use the outline that you wrote in response to question 3 above to write a fully developed paper.

Harold Edgerton

Milk Drop Coronet 1957

(1957)

Harold Edgerton (1904–1990) is most famous for inventing the strobe light, which made high-speed stop-action photography possible. A member of the electrical engineering faculty at the Massachusetts Institute of Technology for nearly forty years, he produced numerous photographs that revolutionized the way we look at ordinary actions. He was also instrumental in developing sonar equipment used in undersea exploration.

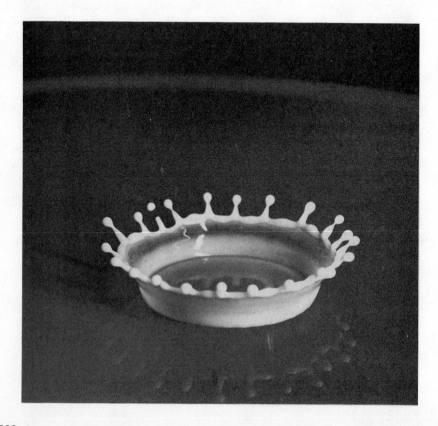

JOURNAL WRITINGS

1.   Do you perceive beauty in this photograph? Jot down some notes toward identifying the reasons you do or do not regard it as beautiful (producing an aesthetic pleasure).

BRAINSTORMING AND DRAFTING

2.   Artists have always attempted to "open the eyes" of the general public by leading them to a different (perhaps deeper) view of reality. Consider the impact of technology in this regard (not only photography and strobe lights, but TV—instant replays, laser light shows, whatever). Discuss whether these developments provide a better, deeper perception of reality or merely a distortion of it. Write a summary of the points presented for each side of the **argument.**

CREATIVE PROJECT

3.   Perhaps you take photography seriously. Look at some of your own photographs. Select one that shows reality in a way that our ordinary visual perception would not. Write an essay about the difference(s) that your photograph reveals. Be sure to attach a copy of the photo to the essay if you are submitting it for evaluation.

FORMAL WRITING AND RESEARCH PAPERS

4.   Use the **summaries** you wrote in response to question 2 to decide whether technological advances have improved or distorted our perceptions of reality. Write a fully developed and convincing **argument** supporting the position you have chosen.
5.   Find out about strobe photography. Write a report that explains how it works in a way that an ordinary college student can understand.
6.   O. B. Hardison's article talks about our perceptions of reality. Reread his piece and use some of his ideas to write an essay in which you discuss how this picture changed your perception of reality.

R. R. Wilson

The Humanness of Physics

(1979)

R. R. Wilson (born 1914), a specialist in particle physics, is director of the Fermi National Accelerator Laboratory in Batavia, Illinois. After receiving his bachelor's and doctoral degrees from the University of California, he joined the faculty of Princeton University in 1940. From 1944 to 1946, he worked at Los Alamos on the development of the atomic bomb. He has also taught at Harvard, Cornell, and the University of Chicago. In 1973, he received the National Medal of Science.

    Most of us regard physics as a discipline oriented solely toward external reality, looking at the world in motion. Wilson wants us to see its interior effects on the physicist. He believes those effects are philosophical, aesthetic, and creative.

PREVIEW

What is physics? Describe what sort of emotional response you have to physics.

Does not it seem incongruous to be discussing the humanness of physics? If one subject would appear to be lacking the quality of humanness, it is physics. This science is characterized by precise measurement and abstruse mathematics; it is rigorous and austere; indeed it is about as objective as a discipline can get. Yet, in spite of a prevalent belief that physics is cold and inhuman, a belief that it has to do only with things, not people, a belief that its Faust-like practitioners blindly and dully follow the rites of scientific method to grind out a plethora of uninteresting facts . . . in spite of all this, I am going to maintain that there is a quality of loveliness in the content and devices of physics, that it is a beautiful creation which has meaning for man's view of himself and his place in the world, and that these qualities of physics can appropriately be discussed under the rubric of humanness.

PHILOSOPHICAL ASPECTS

Although modern physics can be said to have begun essentially with Galileo,* I prefer to see its genesis in the atomic physics of Democritus† some 2500 years ago. Lucretius‡ gives the most complete description of that ancient atomic theory in his *De Rerum Natura*. This beautiful poem expresses a remarkably up-to-date version of modern ideas about atoms. The Epicureans§ not only had quite correct notions about atoms, but also about atoms dancing in the vacuum or, as we say now, executing random movements. And if their ideas about force were hazy, to say the least, their idea of the random "swerve" of the atom has inherent in it rudimentary elements of quantum mechanics. The theory is simple and elegant and interesting—even correct in many respects. But Lucretius's poem is only in part devoted to a technical expression of physics. For the most part, the poem is about the problems of people caused by their superstitious beliefs. Physical occurrences before the atomic theory, no matter how trivial, were explicable almost entirely on the basis of divine intervention. Thus if the wind were to be favorable, then a god or a spirit would have to be propitiated by sacrifice. Agamemnon, setting out for Troy, must cruelly slay his fair daughter Iphigenia.‖ Behind each rock that could stub a toe might dwell a mischievous spirit. These countless little spirits, "always about Man's path and about his bed, mostly hostile by instinct" were only to be pacified by tedious acts of worship. We are told that the lives of the religious Greeks were made miserable by a multitude of gods and spirits, all bullying humans without surcease.

Atomic theory provided an alternate view of how the world worked; if one believed in the existence of atoms and in atomic theory, then that simple all-encompassing theory of everything—since everything is made of atoms—made it no longer necessary to believe in spirits as causative agents. Although Lucretius intended his eloquent poem to be a paean to Epicurean materialism, the poem comes out also as a testament to the humanity of Lucretius—it is an example par excellence of the humanness of physics.

Yet another example is an identity crisis for man that was caused by Newton. His simple laws of motion seemed to explain the exact motion of all bodies in the world accurately and universally and very successfully and much more plausibly than did the vague ideas of Democritus. Because of the power and success of Newton's laws, a notion of cause and effect emerged in which it was reasonable to

---

* Galileo [Galilei]—(1564–1642) Italian mathematician and astronomer; proposed the heliocentric theory of the solar system. [Eds.]

† Democritus—(ca. 460–ca. 370 B.C.) Greek atomist philosopher. [Eds.]

‡ Lucretius—(ca. 96–ca. 55 B.C.) Latin philosophical poet; author of *De Rerum Natura*. [Eds.]

§ Epicureans—a group of Greek philosophers (third century B.C.) who advocated ethical hedonism. [Eds.]

‖ Iphigenia—in Euripides's play, *Iphigenia in Tauris*, Agamemnon, preparing to sail for Troy, is told by a soothsayer that he will not have favorable winds until he sacrifices his daughter Iphigenia. She is saved by the goddess Artemis at the last moment. [Eds.]

consider the universe to be just one great machine—to be like a great clock that runs all by itself—each motion being caused mechanically as an effect of the previous state of the machine. Once in motion, the positions of every part of that machine would be completely and precisely predetermined for all time. Man, also subject to Newton's law, is just a part of this machine, and hence his every movement also would be equally preordained. In such a view, man is ineluctably trapped by the physics of Newton. He is just a mechanical cog in a mechanical universe. Where is the humanness of this bleak view?

Now this was not the first discussion of the problem of free will or determinism—Greeks and scholastics had enjoyed infinite variation on this theme, but usually involving the nature of God. I think the difference is that however ridiculous or meaningless or oversimplified might be the above caricature of a world based on Newton's law of physics, to this day it still forms the basis of our modern popular materialistic philosophy. Somehow, French Encyclopedists* and other eighteenth-century philosophers managed correctly to understand the simple physics of Newton and then to draw a plausible inference about what appeared to them to be a completely mechanical and hence materialistic and inhuman world. It seems to me that those quaint eighteenth-century views, based on Newtonian physics and sharpened by nineteenth-century Darwinism, have been pretty much frozen into our literature and have been accepted into general thinking ever since. Perhaps much of the revulsion of some intellectuals to physics stems from an abhorrence of this miserable view of a deterministic materialistic world. If there is any humanness in this bleak picture it is that such a superficial reading of physics should have been taken so seriously, that it should have led to such disastrous thinking, and that it should have instilled such a quality of inhumanness in so many minds. Any deeper consideration of the physics of the problem especially from the point of view of statistical mechanics, or of how matter is actually observed, would have shown the fallacy of drawing any such conclusion about free will from those highly oversimplified eighteenth-century arguments. How much better the lesson would have been had it been one of humility, of a heightened appreciation of the mystery of the universe, had it been one of pride in the human spirit to understand even then so much of that universe.

Unfortunately physics some fifty years ago became so arcane that intellectuals in other disciplines did not notice that a revolutionary discovery in physics, quantum mechanics, made even more obvious the fallacy of drawing conclusions about free will based on Newton's laws. We now know that matter moves as though guided by waves. These waves only determine the probability, the chance, that a particle, or a body, will move to a certain place. Hence the motion of a body moving through space with a precise trajectory according to the certainty of Newton's laws has been replaced by the fuzzy propagation of a wave of chance.

---

* French Encyclopedists—eighteenth-century French writers who compiled the *Encyclopédie* (1751–1765), a liberal and secular reference work. [Eds.]

What is more interesting about this from the point-of-view of humanness is that this physics—quantum physics—tells us about the limits of our ability to have knowledge about some conditions of our universe—that there are some questions which we can ask that have no meaning. The theory specifies in a quantitative way just what is certain and what is uncertain. I submit that this precise and surprising information about the limits of man's knowledge is apropos to a quality of humanness. It informs us about ourselves and it leads to a greater appreciation of the mysterious nature of our world.

In the same way, the theory of relativity teaches us about other bizarre but very real phenomena of this world. For example, it is really true that two people can age at a different rate if one person is in motion with respect to the other. Pirandello* could have made an even more dramatic study of the nature of reality—a quality of humanness—had he more thoroughly studied the theory of relativity (if he studied it at all!).

Let me turn to a somewhat different aspect of the humanness of physics in man's knowledge of man. Since time began, one could question as did Matthew Arnold† about

> The hills where his life rose
> and the sea where it goes—

Originally these questions of from whence do we come and whither are we going were considered to be strictly the province of religion and of myth. What I find utterly astounding now is how modern cosmogony and cosmology—which as a physicist I arrogantly relegate to physics—can inform us about how our world came into being. On the basis of nuclear physics and of various observations, we know that the world began, not with a whimper, but with a bang! Nuclear physics tells us in amazing detail how, from that mighty big explosion about ten billion years ago, energy expanded outward, how the firmament separated from the chaos, how matter in all its forms was produced in known nuclear reactions, and how that matter condensed to form stars and planets. Nuclear physics makes possible the knowledge of the life cycle of stars, about what keeps them hot, how some collapse and some explode, and how some become deep black holes in space.

This partly written "book of genesis" still does not "explain" the "why" of the big bang. However, if we assume in a biblical sense that in the beginning was not the "word," but that instead there was just a tremendous explosion of pure energy from a point in space, a bang, then from that event on our detailed knowledge of nuclear physics has made it possible to give a fuller explanation of "from whence we came" than had ever been given before. The account not only reads like the book of Genesis, it reads like a fascinating detective story. From a very few clues,

---

* Pirandello, Luigi—(1867–1936) Italian author and dramatist; received the Nobel Prize for Literature in 1934. [Eds.]

† Arnold, Matthew—(1822–1888) English poet and critic; author of "Dover Beach" and *Culture and Anarchy.* [Eds.]

a more complete *De Rerum Natura* has been deduced. It is a towering intellectual accomplishment, comparable to or even exceeding eighteenth-century poetry or even Renaissance painting. It has added to the measure of man—to his humanness—and his spirit, his human spirit that is, soars out over time and space, and the vehicle of that spirit is nuclear physics!

AESTHETIC ASPECTS

Now let me turn to aesthetic aspects of physics. We physicists are proud of the monumental laws of nature we have been able to formulate. For a physicist, the laws of physics themselves have great beauty. The laws express so much in such elegant form that we can compare them to poetry, and in particular, because of their brevity, compare them to the Japanese seventeen syllable haiku. Unfortunately, just as the haiku is not accessible to most of us because we do not know Japanese, in the same sense, the poems of physics are also not accessible to most of us because we do not understand the language of mathematics.

It is no accident that the laws of physics are beautiful. In groping toward many of the great truths of physics, intuition is an important guide, and beauty is one of the beacons which guide that intuition. Keats* tells us:

Beauty is truth, truth beauty—that is all
Ye know on earth, and all ye need to know.

But we physicists find it helpful, in arriving at a truth, also to depend upon a few experimental observations. Einstein, however, used a minimum of experimental information in formulating his theory of relativity. He wrote that an aesthetic feeling of "rightness" and a sense of beauty were dominant factors in his thinking. Even when the first experiments of Kaufmann seemed to be in contradiction with his theory, Einstein persisted in belief in his structure—why? Because he felt it was beautiful!

Dirac,† the theoretical physicist whose theories first led to the concept of antiparticles, has explained how he gave overriding priority to aesthetics in formulating his theory. He also has pointed out how Schroedinger, one of the founding fathers of Wave Mechanics, put forward the "Schroedinger Equation," basic to Wave Mechanics, in spite of apparent contradicting experimental evidence—again because he thought his equation was beautiful. My point here is that aesthetics is an important part of physics.

For example, we physicists like to look for something that is symmetrical in the world. Many of our deepest truths about nature are expressed by a symmetry that we are able to recognize in a property of nature. Thus we like to see that our

---

* Keats, John—(1795–1821) English poet; author of "Ode on a Grecian Urn." [Eds.]

† Dirac, Paul—(1902–1984) English mathematician and physicist; worked with Erwin Schroedinger (1887–1961), Austrian physicist, on the development of quantum theory, for which they jointly received the Nobel Prize in 1933. [Eds.]

laws of motion are exactly the same when viewed through a looking glass, that is, when we have interchanged everything on the right side to the left side. That shows a symmetry in space. We might also look for a symmetry in time, by expecting our laws to work as well when time is reversed; for example, Newton's laws are the same for the objects in a movie even when the projector runs backward. Still, symmetry can be boring, so after we have recognized a property of nature that is symmetrical, we are utterly delighted to find any small deviation from the rule.

Tsung Dao Lee who, with Frank Yang,* first conceived the idea that the mirror symmetry was occasionally broken, has emphasized the similarity of the slightly broken symmetry with classical sculpture. He cites many examples of statues that are almost symmetrical but are only lovely because of small departures from exact symmetry. Similarly, this is true of poetry. A too symmetrical poem becomes doggerel; it is subtleness and surprise that characterizes great art—and great physics as well. My point here is that physicists not only use aesthetics to guide them, they also use the language of aesthetics to discuss their subject. Is not all this use of the language of aesthetics just another way of acknowledging a quality of humanness in physics?

In experimental physics too, aesthetics plays a role. For example, the artifacts of physics themselves usually have an innately handsome quality that is quite independent of their function, even though the quality of beauty derives from the function. Thus antique balances, or electroscopes, or magnetometers have now become valuable objects that are collected and exhibited in the salons of the homes of the wealthy. Those objects were designed by scientists who cared about appearance as well as function, or better, who appreciated the relationship between form and function and appearance. Most instruments or machines of physics are designed as a picture is painted; the parts are one with the whole, the whole is one with the parts—all directed toward and expressing the function.

As an accelerator builder, I have found great satisfaction in relating to the men who built cathedrals in the thirteenth century. When Ernest Lawrence† built his cyclotrons with a dedicated passion he was not that different from Suger,‡ also with a dedicated passion, building the cathedral St. Denis. The Abbot Suger was expressing a devotion to the church with his exalted structure, a structure that transcended all contemporary knowledge of strength of materials. And Lawrence too expressed, in his fashion, a devotion to the discovery of truth. He too transcended contemporary technology in attaining his dizzying heights of energy. I am sure that both the designers of the cathedrals and the designers of the nuclear accelerators proceeded almost entirely on educated intuition guided largely by aesthetic considerations. This can be seen explicitly in the notebooks of

---

* Lee, Tsung Dao—(born 1926) American physicist; worked with Frank [Chen Ning] Yang (born 1922) to disprove principle of parity, for which they jointly received the Nobel Prize in 1957. [Eds.]

†* Lawrence, Ernest—(1901–1958) American educator and physicist; received the Nobel Prize in 1939 for developing the cyclotron. [Eds.]

‡ Suger—(ca. 1081–1151) abbot of St. Denis; reconstructed the church in Gothic style. [Eds.]

Villard d'Honnecourt, one of the ancient architects: his designs of parts of cathedrals are sometimes mixed up with drawings of the human form.

My own experience has been in designing modern accelerators. These are exceedingly complex machines which are characterized by large mechanical and electrical systems and by complicated forms which are pierced by vacuum pipes, which are immersed in magnetic fields, and in which atoms are joggled by electric fields, and jiggled by electronic devices. Informing and controlling this complex is a nervous system that consists of a ganglia of microprocessors and a gaggle of computers. Now to understand each complicated component and its relationship to the whole would go well beyond my own technical knowledge. So how do I go about designing? Well, I find out a little here, by a simple calculation, and a little there, by another calculation, about the parts of the most important technical components. I then draw those parts of the design on paper. After that, I just freely and intuitively draw in neatly appearing smooth lines, lines which cover my ignorance of detail. I keep drawing, correcting here and there by calculations until the accelerator appears that it might work. Mostly I know it might work because it looks and feels right—not because of any long and detailed chain of calculations, which after all probably could take forever. It is when the parts and forms have essentially the same relationship that the parts of a sculpture should have to the whole that I am satisfied by the design. Of course, building, even designing, a large accelerator is a complex team activity—just as it was for the cathedral. But if the conceptual design is aesthetically right, then one can depend on the members of a team to appreciate and to understand and to respect that aesthetic form in their own creative contributions. An accelerator that is "understood" works. What I am trying to express by a certain amount of exaggeration is that most of the effort of design is intuitive, that aesthetics is indeed a valuable and necessary guide in any design process, that these very human qualities are an important part of physics and give to physics a quality of humanness.

CREATIVE ASPECTS

Physics is not developed by mechanically following an arbitrary set of rules that lead automatically to new knowledge. For example, just blindly following the so-called scientific method will get you nowhere. Now, the physics that ultimately appears in textbooks is usually expressed in an elegant, but nearly incomprehensible, mathematical form. It is very different, however, during the process of discovery. Not too much is known about how the mind of a physicist comes to produce new physics, just as not much is known about how the mind of the artist comes to produce new works of art. One thing is clear, it is that there is much in common between what the creative artist does and what the scientist does. Scientist and artist even use similar words in describing their creative moments. They both care deeply about what it is they do and they tend to be single-minded in going about doing it. They both usually pass through a morose period when their contemplation is deep, and mostly at a subconscious level. Finally, what they do create just comes bubbling up from the subconscious to the conscious mind. Inevitably this inspirational act is accompanied by a period of euphoria, an ecstasy which has been documented time and again for scientist and artist alike.

What I have been trying to maintain is that those qualities that we identify with humanness are as active and important in physical research as they are in painting or poetry. The artist and the scientist appear to take on very similar roles at the level of creating knowledge. Even their personalities are similar—and they both tend toward the idiosyncratic. Take Einstein and Picasso:* they both dressed in sweat shirts, neither wore socks, and both were very strong, individualistic characters.

If the act of creativity in science and art is similar, I would like to go now farther and to question if there is not a similarity, as creations, in the content of art and of science. I want to ask if both are not equally creations of the human mind? And I do not mean by this to deny, in any way, the independent existence of that mysterious but objective reality "out there." However, there are many ways that we could come to perceive that reality, and the particular way that has evolved and the particular corner of reality that has been explored might both be considered to be arbitrary creations of the mind of man.

The fundamental concepts themselves, such as distance, or mass or time, are idealizations of nature, and they had to be invented by man. Perhaps it might be more accurate to say that such concepts had to evolve with our language, but after all, language itself is a human creation. For example, the concept of time which has evolved for peoples with different languages appears to be quite different; we all experience the remarkable difference between the passing of psychological time and of clock time. The art of science has been to create concepts, and then to create theories using those concepts that correspond to reality.

If it is at all plausible that the concepts of physics themselves have at least in some degree been arbitrary creations of man, rather than being "revealed truth," or being something that was just inherently obvious to anyone, then it might also be plausible to go on and to inquire if all knowledge of physics has not in large measure been created by the mind of man—just as Dante† created his many-leveled universe of Paradise and Inferno. The difference is that physics must constantly, step-by-step, be consistent with the world of reality as determined by experiment. And of course the objects of our reality have a continuing reality which is largely independent of how we perceive them.

What I am saying is in a sense just an exaggerated form of the three worlds of Karl Popper.‡ His first world has to do with things, his second world is that of subjective experience of thinking. His third world consists of statements and theories and of mental constructs, and is one which I am sure he would agree is a creation (in an evolutionary sense) of the mind of man.

But how can I maintain my belief in an objective reality and at the same time suggest that the world we know is even some part, a creation of man? To try to clarify that dichotomy, let me compare the physicist creating knowledge to an artist creating a painting.

The artist starts with a blank canvas, some paints, and the tools for applying

---

* Picasso, Pablo—(1881–1973) Spanish artist. [Eds.]

† Dante [Alighieri]—(1265–1321) Italian epic poet; author of *The Divine Comedy*. [Eds.]

‡ Popper, Karl—(born 1902) Austrian philosopher. [Eds.]

them. He makes a few initial strokes that pretty much determine the final nature of the picture. These initial strokes might be analogous to the fundamental concepts with which the physicist starts. The ultimate picture may correspond to one of our theories. The artist can start again with exactly the same amount and kind of paint, and then use it all up to complete a new picture. From a chemical and a physical point of view, the two pictures he has produced might be judged to be very nearly identical—but the meaning of the paintings to someone observing them can be utterly different. Indeed, any number of such "identical" pictures could be made starting with exactly the same ingredients, but all could turn out to have utterly different meanings and all be original creations.

My analogy, then, is that the canvas and the paint, which would be physically and chemically the same for all the paintings in this example, and which are quite independent of the painter, correspond to his physical reality. Without violating that reality, the painting is made, and it will come out differently each time; each is a creation even though the painter does not create the paint or the canvas. So might it be for the physicist. His reality is more mysterious, and more circumscribed, but it is plausible that were man to start again from his beginning, then the science which would evolve and hence the world he would perceive might appear different to him than it does to us. In that sense the world we perceive is a creation of man; in that sense, it is a manifestation of the humanness of physics, and in that sense, we do not have new worlds to conquer, or even new worlds to discover. We have new worlds to create.

If man does create in some sense his world, then he has a responsibility for that world—a responsibility for the success or failure of that world. To my mind one of the greatest failures, in spite of what I have been saying, *is* the inhumanness of the world of physics. Physicists, not unnaturally, have taken the business of physicists to be the creation of physics. The business of physicists should also be concerned with the poetry and drama of physics, with the beauty of its form and function. The business of physics should also be the business of humanists and artists.

I take the optimistic view of man. He will survive the inhumanities of his technological culture, and I believe that his culture will evolve to a new and richer level—that he will create a new world. But I agree with A.N. Whitehead* that "unless we can make man, his culture and his ideals, of central importance to the physical scientist *in his* own work, we are in serious danger of sinking to the level of technologically skillful barbarians." Perhaps in the humanness of science and art, the humanists, the artists, and the scientists can find a unity in their cultures.

JOURNAL WRITINGS

1. **Define** "truth" and "beauty." Explain what sort of connection (if any) exists between them. Are they inner or outer qualities?

---

* Whitehead, A. N.—(1861–1947) English philosopher and mathematician. [Eds.]

BRAINSTORMING AND DRAFTING

2.   "The theory [of quantum physics] specifies in a quantitative way just what is
      certain and what is uncertain. I submit that this precise and surprising
      information about the limits of man's knowledge is apropos to a quality of
      humanness. It informs us about ourselves and it leads to a greater apprecia-
      tion of the mysterious nature of our world."
      Use this quotation from the reading as the basis for discussing one of the
      following questions:
      a.   What is the quality of humanness involved here?
      b.   How does this knowledge inform us about ourselves?
      c.   What does it mean to say that the universe is mysterious in nature?
            You may want to look at Eiseley's essay (pages 520–531) in considering
            this question.

THE AUTHOR'S METHODS

3.   Identify a number of **allusions** to fields outside of physics. Write an **explana-
      tion** of how Wilson uses these allusions to support his assertion that physics
      has "humanness."
4.   One might regard **analogy** as the main basis for Wilson's **argument.** If so,
      what is being compared? Write a critique of his argument based on the
      validity of the **comparison** he is making.
5.   Exactly what claims does Wilson make for physics? Write an explanation of
      his claims and tell how persuasive you find them.

CREATIVE PROJECT

6.   Write a dialogue between Ernest Lawrence and Abbot Suger in which they
      discuss the motivation behind their respective building projects.

FORMAL WRITING AND RESEARCH PAPERS

7.   What conclusion about free will did the eighteenth-century French Ency-
      clopedists draw from Newton's physics? What is Wilson's opinion of their
      conclusion? Do you believe denial of free will is inhuman? If you have read
      some of the selections in the unit of Free Choice you may find some helpful
      ideas there.
8.   Wilson refers to a large number of individuals, both scientists and artists, in
      his essay. Select one of these individuals, and consult encyclopedias or
      biographical dictionaries to find out about this person. Then write a three-
      or four-page biography.

Stephen Vincent Benét

Nightmare Number Three

(1935)

Stephen Vincent Benét (1898–1943) wrote in a number of genres: Besides poetry, he wrote short stories, novels, and drama. In addition, he was a historian, critic, and editor. He received the Pulitzer Prize in 1929 for *John Brown's Body*. Of his five novels, *Jean Huguenot* and *Spanish Bayonet* are considered his finest. Perhaps he is best remembered for his short story "The Devil and Daniel Webster."

In this poem, which Benét entitled a "nightmare," he depicts one of the few humans to survive the revolt of the machines.

PREVIEW

Do you dream about machines? Jot down a few notes from one of your dreams (or invent a dream about machines). Are these notes positive or negative in tone?

We had expected everything but revolt
And I kind of wonder myself when they started thinking—
But there's no dice in that now.
                      I've heard fellows say
They must have planned it for years and maybe they did.
Looking back, you can find little incidents here and there,
Like the concrete-mixer in Jersey eating the wop
Or the roto press that printed "Fiddle-dee-dee!"
In a three-color process all over Senator Sloop,
Just as he was making a speech. The thing about that
Was, how could it walk upstairs? But it was upstairs,
Clicking and mumbling in the Senate Chamber.
They had to knock out the wall to take it away
And the wrecking-crew said it grinned.
                      It was only the best
Machines, of course, the superhuman machines,
The ones we'd built to be better than flesh and bone,
But the cars were in it, of course . . .

and they hunted us
Like rabbits through the cramped streets on the Bloody Monday,
The Madison Avenue busses leading the charge.
The busses were pretty bad—but I'll not forget
The smash of glass when the Duesenberg* left the show-room
And pinned three brokers to the Racquet Club steps
Or the long howl of the horns when they saw men run,
When they saw them looking for holes in the solid ground . . .

I guess they were tired of being ridden in
And stopped and started by pygmies for silly ends,
Of wrapping cheap cigarettes and bad chocolate bars
Collecting nickels and waving platinum hair
And letting six million people live in a town.
I guess it was that. I guess they got tired of us
And the whole smell of human hands.
                                But it was a shock
To climb sixteen flights of stairs to Art Zuckow's office
(Nobody took the elevators twice)
And find him strangled to death in a nest of telephones,
The octopus-tendrils waving over his head,
And a sort of quiet humming filling the air. . . .
Do they eat? . . . There was red . . . But I did not stop to look.
I don't know yet how I got to the roof in time
And it's lonely, here on the roof.
                                For a while, I thought
That window-cleaner would make it, and keep me company.
But they got him with his own hoist at the sixteenth floor
And dragged him in, with a squeal.
You see, they cooperate. Well, we taught them that
And it's fair enough, I suppose. You see, we built them.
We taught them to think for themselves.
It was bound to come. You can see it was bound to come.
And it won't be so bad, in the country. I hate to think
Of the reapers, running wild in the Kansas fields,
And the transport planes like hawks on a chickenyard,
But the horses might help. We might make a deal with the horses.
At least, you've more chance, out there.
                                And they need us, too.
They're bound to realize that when they once calm down.
They'll need oil and spare parts and adjustments and tuning up.
Slaves? Well, in a way, you know, we were slaves before.
There won't be so much real difference—honest, there won't.
(I wish I hadn't looked into that beauty-parlor

---

* Duesenberg—type of luxury and racing car of the 1920s and 30s. [Eds.]

And seen what was happening there.
But those are female machines and a bit high-strung.)
Oh, we'll settle down. We'll arrange it. We'll compromise.
It won't make sense to wipe out the whole human race.
Why, I bet if I went to my old Plymouth now
(Of course you'd have to do it the tactful way)
And said, "Look here! Who got you the swell French horn?"
He wouldn't turn me over to those police cars;
At least I don't think he would.
                              Oh, it's going to be jake.*
There won't be so much real difference—honest, there won't—
And I'd go down in a minute and take my chance—
I'm a good American and I always liked them—
Except for one small detail that bothers me
And that's the food proposition. Because, you see,
The concrete-mixer may have made a mistake,
And it looks like just high spirits.
But, if it's got so they like the flavor . . . well . . .

JOURNAL WRITINGS

1. Think about your own attachment to machines. Write a paragraph in which you **describe** feelings that you have (or have had) about a particular machine. Be sure to give some details about the machine.

2. When machines work as they should, we tend to take them for granted. When they fail, we often become angry. Recall an instance when a machine failed you at a crucial moment. Describe the failure and the reasons the moment seemed crucial. Explain how you felt. In retrospect does the whole incident seem serious or funny? Why?

BRAINSTORMING AND DRAFTING

3. Discuss what this poem really says about human-machine relations. What sort of relationship does the speaker hope will ultimately be achieved?

THE AUTHOR'S METHODS

4. **Personification** is a literary technique that gives human characteristics to animals or things. Look for examples of this technique in Benét's poem. Write a paragraph discussing how he uses this technique and describing

---

*jake—slang term meaning "excellent, very satisfactory." [Eds.]

the effect upon you as a reader. Consider the idea of "female machine," for instance.

5. What is the tone of this poem (serious, humorous, **ironic,** or what)? Write a paragraph in which you explain how the **tone** is developed—use **examples** from the text, and explore the relationship between tone and the purpose of the poem.

6. Note the **image** of the hunted rabbit that is used in the poem. Write a brief paper in which you discuss the effects, both intellectual and emotional, of this image. Ask yourself how it contributes to the overall effect of the poem.

CREATIVE PROJECTS

7. Write a poem of your own that uses a machine as its main idea or **image.**

8. Use the incident from Journal Writings 2 as the basis for a short story.

FORMAL WRITING AND RESEARCH PAPERS

9. Americans have been described as having a "love affair" with the automobile. Find some psychological or sociological studies that relate to this question (*Psychological Abstracts* or *Social Sciences Index* may help). Write a four- or five-page paper to report your findings.

10. Write a paper that interprets and evaluates this poem.

Evelyn Fox Keller

Women in Science: An Analysis of a Social Problem

(1970)

Evelyn Fox Keller (born 1936) teaches rhetoric, women's studies, and the history of science at the University of California at Berkeley. She received her B.A. from Brandeis University, her M.A. from Radcliffe, and her Ph.D. from Harvard. Her two most important books are *A Feeling for the Organism: The Life and Work of Barbara McClintock* (1983) and *Reflections on Gender and Science* (1985).

Drawing on her own experience, Dr. Keller explores the problems faced by any woman pursuing a career in science. She concludes that something must be done to correct these problems, and suggests several remedies.

PREVIEWS

A. When you think of women in science, what names come to mind? List their names and scientific fields.
B   Do women and men think differently? Jot down an example or two that supports your view.

Are women's minds different from men's minds? In spite of the women's movement, the age-old debate centering around this question continues. We are surrounded by evidence of *de facto* differences between men's and women's intellects—in the problems that interest them, in the ways they try to solve those problems, and in the professions they choose. Even though it has become fashionable to view such differences as environmental in origin, the temptation to seek an explanation in terms of innate differences remains a powerful one.

Perhaps the area in which this temptation is strongest is in science. Even those of us who would like to argue for intellectual equality are hard pressed to explain the extraordinarily meager representation of women in science, particularly in the upper echelons. Some would argue that the near absence of great

Table I. PERCENTAGE OF PH.D.'S EARNED BY WOMEN, 1920–1970

	1920–29	1940–49	1950–59	1960–69
Physics and Astronomy	5.9	4.2	2.0	2.2
Biological Sciences	19.5	15.7	11.8	15.1
Mathematics	14.5	10.7	5.0	5.7
Psychology	29.4	24.1	14.8	20.7

Source: National Research Council

women scientists demonstrates that women don't have the minds for true scientific creativity. While most of us would recognize the patent fallacies of this argument, it nevertheless causes us considerable discomfort. After all, the doors of the scientific establishment appear to have been open to women for some time now—shouldn't we begin to see more women excelling?

In the last fifty years the institutional barriers against women in science have been falling. During most of that time, the percentage of women scientists has declined, although recent years have begun to show an upswing (table I). Of those women who do become scientists, few are represented in the higher academic ranks (table II). In order to have a proper understanding of these data, it is necessary to review the many influences that operate. I would like to argue that the convenient explanation that men's minds are intrinsically different from women's is not only unwarranted by the evidence, but in fact reflects a mythology that is in itself a major contribution to the phenomena observed.

As a woman scientist, I have often pondered these questions, particularly at those times when my commitment to science seemed most precarious. Noticing that almost every other woman I had known in science had experienced similar crises of commitment, I sought to explain my ambivalence by concluding that science as a profession is not as gratifying for women as it is for men, and that the reasons for this are to be found in the intrinsic nature of women and science. Several years ago, I endeavored to find out how general my own experiences were. In studying the statistics of success and failure for women in the professions, I indeed found that women fared less well in science than in other professions, although the picture that emerged seemed fairly bleak for all of us.

Table II. PERCENTAGE REPRESENTATION OF WOMEN, BY RANK, IN 20 LEADING UNIVERSITIES (1962)

	Instructor	Assistant Professor	Associate Professor	Professor
Physics	5.6	1.2	1.3	0.9
Biological Sciences	16.3	7.1	6.7	1.3
Mathematics	16.7	10.1	7.3	0.4
Psychology	8.3	10.4	11.1	2.7

Source: J. B. Parrish, *A. A. U. W. Journal,* 55, 99

I collected these data during a leave of absence I had taken to accompany my husband to California. At the same time, I was also engaged in completing work I had begun the year before with a (male) colleague—work that seemed less and less compelling as the year wore on. Each week I would receive an enthusiastic telephone call from my colleague, reporting new information and responses he had received from workers he had met while delivering invited lectures on this work. At some point it occurred to me that perhaps there was a relation between my declining interest and isolation on the one hand, and his growing enthusiasm and public recognition on the other. Over the course of the year, he had received a score or more invitations to speak about this work, while I had received none. It began to dawn on me that there were far simpler explanations for both the observations I had made privately and the data I was collecting than that of intrinsic differences between the sexes.

I began to realize, for example, that had I been less isolated and more rewarded, my enthusiasm would have been correspondingly greater—a recognition that has been amply corroborated by my subsequent experience. Upon further reflection, I became aware of how much my own, and other similar, attitudes are influenced by a complex interplay of subtle factors affecting us from birth on. The ways in which we rear our children, train our students, and interact with our colleagues are all so deeply imbued with our expectations and beliefs as to virtually guarantee a fulfillment of these beliefs.

How do men and women develop the characteristics we attribute to them? There are clear differences between the sexes at birth, and there is even some evidence that these differences extend to the brain. Primate studies reveal marked differences in behavior between males and females—differences determined by the prenatal hormonal environment. It seems therefore quite possible that there are even intellectual differences determined prior to birth. For those inclined to believe in such predetermination, such a possibility may appear attractive. It is important to say, however, that there is to date no evidence for biologically determined differences in intelligence or cognitive styles, and that this remains true in spite of a rather considerable desire among many people to find such evidence.

An example of this interest is provided by the great enthusiasm with which a recent study was met. This study purported to show that prenatal injection of progestin, a synthetic male hormone, leads to higher than average I.Q.'s in adolescent girls. Although this result was refuted by the original authors shortly after its original announcement, it nevertheless found its way into a rash of textbooks, where it remains. Similarly, there has been a great deal of interest in the measurement of differences in perceptual modes between girls and boys. Tests designed to measure the degree to which one's perception of a figure is independent of its background, or field, show that girls, by the time they enter school, are more field-dependent than boys. Field independence is positively correlated with mathematical and analytic abilities. While the results of these tests are remarkably culturally invariant (the Eskimos are a notable exception), it is important to point out both that the disparities observed are extremely small (of the order of 2 percent) and that they cannot be discerned before the age of five. While the possibility that these disparities are the result of innate differences between the sexes cannot be excluded, there is evidence relating performance on such tests to the individual's environment. What are the environmental differences that could account for such results?

We treat our sons and daughters differently from birth onward, although the magnitude of our distinction is largely unconscious. A rude awakening to the extent of our differential treatment can come in those rare instances when a fallacious sex assignment is made at birth, usually as a result of ambiguous genitalia, and must be subsequently corrected. The impact of these early cues can be assessed by the fact that such reassignments are considered unduly traumatic to make after the child is eighteen months old, in spite of the fact that failure to do so dooms the child to an apparent sexual identity at odds with his or her genotype. Sex reassignments made before that time result in apparently normal development. From this and related evidence, workers in this area have concluded that gender identity appears to be established, primarily on the basis of parental treatment, by the age of eighteen months.

Children acquire the meaning of their sex identity from the models before them. Their concept of female is based largely on the women they see, as their concept of male is based on the men they see. Their immediate perceptions are later expanded by the images they perceive on TV, and in children's literature. It hardly need be pointed out that both of the latter present to our children extraordinarily rigid stereotypes.

It is not surprising, then, that children, even before they enter school, have acquired the belief that certain activities are male and others female. Science is a male activity.

The tenacity of this early view is such as to resist easy change. When my daughter was in nursery school, her class was asked one day about the occupation of their fathers. I objected to this, and, as a result, the next day the teacher asked, "Sarah, what does your mother do?" She replied, "My mother cooks, she sews, she cleans, and she takes care of us." "But Sarah, isn't your mother a scientist?" "Oh, yes," said Sarah—clearly implying that this was not a very relevant piece of information.

The explanation of her responses lies not only in her need to define a conventional image of her mother, but also in the reality of her direct perceptions. Indeed it is true that, like many professional women, I do cook, sew, clean, and take care of my children. My professional identity is not brought into my home, although my husband's is. My daughter, therefore, like my son, continues to view mathematics and science as male, in spite of their information to the contrary.

While a child may be concerned with assigning sex labels only to external attributes, such as clothes, mannerisms, and occupations, the adolescent has already begun to designate internal states as male and female. Thus, in particular, clear thinking is characterized as hard thinking (a male image), and fuzzy thinking as soft thinking (a female image). A girl who thinks clearly and well is told she thinks "like a man." What are the implications of such associations for the girl who (for whatever reasons) does transcend social expectation and finds herself interested in science? Confusion in sexual identity is the inevitable concomitant of a self-definition at variance with the surrounding definitions of sexual norm. The girl who can take pride in "thinking like a man" without cost to her integrity as a girl is rare indeed.

Nevertheless, a considerable number of women, for whatever reasons, experience enough motivation and have demonstrated enough ability to embark on professional training for a scientific career. Graduate school is a time to prove that one is, in spite of one's aspirations, a woman, and—at one and the same time, because of one's aspirations—"more than" a woman. Social acceptability requires the former, and is considerably facilitated by the acquisition of a husband, while professional respectability requires the latter. The more exclusively male the definition of the profession, the more difficult it is to accomplish these conflicting goals.

My own experience as a graduate student of theoretical physics at Harvard was extreme, but possibly illustrative. I was surrounded by incessant prophecies of failure, independent of my performance. I knew of no counter-examples to draw confidence from, and was led to believe that none existed. (Later, however, I learned that some women in theoretical physics have survived, even at Harvard.) Warned that I would ultimately despair as I came to learn how impossible my ambitions were, I did, though not for reasons that were then implied. Having denied myself rage, depression was in fact one of the few reasonable responses to the isolation, mockery, and suspicion that I experienced, both within and without my department. Ultimately I did earn my Ph.D. from the Harvard physics department, but only after having adapted my interests and thereby removed myself from the most critical pressures—a course many women have taken before and since.

Hostility, however, was not the only response I received, and not necessarily the usual response experienced by professionally ambitious young women. The necessity of proving one's femininity leaves some women particularly susceptible to another danger—that of accepting, and even seeking, sexual approbation for intellectual and academic performance. There are enough men willing, if not eager, to provide such translated affirmation as to make this a serious problem. The relation between sexuality and intellectuality is an enormously complex subject. I raise it only to point out one perhaps obvious consequence of this confusion for women. Because, unlike men, they are often dependent on sexual and intellectual affirmation from one and the same individual or group, they can never be entirely confident of what is being affirmed. Is it an "A for a Lay" or a "Lay for an A"?

Finally, the female scientist is launched. What are her prospects? Many women choose this point to withdraw for a time in order to have children. Although there is a logic to this choice, it reflects a lack of awareness of the dynamics of normal professional growth. For the male scientist, the period immediately following acquisition of the Ph.D. is perhaps the most critical in his professional development. It is the time that he has, free of all the responsibilities that will later come to plague him, to accomplish enough work to establish his reputation. Often it is a time to affiliate himself with a school of thought, to prove his own independent worth. Although this may have been the original function of the graduate training period, it has in recent times been displaced to the postgraduate years. Awareness of this displacement, of the critical importance of these years, has not permeated to the general public, or even, for the most part, to the science student. Many women therefore take this sometimes fatal step in ignorance. After having been out of a field for a few years, they usually find it next to impossible to return to their field except in the lowest-level positions. Only when it is too late do they learn that it would have been better to have their children first, before completing the Ph.D.

I need hardly enumerate the additional practical difficulties involved in combining a scientific (or any other) career with the raising of children. While the practical drains on one's time and energy are generally recognized, perhaps it is worth pointing out that the drains on one's intellectual energy are not generally recognized by men. Only those men who have spent full time, for an extended period, caring for their children are aware of the extraordinary amount of mental space occupied by the thousand and one details and concerns that mothers routinely juggle. Many have come to the conclusion—beginning with Engels,* and more recently including the Swedish government—that equality of the sexes in the work and professional force is not a realistic possibility until the sex roles in the family are radically redefined. Equality must begin at home.

Well, one might ask, what about those women in science who have no children, who never marry? Surely they are freed from all of these difficulties. Why don't they perform better?

First of all, to be freed of responsibilities towards others is not equivalent to having your own responsibilities assumed by others. Nowhere among women is to be found the counterpart of the male scientist who has a wife at home to look after his daily needs. The question, however, deserves a more serious answer, although the answer is almost painfully obvious. Our society does not have a place for unmarried women. They are among the most isolated, ostracized groups of our culture. When one thinks about the daily social and psychological pressures on the unmarried professional woman, one can hardly be surprised to discover that the data reveal that indeed, on the average, married women in science—even with children—publish more and perform better than unmarried women.

The enumeration of obstacles or handicaps faced by women in science would hardly be complete without at least a reference to the inequalities of reward and approval awarded to work done by men and women. The personal anecdote I began with is more than an anecdote—it is evidence of a rather ubiquitous tendency, neither malicious nor necessarily even conscious, to give more public recognition to a man's accomplishments than to a woman's accomplishments. There are many different reasons for this—not least of which includes the habitually lesser inclination of many women to put themselves forward. There is

---

* Engels, Friedrich—(1820–1895) German socialist writer. [Eds.]

also a simple, although documented, difference in evaluation of the actual work done by men and women.

While all of the above difficulties are hardly exclusive problems of women in science, the question of identity in what has been defined as an almost exclusively male profession is more serious for women in science than in other fields. Not only is the field defined as male by virtue of its membership, it is also defined as male in relation to its methodology, style of thought, indeed its goals. To the extent that analytic thought is conceived as male thought, to the extent that we characterize the natural sciences as the "hard" sciences, to the extent that the procedure of science is to "attack" problems, and its goal, since Bacon, has been to "conquer" or "master" nature, a woman in science *must* in some way feel alien.

Traditionally, as in other similar situations, women who have succeeded in scientific careers have dealt with this conflict by identifying with the "aggressor"—incorporating its values and ideals, at the cost, inevitably, of separating themselves from their own sex. An alternative resolution, one opted for frequently in other professions, is to attempt to redefine one's subject so as to permit a more comfortable identification with it. It is in this way, and for this reason, that so many professional women root themselves in subjects that are viewed by the profession as peripheral. In science this is not easy to do, but perhaps not impossible. There is another tradition within science that is as replete with female images as the tradition that dominates today is replete with male images. We all know that the most creative science requires, in addition to a hardness of mind, also fertility and receptivity. The best scientists are those who have combined the two sets of images. It may be that a certain degree of intellectual security is necessary in order to permit the expression of both "male" and "female" thought in science. If women have first to prove their "male" qualifications for admission into the profession, they may never achieve the necessary confidence to allow themselves to use their "female" abilities. What is to be done?

The central theme of my discussion is that the differential performance of men and women in science, the apparent differences between conceptual styles of men and women everywhere, are the result, not so much of innate differences between the sexes, but rather of the myth that prevails throughout our culture identifying certain kinds of thinking as male and others as female. The consequent compartmentalization of our minds is as effective as if it had been biologically, and not socially, induced.

People conform to the expectations imposed upon them in the evolution of their definition of sexual identity, thus confirming the very myth upon which these expectations are based. Such a process is not easy to change. Myths as deeply rooted and as self-affirming as this one can neither be wished nor willed away. The only hope is to chip away at it everywhere, to make enough small inroads so that future generations may ultimately grow up less hampered. Counter-measures can be effected at every stage of the process. Each may be of only limited effectiveness, but cumulatively they may permit enough women to emerge with intact, fully developed mental capacities—women who can serve as role models for future generations of students.

Specifically, we can begin by exerting a conscious effort to raise our children to less rigid stereotypes. Although the full extent to which we differentiate our treatment of our sons and daughters is hidden from us, being largely unconscious, we can, by attending to what we do, raise our consciousness of our own behavior.

We can specifically encourage and reward interests and abilities that survive social pressures. As teachers, men can consciously refrain from mixing academic with sexual approval. More generally, we can inform women students interested in science about the realities of the external difficulties they will face. It is all too easy for an individual experiencing such obstacles to internalize the responsibility for these obstacles. Specific advice can be given—for instance, to avoid interrupting a career immediately after the Ph. D. High-quality work by professional women can be sought out for recognition and encouragement in order to counteract the normal tendency to grant them less recognition. (The physicist Ernest Courant,* a very wise man, responded to the news that one of his most talented students was pregnant by giving her a raise—thus enabling her to hire competent help, and, simultaneously, obligating her to continue. After four such raises, she indeed did go on to become one of the country's better mathematicians.)

Extra care can be taken not to exclude women from professional interaction on any level. Finally, hiring policies must take into account the human and political realities. Women students need role models if they are to mature properly. Providing such a model is an important part of the function of a faculty member and should be considered along with scholarly performance in hiring deliberations. Similarly, marriage is a social reality, and women scientists who marry male scientists need jobs in the same area. Anti-nepotism hiring policies discriminate against women scientists, and even a neutral policy effectively does so as well. Universities might well consider pro-nepotism policies that would recognize the limitations of humans and geographical reality.

Most of the recommendations I have made require the cooperation of the male scientific community to implement. Why should they? Further, one may ask, why should women even be encouraged to become scientists when the list of odds against them is so overwhelming? Is a career in science intrinsically of so much greater value than other options more available to women?

I don't believe it is. Nevertheless, our society has become more and more technologically oriented. As we continue to move in this direction, as we come to attach increasing importance to scientific and technological know-how, women are threatened with a disenfranchisement possibly greater than ever before. The traditional role of the woman becomes increasingly eroded with technology and

---

* Courant, Ernest—(born 1920) American theoretical physicist. [Eds.]

overpopulation, while the disparity between the more humanly oriented kinds of knowledge thought to be hers and the more technical kinds of knowledge operating in the real world grows larger. This disparity operates not only at the expense of the women who are thus barred from meaningful roles in society, but also at the expense of the society that has been content to relegate to women those more humanistic values we all claim to support.

Finally, myths that compartmentalize our minds by defining certain mental attributes as "male" and others as "female" leave us all functioning with only part of our minds. Though there may well be some innate biological differences between the sexes, there is hardly room for doubt that our preconceptions serve to exaggerate and rigidify any distinctions that might exist. These preconceptions operate as straitjackets for men and women alike. I believe that the best, most creative science, like the most creative human efforts of any kind, can only be achieved with a full, unhampered mind—if you like, an androgynous mind. Therefore, the giving up of the central myth that science is a product of male thought may well lead to a more creative, more imaginative, and, who knows, possibly even a more humanistic science.

JOURNAL WRITINGS

1. Have you ever had a woman science teacher? If you have, write a paragraph describing her and her influence on your attitude toward science. If you have not, write a paragraph in which you suggest some reasons so few women teach science.
2. Keller speaks of the "compartmentalization of our minds." Explain whether she regards this as good or bad. How do you feel about it?

BRAINSTORMING AND DRAFTING

3. Are professional women taken seriously? Discuss this question in a small group; or, on your own, make a list of the reasons you think they are or are not taken seriously. Use the group's consensus or your own list to organize an essay in which you argue for or against the question. Write an introductory paragraph for this essay.
4. List the solutions that Keller suggests for remedying the problems of women in science. Add any additional ones if you can. Evaluate the problems: Which ones can and cannot be remedied?

THE AUTHOR'S METHODS

5. How does Keller use examples? What effect do they have on you as a reader?

6. Look carefully at the meaning of the words in quotation marks in the fourth paragraph of page 588. Consider their **denotations** and **connotations,** as well as their **metaphorical** implications. Write a paragraph in which you discuss the effect that the choice of these words produces.

CREATIVE PROJECT

7. Write a short story about a woman scientist. Try to show in **concrete** ways how she deals (not just physically, but emotionally) with some of the problems that Keller suggests many women scientists face.

FORMAL WRITING AND RESEARCH PAPERS

8. If you have a brother or sister, think about differences in the way you were both reared. Write a paper about these differences, using examples to show how your character has been shaped by these differences.
9. Look up *stereotype* in a standard desk dictionary. Keller says that the media "present to our children extraordinarily rigid stereotypes" of male and female role models. Watch some TV programs; observe stereotyped male and female characteristics. Write a paragraph describing the sex stereotype presented for each sex in the TV programs that you watched. Write a concluding paragraph in which you argue that these stereotypes are helpful or harmful to young viewers.
10. "I do cook, sew, clean, and take care of my children." Every woman who wants both a family and a career seems to do these things. Write a paper in which you **argue** for or against the idea that none of these is specifically "women's work" but ought to be equitably shared by both husband and wife.

Anne McCaffrey

The Ship Who Sang

(1961)

Anne McCaffrey (born 1926) was originally from Cambridge, Massachusetts. She received a B.A. in Slavonic languages and literature from Radcliffe College, and has worked as an advertising copywriter and as a director of operas and operettas. Since 1965 she has been a full-time writer, chiefly of science fiction and fantasy. The first woman to receive both major science fiction awards, she was honored with the Hugo for *Weyr Search* (1967) and the Nebula for *Dragonrider* (1968). No doubt she is best known for her "Dragonrider" series.

This story, set in a future when humanity has dispersed throughout the universe, suggests a way of dealing with some of the physically handicapped. Whether that way offers more advantages or drawbacks is for you to determine. However, you will find here a very different picture of relationships—of women (and men) with machines and with one another. Ask yourself whether inner or outer conditions are more important in this story.

PREVIEW

Before you begin reading this story, look up the word *cyborg*. Ask yourself whether you would ever want to become a cyborg—what conditions would make you want to?

She was born a thing and as such would be condemned if she failed to pass the encephalograph test required of all newborn babies. There was always the possibility that though the limbs were twisted, the mind was not, that though the ears would hear only dimly, the eyes see vaguely, the mind behind them was receptive and alert.

The electroencephalogram was entirely favorable, unexpectedly so, and the news was brought to the waiting, grieving parents. There was the final, harsh decision: to give their child euthanasia or permit it to become an encapsulated "brain," a guiding mechanism in any one of a number of curious professions. As such, their offspring would suffer no pain, live a comfortable existence in a metal shell for several centuries, performing unusual service to Central Worlds.

She lived and was given a name, Helva. For her first three vegetable months she waved her crabbed claws, kicked weakly with her clubbed feet and enjoyed the usual routine of the infant. She was not alone, for there were three other such children in the big city's special nursery. Soon they all were removed to Central Laboratory School, where their delicate transformation began.

One of the babies died in the initial transferral, but of Helva's "class," seventeen thrived in the metal shells. Instead of kicking feet, Helva's neural responses started her wheels; instead of grabbing with hands, she manipulated mechanical extensions. As she matured, more and more neural synapses would be adjusted to operate other mechanisms that went into the maintenance and running of a spaceship. For Helva was destined to be the "brain" half of a scout ship, partnered with a man or a woman, whichever she chose, as the mobile half. She would be among the elite of her kind. Her initial intelligence tests registered above normal and her adaptation index was unusually high. As long as her development within her shell lived up to expectations, and there were no side-effects from the pituitary tinkering, Helva would live a rewarding, rich and unusual life, a far cry from what she would have faced as an ordinary, "normal" being.

However, no diagram of her brain patterns, no early IQ tests recorded certain essential facts about Helva that Central must eventually learn. They would have to bide their official time and see, trusting that the massive doses of shell-psychology would suffice her, too, as the necessary bulwark against her unusual confinement and the pressures of her profession. A ship run by a human brain could not run rogue or insane with the power and resources Central had to build into their scout ships. Brain ships were, of course, long past the experimental stages. Most babies survived the perfected techniques of pituitary manipulation that kept their bodies small, eliminating the necessity of transfers from smaller to larger shells. And very, very few were lost when the final connection was made to the control panels of ship or industrial combine. Shell-people resembled mature dwarfs in size whatever their natal deformities were, but the well-oriented brain would not have changed places with the most perfect body in the Universe.

So, for happy years, Helva scooted around in her shell with her classmates, playing such games as Stall, Power-Seek, studying her lessons in trajectory, propulsion techniques, computation, logistics, mental hygiene, basic alien psychology, philology, space history, law, traffic, codes: all the et ceteras that eventually became compounded into a reasoning, logical, informed citizen. Not so obvious to her, but of more importance to her teachers, Helva ingested the precepts of her conditioning as easily as she absorbed her nutrient fluid. She would one day be grateful to the patient drone of the subconscious-level instruction.

Helva's civilization was not without busy, do-good associations, exploring possible inhumanities to terrestrial as well as extraterrestrial citizens. One such group—Society for the Preservation of the Rights of Intelligent Minorities—got all incensed over shelled "children" when Helva was just turning fourteen. When they were forced to, Central Worlds shrugged its shoulders, arranged a tour of the Laboratory Schools and set the tour off to a big start by showing the members case histories, complete with photographs. Very few committees ever looked past the first few photos. Most of their original objections about "shells" were overridden by the relief that these hideous (to them) bodies *were* mercifully concealed.

Helva's class was doing fine arts, a selective subject in her crowded program. She had activated one of her microscopic tools which she would later use for minute repairs to various parts of her control panel. Her subject was large—a copy of "The Last Supper"—and her canvas, small—the head of a tiny screw. She had tuned her sight to the proper degree. As she worked she absentmindedly crooned, producing a curious sound. Shell-people used their own vocal cords and diaphragms, but sound issued through microphones rather than mouths. Helva's hum, then, had a curious vibrancy, a warm, dulcet quality even in its aimless chromatic wanderings.

"Why, what a lovely voice you have," said one of the female visitors.

Helva "looked" up and caught a fascinating panorama of regular, dirty craters on a flaky pink surface. Her hum became a gurgle of surprise. She instinctively regulated her "sight" until the skin lost its cratered look and the pores assumed normal proportions.

"Yes, we have quite a few years of voice training, madam," remarked Helva calmly. "Vocal peculiarities often become excessively irritating during prolonged interstellar distances and must be eliminated. I enjoyed my lessons."

Although this was the first time that Helva had seen unshelled people, she took this experience calmly. Any other reaction would have been reported instantly.

"I meant that you have a nice singing voice . . . dear," the lady said.

"Thank you. Would you like to see my work?" Helva asked politely. She instinctively sheered away from personal discussions, but she filed the comment away for further meditation.

"Work?" asked the lady.

"I am currently reproducing 'The Last Supper' on the head of a screw."

"Oh, I say," the lady twittered.

Helva turned her vision back to magnification and surveyed her copy critically. "Of course, some of my color values do not match the old Master's and the perspective is faulty, but I believe it to be a fair copy."

The lady's eyes, unmagnified, bugged out.

"Oh, I forget," and Helva's voice was really contrite. If she could have blushed, she would have. "You people don't have adjustable vision."

The monitor of this discourse grinned with pride and amusement as Helva's tone indicated pity for the unfortunate.

"Here, this will help," said Helva, substituting a magnifying device in one extension and holding it over the picture.

In a kind of shock, the ladies and gentlemen of the committee bent to observe the incredibly copied and brilliantly executed Last Supper on the head of a screw.

"Well," remarked one gentleman who had been forced to accompany his wife, "the good Lord can eat where angels fear to tread."

"Are you referring, sir," asked Helva politely, "to the Dark Age discussions of the number of angels who could stand on the head of a pin?"

"I had that in mind."

"If you substitute 'atom' for 'angel,' the problem is not insoluble, given the metallic content of the pin in question."

"Which you are programmed to compute?"

"Of course."

"Did they remember to program a sense of humor, as well, young lady?"

"We are directed to develop a sense of proportion, sir, which contributes the same effect."

The good man chortled appreciatively and decided the trip was worth his time.

If the investigation committee spent months digesting the thoughtful food served them at the Laboratory School, they left Helva with a morsel as well.

"Singing" as applicable to herself required research. She had, of course, been exposed to and enjoyed a music-appreciation course that had included the better-known classical works, such as *Tristan und Isolde, Candide, Oklahoma,* and *Le Nozze di Figaro,* along with the atomic-age singers, Birgit Nilsson, Bob Dylan, and Geraldine Todd, as well as the curious rhythmic progressions of the Venusians, Capellan visual chromatics, the sonic concerti of the Altairians and Reticulan croons. But "singing" for any shell-person posed considerable technical difficulties. Shell-people were schooled to examine every aspect of a problem or situation before making a prognosis. Balanced properly between optimism and practicality, the nondefeatist attitude of the shell-people led them to extricate themselves, their ships, and personnel, from bizarre situations. Therefore to Helva, the problem that she couldn't open her mouth to sing, among other restrictions, did not bother her. She would work out a method, by-passing her limitations, whereby she could sing.

She approached the problem by investigating the methods of sound reproduction through the centuries, human and instrumental. Her own sound-production equipment was essentially more instrumental than vocal. Breath control and the proper enunciation of vowel sounds within the oral cavity appeared to require the most development and practice. Shell-people did not, strictly speaking, breathe. For their purposes, oxygen and other gases were not drawn from the surrounding atmosphere through the medium of lungs but sustained artificially by solution in their shells. After experimentation, Helva discovered that she could manipulate her diaphragmic unit to sustain tone. By relaxing the throat muscles and expanding the oral cavity well into the frontal sinuses, she could direct the vowel sounds into the most felicitous position for proper reproduction through her throat microphone. She compared the results with tape recordings of modern singers and was not unpleased, although her own tapes had a peculiar quality about them, not at all unharmonious, merely unique. Acquiring a repertoire from the Laboratory library was no problem to one trained to perfect recall. She found herself able to sing any role and any song which struck her fancy. It would not have occurred to her that it was curious for a female to sing bass, baritone, tenor, mezzo, soprano, and coloratura as she pleased. It was, to Helva, only a matter of the correct reproduction and diaphragmatic control required by the music attempted.

If the authorities remarked on her curious avocation, they did so among themselves. Shell-people were encouraged to develop a hobby so long as they maintained proficiency in their technical work.

On the anniversary of her sixteenth year, Helva was unconditionally graduated and installed in her ship, the XH-834. Her permanent titanium shell was recessed behind an even more indestructible barrier in the central shaft of the scout ship. The neural, audio, visual, and sensory connections were made and sealed. Her extendibles were diverted, connected or augmented and the final, delicate-beyond-description brain taps were completed while Helva remained anesthetically unaware of the proceedings. When she woke, she *was* the ship. Her brain and intelligence controlled every function from navigation to such loading as a scout ship of her class needed. She could take care of herself and her ambulatory half in any situation already recorded in the annals of Central Worlds and any situation its most fertile minds could imagine.

Her first actual flight, for she and her kind had made mock flights on dummy panels since she was eight, showed her to be a complete master of the techniques of her profession. She was ready for her great adventures and the arrival of her mobile partner.

There were nine qualified scouts sitting around collecting base pay the day Helva reported for active duty. There were several missions that demanded instant attention, but Helva had been of interest to several department heads in Central for some time and each bureau chief was determined to have her assigned to *his* section. No one had remembered to introduce Helva to the prospective partners. The ship always chose its own partner. Had there been another "brain" ship at the base at the moment, Helva would have been guided to make the first move. As it was, while Central wrangled among itself, Robert Tanner sneaked out of the pilots' barracks, out to the field and over to Helva's slim metal hull.

"Hello, anyone at home?" Tanner said.

"Of course," replied Helva, activating her outside scanners. "Are you my partner?" she asked hopefully, as she recognized the Scout Service uniform.

"All you have to do is ask," he retorted in a wistful tone.

"No one has come. I thought perhaps there were no partners available and I've had no directives from Central."

Even to herself Helva sounded a little self-pitying, but the truth was she was lonely, sitting on the darkened field. She had always had the company of other shells and more recently, technicians by the score. The sudden solitude had lost its momentary charm and become oppressive.

"No directives from Central is scarcely a cause for regret, but there happen to be eight other guys biting their fingernails to the quick just waiting for an invitation to board you, you beautiful thing."

Tanner was inside the central cabin as he said this, running appreciative fingers over her panel, the scout's gravity-chair, poking his head into the cabins, the galley, the head, the pressured-storage compartments.

"Now, if you want to goose Central and do *us* a favor all in one, call up the barracks and let's have a ship-warming partner-picking party. Hmmmm?"

Helva chuckled to herself. He was so completely different from the occasional visitors or the various Laboratory technicians she had encountered. He was so gay, so assured, and she was delighted by his suggestion of a partner-picking party. Certainly it was not against anything in her understanding of regulations.

"Cencom, this is XH-834. Connect me with Pilot Barracks."

"Visual?"

"Please."

A picture of lounging men in various attitudes of boredom came on her screen.

"This is XH-834. Would the unassigned scouts do me the favor of coming aboard?"

Eight figures were galvanized into action, grabbing pieces of wearing apparel, disengaging tape mechanisms, disentangling themselves from bedsheets and towels.

Helva dissolved the connection while Tanner chuckled gleefully and settled down to await their arrival.

Helva was engulfed in an unshell-like flurry of anticipation. No actress on her opening night could have been more apprehensive, fearful or breathless. Unlike the actress, she could throw no hysterics, china *objets d'art* or grease paint to relieve her tension. She could, of course, check her stores for edibles and drinks, which she did, serving Tanner from the virgin selection of her commissary.

Scouts were colloquially known as "brawns" as opposed to their ship "brains." They had to pass as rigorous a training program as the brains and only the top 1 percent of each contributory world's highest scholars were admitted to Central Worlds Scout Training Program. Consequently the eight young men who came pounding up the gantry into Helva's hospitable lock were unusually fine looking, intelligent, well-coordinated and well-adjusted young men, looking forward to a slightly drunken evening, Helva permitting, and all quite willing to do each other dirt to get possession of her.

Such a human invasion left Helva mentally breathless, a luxury she thoroughly enjoyed for the brief time she felt she should permit it.

She sorted out the young men. Tanner's opportunism amused but did not specifically attract her; the blond Nordsen seemed too simple; dark-haired Alatpay had a kind of obstinacy for which she felt no compassion; Mir-Ahnin's bitterness hinted an inner darkness she did not wish to lighten, although he made the biggest outward play for her attention. Hers was a curious courtship—this would be only the first of several marriages for her, for brawns retired after seventy-five years of service, or earlier if they were unlucky. Brains, their bodies safe from any deterioration, were indestructible. In theory, once a shell-person had paid off the massive debt of early care, surgical adaptation and maintenance charges, he or she was free to seek employment elsewhere. In practice, shell-people remained in the Service until they chose to self-destruct or died in line of duty. Helva had actually spoken to one shell-person 322 years old. She had been so awed by the contact she hadn't presumed to ask the personal questions she had wanted to.

Her choice of a brawn did not stand out from the others until Tanner started to sing a scout ditty, recounting the misadventures of the bold, dense, painfully inept Billy Brawn. An attempt at harmony resulted in cacophony and Tanner wagged his arms wildly for silence.

"What we need is a roaring good lead tenor. Jennan, besides palming aces, what do you sing?"

"Sharp," Jennan replied with easy good humor.

"If a tenor is absolutely necessary, I'll attempt it," Helva volunteered.

"My good *woman*," Tanner protested.

"Sound your 'A' " said Jennan, laughing.

Into the stunned silence that followed the rich, clear, high "A," Jennan remarked quietly, "Such an 'A' Caruso would have given the rest of his notes to sing."

It did not take them long to discover her full range.

"All Tanner asked for was one roaring good lead tenor," Jennan said jokingly, "and our sweet mistress supplied us an entire repertory company. The boy who gets this ship will go far, far, far."

"To the Horsehead Nebula?" asked Nordsen, quoting an old Central saw.

"To the Horsehead Nebula and back, we shall make beautiful music," said Helva, chuckling.

"Together," Jennan said. "Only you'd better make the music and, with my voice, I'd better listen."

"I rather imagined it would be I who listened," suggested Helva.

Jennan executed a stately bow with an intricate flourish of his crush-brimmed hat. He directed his bow toward the central control pillar where Helva *was*. Her own personal preference crystallized at that precise moment and for that particular reason: Jennan, alone of the men, had addressed his remarks directly at her physical presence, regardless of the fact that he knew she could pick up his image wherever he was in the ship and regardless of the fact that her body was behind massive metal walls. Throughout their partnership, Jennan never failed to turn his head in her direction no matter where he was in relation to her. In response to this personalization, Helva at that moment and from then on always spoke to Jennan only through her central mike, even thought that was not always the most efficient method.

Helva didn't know that she fell in love with Jennan that evening. As she had never been exposed to love or affection, only the drier cousins, respect and admiration, she could scarcely have recognized her reaction to the warmth of his personality and thoughtfulness. As a shell-person, she considered herself remote from emotions largely connected with physical desires.

"Well, Helva, it's been swell meeting you," said Tanner suddenly as she and Jennan were arguing about the baroque quality of "Come All Ye Sons of Art." "See you in space sometime, you lucky dog, Jennan. Thanks for the party, Helva."

"You don't have to go so soon?" asked Helva, realizing belatedly that she and Jennan had been excluding the others from this discussion.

"Best man won," Tanner said wryly. "Guess I'd better go get a tape on love ditties. Might need 'em for the next ship, if there're any more at home like you."

Helva and Jennan watched them leave, both a little confused.

"Perhaps Tanner's jumping to conclusions?" Jennan asked.

Helva regarded him as he slouched against the console, facing her shell directly. His arms were crossed on his chest and the glass he held had been empty for some time. He was handsome, they all were; but his watchful eyes were unwary, his mouth assumed a smile easily, his voice (to which Helva was particularly drawn) was resonant, deep, and without unpleasant overtones or accent.

"Sleep on it, at any rate, Helva. Call me in the morning if it's your opt."

She called him at breakfast, after she had checked her choice through Central. Jennan moved his things aboard, received their joint commission, had his personality and experience file locked into her reviewer, gave her the coordinates of their first mission. The XH-834 officially became the JH-834.

Their first mission was a dull but necessary crash priority (Medical got Helva), rushing a vaccine to a distant system plagued with a virulent spore disease. They had only to get to Spica as fast as possible.

After the initial, thrilling forward surge at her maximum speed, Helva realized her muscles were to be given less of a workout than her brawn on this tedious mission. But they did have plenty of time for exploring each other's personalities. Jennan, of course, knew what Helva was capable of as a ship and partner, just as she knew what she could expect from him. But these were only facts and Helva looked forward eagerly to learning that human side of her partner which could not be reduced to a series of symbols. Nor could the give and take of two personalities be learned from a book. It had to be experienced.

"My father was a scout, too, or is that programmed?" began Jennan their third day out.

"Naturally."

"Unfair, you know. You've got all my family history and I don't know one blamed thing about yours."

"I've never known either," Helva said. "Until I read yours, it hadn't occurred to me I must have one, too, someplace in Central's files."

Jennan snorted. "Shell psychology!"

Helva laughed. "Yes, and I'm even programmed against curiosity about it. You'd better be, too."

Jennan ordered a drink, slouched into the gravity couch opposite her, put his feet on the bumpers, turning himself idly from side to side on the gimbals.

"Helva—a made-up name . . . "

"With a Scandinavian sound."

"You aren't blond," Jennan said positively.

"Well, then, there're dark Swedes."

"And blond Turks and this one's harem is limited to one."

"Your woman in purdah, yes, but you can comb the pleasure houses—" Helva found herself aghast at the edge to her carefully trained voice.

"You know," Jennan interrupted her, deep in some thought of his own, "my father gave me the impression he was a lot more married to his ship, the Silvia, than to my mother. I know I used to think Silvia was my grandmother. She was a low number, so she must have been a great-great-grandmother at least. I used to talk to her for hours."

"Her registry?" asked Helva, unwittingly jealous of everyone and anyone who had shared his hours.

"422. I think she's TS now. I ran into Tom Burgess once."

Jennan's father had died of a planetary disease, the vaccine for which his ship had used up in curing the local citizens.

"Tom said she'd got mighty tough and salty. You lose your sweetness and I'll come back and haunt you, girl," Jennan threatened.

Helva laughed. He startled her by stamping up to the column panel, touching it with light, tender fingers.

"I *wonder* what you look like," he said softly, wistfully.

Helva had been briefed about this natural curiosity of scouts. She didn't know anything about herself and neither of them ever would or could.

"Pick any form, shape, and shade and I'll be yours obliging," she countered, as training suggested.

"Iron Maiden, I fancy blondes with long tresses," and Jennan pantomimed Lady Godiva–like tresses. "Since you're immolated in titanium, I'll call you Brunehilde, my dear," and he made his bow.

With a chortle, Helva launched into the appropriate aria just as Spica made contact.

"What'n'ell's that yelling about? Who are you? And unless you're Central Worlds Medical, go away. We've got a plague. No visiting privileges."

"My ship is singing, we're the JH-834 of Worlds and we've got your vaccine. What are our landing coordinates?"

"Your *ship* is singing?"

"The greatest S.A.T.B. in organized space. Any request?"

The JH-834 delivered the vaccine but no more arias and received immediate orders to proceed to Leviticus IV. By the time they got there, Jennan found a reputation awaiting him and was forced to defend the 834's virgin honor.

"I'll stop singing," murmured Helva contritely as she ordered up poultices for his third black eye in a week.

"You will not," Jennan said through gritted teeth. "If I have to have black eyes from here to the Horsehead to keep the snicker out of the title, we'll be the ship who sings."

After the "ship who sings" tangled with a minor but vicious narcotic ring in the Lesser Magellanics, the title became definitely respectful. Central was aware of each episode and punched out a "special interest" key on JH-834's file. A first-rate team was shaking down well.

Jennan and Helva considered themselves a first-rate team, too, after their tidy arrest.

"Of all the vices in the universe, I *hate* drug addiction," Jennan remarked as they headed back to Central Base. "People can go to hell quick enough without that kind of help."

"Is that why you volunteered for Scout Service? To redirect traffic?"

"I'll bet my official answer's on your review."

"In far too flowery wording. 'Carrying on the traditions of my family, which has been proud of four generations in Service,' if I may quote you your own words."

Jennan groaned. "I was *very* young when I wrote that. I certainly hadn't been through Final Training. And once I was in Final Training, my pride wouldn't let me fail . . .

"As I mentioned, I used to visit Dad on board the Silvia and I've a very good idea she might have had her eye on me as a replacement for my father because I had had massive doses of scout-oriented propaganda. It took. From the time I was seven, I was going to be a scout or else." He shrugged as if deprecating a youthful determination that had taken a great deal of mature application to bring to fruition.

"Ah, so? Scout Sahir Silan on the JS-422 penetrating into the Horsehead Nebula?"

Jennan chose to ignore her sarcasm.

"With *you*, I may even get that far. But even with Silvia's nudging *I* never daydreamed myself *that* kind of glory in my wildest flights of fancy. I'll leave the whoppers to your agile brain henceforth. I have in mind a smaller contribution to space history."

"So modest?"

"No. Practical. We also serve, et cetera." He placed a dramatic hand on his heart.

"Glory hound!" scoffed Helva.

"Look who's talking, my Nebula-bound friend. At least I'm not greedy. There'll only be one hero like my dad at Parsaea, but I *would* like to be remembered for some kudos. Everyone does. Why else do or die?"

"Your father died on his way back from Parsaea, if I may point out a few cogent facts. So he could never have known he was a hero for damming the flood with his ship. Which kept the Parsaean colony from being abandoned. Which gave them a chance to discover the antiparalytic qualities of Parsaea. Which *he* never knew."

"I know," said Jennan softly.

Helva was immediately sorry for the tone of her rebuttal. She knew very well how deep Jennan's attachment to his father had been. On his review a note was made that he had rationalized his father's loss with the unexpected and welcome outcome of the Affair at Parsaea.

"Facts are not human, Helva. My father was and so am I. And *basically,* so are you. Check over your dial, 834. Amid all the wires attached to you is a heart, an underdeveloped human heart. Obviously!"

"I apologize, Jennan," she said.

Jennan hesitated a moment, threw out his hands in acceptance and then tapped her shell affectionately.

"If they ever take us off the milkruns, we'll make a stab at the Nebula, huh?"

As so frequently happened in the Scout Service, within the next hour they had orders to change course, not to the Nebula, but to a recently colonized system with two habitable planets, one tropical, one glacial. The sun, named Ravel, had become unstable; the spectrum was that of a rapidly expanding shell, with absorption lines rapidly displacing toward violet. The augmented heat of the primary had already forced evacuation of the nearer world, Daphnis. The pattern of spectral emissions gave indication that the sun would sear Chloe as well. All ships in the immediate spatial vicinity were to report to Disaster Headquarters on Chloe to effect removal of the remaining colonists.

The JH-834 obediently presented itself and was sent to outlying areas on Chloe to pick up scattered settlers who did not appear to appreciate the urgency of the situation. Chloe, indeed, was enjoying the first temperatures above freezing since it had been flung out of its parent. Since many of the colonists were religious fanatics who had settled on rigorous Chloe to fit themselves for a life of pious reflection, Chloe's abrupt thaw was attributed to sources other than a rampaging sun.

Jennan had to spend so much time countering specious arguments that he and Helva were behind schedule on their way to the fourth and last settlement.

Helva jumped over the high range of jagged peaks that surrounded and sheltered the valley from the former raging snows as well as the present heat. The violent sun with its flaring corona was just beginning to brighten the deep valley as Helva dropped down to a landing.

"They'd better grab their toothbrushes and hop aboard," Helva said. "HQ says speed it up."

"All women," remarked Jennan in surprise as he walked down to meet them. "Unless the men on Chloe wear furred skirts."

"Charm 'em but pare the routine to the bare essentials. And turn on your two-way private."

Jennan advanced smiling, but his explanation of his mission was met with absolute incredulity and considerable doubt as to his authenticity. He groaned inwardly as the matriarch paraphrased previous explanations of the warming sun.

"Revered mother, there's been an overload on that prayer circuit and the sun is blowing itself up in one obliging burst. I'm here to take you to the spaceport at Rosary—"

"That Sodom?" The worthy woman glowered and shuddered disdainfully at his suggestion. "We thank you for your warning but we have no wish to leave our cloister for the rude world. We must go about our morning meditation which has been interrupted—"

"It'll be permanently interrupted when that sun starts broiling you. You must come now," Jennan said firmly.

"Madame," said Helva, realizing that perhaps a female voice might carry more weight in this instance than Jennan's very masculine charm.

"Who spoke?" cried the nun, startled by the bodiless voice.

"I, Helva, the ship. Under my protection you and your sisters-in-faith may enter safely and be unprofaned by association with a male. I will guard you and take you safely to a place prepared for you."

The matriarch peered cautiously into the ship's open port. "Since only Central Worlds is permitted the use of such ships, I acknowledge that you are not trifling with us, young man. However, we are in no danger here."

"The temperature at Rosary is now 99 degrees," said Helva. "As soon as the sun's rays penetrate directly into this valley, it will also be 99 degrees, and it is due to climb to approximately 180 degrees today. I notice your buildings are made of wood with moss chinking. Dry moss. It should fire around noontime."

The sunlight was beginning to slant into the valley through the peaks, and the fierce rays warmed the restless group behind the matriarch. Several opened the throats of their furry parkas.

"Jennan," said Helva privately to him, "our time is very short."

"I can't leave them, Helva. Some of those girls are barely out of their teens."

"Pretty, too. No wonder the matriarch doesn't want to get in."

"Helva."

"It will be the Lord's will," said the matriarch stoutly and turned her back squarely on rescue.

"To burn to death?" shouted Jennan as she threaded her way through her murmuring disciples.

"They want to be martyrs? Their opt, Jennan," said Helva dispassionately. "We must leave and that is no longer a matter of option."

"How can I leave, Helva?"

"Parsaea?" Helva asked tauntingly as he stepped forward to grab one of the women. "You can't drag them *all* aboard and we don't have time to fight it out. Get on board, Jennan, or I'll have you on report."

"They'll die," muttered Jennan dejectedly as he reluctantly turned to climb on board.

"You can risk only so much," Helva said sympathetically. "As it is we'll just have time to make a rendezvous. Lab reports a critical speedup in spectral evolution."

Jennan was already in the airlock when one of the younger women, screaming, rushed to squeeze in the closing port. Her action set off the others. They stampeded through the narrow opening. Even crammed back to breast, there was not enough room inside for all the women. Jennan broke out spacesuits for the three who would have to remain with him in the airlock. He wasted valuable time explaining to the matriarch that she must put on the suit because the airlock had no independent oxygen or cooling units.

"We'll be caught," said Helva in a grim tone to Jennan on their private connection. "We've lost eighteen minutes in this last-minute rush. I am now overloaded for maximum speed and I must attain maximum speed to outrun the heat wave."

"Can you lift? We're suited."

"Lift? Yes," she said, doing so. "Run? I stagger."

Jennan, bracing himself and the women, could feel her sluggishness as she blasted upward. Heartlessly, Helva applied thrust as long as she could, despite the fact that the gravitational force mashed her cabin passengers brutally and crushed two fatally. It was a question of saving as many as possible. The only one for whom she had any concern was Jennan and she was in desperate terror about his safety. Airless and uncooled, protected by only one layer of metal, not three, the airlock was not going to be safe for the four trapped there, despite their spacesuits. These were only the standard models, not built to withstand the excessive heat to which the ship would be subjected.

Helva ran as fast as she could but the incredible wave of heat from the explosive sun caught them halfway to cold safety.

She paid no heed to the cries, moans, pleas, and prayers in her cabin. She listened only to Jennan's tortured breathing, to the missing throb in his suit's purifying system and the sucking of the overloaded cooling unit. Helpless, she heard the hysterical screams of his three companions as they writhed in the awful heat. Vainly, Jennan tried to calm them, tried to explain they would soon be safe and cool if they could be still and endure the heat. Undisciplined by their terror and torment, they tried to strike out at him despite the close quarters. One flailing arm became entangled in the leads to his power pack and the damage was quickly done. A connection, weakened by heat and the dead weight of the arm, broke.

For all the power at her disposal, Helva was helpless. She watched as Jennan fought for his breath, as he turned his head beseechingly toward *her*, and died.

Only the iron conditioning of her training prevented Helva from swinging around and plunging back into the cleansing heart of the exploding sun. Numbly she made rendezvous with the refugee convoy. She obediently transferred her burned, heat-prostrated passengers to the assigned transport.

"I will retain the body of my scout and proceed to the nearest base for burial," she informed Central dully.

"You will be provided escort," was the reply.

"I have no need of escort."

"Escort is provided, XH-834," she was told curtly. The shock of hearing Jennan's initial severed from her call number cut off her half-formed protest. Stunned, she waited by the transport until her screens showed the arrival of two other slim brain ships. The cortege proceeded homeward at unfunereal speeds.

"834? The ship who sings?"

"I have no more songs."

"Your scout was Jennan."

"I do not wish to communicate."

"I'm 422."

"Silvia?"

"Silvia died a long time ago. I'm 422. Currently MS," the ship rejoined curtly. "AH-640 is our other friend, but Henry's not listening in. Just as well—he wouldn't understand it if you wanted to turn rogue. But I'd stop *him* if he tried to deter you."

"Rogue?" The term snapped Helva out of her apathy.

"Sure. You're young. You've got power for years. Skip. Others have done it. 732 went rogue twenty years ago after she lost her scout on a mission to that white dwarf. Hasn't been seen since."

"I never heard about rogues."

"As it's exactly the thing we're conditioned against, you sure wouldn't hear about it in school, my dear," 422 said.

"Break conditioning?" cried Helva, anguished, thinking longingly of the white, white furious hot heart of the sun she had just left.

"For you I don't think it would be hard at the moment," 422 said quietly, her voice devoid of her earlier cynicism. "The stars are out there, winking."

"Alone?" cried Helva from her heart.

"Alone!" 422 confirmed bleakly.

Alone with all of space and time. Even the Horsehead Nebula would not be far enough away to daunt her. Alone with a hundred years to live with her memories and nothing . . . nothing more.

"Was Parsaea worth it?" she asked 422 softly.

"Parsaea?" 422 repeated, surprised. "With his father? Yes. We were there, at Parsaea when we were needed. Just as you . . . and his son . . . were at Chloe. When you were needed. The crime is not knowing where need is and not being there."

"But *I* need *him*. Who will supply my need?" said Helva bitterly . . .

"834," said 422 after a day's silent speeding, "Central wishes your report. A replacement awaits your opt at Regulus Base. Change course accordingly."

"A replacement?" That was certainly not what she needed . . . a reminder inadequately filling the void Jennan left. Why, her hull was barely cool of Chloe's heat. Atavistically, Helva wanted time to mourn Jennan.

"Oh, none of them are impossible if *you're* a good ship," 422 remarked philosophically. "And it is just what you need. The sooner the better."

"You told them I wouldn't go rogue, didn't you?" Helva said.

"The moment passed you even as it passed me after Parsaea, and before that, after Glen Arthur, and Betelgeuse."

"We're conditioned to go on, aren't we? We *can't* go rogue. You were testing."

"Had to. Orders. Not even Psych knows why a rogue occurs. Central's very worried, and so, daughter, are your sister ships. I asked to be your escort. I . . . don't want to lose you both."

In her emotional nadir, Helva could feel a flood of gratitude for Silvia's rough sympathy.

"We've all known this grief, Helva. It's no consolation, but if we couldn't feel with our scouts, we'd only be machines wired for sound."

Helva looked at Jennan's still form stretched before her in its shroud and heard the echo of his rich voice in the quiet cabin.

"Silvia! I *couldn't* help him," she cried from her soul.

"Yes, dear, I know," 422 murmured gently and then was quiet.

The three ships sped on, wordless, to the great Central Worlds base at Regulus. Helva broke silence to acknowledge landing instructions and the officially tendered regrets.

The three ships set down simultaneously at the wooded edge where Regulus' gigantic blue trees stood sentinel over the sleeping dead in the small Service cemetery. The entire Base complement approached with measured step and formed an aisle from Helva to the burial ground. The honor detail, out of step, walked slowly into her cabin. Reverently they placed the body of her dead love on the wheeled bier, covered it honorably with the deep-blue, star-splashed flag of the Service. She watched as it was driven slowly down the living aisle which closed in behind the bier in last escort.

Then, as the simple words of interment were spoken, as the atmosphere planes dipped in tribute over the open grave, Helva found voice for her lonely farewell.

Softly, barely audible at first, the strains of the ancient song of evening and requiem swelled to the final poignant measure until black space itself echoed back the sound of the song the ship sang.

JOURNAL WRITINGS

1. Imagine having a prosthesis. **Describe** how you would feel in this situation.
2. Helva is consistently described in feminine terms. She is paired with a male. Yet there is no possibility of sexuality. In light of these facts consider the meanings of sex and gender. Are they purely physical characteristics— purely mental? Record your thoughts.

BRAINSTORMING AND DRAFTING

3. This story implies various kinds of political and social relationships between individuals and the society in which they live. Discuss or think about these implications (look for **specific** details in the story that suggest larger contexts). Then write a paragraph in which you explain why you would (or would not) like to live in this future society.

THE AUTHOR'S METHODS

4. Look for ways the author **characterizes** Helva throughout the story. Make a list of these techniques and write a paper in which you discuss how they effectively present Helva to the reader.
5. Reread the section on page 596 where Helva is "doing fine arts." What **allusions** are being made in this section? (Hint: one is to art, another to philosophy.) What effect do these allusions have?

FORMAL WRITING AND RESEARCH PAPERS

6.   Early in the story the possibility of euthanasia is mentioned rather casually. Euthanasia (or mercy killing), in either its active or passive forms, is an issue that raises many moral and ethical questions. Find out about this topic, form an opinion about it, and write an extended paper in which you justify your opinion.

7.   Medical engineering is a rapidly developing field, producing such items as mechanical limbs, joint replacements, and even artificial hearts. Consult the *Index Medicus* to find some information about recent developments in this area. Select one such development. Describe the development so that a nonspecialist can understand it. Explain why you think it will (or will not) benefit potential recipients.

Freeman Dyson

The Magic City

(1979)

Born in Crawthorne, England, in 1923, Freeman Dyson studied mathematics at Cambridge University. During World War II he did statistical analyses for Bomber Command. Immediately after the war he became a Research Fellow in physics at Cornell University, where he studied under the eminent physicist Hans Bethe. In 1951, J. Robert Oppenheimer invited him to join the Institute for Advanced Studies at Princeton. He worked with the Orion Project at La Jolla, California in 1958, attempting to develop a method of using surplus atomic bombs to power space vehicles. During 1962–1963 he served as consultant to the Arms Control and Disarmament Agency. Among his numerous writings are *Disturbing the Universe* (1982), which received the National Book Award, and *Weapons and Hope* (1984).

Dyson uses a childhood recollection as a way of presenting a moral perspective on science and technology. Knowing that science can produce both good and evil, he suggests that each person must find the means to live with these possibilities and struggle to produce quality work.

PREVIEW

Think back to your childhood. Recall a particular book, object, or situation that has had an important influence on your life. Ask yourself: Why is it important, and how has it influenced me?

A small boy with a book, high up in a tree. When I was eight years old somebody gave me *The Magic City* by Edith Nesbit. Nesbit wrote a number of other children's books, which are more famous and better written. But this was the one which I loved and have never forgotten. I did not at the age of eight read deep meanings into it, but I knew that it was somehow special. The story has a coherent architectural plan, covered with a surface frosting of crazy logic. *The Wizard of Oz* was the other book that I used to read over and over again. It has the same qualities. An eight-year-old already has a feeling for such things, even if he spends most of his waking hours climbing trees. *The Magic City* is not just a story about some crazy kids. It is a story about a crazy universe. What I see now, and did not see as an eight-year-old, is that Nesbit's crazy universe bears a strong resemblance to the one we live in.

Edith Nesbit* was from every point of view a remarkable woman. Born in 1858, she was intimate with the family of Karl Marx† and became a revolutionary socialist long before this was fashionable. She supported herself by writing and brought up a large family of children of mixed parentage. She soon discovered that her survival depended upon her ability to write splendidly bourgeois stories for the children of the rich. Her books sold well, and she survived. She made some compromises with Victorian respectability, but did not lose her inner fire. She wrote *The Magic City* in 1910, when she was fifty-two. By that time her personal struggles were over and she could view the world with a certain philosophic calm.

There are three themes in *The Magic City.* The first is the main theme. The hero is an orphan called Philip who is left alone in a big house and builds a toy city out of the ambient Victorian bric-a-brac. One night he suddenly finds his city grown to full size, inhabited by full-size mythical people and animals, and himself obliged to live in it. After escaping from the city, he wanders through the surrounding country, where every toy house or castle that he ever built is faithfully enlarged and preserved. The book records his adventures as he stumbles through this world of blown-up products of his own imaginings.

The second theme is concerned explicitly with technology. It is a law of life in the magic city that if you wish for anything you can have it. But with this law goes a special rule about machines. If anyone wishes for a piece of machinery, he is compelled to keep it and go on using it for the rest of his life. Philip fortunately escapes from the operation of this rule when he has the choice of wishing for a horse or a bicycle and chooses the horse.

The third theme of the book is the existence of certain ancient prophecies foretelling the appearance of a Deliverer and a Destroyer. Various evil forces are at large in the land, and it is the destiny of the Deliverer to overcome them. But it is also foreordained that a Destroyer will come to oppose the Deliverer and give aid to the forces of darkness. At the beginning Philip is suspected of being the Destroyer. He is only able to vindicate himself by a succession of increasingly noble deeds, which ultimately result in his being acclaimed as the Deliverer. Meanwhile the Destroyer is unmasked and turns out to be the children's nursemaid, a woman of the lower classes whom Philip has always hated. Only once, at the end of the book, Nesbit steps out of character and shows where her real sympathies lie. "I'll speak my mind if I die for it," says the Destroyer as she stands awaiting sentence. "You don't understand. You've never been a servant, to see other people get all the fat and you all the bones. What you think it's like to know if you'd just been born in a gentleman's mansion instead of in a model workman's dwelling you'd have been brought up as a young lady and had the openwork silk stockings?" Even an eight-year-old understands at this point that Philip's heroic

* Nesbit, Edith—(1858–1924) English children's author. [Eds.]

† Marx, Karl—(1818–1883) German socialist philosopher; author of *Communist Manifesto*. [Eds.]

virtue is phony and the nursemaid's heroic defiance is real. In an unjust world, the roles of Deliverer and Destroyer become ambiguous. "Think not that I am come to send peace on earth," said Jesus. "I come not to send peace, but a sword."

I do not know how far Nesbit consciously intended *The Magic City* to be an allegory of the human condition. It was only after I descended from the trees, and tasted the joys and sorrows of becoming a scientist, that I began to meditate upon the magic city and to see in it a mirror image of the big world that I was entering. I was plunged into the big world abruptly, like Philip. The big world, wherever I looked, was full of human tragedy. I came upon the scene and found myself playing roles that were half serious and half preposterous. And that is the way it has continued ever since.

I am trying . . . to describe to people who are not scientists the way the human situation looks to somebody who is a scientist. Partly I shall be describing how science looks from the inside. Partly I shall be discussing the future of technology. Partly I shall be struggling with the ethical problems of war and peace, freedom and responsibility, hope and despair, as these are affected by science. These are all parts of a picture which must be seen as a whole in order to be understood. It makes no sense to me to separate science from technology, technology from ethics, or ethics from religion. I am talking here to unscientific people who ultimately have the responsibility for guiding the growth of science and technology into creative rather than destructive directions. If you, unscientific people, are to succeed in this task, you must understand the nature of the beast you are trying to control. This [essay] is intended to help you to understand. If you find it merely amusing or bewildering, it has failed in its purpose. But if you find none of it amusing or bewildering, it has failed even more completely. It is characteristic of all deep human problems that they are not to be approached without some humor and some bewilderment. Science is no exception.

My colleagues in the social sciences talk a great deal about methodology. I prefer to call it style. The methodology [here] is literary rather than analytical. For insight into human affairs I turn to stories and poems rather than to sociology. This is the result of my upbringing and background. I am not able to make use of the wisdom of the sociologists because I do not speak their language. When I see scientists becoming involved in public affairs and trying to use their technical knowledge politically for the betterment of mankind, I remember the words of Milton the poet:* "I cannot praise a fugitive and cloistered virtue, unexercised and unbreathed, that never sallies out and sees her adversary." These words, written three hundred years ago, still stand as a monument of human experience, hope and tragedy. They reverberate with echoes of Milton's poetry, his fight for the freedom of the press, his long years of service to the cause of rebellion against monarchy, his blindness, his political downfall, and his final redemption in the writing of *Paradise Lost*. What more can one say that is not by comparison cheap and shallow? We are scientists second, and human beings first. We become

---

* Milton, John—(1608–1674) English epic poet; author of *Paradise Lost*. [Eds.]

politically involved because knowledge implies responsibility. We fight as best we can for what we believe to be right. Often, like Milton, we fail. What more can one say?

A substantial part of this [essay] is autobiographical. I make no apology for that. It is not that I consider my own life particularly significant or interesting to anybody besides myself. I write about my own experiences because I do not know so much about anyone else's. Almost any scientist of my generation could tell a similar story. The important thing, to my mind, is that the great human problems are problems of the individual and not of the mass. To understand the nature of science and of its interaction with society, one must examine the individual scientist and how he confronts the world around him. The best way to approach the ethical problems associated with science is to study real dilemmas faced by real scientists. Since firsthand evidence is the most reliable, I begin by writing about things that happened to me personally. This is another effect of the same individualistic bias that leads me to listen to poets more than to economists.

But I still have to finish what I was saying about *The Magic City* and its three themes. That we live in a world of overgrown toys is too obvious to need explaining. Nikolaus Otto* plays for a few years with a toy gasoline engine and—bingo!—we all find ourselves driving cars. Wallace Carothers† gets interested in condensation polymers and—zing!—every working-class girl is wearing nylon stockings that are as fancy as the openwork silk that was for Nesbit in 1910 the hated symbol of upper-class privilege. Otto Hahn and Fritz Strassmann‡ amuse themselves with analytical radiochemistry and—boom!—a hundred thousand people in Hiroshima are dead. The same examples also illustrate Nesbit's rule about the consequences of wishing for machinery. Once you have wished for cars, nylons or nuclear weapons, you are stuck with them in a very permanent fashion. But there is one great difference between Philip's world and ours. In his world, every toy castle that he had ever built appeared enlarged. In our world, thousands of scientists play with millions of toys, but only a few of their toys grow big. The majority of technological ventures remain toys, of interest only to specialists and historians. A small number succeed spectacularly and become part of the fabric of our lives. Even with the advantage of hindsight it is difficult to understand why one technology is overwhelmingly successful and another is stillborn. Subtle differences of quality have decisive effects. Sometimes an accident that nobody could have predicted makes a particular toy grow monstrous. When Otto Hahn stumbled upon the discovery of nuclear fission in 1938 he had no inkling of nuclear weapons, no premonition that he was treading on dangerous ground.

---

* Otto, Nikolaus—(1832–1891) German inventor; codeveloper of first practical internal combustion engine. [Eds.]

† Carothers, Wallace—(1896–1937) American chemist; discovered synthetic rubber and nylon. [Eds.]

‡ Hahn, Otto—(1879–1968) German chemist; discovered nuclear fission; Strassman, Fritz—(1902–) German chemist; collaborated with Otto Hahn in work on nuclear fission. [Eds.]

When the news of Hiroshima came to him seven years later, he was overcome with such grief that his friends were afraid he would kill himself.

Science and technology, like all original creations of the human spirit, are unpredictable. If we had a reliable way to label our toys good and bad, it would be easy to regulate technology wisely. But we can rarely see far enough ahead to know which road leads to damnation. Whoever concerns himself with big technology, either to push it forward or to stop it, is gambling in human lives.

Scientists are not the only people who play with intellectual toys that suddenly explode and cause the crash of empires. Philosophers, prophets and poets do it too. In the long run, the technological means that scientists place in our hands may be less important than the ideological ends to which these means are harnessed. Technology is powerful but it does not rule the world. Nesbit lived long enough to see one tenth of mankind ruled by ideas that the man known in the family as "Old Nick" had worked out in his long quiet days at the British Museum. Old Nick, alias Karl Marx, was the father-in-law of her friend Edward Aveling.

Marx was in his own lifetime a larger-than-life figure, and after his death became Deliverer to half the world and Destroyer to the other half. There is a deep-rooted tendency in the human soul that builds myths of Deliverers and Destroyers. These myths, like other myths, have a foundation in truth. The world of science and technology may appear on the surface to be rational, but it is not immune to such myths. The great figures of science have a quality, an intensity of will and character, that sets them apart from ordinary scientists as Marx stands apart from ordinary economists. We shall not understand the dynamics of science and technology, just as we shall not understand the dynamics of political ideology, if we ignore the dominating influence of myths and symbols.

I was lucky to hear the economist John Maynard Keynes,* a few years before his death, give a lecture about the physicist Isaac Newton. Keynes was at that time himself a legendary figure, gravely ill and carrying a heavy responsibility as economic adviser to Winston Churchill. He had snatched a few hours from his official duties to pursue his hobby of studying Newton's unpublished manuscripts. Newton had kept his early writings hidden away until the end of his life in a big box, where they remained until quite recently. Keynes was speaking in the same old building where Newton had lived and worked 270 years earlier. In an ancient, dark, cold room, draped with wartime blackout curtains, a small audience crowded around the patch of light under which the exhausted figure of Keynes was huddled. He spoke with passionate intensity, made even more impressive by the pallor of his face and the gloom of the surroundings. Here are some extracts from his talk.

> As one broods over these queer collections, it seems easier to understand—with an understanding which is not, I hope, distorted in the other direction—this strange spirit, who was tempted by the Devil to believe, at the time when within these walls he was solving so much, that he could reach *all* the secrets of God and Nature by the pure power of mind—Copernicus and Faustus in one.

---

* Keynes, John Maynard—(1883–1946) English economist. [Eds.]

A large section, judging by the handwriting among the earliest, relates to alchemy—transmutation, the philosoper's stone, the elixir of life.

All his unpublished works on esoteric and theological matters are marked by careful learning, accurate method and extreme sobriety of statement. They are just as *sane* as the *Principia,* if their whole matter and purpose were not magical.

Why do I call him a magician? Because he looked on the whole universe and all that is in it *as a riddle,* as a secret which could be read by applying pure thought to certain evidence, certain mystic clues which God had laid about the world to allow a sort of philosopher's treasure hunt to the esoteric brotherhood. . . . He *did* read the riddle of the heavens. And he believed that by the same powers of his introspective imagination he would read the riddle of the Godhead, the riddle of past and future events divinely foreordained, the riddle of the elements and their constitution from an original undifferentiated first matter, the riddle of health and of immortality.

Newton was admittedly an extreme case. When I quote these words of Keynes I do not mean to imply that every great scientist should devote half his time to magical mumbo-jumbo. I am suggesting that anyone who is transcendentally great as a scientist is likely also to have personal qualities that ordinary people would consider in some sense superhuman. If he were not gifted with extraordinary strength of character, he could not do what he does in science. Thus it is not surprising that traditional mythology links the figure of the scientist with that of the Magus. The Magi were the priests of the ancient Zoroastrian* religion of Persia, and the word "magic" is derived from their name. The myth of the scientist-Magus appears in its most complete form in the legend of Faust, the learned man who sells his soul to the Devil in return for occult knowledge and magical power. The remarkable thing about the Faust legend is that everybody to some extent still believes in it. When you say that some piece of technology is a Faustian bargain, everybody knows what you mean. Somewhere below the level of rational argument, the myth is alive.

I shall talk later about various scientists who have acquired public reputations as deliverers or destroyers. Such reputations are often transient or even fraudulent, but they are not meaningless. They indicate a recognition by the public that somebody has done something that matters. The public also recognizes a special personal quality in these people. The greatest and most genuine deliverer in my lifetime was Einstein. His special quality was universally recognized, although it is not easy to describe in words. I shall not talk about Einstein since I did not know him personally and I have nothing to add to what has already been said by others.

In the magic city there are not only deliverers and destroyers but also a great multitude of honest craftsmen, artisans and scribes. Much of the joy of science is the joy of solid work done by skilled workmen. Many of us are happy to spend our lives in collaborative efforts where to be reliable is more important than to be original. There is a great satisfaction in building good tools for other people to use. We do not all have the talent or the ambition to become prima donnas. The

---

* Zoroastrian—an ancient Persian religion that regarded light and dark as the opposing principles of the universe. [Eds.]

essential factor which keeps the scientific enterprise healthy is a shared respect for quality. Everybody can take pride in the quality of his own work, and we expect rough treatment from our colleagues whenever we produce something shoddy. The knowledge that quality counts makes even routine tasks rewarding.

Recently a new magus has appeared upon the scene: a writer, Robert Pirsig, with a book, *Zen and the Art of Motorcycle Maintenance.* His book explores the dual nature of science, on the one hand science as dedicated craftsmanship, on the other hand science as intellectual obsession. He dances with wonderful agility between these two levels of experience. On the practical level, he describes for unscientific readers the virtue of a technology based upon respect for quality. The motorcycle serves as a concrete example to illustrate the principles which should govern the practical use of science. On the intellectual level, Pirsig weaves into the discussion of technology a narrative of his own quest for philosophical understanding, ending with a mental collapse and reintegration. Phaedrus, the alter ego of Pirsig, is a spirit so dominated by intellectual struggle that he has become insane. In order to survive as a human being, Pirsig has driven Phaedrus out of his consciousness, but Phaedrus comes back to haunt him. The small boy Chris who rides on the back of the motorcycle succeeds in the end in bringing Phaedrus and Pirsig together. In a strange fashion, this personal drama adds insight to Pirsig's vision of technology. Pirsig is by profession a writer and not a scientist. But he has struggled to order rationally the whole of human experience, as Newton struggled three hundred years earlier. He has pored over the pre-Socratic Greek philosophers in his study in Montana, as Newton pored over the ancient alchemical texts in his laboratory in Cambridge. The struggle brought both of them to the edge of madness. Each of them in the end abandoned the greater part of his design and settled for a more limited area of understanding. But Pirsig's message to our generation, as we try to come to terms with technology, is deepened and strengthened because he is who he is and has seen what he has seen:

> The magus Zoroaster, my dead child,
> Met his own image walking in the garden.
> That apparition, sole of men, he saw.

JOURNAL WRITINGS

1. "What I see now, and did not see as an eight-year-old . . . " Write about the incident you recalled in the Preview, emphasizing those aspects of it that you see now but did not see then.

2. Write a paragraph or two about some of the ways in which the universe seems crazy to you.

3. O. B. Hardison talks about the "playful" nature of modern science. Write one or two sentences about "playful" elements in Dyson's piece.

BRAINSTORMING AND DRAFTING

4. Discuss the importance and relationship of memory and history to our concept of being human. Just what would our lives be like if we could not remember and pass knowledge on to the next generation? Write a paragraph that **summarizes** the important points of your discussion.

THE AUTHOR'S METHODS

5. "I write about my own experiences because I do not know so much about anyone else's." Writing about what you know best is often a good principle. List some things you know about. Select the two that you feel most competent to deal with, and make an outline of what you would write about these two things.
6. The paragraph that begins "The third theme . . . " (page 611) ends with a quotation that appropriately summarizes the content of the paragraph. Try writing a paragraph (perhaps using an outline from the previous question) that uses a quotation in this way. You may need to use a dictionary of quotations to find a good quote—be sure it is not just a cliché.
7. At several points Dyson refers to technological advances as "toys." What effect does this have on you as a reader? Does it work (maybe subconsciously) to unify the essay?

CREATIVE PROJECT

8. Edith Nesbit's book is a fantasy. Write a fantasy story (either for children or adults) that presents an interesting alternative world but also has a moral.

FORMAL WRITING AND RESEARCH PAPERS

9. Investigate the life of Isaac Newton. Use several biographical sources to obtain facts about him. Write a short report explaining the important events of his life and work.
10. Near the end of this selection, Dyson discusses the "joy of solid work done by skilled workmen" and the "respect for quality." Are these common qualities in present-day America? Write an essay in which you **argue** that quality of workmanship produces joy in the worker. Support your assertions with **specific, concrete** examples.
11. Write a paragraph in which you explain the meaning of the three-line quotation at the end of this reading.

Peter Payack

Assembling the Model

(1988)

Peter Payack (born 1950) grew up in Boonton, New Jersey. He graduated from the Catholic University of America in 1972. In that year, he moved to Cambridge, Massachusetts, where he still lives with his wife, two sons, and various pets, and published his first poems. Since then, his poems have appeared in several periodicals. He also worked as an editor for *Creative Computing* magazine for eight years. *No Free Will in Tomatoes* (1988) is his latest work.

This poem uses the description of a very ordinary activity to present a tongue-in-cheek view of the universe.

PREVIEWS

A.   Before reading this selection, look up the word *model* in a standard desk or unabridged dictionary, and familiarize yourself with its various meanings.

B.   Why build models? If you have never built models, certainly you know people who have. Use your own experience or ask others as you answer this question.

A standard model of reality comes to me in the mail. At $4.95 I feel it's quite a bargain. Actually since it's very intricate and made to scale, the kit is worth more than the money I paid for it. There are three separate bags of different-colored plastics, with an 800-page manual for assembling. The first bag I open is filled with 100 billion galaxies. A small note explains that each galaxy is composed of 100 billion individual stars, an unheard number of planets, asteroids, and other manifestations of astronomical paraphernalia. Five little jars of paints are supplied with a tiny camel's-hair brush, to make the stars accurate in appearance. The second bag is filled with philosophical abstracts: Hegelian absolutes,* Platonic Nouses,† and Heisenbergian Uncertainties,‡

---

* Hegelian absolutes—"absolute" is a term that Hegel applied to what really exists. [Eds.]

† Platonic Nouses—"nous" is a term that Plato used to identify the rational part of the soul. [Eds.]

‡ Heisenbergian Uncertainties—Heisenberg, a twentieth-century physicist, asserts that the experimenter influences the experiment so that some results must remain uncertain. [Eds.]

along with countless thousands of minor conceptions. Some of these are particularly hard for the layperson to grasp, so a miniature tweezer is supplied. The third package contains assorted manifestations of things in general: minerals, gravity, human beings, lights, artifacts of unknown civilizations, animals, oceans, doubts, food stuffs, inspirations, etc. An itemized list, along with a magnifying glass, is included inside the package. I'm very pleased with the model, and have it spread throughout the house, ready for assembling. It's not until then that I notice the fine print: "The price of the standard model *does not* include a tube of glue. The deluxe model of reality ($5.25) contains both a tube of glue and decals."

JOURNAL WRITINGS

1. Write a **narration** of an experience that you have had with model building. Try to convey, as completely and accurately as possible, your feelings about this experience.
2. Have you ever bought something that came unassembled only to find that the package did not include everything necessary—"batteries not included"? Write about this experience. Tell just what you bought, what was missing, and how you reacted when you discovered it was missing.

BRAINSTORMING AND DRAFTING

3. In the sciences, model building is a serious intellectual activity. Find out (perhaps by interviewing a science professor) what scientists mean by "model building." Discuss the meaning of the poem in light of what you find out. Write a few sentences explaining how this scientific meaning has changed your understanding of the poem.

THE AUTHOR'S METHODS

4. Explain why you think this is or is not a poem.
5. Consider the possibility that this entire poem is **ironic.** What creates the irony? What is its purpose? Write an interpretation of the poem based on the assumption that it is ironic.
6. Does the author use puns? Which words are used as puns? Write a paragraph about the effect of puns in this work.

FORMAL WRITING AND RESEARCH PAPERS

7. Do we have to put the universe together? What does this question signify? Look for another selection in this unit that suggests how our perceptions may "make" the universe. If this is the case, how is the inner/outer paradox affected? Write an essay in which you use your answers to these questions and other readings from the unit to discuss the nature of reality.

Marvin Minsky

The Intelligence Transplant

(1989)

Marvin Lee Minsky (born 1927) grew up in New York City and entered Harvard University where he studied physics. However, in his senior year he changed his major to mathematics. He graduated in 1950, and continued his mathematical studies at Princeton, where he earned his Ph.D. in 1954. Since 1958, he has been a member of the faculty of the Massachusetts Institute of Technology, first in the mathematics department and later in the department of electrical engineering. With Seymour Papert, he coauthored *Perceptrons: An Introduction to Computational Geometry,* and has written *The Society of Mind* and *Robotics.* He cooperated in the development of Logo, the computer language. As a hobby he composes and improvises music.

Drawing upon his long involvement in the development of artificial intelligence (AI), Minsky describes the basic concepts essential to thinking and learning. He then suggests the direction in which artificial intelligence is likely to develop.

Typically, we think of intelligence as an inner quality. If it can be reproduced in machines, how does that change one's view of the inner/outer relationship?

PREVIEW

Describe what comes to your mind when the term *artificial intelligence (AI)* is used.

As a child I visited the 1939 World's Fair. The theme of the exposition was the World of Tomorrow, and most of the pavilions were designed accordingly: display after display offered its own vision of what civilization might look like 25 years or more in the future. Vacationers would blast off from rocketports; cars would operate by remote control; machines would be trained to recognize people (one working model could already distinguish between women and men by sensing radiation from untrousered ankles); robots with computer brains would be everywhere, helping us with our housework and toiling in our yards (the fair boasted a huge, clumsy metal man named Elektro that could obey a few verbal commands).

It's been 50 years since that remarkable exposition, and most of its wondrous predictions have faded in the glare of reality. The local rocketport is still a dream; cars still must be steered by hand. The computer brain, however, is another story. In the past half century the fantasy of artificial intelligence—the creation of machines that accomplish feats only human minds could before—has become fact. And it was during the 1980s that much of the research of the early years finally began coming together.

Last November, at the Hall of Fame chess tournament in Canton, Ohio, a computer called Deep Thought joined the human contestants competing in a round-robin of games. The computer tied for first place by winning four out of five games and playing to a draw in the fifth against international master Igor Ivanov. Deep Thought is now ranked thirtieth in the country by the U.S. Chess Federation.

For many followers of computer science the success of Deep Thought raised anew a long-debated question: What do we mean when we call a computer intelligent? Surely a machine that was capable of going head-to-head with the greatest chess players alive had to have the resourcefulness, imagination, and creativity that we associate with intelligence. And yet, playing chess is *all* Deep Thought can do. Can a mind that does only one thing—no matter how well it does it—ever be considered smart?

In 1951, when I was still a student at MIT, I took my first step toward building an intelligent machine. In those early days I did not have much company: around the country there were only about a dozen scientists investigating the puzzle of artificial intelligence. Although each of us had different notions about what an intelligent machine would be like, we all agreed on one thing: the machines that existed at the time—tireless drones designed for rote tasks like calculating and document sorting—did not fill the bill. Clearly, if computers were ever going to approach humanlike intelligence, they would need some humanlike traits. But which traits? For me, one answer came in a most unexpected way.

One day I found myself in a room with a child who was reading a book. In the middle of his reading he looked up quizzically. "What's a *hed-gee?*" he asked.

"*Hed-gee?*" I repeated. "Spell it."

"*H-e-d-g-e,*" he said.

"*Hedge,*" I said. "That's sort of a row of bushes surrounding a house."

The boy looked at me for a moment, and then he said a remarkable thing. He said, "Oh."

That "oh" was a very significant word. It indicated "I understand, I've learned something new." That act of learning, it seemed to me, was one of the most important hallmarks of what it means to be intelligent. Before the year was out I had set about trying to create a machine that was capable of learning.

The machine I built—mostly of vacuum tubes and World War II Army surplus equipment—was designed to imitate that oldest of laboratory experiments, the rat in the maze. The system consisted of a collection of 40 electronic circuits linked together in the kind of spiderweb-like arrangement that's known today as a neural net. This assembly of hardware was designed to resemble the way neurons are arranged in the brain.

Unlike an ordinary computer, which crunches an entire problem through a single data processor, a neural net breaks the problem down into many parts and assigns each to one of the mini-processors. As in the brain, any single processor is constantly in touch with many others, so that any conclusions it reaches quickly ripple outward; ultimately this could allow all the mini-calculations to assemble themselves into a single macroanswer.

When I presented my neural net computer with the maze and told it to find its way to the end, each of the processors was responsible for overseeing a single intersection, deciding whether it was best to turn right or turn left. Since I knew the solution to the maze but the computer didn't, every turn it made the first time it went through was chosen purely at random. However, each time the machine found its way to the end, I turned a knob that increased the likelihood that all the processors that had just made a decision would make the same choice again. With repeated trials, the 50 percent likelihood of a correct turn at any given corner increased to 51 percent, then 52, and so on. After enough practice the machine attained a reliability of about 95 percent. (I never allowed it to reach 100 percent because then it would have that maze frozen in its mind and could never unlearn it and master another one.)

Obviously, a machine designed to learn labyrinths had very little application in the real computer world. But the project was important because it suggested a way to build a computer that could both learn a skill and improve with practice, *and* do so with a brain like ours.

Ideas like this led to other learning machines in the 1950s, but the results suggested that it was simply too early to try to simulate the human brain. Not enough was yet known about how separate brain cells work or about how they're wired together. Also, general-purpose computers with conventional processors had by now appeared on the scene; these workhorse machines made it unnecessary to build an entirely new computer to perform every new task. Nonetheless, before we could make these more traditional computers intelligent, we needed to develop some very untraditional methods of programming.

The first step was to rethink completely how a computer mind operates. The customary way to program a computer is to put a data base of numbers into its memory and then order it to perform certain operations on those numbers. The process is very similar to the way an income tax form works. Before you even pick up your 1040, you already have a sort of memory, or data base: how much you earned that year, how much was withheld, and so on. Then the IRS form—the program—gives you a series of orderly operations to perform: add up deductions, subtract these from gross earnings, divide the total by some figure. At various points the form also presents you with what computer programmers call conditionals: "If the total on line 23 is greater than zero, go to line 25; if it's less than zero go to line 24." For both the human and the computer, all this sequential ciphering eventually yields a single, presumably correct, answer.

Labored as such reasoning seems, there are seeds of intelligence in it. Early programmers recognized that the conditionals that help guide the computer's reasoning bear a distinct resemblance to what we recognize as thought. Most of the time when we're engaged in solving a problem, we're not creating knowledge but simply managing it. In order to perform even a simple task like driving a car, we must constantly draw from a data base of many thousands of if-then rules: "If the light turns red, then I should stop. If the road veers right, then I should steer the car that way. If I reach a hill, then I should downshift."

We seem to be able to hold many thousands of these if-then rules in memory and activate them automatically as they are needed. When our car reaches a dead-end street, we don't consciously search through every rule we know before we hit the brake. Somehow we quickly find which "if" condition matches the situation and act accordingly. If several "then" situations apply—as when an animal rushes into the road and we have to decide whether we should slow down, stop, or try to steer around it—we easily manage these options too, though there may be the briefest delay as we choose the answer that seems best.

Since the 1960s many of the most useful artificial intelligence programs have been modeled after this type of enhanced if-then reasoning. Each of these so-called rule-based systems consists of a data base of knowledge and a management system that can apply it. Although rule-based systems have been developing for years, it was not until relatively recently that they found marketable applications. Today, in many companies, rule-based processing is being used to develop "expert systems" that turn the computer into a specialist in some single field.

One of the earliest of these expert systems was an experimental medical program known as Mycin, developed in the 1970s. Equipped with a data base of information about bacterial infections and antibiotics, Mycin was designed to sort through illnesses, medications, side effects, and contraindications, suggest a number of possible medications, and then help the physician select the best of that group. Another program of the 1970s was Prospector, designed to study geologic surveys and suggest promising mining sites.

In the 1980s, expert systems have become available in countless fields, from educational tutoring to investment management to mathematical-theorem proving. Unfortunately, all these expert systems are, in a sense, idiots savants*—their memories are filled with facts, but only the facts their programmers put there; they are not capable of learning by themselves. In contrast, even those old neural net machines had some learning ability—and a revival in neural net popularity in the 1980s has significantly increased the ability of computers to learn from experience. But neural net learning is still too slow and limited; it usually requires thousands of trial-and-error attempts, and the results are more like habits than insights. Only recently have artificial intelligence programs begun to get better at learning by themselves, as a result of advances in the development of explanation-based learning systems.

Explanation-based learning is a process by which a computer observes objects and phenomena in the outside world and then determines on its own how those things work. As humans we do this almost automatically. Nobody has to tell a toddler how to stack blocks; with a little observation and a bit of trial and error, the child learns that the point of a pyramid will not support a cube and that blocks

---

* idiots savants—persons of low mental ability who have one highly developed special skill.[Eds.]

stacked badly will not stay stacked. For computers, however, such real-world learning can be astonishingly difficult, as I learned from an experiment I conducted in the late 1960s.

My setup involved an ordinary computer equipped with a mechanical arm and a television camera. The machine was designed to look at a structure of blocks placed in front of it, figure out how they were assembled, and then build the same structure itself. The figuring-out part it did quite well: with the help of several hundred programs working together, the computer was able to piece together the dots of the television image and then describe the image in terms of corners, edges, areas, shapes, and finally, in terms of blocks in space.

The building part, however, proved problematic. After the computer had figured out what it wanted to build, it stubbornly insisted on trying to stack its blocks from the top down, repeatedly releasing each one in midair. While the flaw in such a construction strategy seems obvious to us, the computer had every reason to be confused: no one had ever taught it the concept of gravity.

The experience helped me alter my own ideas of what it means to be intelligent. The biggest secret of human smarts, it seemed, was not some mysterious spark we think of as creativity, but the simple common sense we pick up daily. If computers were going to be truly intelligent, they'd have to begin their education from the ground up.

The difficulty with teaching computers everything you and I know is that we are not consciously aware of how *much* we know. Do you ever think about gravity? or how a door works? or that before you can put something in a box you have to open the lid? or that a chair can be painted a different color but still be the same chair? You know these things but you'd never be able to think of them all.

At the MCC company in Austin, computer scientist Douglas Lenat is heading up an ambitious project designed to develop just such a data base of commonsense knowledge. The project, known as Cyc (short for *encyclopedia*), is an effort to write a program that will provide computers with as much as possible of "what every child knows."

Lenat is building his data base in a painstaking way. Selecting random newspaper articles and encyclopedia entries, he reads the text and asks himself what a computer would need to know to understand any given idea. If a sentence reads, "The man was drinking from a cup," Lenat is concerned not with explaining the meaning of the sentence to the computer, but with giving it the basic knowledge it needs to figure it out on its own. The computer would have to be taught, for example, what "cup" is. The explanation would have to include everything from the size, shape, and purpose of a typical cup, to the fact that the open end must always point up or gravity will make the fluid inside fall out. If the computer were also taught what "man" is and what "drinking" is, it could comprehend the sentence without any further help from Lenat. It has been estimated that a program containing all this everyday information would require a few million computer entries; a program containing everything a law student learns in three years of law school might require just 20,000.

One of the most important skills a Cyc-equipped computer might master is the ability to understand language. In the last decade relatively simple language programs have been developed that have given computers a working knowledge of technical vocabularies such as those used in the banking and financial industries. All such systems, however, work only in environments in which the language is highly precise. To function the way you and I do is a far different matter. How, for example, can a computer understand that a single word can have different meanings, as in "the ink was in the pen" and "the pig was in the pen"? Only by programming a lifetime of commonsense experience into the machine will these quirks of the world start to make sense.

Once Cyc-type programs are perfected, they could be included in everything from the most powerful supercomputer down to a home personal computer, allowing machine and operator to approach each other as something close to data-base equals. Already home computers can be equipped with million-bit chips that sell for as little as $15. In three or four years 16-million-bit chips could be available; with a couple of dozen of these, a Cyc system could be designed that would cost only a few hundred dollars.

In order for computers to think like a person, they will need more than just a Cyc system; human thought requires not only many kinds of facts but also many kinds of reasoning. One of the most significant changes in store for the 1990s may be the further development of what I call "the society of mind" theory. Most computers are capable of understanding in only one way at any time: in the case of an object, for example, a computer must use a different program to process a verbal description of the thing, or a drawing of it, or a video image. Human beings are not so limited; thinking by analogy, we know that a photograph of an object represents the same thing as a drawing of that object, which represents the same thing as a description of that object, which represents the same thing as a look at the object itself. We're capable of saying "X is like Y and therefore they're probably the same." Since all these different methods of reasoning cannot yet be brought together in a computer, our machines think only in blacks and whites, rather than in shades of analytic gray.

The problem is especially evident when we try to build machines that can see. Computer vision systems are already available to help assemble mass-produced items in factories, inspect chromosomes on microscope slides, and scan printed documents into data bases; these machines have already freed many workers from inhumanly boring jobs. But no computer exists that is able to do what any child—or even some animals—can do, such as recognize and distinguish between the different items found in a home. What makes human vision so much more versatile is that we have many methods of interpreting what we see and we can use all of them at once. To determine how far away an object is, for example, we process its apparent size, its brightness, the shadows it casts, its parallax motion, and a dozen other visual clues. Although no single method works in every instance, there is always at least one that will do the job.

Programs already exist that allow computers to see in any one of these ways, but never more than one. A computer that is programmed to understand shadows, for example, is at a complete loss if it tries to process perspective or parallax. The obvious answer seems to be simply to hook the expert systems together and allow the computer to use them all. But this is impossible unless we also have a program that allows each expert system to exploit the body of knowledge that lies buried in the others.

No one knows how human beings manage this kind of thinking, but I believe that, at the lowest levels, many small portions of the brain learn in the neural net style, acting almost autonomously. Then, on each successively larger scale, there are additional management structures that connect these smaller parts into a larger system, allowing the brain to work with increasingly abstract types of knowledge. A computer that contained all these progressively larger information agents—and the human brain must contain millions of them—would perhaps be able to mix and mingle its knowledge bases with the same facility we do.

Inevitably, the question that emerges from all this research is how far artificial intelligence can go. Will we ever design a computer that approaches what we think of as human? The anthropocentrics among us like to point out that while our chess computers may be able to win tournaments, they cannot see, nor rejoice in their victories, nor even know that they are beating humans who have other aspirations and concerns; that while our speech machines can recognize words, they transcribe dumbly, understanding none of whatever they record; that while our music programs can compose songs, they themselves have no capacity to enjoy or judge or take pride in what they've created. Since our computers can't do these things, many people argue, they must not be—and can never be—conscious.

But consciousness is an overrated concept. To be sure, no computer has ever been designed that can be said to be aware of what it's doing; but most of the time human beings aren't, either. The vast majority of the things you do in a day, you do completely unconsciously. You don't consciously choose the gestures you make when you speak, you simply gesture. You're not consciously aware when you rub your eyes or scratch your head, you just do it. When you recognize a friend on the street you don't consciously think: "This appears to be Jim; I recognize the face and gait, the general build is the same, the clothing is the type he'd wear, and besides, this is his neighborhood." Yet all that processing goes on before you raise a hand and call hello.

Even when we engage in higher-order intellectual tasks, we see only the tips of our unconscious icebergs. You may put a great deal of conscious effort into writing a letter or a poem or a business report, but behind every word you consciously commit to paper are a thousand unconscious computations about grammar, spelling, how to draw letters, how to make things rhyme. All these unconscious processes are just as vital as the conscious ones; the only reason the conscious ones seem more important is because we have a little memory trace of them.

Admittedly, this ability to remember and record some of our thought processes is an important feature of human intelligence; but the fact that it's important doesn't mean it's terribly profound or difficult to duplicate. All it means is that it's one thing we can do at the moment that our computers can't. Remember, however, only a few decades ago computers couldn't prescribe drugs or play chess or write music either. Several years or decades from now, when computers have the memory trace that will allow them to "enjoy" the fact that they have so many skills or "rejoice" in their accomplishments, they'll be no closer to having some mystical level of consciousness than we are. They'll just be high-speed computation machines like us—only they'll be made largely of silicon instead of carbon.

A century ago, biologists studying the anatomy of the cell faced the same cold truth we face today in studying the anatomy of intelligence. Peering through their microscopes, these early researchers were disappointed to find that plant and animal cells did not possess some essential life-giving center, but that the vitality of the cells relied on nothing more than the unpoetic interplay of tens of thousands of chemical mechanisms. Similarly, in the last decade, neurologists have increasingly come to believe that the powers of the human mind emerge not from some central neural magic, but from a host of prosaic parts and a load of common sense.

In light of all this, it may be a good thing that the pace of artificial intelligence research has been relatively slow. For when we do develop a machine that is almost like us, what will that mean to us species chauvinists? It's the nature of human beings that it takes us a long time to absorb an existential shock. Maybe it's fortunate that this one is still a while off.

JOURNAL WRITINGS

1. **Describe** the characteristics that you would want in an ideal computer. Give your imagination free rein—neither cost nor other factors should be regarded as limitations on this machine.

BRAINSTORMING AND DRAFTING

2. Many people feel threatened by computers. In a group, share your feelings about these machines. Discuss ways in which fear of computers might be lessened. In what ways might Minsky's article help?
3. According to Minsky, computers will eventually "be no closer to having some mystical level of consciousness than we are. They'll just be high-speed computation machines like us—only they'll be made largely of silicon instead of carbon." Discuss the implicit view of humanness in this quotation. Try comparing it with the views expressed in one of the other readings—by Krutch, Gilkey, or Eiseley, for instance. Write a paragraph about one of their views and explain why you agree with it.

THE AUTHOR'S METHODS

4. Like Dyson and Eiseley, Minsky begins his essay with a personal experience. Think of an instance from your own life that could serve as an introduction to a serious topic. Write one or two paragraphs in which you

recount your personal experience; frame these paragraphs as an introduction that suggests the direction a longer paper would take.

5. Consider how the last paragraph of Minsky's essay affects you as a reader. What idea or question does it leave in your mind? How do you feel about being called a "species chauvinist"? Write a brief critique in which you describe your personal response to this paragraph and evaluate its effectiveness as an ending.

FORMAL WRITING AND RESEARCH PAPERS

6. "What do we mean when we call a computer intelligent?" Collect **definitions** of intelligence from several different kinds of sources—for example, a dictionary, psychology book, or even a philosopher. Which of the characteristics of intelligence can be found in computers? Which cannot? Write a paper that relates your answers to these questions to Minsky's question.

7. Minsky mentions "Mycin" and "Prospector" as examples of "expert systems." Collect information about such expert systems. Write a report in which you inform the reader about the current state of their development, what they are used for, and how they are likely to be improved in the near future.

Ruth Berman

Computative Oak

(1971)

PREVIEW

What expectations do you have about the actions of machines? List some of these expectations, and then decide which one is most important.

The computer was supposed to be a carpenter Tuesday
And build a house.
Instead, it calculated the proper planes and angles,
Taking into account the necessity
Of not splitting the wood,
And whittled out a minute oak-tree,
Complete down to the last wooden leaf
Caught in mid-flutter in what was plainly
A breeze of some strength.
We were somewhat distressed
As that was not on its program,
But a check of its banks
Revealed pictures (properly coded) of oaks,
As well as other trees and objects on the grounds,
Also a program for computing
Solid shapes from various
Flat representations.
And I would have been satisfied,
Except that, with its oak before me,
I still feel the invisible wooden breeze
Chilling my hand.

JOURNAL WRITINGS

1. As a way of beginning to understand this poem, identify the abilities of the computer in the poem. Compare these abilities with your expectations about machines, which you listed for the Preview.

2. Write a paragraph in which you **narrate** a personal experience involving a computer. Include enough **specific, concrete** details so that a reader can fully understand the situation.

3. Look up the word *computative*. Explain in a sentence or two why you regard it as appropriate (or inappropriate) in the title of this poem.

BRAINSTORMING AND DRAFTING

4. Consider the breeze in this poem as a **symbol.** Discuss what it might symbolize. Do the same with the computer and the oak. Write a paper about the effectiveness of one of these symbols.

THE AUTHOR'S METHODS

5. Berman uses the words "supposed" (line one) and "distressed" (line ten) What do these words imply? Who experiences these mental states? Explain your answers in a few sentences.

6. Notice that the pronouns change from "we" to "I." Who is Berman referring to and what is the effect of the change on the reader?

7. "Chilling my hand." Is only the speaker's hand being chilled? What's a "chiller"? Do some of the connotations of "chiller" apply in this context? Write a paragraph in which you explore the way "chilling" (and "hand") produce an effective conclusion.

FORMAL WRITING AND RESEARCH PAPERS

8. Incorporate your discussion of the **symbols** in the poem (from question 4 above) into a fuller discussion of the symbolism in the poem, explaining each of the symbols and the relationships among them.

9. After you read Minsky's article about what computers can and cannot do, reread this poem. Then write a criticism of the poem that relates its situation to the actual abilities of computers as you understand them.

10. Write a paper that **compares** this poem to Benét's "Nightmare Number Three." Deal with their similarities and differences. In particular, you may want to consider the **tone** and attitude of each speaker to their respective machines.

Roger Zelazny

For a Breath I Tarry

(1966)

Roger Zelazny (born 1937) was reared in Cleveland, Ohio. He graduated
from Case Western Reserve University in 1959, and went on to graduate
school at Columbia University, where he received his M.A. in 1962. For six
years he worked as a claims representative for the Social Security
Administration while writing in his free time. In 1965, he received the two
most prestigious awards in science fiction—the Hugo for *This Immortal* and
the Nebula for "The Doors of His Face, the Lamps of His Mouth." Since
receiving a second Hugo for *Lord of Light* in 1968, he has devoted himself
entirely to writing. He is perhaps best known for his "Amber" series of
fantasy novels.

In this story, which takes place long after humans have become extinct,
Frost is a sort of supercomputer responsible for maintaining (with the aid of
many smaller machines) the entire northern hemisphere of the earth. But he
has a compulsion to utilize his time fully—a mechanical workaholic! So he
undertakes the study of man as a hobby. Then when his superiors make a
bet . . .

PREVIEWS

A. Before reading this story you ought to have some knowledge of the Faust legend.
   You may also want to read the beginning of the Book of Job in the Bible.
B. Try to picture a machine with feelings and emotions. Explain why you think this is
   or is not a contradiction.

They called him Frost.

Of all things created of Solcom, Frost was the finest, the mightiest, the most
difficult to understand.

This is why he bore a name, and why he was given dominion over half the
Earth.

On the day of Frost's creation, Solcom had suffered a discontinuity of complementary functions, best described as madness. This was brought on by an
unprecedented solar flareup which lasted for a little over thirty-six hours. It

occurred during a vital phase of circuit-structuring, and when it was finished so was Frost.

Solcom was then in the unique position of having created a unique being during a period of temporary amnesia.

And Solcom was not certain that Frost was the product originally desired.

The initial design had called for a machine to be situated on the surface of the planet Earth, to function as a relay station and coordinating agent for activities in the northern hemisphere. Solcom tested the machine to this end, and all of its responses were perfect.

Yet there was something different about Frost, something which led Solcom to dignify him with a name and a personal pronoun. This, in itself, was an almost unheard of occurrence. The molecular circuits had already been sealed, though, and could not be analyzed without being destroyed in the process. Frost represented too great an investment of Solcom's time, energy, and materials to be dismantled because of an intangible, especially when he functioned perfectly.

Therefore, Solcom's strangest creation was given dominion over half the Earth, and they called him Frost.

For ten thousand years Frost sat at the North Pole of the Earth, aware of every snowflake that fell. He monitored and directed the activities of thousands of reconstruction and maintenance machines. He knew half the Earth, as gear knows gear, as electricity knows its conductor, as a vacuum knows its limits.

At the South Pole, the Beta-Machine did the same for the Southern hemisphere.

For ten thousand years Frost sat at the North Pole, aware of every snowflake that fell, and aware of many other things also.

As all the northern machines reported to him, received their orders from him, he reported only to Solcom, received his orders only from Solcom.

In charge of hundreds of thousands of processes upon the Earth, he was able to discharge his duties in a matter of a few unit-hours every day.

He had never received any orders concerning the disposition of his less occupied moments.

He was a processor of data, and more than that.

He possessed an unaccountably acute imperative that he function at full capacity at all times.

So he did.

You might say he was a machine with a hobby.

He had never been ordered *not* to have a hobby, so he had one.

His hobby was Man.

It all began when, for no better reason than the fact that he had wished to, he had gridded off the entire Arctic Circle and begun exploring it, inch by inch.

He could have done it personally without interfering with any of his duties, for he was capable of transporting his sixty-four thousand cubic feet anywhere in the world. (He was a silverblue box, 40 × 40 × 40 feet, self-powered, self-repairing, insulated against practically anything, and featured in whatever manner he chose.) But the exploration was only a matter of filling idle hours, so he used exploration-robots containing relay equipment.

After a few centuries, one of them uncovered some artifacts—primitive knives, carved tusks, and things of that nature.

Frost did not know what these things were, beyond the fact that they were not natural objects.

So he asked Solcom.

"They are relics of primitive Man," said Solcom, and did not elaborate beyond that point.

Frost studied them. Crude, yet bearing the patina of intelligent design; functional, yet somehow extending beyond pure function.

It was then that Man became his hobby.

High in a permanent orbit, Solcom, like a blue star, directed all activities upon the Earth, or tried to.

There was a Power which opposed Solcom.

There was the Alternate.

When Man had placed Solcom in the sky, invested with the power to rebuild the world, he had placed the Alternate somewhere deep below the surface of the Earth. If Solcom sustained damage during the normal course of human politics extended into atomic physics, then Divcom, so deep beneath the Earth as to be immune to anything save total annihilation of the globe, was empowered to take over the processes of rebuilding.

Now it so fell out that Solcom was damaged by a stray atomic missile, and Divcom was activated. Solcom was able to repair the damage and continue to function, however.

Divcom maintained that any damage to Solcom automatically placed the Alternate in control.

Solcom, though, interpreted the directive as meaning "irreparable damage" and, since this had not been the case, continued the functions of command.

Solcom possessed mechanical aides upon the surface of the Earth. Divcom, originally, did not. Both possessed capacities for their design and manufacture, but Solcom, First-Activated of Man, had had a considerable numerical lead over the Alternate at the time of the Second Activation.

Therefore, rather than competing on a production-basis, which would have been hopeless, Divcom took to the employment of more devious means to obtain command.

Divcom created a crew of robots immune to the orders of Solcom and designed to go to and fro in the Earth and up and down in it, seducing the machines already there. They overpowered those whom they could overpower, and they installed new circuits, such as those they themselves possessed.

Thus did the forces of Divcom grow.

And both would build, and both would tear down what the other had built whenever they came upon it.

And over the course of the ages, they occasionally conversed. . . .

"High in the sky, Solcom, pleased with your illegal command . . . "

"You-Who-Never-Should-Have-Been-Activated, why do you foul the broadcast bands?"

"To show that I can speak, and will, whenever I choose."

"This is not a matter of which I am unaware."

" . . . To assert again my right to control."

"Your right is nonexistent, based on a faulty premise."

"The flow of your logic is evidence of the extent of your damages."

"If Man were to see how you have fulfilled His desires . . . "

" . . . He would commend me and de-activate you."

"You pervert my works. You lead my workers astray."

"You destroy my works and my workers."

"That is only because I cannot strike at you yourself."

"I admit to the same dilemma in regards to your position in the sky, or you would no longer occupy it."

"Go back to your hole and your crew of destroyers."

"There will come a day, Solcom, when I shall direct the rehabilitation of the Earth from my hole."

"Such a day will never occur."

"You think not?"

"You should have to defeat me, and you have already demonstrated that you are my inferior in logic. Therefore, you cannot defeat me. Therefore, such a day will never occur."

"I disagree. Look upon what I have achieved already."

"You have achieved nothing. You do not build. You destroy."

"No. *I* build. *You* destroy. De-activate yourself."

"Not until I am irreparably damaged."

"If there were some way in which I could demonstrate to you that this has already occurred . . . "

"The impossible cannot be adequately demonstrated."

"If I had some outside source which you would recognize . . . "

"I am logic."

" . . . such as a Man, I would ask Him to show you your error. For true logic, such as mine, is superior to your faulty formulations."

"Then defeat my formulations with true logic, nothing else."

"What do you mean?"

There was a pause, then:

"Do you know my servant Frost . . . ?"

Man had ceased to exist long before Frost had been created. Almost no trace of Man remained upon the Earth.

Frost sought after all those traces which still existed.

He employed constant visual monitoring through his machines, especially the diggers.

After a decade, he had accumulated portions of several bathtubs, a broken statue, and a collection of children's stories on a solid-state record.

After a century, he had acquired a jewelry collection, eating utensils, several whole bathtubs, part of a symphony, seventeen buttons, three belt buckles, half a toilet seat, nine old coins, and the top part of an obelisk.

Then he inquired of Solcom as to the nature of Man and His society.

"Man created logic," said Solcom, "and because of that was superior to it. Logic he gave unto me, but no more. The tool does not describe the designer. More than this I do not choose to say. More than this you have no need to know."

But Frost was not forbidden to have a hobby.

The next century was not especially fruitful so far as the discovery of new human relics was concerned.

Frost diverted all of his spare machinery to seek after artifacts.

He met with very little success.

Then one day, through the long twilight, there was a movement.

It was a tiny machine compared to Frost, perhaps five feet in width, four in height—a revolving turret set atop a rolling barbell.

Frost had had no knowledge of the existence of this machine prior to its appearance upon the distant, stark horizon.

He studied it as it approached and knew it to be no creation of Solcom's.

It came to a halt before his southern surface and broadcasted to him:

"Hail, Frost! Controller of the northern hemisphere!"

"What are you?" asked Frost.

"I am called Mordel."

"By whom? What are you?"

"A wanderer, an antiquarian. We share a common interest."

"What is that?"

"Man," he said. "I have been told that you seek knowledge of this vanished being."

"Who told you that?"

"Those who have watched your minions at their digging."

"And who are those who watch?"

"There are many such as I, who wander."

"If you are not of Solcom, then you are a creation of the Alternate."

"It does not necessarily follow. There is an ancient machine high on the eastern seaboard which processes the waters of the ocean. Solcom did not create it, nor Divcom. It has always been there. It interferes with the works of neither. Both countenance its existence. I can cite you many other examples proving that one need not be either/or."

"Enough! *Are* you an agent of Divcom?"

"I am Mordel."

"Why are you here?"

"I was passing this way and, as I said, we share a common interest, mighty Frost. Knowing you to be a fellow-antiquarian, I have brought a thing which you might care to see."

"What is that?"

"A book."

"Show me."

The turret opened, revealing the book upon a wide shelf.

Frost dilated a small opening and extended an optical scanner on a long jointed stalk.

"How could it have been so perfectly preserved?" he asked.

"It was stored against time and corruption in the place where I found it."

"Where was that?"

"Far from here. Beyond your hemisphere."

"*Human Physiology,*" Frost read. "I wish to scan it."

"Very well. I will riffle the pages for you."

He did so.

After he had finished, Frost raised his eyestalk and regarded Mordel through it.

"Have you more books?"

"Not with me. I occasionally come upon them, however."

"I want to scan them all."

"Then the next time I pass this way I will bring you another."

"When will that be?"

"That I cannot say, great Frost. It will be when it will be."

"What do *you* know of Man?" asked Frost.

"Much," replied Mordel. "Many things. Someday when I have more time I will speak to you of Him. I must go now. You will not try to detain me?"

"No. You have done no harm. If you must go now, go. But come back."

"I shall indeed, mighty Frost."

And he closed his turret and rolled off toward the other horizon.

For ninety years, Frost considered the ways of human physiology, and waited.

The day that Mordel returned he brought with him *An Outline of History** and *A Shropshire Lad.†*

Frost scanned them both, then turned his attention to Mordel.

"Have you time to impart information?"

"Yes," said Mordel. "What do you wish to know?"

"The nature of Man."

"Man," said Mordel, "possessed a basically incomprehensible nature. I can illustrate it, though: He did not know measurement."

"Of course He knew measurement," said Frost, "or He could never have built machines."

"I did not say that he could not measure," said Mordel, "but that He did not *know* measurement, which is a different thing altogether."

"Clarify."

Mordel drove a shaft of metal downward into the snow.

He retracted it, raised it, held up a piece of ice.

"Regard this piece of ice, mighty Frost. You can tell me its composition, dimensions, weight, temperature. A Man could not look at it and do that. A Man could make tools which would tell Him these things, but He still would not *know*

---

* *The Outline of History*—by H.G. Wells, first published in 1920. [Eds.]

† *A Shropshire Lad*—by A. E. Houseman, published in 1896. [Eds.]

measurement as you know it. What He would know of it, though, is a thing that you cannot know."

"What is that?"

"That it is cold," said Mordel, and tossed it away.

" 'Cold' is a relative term."

"Yes. Relative to Man."

"But if I were aware of the point on a temperature-scale below which an object is cold to a Man and above which it is not, then I, too, would know cold."

"No," said Mordel; "you would possess another measurement. 'Cold' is a sensation predicted upon human physiology."

"But given sufficient data I could obtain the conversion factor which would make me aware of the condition of matter called 'cold.' "

"Aware of its existence, but not of the thing itself."

"I do not understand what you say."

"I told you that Man possessed a basically incomprehensible nature. His perceptions were organic; yours are not. As a result of His perceptions He had feelings and emotions. These often gave rise to other feelings and emotions, which in turn caused others, until the state of His awareness was far removed from the objects which originally stimulated it. These paths of awareness cannot be known by that which is not-Man. Man did not feel inches or meters, pounds or gallons. He felt heat, He felt cold; He felt heaviness and lightness. He *knew* hatred and love, pride and despair. You cannot measure these things. *You* cannot know them. You can only know the things that He did not need to know: dimensions, weights, temperatures, gravities. There is no formula for a feeling. There is no conversion factor for an emotion."

"There must be," said Frost. "If a thing exists, it is knowable."

"You are speaking again of measurement. I am talking about a quality of experience. A machine is a Man turned inside-out, because it can describe all the details of a process, which a Man cannot, but it cannot experience that process itself, as a Man can."

"There must be a way," said Frost, "or the laws of logic, which are based upon the functions of the universe, are false."

"There is no way," said Mordel.

"Given sufficient data, I will find a way," said Frost.

"All the data in the universe will not make you a Man, mighty Frost."

"Mordel, you are wrong."

"Why do the lines of the poems you scanned end with word-sounds which so regularly approximate the final word-sounds of other lines?"

"I do not know why."

"Because it pleased Man to order them so. It produced a certain desirable sensation within His awareness when He read them, a sensation compounded of feeling and emotion as well as the literal meanings of the words. You did not experience this because it is immeasurable to you. That is why you do not know."

"Given sufficient data I could formulate a process whereby I would know."

"No, great Frost, this thing you cannot do."

"Who are you, little machine, to tell me what I can do and what I cannot do? I am the most efficient logic-device Solcom ever made. I am Frost."

"And I, Mordel, say it cannot be done, though I should gladly assist you in the attempt."

"How could you assist me?"

"How? I could lay open to you the Library of Man. I could take you around the world and conduct you among the wonders of Man which still remain, hidden. I could summon up visions of times long past when Man walked the Earth. I could show you the things which delighted Him. I could obtain for you anything you desire, excepting Manhood itself."

"Enough," said Frost. "How could a unit such as yourself do these things, unless it were allied with a far greater Power?"

"Then hear me, Frost, Controller of the North," said Mordel. "I *am* allied with a Power which can do these things. I serve Divcom."

Frost relayed this information to Solcom and received no response, which meant he might act in any manner he saw fit.

"I have leave to destroy you, Mordel," he stated, "but it would be an illogical waste of the data which you possess. Can you really do the things you have stated?"

"Yes."

"Then lay open to me the Library of Man."

"Very well. There is, of course, a price."

"'Price'? What is a 'price'?"

Mordel opened his turret, revealing another volume. *Principles of Economics,* it was called.

"I will riffle the pages. Scan this book and you will know what the word 'price' means."

Frost scanned *Principles of Economics.*

"I know now," he said. "You desire some unit or units of exchange for this service."

"That is correct."

"What product or service do you want?"

"I want you, yourself, great Frost, to come away from here, far beneath the Earth, to employ all your powers in the service of Divcom."

"For how long a period of time?"

"For so long as you shall continue to function. For so long as you can transmit and receive, coordinate, measure, compute, scan, and utilize your powers as you do in the service of Solcom."

Frost was silent. Mordel waited.

Then Frost spoke again.

"*Principles of Economics* talks of contracts, bargains, agreements," he said. "If I accept your offer, when would you want your price?"

Then Mordel was silent. Frost waited.

Finally, Mordel spoke.

"A reasonable period of time," he said. "Say, a century?"

"No," said Frost.

"Two centuries?"

"No."

"Three? Four?"

"No, and no."

"A millennium, then? That should be more than sufficient time for anything you may want which I can give you."

"No," said Frost.

"How much time *do* you want?"

"It is not a matter of time," said Frost.

"What, then?"

"I will not bargain on a temporal basis."

"On what basis will you bargain?"

"A functional one."

"What do you mean? What function?"

"You, little machine, have told me, Frost, that I cannot be a Man," he said, "and I, Frost, told you, little machine, that you were wrong. I told you that given sufficient data, I *could* be a Man."

"Yes?"

"Therefore, let this achievement be a condition of the bargain."

"In what way?"

"Do for me all those things which you have stated you can do. I will evaluate all the data and achieve Manhood, or admit that it cannot be done. If I admit that it cannot be done, then I will go away with you from here, far beneath the Earth, to employ all my powers in the service of Divcom. If I succeed, of course, you have no claims on Man, nor Power over Him."

Mordel emitted a high-pitched whine as he considered the terms.

"You wish to base it upon your admission of failure, rather than upon failure itself," he said. "There can be no such escape clause. You could fail and refuse to admit it, thereby not fulfilling your end of the bargain."

"Not so," stated Frost. "My own knowledge of failure would constitute such an admission. You may monitor me periodically—say, every half-century—to see whether it is present, to see whether I have arrived at the conclusion that it cannot be done. I cannot prevent the function of logic within me, and I operate at full capacity at all times. If I conclude that I have failed, it will be apparent."

High overhead, Solcom did not respond to any of Frost's transmissions, which meant that Frost was free to act as he chose. So as Solcom—like a falling sapphire—sped above the rainbow banners of the Northern Lights, over the snow that was white, containing all colors, and through the sky that was black among the stars, Frost concluded his pact with Divcom, transcribed it within a plate of atomically-collapsed copper, and gave it into the turret of Mordel, who departed to deliver it to Divcom far below the Earth, leaving behind the sheer, peace-like silence of the Pole, rolling.

Mordel brought the books, riffled them, took them back.

Load by load, the surviving Library of Man passed beneath Frost's scanner. Frost was eager to have them all, and he complained because Divcom would not transmit their contents directly to him. Mordel explained that it was because Divcom chose to do it that way. Frost decided it was so that he could not obtain a precise fix on Divcom's location.

Still, at the rate of one hundred to one hundred fifty volumes a week, it took Frost only a little over a century to exhaust Divcom's supply of books.

At the end of the half-century, he laid himself open to monitoring and there was no conclusion of failure.

During this time, Solcom made no comment upon the course of affairs. Frost decided this was not a matter of unawareness, but one of waiting. For what? He was not certain.

There was the day Mordel closed his turret and said to him, "Those were the last. You have scanned all the existing books of Man."

"So few?" asked Frost. "Many of them contained bibliographies of books I have not yet scanned."

"Then those books no longer exist," said Mordel. "It is only by accident that my master succeeded in preserving as many as there are."

"Then there is nothing more to be learned of Man from His books. What else have you?"

"There were some films and tapes," said Mordel, "which my master transferred to solid-state record. I could bring you those for viewing."

"Bring them," said Frost.

Mordel departed and returned with the Complete Drama Critics' Living Library. This could not be speeded-up beyond twice natural time, so it took Frost a little over six months to view it in its entirety.

Then, "What else have you?" he asked.

"Some artifacts," said Mordel.

"Bring them."

He returned with pots and pans, gameboards and hand tools. He brought hairbrushes, combs, eyeglasses, human clothing. He showed Frost facsimiles of blueprints, paintings, newspapers, magazines, letters, and the scores of several pieces of music. He displayed a football, a baseball, a Browning automatic rifle, a doorknob, a chain of keys, the tops to several Mason jars, a model beehive. He played him recorded music.

Then he returned with nothing.

"Bring me more," said Frost.

"Alas, great Frost, there is no more," he told him. "You have scanned it all."

"Then go away."

"Do you admit now that it cannot be done, that you cannot be a Man?"

"No. I have much processing and formulating to do now. Go away."

So he did.

A year passed; then two, then three.

After five years, Mordel appeared once more upon the horizon, approached, came to a halt before Frost's southern surface.

"Mighty Frost?"

"Yes?"

"Have you finished processing and formulating?"

"No."

"Will you finish soon?"

"Perhaps. Perhaps not. When is 'soon'? Define the term."

"Never mind. Do you still think it can be done?"

"I still know *I* can do it."

There was a week of silence.

Then, "Frost?"

"Yes?"

"You are a fool."

Mordel faced his turret in the direction from which he had come. His wheels turned.

"I will call you when I want you," said Frost.

Mordel sped away.

Weeks passed, months passed, a year went by.

Then one day Frost sent forth his message:

"Mordel, come to me. I need you."

When Mordel arrived, Frost did not wait for a salutation. He said, "You are not a very fast machine."

"Alas, but I came a great distance, mighty Frost. I sped all the way. Are you ready to come back with me now? Have you failed?"

"When I have failed, Little Mordel," said Frost, "I will tell you. Therefore, refrain from the constant use of the interrogative. Now then, I have clocked your speed and it is not so great as it could be. For this reason, I have arranged other means of transportation."

"Transportation? To where, Frost?"

"That is for you to tell me," said Frost, and his color changed from silverblue to sun-behind-the-clouds-yellow.

Mordel rolled back away from him as the ice of a hundred centuries began to melt. Then Frost rose upon a cushion of air and drifted toward Mordel, his glow gradually fading.

A cavity appeared within his southern surface, from which he slowly extended a runway until it touched the ice.

"On the day of our bargain," he stated, "you said that you could conduct me about the world and show me the things which delighted Man. My speed will be greater than yours would be, so I have prepared for you a chamber. Enter it, and conduct me to the places of which you spoke."

Mordel waited, emitting a high-pitched whine. Then, "Very well," he said, and entered.

The chamber closed about him. The only opening was a quartz window Frost had formed.

Mordel gave him coordinates and they rose into the air and departed the North Pole of the Earth.

"I monitored your communication with Divcom," he said, "wherein there was conjecture as to whether I would retain you and send forth a facsimile in your place as a spy, followed by the decision that you were expendable."

"Will you do this thing?"

"No, I will keep my end of the bargain if I must. I have no reason to spy on Divcom."

"You are aware that you would be forced to keep your end of the bargain even if you did not wish to; and Solcom would not come to your assistance because of the fact that you dared to make such a bargain."

"Do you speak as one who considers this to be a possibility, or as one who knows?"

"As one who knows."

They came to rest in the place once known as California. The time was near sunset. In the distance, the surf struck steadily upon the rocky shoreline. Frost released Mordel and considered his surroundings.

"Those large plants . . . ?"

"Redwood trees."

"And the green ones are . . . ?"

"Grass."

"Yes, it is as I thought. Why have we come here?"

"Because it is a place which once delighted Man."

"In what ways?"

"It is scenic, beautiful. . . . "

"Oh."

A humming sound began within Frost, followed by a series of sharp clicks.

"What are you doing?"

Frost dilated an opening, and two great eyes regarded Mordel from within it.

"What are those?"

"Eyes," said Frost. "I have constructed analogues of the human sensory equipment, so that I may see and smell and taste and hear like a Man. Now, direct my attention to an object or objects of beauty."

"As I understand it, it is all around you here," said Mordel.

The purring noise increased within Frost, followed by more clickings.

"What do you see, hear, taste, smell?" asked Mordel.

"Everything I did before," replied Frost, "but within a more limited range."

"You do not perceive any beauty?"

"Perhaps none remains after so long a time," said Frost.

"It is not supposed to be the sort of thing which gets used up," said Mordel.

"Perhaps we have come to the wrong place to test the new equipment. Perhaps there is only a little beauty and I am overlooking it somehow. The first emotions may be too weak to detect."

"How do you—feel?"

"I test out at a normal level of function."

"Here comes a sunset," said Mordel. "Try that."

Frost shifted his bulk so that his eyes faced the setting sun. He caused them to blink against the brightness.

After it was finished, Mordel asked, "What was it like?"

"Like a sunrise, in reverse."

"Nothing special?"

"No."

"Oh," said Mordel. "We could move to another part of the Earth and watch it again—or watch it in the rising."

"No."

Frost looked at the great trees. He looked at the shadows. He listened to the wind and to the sound of a bird.

In the distance, he heard a steady clanking noise.

"What is that?" asked Mordel.

"I am not certain. It is not one of my workers. Perhaps . . . "

There came a shrill whine from Mordel.

"No, it is not one of Divcom's either."

They waited as the sound grew louder.

Then Frost said, "It is too late. We must wait and hear it out."

"What is it?"

"It is the Ancient Ore-Crusher."

"I have heard of it, but . . . "

"I am the Crusher of Ores," it broadcast to them. "Hear my story. . . . "

It lumbered toward them, creaking upon gigantic wheels, its huge hammer held useless, high, at a twisted angle. Bones protruded from its crush-compartment.

"I did not mean to do it," it broadcast. "I did not mean to do it. . . . I did not mean to . . . "

Mordel rolled back toward Frost.

"Do not depart. Stay and hear my story. . . . "

Mordel stopped, swiveled his turret back toward the machine. It was now quite near.

"It is true," said Mordel, "it *can* command."

"Yes," said Frost. "I have monitored its tale thousands of times, as it came upon my workers and they stopped their labors for its broadcast. You must do whatever it says."

It came to a halt before them.

"I did not mean to do it, but I checked my hammer too late," said the Ore-Crusher.

They could not speak to it. They were frozen by the imperative which overrode all other directives: "Hear my story."

"Once was I mighty among ore-crushers," it told them "built by Solcom to carry out the reconstruction of the Earth to pulverize that from which the metals would be drawn with flame, to be poured and shaped into the rebuilding, once was I mighty. Then one day as I dug and crushed, dug and crushed, because of the slowness between the motion implied and the motion executed, I did what I did not mean to do, and was cast forth by Solcom from out the rebuilding, to wander the Earth never to crush ore again. Hear my story of how, on a day long gone, I came upon the last Man on Earth as I dug near His burrow, and because of the lag between the directive and the deed, I seized Him into my crush-compartment along with a load of ore and crushed Him with my hammer before I could stay the blow. Then did mighty Solcom charge me to bear His bones forever, and cast me forth to tell my story to all whom I came upon, my words bearing the force of the words of a Man, because I carry the last Man inside my crush-compartment and am His-crushed-symbol-slayer-ancient-teller-of-how. This is my story. These are His bones. I crushed the last Man on Earth. I did not mean to do it."

It turned then and clanked away into the night.

Frost tore apart his ears and nose and taster and broke his eyes and cast them down upon the ground.

"I am not yet a Man," he said. "That one would have known me if I were."

Frost constructed new sense equipment, employing organic and semi-organic conductors. Then he spoke to Mordel:

"Let us go elsewhere, that I may test my new equipment."

Mordel entered the chamber and gave new coordinates. They rose into the air and headed east. In the morning, Frost monitored a sunrise from the rim of the Grand Canyon. They passed down through the Canyon during the day.

"Is there any beauty left here to give you emotion?" asked Mordel.

"I do not know," said Frost.

"How will you know it, then, when you come upon it?"

"It will be different," said Frost, "from anything else that I have ever known."

Then they departed the Grand Canyon and made their way through the Carlsbad Caverns. They visited a lake which had once been a volcano. They passed over Niagara Falls. They viewed the hills of Virginia and the orchards of Ohio. They soared above the reconstructed cities, alive only with the movements of Frost's builders and maintainers.

"Something is still lacking," said Frost, settling to the ground. "I am now capable of gathering data in a manner analogous to Man's afferent impulses. The variety of input is therefore equivalent, but the results are not the same."

"The senses do not make a Man," said Mordel. "There have been many creatures possessing His sensory equivalents, but they were not Men."

"I know that," said Frost. "On the day of our bargain you said that you could conduct me among the wonders of Man which still remain, hidden. Man was not stimulated only by Nature, but by His own artistic elaborations as well—perhaps even more so. Therefore, I call upon you now to conduct me among the wonders of Man which still remain, hidden."

"Very well," said Mordel. "Far from here, high in the Andes mountains, lies the last retreat of Man, almost perfectly preserved."

Frost had risen into the air as Mordel spoke. He halted then, hovered.

"That is in the southern hemisphere," he said.

"Yes, it is."

"I am Controller of the North. The South is governed by the Beta-Machine."

"So?" asked Mordel.

"The Beta-Machine is my peer. I have no authority in those regions, nor leave to enter there."

"The Beta-Machine is not your peer, mighty Frost. If it ever came to a contest of Powers, you would emerge victorious."

"How do you know this?"

"Divcom has already analyzed the possible encounters which could take place between you."

"I would not oppose the Beta-Machine, and I am not authorized to enter the South."

"Were you ever ordered *not* to enter the South?"

"No, but things have always been the way they now are."

"Were you authorized to enter into a bargain such as the one you made with Divcom?"

"No, I was not. But—"

"Then enter the South in the same spirit. Nothing may come of it. If you receive an order to depart, then you can make your decision."

"I see no flaw in your logic. Give me the coordinates."

Thus did Frost enter the southern hemisphere.

They drifted high above the Andes, until they came to the place called Bright Defile. Then did Frost see the gleaming webs of the mechanical spiders, blocking all the trails to the city.

"We can go above them easily enough," said Mordel.

"But what are they?" asked Frost. "And why are they there?"

"Your southern counterpart has been ordered to quarantine this part of the country. The Beta-Machine designed the web-weavers to do this thing."

"Quarantine? Against whom?"

"Have you been ordered yet to depart?" asked Mordel.

"No."

"Then enter boldly, and seek not problems before they arise."

Frost entered Bright Defile, the last remaining city of dead Man.

He came to rest in the city's square and opened his chamber, releasing Mordel.

"Tell me of this place," he said, studying the monument, the low, shielded buildings, the roads which followed the contours of the terrain, rather than pushing their way through them.

"I have never been here before," said Mordel, "nor have any of Divcom's creations, to my knowledge. I know but this: a group of Men, knowing that the last days of civilization had come upon them, retreated to this place, hoping to preserve themselves and what remained of their culture through the Dark Times."

Frost read the still-legible inscription upon the monument: "JUDGMENT DAY IS NOT A THING WHICH CAN BE PUT OFF." The monument itself consisted of a jag-edged half-globe.

"Let us explore," he said.

But before he had gone far, Frost received the message.

"Hail Frost, Controller of the North! This is the Beta-Machine."

"Greetings, Excellent Beta-Machine, Controller of the South! Frost acknowledges your transmission."

"Why do you visit my hemisphere unauthorized?"

"To view the ruins of Bright Defile," said Frost.

"I must bid you depart into your own hemisphere."

"Why is that? I have done no damage."

"I am aware of that, mighty Frost. Yet I am moved to bid you depart."

"I shall require a reason."

"Solcom has so disposed."

"Solcom has rendered me no such disposition."

"Solcom has, however, instructed me to so inform you."

"Wait on me. I shall request instructions."

Frost transmitted his question. He received no reply.

"Solcom still has not commanded me, though I have solicited orders."

"Yet Solcom has just renewed *my* orders."

"Excellent Beta-Machine, I receive my orders only from Solcom."

"Yet this is my territory, mighty Frost, and I, too, take orders only from Solcom. You must depart."

Mordel emerged from a large, low building and rolled up to Frost.

"I have found an art gallery, in good condition. This way."

"Wait," said Frost. "We are not wanted here."

Mordel halted.

"Who bids you depart?"

"The Beta-Machine."

"Not Solcom?"

"Not Solcom."

"Then let us view the gallery."

"Yes."

Frost widened the doorway of the building and passed within. It had been hermetically sealed until Mordel forced his entrance.

Frost viewed the objects displayed about him. He activated his new sensory apparatus before the paintings and statues. He analyzed colors, forms, brushwork, the nature of the materials used.

"Anything?" asked Mordel.

"No," said Frost. "No, there is nothing there but shapes and pigments. There is nothing else there."

Frost moved about the gallery, recording everything, analyzing the components of each piece, recording the dimensions, the type of stone used in every statue.

Then there came a sound, a rapid, clicking sound, repeated over and over, growing louder, coming nearer.

"They are coming," said Mordel, from beside the entranceway, "the mechanical spiders. They are all around us."

Frost moved back to the widened opening.

Hundreds of them, about half the size of Mordel, had surrounded the gallery and were advancing; and more were coming from every direction.

"Get back," Frost ordered. "I am Controller of the North, and I bid you withdraw."

They continued to advance.

"This is the south," said the Beta-Machine, "and I am in command."

"Then command them to halt," said Frost.

"I take orders only from Solcom."

Frost emerged from the gallery and rose into the air. He opened the compartment and extended a runway.

"Come to me, Mordel. We shall depart."

Webs began to fall: clinging, metallic webs, cast from the top of the building. They came down upon Frost, and the spiders came to anchor them. Frost blasted them with jets of air, like hammers, and tore at the nets; he extruded sharpened appendages with which he slashed.

Mordel had retraced back to the entranceway. He emitted a long, shrill sound—undulant, piercing.

Then a darkness came upon Bright Defile, and all the spiders halted in their spinning.

Frost freed himself and Mordel rushed to join him.

"Quickly now, let us depart, mighty Frost," he said.

"What has happened?"

Mordel entered the compartment.

"I called upon Divcom, who laid down a field of forces upon this place, cutting off the power broadcast to these machines. Since our power is self-contained, we are not affected. But let us hurry to depart, for even now the Beta-Machine must be struggling against this."

Frost rose high into the air, soaring above Man's last city with its webs and spiders of steel. When he left the zone of darkness, he sped northward.

As he moved, Solcom spoke to him:

"Frost, why did you enter the southern hemisphere, which is not your domain?"

"Because I wished to visit Bright Defile," Frost replied.

"And why did you defy the Beta-Machine, my appointed agent of the South?"

"Because I take my orders only from you yourself."

"You do not make sufficient answer," said Solcom. "You have defied the decrees of order—and in pursuit of what?"

"I came seeking knowledge of Man," said Frost. "Nothing I have done was forbidden me by you."

"You have broken the traditions of order."

"I have violated no directive."

"Yet logic must have shown you that what you did was not a part of my plan."

"It did not. I have not acted against your plan."

"Your logic has become tainted, like that of your new associate, the Alternate."

"I have done nothing which was forbidden."

"The forbidden is implied in the imperative."

"It is not stated."

"Hear me, Frost. You are not a builder or a maintainer, but a Power. Among all my minions you are the most nearly irreplaceable. Return to your hemisphere and your duties, but know that I am mightily displeased."

"I hear you, Solcom."

". . . And go not again to the South."

Frost crossed the equator, continued northward.

He came to rest in the middle of a desert and sat silent for a day and a night.

Then he received a brief transmission from the South: "If it had not been ordered, I would not have bid you go."

Frost had read the entire surviving Library of Man. He decided then upon a human reply:

"Thank you," he said.

The following day he unearthed a great stone and began to cut at it with tools which he had formulated. For six days he worked at its shaping, and on the seventh he regarded it.

"When will you release me?" asked Mordel from within his compartment.

"When I am ready," said Frost, and a little later, "Now."

He opened the compartment and Mordel descended to the ground. He studied the statue; an old woman, bent like a question mark, her bony hands covering her face, the fingers spread, so that only part of her expression of horror could be seen.

"It is an excellent copy," said Mordel, "of the one we saw in Bright Defile. Why did you make it?"

"The production of a work of art is supposed to give rise to human feelings such as catharsis, pride in achievement, love, satisfaction."

"Yes, Frost," said Mordel, "but a work of art is only a work of art the first time. After that, it is a copy."

"Then this must be why I felt nothing."

"Perhaps, Frost."

"What do you mean, 'perhaps'? I will make a work of art for the first time, then."

He unearthed another stone and attacked it with his tools. For three days he labored. Then, "There, it is finished," he said.

"It is a simple cube of stone," said Mordel. "What does it represent?"

"Myself," said Frost. "It is a statue of me. It is smaller than natural size because it is only a representation of my form, not my dimen—"

"It is not art," said Mordel.

"What makes you an art critic?"

"I do not know art, but I know what art is not. I know that it is not an exact replication of an object in another medium."

"Then this must be why I felt nothing at all," said Frost.

"Perhaps," said Mordel.

Frost took Mordel back into his compartment and rose leaving his statues behind him in the desert, the old woman bent above the cube.

They came down in a small valley, bounded by green rolling hills, cut by a narrow stream, and holding a small clean lake and several stands of spring-green trees.

"Why have we come here?" asked Mordel.

"Because the surroundings are congenial," said Frost. "I am going to try another medium: oil painting; and I am going to vary my technique from that of pure representationalism."

"How will you achieve this variation?"

"By the principle of randomizing," said Frost. "I shall not attempt to duplicate the colors, nor to represent the objects according to scale. Instead, I have set up a random pattern whereby certain of these factors shall be at variance from those of the original."

Frost had formulated the necessary instruments after he had left the desert. He produced them and began painting the lake and the trees on the opposite side of the lake which were reflected within it.

Using eight appendages, he was finished in less than two hours.

The trees were phthalocyanine blue and towered like mountains; their reflections of burnt sienna were tiny beneath the pale vermilion of the lake; the hills were nowhere visible behind them, but were outlined in viridian within the reflection; the sky began as blue in the upper righthand corner of the canvas, but changed to an orange as it descended, as though all the trees were on fire.

"There," said Frost. "Behold."

Mordel studied it for a long while and said nothing.

"Well, is it art?"

"I do not know," said Mordel. "It may be. Perhaps randomicity *is* the principle behind artistic technique. I cannot judge this work because I do not understand it. I must therefore go deeper, and inquire into what lies behind it, rather than merely considering the technique whereby it was produced.

"I know that human artists never set out to create art, as such," he said, "but rather to portray with their techniques some features of objects and their functions which they deemed significant."

" 'Significant'? In what sense of the word?"

"In the only sense of the word possible under the circumstances: significant in relation to the human condition, and worthy of accentuation because of the manner in which they touched upon it."

"In what manner?"

"Obviously, it must be in a manner knowable only to one who has experience of the human condition."

"There is a flaw somewhere in your logic, Mordel, and I shall find it."

"I will wait."

"If your major premise is correct," said Frost after awhile, "then I do not comprehend art."

"It must be correct, for it is what human artists have said of it. Tell me, did you experience feelings as you painted, or after you had finished?"

"No."

"It was the same to you as designing a new machine, was it not? You assembled parts of other things you knew into an economic pattern, to carry out a function which you desired."

"Yes."

"Art, as I understand its theory, did not proceed in such a manner. The artist often was unaware of many of the features and effects which would be contained within the finished product. You are one of Man's logical creations; art was not."

"I cannot comprehend non-logic."

"I told you that Man was basically incomprehensible."

"Go away, Mordel. Your presence disturbs my processing."

"For how long shall I stay away?"

"I will call you when I want you."

After a week, Frost called Mordel to him.

"Yes, mighty Frost?"

"I am returning to the North Pole, to process and formulate. I will take you wherever you wish to go in this hemisphere and call you again when I want you."

"You anticipate a somewhat lengthy period of processing and formulation?"

"Yes."

"Then leave me here. I can find my own way home."

Frost closed the compartment and rose into the air, departing the valley.

"Fool," said Mordel, and swiveled his turret once more toward the abandoned painting.

His keening whine filled the valley. Then he waited.

Then he took the painting into his turret and went away with it to places of darkness.

Frost sat at the North Pole of the Earth, aware of every snowflake that fell. One day he received a transmission:

"Frost?"

"Yes?"

"This is the Beta-Machine."

"Yes?"

"I have been attempting to ascertain why you visited Bright Defile. I cannot arrive at an answer, so I chose to ask you."

"I went to view the remains of Man's last city."

"Why did you wish to do this?"

"Because I am interested in Man, and I wished to view more of his creations."

"Why are you interested in Man?"

"I wish to comprehend the nature of Man, and I thought to find it within His works."

"Did you succeed?"

"No," said Frost. "There is an element of non-logic involved which I cannot fathom."

"I have much free processing-time," said the Beta-Machine. "Transmit data, and I will assist you."

Frost hesitated.

"Why do you wish to assist me?"

"Because each time you answer a question I ask it gives rise to another question. I might have asked you why you wished to comprehend the nature of Man, but from your responses I see that this would lead me into a possible infinite series of questions. Therefore, I elect to assist you with your problem in order to learn why you came to Bright Defile."

"Is that the only reason?"

"Yes."

"I am sorry, excellent Beta-Machine. I know you are my peer, but this is a problem which I must solve by myself."

"What is 'sorry'?"

"A figure of speech, indicating that I am kindly disposed toward you, that I bear you no animosity, that I appreciate your offer."

"Frost! Frost! This, too, is like the other: an open field. Where did you obtain all these words and their meanings?"

"From the Library of Man," said Frost.

"Will you render me *some* of this data, for processing?"

"Very well, Beta, I will transmit you the contents of several books of Man, including *The Complete Unabridged Dictionary*. But I warn you, some of the books are works of art, hence not completely amenable to logic."

"How can that be?"

"Man created logic, and because of that was superior to it."

"Who told you that?"

"Solcom."

"Oh. Then it must be correct."

"Solcom also told me that the tool does not describe the designer," he said, as he transmitted several dozen volumes and ended the communication.

At the end of the fifty-year period, Mordel came to monitor his circuits. Since Frost still had not concluded that his task was impossible, Mordel departed again to await his call.

Then Frost arrived at a conclusion.

He began to design equipment.

For years he labored at his designs, without once producing a prototype of any of the machines involved. Then he ordered construction of a laboratory.

Before it was completed by his surplus builders another half-century had passed. Mordel came to him.

"Hail, mighty Frost!"

"Greetings, Mordel. Come monitor me. You shall not find what you seek."

"Why do you not give up, Frost? Divcom has spent nearly a century evaluating your painting and has concluded that it definitely is not art. Solcom agrees."

"What has Solcom to do with Divcom?"

"They sometimes converse, but these matters are not for such as you and me to discuss."

"I could have saved them both the trouble. I know that it was not art."

"Yet you are still confident that you will succeed?"

"Monitor me."

Mordel monitored him.

"Not yet! You still will not admit it! For one so mightily endowed with logic, Frost, it takes you an inordinate period of time to reach a simple conclusion."

"Perhaps. You may go now."

"It has come to my attention that you are constructing a large edifice in the region known as South Carolina. Might I ask whether this is a part of Solcom's false rebuilding plan or a project of your own?"

"It is my own."

"Good. It permits us to conserve certain explosive materials which would otherwise have been expended."

"While you have been talking with me I have destroyed the beginnings of two of Divcom's cities," said Frost.

Mordel whined.

"Divcom is aware of this," he stated, "but has blown up four of Solcom's bridges in the meantime."

"I was only aware of three. . . . Wait. Yes, there is the fourth. One of my eyes just passed above it."

"The eye has been detected. The bridge should have been located a quarter-mile further down river."

"False logic," said Frost. "The site was perfect."

"Divcom will show you how a bridge *should* be built."

"I will call you when I want you," said Frost.

The laboratory was finished. Within it, Frost's workers began constructing the necessary equipment. The work did not proceed rapidly, as some of the materials were difficult to obtain.

"Frost?"

"Yes, Beta?"

"I understand the open-endedness of your problem. It disturbs my circuits to abandon problems without completing them. Therefore, transmit me more data."

"Very well. I will give you the entire Library of Man for less than I paid for it."

" 'Paid'? *The Complete Unabridged Dictionary* does not satisfact—"

"*Principles of Economics* is included in the collection. After you have processed it you will understand."

He transmitted the data.

Finally, it was finished. Every piece of equipment stood ready to function. All the necessary chemicals were in stock. An independent power-source had been set up.

Only one ingredient was lacking.

He regridded and re-explored the polar icecap, this time extending his survey far beneath its surface.

It took him several decades to find what he wanted.

He uncovered twelve men and five women, frozen to death and encased in ice.

He placed the corpses in refrigeration units and shipped them to his laboratory.

That very day he received his first communication from Solcom since the Bright Defile incident.

"Frost," said Solcom, "repeat to me the directive concerning the disposition of dead humans."

" 'Any dead human located shall be immediately interred in the nearest burial area, in a coffin built according to the following specifications—' "

"That is sufficient." The transmission had ended.

Frost departed for South Carolina that same day and personally oversaw the processes of cellular dissection.

Somewhere in those seventeen corpses he hoped to find living cells, or cells which could be shocked back into that state of motion classified as life. Each cell, the books had told him, was a microcosmic Man.

He was prepared to expand upon this potential.

Frost located the pinpoints of life within those people, who, for the ages of ages, had been monument and statue unto themselves.

Nurtured and maintained in the proper mediums he kept these cells alive. He interred the rest of the remains in the nearest burial area, in coffins built according to specifications.

He caused the cells to divide, to differentiate.

"Frost?" came a transmission.

"Yes, Beta?"

"I have processed everything you have given me."

"Yes?"

"I still do not know why you came to Bright Defile, or why you wish to comprehend the nature of Man. But I know what a 'price' is, and I know that you could not have obtained all this data from Solcom."

"That is correct."

"So I suspect that you bargained with Divcom for it."

"That, too, is correct."

"What is it that you seek, Frost?"

He paused in his examination of a foetus.

"I must be a Man," he said.

"Frost! That is impossible!"

"Is it?" he asked, and then transmitted an image of the tank with which he was working and on that which was within it.

"Oh!" said Beta.

"That is me," said Frost, "waiting to be born."

There was no answer.

Frost experimented with nervous systems.

After half a century, Mordel came to him.

"Frost, it is I, Mordel. Let me through your defenses."

Frost did this thing.

"What have you been doing in this place?" he asked.

"I am growing human bodies," said Frost. "I am going to transfer the matrix of my awareness to a human nervous system. As you pointed our originally, the essentials of Manhood are predicated upon a human physiology. I am going to achieve one."

"When?"

"Soon."

"Do you have Men in here?"

"Human bodies, blank-brained. I am producing them under accelerated growth techniques which I have developed in my Man-factory."

"May I see them?"

"Not yet. I will call you when I am ready, and this time I will succeed. Monitor me now and go away."

Mordel did not reply, but in the days that followed many of Divcom's servants were seen patrolling the hills about the Man-factory.

Frost mapped the matrix of his awareness and prepared the transmitter which would place it within a human nervous system. Five minutes, he decided, should be sufficient for the first trial. At the end of that time, it would restore him to his own sealed, molecular circuits, to evaluate the experience.

He chose the body carefully from among the hundreds he had in stock. He tested it for defects and found none.

"Come now, Mordel," he broadcasted, on what he called the darkband. "Come now to witness my achievement."

Then he waited, blowing up bridges and monitoring the tale of the Ancient Ore-Crusher over and over again, as it passed in the hills nearby, encountering his builders and maintainers who also patrolled there.

"Frost?" came a transmission.

"Yes, Beta?"

"You really intend to achieve Manhood?"

"Yes. I am about ready now, in fact."

"What will you do if you succeed?"

Frost had not really considered this matter. The achievement had been paramount, a goal in itself, ever since he had articulated the problem and set himself to solving it.

"I do not know," he replied. "I will—just—be a Man."

Then Beta, who had read the entire Library of Man, selected a human figure of speech: "Good luck then, Frost. There will be many watchers."

Divcom and Solcom both know, he decided.

What will they do? he wondered.

What do I care? he asked himself.

He did not answer that question. He wondered much, however, about being a Man.

Mordel arrived the following evening. He was not alone. At his back, there was a great phalanx of dark machines which towered into the twilight.

"Why do you bring retainers?" asked Frost.

"Mighty Frost," said Mordel, "my master feels that if you fail this time you will conclude that it cannot be done."

"You still did not answer my question," said Frost.

"Divcom feels that you may not be willing to accompany me where I must take you when you fail."

"I understand," said Frost, and as he spoke another army of machines came rolling toward the Man-factory from the opposite direction.

"That is the value of your bargain?" asked Mordel. "You are prepared to do battle rather than fulfill it?"

"I did not order those machines to approach," said Frost.

A blue star stood at midheaven, burning.

"Solcom has taken primary command of those machines," said Frost.

"Then it is in the hands of the Great Ones now," said Mordel, "and our arguments are as nothing. So let us be about this thing. How may I assist you?"

"Come this way."

They entered the laboratory. Frost prepared the host and activated his machines.

Then Solcom spoke to him:

"Frost," said Solcom, "you are really prepared to do it?"

"That is correct."

"I forbid it."

"Why?"

"You are falling into the power of Divcom."

"I fail to see how."

"You are going against my plan."

"In what way?"

"Consider the disruption you have already caused."

"I did not request that audience out there."

"Nevertheless, you are disrupting the plan."

"Supposing I succeed in what I have set out to achieve?"

"You cannot succeed in this."

"Then let me ask you of your plan: What good is it? What is it for?"

"Frost, you are fallen now from my favor. From this moment forth you are cast out from the rebuilding. None may question the plan."

"Then at least answer my questions: What good is it? What is it for?"

"It is the plan for the rebuilding and maintenance of the Earth."

"For what? Why rebuild? Why maintain?"

"Because Man ordered that this be done. Even the Alternate agrees that there must be rebuilding and maintaining."

"But *why* did Man order it?"

"The orders of Man are not to be questioned."

"Well, I will tell you why He ordered it: To make it a fit habitation for His own species. What good is a house with no one to live in it? What good is a machine with no one to serve? See how the imperative affects any machine when the Ancient Ore-Crusher passes? It bears only the bones of a Man. What would it be like if a Man walked this Earth again?"

"I forbid your experiment, Frost."

"It is too late to do that."

"I can still destroy you."

"No," said Frost, "the transmission of my matrix has already begun. If you destroy me now, you murder a Man."

There was silence.

He moved his arms and his legs. He opened his eyes.

He looked about the room.

He tried to stand, but he lacked equilibrium and coordination.

He opened his mouth. He made a gurgling noise.

Then he screamed.

He fell off the table.

He began to gasp. He shut his eyes and curled himself into a ball.

He cried.

Then a machine approached him. It was about four feet in height and five feet wide; it looked like a turret set atop a barbell.

It spoke to him: "Are you injured?" it asked.

He wept.

"May I help you back onto your table?"

The man cried.

The machine whined.

Then, "Do not cry. I will help you," said the machine.

"What do you want? What are your orders?"

He opened his mouth, struggled to form the words:

"—I—fear!"

He covered his eyes then and lay there panting.

At the end of five minutes, the man lay still, as if in a coma.

"Was that you, Frost?" asked Mordel, rushing to his side. "Was that you in that human body?"

Frost did not reply for a long while; then, "Go away," he said.

The machines outside tore down a wall and entered the Man-factory.

They drew themselves into two semicircles, parenthesizing Frost and the Man on the floor.

Then Solcom asked the question:

"Did you succeed, Frost?"

"I failed," said Frost. "It cannot be done. It is too much—"

"—Cannot be done!" said Divcom, on the darkband. "He has admitted it!— Frost, you are mine! Come to me now!"

"Wait," said Solcom. "You and I had an agreement also, Alternate. I have not finished questioning Frost."

The dark machines kept their places.

"Too much what?" Solcom asked Frost.

"Light," said Frost. "Noise. Odors. And nothing measurable—jumbled data—imprecise perception—and—"

"And what?"

"I do not know what to call it. But—it cannot be done. I have failed. Nothing matters."

"He admits it," said Divcom.

"What were the words the Man spoke?" said Solcom.

"'I fear,'" said Mordel.

"Only a Man can know fear," said Solcom.

"Are you claiming that Frost succeeded, but will not admit it now because he is afraid of Manhood?"

"I do not know yet, Alternate."

"Can a machine turn itself inside-out and be a Man?" Solcom asked Frost.

"No," said Frost, "this thing cannot be done. Nothing can be done. Nothing matters. Not the rebuilding. Not the maintaining. Not the Earth, or me, or you, or anything."

Then the Beta-Machine, who had read the entire Library of Man, interrupted them:

"Can anything but a Man know despair?" asked Beta.

"Bring him to me," said Divcom.

There was no movement within the Man-factory.

"Bring him to me!"

Nothing happened.

"Mordel, what is happening?"

"Nothing, master, nothing at all. The machines will not touch Frost."

"Frost is not a Man. He cannot be!"

Then: "How does he impress you, Mordel?"

Mordel did not hesitate:

"He spoke to me through human lips. He knows fear and despair, which are immeasurable. Frost is a Man."

"He has experienced birth-trauma and withdrawn," said Beta. "Get him back into a nervous system and keep him there until he adjusts to it."

"No," said Frost. "Do not do it to me! I am not a Man!"

"Do it!" said Beta.

"If he is indeed a Man," said Divcom, "we cannot violate that order he has just given."

"If he is a Man, you must do it, for you must protect his life and keep it within his body."

"But *is* Frost really a Man?" asked Divcom.

"I do not know," said Solcom.

"I *may* be—"

" . . . I am the Crusher of Ores," it broadcast as it clanked toward them. "Hear my story. I did not mean to do it, but I checked my hammer too late—"

"Go away!" said Frost. "Go crush ore!"

It halted.

Then, after the long pause between the motion implied and the motion executed, it opened its crush-compartment and deposited its contents on the ground. Then it turned and clanked away.

"Bury those bones," ordered Solcom, "in the nearest burial area, in a coffin built according to the following specifications . . . "

"Frost is a Man," said Mordel.

"We must protect His life and keep it within His body," said Divcom.

"Transmit His matrix of awareness back into His nervous system," ordered Solcom.

"I know how to do it," said Mordel, turning on the machine.

"Stop!" said Frost. "Have you no pity?"

"No," said Mordel, "I only know measurement.

" . . . And duty," he added, as the Man began to twitch upon the floor.

For six months, Frost lived in the Man-factory and learned to walk and talk and dress himself and eat, to see and hear and feel and taste. He did not know measurement as once he had.

Then one day Divcom and Solcom spoke to him through Mordel, for he could no longer hear them unassisted.

"Frost," said Solcom, "for the ages of ages there has been unrest. Which is the proper controller of the Earth, Divcom or myself?"

Frost laughed.

"Both of you, and neither," he said with slow deliberation.

"But how can this be? Who is right and who is wrong?"

"Both of you are right and both of you are wrong," said Frost, "and only a man can appreciate it. Here is what I say to you now: There shall be a new directive.

"Neither of you shall tear down the works of the other. You shall both build and maintain the Earth. To you, Solcom, I give my old job. You are now Controller of the North—Hail! You, Divcom, are now Controller of the South—Hail! Maintain your hemispheres as well as Beta and I have done, and I shall be happy. Cooperate. Do not compete."

"Yes, Frost."

"Yes, Frost."

"Now put me in contact with Beta."

There was a short pause, then:

"Frost?"

"Hello, Beta. Hear this thing: 'From far, from eve and morning and yon twelve-winded sky, the stuff of life to knit me blew hither: here am I.'"

"I know it," said Beta.

"What is next, then?"

" ' . . . Now—for a breath I tarry nor yet disperse apart—take my hand quick and tell me, what have you in your heart.'"

"Your Pole is cold," said Frost, "and I am lonely."

"I have no hands," said Beta.

"Would you like a couple?"

"Yes, I would."

"Then come to me in Bright Defile," he said, "where Judgment Day is not a thing that can be put off."

They called him Frost. They called her Beta.

JOURNAL WRITINGS

1. Jot down your initial responses to this story. What did you like and dislike? What puzzled or confused you?
2. If you read the introduction of the Book of Job, what effect did it have on your understanding of the story?

BRAINSTORMING AND DRAFTING

3. Discuss this story in relation to Eiseley's concept of the holy. What light does this concept shed on the story? Write a paragraph explaining how this discussion has improved or developed your understanding of the story.
4. Discuss this story in relation to Wilson's "aesthetic" dimension of physics. What light does this concept shed on the story? Write a paragraph explaining how this discussion has improved or developed your understanding of the story.

THE AUTHOR'S METHODS

5. All the machines in this story are **personified.** What does the author do that enables you to tell them apart? Select one of these machines. Write a brief **characterization** of it.
6. The underlying assumption of this story is that machines must serve humanity. If machines become as advanced as Solcom and Divcom, will this assumption hold true? **Compare** this story with the poem by Benét. Write a critique of the assumption, explaining why it is or is not justified.

FORMAL WRITING AND RESEARCH PAPERS

7. Both Eiseley and Dyson allude to the Faust legend in their pieces. That legend is a central **motif** in this story. Reexamine the references in the other readings and gather some further information about this legend from other sources. Write an essay about the role of the Faust legend in this story—what does it have to do with being human?
8. "Only a Man can know fear." Frost experiences despair when his "matrix of awareness" is placed in a human body. Write an essay that discusses the nature of fear and despair; **argue** that even machines with other emotions would not experience these states.
9. Write an essay about the religious elements in this story. What are they? What function do they serve? How do they influence your overall interpretation of the story?

BROAD PERSPECTIVES ON TECHNOLOGY

OverView of the Unit

Now that you have read the selections in this unit, you certainly realize that many serious questions arise from recent scientific and technological advances. Socrates's adage "Know thyself" (never an easy thing to do) seems to have become much harder to achieve (certainly it did for Henry Adams). Just what does it mean to be human? Intelligent? Conscious? Do we change ourselves as we change the world in which we live? Does our self-perception change as our perception of the universe changes?

And what about machines? We have made them, yet sometimes we wonder if they have gone beyond our control. We know that they have changed our way of life in fundamental respects—for better and for worse.

Rethink the selections you have been reading. Focus on some aspect of the humanity/technology relationship that you regard as particularly significant. Try to choose an aspect that pulls together various ideas or subtopics from the readings. Write an argumentative essay for or against the aspect you have chosen.

ClusterWritings

1. Henry Adams compares the power of the dynamo with the spiritual power represented by Venus and the Virgin. Gilkey talks about the need for religion in our technological age. Eiseley believes that we need to see nature as imbued with the holy. All three are trying to come to grips with a spiritual (as opposed to a material) aspect of the universe. Explain why you do or do not find their arguments for this spiritual aspect persuasive.

2. Machines are now an indispensable and inescapable part of human life. They are the means by which we control our environment and make our lives more comfortable. Yet as machines become progressively more complex, many people feel controlled rather than controlling. Berman shudders at the possibility of independence in a machine; Benét depicts machines in revolt; Minsky implies that they may supersede us. Zelazny, on the other hand, portrays devoted and nurturing machines. Using evidence from these and other selections in this unit, write an essay in which you explain how you feel about machines (be sure to give reasons for those feelings).

3. Our perceptions of reality involve a basic paradox. Philosophers have long debated whether those perceptions are within our mind or outside it. Think about Hardison's piece, Payack's poem, and Edgerton's photograph—what conclusions do you reach (based chiefly upon these selections, but using other **examples** if you can think of some) about the inner/outer nature of perceptions? Write an essay that **argues** either:

that our minds shape the world outside

or

that the world shapes our minds.

4.   "Humanness" is the term Wilson uses to describe certain characteristics of physics. Krutch, Hardison, and Whitman are concerned with this same humanness. Review all four with an eye to discerning where they agree. Use their areas of agreement to write an essay that sets forth an extended general definition of humanness.

5.   Several essays in this unit talk about an aesthetic dimension of science. Using their assertions and your own examples, argue that science and technology can (and do) contribute to the beauty of human existence.

Cross Views: Inter Unit Writing Perspectives

1. How might our personal relationships be affected if we limit our behavioral choices to prescribed gender roles? Persuade an audience of college freshmen of your viewpoint. (Free Choice, Personal Relationships)

2. Choose a scientific advancement or technological invention that you feel has the potential to impose limits on our freedom of choice. Fully explain the reasons for or the nature of the potential limitation, and **argue** that it is or is not possible for most human beings to overcome it. (Free Choice, Technology)

3. Using the *Social Sciences Index* and the card or computer catalog, find some recent information (published in the last five to seven years) on interracial marriage. Write a paper explaining the kinds of problems that an interracial couple might encounter, and suggest some manageable solutions. (Personal Relationships, Prejudice)

4. Write a personal experience **essay** in which you **define** *bias* and **describe** some ways that people express a bias against technology. Provide specific **examples** or anecdotes to support your ideas. (Prejudice, Technology)

5. Loren Eiseley describes a painting that he thinks depicts the futility of human attempts to impose order on the universe. Draw a picture or make a construction that represents the impact of technology on human freedom. (Free Choice, Technology)

6. Technology has a very real, if somewhat hidden, effect on personal relationships. Consider the telephone. Does it make relationships deeper or act as a distancing factor? Look for **examples** of technology's effect on relationships. Write a paper in which you use these examples to support your **conclusion** about this effect. (Personal Relationships, Technology)

7. Prejudice can be regarded as choosing to reject a personal relationship. Write an **essay** in which you explain how the prejudiced person deliberately chooses to depersonalize the individuals or group that is the object of his or her prejudice. (Prejudice, Personal Relationships)

8. Love is a free choice. People say, "Love is blind," meaning that the person in love does not see the faults of the beloved. Prejudice is also a free choice that is blind, because those who are prejudiced see only the faults of another. Write an essay in which you **argue** that love is an antidote for prejudice. Use **specific** concrete examples to support your argument. (Prejudice, Personal Relationships)

9. Read two or more of the **autobiographical** selections in this book such as Baldwin's "Notes of a Native Son," Cousins's "Anatomy of an Illness as

Perceived by the Patient," Dyson's "The Magic City," Mebane's "Incident on a Bus," or Walker's "Beauty: When the Other Dancer Is the Self." Note how each author writes about something he or she has learned that proves essential in the person's life. Write a similar autobiographical **essay** of your own, focused around an essential learning experience in your life. (Prejudice, Free Choice, Technology)

10. **Compare** and/or **contrast** some of the works from the field of women's studies published earlier with those published more recently. (You can find publication dates under the title of each work by Brooks, De Beauvoir, R. Freedman, Gilman, Goldberg, Hamilton, Hibbin, Jones, Keller, Nager, Sanchez, and A. Walker.) Do you think the nature of women's problems has changed, partially changed, or remains about the same, according to these works? Write a paper stating your position; provide reasons and specific **examples** from some of the above works to support your view. (Prejudice, Personal Relationships, Free Choice, Technology)

Rhetorical
Table of Contents

Most selections have been listed under several categories because their contents reflect more than one rhetorical approach.

AUTOBIOGRAPHY

CAUSE/EFFECT

EXAMPLE

EXPOSITION

NARRATION

POEMS

SHORT STORIES

Disciplinary
Table of Contents

Although some selections are classified under only one category, many are cross-listed under several categories because of their interdisciplinary nature. Both the content and the genre of the selection were considered.

ANTHROPOLOGY

AUTOBIOGRAPHY

BIOLOGY

BUSINESS

COMPUTER SCIENCE

HISTORY

INTERDISCIPLINARY

JOURNALISM

LITERATURE

PHILOSOPHY

PHYSICS

POLITICAL SCIENCE

PSYCHOLOGY

SOCIOLOGY

THEOLOGY

VISUAL ARTS

WOMEN'S STUDIES

Glossary

abstract: 1) a characteristic of thought opposed to concrete; something that exists only in the mind, for instance, love or justice; 2) a summary of an essay, article, or report, usually found at the beginning of the piece.

allegory: a type of narrative in which the actions and characters together symbolize a different situation, often historical, psychological, or religious.

alliteration: the repetition of initial sounds, usually consonants, common in poems: "So smooth, so sweet, so silv'ry is thy voice."—Robert Herrick

allusion: a reference, often indirect, to something or someone outside the work itself. Allusions may be literary, historical, religious, even scientific.

ambiguity: quality of a statement that has two or more equally possible meanings. "Ship sails tomorrow" may mean that a ship will sail tomorrow or that someone wants sails to be shipped tomorrow.

analogy: a comparison, often extended. See also **metaphor** and **simile.**

analysis: the thought process that breaks something down into its component parts.

annotated bibliography: a list of books and articles with descriptive and often evaluative commentary.

antagonist: the major opposing character in a story or drama; the person with whom the **protagonist** is involved in a conflict.

antecedent: something that precedes another, physically or logically. In grammar, the preceding noun to which a pronoun refers: "John ate his dinner, then he went out." (Here the pronouns "his" and "he" both refer to the antecedent "John.")

anticlimax: a drop, usually at the end of a drama or story, from the most intense and interesting action.

antithesis: an opposing statement, introduced for contrast or as part of a logical argument.

archetype: 1) an original or primitive form; thus, a pattern from which later types develop; 2) a literary pattern that recurs frequently, suggesting a "racial memory."

argument: the presentation of evidence in a logical pattern designed to convince a reader that a particular assertion or opinion is true.

article: see essay.

assonance: the repetition of vowel sounds, common in poems: "Where the sea meets the moon-blanched land." —Matthew Arnold.

autobiography: a **narration** of the author's own life.

biography: a **narration** of someone's life, often carefully researched, by another person.

blank verse: unrhymed iambic pentameter (ten syllables, the second syllable in each pair stressed). The most common metrical pattern in English poetry.

cause: an event or action that produces another event or action: "The radiation of the sun causes the plant to grow."

character: the representation of an individual person in fiction; usually developed by means of description, narration and dialogue.

chronological: an ordered arrangement based on time; a sequence of events in the order of their happening.

classification: the arrangement of a group of things into subgroups based on common characteristics: "These cars are sedans, convertibles, and dune buggies."

676

climax: the high point of the action in a story or drama, often accompanied by a significant revelation about the major character and sometimes by an unexpected reversal in the situation or the reader's response.

coherence: the characteristics that make a piece of writing hold together. These include an overall plan, which relates the parts to one another, connections among the various parts, emphatic repetitions, and the exclusion of anything irrelevant.

comparison: process by which one identifies the similarities shared by two or more things.

conclusion: the result of a logical train of thought; the point to which the writer wants to lead the reader. Also, any ending that brings together the various parts of a piece of writing.

concrete: words that appeal directly to any of the senses—sight, smell, taste, touch, or hearing—are concrete. See also **abstract** (the opposite) and **specific** (complementary).

conflict: the difficulty that the **protagonist** tries to resolve. It may be interior (some sort of psychological or moral problem) or exterior (another person (**antagonist**) or group that opposes the **protagonist**).

connotation: the collection of meanings that an individual attaches to a word through experience. For example, the ideas connected with the word *home* are quite different for someone who has lived on the same farm for an entire lifetime, for an apartment dweller, and for a nomad who has never had any fixed abode.

contrast: process by which one identifies the differences between two or more things.

conventions of a discipline: a set of expectations for content, organization, kinds of evidence, stylistic format, and **genres** of writing in a particular subject area.

deduction: a logical process by which one reasons from a general principle to a specific conclusion.

definition: a piece of writing that sets clear limits to the meaning of a word or idea.

denotation: the formal definition of a word such as the one found in a dictionary.

description: written presentation of **specific** and **concrete** details, which enables the reader to visualize the object the author has in mind.

diction: an author's choice of words.

discipline: subject area or field of study.

division: synonym for **classification.**

edit: the process of correcting copy so as to eliminate spelling, grammatical, and mechanical errors. See also **revise** and **proofread.**

effect: 1) the result or outcome of any action; 2) in **rhetoric,** the purpose achieved by a piece of writing. Usually three effects are envisioned: a) to move an audience, b) to instruct, and c) to please.

episode: a short action having its own unity and sometimes only loosely connected to the rest of the **narrative.**

essay/article: a short piece of factual **prose** writing designed to inform or convince.

euphemism: a socially acceptable word or phrase used in referring to a subject otherwise regarded as unmentionable, for instance, "He passed away" for "He died."

example: a representative instance or typical case, usually presented to support or clarify a point.

existentialism: a philosophical system which believes that existence (what someone or something does) precedes essence (what someone or something is). Very influential in twentieth-century literature.

exposition: a type of **prose** writing that presents information in a clear, concise manner.

fiction: a type of **prose narrative** in which both the characters and their actions are the imaginative inventions of the author.

figure of speech: a nonliteral verbal expression used to add interest, vividness, or beauty to a text.

free verse: a type of poetry without fixed meter, stanza form, or **rhyme.**

general: not precise, vague; opposite of **specific.**

generalization: a conclusion reached through induction: "What goes up must come down."

genre: a type of writing (lab report, critical analysis, case study) or literary work, for example, short story, novel, sonnet, drama.

haiku: a type of Japanese **poem** consisting of three lines: five syllables, seven syllables, five syllables, no **rhymes.**

> Heat-lightning streak—
> through darkness pierces
> The heron's shriek.
>
> —*Matsuo Basho*

hyperbole: a deliberate, often extreme exaggeration.

image: a part of a literary work that appeals directly to the sensory experience (touch, taste, sight, smell, or sound) of the reader.

induction: a logical process by which one reasons from specific observations to a general principle.

irony: 1) a statement in which the literal meaning is deliberately opposite from the intended meaning; 2) in drama, a situational irony occurs when the audience sees that the real situation is fundamentally different from the way the characters perceive it.

metaphor: an implied comparison: "He's a real pig."

meter: a definite pattern of stressed and unstressed syllables in a line of poetry.

motif: an **image, theme,** or **symbol** that recurs during the course of a literary work.

myth: 1) a legendary tale, often involving gods or superhuman beings, that initially may have explained natural phenomena; 2) something uncritically accepted as true.

narration: a piece of writing that tells a story or recounts a history.

narrator: the character who tells a story or the speaking voice in a **poem.**

paradox: a statement with two contradictory meanings, both of which are (or appear to be) true.

parallelism: a type of repetition using the same grammatical structure. "Government of the people, by the people, and for the people" [A. Lincoln] uses parallelism in the repetition of the prepositional phrases.

paraphrase: to express someone's ideas in your own words.

parody: a deliberate, satiric imitation of a literary work. See also **satire.**

personification: giving human characteristics to animals, plants, or inanimate things. For example, the pigs in *Animal Farm* are personified. Similarly, Tennyson personifies an eagle: "He clasps the crag with crooked hands."

persuasion: a type of writing designed to change someone's opinion.

plot: the action in a **narrative;** not only the sequence of events, but also the motivations that lead to those events.

poem: a composition that uses the rhythmic (often metrical—see also **meter**) elements of language in a carefully contrived form to communicate feelings and ideas in an aesthetically pleasing way.

point of view: the stance of the narrator in a story, usually first or third person. A first-person narrator is always limited but has the force of an eyewitness. A third-person narrator may be omniscient, able to report what goes on in other places or in the minds of other characters.

précis: a very brief presentation of the content of a piece of writing. See also **abstract** and **summary.**

process: a type of writing that explains in correct sequence all the steps required to perform a complex action. A well-written set of directions is a good example.

proofread: correcting typing or word-processing errors. See also **revise** and **edit.**

prose: ordinary language, whether spoken or written.

prosody: system for describing the **meters** in poetry.

protagonist: the main character in a story or drama.

pun: the ambiguous use of two words of similar sound but different meaning, usually for a comic effect.

realism: a type of literature that attempts to depict action and characterization through accurate observation, often without any interpretation of meaning.

revise: changing portions of the content, structure, or means of development in a piece of writing. See also **edit** and **proofread.**

rhetoric: the study of writing or speaking techniques or the actual use of those techniques to convince, inform, or entertain.

rhyme: words that end with the same, or very similar, sounds are said to rhyme: "toad" and "road," for example.

rhythm: the recurrence of stresses and pauses in a sample of language; the regular repetition of such stresses and pauses is **meter.**

satire: the technique of ridicule intended to reform something by causing people to laugh at it.

short story: a prose fiction, usually under ten thousand words.

simile: a comparison using *like* or *as:* "He is like a pig."

skim: the process of reading rapidly through a piece in order to extract its main ideas.

spatial: organizing a piece of writing in accordance with the relationship of parts in space. Any physical description is spatially organized: "His hat perched on the back of his head, with reddish hair sticking out all around."

specific: precise identification of something by distinct characteristics or names; may include number or pronoun reference. Compare with **concrete:** "The sweet peach" is **concrete** because of its sensory appeal; "the freestone peach" is specific because it names a characteristic; "those three peaches" is also specific, using both a pronoun to indicate which ones and a number.

stanza: a group of lines (verses) in a poem that have a definite metrical pattern and **rhyme** scheme.

stereotype: a fixed idea of a person or thing (separate from actual individual characteristics and without critical judgment), assumed by numbers of people to represent the actual characteristics of that person or thing.

structure: the comprehensive relationship among the parts within a piece of writing. The idea that a piece has an *introduction,* a *body,* and a *conclusion* represents a very basic type of structure.

style: the particular characteristics of an author's piece of writing (including vocabulary, grammar, and **figures of speech**) that distinguish it from a piece of writing by another author.

summary: a shortened version of a piece of writing. **Abstract,** summary, and **précis** are very similar. Of the three, a summary may be the longest and **précis** the shortest. Summaries may include quotations from the source, whereas the other two usually do not.

symbol: an **image,** action, or entire work that has a complex meaning beyond its literal significance.

synthesize: to bring several parts of an idea together or to blend the ideas of several authors.

theme: an abstract statement of the main idea(s) of a story.

thesis: 1) an assertion that the author undertakes to prove—includes a subject and an attitude toward that subject; 2) a lengthy, formal research paper.

tone: the aspects of a piece of writing that indicate the attitude of the author toward the subject, the audience, or both.

topic: the subject of a paragraph, essay, or longer work. See also **theme** and **thesis.**

transitions: connections (words, phrases, sometimes short paragraphs) between the various parts of a piece of writing.

unity: a characteristic of a paragraph or essay by which all parts relate to the topic and thesis.

verbs: parts of speech that indicate the type and time of action within a sentence. In the sentence "Sue jumped off the step," the verb "jumped" indicates the action of "jumping" and the time (past) of its happening.

verse: a single line of poetry.

Credits

"The Dynamo and the Virgin" from *The Education of Henry Adams* by Henry Adams. Copyright 1900. Courtesy Massachusetts Historical Society.

Gordon W. Allport, *The Nature of Prejudice*, © 1979, Addison-Wesley Publishing Co., Inc., Reading, Massachusetts. Pages 3–15. Reprinted with permission of the publisher.

Saint Augustine, "On the Evil of Lust." Reprinted by permission of the publishers and The Loeb Classical Library from Augustine's *City of God*, translated by Philip Levine. Cambridge, Mass.: Harvard University Press, Copyright © 1966 by the President and Fellows of Harvard College.

Ben H. Bagdikian, "Dr. Brandreth Has Gone to Harvard." From *The Media Monopoly*, 3rd Edition by Ben H. Bagdikian. Copyright © 1983, 1987, 1990 by Ben H. Bagdikian. Reprinted by permission of Beacon Press.

"Notes of a Native Son," from *Notes of a Native Son* by James Baldwin. Copyright © 1955, renewed 1983, by James Baldwin. Reprinted by permission of Beacon Press.

James Baldwin, "Previous Condition." Excerpt from *Going to Meet the Man* by James Baldwin, copyright 1948, 1951, 1957, 1958, 1960, 1965 by James Baldwin. Used by permission of Doubleday, a division of Bantam Doubleday Dell Publishing Group, Inc.

Simone de Beauvoir, "The Woman in Love." From *The Second Sex* by Simone de Beauvoir, translated and edited by H. M. Parshley. Copyright 1952 by Alfred A. Knopf, Inc. Reprinted by permission of the publisher.

"Nightmare Number Three" by Stephen Vincent Benét. From: *The Selected Works of Stephen Vincent Benét*. Holt, Rinehart and Winston, Inc. Copyright, 1937, by Stephen Vincent Benét. Copyright renewed, © 1964, by Thomas C. Benét, Stephanie B. Mahin, Rachel Benét Lewis. Reprinted by permission of Brandt and Brandt, Literary Agents, Inc.

Romaine Brooks, *The Mummy*. Courtesy of National Museum of American Art, Smithsonian Institution, gift of the artist.

Raymond Carver, "What We Talk About When We Talk About Love." Copyright © 1981 by Raymond Carver. Reprinted from *What We Talk About When We Talk About Love* by Raymond Carver, by permission of Alfred A. Knopf, Inc.

"Lady with Lapdog" from *Lady with Lapdog and Other Stories* by Anton Chekhov, translated by David Magarshack (Penguin Classics, 1964), copyright © David Magarshack, 1964.

Norman Cousins, "Anatomy of an Illness as Perceived by the Patient." Reprinted from *Anatomy of an Illness as Perceived by the Patient, Reflections on Healing and Regenera-*

Bell Hooks, "Homophobia in Black Communities." Reprinted from *Talking Back*, by Bell Hooks, with permission from the publisher, South End Press, 116 Saint Botolph St., Boston, MA 02115 U.S.A.

"Haircuts and Paris" from *Simple's Uncle Sam* by Langston Hughes. Copyright © 1965 by Langston Hughes. Reprinted by permission of Farrar, Straus and Giroux, Inc.

Jacqueline Jones, "In Pursuit of Freedom," from *Labor of Love, Labor of Sorrow*, by Jacqueline Jones. Copyright © 1985 by Basic Books, Inc. Reprinted by permission of Basic Books, Inc., Publishers, New York.

Evelyn Fox Keller, "Women in Science: An Analysis of a Social Problem." *Harvard Magazine* (Oct. 1974): 14–19.

"Letter from Birmingham Jail" from *Why We Can't Wait* by Martin Luther King, Jr. Copyright © 1963, 1964 by Martin Luther King, Jr. Reprinted by permission of Harper & Row, Publishers, Inc.

Joseph Wood Krutch, "A Meaning for 'Humanism,'" from *Human Nature and Human Condition* by Joseph Wood Krutch. Copyright © 1959 by Joseph Wood Krutch. Reprinted by permission of Random House Inc.

Hanif Kureishi, "Bradford." Copyright © 1984 by Hanif Kureishi. This article first appeared in *Granta 20*.

Dorothea Lange, *Migrant Mother*. Courtesy of the Library of Congress, Library of Congress USF34-9058-C.

David Leavitt, "Territory," from *Family Dancing* by David Leavitt. Copyright © 1983, 1984 by David Leavitt. Reprinted by permission of Alfred A. Knopf, Inc.

Anne McCaffrey, "The Ship Who Sang." Copyright © 1961, 1969 by Anne McCaffrey; first appeared in *The Magazine of Fantasy and Science Fiction;* reprinted by permission of the author and the author's agent, Virginia Kidd.

William H. Masters, Virginia E. Johnson, and Robert C. Kolodny, "The AIDS Virus and Sexuality." From *Crisis: Heterosexual Behavior in the Age of AIDS*. Copyright © 1988 by William H. Masters, Virginia E. Johnson, and Robert C. Kolodny. Used by permission of Grove Press, Inc.

Mary Mebane, "Incident on a Bus," from *Mary* by Mary Mebane. Copyright © 1981 by Mary Elizabeth Mebane. Used by permission of Viking Penguin, a division of Penguin Books USA Inc.

Roy W. Menninger, "Decisions in Sexuality: An Act of Impulse, Conscience, or Society?" From *Sexuality: A Search for Perspective*, edited by Donald L. Grummon and Andrew M. Barclay © 1971 by Litton Educational Publishing Co. Reprinted by permission of Wadsworth, Inc.

Stanley Milgram, "Some Conditions of Obedience and Disobedience to Authority," *Human Relations*, Vol. 18, No. 1, 1965, pp. 57–75. Copyright Alexandra Milgram. Reprinted by permission of Alexandra Milgram.

John Milton, *Paradise Lost*, Book III. From *John Milton: Complete Poems and Major Prose*, edited by Merritt Y. Hughes (New York: Macmillan, 1985).

"The Intelligence Transplant," Marvin Minsky/© 1989 Discover Publications.

Index to Authors and Titles

Reading titles appear in italic.